AF775888

Scarcity and the State I

The Allocation of Limited Rights by the Administration

Editors:
Paul Adriaanse,
Frank van
Ommeren,
Willemien den
Ouden and Johan
Wolswinkel

Scarcity and the State I

The Allocation of Limited Rights by the Administration

intersentia

METRO

Ius Commune Europaeum

Intersentia Ltd
Sheraton House | Castle Park
Cambridge | CB3 0AX | United Kingdom
Tel.: +44 1223 370 170 | Fax: +44 1223 370 169
Email: mail@intersentia.co.uk
www.intersentia.com | www.intersentia.co.uk

Distribution for the UK and Ireland:
NBN International
Airport Business Centre, 10 Thornbury Road
Plymouth, PL6 7 PP
United Kingdom
Tel.: +44 1752 202 301 | Fax: +44 1752 202 331
Email: orders@nbninternational.com

Distribution for Europe and all other countries:
Intersentia Publishing nv
Groenstraat 31
2640 Mortsel
Belgium
Tel.: +32 3 680 15 50 | Fax: +32 3 658 71 21
Email: mail@intersentia.be

Distribution for the USA and Canada:
International Specialized Book Services
920 NE 58th Ave. Suite 300
Portland, OR 97213
USA
Tel.: +1 800 944 6190 (toll free) | Fax: +1 503 280 8832
Email: info@isbs.com

ISBN 978-1-78068-347-8
D/2016/7849/72
NUR 823

British Library Cataloguing in Publication Data. A catalogue record for this book is available from the British Library.

FOREWORD

This is an important, ambitious and timely book in an area of huge economic importance. It is directed to legislators, administrators and the courts. Its subject is one which has not, so far as I know, been comprehensively covered by any other, namely, the allocation to economic actors of limited rights by the European Union and Member States – rights to receive a subsidy or to licences to carry on an activity which can not lawfully be carried on without such a licence. A careful reading of the first chapter gives a good insight into what is being attempted by the authors.

The book does not walk again down well trodden paths but rather exposes and discusses a collection of often overlapping and at times conflicting Treaty provisions, Directives, Regulations, legal decisions and economic and political desiderata. It seeks to identify tools which will help to construct something orderly.

As a former judge of the Court of Justice of the European Union who has had to try with his colleagues to find a path through inconsistent case law and concepts it was a joy on being asked whether I would write this preface, to come across – alas too late – a draft of this book. It should help my successors to find a conceptually coherent approach to drafting judgments in a particular field so that they do not conflict with other judgments in overlapping fields.

The law is currently being developed and is still sufficiently flexible and uncrystallised for this book to be in a position to make a significant contribution to that development. I hope that in due course it will be found possible to translate it into French – still the working language of the CJEU.

Konrad Schiemann
Former Judge of the Court of Justice of the European Union

Editors:
Paul Adriaanse,
Frank van Ommeren,
Willemien den Ouden and Johan Wolswinkel

Scarcity and the State I

The Allocation of Limited Rights by the Administration

intersentia

METRO

Intersentia Ltd
Sheraton House | Castle Park
Cambridge | CB3 0AX | United Kingdom
Tel.: +44 1223 370 170 | Fax: +44 1223 370 169
Email: mail@intersentia.co.uk
www.intersentia.com | www.intersentia.co.uk

Distribution for the UK and Ireland:
NBN International
Airport Business Centre, 10 Thornbury Road
Plymouth, PL6 7 PP
United Kingdom
Tel.: +44 1752 202 301 | Fax: +44 1752 202 331
Email: orders@nbninternational.com

Distribution for Europe and all other countries:
Intersentia Publishing nv
Groenstraat 31
2640 Mortsel
Belgium
Tel.: +32 3 680 15 50 | Fax: +32 3 658 71 21
Email: mail@intersentia.be

Distribution for the USA and Canada:
International Specialized Book Services
920 NE 58th Ave. Suite 300
Portland, OR 97213
USA
Tel.: +1 800 944 6190 (toll free) | Fax: +1 503 280 8832
Email: info@isbs.com

Scarcity and the State I. The Allocation of Limited Rights by the Administration

ISBN 978-1-78068-347-8
D/2016/7849/72
NUR 823

British Library Cataloguing in Publication Data. A catalogue record for this book is available from the British Library.

EDITORS' PREFACE

This book is the result of a Europe-wide exploration of building blocks for a consistent and general legal theory on the allocation of limited rights by administrative authorities. The idea of an international book project on this theme was launched at an inspiring international conference, organised by researchers from the Departments of Constitutional and Administrative law of Leiden University and VU University Amsterdam, the Netherlands. The project has been realised with the help of many researchers from various EU Member States. The contributions in this book deal with the subject from a general perspective, as well as from an EU law perspective and a comparative law perspective. These contributions have been enriched by the information provided by national reports on the allocation of gambling licences, radio frequencies and CO_2 emission permits in seven EU Member States: France, Germany, Greece, Italy, the Netherlands, Romania and Spain.[1] Together, all these contributions have resulted in a valuable and interesting collection of legal scholarship, which sheds light on various complex issues concerning the allocation of limited rights by administrative authorities. We sincerely hope that, based on these building blocks, further research in this field can be carried out. We wish to thank all the authors for their efforts and contributions to this book project.

Paul Adriaanse, Frank van Ommeren, Willemien den Ouden and Johan Wolswinkel
Leiden/Amsterdam, November 2015

1 See P. Adriaanse, F. van Ommeren, W. den Ouden and J. Wolswinkel, *Scarcity and the State II. Member State Reports on Gambling Licences, Radio Frequencies and CO_2 Emission Permits*, Intersentia, Antwerp 2016.

CONTENTS

PART II. EU LAW PERSPECTIVES

PART I

GENERAL PERSPECTIVES

Paul Adriaanse,
Frank van
Ommeren,
Willemien den
Ouden and Johan
Wolswinkel*

CHAPTER 1.
THE ALLOCATION OF LIMITED RIGHTS BY THE ADMINISTRATION: A QUEST FOR A GENERAL LEGAL THEORY

1. Introduction

Managing scarcity to serve the public interest is a classic task of government. Whereas economic and political theory have paid much attention to the allocation of scarce goods and rights, until now a consistent and general legal theory of 'the allocating government' has been more or less absent. In fact, the law of public administration seems to assume that every party shall be granted a good or right once it satisfies all the necessary conditions.[1] This assumption neglects the fact that in several areas of government regulation, individual rights such as authorisations and (financial) claims are available only in a limited quantity. As a result of this limited availability, certain applications for those rights must be denied even though the applicants satisfy all the necessary conditions. In other words, there may not be enough rights available to satisfy all qualified parties.

This idiosyncratic feature of limited rights can be illustrated using a number of examples. First, it is worth mentioning the auctions of the 4G spectrum in several Member States as an example of rights which are scarce for natural reasons. With revenues running up to billions of euros, the financial importance of these frequencies for both the allocating authorities and the bidding undertakings is clear from the outset. In the area of gambling law, an area entirely different from telecommunications law at first sight, scarcity exists as well: in order to ensure the protection of consumers and to combat crime and gambling addiction, many Member States artificially restrict the number of authorisations that are available to be granted. The same holds true for financial grants, although the background is different: in order to restrict expenditure,

* Paul Adriaanse is Associate Professor of constitutional and administrative law at Leiden University and practising lawyer at Justion Advocaten, the Netherlands. Frank van Ommeren is Professor of constitutional and administrative law at VU University Amsterdam, the Netherlands. Willemien den Ouden is Professor of administrative law at Leiden University, the Netherlands. Johan Wolswinkel is Associate Professor of administrative law at Tilburg University, the Netherlands.

1 See e.g. Article 10(5) Directive 2006/123/EC of the European Parliament and of the Council of 12 December 2006 on services in the internal market [2006] OJ L 376/36 (hereinafter: Services Directive): 'The authorisation shall be granted as soon as it is established, in the light of an appropriate examination, that the conditions for authorisation have been met.'

most kinds of financial grants and subsidies are available in limited budget only, both at the European level and at the level of the Member States. Last but not least, we mention the many procurement procedures being performed in order to conclude supply contracts with market parties.

This book seeks to demonstrate the need for a consistent and general theory on the allocation of limited rights by administrative authorities from a legal perspective. Since all these limited rights are usually of great importance to applicants – they represent significant economic value, and it is often not possible for the applicant to perform the intended activities without the requested permit, authorisation or subsidy – decisions concerning the allocation of limited public rights often lead to disputes, for example on the lack of transparency, the selected allocation procedure or the renewal of limited rights to the detriment of new entrants in the market.

Since many limited rights have a European origin or a cross-border impact, the allocation of these rights is subject to a process of Europeanisation and consequent economisation of administrative law.[2] Although European Union law has always been aimed at establishing and ensuring the functioning of an internal market (an area without internal frontiers in which the free movement of goods, persons, services and capital is ensured)[3] over the years the corpus of EU law has extended in volume and detail. Not surprisingly, this offers new possibilities for undertakings and other applicants to contest the allocation of limited rights, even in cases falling outside the (direct) scope of EU law. Arguments derived from European law, be it primary EU law or (specific) secondary legislation, can sometimes be invoked successfully before the national courts in cases where national law offers less protection of the interests of competing applicants, or none at all. By doing so EU law concepts are introduced in disputes in policy fields that have been governed traditionally by national law only.

Furthermore – and more importantly – many of the above-mentioned legal issues are not exclusively linked to a particular policy field, but – on the contrary – seem to be characteristic of *any* allocation of limited rights by administrative authorities. Therefore, solutions to these legal problems may be available not only in the area at stake, but also in other areas that are confronted with limited rights. This calls for a *general* legal theory of the allocation of limited public rights. This view is supported by the fact that both national courts and the Court of Justice of the European Union (hereinafter: CJEU) are increasingly willing – in the absence of specific legislation – to consider the allocation of limited rights in various fields of law under general legal principles, like the fundamental freedoms or the principle of equal treatment. To illustrate this point,[4] reference can be

2 See on the economisation of administrative law also M. Ruffert (ed.), *The Transformation of Administrative Law in Europe*, Sellier European Law Publishers, Münich 2007, p. 24 ff. More in general on the Europeanization of administrative law, see J. Schwarze, *European Administrative Law*, Sweet & Maxwell, London 2006, and H.C.H. Hofmann, G.C. Rowe and A.H. Türk, *Administrative Law and Policy of the European Union*, OUP, Oxford 2011.

3 Article 26 TFEU.

4 For the Dutch context, this point was established during two expert meetings in 2010, followed by a book: F.J. van Ommeren, W. den Ouden, C.J. Wolswinkel (eds.), *Schaarse publieke rechten*, Boom

made to judgments by the CJEU in the field of public procurement,[5] gambling,[6] telecommunications,[7] petrol stations,[8] pharmacies[9] and opticians[10], as well as judgments by national courts in different Member States on issues like limited licences for 'Sunday night stores',[11] gambling,[12] and CO_2 emission allowances.[13]

The search for a general legal theory of limited rights fits in broader thinking throughout the EU and its Member States concerning the development and codification of general principles of law governing composite administration at the European and national level. Using these general principles, gaps can be filled in specific legislation or when legislation is lacking altogether. General principles can also serve as landmarks when developing new legislation. As such, they could even have a harmonising effect. Legal practice will also be aided by a general legal theory since the wheel does not have to be re-invented everywhere, thereby contributing to legal certainty and efficiency. Not only legislatures, administrative bodies and judges, but also the various applicants for limited rights and their competitors will therefore benefit from a general legal theory of this phenomenon. This makes the attempt to arrive at such an overall theory all the more challenging.

In order to support and expand a generalised analysis of the allocation of limited rights from a legal perspective, the following question will be the focus of this introductory chapter and further in the other contributions in this book:

> *What rules and principles are relevant for a consistent and general legal theory on the allocation of limited rights by administrative authorities in the EU and its Member States?*

Juridische uitgevers, The Hague 2011. See also C.J. Wolswinkel, 'The Allocation of a Limited Number of Authorisations. Some General Requirements from European Law' (2009) 2(2) *Review of European Administrative Law*, 61; F. Wollenschläger, *Verteilungsverfahren*, Mohr Siebeck, Tübingen 2010; L. Arroyo Jiménez and D. Utrilla Fernández-Bermejo (eds.), *La administración de la escasez*, Marcial Pons, Madrid 2015, and F. Wollenschläger, 'EU Law Principles for Allocating Scarce Goods and the Emergence of an Allocation Procedure. Identifying Substantive and Procedural Standards and Developing a New Type of Administrative Procedure' (2015) 8 (1) *Review of Administrative Law*, 205.

5 Joined Cases C-147/06 and C-148/06, *SECAP and Santorso* [2008] ECR I-3565.

6 Case C-203/08, *Sporting Exchange* [2009] ECR I-4695; Case C-64/08, *Engelmann* [2010] ECR I-8219; Joined Cases C-72/10 and C-77/10, *Costa and Cifone* [2012] ECLI:EU:C:2012:80.

7 Case C-375/11, *Belgacom* [2013] ECLI:EU:C:2013:185.

8 Case C-384/08, *Attanasio Group* [2010] ECR I-2055.

9 Joined Cases C-570/07 and C-5712/07, *Blanco Pérez and Chao Gómez* [2010] ECR I-4629.

10 Case C-539/11, *Ottica New Line* [2013] ECLI:EU:C:2013:591.

11 See for example the Judgment of the Dutch Trade and Industry Appeals Tribunal of 24 August 2012, *Vomar Voordeelmarkt B.V.*, *AB* 2012, 373.

12 See for example the Judgment of the Austrian *Landesgericht Linz* of 23.01.2008, *Engelmann*, with reference for a preliminary ruling from the Court of Justice (see Case C-64/08, [2010] ECR I-8219).

13 See for example the Judgment of the Regional Court of Lazio, II-bis, 3313/2010, *Soc. Columbian Carbon Europa vs. Ministry of Environment.*

This introductory chapter is structured as follows. After demonstrating the need for a consistent and general legal perspective to the allocation of limited rights by administrative authorities in addition to economic and political theory (Section 2), we elaborate on the legal approaches that can be adopted in order to disentangle the phenomenon of limited rights (Section 3). We then go on to identify three approaches that are useful in this regard: a conceptual approach, a top-down approach and a bottom-up approach. The *conceptual* approach aims to distinguish the general elements characterising any allocation of limited rights (Section 4). The *top-down* approach addresses the relevance of EU law for (general) rules and principles on the allocation of limited rights (Section 5). Finally, the *bottom-up* approach takes a reverse perspective by focusing on the ways Member States use the freedom left by EU law to regulate the allocation of limited rights in several areas of government intervention (Section 6). In these three sections, we outline the relevance of the various chapters in this book as 'building blocks' for a general legal theory on the allocation of limited rights in the EU and its Member States. In the concluding remarks (Section 7), we reflect briefly on this theory and the next steps to be taken.

2. Economic, Political and Legal Issues

The allocation of limited rights by administrative authorities can be analysed using several academic disciplines.[14] When focusing on the aspects of 'allocation' and 'scarcity', the allocation of limited rights falls firstly within the scope of economics. In his seminal *Essay on the Nature & Significance of Economic Science*, Robbins defined economics as the science which studies human behaviour as a relationship between ends and scarce means which have alternative uses.[15] This definition perfectly fits our subject matter: since only a limited number of rights is available to be granted, the number of applicants may exceed this number of rights as a result of which these rights have alternative recipients. Several branches of economic theory deal explicitly with the allocation of scarce resources, like resource allocation theory and auction theory.[16] However, since economic theory used to claim to be neutral with regard to the ends of allocation,[17] the question concerning which allocation principles should guide the allocation remains, at least partly, an open question in economics.

This question has been debated in philosophical and political theories on distributive justice, addressing the issue of which allocation principles, like efficiency, merit or need, should be decisive in the allocation of scarce resources.[18] These philosophical theories, like the approach in economic theory, usually abstract from the specific (legal) context

14 For more detail, see C.J. Wolswinkel, 'An Allocation Perspective to Public Law: Limited Public Rights and Beyond' (2014) 5 *Law & Method*, DOI:10.5553/REM/.000004.

15 L. Robbins, *An Essay on the Nature & Significance of Economic Science*, MacMillan, London 1952, p. 16.

16 See for example M.C.W. Janssen (ed.), *Auctioning Public Assets. Analysis and Alternatives*, Cambridge University Press, Cambridge 2004.

17 Robbins 1952, p. 24.

18 At a local level, see with further references for example J. Elster, *Local Justice. How Institutions Allocate Scarce Goods and Necessary Burdens*, Russell Sage Foundation, New York 1992.

for a particular allocation of scarce resources and therefore do not take into account existing legal constraints on the design of allocation mechanisms.

In contrast to economics and distributive justice theory, such a pre-eminent role for scarcity and allocation issues seems to be lacking in law, at least in administrative law. To put it somewhat simplistically, as mentioned in the introduction, the 'default' legal approach to granting rights is that public authorities should grant a right whenever an applicant meets the conditions necessary to be granted that right. This does not mean that legal doctrine is totally unaware of the phenomenon of limited rights. In particular – and not surprisingly – there is a huge branch of law & economics literature with regard to public regulation, including monopoly regulation and public franchising. It is worth emphasising that Coase's founding articles on law & economics, 'The Federal Communications Commission' (1959) and 'The Problem of Social Cost' (1960),[19] addressed in particular the use of pricing mechanisms by administrative authorities for the allocation of scarce resources (broadcasting frequencies and pollution rights).[20] In recent literature on law and economics, this explicit attention to market mechanisms on the allocating of scarce resources is still clearly present.[21] However, because of the *instrumental* approach in literature on law and economics and the strong emphasis on law as a *tool* for public regulation,[22] there is hardly any attention for the more doctrinal issue of how the allocation of these limited rights should be incorporated into a consistent and general legal framework. Shifting our perspective from an instrumental function of law to a more *protective* one,[23] focusing on the protection of individual citizens' interests and – conversely – the need for proper or sound administration, the literature remains even more silent, at least with respect to fundamental *legal* principles that should guide the allocation of limited rights and thereby give due care to the interests of market parties.

This chapter therefore aims to address relevant *legal* questions in order to establish general allocation rules and principles and to identify best legal practices applying to any allocation of limited rights. The resulting legal framework should be fitted into the classic, 'non-limited' part of administrative law in order to create a coherent and consistent system of legal protection, applying to any granting of rights by administrative

19 R.H. Coase, 'The Federal Communications Commission' (1959) *The Journal of Law & Economics*, 1, and R.H. Coase, 'The Problem of Social Cost' (1960) *The Journal of Law & Economics*, 1.

20 However, it was not until the nineties of the previous century that the auctions of broadcasting frequencies took place in the United States. See J. McMillan, 'Selling Spectrum Rights' (1994) *Journal of Economic Perspectives*, 145.

21 See for example R. Posner, *Economic Analysis of Law*, Aspin Publishers, New York 2007, 47–48.

22 See for example A.I. Ogus, *Regulation: Legal Form and Economic Theory*, Hart Publishing, Oxford 2004, p. 214 and 318, distinguishing from an instrumental point of view between 'prior approval' licences (*i.e.* 'non-limited authorisations') and 'public franchises' ('limited authorisations').

23 See for this distinction between the instrumental and the protective function of law: W. van den Burg, 'The expressive and communicative functions of law, especially with regard to moral issues' (2001) *Law and Philosophy*, 34, with reference to Dworkin's distinction between principle and policy (R. Dworkin, *Taking Rights Seriously*, Cambridge University Press, Cambridge 1978, p. 22).

authorities. At the same time, this framework functions in addition to literature on law and economics, and economic and philosophical insights on the allocation of limited rights, and thereby contributes to a profound and multidisciplinary analysis of the phenomenon of limited rights.

3. Legal Approaches

Above all, it is necessary to introduce general terminology that will facilitate a generalised analysis of the allocation of limited rights by administrative authorities. This 'conceptual' approach[24] precedes any other legal approach to limited rights that aims to develop a consistent and general legal theory on this matter. The conceptual approach takes account of the specific characteristics of, on the one hand, the 'resources' that are to be allocated, *i.e.* rights awarded by administrative authorities, and, on the other hand, the allocation procedures facilitating a relative comparison of applicants. Thus, this conceptual approach should be followed in close connection with similar definitions in economic theory and theories of distributive justice. The resulting conceptual framework might facilitate *any* legal system, either at the EU level or at the national level, to adopt general rules and principles on the allocation of limited rights.

Next, considering the relationship between the EU level and the level of the Member States in more detail, two opposite approaches can be distinguished: a top-down approach and a bottom-up approach. In the top-down approach, we examine the influence of EU law on the design of allocation systems, both at an EU level and at a national level. Therefore, the relevant question becomes: Which elements of a general legal theory on the allocation of limited public rights follow from European Union law?[25] This approach highlights the guiding role of the European institutions, including the Court of Justice, in the development of requirements applying to the allocation of limited rights. This guidance may vary in its general or specific character, depending on the question whether it applies to a particular area of policy regulation (e.g. telecommunications law, gambling law) or has a more general scope (e.g. services). Thus, it should be emphasised that this top down approach is not restricted to a deductive exercise starting with the general principles of EU law, but may also cover more specific allocation rules resulting from EU law.[26]

In the absence of exhaustive and crystallised top-down regulation with regard to the allocation of limited rights, there is a need for a bottom-up approach as well. This bottom-up approach aims to identify common principles or rules to the allocation of limited rights that apply in the absence of or in addition to EU regulations. This inductive approach, which is complementary to the top-down approach, requires a *comparative* view on the subject matter and aims at identifying some *ius commune* or

24 This conceptual approach is identical to the analytical approach adopted by Arroyo and Utrilla in their chapter to this book.

25 In fact, legal rules may result from other supranational sources as well, e.g. the European Charter on Human Rights. See the chapter by den Ouden and Tjepkema.

26 This top-down approach overlaps with the constitutional approach of Arroyo and Utrilla as far as allocation rules are derived from general principles of EU law.

best legal practices.[27] We find it helpful to distinguish two dimensions within this bottom-up approach. In the first place, it is useful to analyze several areas of public regulation with limited rights (e.g. telecommunications law, gambling law and subsidy law) with the intention of identifying similarities and differences across these areas that may contribute to common rules or principles. In the second place, within these particular areas of public regulation, it is useful to compare Member States' practices with each other concerning their use of discretion as left by EU law. This bottom-up approach therefore serves to identify a common, though minimal, legal core of allocation rules, while respecting Member States' discretion in the allocation of limited rights.

In the following sections, the implications of these three approaches are sketched briefly by highlighting some general developments and pointing out some important findings in the other chapters to this book. In fact, these three sections show that these approaches should go hand-in-hand. Therefore, the three parts of the book follow the three distinctive approaches identified above, but only to a certain extent.

4. Conceptual Approach: Definitions and Characteristics

Right from the outset, it is necessary to introduce some uniform terminology on the subject matter in order to have a clear understanding of limited rights. To explain this phenomenon accurately, it is useful to make a conceptual distinction between (i) the object of allocation (*the 'what' question*), (ii) the method of allocation (*the 'how' question)* and (iii) the legal form of the allocation (*the 'form' question*). The advantage of these conceptual distinctions is that they generate general tools to explain the essential features of the allocation of limited public rights. Moreover, these distinctions could prevent us from some rather complicated misunderstandings.

4.1. Object of Allocation: Limited Rights

Let us first address the object of allocation. In other words: how do we conceptualise the notion of limited rights? An answer to this question also offers a first glimpse of the scope of this book. With the term 'rights' we designate individual rights granted by an administrative authority. These 'public' rights can be subdivided into two main categories: 'authorisations' and 'claims'.[28]

An 'authorisation' covers any administrative decision creating an individual exception to a statutory prohibition or injunction. It concerns various types of government approvals that exist in legal practice, such as licences or permits. As an overarching characteristic, all these approvals imply a permission from an administrative authority to engage in a certain (usually economic) activity which is otherwise prohibited.

27 See more extensively on the emergence of European administrative law through comparative method: J. Schwarze, *European Administrative Law*, Sweet & Maxwell, London 2006, p. clxxxi ff and 76 ff.

28 For this distinction in general see R. Alexy, *A theory of constitutional rights*, OUP, Oxford 2002, p. 133 ff.

Claims result from administrative decisions awarding rights to a *positive* act of an administrative authority.[29] The main types of claims are financial grants (subsidies) on the one hand and governmental commissions on the other. Financial grants or subsidies of an administrative authority do not merely concern government approval but rather governmental incentives or support. Governmental commissions, by contrast, create a claim for a private party against the commissioning government to something in return for the supply of goods and services. Usually this reciprocity or consideration consists of payment, but this reciprocity may also consist of the right to exploit these goods or services.

The next issue is what we mean by *limited*. Stripped of most of the complexities, (public) rights are limited if they are available in a limited quantity. Therefore, limited rights presuppose a *maximum* – often referred to as a *ceiling* – indicating the maximum number of rights that can be granted (within a given period). There may be numerous reasons for administrative authorities to set such a ceiling: it may result from scarcity of natural resources, like the radio spectrum or mineral resources, but can also be inspired by legitimate 'artificial' reasons, like consumer protection or public order. Of course, it should also not be neglected that allocating authorities might pursue their own interests as 'necessary side-effects', like collecting extra revenues.

At this point, it should be stressed that the governmental task of managing scarcity is not restricted to the allocation of limited rights. For example, the government can assign alternative modes of use to several parts of a certain scarce resource (e.g. radio spectrum) in order to balance the various interests involved in the use of this resource *without* introducing a (*limited*) authorisation scheme.

Several characteristics of limited rights are relevant for the allocation of these rights. The first aspect to be highlighted is the *duration* of rights. Exactly because a ceiling allows only a limited number of parties to conduct certain activities, the disadvantages of the rejection of applications and the prevention of parties entering the market would be 'eternal' if these limited rights were granted for an indefinite period.

Next, it is important whether these limited rights are *tradable* or not.[30] If rights can be transferred,[31] applicants missing out in the allocation procedure are not banned forever from obtaining this limited right. This transferability of rights is especially appealing when these rights represent a significant financial value, which is often the case with rights that are available in a limited number only.

In sum, the object of allocation raises a number of issues that are relevant for the allocation of limited rights, *inter alia* (i) when may or should the number of public rights be limited, (ii) how are these limitations constructed legally and (iii) does it make any

29 Alexy 2002, p. 120, describes claims as 'rights to something'.

30 See e.g. the chapters by Wolswinkel and Adriaanse in this book.

31 Some limited rights are known in the jargon as 'tradable permits', with the specific feature that they are (by definition) transferable: the possessor may transfer this right to a successor, as in the case of emission rights.

legal difference, which subject (e.g. radio frequencies, CO_2 emissions or gambling activities) these limited rights concern? Answering these kinds of questions with regard to the object of allocation might be a first step in the development of a consistent and general legal theory on the allocation of limited rights.

4.2. Allocation Procedures

Scarcity is a relative notion that binds supply and demand. Thus, whenever the total number of applicants exceeds the number of available rights, these limited rights are called scarce. In those circumstances of scarcity, limited rights have to be granted by means of a so-called *allocation* procedure. Following this terminology, an *allocation* is understood as the resulting award of *limited* rights to individual applicants, thereby excluding other applicants from obtaining these rights.[32]

There are several allocation methods or procedures of allocation that can be applied by an administrative authority. The allocation procedures commonly used are:[33]

- the order of receipt of the applications ('first come first served');
- the drawing of lots;
- an auction;
- a comparative assessment (also called 'beauty contest' or 'tender');
- a proportional division.

This list of allocation procedures is not meant to be exhaustive. For example, it is sometimes useful to distinguish public procurement as a separate allocation procedure, because it is the most regulated and detailed procedure to allocate limited rights.[34] Nonetheless, as indicated by Jansen in this book, public procurement may be classified either as an auction or as a comparative assessment dependent on the applicable 'award criteria'.

Anyway, characteristic of any of these allocation procedures is that these procedures have a *relative* character: applications are compared by means of one or more allocation criteria. For example, in the case of allocation in order of receipt of applications it is decisive which application was received first by the awarding authority. However, in the case of an auction, the applicant with the highest financial bid determines the outcome. Consequently, each allocation procedure has its own characteristics.

32 In this respect, there is no uniform terminology. Instead, a wide variety of terms and definitions can be distinguished. In the area of radio spectrum policy, e.g., frequency distribution to several services (broadcasting, mobile communications, etcetera) is called 'allocation', where the subsequent frequency distribution to individual undertakings is called 'assignment' (Article 1 ITU Radio Regulations 2012). See into more detail the chapter by Oberst in this book.

33 Elster 1992, p. 67 ff.

34 See the chapter by Van Ommeren.

When considering the allocation of limited rights, attention should not be restricted to the so-called 'initial' allocation. For example, if the initial allocation has been accompanied by a waiting list, limited rights that have been withdrawn afterwards, will be granted to the initially unsuccessful applicants. Moreover, an important issue is whether rights that have been granted can be modified, extended or renewed without applying a new allocation procedure. In particular, in relationship to the duration of limited rights mentioned above, the issue of prolongation turns out to be highly relevant: as a result of prolongation, newcomers who will reckon with the limited duration of limited rights, might (once again) not be able to compete for these rights in the future. Finally, after the expiry of limited rights, these rights become available again to grant, provoking the debate whether new entrants should be put at an advantage *vis-à-vis* incumbents.

Thus, in addition to the issues raised by the object of allocation, a generalised analysis of the allocation procedure provokes a number of additional questions, e.g. (i) when should limited rights be allocated by a competitive method, (ii) what kind of objective allocation criteria are used in order to prevent favouritism and nepotism, and (iii) how can the equal treatment of long-established parties and newcomers be ensured? Whereas general or uniform answers to these questions should not always be expected, differences between allocation procedures should still be justified by some consistent legal theory on the allocation of limited rights.

4.3. Legal Form

Apart from the object and the procedure, the legal form of the allocation should be distinguished. The legal form of an allocation refers to the public or private form in which the limited right at stake is granted. Generally, administrative authorities grant public rights by unilateral single case decision-making or by a contract. Although a public right will usually be allocated unilaterally, it is sometimes necessary that the other (receiving) party agrees with this grant and that there is some kind of bilateral or multilateral legal form to express this reciprocity. In particular, this kind of agreement – a bilateral or multilateral "public" contract – is needed when the administrative authority lacks the power to grant the public right unilaterally. "Public" contracts in this broad sense, i.e. contracts of which at least one of the parties is a public authority,[35] are conceptualised very differently in several EU Member States: in some jurisdictions, these public contracts are understood to be administrative agreements under public law while in other jurisdictions as civil law contracts.[36]

35 This definition of public contracts includes, but does not coincide with the definition of 'public contracts' in Article 1(2)(a) Directive 2004/18/EC of the European Parliament and of the Council of 31 March 2004 on the coordination of procedures for the award of public works contracts, public supply contracts and public service contracts [2004] OJ L 134/114: 'contracts for pecuniary interest concluded in writing between one or more economic operators and one or more contracting authorities and having as their object the execution of works, the supply of products or the provision of services'.

36 See R. Noguellou and U. Stelkens (ed.), *Droit comparé des Contrats Publics. Comparative Law on Public Contracts*, Bruylant, Bruxelles 2010.

Although this is not necessarily the same in every legal system, a certain kind of limited right does not automatically imply a certain allocation procedure, nor does a certain kind of allocation procedure imply a certain legal form. For example, a licence is more than once issued on a first come first served basis, but can be subject to an auction as well. Licences are often issued unilaterally, but sometimes it is necessary that the licence is accepted by the other party to have legal force. Similarly, the allocation procedure of a comparative assessment ('beauty contest') can result in both a unilateral decision and a (public) contract. Nor can we equate every governmental commission with a public contract, because not every governmental commission has a bilateral nature. The same holds for the public procurement procedure: most often, this allocation results in a bilateral public contract, but this is not necessarily the case; the public procurement procedure may also be used in the case of unilateral decision-making.[37]

Therefore, in addition to the questions raised by the object of allocation and by the allocation procedure, it is necessary to address issues relating to the legal form of the allocation, e.g. (i) does EU law prescribe a preferred legal form of limited rights, (ii) which judge (civil, administrative or otherwise) has jurisdiction with regard to the various legal forms of limited rights, and (iii) to what extent do the various legal forms of limited rights entail specific problems of legal protection? These issues on the legal form of the allocation already mark the need for a comparison between EU Member States (below Section 6), as different legal systems might result in different answers.

4.4. *Reflection*

Part I of this book shows first of all the merits of a conceptual approach. In this respect, as Arroyo and Utrilla make clear in their chapter, the use of clear 'allocation' terminology is necessary to unveil the typical characteristics of an allocation of limited rights. Moreover, uniform terminology should be preferred as much as possible, although differences in terminology might be justified. This allocation terminology facilitates the analysis of the importance of general principles of law for the identification of specific allocation rules. Arroyo and Utrilla illustrate this with their constitutional approach to limited rights, characterised by the deduction of normative findings from a set of higher principles which operate as structural building blocks of a legal system for the allocation of limited rights.

37 See explicitly Regulation (EC) No 1370/2007 of the European Parliament and of the Council of 23 October 2007 on public passenger transport services by rail and by road and repealing Council Regulations (EEC) Nos 1191/69 and 1107/70 [2007] OJ L 315/1: whereas the competent authorities are required to award public service contracts on the basis of a *competitive tendering procedure* (Article 5(3)), these public service contracts are defined as 'one or more legally binding acts confirming the agreement between a competent authority and a public service operator to entrust to that public service operator the management and operation of public passenger transport services subject to public service obligations'. Depending on the law of the Member State, this contract may also consist of 'a decision adopted by the competent authority *taking the form of an individual legislative or regulatory act*' (Article 2(i)) (emphasis added by the authors).

In legal practice, however, there is still much work to be done. Buijze notes that the EU legislature does not contribute to the allocation of limited rights with a detailed set of general allocation rules. The EU legislature has more than one reason to be interested in the allocation of limited rights, *i.e.* the proper functioning of the internal market and the potential of limited rights as an instrument to give effect to EU policy within the environmental or the social domain for example. As a result, EU law does respect the fact that the allocation of limited rights can also serve other (general) objectives than efficiency and competition within the internal market. However, the question *how* these objectives are being pursued, is primarily a matter of the Member States; EU law provides only guidance with some 'broad principles', for example on subsidiarity and proportionality. While it is far from easy to determine what these broad principles require in practice, more detailed rules at the EU level are not the solution according to Buijze. Instead, the national legislature should address this issue.

As to this role of the national legislature, Van Ommeren points out that in order to be fruitful, any such legislative attempt should balance between principle-based regulation and rule-based regulation. While several principles have shown to be very powerful in the regulation of the allocation of limited rights, rule-based legislation remains necessary. In particular, this rule-based regulation should take into account key features of the allocation of limited rights, such as the power to set a ceiling, the choice between allocation procedures and the (limited) duration and transferability of limited rights. Moreover, the national legislature should make explicit its allocation objective, thereby completing the wide range of discretion left to it by the EU legislature.

The idiosyncratic features of limited rights also come to the fore with regard to questions of judicial protection. First of all, disappointment is inherent to any allocation of limited public rights: the award of one application implies the rejection of another. Consequently, allocation decisions have a dispute-triggering character: parties are not inclined to consider an allocation procedure as being fair, when they did not receive what they applied for because the available rights were issued to another party. Another relevant characteristic for many allocation procedures is the phenomenon of 'phased decision making'. As a result, there are usually several moments for interested parties to seek legal protection. It should not be surprising that if the allocation procedure takes longer, it becomes more difficult for a judge to intervene. In this regard, Wollenschläger states that allocation procedures do not follow the classic bipolar citizen-state paradigm on which many rules and institutions of administrative law are based. The multipolar paradigm that is necessary instead to capture the allocation of limited rights, poses a challenge to legal doctrine and jurisprudence. For example, the need for so-called 'stability' of allocation decisions, ruling out their ex-post repeal once allocation procedures have been executed, results in the substitution of ex-post remedies by preventive or prospective remedies, on the one hand, and in the complete exclusion of primary legal remedies (annulments of allocation decisions) with a limitation to secondary legal remedies (damages) on the other hand.

In sum, the conceptual approach sketched above provides for the tools necessary to unveil the peculiar characteristics of the allocation of limited rights within the domain of (administrative) law. The resulting legal concepts can be used in both a top-down approach and a bottom-up approach, as these concepts abstract from the particular allocation context.

5. Top-Down Approach: EU Law Perspectives

5.1. Introductory Observations

Many of the current legal issues on the allocation of limited rights have been influenced, in one way or another, by developments in EU law. In order to elaborate on this point, it is useful to distinguish several levels of EU regulation. While some allocation rules apply to *EU institutions* only, EU law may also prescribe specific rules for the allocation of limited rights by *Member States*. Between those two extremes, several kinds of intermediate forms of influence of EU rules and principles can be traced with regard to allocation issues in the Member States or, in a wider perspective, in the European composite administration.[38] Below, we will outline some important developments in EU law that we regard as being most relevant to a generalised approach to allocations of limited rights, both at EU level and at national level.

5.2. Allocation at EU Level

Several limited rights are granted by EU institutions. Examples include the granting of subsidies and the award of public contracts by the European Commission, but also limited authorisations that have been awarded occasionally at an EU level.[39] Currently, the most relevant provisions on these so-called 'EU limited rights' are laid down in the Financial Regulation[40] and the corresponding Delegated Regulation of the Commission.[41] The chapter by Van den Brink describes accurately how the allocation of EU subsidies has evolved during the most recent 'programme periods' of the EU. In particular, the current Financial Regulation and the corresponding Delegated Regulation contain rather specific provisions on allocation criteria, in particular prescribing the tender procedure as the allocation procedure to be applied. The impact of EU law on the allocation of limited subsidies can be characterised as a manifestation of a sliding scale:

38 See on composite administration O.J.D.M.L. Jansen and B. Schöndorf-Haubold (eds.), *The European Composite Administration*, Intersentia, Antwerp 2011; A. Von Bogdandy and Ph. Dann, 'International Composite Administration: Conceptualizing Multi-Level and Network Aspects in the Exercise of International Public Authority' (2008) *German Law Journal*, 2013; H.C.H. Hofmann and A.H. Türk (eds.), *Legal Challenges in EU Administrative Law*, Edward Elgar, Cheltenham 2009.

39 See for the award of frequencies for mobile satellite services at an EU-wide level the chapter by Oberst in this book.

40 Regulation (EU, Euratom) No 966/2012 of the European Parliament and of the Council of 25 October 2012 on the financial rules applicable to the general budget of the Union and repealing Council Regulation (EC, Euratom) No 1605/2002 [2012] OJ L 298/1 (hereinafter Financial Regulation).

41 Commission Delegated Regulation (EU) No 1268/2012 of 29 October 2012 on the rules of application of Regulation (EU, Euratom) No 966/2012 of the European Parliament and of the Council on the financial rules applicable to the general budget of the Union [2012] OJ L 362/1 (hereinafter Delegated Regulation).

whereas until recently, the rules of the Financial Regulation covered 'direct administration' by EU institutions only, the current rules include 'shared management' by national authorities as well,[42] although it is still unclear what this extension means exactly for national authorities when allocating (European) subsidies. Although there is still a difference in regulatory intensity as to the granting of subsidies *vis-à-vis* the award of public contracts,[43] both the granting of subsidies and the award of public contracts are governed by some general budgetary principles, e.g. the principle of sound financial management (including the principles of economy, efficiency and effectiveness[44]) and the principle of transparency, which may shed particular light on the allocation of these categories of limited rights.[45]

Outside the scope of the Financial Regulation, European administrative law is constantly changing as well. Relevant in this respect is the European Parliament resolution concerning a Law of Administrative Procedure of the European Union.[46] This resolution requests the Commission to submit a proposal for a regulation on a European Law of Administrative Procedure, which should apply to the Union's institutions, bodies, offices and agencies ('the Union's administration') in their relations with the public.[47] According to this resolution, the intended regulation should at least include the principle of equal treatment and non-discrimination and the principle of transparency. However, the regulation may even include more detailed general provisions on the allocation of limited rights, as the ReNEUAL Model Rules on EU Administrative Procedure show.[48]

It follows from the developments described above that *spillover* effects to allocations of limited rights by administrative authorities in Member States should not be excluded. As for the Financial Regulation, one can assume that these rules influence national subsidy practice as well, given the fact that national authorities executing national subsidy schemes are often selected to implement European subsidy schemes as well, while (partly) using the same procedural rules for both tasks. Therefore, these rules, though directed towards the EU institutions may serve as a starting point for the design of allocation procedures by Member States in order to comply with fundamental principles of equal treatment and transparency. Likewise, the European Parliament has emphasised that a European Law of Administrative Procedure could strengthen a

42 Article 59(1) Financial Regulation.

43 The rules on procurement are laid down in title V of the Financial Regulation, the rules on grants are to be found in Title VI.

44 Article 30 Financial Regulation.

45 With regard to budgetary matters, this obligation of transparency is essentially intended to preclude any risk of favouritism or arbitrariness on the part of the budgetary authority. Cf. Article 31 Financial Regulation. According to the General Court, this principle of transparency, because of its *fundamental* nature, applied to the procedure for awarding grants from the Community budget even although the applicable Financial Regulation of 21 December 1977 did not mention this principle expressly (Case T-297/05, *IPK International* [2011] ECR II-1859, para. 123).

46 European Parliament resolution concerning a Law of Administrative Procedure of the European Union of 15 January 2013 with recommendations to the Commission on a Law of Administrative Procedure of the European Union (2012/2024(INL)).

47 See further P. Craig, 'A General Law on Administrative Procedure, Legislative Competence and Judicial Competence' (2013) *European Public Law*, 503.

48 For more detail, see the chapter by Van Ommeren.

spontaneous convergence of national administrative law and thus strengthen the process of integration.[49]

5.3. *Allocation by Member States*

EU law may, either by way of specific rules or by general principles, directly influence the allocation of limited rights by Member States' authorities, irrespective of whether these limited rights have a national or a European origin. With regard to limited rights with a national origin, like gambling licences, Member States will 'only' have to respect basic EU principles while designing their authorisation scheme and taking allocation decisions. The key issue is how these basic EU principles should be translated into more specific allocation rules. This issue will be considered separately below for public procurement law, internal market law and competition law (including State aid), although these areas overlap each other in practice.

5.3.1. Public Procurement Law

Both chronologically and analytically, public procurement law might be a very useful starting point to explore the possibilities for a generalised legal theory on the allocation of limited rights. While starting in the 1970s with some (general) requirements on the award of public contracts,[50] the 1990s showed not only a modernised and detailed update of the old directives,[51] but also an extension of these rules to public contracts for the provision of services.[52] The adoption in 2004 of one general directive on the award of public contracts seemed to complete this process of generalisation,[53] but the recent adoption of a new directive on the award of public contracts[54] and a separate Concessions Directive[55] show that the process of generalisation and fine-tuning is an ongoing process.

49 European Parliament resolution concerning a Law of Administrative Procedure of the European Union of 15 January 2013 with recommendations to the Commission on a Law of Administrative Procedure of the European Union (2012/2024(INL)).

50 Council Directive 71/305/EEC of 26 July 1971 concerning the co-ordination of procedures for the award of public works contracts [1971] OJ L 185/5, and Council Directive 77/62/EEC of 21 December 1976 coordinating procedures for the award of public supply contracts [1977] OJ L 13/1.

51 Council Directive 93/36/EEC of 14 June 1993 coordinating procedures for the award of public supply contracts [1993] OJ L 199/54, and Council Directive 93/37/EEC of 14 June 1993 concerning the coordination of procedures for the award of public works contracts [1993] OJ L 199/54.

52 Council Directive 92/50/EEC of 18 June 1992 relating to the coordination of procedures for the award of public service contracts [1992] OJ L 209/1.

53 Directive 2004/18/EC of the European Parliament and of the Council of 31 March 2004 on the coordination of procedures for the award of public works contracts, public supply contracts and public service contracts [2004] OJ L 134/114. A special directive has been adopted for procurement procedures of entities operating in the water, energy, transport and postal services sectors: Directive No 2004/17/EC [2004] OJ L 134/1.

54 Directive 2014/24/EU of the European Parliament and of the Council of 26 February 2014 on public procurement and repealing Directive 2004/18/EC [2014] OJ L 94/65.

55 Directive 2014/23/EU of the European Parliament and of the Council of 26 February 2014 on the award of concession contracts [2014] OJ L 94/1.

Despite the appeal to extrapolate the extensive set of public procurement rules to other areas of limited rights, Jansen points out in his contribution that allocation rules cannot be fully understood without their particular context. In the case of public procurement law, this particular context is determined by public contracts. These public contracts consist of 'payment rights' that are awarded to market parties as consideration for the supply of goods or services. In this regard, it is necessary to keep in mind that the specific two-fold objective of the EU rules in the field of public procurement has always been to ensure the free movement of services and the opening up to undistorted competition in the Member States.[56] Consequently, only in as far as other areas of limited rights have these objectives in common, the rules on public procurement might be a useful starting point to develop a more general and consistent theory on the allocation of limited rights.

To illustrate this tendency of extrapolation *and* its restrictions,[57] the Court's case-law on the obligation of transparency is illuminating. Within the public procurement directives, rather detailed rules on transparency and advertising have always played a prominent role in order to guarantee potential tenderers equal opportunities to win the tender. However, the CJEU has held that a similar obligation of transparency applies – as a corollary of the fundamental freedoms in general (Articles 49 and 56 TFEU) and the principle of equal treatment in particular – outside the scope of public contracts as well, first to service concessions (2000)[58] and recently to limited authorisations (2011). According to the CJEU, this obligation of transparency is a 'mandatory prior condition' of the right of a Member State to award to an operator the exclusive right to carry on an economic activity, irrespective of the method of selecting that operator, since the effects of an exclusive licence on undertakings established in other Member States and potentially interested in that activity are the same as those of a service concession contract.[59] However, although this obligation of transparency excludes the absence of any call for competition,[60] it does not require an invitation to tender as prescribed by the public procurement directives. Instead, it is sufficient in case of limited authorisation schemes that the criteria of these schemes are *sufficiently advertised*.[61]

With regard to legal protection, public procurement law plays a similar catalysing role. The remedies directive in public procurement law seeks to combine the need for effective and rapid remedies in procurement procedures with general EU principles of

56 Case 26/03, *Stadt Halle and RPL Lochau* [2005] ECR I-1, para. 44; Case C-454/06, *Pressetext Nachrichtenagentur* [2008] ECR I-4401, para. 31.

57 Into more detail on the relationship between public contracts, concessions and limited authorisations, See C.J. Wolswinkel, 'From public contracts to limited authorisations and vice versa. Exploring general award requirements from the EU Court's corollary approach' (2015) 24 (5) *Public Procurement Law Review*, 137.

58 Case C-324/98, *Telaustria and Telefonadress* [2000] ECR I-10745, paras. 61–62.

59 Case C-203/08, *Sporting Exchange* [2009] ECR I-4695, para. 47, and Case C-64/08, *Engelmann* [2010] ECR I-8219, para. 53.

60 Case C-458/03, *Parking Brixen* [2005] ECR I-8585, para. 50.

61 Case C-203/08, *Sporting Exchange* [2009] ECR I-4695, paras. 51–55.

effective legal protection, effectiveness and equivalence.[62] Solutions found in this area of law may inspire more general reflections on legal protection issues concerning the allocation of limited rights.

5.3.2. Internal Market Law

The fundamental freedoms of movement, especially the freedom to provide services (Article 56 TFEU) and the freedom of establishment (Article 49 TFEU) have proven to be very important in the regulation of the allocation of limited rights, in particular limited authorisations. This holds first of all for sector-specific directives that have been adopted in order to facilitate the freedoms of service provision or establishment in a particular area. These directives identify limited authorisation schemes as a *separate* category of authorisation schemes with an additional set of requirements.[63] However, limited authorisation schemes have also been evaluated under the general provisions of the TFEU. However, as the chapter by Hatzopoulos unveils, what matters for the CJEU is the impact on the freedom of movement. Consequently, the dividing line between non-limited and limited authorisations has not always been drawn very clearly by the CJEU, just like the line between public contracts, concessions and (limited) authorisations. Moreover, this chapter gives rise to the conjecture that important EU 'principles' like the principle of mutual recognition, cannot be applied one-on-one in the case of limited authorisation schemes, as mutual recognition of authorisations might thwart a limited authorisation scheme in a Member State.

Whereas we saw already in Section 4 that the EU legislature does not seem to contribute much to the development of detailed rules on the allocation of limited rights, the role of the CJEU seems to be expanding. First of all, case law has made clear that a ceiling should be considered a restriction to the freedom of movement *additional* to the restriction following from a prior authorisation scheme as such: an undertaking satisfying all other granting criteria may be refused an authorisation with single reference to this limitation.[64] In order to be justified, this limitation should comply with the general requirements of non-discrimination, justification by an overriding reason of public interest, suitability and necessity. Although the exact relevance of these requirements in practice is far from clear when it comes to a limitation of the number of available authorisations, Wolswinkel shows that the CJEU seems to be increasingly prepared to translate the general requirements of suitability and necessity into more specific allocation rules to evaluate the allocation of limited rights. However, it would go too far to derive a general hierarchy between allocation procedures from the fundamental

62 Directive 2007/66/EC of the European Parliament and of the Council of 11 December 2007 amending Council Directives 89/665/EEC and 92/13/EEC with regard to improving the effectiveness of review procedures concerning the award of public contracts [2007] OJ L 335/31.

63 See for example Directive 94/22/EEC of the European Parliament and of the Council of 30 May 1994 on the conditions for granting and using authorisations for the prospection, exploration and production of hydrocarbons [1994] OJ L 164/3.

64 Joined Cases C-570/07 and C-571/07, *Blanco Pérez and Chao Gómez* [2009] ECR I-4629, paras. 54–61.

freedoms, as such a hierarchy would be liable to restrict the fundamental freedoms even more.

The Services Directive, which applies to almost all services, gives no reason to assume such a general hierarchy either. Nonetheless, it is worth emphasising that this directive contains some general provisions on limited authorisation schemes, in particular with regard to the need for a transparent and impartial selection procedure and to the duration of limited authorisations. With regard to duration, the general rule is that limited authorisations – in *contrast* with non-limited authorisations – should be granted for a *limited* period of time.[65] Although several other allocation issues remain unanswered in the Services Directive, e.g. the tradability of limited authorisations, this directive endorses at least the need for *and* the possibilities of a generalised theory of the allocation of limited rights.

Both the CJEU in its case-law under the fundamental freedoms and the EU legislature in the Services Directive seem to worry most about discrimination of new entrants. This is not surprising, as new entrants will usually be undertakings from other Member States, as a result of which discrimination of new entrants amounts to discrimination on grounds of nationality, which affects the cornerstone of the fundamental freedoms. Interestingly, the chapter by Den Ouden and Tjepkema shows that the ECHR seems to give more weight to the interests of current holders of limited rights, usually incumbent parties *vis-à-vis* the interests of new entrants, at least if (limited) authorisations are withdrawn and subsequently re-allocated. Thus, the legal regime of Article 1 First Protocol on protection of property might give rise to the development of additional rules on the allocation of limited rights, supplementary to, or even conflicting with, the allocation rules deriving from the EU fundamental freedoms of movement.

5.3.3. Competition Law (Including State Aid Law)

Apart from internal market law and the fundamental freedoms of movement, competition law may be relevant for the allocation of limited rights. First, according to Article 106(1) TFEU, Member States shall neither enact nor maintain in force any measure contrary to the rules contained in the Treaties – in particular the prohibition of discrimination on grounds of nationality[66] and the rules on competition[67] – in the case of undertakings to which Member States grant *special or exclusive* rights. Since limited rights (might) classify as special or exclusive rights, this Treaty provision seems to cover limited rights in particular. Although the granting of limited rights does not as such result in abuse, for example, by one or more undertakings of a dominant position within (a substantial part of) the internal market,[68] it should be realised that such an abuse might occur more

[65] See the Articles 11 and 12 Services Directive. For more on these provisions in the Services Directive: C.J. Wolswinkel, 'The Allocation of a Limited Number of Authorisations. Some General Requirements from European Law' (2009) 2(2) *Review of European Administrative Law*, 61.

[66] Article 18 TFEU.

[67] Articles 101 to 109 TFEU.

[68] Article 102 TFEU.

easily in the case of limited rights. In order to avoid such an abuse, the CJEU has emphasised the need for 'equality of opportunity', which may have important consequences for a consistent design of allocation procedures *over time*, apart from the need for transparent allocation procedures at a specific moment.

The need for transparency has also emerged in the area of State aid law.[69] Although the well-known criteria applying to the classification of measures as State aid, do not refer to allocation issues explicitly, this area cannot be neglected when developing a general legal theory on the allocation of limited rights. For rights which are fully or partly regulated by EU law, the possible influence of the EU State aid rules may follow explicitly from the applicable EU legal framework, as is for example the case for emission rights[70] and European subsidies.[71] But also by lack of such explicit reference in EU legislation, or when limited rights are not regulated by EU legislation, the State aid rules will have to be taken into account when allocating these rights. According to consistent case law of the CJEU, the concept of State aid 'embraces not only positive benefits, such as subsidies, but also measures which, in various forms, mitigate the charges which are normally included in the budget of an undertaking and which, therefore, without being subsidies in the strict sense of the word, are similar in character and have the same effect'.[72] Thus, this broad interpretation of State aid may cause the allocation of limited rights to come within the realm of State aid law. In fact, a variety of allocation scenarios can come within the scope of State aid, e.g. free allocation of rights instead of selling or auctioning them,[73] over-allocations of tradable rights, allocations based on discretionary powers without objective criteria or based on preferential terms for certain undertakings or sectors[74] and allocations of comparable limited authorisations with different fees.[75] Adriaanse shows, however, that it is still hard to draw some general conclusions from the CJEU's case-by-case approach. The 2014 draft Commission Communication on the definition of State aid law may provide more guidance in this respect, emphasising the need for transparent and competitive allocation procedures in order to *prevent* State aid. In sum, it can be concluded that State aid law is still waiting for a hallmark judgment on the allocation of limited rights.

At the same time, Adriaanse shows that State aid law sheds some interesting light on issues of legal protection. If a measure qualifies as State aid, a whole proactive set of rules,

69 Article 107 and further TFEU.

70 See para. 49 of the preamble of Directive 2009/29/EC of 23 April 2009 amending Directive 2003/87/EC so as to improve and extend the greenhouse gas emission allowance trading scheme of the Community [2009] OJ L 140/63.

71 See Regulation (EC) No 1083/2006 of 11 July 2006 laying down general provisions on the European Regional Development Fund, the European Social Fund and the Cohesion Fund and repealing Regulation (EC) No 1260/1999 [2006] OJ L 2010/25. In the same way the proposal from the Commission to amend this regulation (COM (2013) 246 final).

72 See Case C-73/11 P, *Frucona Košice a.s v. Commission*, ECLI:EU:C:2013:32, para. 69.

73 See Case C-279/08 P, *Commission v. The Netherlands* [2011] ECR I-7671.

74 See A.T. Seinen, 'State aid aspects of the EU Emission Trading Scheme: the second trading period' (2007) 3 *Competition Policy Newsletter*, pp. 100–105.

75 See Case C-431/07 P, *Bouygues and Bouygues Télécom v. Commission* [2009] ECR I-2665.

procedures and powers enters into force.[76] The following procedure, during which the Member State concerned is not allowed to put its proposed measures into effect, may take at least a few months. Especially in allocation procedures on limited rights, in which different parties with parallel or opposite interests often have an interest in an early outcome, this delayed decision-making may cause problems. However, breaching the procedural State aid rules could cause even bigger problems, since unlawfully granted State aid plus interest may have to be recovered from the beneficiaries, and damages might have to be paid. The rigorous case law of the CJEU in this respect limits the opportunities for recipients of unlawful State aid to oppose recovery.[77] Simultaneously, the CJEU's case law offers opportunities for competitors of State aid recipients to rely on directly effective EU law provisions before national courts in order to appeal against unlawful State aid.[78] In the search for general rules and principles underlying the possibilities for legal protection when allocating limited rights, this State aid case law has to be taken into account.

6. Bottom-Up Approach: Comparative Law Perspectives

The top-down approach adopted in the previous section shows, on the one hand, that several legal concepts of EU law are relevant for (a consistent approach to) the allocation of limited rights, but, on the other hand, that the limitations resulting from EU law should not be overstated. In other words, even if spillover effects of more detailed provisions in EU law are certainly not to be excluded, Member States are not entirely bound by EU law in the ways they limit the number of rights available and how they allocate these limited rights. Consequently, Member States still enjoy an (extensive) amount of discretion as to the design of allocation procedures for limited rights.

These conclusions mark the need for a *comparative* view in addition to the top-down approach followed in the previous section. This bottom-up approach completes our search for relevant rules and principles for a general legal theory on the allocation of limited rights: as far as general rules in EU law on the allocation of limited rights are lacking, 'best performances' derived from practices in different Member States or specific areas of law, may be helpful in optimising the authorities' discretion with regard to the allocation of a certain limited right.

In order to facilitate the identification of best practices under a comparative bottom-up approach, we distinguish two levels of comparison. First, it is useful to distinguish between several limited rights with regard to their 'degree of Europeanisation', *i.e.* the extent to which the allocation of these rights is subject to (specific) EU law. At one end of this sliding scale, there are limited rights which are entirely governed by EU law and therefore leave no room for discretion to Member States. An example of this is the granting of subsidies in the case of 'direct management' (Section 5.2). At the other end of

76 Article 108 TFEU.

77 Case C-24/95, *Land Rheinland-Pfalz v Alcan Deutschland Gmb* [1997] ECR I-1591.

78 Case C-39/94, *Syndicat français de l'Express international (SFEI) and others v La Poste and others* [1996] ECR I-3547.

this scale, there are limited rights that lack any connection with relevant EU rules, e.g. limited rights with regard to rules on business opening hours[79] or national authorisations or subsidies without any cross-border impact.[80] In the absence of any boundaries imposed by EU law, the allocation of such limited rights is to be guided by national legal rules and principles, like the principle of legal certainty or the principle of due care.[81]

In addition to this *first* level of comparison between sector-specific areas of law, the *second* level of comparison is that of the Member States: how do they use their discretion within a sector-specific area of law? Given the existence of more or less discretion as to the design of allocation procedures, a comparison between countries may generate interesting and fruitful insights for an optimal design of allocation procedures.

Within this book, as to the first dimension of comparison, three kinds of limited rights have been selected on the basis of their degree of Europeanisation: emission allowances, authorisations for the use of frequency space and gambling licences. With regard to these three areas of law, reports on allocation practices in seven Member States have been collected: France, Germany, Greece, Italy, the Netherlands, Romania and Spain.[82] This selection does not only provide a rich variety of allocation practices, but also allows taking into account the different legal traditions that might be relevant from a conceptual point of view.

As regards the allocation of emission allowances, the overview chapter by Rønne shows clearly the intensity of EU legislation that has governed the EU Emissions Trading System from its very start. It is worth pointing out that this regulatory framework has been adopted to pursue environmental objectives rather than to ensure the functioning of the internal market. Nonetheless, there are still new tendencies towards a more centralised allocation of allowances. One example is the uniform prescription of the auction as the allocation procedure to be applied. Moreover, the relevant EU legislation provides for one uniform auction platform which facilitates the allocation of emission allowances at an EU-wide level.

A similar development towards a more centralised regulatory framework for the allocation of limited rights seems to be taking place in the area of radio spectrum management. Currently, this area is governed by a set of directives, known as the 'new common regulatory framework', which still leaves room for Member States to make

79 These rules classify as selling arrangements falling outside the scope of the free movement of goods (Article 34 TFEU). Cf. Joined Cases C-401/92 and C-402/92, *Tankstation 't Heukske and Boermans* [1994] ECR I-2199, paras. 12–14, and especially Joined Cases C-69/93 and C-258/93, *Punto Casa and PPV* [1994] ECR I-2355, paras. 12–14.

80 EU law provisions on the fundamental freedoms do not apply to situations where all the relevant facts are confined within a single Member State. Cf. Case C-245/09, *Omalet* [2010] ECR I-13771, para. 12.

81 See the chapter by Van Ommeren in this book.

82 See the accompanying book P. Adriaanse, F. van Ommeren, W. den Ouden and J. Wolswinkel (eds.), *Scarcity and the State II. Member State Reports on Gambling Licences, Radio Frequencies and CO_2 Emission Permits*, Intersentia, Antwerp 2016. The only Member State report lacking in this book is a report on gambling law in Italy, since this Italian legislation has been described already quite abundantly in the numerous cases of the CJEU in the last decade. For more detail, see also the chapter by Van den Bogaert and Cuyvers in this book.

their own choices in the allocation of individual rights of use for radio frequencies. However, Oberst sketches several recent developments in the EU regulation of spectrum management that might foster further harmonisation. At the same time, this area of law still shows diverging choices between Member States, for example on the treatment of new entrants versus incumbents. After all, it seems that – as a paradox – more detailed regulation at EU level does not necessarily imply a restriction of the regulatory choices of the Member States.

In the absence of any secondary legislation, the area of gambling law, by contrast, is governed by primary EU law only, in particular the freedom to provide services and the freedom of establishment. Given this rather general legal framework, it should not be surprising that Member States are allowed to make diverging choices with regard to the limitation and allocation of gambling authorisations, e.g. by maintaining legal monopolies or by introducing limited authorisation schemes with minimal geographic distances between establishments. Nonetheless, Member States' discretion is not unlimited. In this respect, Van den Bogaert and Cuyvers show that the CJEU is prepared to tighten up when applying the general requirements of suitability and necessity: gambling activities that are subject to a limited authorisation scheme, should be restricted in a consistent and coherent manner in order to avoid hypocrisy in the allocation policy.

The first contours resulting from the description of these three areas of law are a useful starting point to develop a more complete picture of the allocation of limited rights in different areas of EU law. In particular, by considering these three kinds of limited rights as specific points on a sliding scale, other limited rights[83] could be compared with these examples as well. By doing so, it is not only possible to identify best practices in other areas of law, but also to develop general principles that reappear in any allocation of limited rights, irrespective of the sector-specific legislation and irrespective of the Member States. These principles may contribute to the development of a general legal theory on the allocation of limited public rights in addition to the elements resulting from the top-down approach.

7. Concluding Remarks

This introductory chapter to the book *Scarcity and the State* seeks to demonstrate the need for a consistent and general legal theory on the allocation of limited rights by administrative authorities. In this regard, we have started from two fundamental assumptions. First, EU law plays an important role in the allocation of limited public rights, both at EU level and at national level. Secondly, all EU Member States deal with the allocation of limited public rights in various policy fields. In order to identify allocation rules and principles facilitating a general legal theory of the allocation of limited rights in the EU and its Member States, we have elaborated on these two

83 Examples include the granting of authorisations for exploring and producing hydrocarbons, the award of rights of use with regard to water as a scarce resource and the grant of concessions for public transport.

assumptions by way of a threefold approach: a conceptual perspective, a top-down (EU law) perspective and a (comparative) bottom-up perspective.

From this introductory analysis we can conclude that although several legal concepts of EU law appear to be relevant for (a consistent and general theory of) the allocation of limited rights, and tendencies of harmonisation can be observed in particular fields of law, the guidance provided by EU law should not be overstated. Influences from EU law occur in different ways, but are fragmented rather than structured. In some areas of law, European institutions or national authorities should comply with specific allocation rules explicitly provided for, whereas in other areas influence comes along the lines of the basic TFEU provisions on the internal market and competition. In other words, Member States are not entirely bound by EU law in the ways in which they limit the number of rights available and how they allocate these limited rights. Having said that, spillover effects from more detailed provisions are certainly not to be excluded. Moreover, this introductory analysis makes clear that a *consistent* analysis of the allocation of limited rights does not necessarily entail the application of the same *uniform* set of rules to all allocation issues. Instead of generalising without any restraint specific allocation rules applicable in certain policy fields or certain Member States, the particularities of each allocation context may limit the possibilities for expansion.

In more general terms, we submit that the scarcity perspective provided for by the allocation of limited rights offers new and surprising insights; not only into allocation topics, but also into other traditional topics of administrative law, for example legal protection or mutual recognition. While transparency is an essential focal point within this scarcity perspective, this chapter demonstrates that allocation concerns more than just transparency.

It is clear that the lens provided by this scarcity perspective, needs to be polished even further. To that end, the comparative exercises on the allocation of limited rights, both between areas of law and between Member States (as well as between Member States and the EU), are worth continuing within legal *academia*. What is more, however, both the legislature and the judiciary can play an important role in developing a general legal theory on the allocation of limited rights that takes into account the peculiar characteristics of these rights.

Luis Arroyo Jiménez
and Dolores Utrilla
Fernández-Bermejo*

CHAPTER 2. THE ALLOCATION OF LIMITED PUBLIC RIGHTS: AN ANALYTICAL AND CONSTITUTIONAL APPROACH

1. Introduction

The protection and neat allocation of certain categories of scarce resources has traditionally been a defining task for public authorities. Both in the EU and in its Member States, administrative law regulates the creation and the allocation of different types of limited public rights in rather diverse policy areas. To illustrate the extent to which this is a widespread and heterogeneous reality, several examples can be brought up: allocation of greenhouse gas emission permits; award of public contracts; concession of subsidies and other State aids; the granting of public employment places; procedures for alienation of certain public assets; and, finally, the allocation of scarce entitlement administrative decisions (authorizations, licences, quotas, permits, concessions and so on), the object of which can also be quite diverse: provision of a (public) service, utilization of public goods, production of a certain amount of goods or, more generally, the development of a given activity under certain conditions.

These manifestations of the administrative activity of allocation of limited public rights are subject to their own specific legal regime. The pluralism in the regulation of the corresponding administrative procedures and decisions stems from the existing differences among the rights to be allocated in each case (contracts, authorizations, property rights, subsidies, public benefits...). Even within each of these manifestations, the regulation of this kind of administrative activity must conform, both to the specific features of the sector in which it develops, as well as to the relevant demands it imposes on administrative law understood as an instrument of social direction (*Steuerungsinstrument*). The differential treatment of this administrative activity can also find its basis on EU law (for instance, with regards to public procurement: Directives 23, 24 and 25/2014/EU), or in the relevant domestic constitution of each Member State [for

* Luis Arroyo Jiménez is Professor of administrative law at University of Castilla-La Mancha, Spain. Dolores Utrilla Fernández-Bermejo is Assistant of administrative law and research fellow of the Center for European Studies at University of Castilla-La Mancha, Spain.

example, Articles 103(3) and 45 of the Spanish Constitution define specific requirements in relation to access to public sector posts and the rational use of natural resources].

In spite of the fact that these regulations have been produced from a sector-based perspective, it can be noticed that the various kinds of limited public rights to which they refer raise some common regulatory problems. In addition, the solutions provided in response thereto by special administrative law tend to converge, at least to a certain extent. This can be explained by the fact that in all of these areas the Administration performs a similar activity consisting in the allocation of scarce resources in situations of concurrency. Due to this structural similarity, the legal regime of these different manifestations of administrative action tends to present some similar characteristics, yet it still features diversity and pluralism. Moreover, from a normative standpoint, it can be argued that these transversal elements account for the embodiment of certain constitutional principles, and thus they should be regarded and systematically developed as part of general administrative law.[1]

Indeed, the proper dogmatic treatment of this type of administrative activity requires the development of proposals for interpretation and improvement of the sector-based regulation corresponding to each of the manifestations of the relevant category. However, alongside this it is also necessary to incorporate the administrative activity of allocation of limited public rights to the system of administrative law. Such an approach will provide a better understanding of current law as well as useful items for its review and improvement. With that aim, this contribution is specifically focused on the analytical and constitutional premises for the development of a comprehensive theory on the administrative allocation of limited public rights. Therefore, both the scope and the main forms of this kind of administrative activity (Section 2) and some of its main constitutional requirements (Section 3) will next be tackled.

2. Analytical Approach

The boundaries of the administrative activity of allocation of limited public rights are to be marked by taking into account two criteria. The first one refers to the subject matter or object[2] of the rights to be allocated (below 2.1), while the second alludes to how these legal positions are awarded to the selected candidates (below 2.2). The combination of both elements allows for a complete picture of the type of administrative activity under examination, enabling its differentiation from other kinds of administrative action that may seem somewhat similar.[3] These conceptual or analytical elements, which have

1 On the methodological premises, see E. Schmidt-Aßmann, *Das Allgemeine Verwaltungsrecht als Ordnungsidee*, Springer, Berlin 2004, pp. 10 ff., 43 ff.

2 The terms 'subject matter' and 'object' will henceforward be used as synonymous (so for instance R. Alexy, 'Rights and liberties as concepts' in M. Rosenfeld and A. Sajó (eds.), *The Oxford Handbook of Comparative Constitutional Law*, OUP, Oxford 2012, p. 285).

3 On these analytical premises, see L. Arroyo and D. Utrilla, 'La actividad administrativa de adjudicación de derechos limitados en número. Bases conceptuales y metodológicas' in L. Arroyo and D. Utrilla (eds.),

already been briefly described in the introductory Chapter of this book, are next examined in order to define the contours and the main manifestations of the administrative activity of allocation of limited public rights.

2.1. *Limited Public Rights*

From the perspective of its object, the administrative activity under consideration is characterized by reference to the attribution of legal positions which simultaneously show two main features: they are subjective public rights and they are limited in number.[4]

2.1.1. Subjective public rights

Within this context, the notion of subjective public right is used in its broadest sense, to refer to any active legal position held by a subject *vis-à-vis* public authorities, irrespective of their structure and of the degree of protection they provide to the rightholders. It is necessary to separately refer to these three dimensions of the right to be allocated: its public character, the degree of protection that it provides, and its legal structure.

A subjective right has a public character if the holder of the reciprocal legal obligation is a public subject (or a private person who is assigned the exercise of a public function or service for and behalf of its holder). Sometimes the law enables the transfer of the awarded rights to third parties. In certain circumstances, the creation of a secondary market is precisely the goal pursued by public authorities when they decide to limit the number of rights to allocate.[5] However, this does not turn the awarded right in a legal position of a private nature, because what is incorporated into the private law domain is a subjective right *vis-à-vis* a public authority.

Secondly, once it has been granted (*ex post* perspective), the active legal position can provide different degrees of protection to its holder. The allocated position may have a full character (perfect subjective right), or it may be conditioned (mere legitimate interest). However, the limitation in the number of rights to grant brings along that prior to the allocation (*ex ante* perspective), the legal position of the applicants is always defined as a legitimate interest, since scarcity prevents such positions from functioning as definitive reasons, i.e., regardless of the outcome of the allocation procedure. This applies regardless of the fact that, at times, such interest is connected with the exercise of a pre-existing right, eventually with constitutional rank (for example, the position of a college applicant where education is a constitutional right, or of an applicant for an authorization related to the exercise of a constitutional freedom).

La administración de la escasez. Fundamentos de la actividad administrativa de adjudicación de derechos limitados en número, Marcial Pons, Madrid 2015, pp. 25 ff.

4 See the chapter by Adriaanse, van Ommeren, den Ouden and Wolswinkel in this book.

5 J. Esteve Pardo, 'El mercado de títulos administrativos' in L. Cosculluela (ed.), *Estudios de derecho público económico. Libro homenaje al prof. Dr. D. Sebastián Martín-Retortillo*, Civitas, Madrid 2003, pp. 743 ff.

Thirdly, it is here immaterial whether the public right has its correlate in an obligation to do something, to refrain from doing something or to give something on the part of a public entity. The examples offered at the beginning of this work demonstrate the considerable heterogeneity of legal positions that may be subject to an administrative decision of allocation. One possible systematization could be the following:[6]

(i) Allocation of faculties for the exercise of freedoms, i.e. rights to negative actions of a public power. In spite of the different names used by special administrative law to refer to them (authorizations, concessions, licences, permits, waivers, allowances, etc.), they can be labelled as limited authorizations in the broad sense,[7] or, more precisely, as limited entitlement administrative decisions.[8] Their legal regime is characterized by a great diversity, but they all are legal entitlements conferred on a firm or individual by the public Administration through the use of a public power prerogative. The exercise of the freedom triggered by the right to be allocated may refer to starting an activity (entitlement administrative decisions in the strict sense), or may refer to a particular way of developing it, defined by reference to a certain volume of activity, production or external effects. As further references within this study will show, limited entitlement administrative decisions are a qualified reference field for the development of a general theory on the allocation of limited public rights.
(ii) Allocation of public benefits or services, i.e. rights to positive actions by a public power where the potential demand for them exceeds the available supply, so that the Administration assumes the task of their assignment (for instance, selection procedures for admission to colleges or for the provision of certain medical services).
(iii) Allocation of *in rem* rights of use and enjoyment exercised over third-party property,[9] like those that entitle their holders to use public goods (for example, rights for the privative use of the spectrum where it is set up as a public good).
(iv) Allocation of credit claims, such as subsidies or other types of aids offered by a public body.
(v) Allocation of complex legal positions that comprise both rights and duties, obligations or charges (for example, the position of the recipient of a grant, the winner of a public contract or a public employee).

6 A partially different one in the chapter by Adriaanse, Van Ommeren, Den Ouden and Wolswinkel in this book.

7 European Parliament and Council Directive 2006/123/EC of 12 December 2006 on services in the internal market [2006] OJ L376/36, Recital (39): 'The concept of "authorization scheme" should cover, inter alia, the administrative procedures for granting authorizations, licences, approvals or concessions, and also the obligation, in order to be eligible to exercise the activity, to be registered as a member of a profession or entered in a register, roll or database, to be officially appointed to a body or to obtain a card attesting to membership of a particular profession'.

8 The use of this expression in a research on general administrative law in Europe can be useful due to the pluralism of European administrative law traditions within this context: while in EU law and in some national legal orders (e.g. UK) all administrative decisions with such an entitlement effect are called "authorizations" or "licences", in other Member States (e. g. Germany, France, Spain or Italy) the term "authorization" is reserved for a specific kind of them.

9 L. Diez-Picazo, *Fundamentos del Derecho civil patrimonial, vol. I*, Civitas, Madrid 2007, pp. 75 ff.

2.1.2. Scarcity

The second distinctive feature of the object of the administrative activity under consideration is that the rights to grant are limited in number, and therefore the Administration must allocate them within a context of concurrence. The reasons explaining the scarcity (and which may justify it, where appropriate) can be systematized in a threefold scheme.[10] Firstly, the exercise of some activities requires the use of certain resources that are scarce due to natural or technical reasons. This can lead public authorities to exclude decisions on their allocation from the scope of private autonomy and to subject them to public law regimes in order to ensure they are used efficiently. The configuration of natural scarcity and its management may be heterogeneous: the relevant scarce resource can be a public good (for example, the spectrum), a private property (such as a private infrastructure), or a good not amenable to appropriation (for example, the environmental capacity of reception of greenhouse gases, which can be regarded as a *res nullius*). Secondly, scarcity may result from a decision adopted by public authorities to correct the relevant market's functioning. Scarcity arises here from a political decision based on a certain interpretation of the requirements stemming from the public interest, such as the need to correct a market failure related to the efficient allocation of resources (for example, a natural monopoly, a situation of excessive competition or an externality) or to ensure justice in their distribution (securing a certain volume and quality of supply in a given territory, for example).[11] Finally, scarcity may also be rooted in the limited amount of resources demanded or offered by public authorities.[12] In contrast to the preceding cases, in the latter the Administration affects the activity involving the use of scarce resources from the inside of the market where such resources are exchanged. This form of scarcity has two variants, depending on the role played by the Administration in each case. On the one hand, public contracts and public employment places are examples of goods which are scarce due to the restricted nature of the administrative needs to be covered. On the other hand, scarcity may stem from the finite character of the public resource to grant, as exemplified by public subsidies and other monetary transfers as well as by public services the amount or volume of which has been previously limited.

After identifying the different causes of scarcity, attention must also be paid to the way in which it is expressed. First, subjective public rights are limited if the total amount of available rights has been limited in advance and if such an amount is exceeded by the sum of requested rights.[13] In the simplest case each applicant can obtain a single right and scarcity emerges when the number of applicants exceeds the number of rights to grant (e.g. public employment

10 D. Kupfer, *Die Verteilung knapper Ressourcen im Wirtschaftsverwaltungsrecht*, Nomos, Baden-Baden 2005, pp. 103 ff.; M. Martini, *Der Markt als Instrument hoheitlicher Verteilungslenkung. Möglichkeiten und Grenzen einer staatlichen Verwaltung des Mangels durch Marktmechanismen*, Mohr Siebeck, Tübingen 2008, pp. 19 ff.; F. Wollenschläger, *Verteilungsverfahren*, Mohr Siebeck, Tübingen 2010, pp. 1 ff.

11 L. Arroyo, *Libre empresa y títulos habilitantes*, CEPC, Madrid 2004, pp. 444 ff.; A. Ogus, *Regulation. Legal form and economic theory*, Hart, Oxford 2004, pp. 320 ff.

12 Kupfer 2005, pp. 113 ff.

13 Adriaanse, Van Ommeren, Den Ouden and Wolswinkel, Chapter 1 of this book.

places, public contracts). On the contrary, if each applicant can get more than one of such rights, the decisive factor is not the number of applicants but the volume or amount of requested legal positions (e.g. greenhouse emission rights), or the existence of qualitative differences among the needs satisfied by the rights to allocate (e.g. school admissions). Thus, for the purpose of marking boundaries for this kind of administrative activity what matters is that the resource is either limited in the strict (quantitative) sense, so that only some applicants can obtain the requested number of rights, or that it is heterogeneous in nature, i.e., that all applicants may receive rights but these can meet their preferences to a different extent.[14] Scarcity is apparent in case of allocation of public employment places, public contracts, or shares in state companies' capital. Similarly, the prior establishment of a ceiling and its subsequent progressive reduction is one of the central elements of the European trading scheme for greenhouse gases allowances. A previous quantitative limitation also characterizes the granting of subsidies and the admission of users of public services to those centres and facilities the capacity of which is subject to a *numerus clausus* system.

Hence, scarcity is a real premise for the allocation activity and not the mere result of the exercise of the relevant administrative authority. This criterion allows for distinguishing limited public rights schemes from those administrative procedures where the public body is empowered to grant or reject the requested right on a discretionary basis, thus enjoying a scope for assessment which is sometimes called *Entschliessungsermessen*[15] or discretion regarding the *an* of the prerogative.[16] *A priori* limited public rights schemes shall also be differentiated from admission procedures, in which the Administration simply checks whether the applicants meet a set of predetermined requirements, awarding the requested right to each an every applicant who complies with the said requirements.[17] There is no allocation, yet there is admission, where rules governing the attribution of a right set a requirement which only certain applicants meet (for example, a certain degree of expertise or solvency),[18] as long as all subjects in compliance with such a requirement perceive one of the rights to grant.

2.2. *Administrative Allocation*

2.2.1. Scope

The administrative activity analysed herein is conducive to administrative decisions adopted in the exercise of authority powers and through an administrative procedure by

14 J. Elster, *Local Justice. How Institutions Allocate Scarce Goods and Necessary Burdens*, Cambridge University Press, Cambridge 1992, pp. 21 ff.

15 H. Maurer, *Allegemeines Verwaltungsrecht,* C.H. Beck, Munich 2009, pp. 135 ff.

16 J.L. Villar Palasí, *La intervención administrativa en la industria*, Instituto de Estudios Políticos, Madrid 1964, p. 381.

17 W.K.B. Hofstee, 'Allocation by lot: a conceptual and empirical analysis' (1990) 29 (4) *Social Science Information*, 745 ff.; Elster 1992, p. 25.

18 C.J. Wolswinkel, 'The allocation of a limited number of authorisations. Some general requirements from EU law' (2009) 2 *Review of European Administrative Law* 61, 65.

which the Administration grants the available number of rights to one or more applicants. For the purposes of conceptual demarcation of this kind of administrative activity, it is immaterial whether the relevant administrative authority is discretionary or not, in what legal form it is exercised and whether the procedure has a multipolar or bipolar structure (i.e., if all competitors take place in the same allocation procedure, or if the Administration simultaneously conducts several procedures in which only one applicant participates).[19] What characterizes this kind of administrative activity is the existence of a situation of concurrence among applicants the resolution of which rests with the public Administration.

This feature allows to differentiate the allocation of limited public rights from two other close yet different forms of administrative activity. The first one relates to cases where the problem of scarcity is not managed through the limitation of the number of rights and their subsequent administrative allocation, but rather by means of admission procedures such as the ones which have already been mentioned.[20] A clear example is the administrative grant of public benefits or services which entails a distribution of scarce public resources among those subjects who meet the legally required conditions. As can be observed, in this kind of scenarios the Administration identifies the beneficiaries of the services or benefits at stake, but in doing so it does not resolve a situation of genuine concurrence. The reason is that in these sort of contexts the problem of scarcity has already been solved by the law through the definition of the subjective and objective scope of the relevant rights, so that in the subsequent administrative procedure each applicant meeting the relevant conditions will receive a quota or predetermined portion of the granting rights. The second type of contexts are those of allocation of limited public rights by private subjects. Secondary commerce of the awarded rights falls outside the scope of the administrative allocation activity, even when both are closely connected from a substantive standpoint. As regards primary allocation, the decisive criterion is not the public or private nature of the decision-making subject, nor the legal regime (whether public or private law) by which it may be governed in sector-based legislation, but rather the fact that the resources to allocate are public rights. Therefore, there may exist administrative activity of allocation exerted by a private subject to whom such activity has been delegated (for example, a public subsidy indirectly managed by a private collaborating entity).

2.2.2. Allocation criteria

The administrative allocation of scarce resources can be accomplished through the implementation of very different rules. Allocation criteria can be split into two categories, depending on whether the allocation decisions are adopted taking into account the characteristics of the right to assign or those of the different applicants (substantive

19 On the structure of allocation procedures, see the chapters of Wollenschläger and Van Ommeren in this book.

20 Wollenschläger 2010, p. 4.

criteria) or without regard to such considerations (formal criteria).[21] Each of these criteria has specific advantages and disadvantages, particularly from the perspective of their constitutional foundations, and depending *inter alia* on the features of the limited public right at stake and the context where its allocation takes place. It must be taken into account that in most cases the applicable allocation criteria are intensely predetermined by the kind of allocation procedure to be conducted, so that certain procedures distinguish from others precisely based on the relevant allocation criteria.[22]

Some of the most widespread formal criteria are the following: (i) allocation by heads or quotas, so each applicant obtains the same portion of the scarce right, the amount of which is fixed by reference to the total amount of rights to allocate and the number of applicants; (ii) proportional or *pro rata* allocation, according to which scarce rights are distributed among the different candidates on the basis of a common parameter, so that they do not all get an equal amount of resource, but rather an amount proportional to the one applied for in each instance; (iii) drawing of lots or lottery, whereby the scarce rights are randomly allocated, be it directly or alternatively (i.e. as a consequence of the failure of other criteria to justify an allocation decision); (iv) principle of temporal priority ('first come first served'), that results in allocations based on the order of receipt of the different applications and which can also be used in a direct or alternative fashion.

In contrast with formal criteria, material or substantive ones take into account the particular characteristics of the candidates and/or of the project they lodge with regard to the utilization of the resource at stake. The most common substantive criteria account for derivations from the notions of necessity or capacity. On the one hand, limited resources may be allocated to those applicants demonstrating a higher degree of necessity concerning their utilization. This criterion is usual in contexts where the allocation of limited public rights has become independent from the criterion of formal equality, as happens with the public provision of certain welfare services (e.g. housing benefits). On the other hand, the allocation may be performed according to the applicants' aptitude to make better use of the scarce resource from the perspective of one or more given parameters. The comparative assessment ('beauty contest') usually takes into account one or more characteristics of the candidates and/or of their applications (technical ability, reliability...), the relative weight of which can be configured in many different ways. Two allocation criteria regarding the idea of aptitude shall be pointed out. The first one links the ability to efficiently use the scarce resource to temporal parameters, which can refer to the applicants' age, to their experience or to their previous exercise of the same limited public right. The second criterion, which accounts for a defining feature of auctions, connects the aptitude of efficient use of the scarce right with the willingness to pay on the part of the applicants.

21 Martini 2008, pp. 94 ff.; Wollenschläger 2010, pp. 554 ff.

22 For example, the order of receipt of applications is at the same time an allocation criterion and a type of allocation procedure. On the main kinds of allocation procedures, see Chapter 1 in this book by Adriaanse, Van Ommeren, Den Ouden and Wolswinkel.

The diversity of the mentioned criteria clearly shows that the allocation of limited public rights, broadly understood, comprises two subcategories, which lead to different outcomes and the use of which raises different regulatory and constitutional issues. On the one hand, when limited public rights are indivisible their allocation will consist in the selection of one or more applicants, so that the rest of them will be totally rejected. Public contracts, public employment places, entitlement administrative decisions and certain public benefits or services (such as transplants) are clear examples of this category. On the other hand, if the scarce resource is divisible its allocation may also take place through its distribution among the different applicants, so that they all receive a given portion measured in units (e.g. pro rata allocation of a grant) or in time (e.g. turnover among the applicants).[23] These two types of allocation in the broad sense may be designated as, respectively, allocation in the strict sense (or selection), and distribution of limited public rights. When the rights to allocate refer to heterogeneous subject-matters, the distinction between distribution and selection fades away, because even if all interested parties get a portion of the resource, it does not necessarily satisfy their preferences to the same extent.

3. Constitutional Approach

3.1. Justification

The constitutional approach to limited public rights schemes consists in the deduction of normative findings from a set of higher principles which operate as structural building blocks of the legal system to which they belong.[24] Those principles do not only contain legal requirements of administrative regulation, but they also have a systematic function and thus an important role in the development of general administrative law.[25] For that reason, we suggest that this constitutional approach might be useful for the development of a limited public rights general legal framework. As will be observed, this view largely corresponds to what has been termed 'top down approach' to the allocation of limited public rights,[26] even when here the analysis is not restricted to EU law, but extends also to national constitutional law.

In EU Member States, limited public rights schemes are subject to certain constitutional requirements stemming from both EU law and each relevant domestic Constitution. Academic literature has mainly focused on the former, probably due to the fact that the main transformations suffered by the legal framework of this kind of administrative action have their origin in the evolution of EU law, particularly of secondary legislation,[27] and of

23 On the divisibility of the resource, see Elster 1992, p. 22.

24 On the methodological premises, see, among others, A. von Bogdandy, 'Constitutional Principles' in A. von Bogdandy and J. Bast (eds), *Principles of European Constitutional Law*, Hart Publishing, Oxford 2005, pp. 3 ff.

25 Schmidt-Aßmann 2004, pp. 11 ff.

26 See Chapter 1 in this book by Adriaanse, Van Ommeren, Den Ouden and Wolswinkel.

27 Alongside the Public Procurement Directives, see the Services Directive (above n 7); European Parliament and Council Directive 2003/87/EC of 13 October 2003 establishing a scheme for greenhouse

case-law on gambling,[28] and on services concessions.[29] Nonetheless, such transformations have been primarily faced from the perspective of sector-based regulation, competition law, and the internal market, while that of constitutional principles remain less widespread.[30] It is important to note at this point that EU law does not affect the administrative allocation of every limited public right, but only the allocation of some of such rights, and particularly of those which have a greater impact on the functioning of the internal market: public contracts, concessions, authorizations and, to a lesser extent, subsidies.

On the other hand, Member States Constitutions do also contain some general principles which provide for the obligation to design and implement the administrative allocation of limited public rights according to certain criteria.[31] These constitutional principles primarily bind the legislature as long as it is called upon to produce administrative law in the first place, but they also do bind the Administration itself where their decisions cannot be regarded as the plain execution of the legislator's will. Therefore, this set of constitutional principles is also directly binding on the public Administration where

gas emission allowance trading within the Community and amending Council Directive 96/61/EC [2003] OJ L275/32; European Parliament and Council Directive 2009/29/EC of 23 April 2009 amending Directive 2003/87/EC so as to improve and extend the greenhouse gas emission allowance trading scheme of the Community [2009] OJ L140/63; and European Parliament and Council Directive 2002/20/EC of 7 March 2002 on the authorisation of electronic communications networks and services [2002] OJ L108/21.

28 Among the most relevant judgments relating to gambling, see Case C-42/07, *Liga Portuguesa de Futebol Profissional and Bwin International Ltd. v. Departamento de Jogos da Casa da Misericórdia de Lisboa* [2009] ECR I-7633; Case C-64/08, *Ernst Engelmann* [2010] ECR I-8219; and Case 203/08 *Betfair* [2010] ECR I-4695. See also S. van den Bogaert and A. Cuyvers, '"Money for nothing": The case-law of the EU Court of Justice on the regulation of gambling' (2011) 48 *Common Market Law Review*, pp. 1175 ff.

29 See, among others, Case C-324/98, *Telaustria Verlags GmbH and Telefonadress GmbH v. Telekom Austria AG* [2000] ECR I-10745; Case C-231/03, *Coname* [2005] ECR I-7287; Case C-458/03, *Parking Brixen GmbH* [2005] ECR I-8585; Case C-410/04, *Associazione Nazionale Autotrasporto Viaggiatori (ANAV) v. Comune di Bari, AMTAB Servizio SpA* [2006] ECR I-3303; Case C-507/03, *Commission v. Ireland* [2007] ECR I-9777; Case 412/04, *Commission v. Italy* [2008] ECR I-619; Case C-220/06, *Asociación Profesional de Empresas de Reparto y Manipulado de Correspondencia v. Administración General del Estado* [2007] ECR I-12175; Case C-347/06, *ASM Brescia SpA v. Comune di Rodengo Saiano* [2008] ECR I-5641.

30 See for example S. Prechal and M.E. de Leeuw, 'Transparency: A General Principle of EU Law?' in U. Bernitz, J. Nergelius and C. Cardner (eds.), *General Principles of EC Law in a Process of Development*, Kluwer Law International, Alphen aan den Rijn 2008, pp. 201 ff. For a recent and comprehensive study, see F. Wollenschläger, 'EU Law Principles for Allocating Scarce Goods', *Review of European Administrative Law*, 2015-1, pp. 205 ff.

31 This approach has been particularly used in Germany. Among recent contributions see Wollenschläger 2010; N. Malaviya, *Verteilungsentscheidungen und Verteilungsverfahren. Zur staatlichen Güterverteilung in Konkurrenzsituationen*, Mohr Siebeck, Tübingen 2010; H.C. Röhl, 'Ausgewählte Verwaltungsverfahren', in W. Hoffmann-Riem, E. Schmidt-Aßmann and A. Vosskuhle, *Grundlagen des Verwaltungsrechts II*, C. H. Beck, Munich 2008, pp. 696 ff. See also C. Koenig, *Die öffentlich-rechtliche Verteilungslenkung. Grund und Grenzen einer Deregulierung am Beispiel der Vergabe von Konzessionen, Kontingenten und Genehmigungen zur unternehmerischen Nutzung öffentlich verwalteter Güter*, Duncker & Humblot, Berlin 1994, and M. Schmidt-Preuss, *Kollidierende Privatinteressen im Verwaltungsrecht*, Duncker & Humblot, Berlin 2005.

there is no parliamentary piece of law or where it does exist yet it lacks a comprehensive regulation of the administrative decision. The national constitutional basis of the administrative allocation can also be of interest in terms of EU law for two reasons. Firstly, they guarantee the application of certain legal requirements that are also enshrined in EU law, even when the conditions for the application of the latter are not met, thus contributing to the prevention of asymmetries between EU and non-EU law cases. Secondly, these principles are also contained in EU primary law (Article 6 TFEU) and even though as a part of it they have to be interpreted autonomously, national sources are also of interest with respect to the development of such an interpretation.[32]

The requirements deriving from EU law and from national Constitutions with respect to limited public rights schemes deploy over public decisions limiting the number of rights to grant, over the scheme's regulation and over the administrative allocation itself. Such requirements can be divided into two groups, depending on their scope. On the one hand, there are certain general principles which apply to the allocation of any limited public right, irrespective of their object and legal nature. Such general requirements can be traced back to the principles of transparency, equality, impartiality, objectivity and efficacy (below 3.2). On the other hand, EU law and some national Constitutions enshrine some principles which set limits on the allocation of certain specific types of limited public rights, depending on their subject-matter (below 3.3).[33] In the sections below, Spanish and German law will be used in an instrumental way.

3.2. *General Requirements*

3.2.1. Transparency

One of the main general requirements for the allocation of limited public rights stemming from EU law and from national Constitutions is the need to grant those rights by means of transparent administrative procedures. Transparency is quite an open and ambiguous legal concept which has been described as an umbrella notion.[34] However, when it comes to allocating scarce resources, transparency can be assessed, at least, at three different moments. First, before the allocation begins transparency seems to call for some kind of *ex ante* publicity or information about the procedure at stake. Secondly, transparency can also be weighted within the allocation procedure both with respect to those taking part in it, and to the public. Finally, transparency also has a great deal to do with the content and form of the administrative decision once it has been taken, as is clearly shown by the duty to give reasons. Transparency is expressly enshrined as a constitutional

32 Von Bogdandy 2005, p. 10.

33 A further development of these issues from the point of view of Spanish law in L. Arroyo, 'Las bases constitucionales de la actividad administrativa de adjudicación de derechos limitados en número' in L. Arroyo and D. Utrilla (eds.), *La administración de la escasez. Fundamentos de la actividad administrativa de adjudicación de derechos limitados en número*, Marcial Pons, Madrid 2015.

34 See Prechal and De Leeuw 2008. See also A. Buijze, *The principle of transparency in EU law*, Utrecht University, Utrecht 2013.

principle in some Member States (e.g., Articles 1(1) and 105 Spanish Constitution), and at least in its *ex ante* dimension it can be traced back to other general principles of EU law (for example, the fundamental freedoms) and national constitutional law (in particular, the principles of equality, impartiality, and objectivity).

EU law is going through a noteworthy evolution in this context, especially regarding the obligation of *ex ante* transparency. On the one hand, taking as a starting point the freedoms of establishment and to provide services (Articles 49 and 56 TFEU) the EUCJ has developed this dimension of transparency with respect to service concessions,[35] in a process which has recently culminated with the codification of this requirement (Articles 3 and 30 *et seq.* Directive 23/2014/EU). On the other hand, the requirement of *ex ante* transparency has been provided for by Article 12(1) of the Services Directive with respect to a specific kind of limited entitlement administrative decisions (authorisations limited in number because of the scarcity of available natural resources or technical capacity). For these cases, the aforementioned provision requires publicity to refer to 'the launch, conduct and completion of the procedure', so that the kind of allocation procedure has to be previously specified and adequately announced. Moreover, the Preamble of the Services Directive requires this procedure to include some kind of 'open competition'.[36] Finally, the EUCJ has extended the scope of the transparency requirement to other limited authorisations schemes which are not covered by the Services Directive.[37] From the foregoing it follows that both secondary legislation and case-law of the EUCJ have extended the obligation of transparency from the field of public procurement and services concessions to the allocation of other types of limited public rights, and specifically to the allocation of limited entitlement administrative decisions.[38] It should be taken into account that the legal regime of such a requirement is by no means identical in all those contexts, since important differences between them regarding scope, contents and admissible exceptions still remain.

3.2.2. Equality

One of the main features of limited public rights is that, as a result of scarcity, their allocation implies that interested individuals or firms will usually be treated differently by public authorities: whereas some of the applications will be accepted, others will be (at least partially) rejected. This confirms the need to explore the legal consequences of the equality principle with respect to the adoption of allocation administrative decisions, as well as the regulation of both allocation criteria and procedures.

35 Case C-324/98, *Teleaustria Verlags GmbH and Telefonadress GmbH v. Telekom Austria AG* [2000] ECR I-10745, paras. 61–62; Case C-231/03, *Consorzio Aziende Metano (Coname) v. Comune di Cingia de' Botti* [2005] ECR I-7287, paras. 17–21; Case C- 458/03, *Parking Brixen GmbH v. Gemeinde Brixen and Stadtwerke Brixen AG* [2005] ECR I-8585, para. 50.

36 Recital (62).

37 Case C-64/08, *Ernst Engelmann* [2010] ECR I-8219, para 58, and case 203/08 *Sporting Exchange Ltd (Betfair) v. Minister van Justitie* [2010] ECR I-4695, para 54. See Van den Bogaert and Cuyvers 2011, pp. 1187 ff.

38 Wolswinkel 2009, p. 96. See also Prechal and De Leeuw 2008, p. 229; Wollenschläger 2015, pp. 250 ff.

Equality is acknowledged as a fundamental constitutional principle both in Member States and in EU law. For example, in Article 3(1) of the German Constitution equality is expressly enshrined as a fundamental right with a twofold nature, thus operating both as a subjective right of individuals and as an objective norm.[39] Similarly, Article 14 of the Spanish Constitution ensures the protection of equality as a fundamental right and therefore, according to the same view, as an individual guarantee and an essential element for the objective order of the community.[40] Within the academic literature of these two Member States, the equality principle is deemed as being one of the main substantive building blocks of the rule of law [Article 20(1) of the German Constitution and Article 1(1) of the Spanish Constitution].[41] In EU law, the principle of equality is nowadays enshrined as one of the Union's founding principles, i.e. as one of the values common to the Member States in which the EU is founded (Article 2 TEU) and as a fundamental right (Articles 20 and 21 CFREU). The principle of equality is recognized in EU law in a very broad sense, not only from the point of view of its scope, which moves beyond the particular areas of law in which the Treaties have established a specific non-discrimination clause,[42] but also from the perspective of its functions, since it has been pointed out that the principle of equal treatment plays at least three basic roles within the EU legal order: it first performs an instrumental role as a market unifier, it also plays a regulatory role, and finally, equality acts as an autonomous constitutional principle.[43] The principle of equality has also been connected by the EUCJ with the rule of law.[44]

When setting up the content and scope of the principle of equality, the EUCJ has relied primarily on Member States law,[45] and this circumstance explains why the general content of the principle tends to be homogeneous in these jurisdictions. Such content results in a mandate pursuant to which similar situations are treated in a similar manner, as well as the corresponding prohibitions of treating differently such situations which are analogous,[46] and of treating similarly situations which are different,[47] unless exceptions are grounded on objective criteria. The absence of an objective and rational justification

39 In reference to this double nature of fundamental rights in Germany see the Judgment of the Federal Constitutional Court in the *Lüth* case (BVerfGE 7, 198).

40 See the Judgment of the Spanish Constitutional Court no. 25/1981, para 5.

41 See, for example, M. Sachs, 'Art. 20' in M. Sachs (ed.), *Grundgesetz Kommentar*, C.H. Beck, Munich 2009, and L.M. Díez-Picazo, 'Sobre la igualdad ante la Ley' in F. Rey Martínez and others (eds.), *La democracia constitucional. Estudios en homenaje al Profesor Francisco Rubio Llorente. Vol. I*, Centro de Estudios Políticos y Constitucionales, Madrid 2002, pp. 469 ff.

42 J. Schwarze, *European Administrative Law*, Sweet & Maxwell, London 2006, pp. 625 ff.

43 See G. De Búrca, 'The Role of Equality in European Community Law', and C. Barnard 'P v. S: Kite Flying or a New Constitutional Approach?', both in A. Dashwood and S. O'Leary (eds.), *The Principle of Equal Treatment in EC Law*, Sweet & Maxwell, London 1997, pp. 13 ff., 59 ff.; and G. More, 'The Principle of Equal Treatment: From Market Unifier to Fundamental Right?' in P. Craig and G. De Búrca (eds.), *The Evolution of EU Law*, OUP, Oxford 1999, pp. 517 ff.

44 T. Tridimas, *The General Principles of EU Law*, OUP, Oxford 2006, pp. 4 ff.

45 Tridimas 2006, p. 6.

46 Joined Cases 117/76 and 16/77, *Albert Ruckdeschel & Co. and Others v. Hauptzollamt Hamburg St. Annen* [1977] ECR I-1753, para. 7.

47 Case 106/83, *Sermid v. Cassa Conguaglio Zucchero* [1984] ECR 4209, para. 28.

of different treatment leads to arbitrariness and thus to an infringement of the principle of equality. This is a wide spread understanding of equality,[48] which in some jurisdictions is nevertheless being transformed as to additionally including a proportionality test, so that the measure does not only have to rest in objective reasons but also provide for a proportional difference of treatment.[49] Equality has its negative counterpart in the prohibition of discrimination.[50] This negative dimension is particularly apparent in EU law, especially within the rules on free movement – which are particular manifestations not only of the principle of non-discrimination based on nationality, but also of the general principle of equality, and thus they do not only prohibit direct discrimination on grounds of nationality, but also any other form of discrimination –[51] and in the context of the rules on competition – where the lack of equality is expressed in distortions of competition.[52] It is important to note that both sets of rules are specifically qualified in Article 106(1) TFUE as amenable to being infringed in the process of granting special or exclusive rights.[53]

The creation of a limited rights allocation scheme necessarily gives raise to a different treatment of cases falling inside and outside its scope of application and, therefore, it has to comply with the said constitutional and EU law requirements.[54] Furthermore, with respect to the allocation (in its strict sense) of limited public rights, scarcity drives to the need of selecting amongst applicants and therefore of treating them differently. Such differentiation is not in itself inconsistent with the principle of equality, but this constitutional requirement sets some conditions on the definition of the selection criteria. On the one hand, allocation cannot give rise to discrimination and consequently it must be based on reasonable and objective criteria and shall eventually comply with the principle of proportionality. On the other hand, the definition of such criteria must drive to equal or at least comparable conditions of applying for such resources for all operators concerned. In order to meet the requirements deriving from the principle of equality, allocation criteria must be feasible – i.e. giving all undertakings the real opportunity to comply with them –, verifiable – i.e. enabling the reliable verification of

48 See, e. g., T.R.S. Allan, *Constitutional justice. A liberal theory of the rule of law*, OUP, Oxford 2001, p. 21; L. Favoreu, *Droit constitutionnel*, Dalloz, Paris 2004, pp. 860 ff.; G. de Vergottini, *Diritto Costituzionale*, Cedam, Milano 2008, p. 288; J.J. Gomes Canotilho, *Direito Constitucional e Teoria da Constituçao*, Almedina, Coimbra 2003, pp. 1295 ff.

49 On the differences between the 'old' and the 'new test' in Germany, see L. Orterloh, 'Art. 3' in M. Sachs (ed.), *Grundgesetz Kommentar*, pp. 8 ff.

50 Schwarze 2003, p. 562.

51 See Case 152/73, *Giovanni Maria Sotgiu v. Deutsche Bundespost* [1974] ECR 153, para. 11; Case C-279/93, *Finazamt Köln-Altstadt v. Roland Schumacker* [1995] ECR I-225, para. 26; Case C-381/93, *Commission v. French Republic* [1994] ECR I-5145, para. 17; Case C-55/94, *Reinhard Gebhard v. Consiglio dell'Ordine degli Avvocati e Procuatori di Milano* [1995] ECR I-4165, para. 37; Case C-367/98, *Commission v. Portugal* [2002] ECR I-4731, para. 45; Case C-110/05, *Commission v. Italy* [2009] ECR I-519, para. 37; Case C-383/05, *Raffaele Talotta v. État belge* [2007] ECR I-2555, para. 17.

52 Tridimas 2006, pp. 75 ff.

53 See in this respect chapter 7 by Hatzopoulos in this book.

54 Case 127/07, *Société Arcelor Atlantique et Lorraine* [2008] ECR I-9895.

whether in a given instance they are in fact fulfilled –, mostly linked to the subject of the resource that is being awarded –since the farther and more loosely the criteria are connected with the subject-matter of the resource in question, the greater the risk that they would be set arbitrarily –, sufficiently clear and precise, and applied in accordance with uniform legal standards.[55] According to the case-law of the EUCJ, when national authorities have to base their allocation decisions on objective and non-discriminatory criteria, their discretion is subsequently circumscribed in such a way that it cannot be regarded as arbitrary.[56]

Alongside these constraints related to the creation of the allocation scheme and to the definition of allocation criteria, from the principle of equality certain consequences with respect to the configuration and the execution of allocation procedures can also be derived.[57] Given that allocation procedures are a sort of multi-polar legal relations, where inasmuch as what benefits one, burdens the other, equality in the sense of equal outcomes for all applicants is hardly feasible. However, in some jurisdictions equality is guaranteed at an earlier stage as equality of opportunities for all the potentially interested subjects.[58] From this perspective, the principle of equality requires the granting authority to treat all the interested operators on an equal basis regarding the factual and legal conditions and circumstances tied to the very participation in the allocation procedure. This interpretation of the principle of equality as equality of opportunities underlies the requirement of transparency, which comprises a specific dimension in the sphere of selection procedures, amounting to the need to ensure a degree of *ex ante* advertising sufficient to allow for all the potential applicants to participate in the procedure on an equal footing. As has been pointed out, the EUCJ has adopted this view regarding service concessions.[59] As for limited entitlement administrative decisions, the Court has also clearly stated that 'compliance with the principle of equal treatment and with the consequent obligation of transparency necessarily means that the objective criteria enabling the Member States' competent authorities' discretion to be circumscribed must be sufficiently advertised'.[60]

It is thus apparent that the transparency requirement and the resulting obligation of prior advertising have in EU law a strong connection with the principle of equality which lies in the understanding of the latter as equality of opportunities. In accordance

55 M. Szydlo, 'The Process of Granting Exclusive Rights in the Light of Treaty Rules on Free Movement' (2011) 12 (7) *German Law Journal*, 1429, 1048. See also Wollenschläger 2010, pp. 35 ff.

56 See among others Case C-205/99, *Asociación Profesional de Empresas Navieras de Líneas Regulares (Analir) and Others v. Administración General del Estado* [2001] ECR I-1271, para. 38; Case C-389/05, *Commission v French Republic* [2008] ECR I-5337, para. 94; Case 203/08, *Betfair* [2010] ECR I-4695, para. 50; Case C-64/08, *Ernst Engelmann* [2010] ECR I-8219, para. 55.

57 Judgment of the German Federal Constitutional Court in the *Gleichheit im Vergaberecht* case (BVerfG 116, 135 [153]). See Wollenschläger 2010, pp. 34 ff.

58 Wolswinkel 2009, pp. 38 ff.

59 Case C-231/03, *Coname* [2005] ECR I-7287, paras. 17 ff.

60 Case 203/08, *Betfair* [2010] ECR I-4695, para. 50. See also Case C-64/08, *Ernst Engelmann* [2010] ECR I-8219, paras. 55–57.

with these grounds, certain conclusions can be drawn as to the scope of the obligation: on the one hand, the information must be appropriate, adequate, and adapted to the characteristics of the right to grant;[61] and on the other hand, it must include a reference to the future allocation procedure, the features of the rights that are to be allocated, the terms and forms of participation in the procedure, and the allocation criteria.[62] An obligation of transparency with such a minimum content can be rationally regarded as a condition of the existence of truly equal opportunities and therefore as a duty arising from the principle of equality in its condition as an EU law principle. The same can be said as for German public law: Article 3(1) of the Constitution has been interpreted both by the academic literature and the courts as enshrining a subjective right to participate in an allocation procedure ruled by the principle of equal opportunities (*Recht auf chancengleiche Teilnahme*),[63] which comprises an obligation of *ex ante* transparency.[64]

Such a wide interpretation of the equality principle is grounded on particular reasons in both legal systems: the role of equality as a market integration clause in EU law and the scope of the right to effective judicial protection (*Schutznorm* doctrine) in the German Constitution (Article 19 IV). This is the reason why in other national legal orders the principle of equality is interpreted in a narrower manner, as a plain prohibition of different treatment and not enshrining an obligation of *ex ante* transparency. An example is Spanish law, where this obligation can be connected with other constitutional mandates (objectivity, efficacy and transparency itself) but it has not been regarded yet as a consequence of the principle of equality in non-EU law cases.

On the contrary, it is not at all evident that the principle of equality demands a specific type of allocation procedure, neither in EU nor in national law. Provided that the selection rests on objective criteria, equality does not require that the allocation procedure has a comparative nature based on material criteria. Granting limited public rights according to the rule 'first come, first served' does not entail a comparison of the applications, projects, or subjective features of the interested individuals or firms, but it undoubtedly rests on an objective criterion – *prior in tempore* – which excludes the shadow of arbitrariness and discrimination. To sum up, while the obligation of transparency can be rationally regarded, at least in EU law and some Member States, as connected with the principle of equality – understood as equality of opportunities –, the need of a competitive procedure shall necessarily be founded on a different constitutional principle.

61 See Case C-231/03, *Coname* [2005] ECR I-7287, para. 21; Case C-507/03, *Commission v. Ireland* [2007] ECR I-9777, para. 32; Case C- 458/03, *Parking Brixen GmbH* [2005] ECR I-8585, para. 50.

62 Wolswinkel 2009, pp. 88 ff.; Szydlo 2011, pp. 1433 ff.

63 Judgment of the German Federal Constitutional Court in the *Gleichheit im Vergaberecht* case (BVerfG 116, 135 [153]).

64 Wollenschläger 2010, pp. 34 ff.

3.2.3. Impartiality and objectivity

When it comes to the allocation of limited public rights, preclusion of favouritism and nepotism plays an important role.[65] Taking into account that in such contexts public authorities decide on the distribution of a scarce resource and thus benefit some subjects with respect to others, the risk of being partial on the part of public bodies and public officials and agents is apparent. This explains the relevance of the analysis of the requirements deriving from the idea of impartiality in this context.

The requirement for impartiality in administrative action falls into the main principles of administrative law. In fact, in some Member States it enjoys constitutional status. For example, Article 103 of the Spanish Constitution recognizes both objectivity and impartiality as constitutional mandates with the same content and different addressees: while objectivity imposes structural requirements on administrative organization, regarding impartiality certain constraints related to individual officials are derived thereto. As for the contents of those requirements, which in Spain are usually connected with the principle of democracy,[66] objectivity and impartiality have two dimensions which have been subsequently specified under the general Administrative Procedure Act.[67] On the one hand, impartiality forbids administrative decisions which unduly favour or work against private interests, and consequently sets conditions on the administrative decision-making and prevents the intervention in the procedure of civil servants and other administrative agents when a conflict of interests is apparent (Articles 28 and 29 of the Administrative Procedure Act). On the other hand, the principles of objectivity and impartiality also require that administrative decisions are taken after a due and fair balance of the different interests at issue [Article 4(1)c of the Administrative Procedure Act], thus entailing certain obligations in terms of administrative organization and procedure, particularly concerning advertising, participation and transparency [Articles 3 and 35 *et seq.* of the Administrative Procedure Act].

Although it is not expressly enshrined in the German Constitution, impartiality is a well-established principle of German public law, the main contents of which are included in the German Federal Act on Administrative Procedure:[68] Articles 20 and 21 forbid the action of certain public officials acting on behalf of the Administration by reason of their connection with the parties or with the subject-matter of the procedure. A general principle has been inferred from these provisions, according to which the State must act with neutrality in administrative procedures.[69] It has been particularly highlighted that the goal of Articles 20 and 21 of the Federal Act on Administrative Procedure is to prevent

65 Adriaanse, Van Ommeren, Den Ouden and Wolswinkel, Chapter 1 of this book.

66 See J.A. Santamaría Pastor, *Principios de Derecho Administrativo General I*, Iustel, Madrid 2009, pp. 82 ff.

67 *Ley 30/1992, de 30 de septiembre, de Régimen Jurídico de las Administraciones Públicas y del Procedimiento Administrativo Común.*

68 *Verwaltungsverfahrensgesetz* of 25.05.1976 (last amendment of 11.12.2008).

69 V. Nessler, 'Der Neutralitätsgrundsatz im Vergaberecht' (1999) *NVwZ* (*Neue Zeitschrift für Verwaltungsrecht*), 1081.

the influence in administrative procedures of private interests which are unconnected with its subject-matter, and consequently to enable that the procedure and its outcome are fair, objective, and impartial.[70] These requirements have sometimes been traced back to the constitutional principle of democracy,[71] whilst other authors connect them primarily with the rule of law and, specifically, with the general principle of equality.[72] On the contrary, the need for a due and fair balance of the different interests affected by an administrative decision has not been understood in Germany as a consequence of the principle of impartiality. Nevertheless, it has been regarded as a general requirement of rational administrative action materially linked to the rule of law.[73]

Regarding EU law, both the EUCJ and the General Court (hereinafter referred to as EUGC) have laid down the existence of the principle of impartiality as an element of the principle of good administration.[74] According to the EUGC in the *max.mobil* case, the principle of impartiality derives from the principle of good administration, which is itself traceable to the rule of law.[75] As for its content, the principle presumes both the removal of those officials who have a personal interest in the outcome of the administrative procedure, and the duty of administrative bodies to carefully and impartially examine the relevant facts, interests and questions of law before adopting a decision.[76] Therefore, the two dimensions of impartiality and objectivity which have been identified with respect to the (in this respect somewhat different) national legal orders can be also noticed in EU law and particularly in the right to good administration.

These requirements have been expressly recognised as a part of the right to good administration enshrined in Article 41(1) CFREU, according to which 'every person has the right to have his or her affairs handled impartially, fairly and within a reasonable time by the institutions, bodies, offices and agencies of the Union'. This right to good administration does not only bind the EU authorities but also the authorities of the Member States in so far as they implement EU law [Article 51(1) CFREU]. The content of the principle of good administration was nevertheless stipulated even before the

70 F.O. Kopp, *Verwaltungsverfahrensgesetz*, C.H. Beck, Munich 1996, pp. 334 ff.

71 E. Schmidt-Aßmann, 'Verwaltungsverfahren und Verwaltungsverfahrensgesetz: Perspektiven der Systembildung' in W. Hoffmann-Riem and E. Schmidt-Aßmann (eds.), *Verwaltungsverfahren und Verwaltungsverfahrensgesetz*, Nomos, Baden-Baden 2002, p. 454.

72 Nessler 1999, p. 1082. See also Kopp 1996, pp. 334 ff.

73 Schmidt-Aßmann 2004, pp. 84 ff.

74 See, among others, Case C-255/90, *Jean-Louis Burban v. European Parliament* [1992] ECR I-02253; Case T-167/94 *Detlef Nölle v. Council and Commission* [1995] ECR II-02589. Regarding this case law see J. Schwarze, 'The Principle of Proportionality and the Principle of Impartiality in European Administrative Law' (2003) 1 *Rivista Trimestrale di Diritto Pubblico*, 53.

75 See Case T-54/99, *max.mobil Telekommunikation Service GmbH v. Commission* [2002] ECR II-00313, para. 48. This judgment was later set aside by the ECJ, which did not however put into question the argumentation concerning the character and the ground of the principle of impartiality (Case C-141/02, *Commission v. T-Mobile Austria GmbH* [2005] ECR I-01283).

76 See Case C-269/90, *Technische Universität München v. Hauptzollamt München-Mitte* [1991] ECR I-5469; see also Case T-71/93, *Langnese v. Iglo GmbH* [1995] ECR II-1533, and Case T- 14/96, *Bretagne Angleterre Irlande (BAI) v. Commission* [1999] ECR II-139.

incorporation of the Charter to EU law. Therefore, its meaning had been specified in various soft law instruments, such as the Ombudsman's Code of Good Administrative Behaviour, which was adopted by the European Parliament through Resolution of 6 September 2001. The Code remarks, on the one hand, the notion of impartiality, according to which the official 'shall be impartial and independent', 'shall abstain from any arbitrary action adversely affecting members of the public, as well as from any preferential treatment on any grounds whatsoever', his conduct 'shall never be guided by personal, familiar or national interest or by political pressure', and he 'shall not take part in a decision in which he or she, or any close member of his or her family, has a financial interest' (Article 8); and on the other hand, the notion of objectivity, according to which 'when taking decisions, the official shall take into consideration the relevant factors and give each of them its proper weight in the decision, whilst excluding any irrelevant element from consideration' (Article 9).

With respect to the allocation of limited public rights, the requirements of impartiality and objectivity purport a prohibition of adopting allocation decisions based on private interests of the public agents who are competent to take the allocation decision, as well as an obligation of carefully and impartially taking into consideration the relevant facts and interests at stake. Indeed, two kinds of interrelated requirements can be inferred from objectivity, the ultimate aim of which is to limit the margin of discretion of public authorities and to allow for controlling its exercise. On the one hand, it calls for a clear wording of the standards and criteria governing the allocation, which shall be accurate and unambiguous. In addition, such standards and criteria shall also be interpreted and applied in a homogeneous and consistent manner throughout the entire allocation procedure. On the other hand, out of the principle of objectivity arises a requirement for transparency in order to make possible that the granting authority takes due care of the relevant interests affected by the decision and to enable the review of the exercise of administrative discretion. This connection between objectivity and transparency is especially apparent in view of Article 12(1) of the Services Directive and the EUCJ's case-law on the allocation of public contracts falling outside the scope of the secondary legislation on public procurement.[77]

Therefore, the obligations of advertisement and *ex ante* transparency deriving from the general principle of equality are also a means to achieve the guarantees of impartiality and –especially– objectivity of administrative action. From this perspective it has indeed been stated that transparency, 'both in the design and in the conduct of the selection procedure, contributes to reviewing the impartiality of the selection procedure', and that the 'impartiality requirement is closely related or even part of the principle of equal treatment: impartiality is necessary to guarantee equal treatment'.[78] In turn, some authors have argued that the fact that transparency is intended to protect impartiality

[77] Case C-324/98, *Telaustria and Telefonadress* [2000] ECR I-10745, para 62. See also Case C- 458/09, *Parking Brixen* [2005] ECR I-8585, para. 49.

[78] Wolswinkel 2009, p. 91.

proves that 'it can be separated from equal treatment' and that they have '– partly – independent nature'.[79] In our view, the requirements of equality, transparency, objectivity and impartiality overlap only to a certain extent. The relationship between equality and impartiality within allocation procedures becomes particularly apparent in EU law due to the case-law of the EUCJ, where freedoms of movement and non-discrimination are of central importance. Notwithstanding, some of the national experiences we have dealt with show a weaker connection between these constitutional mandates. Furthermore, the Charter provides a framework which will probably facilitate an autonomous role of impartiality, objectivity and good administration in this respect.

Regarding the type of allocation procedure, the distinction between the two dimensions of impartiality and objectivity seems to be of importance. The need for impartial behaviour of public authorities does not require that the allocation procedure has a comparative or competitive nature, because it can be satisfied through lottery or a 'first come, first served' procedure. On the contrary, the duty of administrative bodies to carefully examine the relevant facts and interests at stake can eventually require that the type of procedure enables some kind of comparison or competition among the individuals and firms interested in accessing the relevant market or in the exercise of a right. Depending on the features of the activity or right concerned, this second dimension of impartiality – objectivity, in the wording of the Code of Good Administrative Behaviour – may call for some kind of comparative allocation procedure.

3.2.4. Efficacy

EU law imposes a general requirement of effectiveness on the Member States according to which national authorities have to give to the former adequate effect. Nonetheless, EU law does not contain a general principle of efficacy of administrative action in itself. Moreover, efficacy does not operate as a directive of administrative allocation decisions. EU law on public procurement is clear proof of this. On the one hand, the EUCJ has historically focused on the consequences of public procurement over the internal market and competition, paying almost no attention to the way in which administrative procedures and decisions in the area of public procurement favour the public interest. On the other hand, EU secondary legislation has dealt with the specification of those requirements which are necessary to prevent public procurement from having a negative effect on the fundamental freedoms and the rules on competition, the obligation of effectiveness being of great importance within this context. In contrast, the understanding of public procurement law as an instrument to improve the efficacy of other public policies as well as of public procurement decisions is rather new. The recent Directive 2014/24/EU on public procurement seeks to complement the traditional rationale of public procurement regulation with two supplementary objectives: increasing 'the efficiency of public spending to ensure the best possible procurement outcomes in terms of value for money' and to allow 'procurers to make better use of public procurement in

79 Prechal and De Leeuw 2008, p. 231.

support of common societal goals such as protection of the environment, higher resource and energy efficiency, combating climate change, promoting innovation, employment and social inclusion and ensuring the best possible conditions for the provision of high quality social services'.[80] In short, the manner and the extent to which public procurement satisfies the public interest is increasingly important, although efficacy of administrative action is not a general principle of EU law, but a requirement having a governing role which remains circumscribed to those legal frameworks where it has already been incorporated.

On the contrary, in some national legal orders efficacy operates as a general principle of public law. In Germany efficacy had deserved little attention outside well defined areas of administrative law, such as the execution of administrative acts. However, academic literature has recently noticed its important contribution to the development of general administrative law as a general principle stemming from the rule of law [Article 20(1) of the German Constitution]: administrative law and administrative action are instruments of social direction, the efficacy of which matters from a constitutional standpoint.[81] The Spanish Constitution expressly proclaims that the public Administration is obliged to protect and pursue with efficacy [Article 103(1)] and efficiency [Article 31(2)] those interests which have been qualified as public interests by the law. Hence, optimization of scarce public resources becomes a constitutional requirement, while efficacy turns into a source of legitimacy of a public Administration which, as the bureaucratic organisation of a social State (Article 1 of the Spanish Constitution), is called to shape the social order subject to the public interest.[82] Moreover, as has been pointed out, these constitutional mandates do not only bind the public Administration in the exercise of its discretionary powers, but also directly bind the Parliament insofar as it is primarily concerned with the development of administrative law.[83]

According to this understanding, the principle of efficacy has an effect on the whole range of administrative activities since they are devoted to the fulfilment of public interest requirements. It also has an impact on the allocation of limited public rights, as long as the limitation in itself of these legal positions as well as the selection among those private parties interested in obtaining them are measures designed to achieve different public interests. The scope and content of the principle of efficacy within this context shall be analysed on a separate basis. As for its scope, efficacy operates as a constitutional directive whenever the allocation decision is relevant to public interests. It is possible that, once the limitation of the number of rights to grant has been executed, the selection among those who aim at obtaining them lacks any potential impact on the relevant public interest, thus making it essentially neutral from this perspective. In these circumstances the regulation of the allocation procedure might

80 Recitals (2) and (47).

81 See Schmidt-Aßmann 2004, pp. 56 ff.

82 See L. Parejo Alfonso, *Eficacia y Administración. Tres estudios*, Instituto Nacional de Administración Pública, Madrid 1995.

83 L. Arroyo, 'Ponderación, proporcionalidad y Derecho administrativo' (2009) 2 *InDret*.

be constitutionally conditioned by virtue of other mandates but not by the principle of efficacy. In contrast, when the selection does have those effects, efficacy gains importance. However, such importance might have various degrees, depending on the following criteria: first, the public interest can work as an external limitation in the exercise of the allocated right (e.g. an authorization for the provision of gambling services) and secondly, the exercise of such right can be directly aimed at the execution of the public interest (e.g. a public contract). Despite not being able to establish an absolute connection in this respect, it seems reasonable that the requirements of the principle of efficacy regarding the regulation of the allocation procedure will be higher in the last of these two situations.

With respect to the substantive requirements, in the context of allocation procedures the principle of efficacy basically has two relevant dimensions: from a negative perspective, it forbids the administrative authority to grant the rights at stake to those individuals or firms who are not in an adequate condition to respect or to eventually comply with the requirements of public interests, and positively, it compels rights to be granted to those who could better comply, from an objective standpoint, with the demands of public interests, both in terms of the extent of their implementation (efficacy) and of the optimization of scarce resources (efficiency). Administrative law must therefore shape not only the selection criteria, but also the allocation procedures in a way that makes it possible to evaluate the capacities, strengths and limitations of the potential applicants and their projects, according to the particular features of the limited public rights at issue.[84] Two consequences can be deduced in this respect: first, when efficacy matters *ex ante* transparency should always be obligatory because of its decisive contribution to the selection of potential candidates; and secondly, when efficacy matters genuine comparative or competitive procedures should enjoy *prima facie* priority over other selection mechanisms which do not allow a particular scrutiny of candidates. Indeed, allocation procedures such as lottery or 'first come, first served' can satisfy the requirements stemming from the principle of equality, but as it has also been said regarding objectivity, if the principle of efficacy comes into play the allocation procedure must foresee competitive, or at least comparative, selection mechanisms.[85]

3.3. *Specific Requirements*

The aforementioned constitutional principles affect the legal regime and the development of the administrative activity of allocation of limited public rights in a general way, i.e., regardless the object of such rights. However, EU law and domestic constitutional law impose some additional requirements on certain limited public rights schemes due to their content and/or the context in which their allocation takes place. In this regard two

84 For other dimensions of the relationship between transparency and the quality of administrative decisions, see Buijze 2013, pp. 45 ff.

85 Szydlo 2011, p. 1445, with respect to the granting of exclusive rights. For additional references to Dutch law, see Wolswinkel 2009, p. 92.

main scenarios should be separately mentioned: the administrative allocation of legal positions covered by a given constitutional freedom, and the administrative allocation of public benefits or services which have constitutional relevance.

The first group of cases refers to the creation and subsequent allocation of a limited number of entitlement administrative decisions which enable the exercise of a constitutional freedom, normally (but not always) the freedom to conduct a business (Articles 14 and 15 CFREU, Article 38 of the Spanish Constitution, Article 12 of the German Constitution). The decision to limit the number of entitlement administrative decisions and the definition of the allocation criteria entail a restriction of the content of the relevant freedoms. Therefore, they must meet the constitutional requirements applying to the limitation of such legal positions. These requirements include *inter alia* the intervention of the Parliament (*Gesetzesvorbehalt* or *reserva de ley*) and, more generally, the principle of prior normative programming (i.e., the requirement on regulatory authorities to predetermine to a certain extent the content and procedure for the adoption of singular administrative decisions before they are taken). The limitation of the number and the allocation criteria must also be justified in the pursuance of a legitimate purpose, satisfy the principle of proportionality and may not infringe the essential content or substance of the right [Article 52(1) CFREU, Article 53.2 of the Spanish Constitution and Article 19(2) of the German Constitution concerning the core content guarantee[86]].

As for the limitation of the number of entitlement administrative decisions for the development of economic activities, the influence of EU primary law shall be highlighted, which in this context is quite sharp and derives from at least three set of rules. The first one is that of the freedoms recognized in the Charter, and in particular the freedom to conduct a business (Article 16 CFREU). Secondly, in this kind of scenarios some other specific requirements arise from the fundamental freedoms of the Treaty whenever the limited entitlement decisions scheme falls within their scope, essentially due to its cross-border character.[87] Indeed, the quantitative limitation of the entitlement administrative decisions to grant involves a restriction of the fundamental freedoms which is additional to that resulting from the very requirement of an authorization. Such a restriction can be justified if it aims at protecting certain interests or objectives (mandatory requirements, overriding reasons of public interest, etc.) and if, in doing so, it passes a proportionality test (Articles 49 and 56 TFEU).[88] The scope and structure of such requirements depend on whether or not the concerned sector is governed by secondary legislation (as is the case of services, hydrocarbons,

86 On German law, see also, e.g., the Judgments of the German Federal Constitutional Court of 11.06.1958 (BVerfGE 7, 377) and of 28.03.2006 (1 BvR 1054/01).

87 See, e. g., Joined Cases C-570/07 and C-571/07, *Blanco Pérez and Chao Gómez* [2010] ECR I-4629, paras. 55 ff.; Case C-169/07, *Hartlauer* [2009] Rec I-7633, para. 36.

88 See on this point, e.g., Case C-42/07, *Liga Portuguesa de Futebol Profissional and Bwin International Ltd. v. Departamento de Jogos da Casa da Misericórdia de Lisboa* [2009] ECR I-7633, para. 56; Case C-64/08, *Ernst Engelmann* [2010] ECR I-8219, para. 45.

electronic communications, or transport sectors): if there is some harmonization of the relevant area, the national measure will be primarily confronted with the relevant piece of secondary legislation.[89] Thirdly, the TFUE rules on special and exclusive rights also have an impact on public decisions limiting the number of entitlement administrative decisions to grant, since the allocation of the later results in the attribution of special or exclusive rights to their holders. As a consequence, the decision concerning the limitation of the number of this kind of public rights may be brought under any of the prohibitions built by the EUCJ when interpreting Article 106(1) TFEU, which would make necessary a justification through the general exception of Article 106(2) TFEU.[90]

Secondary EU legislation is also of importance with respect to the definition of a scheme of limited entitlement administrative decisions. On the one hand, there are Directives which face the regulation of limited entitlement administrative decisions from a sector-based perspective and some of them are studied in depth in this collective work, namely those regulating greenhouse gas emission permits[91] and radio frequencies.[92] On the other hand, the Services Directive establishes a general legal framework for limited authorisations schemes which applies to entitlement administrative decisions, irrespective of them being technically administrative authorisations, concessions, or waivers, whenever they refer to services (and not goods) of any kind, except those that are excluded from its scope in Article 2. Firstly, Article 15(2) requires Member States to examine whether their legal system makes access to a service activity or the exercise of it subject to 'quantitative or territorial restrictions, in particular in the form of limits fixed according to population or of a minimum geographical distance between providers'. Secondly, Article 15(3) states that those restrictions shall comply with some conditions: (i) they must be neither directly nor indirectly discriminatory on the basis of nationality nor on the basis of the registered office location; (ii) they must be necessary in terms of being justified by an overriding reason relating to the public interest; and (iii) they must be proportional, in the sense that the restrictions are suitable for securing the attainment of the objective pursued, that they do not go beyond what is necessary to attain that objective and that it is not possible to replace those requirements with other, less restrictive measures which attain the same result. Thirdly, Article 11 forbids those authorisations that are granted for a limited period, except where 'the number of available authorisations is limited by an overriding reason relating to the public interest'. Finally, Article 12 contains rules on the allocation procedure, duration and renewal of

89 See C. Barnard, *The Substantive Law of the EU: The Four Freedoms*, OUP, Oxford 2010, pp. 149 ff., 479 ff.

90 Arroyo 2004, pp. 467 ff.

91 European Parliament and Council Directive 2003/87/EC of 13 October 2003 establishing a scheme for greenhouse gas emission allowance trading within the Community and amending Council Directive 96/61/EC [2003] OJ L275/32.

92 European Parliament and Council Directive 2002/20/EC of 7 March 2002 on the authorisation of electronic communications networks and services [2002] OJ L108/21.

authorisations whose number 'is limited because of the scarcity of available natural resources or technical capacity'.

With regard to the allocation of the entitlement administrative decisions, once their number has been validly limited the concerned constitutional freedom turns into a right to participate in the allocation procedure, and to do so with certain guarantees: the requirement of Parliamentary legislation spreads to the regulation of the administrative procedure of allocation, the Administration is required to give adequate publicity to the call and, if necessary, to complete and to concrete the allocation program (so-called *Konzeptpflicht* within the German academic literature).[93] Finally, the constitutional freedom held by all applicants does not ensure that they will all obtain the entitlement administrative decision, but it does include the guarantee that the administrative decision results from a proper and accurate implementation of the allocation program. In general terms, the obligation of correctness of administrative action stems from the rules governing such action, but in cases like these such an obligation finds a specific constitutional basis, which vanishes when the subject-matter of the allocation is not a legal position protected by the Constitution.

As stated above, the second set of cases is that of the allocation of constitutionally relevant public benefits or services. Such relevance can derive from the fact that the benefit to allocate is the subject-matter of a constitutional right [e.g., the right to education in Article 27(1) of the Spanish Constitution], or it may result from the circumstance that the affected benefit or service is the object of a constitutional directive, i.e. a mandate of optimization imposed on the public authorities by the Constitution without directly acknowledging a corresponding subjective public right to citizens [e.g. the mandates of protection of health, housing, disabled and elderly people in Articles 43, 47, 49 and 50 in connection to Article 53(3) of the Spanish Constitution]. The scarcity of public resources available for the satisfaction of these benefits or services can be managed either through the restrictive configuration of their scope and/or of the requirements for accessing them and the subsequent establishment of admission procedures, or by means of the limitation of the number of benefits and their further administrative allocation. When the latter alternative is chosen, the limitation on the number of benefits, the demarcation of their scope and the definition of the allocation criteria are constitutionally relevant,[94] to the extent that they will have to pass a proportionality test from the perspective of the prohibition of insufficient actions (*Untermassverbot*). Likewise, as a result of the quantitative limitation of resources to allocate, the right or interest in obtaining the benefit in question turns into a right to participate in a procedure with certain guarantees. Which ones these are depends largely, however, on whether the constitutional provision configures the service or benefit directly as a right [as happens with the right to education in Article 27(1) of the Spanish Constitution] or as a mere mandate for public authorities

93 See Wollenschläger 2010, pp. 536 ff.

94 See e.g. the Judgement of the Case *Tarantino and others v. Italy* ECtHR 2.04.2013 regarding the right to education.

in compliance of which the corresponding rights are set out [e.g., the rights to access health services or to a subsidized housing in Articles 43 and 47 of the Spanish Constitution].[95]

4. Closing Remarks

The creation and the administrative allocation of limited public rights, although traditionally governed by heterogeneous legal regimes, raise certain common regulatory problems which make necessary to incorporate this kind of activity to the system of general administrative law. To that end, it is first necessary to conceptually demarcate it as well as to identify its main manifestations. The analytical tools resulting from this approach are the basis for the systematic construction of the administrative activity of allocation of limited public rights, which must be developed both deductively and inductively. The deductive or *top down* perspective,[96] which is the one on which this paper has focused, allows for identifying certain horizontal requirements on the administrative activity under examination, which stem both from EU law and national constitutional law. Academic literature has mainly focused on the scope and particularities of the limitations arising from the fundamental freedoms as well as from both general and sector-based secondary EU law. Nevertheless, the development of a doctrine on the allocation of limited public rights as a part of general administrative law demands widening the perspective in order to explore the requirements on this kind of administrative activity, which derive from a set of constitutional principles, such as impartiality, objectivity, efficacy, transparency and equality, the two latter being of special strength from the point of view of EU law. These principles go beyond the law of the internal market and operate as a bridge between the law of the Union and the constitutional orders of its Member States. From this perspective, it should be noticed that, as long as some of these principles ensure the application of certain legal requirements that are also enshrined in EU law even in the cases where the conditions for the application of the later are not met, they contribute to the prevention of asymmetries between EU and non-EU law cases.

EU and national constitutional law impinge on two main aspects of limited public rights schemes. The first one refers to the limitation on the number of rights to be allocated. When such rights are related to the exercise of a subjective legal position with a constitutional rank, the limitation of their number may involve a restriction of the corresponding constitutional right and must therefore fulfil the requirements that the CFREU and/or the relevant domestic Constitution imposes on such kind of restrictions. This particularly applies to limited entitlement administrative decisions as well as to limited public benefits with constitutional relevance. Moreover, the limitation on the number of entitlement administrative decisions for the development of economic activities raises concerns from the standpoint of the EU law rules on fundamental

95 Arroyo 2015.

96 See Chapter 1 in this book by Adriaanse, Van Ommeren, Den Ouden and Wolswinkel.

freedoms and on special and exclusive rights, and must therefore conform to the corresponding justifications provided for by EU law in this context.

The second element concerns the administrative allocation procedure and the allocation criteria. Apart from the specific requirements that may exist on this field depending on the content of the right to be allocated, both EU law and domestic constitutional law impose a general mandate that the allocation procedure and criteria meet certain requirements of transparency, equality and non-discrimination, objectivity, impartiality and efficacy. The scope of these requirements and the specific techniques through which they must be carried out, as well as their constitutional basis, vary depending on the kind of right to grant and the context of its allocation, yet their acknowledgement is an indisputable trend in relation to almost all of them.

Finally, some closing remarks shall be made with respect to these procedural requirements. Firstly, they have been regarded as outcomes of certain legal principles, some of them being fundamental rights both at EU and national level (e.g. equality and good administration) while others are policies without a subjective nature, and even without constitutional status in some jurisdictions (e.g. efficacy and efficiency). Furthermore, it has been confirmed that these specific procedural requirements can be simultaneously connected with more than one of these principles, as is particularly true for *ex ante* transparency. Secondly, as long as they are legal principles their legal force has to be analysed from two different perspectives: on the one hand, these procedural regulations are *prima facie* required by the respective constitutional principles but on the other hand, they can eventually be displaced by other opposing principles under certain conditions. Finally, these procedural requirements enjoy the legal force which comes from the norm at stake (e.g. EU primary law, national constitutional law, etc.). However, they perform a genuine constitutional function which consists in providing structural criteria for the systematic construction of general administrative law, and, in particular, for the development of a general theory on the allocation of limited public rights.

Anoeska Buijze*

CHAPTER 3. THE ALLOCATION OF LIMITED PUBLIC RIGHTS FROM THE PERSPECTIVE OF THE EU LEGISLATOR

1. Introduction

This contribution deals with the allocation of limited public rights by authorities in the EU member states – an issue that touches upon the core business of the EU legislator. On the one hand, the allocation of such rights by public authorities in the member states has the potential to do serious damage to the common market. On the other hand, the proper allocation of such rights could contribute to an efficient allocation of scarce resources and thus to the overall welfare of EU citizens as well as to a host of other EU policy goals. Despite these incentives to regulate, general rules on how member state authorities should allocate limited rights are mostly lacking. Only the allocation of specific rights is regulated in any detail. This contribution explores the reasons the EU legislator has to intervene in the allocation of limited rights by the authorities of the member states, or to refrain from intervening, and addresses the question of whether the EU legislator should adopt a more active approach to the issue. The allocation of limited rights by the EU institutions themselves falls outside of the scope of this contribution.[1]

The role of the EU legislator in the discourse on limited rights has so far been modest. A lot of attention has gone to the Court of Justice, which tends to say interesting things on the matter.[2] But one would certainly expect limited rights to pique the interest of the legislator as

* Anoeska Buijze is currently working as Assistant Professor of administrative law at the Institute for Constitutional and Administrative Law and Legal Theory at Utrecht University, the Netherlands. Any comments or thoughts on this article can be addressed to a.buijze@uu.nl.

1 As far as European subsidies are concerned the interested reader is referred to the chapter by Van den Brink in this book.

2 On the award of service concessions see e.g. Case C-260/04, *Commission v. Italy* [2007] ECR I-7083. On the award of licences required to provide services see joined cases C-203/08 and C-258/08, *Betfair/ Ladbrokes* [2010] ECR I04695; Case C-64/08, *Engelmann* [2010] ECR I-8219; Case C-347/09, *Dickinger and Ömer* [2011] ECR I-0000. See C.J. Wolswinkel, 'The Allocation of a Limited Number of Authorisations,' (2009) 2 (2) *REALaw (Review of European Administrative Law)* 61, for a more comprehensive treatment of the status of EU law on the allocation of limited public rights that takes into account both secondary legislation the case law of the Court of Justice.

well: EU law reflects a very outspoken view on how scarcity is best dealt with. Whether it is goods, services, or the labour and capital needed to produce them, the best way to allocate scarce resources is through a properly functioning, competitive market. It is one of the tasks of the legislator to develop this market, to the benefit of all EU citizens. Limited public rights are problematic in this philosophy, since they are not bought and sold on markets, but granted by public authorities who may have all sorts of nefarious, economically irrelevant reasons for their decisions. The manner in which they allocate resources might deviate considerably from how a perfect market would have done it, and no matter how well their intentions were, this will detract from efficiency. Yet, when we address the issue of limited rights from the perspective of the European legislator, we are confronted with two questions. We must look at the reasons it would have to regulate the allocation of limited rights in a particular manner – and the grating lack of efficiency that may result when the matter is left to the member states may play a role there – but in addition, we must consider whether it has the competence and the capacity to do so. The answers to these questions can vary with the nature of the allocated right, and appear to be responsible for at least some of the variation we see in the regulation of allocation procedures, especially with regard to the level of detail it contains.

In this article I will address i.a. the view of the EU legislator on when it is acceptable to artificially limit the number of public rights that are available, and how the subject of a limited right determines the intensity of EU regulation. I will touch upon how ceilings should be set, on whether there should be special rules for newcomers, and on various other issues that deal with the design of allocation procedures. A word of caution is in order though: the EU-legislator has not regulated these issues in any detail, and high-strung expectations about the insight it provides in these matters should be avoided. Nevertheless, its lack of activity is in itself telling, and attracts attention to a number of important issues with regard to the allocation of limited rights.

Below, I will set out to give an overview of the manner in which allocation procedures can be used to achieve a number of policy goals. I will then proceed to address the extent to which those goals are relevant to EU law. For some of these goals, the EU legislator might want to promote their realisation. For others, it may want to prevent the member states from doing so. After a short discussion of the competence of the EU legislator to achieve both these things, we will look at the manner in which it has regulated the procedures for allocating a number of resources. We will see how the policy goals that can be achieved through the allocation of certain public rights as well as the competence of the EU legislator appear to affect the level of regulation of the allocation procedure. After concluding that the EU legislator usually practices considerable restraint when legislating on the allocation of limited public rights, I will discuss shortly whether the current situation needs to be changed.

2. Allocating Limited Public Rights: What can be Achieved

Limited rights are a versatile tool in the hands of public authorities, both on the national and the European level. This is true both with regard to rights that are naturally scarce and those whose scarcity is artificial. The latter category are made scarce for a reason, and the scarcity itself is the effect of a policy choice rather than a given. Once the scarcity of the right has been established, the issue of how the limited right must be allocated is very similar. The value that limited public rights have to policy makers lies in their scarcity. The recipient of a limited right receives something that is of value to him, while others are left empty-handed, and that makes the ability to decide who will get such a right a powerful one. The allocation of limited rights opens the door to nepotism as well as confirmative action, but public authorities can also use more 'neutral' criteria, like first come, first serve, or have lotteries. Such neutral procedures ensure that the rights get allocated, but serve no additional policy purpose.[3] Because limited rights represent economic value, and because their exact value will tend to differ between potential candidates, public authorities also have the option to distribute them in what they think is the most economically efficient way. In other words, they can attempt to give rights to those candidates to whom they have the highest value. Normally, the market is the best way to achieve an efficient distribution of scarce resources: it effortlessly ensures that goods end up with those that value them the most, and that resources are used by those who create the greatest value from them – at least theoretically.[4] By mimicking the allocation that a perfect free market would arrive at, public authorities can ensure that the rights they distribute will contribute the most to the general welfare.[5] Mimicking a perfect market can be done in several ways, but it will always require some mechanism to establish the value a limited right has to potential recipients. One way to determine this is by measuring their willingness to pay for a public right, for example through an auction.[6] After all, the distinguishing characteristic of a market is that it ensures that goods end up with those who are willing to pay the most for them.[7] Alternatively,

3 Provided they are open to everyone, both in legal and practical terms. It is quite possible to design lotteries and first come, first serve systems that in practice result in nepotism. However, if a public authority consciously chooses one of these systems for the allocation of scarce rights, it should be indifferent to who gets the rights, as long as someone gets it.

4 The conclusion that markets lead to optimal efficiency is subject to a lot of conditions. Competition must be perfect, information must be complete, people must act rational, and there may be no externalities. In practice, these conditions never apply. R. Cooter and T. Ulen, *Law and Economics* (ed.), Pearson/Addison-Wesley, Boston 2004, p. 38. The argument that the market is the best means to allocate resources remains forceful though, mostly because we have no alternative means to determine how much people value things. See F. von Hayek, *The Road to Serfdom*, Routledge, London 1944, pp. 42–43 for a particularly elegant rendition of the argument. R. Cooter and T. Ulen, *Law and Economics*, 6th ed., Pearson/Addison-Wesley, Boston 2011, p.19. My purpose in this paper is not to argue with free market theory though. Suffice to say that many policy makers have embraced the idea that the market is the best means to allocate resources, at least in principle, including the EU.

5 Although one can argue that there is a market for limited rights, with public authorities being the suppliers and parties interested in acquiring the rights being the demand side, such a market does not come close to the perfection of the theoretical model. There is no competition on the supply side, often only limited competition on the demand side, information is far from complete, and actors will not necessarily act like one would expect from homo economicus.

6 Designing an auction in a way that accurately measures candidates' willingness to pay is quite the challenge though. E. Maasland, *Essays in Auction Theory*, dissertation, University of Tilburg, 2012, pp. 27, 30, 33, 63.

7 Cooter and Ulen 2012, p. 19.

public authorities can attempt to assess the added value that a candidate will produce when the right is awarded to it. This will require it to design a comparative test to assess the merits of the plans that candidates have to make use of the public right, akin to the best value for money criterion used in procurement law.[8]

Although generally speaking markets produce the most efficient results, they do not always function perfectly,[9] and public authorities might want to design allocation procedures in a way that corrects these failures. Indeed, liberal authors traditionally hold the view that the state should only act to take care of a certain matter if the market fails, and then only if it has the ability to perform better than the admittedly flawed market.[10] If public authorities adhere to this adage, and design their allocation procedures to improve on the outcome produced by a failing market, efficiency is still the goal. The difference is that public authorities try to improve upon the outcome of the market rather than that they only try to copy it. Allocation procedures can help to circumvent market failures in a number of ways. If in a particular market producers need public rights to be able to make their product – like radio stations need frequencies to be able to make programmes – it will be difficult to enter the market for newcomers. Competition will be imperfect[11] and existing market players may be able to gather rent, a premium on market inefficiencies that does not represent any added value.[12] Public authorities that allocate such rights can try to gather this rent for themselves. This requires a procedure where rights are sold by public authorities, such as an auction.[13] Another way to tackle the problem of limited competition is to divide rights over a relatively large number of market actors. By making sure there are a sufficient number of players on the supply side, the public authority can promote a competitive market, whereas when they allow one player to buy all available rights, they create a monopolist who can then proceed to charge monopoly prices to his customers. Public authorities can also design allocation procedures in a way that enables or actively promotes newcomers to enter a market. They will be most likely to attach importance to this when the performance of current market players is unsatisfactory. The possibility of new entrants in a market is necessary to ensure competition, to keep prices low and quality high and to ensure innovation.[14] If any of these things appear to be lacking, new players can give an impetus to the market.

All too ambitious public authorities should restrain their enthusiasm though. Neither mimicking the market nor correcting its failures is easy. The market in practice falls

8 See the chapter by Jansen.

9 Cooter and Ulen 2012, pp. 39–42.

10 R. Posner, *Economic Analysis of Law*, 6th ed., Aspen Publishers, New York 2003, p. 50.

11 Normally, new entrant will be attracted to a market where prices are high and profit margins larger than usual. The increase in supply will cause prices to fall until they reach the normal level. R. Cooter and T. Ulen 2012, p. 28. If entry is difficult, this mechanism will fail.

12 See, D.M. Ricci, 'Fabian Socialism: A Theory of Rent as Exploitation,' (1969) 9 (1) *Journal of British Studies*, 105, 106, who uses the straightforward formulation that rent allows one to get something for nothing.

13 Maasland 2012, p. 10, 94.

14 Cooter and Ulen 2012, p. 28.

short of realising efficiency, but governments should not assume they can do better. How could they, with their limited knowledge and resources, establish the value of goods and services any better than the market can?[15] To illustrate the difficulty in figuring out how to design an allocation procedure I refer to Maasland, who shows in detail how complicated it is to properly design an auction procedure that will answer the government's needs. Also noteworthy is that the proper design will in part depend on the specific characteristics of a market, which can vary through time and place.[16] This means there is no one right way to auction these rights, but that procedures must be designed for a specific case to maximise their contribution to the realisation of public policy goals. Details like the number of rounds in which to bid or whether and when the number of participants in auction is announced before the bidding take place can have a great impact on the outcome of the procedure.

Limited rights are more than just tools to improve efficiency. They can also present public authorities with a means to gain revenue.[17] They can sell the rights. They can even create artificial scarcity and then attempt to make money from that, e.g. by limiting the number of licences available to super markets for Sunday openings and selling them to the highest bidder. Artificial scarcity can also be used to restrict a harmful activity, or one that is harmful in large quantities, such as the running of gambling joints or CO_2 emissions. This goal is achieved by setting a proper ceiling, and the design of the allocation procedure need not be affected by it. Alternatively, public authorities can try to reduce the harmfulness of an otherwise necessary activity by awarding rights to the least harmful candidate or candidates. This requires artificial scarcity, and thus a ceiling, but also requires a procedure to select the candidate who is best able to reduce harm, or in other words, has low costs associated with reducing harm. In the long run, such policies may result in innovations that limit the harm associated with the activity even further.[18]

Allocation procedures can also be used to favour certain groups, and as said they offer an opportunity for both nepotism and confirmative action. This allows them to be used for a wide range of policy goals. Subsidies for innovative entrepreneurs could be awarded to women only. Access to radio frequencies could be reserved for stations that cater to the needs of certain minorities. Disabled and elderly people could be given priority when dividing parking licences. Such measures necessarily detract from efficiency. The innovation subsidy will not go to a male entrepreneur, even if his innovations would

15 R. Posner, *Economic Analysis of Law*, 6th ed., Aspen Publishers, New York 2003, p. 50 argues that governments should refrain from acting if they are not sure they can improve upon the outcome achieved by the market, even if they know this outcome is less than efficient.

16 Maasland 2012.

17 Maasland 2012, p. 92.

18 C. Kettner, A. Köppl and S. Schleicher, 'The EU Emission Trading Scheme: Insights from the First Trading Years with a Focus on Price Volatility', *WIFO Working Papers no. 368*, 2010, argue that the lack of real scarcity under the first phase of the European emission trading system resulted in a lack of incentives to invest in technologies to lower emissions. High prices on the other hand would have provided such an incentive.

contribute much more to society. The minority station might take the frequency of a potentially highly successful radio station that would have been able to generate triple the advertising income and would have many more listeners. But even though these approaches may not be the most efficient way to allocate resources, they can certainly be justified. A particularly ill-advised strategy on the other hand, is to use limited rights to favour one's own nationals. Although such a policy would initially give domestic players a competitive edge, and benefit the national economy at the expense of that of other countries, in the long run those other countries are likely to retaliate by favouring their own domestic industries.[19] Eventually, all economies will suffer. Even if all countries know that this is true, it unfortunately still makes sense for a state to favour its domestic industry. If other states do not favour their domestic industry, they are the only state that does so and it will benefit their domestic industry. If other states discriminate as well, their economy will suffer less if they favour their domestic industry than if they are the only state that does not. Hence, states are confronted with a coordination problem: even if they agree to act in their mutual benefit and refrain from supporting their domestic industries, there is always an incentive to be the first, and hopefully the only one, to break the agreement. To prevent this from happening, a neutral third party should oversee their behaviour.[20]

So, although discrimination against non-nationals is not the best of ideas, public authorities can still use allocation procedures for a variety of purposes. They can try to achieve an efficient allocation of the public rights they must divide. They can try to create competitive markets. They can try to enable newcomers to enter a market. They can favour particular groups. They can try to make money from selling off public rights. They can try to reduce the harm associated with certain activities. They can even try to favour their domestic industries at the expense of foreign economies, although the attempt is probably doomed to fail. But although allocation procedures can contribute to all these things, the different goals are not necessarily compatible. Maximising the revenue gained through an auction requires a different kind of auction than creating a competitive market for example, because suppliers would be willing to pay most for a monopoly.[21] Likewise, maximising efficiency is at odds with confirmative action. Public authorities will need to set their priorities and design a procedure accordingly. To maximise the contribution that an allocation procedure can make to the policy goals the public authority has settled on, it has to design the specifics of the procedure taking into account the current circumstances on the market as well as the nature of the right. It is clear then that limited public rights are a versatile policy tool, and any legislator worth his salt should show a keen interest in them. They are also a delicate tool: although public

19 H.W. Friederiszick, L.H. Röller and V. Verouden, 'European State Aid Control: an economic framework' in P. Buccirossi (ed.), *Handbook of Antitrust Economics*, MIT Press, Cambridge Mass. 2007, explain the mechanism in the context of state aid, but it is valid for all measures that favour domestic undertakings at the expense of foreign ones.

20 Friederiszick et al. 2006.

21 Maasland 2012, p. 92 shows that auctioneers may elect to select only a happy few to ensure they collect enough revenue.

authorities can achieve many things through the way in which they allocate limited rights, the details in the design of their procedure will determine whether they succeed.

3. EU Law and the Allocation of Limited Public Rights

Limited rights are relevant to all jurisdictions, but perhaps even more to the EU legislator, due to its focus on the internal market. The EU legislator is concerned with many things, from monetary policy to agriculture to gender equality and human rights. Originally though, the EU was an economic project, and the purpose of creating a common European market has shaped much of what it has done, and of what it is doing. The internal market is a strong force in European law, as well as a reason to take legislative action, as reflected in Article 26 TFEU, which assigns the Union the task to adopt measures with the aim of establishing or ensuring the functioning of the internal market. The internal market, one without barriers to intra-community trade, is not a goal in itself though. It is to lead to prosperity for all EU citizens, and is believed to lead to a higher standard of living, harmonious economic development, and to promote closer relations between the member states.[22] The belief that a properly functioning market leads to an efficient allocation of resources, and to welfare for all, is reflected both in provisions that prohibit interference in that market, like the free movement rules and the prohibition of state aid, and the competition rules, that aim to prevent the market failures of monopoly and oligopoly.[23]

When we keep in mind how limited rights can be used, or, from the EU perspective, abused, the relevance of those rights for EU law becomes clear. In the previous paragraph we saw that the allocation of limited rights can have an effect on the internal market. It can either help that market to function more smoothly, or interfere with it. From the perspective of the internal market, allocation procedures that mimic the market or aim to correct market failures resulting from limited competition are to be valued positively. Allocation procedures that favour particular groups are suspect, because they interfere in the functioning of the common market. However, it is well-established that such interferences may be justifiable. Allocation procedures that favour the nationals of one of the member states are anathema to EU law. Artificially induced scarcity is a trade barrier, and may be problematic under the free movement rules, but again, such barriers may be justifiable.[24] Legislation that aims to ensure the functioning of the internal market would thus be either legislation that attempts to prevent that allocation procedures hamper the internal market or that clarifies when such allocation procedures are justifiable, or legislation that promotes allocation procedures that work in concert with

22 See P. Craig and G. De Búrca, *EU Law: Text, Cases and Materials,* 4th ed., Oxford University Press, Oxford 2007, pp. 10–11.

23 Craig and De Búrca 2007, p. 11.

24 See also Wolswinkel 2009, p. 65, who qualifies artificially limited authorisations as quantitative restrictions in the meaning of Article 28 EC, now Article 34 TFEU. However, authorisation systems as such already qualify as a restriction of one of the treaty freedoms, p. 69.

the internal market to achieve an efficient allocation of resources. Additionally, there might be legislation on when artificial scarcity is acceptable.

On the other hand, although these matters are relevant for EU law, not all of them need to concern the legislator. We already know that barriers to the free movement of goods, services, labour and capital are in principle prohibited under primary EU law. We know that exceptions to this prohibition can be justified under the Treaty or under the rule of reason. Likewise, discrimination of non-nationals is already prohibited. Allocation procedures that favour domestic candidates thus violate primary EU law.[25] We already know, thanks to the Court of Justice, that allocation procedures have to comply with the principles of equal treatment, transparency, and objectiveness to ensure that they do not disturb the market.[26] Still, not all issues have been resolved: it is not always clear what is required in concrete cases to ensure compliance with those principles. If the legislator would draw up more detailed rules, it could bring an end to a lot of insecurity.

As with any legislator, the EU legislator can consider allocation procedures for limited rights to be a policy instrument in the hands of the EU institutions, which can use them to correct market failures or achieve a number of other goals in the fields of social, cultural, or environmental policy. This can provide an additional incentive to regulate allocation procedures when doing so can contribute to the realisation of some other policy goal, in addition to concerns for the market.

4. The Competence of the EU Legislator

The allocation of limited rights is an important policy tool that is both versatile and delicate. Allocation procedures can work in concert with the common market, or they can interfere with its proper working. Especially allocation procedures that favour nationals have the potential to do serious harm to the internal market. The EU legislator, whose goal it is, i.a., to increase the overall welfare of European citizens through the completion of the internal market, clearly has reasons to regulate such procedures. This holds true for all procedures that have the potential to affect the internal market, and more so for those procedures that can be used to accomplish policy goals that fall under the competence of the EU. But even though the EU may want to legislate about the allocation of limited public rights, this does not necessarily mean it has the competence to do so. Its powers are limited by the principle of conferred powers, so that it can only legislate on an issue if the Treaties confer the power to do so.[27] Even when the EU has the power to legislate on a given subject, it is still bound by the principles of subsidiarity

25 For an overview of the obligations that must be complied with when allocating limited rights that follow from primary EU law, see F. Wollenschläger, 'EU Law Principles for Allocating Scarce Goods and the Emergence of an Allocation Procedure' (2015) 8 (1) *Review of European Administrative Law* 205, 256.

26 E.g. Case C-496/99, P *Succhi di frutta* [2004] ECR I-3801; Case C-470/99, *Universale Bau* [2002] ECR I-11617; Case C-458/03, *Parking Brixen* [2005] ECR I-8612.

27 Article 5(1) TEU.

and proportionality.[28] This means that in fields where the EU shares its competence with the member states, it may only act if and in so far as the objectives of the proposed action cannot be sufficiently achieved by the Member States, either at central level or at regional and local level, but can rather, by reason of the scale or effects of the proposed action, be better achieved at Union level.[29] In addition, the content and form of Union action shall not exceed what is necessary to achieve the objectives of the Treaties.[30]

The shared competences that the principle of subsidiarity applies to can be found in Article 4(2) TFEU. Clearly, the issue most relevant here is the internal market, but the EU also shares with the member states the competence to regulate on the environment, and on social policy. Since the allocation of limited rights has the potential to disturb the functioning of the internal market as well as to enhance it, the competence of the EU legislator is a given. In addition, it would be competent to legislate on limited rights for other purposes, such as environmental protection or the emancipation of vulnerable groups. That does not mean it gets a free pass to do as it pleases though. Because we are talking about shared competences, the member states can pass legislation on these subjects as well, and because the principle of subsidiarity applies, the EU can only regulate if national regulation is insufficient and the EU legislator can improve on the situation. Because it is also bound by the principle of proportionality, the EU legislator should practice restraint when legislating on the allocation of limited rights. Allocation procedures are an important tool for the public authorities in the member states, and detailed regulation on the EU level will rob them of a useful policy instrument. Thus, EU law should not be so restrictive that the member states are hampered in their ability to make policy in those areas that fall under their competence, provided their goals are justifiable and their means proportionate.

Thinking back to the policies that can be pursued through the allocation of limited rights, I would argue that one issue falls clearly within the competence of the EU, without further arguments needed. This is of course the prevention of member states adopting the beggar-thy-neighbour approach. Because national governments will always have an incentive to adopt this policy, the prevention of the destructive cycle of discrimination is best done at the EU-level.

As regards the other policy goals that public authorities may pursue through allocation procedures, the matter is less clear. Although the EU is competent to further improve the internal market, and to regulate on social and environmental issues, the argument that these matters are better regulated at the EU level than at the national level cannot be made in general. The EU legislator will always be competent to regulate the allocation of limited rights in a way that promotes the functioning of the internal market, but it can only do so when it notices a problem that the member states are unable to

28 Article 5(1) TEU.

29 Article 5(2) TEU. See also A. Buijze, 'Shared regulatory regimes through the lens of subsidiarity: Towards a substantive approach' (2014) 5 *Utrecht Law Review* 67, 79.

30 Article 5(3) TEU.

resolve. If there is no existing shortcoming, the EU legislator cannot act.[31] Whether it can act to realise policy goals that are not directly related to the internal market will depend both on whether it is competent in respect of the subject of a particular right as well as on its ability to identify an existing shortcoming that the member states fail to resolve. Because allocation procedures can serve so many different goals, some of them simultaneously, all of them justifiable, and because the design needed to accomplish these goals will in part depend on local circumstances, the starting point perhaps should be to give member states some space to make their own choices. Much will depend on the specific rights, and the purposes that are to be served by their allocation.

5. EU Legislation on the Allocation of Limited Public Rights

Based on the previous paragraph, one would expect to see some variety in the manner in which the allocation of limited rights is regulated. Across the board, one would expect to see an emphasis on regulation aiming to ensure non-discrimination. In particular areas, where more far-reaching EU interference can be justified, we may see more detailed regulation with specific aims. Below, I will shortly address the regulation in the fields that take centre stage in part III of this book: gambling licences, CO_2 emission permits, and radio frequencies – or at least, the division of scarce resources under the telecom directives. In addition, and because regulation on gambling licences is in fact non-existent, I will discuss the services directive.[32]

5.1. Gambling Licences and the Services Directive

The case law of the Court of Justice on the issuing of gambling licences has provided much input for the debate on limited public rights.[33] However, the judgments of the Court have been based on primary EU law, in particular Article 57 TFEU and the principles of equal treatment and transparency.[34] The legislator has not contributed much to this debate.[35] Indeed, gambling licences fall outside of the scope of the Services Directive, which is otherwise concerned with issuing licences to provide services. Because gambling is a sensitive area, where member states try to balance public health, public security, and economic interests, while trying to battle money laundering and the like, the restraint of

[31] J. Wuermeling, 'Draft Constitution of the European Union: the new division of competences,' in H.J. Blanke and S. Mangiameli (eds.), *Governing Europe Under a Constitution*, Springer, Berlin 2006, p. 298, 302.

[32] Directive 2006/123/EC of the European Parliament and of the Council of 12 December 2006 on services in the internal market [2006] OJ L376/36.

[33] See the chapter by Van den Bogaert and Cuyvers in this book.

[34] See Betfair/Ladbrokes cited above. Note though that the Court leaves ample room to the member states to decide on the exact details of the procedure, as long as they comply with the principles of equal treatment and transparency.

[35] This will probably not change soon. The Commission concluded there is no support for EU-wide regulation of the issue. Commission Communication of 23.10.2012, 'Towards a comprehensive European framework for online gambling,' COM 2012 (596) final.

the legislator is perhaps understandable: the obligation to observe primary EU law is in itself enough to ensure that discriminatory practices are prohibited. The exact manner in which to achieve this, and how to reconcile it with the other policy goals the member states may have in regulating their gambling markets, is perhaps best left to national governments.

The Services Directive, which aims to further open up the internal market for services, does contain a specific regime for limited rights. Article 12 is concerned with the situation where the number of authorisations available for a given activity is limited. The procedure for the selection of candidates must provide full guarantees of impartiality and transparency, including, in particular, adequate publicity about the launch, conduct and completion of the procedure. Paragraph 2 prohibits authorisations for an unlimited period as well as automatic renewals, as well as any other advantage conferred on a service provider whose authorisation has just expired as well as any person having any links with that provider. This provision goes a bit further than merely ensuring non-discrimination or equal treatment, since it explicitly promotes competition amongst service providers. Nevertheless, member states are free to reconcile this purpose with other policy goals, since allocation procedures may, according to paragraph 3, take considerations of public health, social policy objectives, the health and safety of employees or self-employed persons, the protection of the environment, the preservation of cultural heritage and other overriding reasons relating to the public interest into account.

The Services Directive goes slightly further than only preventing discrimination, since it obliges the member states to promote competition – something they are not obliged to do when issuing gambling licences.[36] In addition, it gives rules about publicity, although these do not tell us much we did not already know. All in all, it remains very general, and the Directive leaves it to the member states to design specific allocation procedures. The legislator has not availed itself of the opportunity to specify in any detail what compliance with the principles developed in the case law requires.

Article 12 of the Services Directive refers only to situations where the number of authorisations is limited because of the scarcity of natural resources or technical capacity.[37] The Directive gives no extensive answer as to when artificial scarcity is allowed, and only limited guidance on how procedures to allocate artificially scarce rights should be designed. Artificial scarcity is certainly an option. The case law of the Court of Justice makes it clear that justifications for such a policy can exist, recital 62 of the preamble to the Services Directive ensures Article 12 does not prevent member states from limiting the number of authorisations for reasons other than scarcity of natural resources or technical capacity, and Article 11(1)b of the Services Directive makes explicit reference to the situation in which the number of authorisations is limited by an overriding reason relating to the public interest.

36 The Court of Justice leaves this option open in its *Betfair* judgment.

37 See Wolswinkel 2009, p. 84–87 for an extensive treatment of the relation between technical or natural scarcity and artificial scarcity under the Services Directive.

Limited authorisation schemes of this kind do not fall under the scope of Article 12, but they must still comply with a number of requirements. Article 9 provides that member states can only require that service providers have an authorisation for providing a particular service when such schemes are not discriminatory and are justified by an overriding reason relating to the public interest. Such authorisation schemes must moreover be proportionate, meaning that the objective cannot be attained by a less restrictive measure. Because a limited number of authorisations is more restrictive than the requirement to have an authorisation as such, the justification for such a system will need to be convincing. Allocation procedures for artificially limited rights will also have to comply with Article 10 of the Directive, meaning they must be non-discriminatory, justified by an over-riding public interest, proportionate, clear and unambiguous, objective, made public in advance, and transparent and accessible. In addition, according to Article 15, member states must examine any quantitative restrictions to the provisions of services that exist in their national legal systems, and ensure that they are non-discriminatory, necessary and proportionate. These broad criteria offer slightly more wiggle room to the member states than those in Article 12. In particular the obligation to issue limited authorisations for a limited period of time does not seem to apply. Whereas Article 12(2) prohibits authorisations for an unlimited period and automatic renewals in situations of natural scarcity, Article 11 allows for an exception to the obligation to issue authorisations for an unlimited period of time if a limited number of authorisations are available because of an overriding reason related to the public interest.

5.2. *CO_2 Emission Permits*

In the case of CO_2 emission permits, matters are quite different. In this field, we find detailed regulation on how the member states should allocate rights,[38] and the EU reserves some competences in relation to the procedure for itself. I will not discuss the procedure for allocating emission rights in great detail, others have already done that.[39] Rather, I will attempt to illustrate the relation between the level of detail of the Regulation and the goal the EU legislator was trying to achieve in combination with its competence to do so in the face of the inability of the member states to tackle this issue.

The EU has a shared competence when it comes to environmental protection. It is 'to preserve, protect and improve the quality of the environment, to contribute towards protecting human health, and to ensure a prudent and rational utilization of natural resources,' subject to the principle of subsidiarity.[40] Thus, the EU can only act if this goal cannot be achieved at the national or local level, and if it is itself better able to achieve it. With regard to CO_2 emissions, there is a broad consensus that individual nations are ill-

38 Directive 2009/29/EC of the European Parliament and of the Council of 23 April 2009 amending Directive 2003/87/EC so as to improve and extend the greenhouse gas emission allowance trading scheme of the Community [2009] OJ L140/63 and Directive 2003/87/EC of the European Parliament and of the Council of 13 October 2003 establishing a scheme for greenhouse gas emission allowance trading within the Community and amending Council Directive 96/61/EC [2003] OJ L275/32.

39 See the chapter by Rønne for a more comprehensive overview of the CO_2 emission trading system.

40 P.P. Craig, *EU Administrative Law*, 2nd ed., Oxford University Press, Oxford 2012, p. 11.

suited to resolve this problem. The EU legislator itself promotes the view that the reduction of CO_2 emission levels that it has committed to under the Kyoto protocol can only be achieved through a scheme operated with the highest possible degree of economic efficiency and on the basis of fully harmonised conditions of allocation within the Community.[41] The solution the EU has chosen, a Union-wide system of emission rights trading, most certainly needs to be created on the EU level. As I will argue below, the member states are probably unable to reach the desired reduction on their own, if only because they have a powerful incentive to give too many emission rights to their own nationals. Thus, it is only proper that the EU sets the ceiling. However, the manner in which they must allocate the rights given to them is also heavily regulated to ensure that the necessary reductions are achieved in the most efficient manner possible. Hence, the primary goal of reducing emissions is married expertly to the all-pervasive concern for an efficient market. The goal of the Directive is to promote reductions of greenhouse gas emissions in a cost-effective and economically efficient manner,[42] and the manner in which emission rights must be allocated must create this efficiency.

The member states have significantly less freedom to design their own procedures. The EU sets the ceiling, and determines the level of emissions for each country.[43] This is a textbook case of a competence that is better exercised at the supranational level. If member states are to set emission levels themselves, they will be tempted to free ride and set the emission levels for their national industry too high. They know this will matter little if all others comply. The impact of their transgression on the total level of emissions will be limited, they will still profit from the lower emission levels, and their national industry gains a competitive edge. If others do not comply, they will not want to hamper their national industry by imposing restrictions on them that will do no good anyway, because other member states retain high emission levels. So, independent of the behaviour of all the others, member states will have an incentive to set the emission level too high. This danger is not merely theoretical, as shown by the first periods of emission trading.[44] Because there were too many emission rights to begin with, their price was low, and the trading system did not really work. The EU legislator had good reasons to be convinced it was acting in compliance with the principle of subsidiarity when attributing the power to set the ceiling to the Commission.

The allocation of emission rights is regulated as well, and should take place through a fairly complex system of grandfathering cum auction. In addition, rights are tradable. The EU legislator has decided on auctioning as the basic principle for allocation, because 'it is the simplest, and generally considered to be the most economically efficient system.' It should 'eliminate windfall profits and put new entrants and economies growing faster than average on the same competitive footing as existing installations.'[45] The manner in

41 Para. 15 of the preamble to Directive 2009/29/EC.
42 Directive 2009/29/EC, para. 1 of the preamble.
43 Directive 2009/29/EC Article 9.
44 Kettner et al. 2010, p. 1.
45 Directive 2009/29/EC, para. 15 of the preamble.

which auctions should be organised is further defined in a separate regulation adopted pursuant to Article 10(4).[46] More detailed rules are probably quite welcome to the member states, who see themselves confronted with the task of designing auctions that ensure that operators, in particular any SMEs covered by the Community scheme, have full, fair and equitable access, that all participants have access to the same information at the same time and that participants do not undermine the operation of the auction, that the organisation and participation in auctions is cost-efficient and undue administrative costs are avoided, and that access to allowances is granted for small emitters.[47] The EU legislator has also addressed the issue of new entrants. It decided to harmonise this issue 'in order to maintain the environmental and administrative efficiency of the Community scheme,' and 'to avoid distortions of competitions and the early depletion of the entrant's reserve.'[48]

As said, the EU legislator justifies these fairly intrusive rules with the argument that the only way in which the Union can meet its obligations under the Kyoto agreement is to reduce emissions in as efficient a manner as possible. If the goal is to be achieved at all, there is only one way of doing it: the Directive's way.

5.3. Radio Frequencies and the Electronic Communication Directives

As regards the division of radio frequencies, the EU legislator is once again practicing restraint.[49] Deciding on the best way to allocate these resources is not a simple feat, as evidenced by some of the other contributions in this book. EU law provides only limited guidance. Article 9(1) of the Framework Directive[50] requires that the allocation and assignment of radio frequencies for electronic communication services are based on objective, transparent, non-discriminatory and proportionate criteria. The details are not expanded upon in the Directive. Likewise, Article 5(2) of the Authorization Directive[51] requires that rights of use of radio frequencies to providers of radio or television broadcast content services shall be granted through open, transparent, and non-discriminatory procedures, and if the number of rights of use to be granted for radio frequencies is limited, again these rights should be granted on the basis of selection

46 Commission Regulation (EU) No. 1031/2010 of 12 November 2010 on the timing, administration and other aspects of auctioning of greenhouse gas emission allowances pursuant to Directive 2003/87/EC of the European Parliament and of the Council establishing a scheme for greenhouse gas emission allowances trading within the Community [2010] OJ L302/2.

47 Directive 2009/29/EC Article 10(4).

48 Directive 2009/29/EC para. 16 of the preamble.

49 See the chapter by Oberst in this book for a more detailed treatment of the allocation of radio frequencies.

50 Directive 2002/21/EC of the European Parliament and of the Council of 7 March 2002 on a common regulatory framework for electronic communications networks and services (Framework Directive) [2002] OJ L 108/33.

51 Directive 2003/87/EC of the European Parliament and of the Council of 7 March 2002 on the authorisation of electronic communications networks and services [2003] OJ L 108/21.

criteria which must be objective, transparent, non-discriminatory and proportionate.[52] They must also take into account the achievement of the objectives mentioned in Article 8 of the Framework Directive, i.e.: promoting competition in the provision of electronic communications networks, electronic communications services and associated facilities and services; contributing to the development of the internal market; and promoting the interests of the citizens of the EU. The inclusion of these elements that must be taken into account when designing an allocation procedure means the telecom Directives go a little further than the Services Directive. When allocating frequencies, service obligations, or authorisations, public authorities must heed the goals of creating competition, promoting the internal market, and promoting the interests of the citizens. The latter point includes ensuring that all citizens have access to electronic communication services at a reasonable price.[53]

If the Member States decide to impose universal service obligations as per the Universal Service Directive,[54] the addressee of the obligations must be assessed in an open, transparent and non-discriminatory procedure. This obligation is commemorative of the principle of transparency as it has been developed in public procurement law and in relation to service concessions.

The allocation of radio frequencies and other scarce resources under the telecom Directives has to take different objectives into account, and must balance social interests against the interest in having a competitive internal market. In this respect it is not so different from the allocation of emission rights. The difference in the manner in which the allocation procedure is regulated is significant though. The telecom Directives only provide a number of principles that must be observed, and a number of goals that must be taken into account. It is left to the member states to balance these goals, or at least to determine what procedures are best suited to achieve those goals in their national market. There is not one right way in which to achieve a goal that is shared by the Community as a whole. Instead, the EU legislator shows restraint, and allows the member states to adapt allocation procedures to their national circumstances. The reason for the restraint practiced by the EU legislator can be found in the principle of subsidiarity. The telecom Directives, like most EU regulation, attempt to improve the functioning of the market. In addition, they aim to ensure that all EU citizens have access to reasonably priced communication services. The latter goal differs from the reduction of CO_2 emissions: there is no evident reason why it cannot be accomplished at the national level, without the EU legislator stepping in to give detailed rules about how it should be done.

52 See also Article 4(2) of Commission Directive 2002/77/EC of 16 September 2002 on competition in the markets for electronic communications networks and services [2002] OJ L249/21 (the Competition Directive) which requires such decision to be based on objective, transparent, non-discriminatory and proportionate criteria.

53 See para. 4 of the preamble to the Framework Directive, as well as the Universal Service Directive.

54 Directive 2002/22/EC of the European Parliament and of the Council of 7 March 2002 on universal service and users' rights relating to electronic communications networks and services (Universal Service Directive) [2002] OJ L108/51.

Nor would anyone make the argument that the only way to achieve a basic level of service provision is through a flawless, optimally efficient, EU-wide market. Indeed, the tenet of the telecom Directives appear to be that the EU legislator recognises that the member states are better able to assess the circumstances on their national markets, and to determine what concrete measures best serve the purposes of the Directives.[55]

6. Conclusions

We have seen that the allocation of limited rights is a versatile and delicate policy tool. Limited rights can be used to achieve a variety of policy goals, some of them laudable, some of them less so. Public authorities can distribute limited rights in a manner that contributes to the overall efficiency of the economy and maximises welfare, or to the resolution of market failures. They can use them to stimulate the economic development of vulnerable groups or as a trade barrier against foreign undertakings, or they can simply sell them to earn money. A number of these goals can be achieved simultaneously, others conflict. Whether and to what extent a particular allocation procedure contributes to the realisation of a given policy goal will depend on the details of its design as well as the circumstances on the market.

The EU legislator has two reasons to be interested in the allocation of limited public rights. First, allocation procedures can interfere with the proper functioning of the market, especially when rights are awarded pursuant to discriminatory criteria. Second, the EU legislator may want to use limited rights as an instrument when it is trying to give effect to EU policy. In either case, it is limited by the principles of conferred powers, subsidiarity and proportionality. It may only enact legislation on a particular subject when the competence to do so has been given to it in the Treaties. It can only use this competence when the member states fail to resolve an issue on the national level, and when it can provide a better solution than they can. Even so, its legislation cannot go any further than is necessary to achieve that particular goal. The most important competence in regard to limited public rights is the EU's power to legislate on the internal market. However, environmental protection and social issues, areas where it also shares legislative competence with the member states, can be relevant as well.

Because limited public rights have economic value, their allocation invariably has the potential to affect the internal market. Thus, the EU legislator is always competent. From the perspective of the internal market, there is one worst way to allocate limited rights: they should never be used to favour nationals over non-nationals. Not only do such practices interfere with the market at the expense of non-nationals, in the long run they

55 The downside of this approach is that the completion of the internal market is delayed. The Commission has issued a proposal for a new regulation to finally realize a single market for electronic communication services. Proposal Com 2013 (627) of 11.09.2013 for a Regulation of the European Parliament and of the Council laying down measures concerning the European single market for electronic communications and to achieve a connected Continent. However, the guidance provided on how to allocate limited rights remains scarce.

are also harmful to the national economy itself. In other words: they do not achieve their goal, and the economy of the EU as a whole suffers from such practices. Because national authorities have an incentive to engage in these practices despite their destructiveness, the competence of the EU legislator to resolve this issue is a given. However, discriminating against non-nationals is already prohibited in primary EU-law. The Courts have played an important role in applying this principle to the allocation of limited rights, and the role of the legislator in this respect has been modest.

The internal market benefits most from one particular way of allocating limited rights. The 'best' way to allocate rights, when by 'best' we mean most efficient, is to give them to those candidates who value them the most, measured by their willingness to pay, or their ability to generate profit from them. Such a division mimics the one a perfect market would arrive at, is the most efficient, and therefore best in terms of general welfare. But although the internal market points in the direction of allocation procedures that emphasize efficiency and contribute to competition, EU law does respect the fact that the allocation of limited public rights can also serve other goals, and these goals have to be balanced against the interest in efficiency. These goals may be relevant to the EU as a whole, but they might as well vary between member states. Even when the goals are clear, the manner in which an allocation procedure works out will in part depend on the circumstances of what might well be a national or regional market, and the member states will often be better able to decide on how to design allocation procedures in the manner that achieves these goals best than the EU. In accordance with the principle of subsidiarity, the EU legislator leaves these tasks to the member states and only steps in when he deems primary EU law to be insufficient for some reason.

Even when there is additional regulation, this will often be general. The Services Directive and the telecom Directives suffice for the most part with identifying a number of principles that allocation procedures must comply with. The Services Directive contains a small number of slightly more concrete obligations, and the telecom Directives identify a number of goals that must be taken into account when designing allocation procedures. Even so, the exact details of the procedure are left to the authorities of the member states. Again, although the EU legislator prescribes a number of goals that must be taken into account, it appears to recognise that national authorities are in a better position to balance these goals, or at least to assess the relevant circumstances on their national markets that would warrant this allocation procedure or that.

The EU legislator does not contribute much on the issue of artificial scarcity. Limiting the number of public rights that are available is allowed under EU law, although such limitation will have to comply with a number of criteria. The EU legislator has not provided much detail on when a system like that will be justifiable. It does recognise the usefulness of artificial ceilings, as evidenced by its use of them in the field of emission trading. Indeed, CO_2 emissions show us that the EU legislator will take it upon itself to set an appropriate ceiling if it feels the member states themselves are unable to do so.

Occasionally, the EU legislator does provide detailed regulation. Emission rights are once again a prominent example. Here, the EU legislator argues that the only way to realise sufficiently low emission levels is through the relatively uniform system it has imposed. It has taken firm decisions on what it considers the most efficient way to allocate these rights, and has expanded considerable time and energy on designing detailed rules that auctions must comply with. I would argue that the importance of such regulation for the allocation of rights that do not fall under its scope is fairly limited. The emphasis on efficiency is only justified because it is required to achieve environmental goals, not because an efficient internal market is in itself a requirement, and the rules for the design of the auction procedure depend on the particular right involved and the characteristics of the market for that right. Neither the demand for highly efficient procedures nor the design details that are to achieve this efficiency can be easily transferred to other fields. I expect the approach where the EU legislator practices restraint and leaves it to national authorities to assess which allocation methods will get the best results given the circumstances they observe will usually be the wiser.

Unfortunately, such an approach does little to resolve the current confusion resulting from the case law on limited rights. Although I firmly believe that the member states should cherish the relative freedom they enjoy to design allocation procedures in a manner that allows them to pursue their own policies, as long as they comply with certain broad principles, I also know that it is far from easy to determine what these broad principles require in practice. When one sees the time and energy that is expended to design an auction to divide radio spectrum, it is hard not to doubt the ability of small local authorities to design allocation procedures that successfully merge the requirements from EU law with their own policy objectives. More detailed rules on the EU level are not the solution though. They would diminish the flexibility of allocation procedures, and hence member states' ability to pursue their own policy goals, as well as their ability to adapt procedures to local circumstances to maximise their contribution to both their own goals and those of the EU. I see two alternative solutions. First, the issue could be addressed by the national legislator. This would allow for some adaptation to local circumstances, but would still diminish flexibility. Alternatively, the Commission could issue guidelines on one or more basic procedures that comply with EU law, and that provide a safety net to public authorities that are at a loss as to how they should design an allocation procedure. That way, public authorities that do not have the resources to design a procedure from scratch could just pick one of the safe procedures, and rest assured that even though they have not optimised their procedure, at least they are complying with EU law.

Frank van Ommeren*

CHAPTER 4. CHALLENGES FOR THE NATIONAL LEGISLATOR: THE ALLOCATION OF LIMITED RIGHTS BY THE ADMINISTRATION

1. Introduction

The idea that limited authorisations – and to a lesser extent: limited grants – might be allocated in a different way than in the order of the receipt of the applications, is an idea that in the world of general administrative law still does not get sufficient attention. Many licensing public authorities are unsure or have no idea of what is possible – at least in theory. One of the most important measures to offer more insights and certainties is a smart applicable national regulatory framework. The aim of this piece is to deliver a prime and modest contribution to this, by developing a general regulatory framework that can serve as a template.

As stated in the introductory Chapter of this book, with *limited* authorisations and grants I mean that the number of authorisations and grants has been limited to a certain maximum.[1] This limited character raises the fundamental question how the administration should allocate these public rights.

The allocation of limited authorisations and grants confronts the national legislator with new questions; questions which until now had been overlooked or left unconsidered. In any event, the allocation of limited authorisations and grants will give the legislator much to think about. To prevent misunderstandings, with the national legislator I mean every qualified legislator within a national context. This can be the authorized legislator at a state level, but also a competent regional or local public authority with the power to legally establish general binding rules, delegated rulemaking included. This piece goes neither into the room the EU legislator leaves to the national legislator nor into the national obligation to implement EU directives that regard limited rights. The role of the EU legislator in the discourse on limited authorisations and grants has thus far been rather modest.[2]

* Frank van Ommeren is full professor of constitutional and administrative law at the VU University Amsterdam, the Netherlands. Any comments or thoughts on this contribution can be addressed to f.j.van.ommeren@vu.nl.

1 See Chapter 1 by Adriaanse, van Ommeren, den Ouden and Wolswinkel in this book.

2 See the chapter by Buijze in this book.

For this contribution I take a general perspective, independent of the legal system of a certain state, although I will give a few examples from the Dutch legislative practise. Writing in general terms about national regulations confronts us with a well-known difficulty: every legal system has its own specific characteristics. To overcome this problem I will use a few insights that are recognizable from general regulatory doctrine.[3] Without those notions it would be almost impossible to paint a picture of a general regulatory framework.

I will take the position that a national general regulatory framework on the allocation of authorisations and grants should consist of both principles-based and rules-based regulations and that it is worthwhile to distinguish clearly between both kinds of provisions. At the same time it is very important to avoid from the start the risk of overregulation.

Writing – from direct experience – as a lawyer who used to draft national legislation, I will now first focus on problems and questions close to home. Of course, I will also make use of experiences that originate from my earlier national publications on limited authorisations as an academic.[4] Moreover, there are the experiences with the VU University Amsterdam and Leiden University research project and national expert meetings on this subject in the recent past.[5] And finally I had the opportunity to use the distinct and fine contributions to this book.

2. Problematic Experiences

As often in the world of law and regulation, it is useful to start with a problematic experience. I would like to start with the Betfair gambling case, a Dutch case originally, which most readers are probably familiar with. Right from the outset, I should say that I am not so much interested in the juridical merits of this specific case, but rather in the consequences of a case like this for the legislator.

The Betfair case bears upon the *Stichting de Nationale Sporttotalisator ('De Lotto')*, which is a non-profit-making foundation governed by private law. De Lotto has held the licence for the organisation of sports-related prize competitions, the lottery and numbers games since 1961. The licence for the organisation of a totalisator on the outcome of horse races was granted to a company called Scientific Games Racing BV ('SGR'). For years, a practise of automatic renewal of these licences has existed. The Minister for Justice renewed the licence of De Lotto and that granted to SGR, without any competitive

3 See on this approach in general e.g.: R. Baldwin and M. Cave, *Understanding Regulation: Theory, Strategy and Practice*, Oxford, Oxford University Press 1999. B. Morgan and K. Yeung, *An Introduction to Law and Regulation*, Cambridge, Cambridge University Press 2007. See also the impressive volume: D. Levi-Faur (ed.), *Handbook on the Politics of Regulation*, Cheltenham, Edward Elgar 2011.

4 Incl. F.J. van Ommeren, *Schaarse vergunningen. De verdeling van schaarse vergunningen als onderdeel van het algemene bestuursrecht*, (inaugural lecture VU University Amsterdam), Deventer: Kluwer 2004. I supervised the PhD-dissertation of C.J. Wolswinkel, *De verdeling van schaarse publiekrechtelijke rechten*, (diss. VU Amsterdam), Boom Juridische uitgevers, The Hague 2013.

5 F.J. van Ommeren, W. den Ouden and C.J. Wolswinkel (eds.), *Schaarse publieke rechten*, Boom Juridische uitgevers, The Hague 2011.

tendering procedure. The services of the British company Betfair are provided solely via the internet and by telephone. Betfair wished to actively offer its services on the Netherlands market. However, the Minister denied the access to this market.

The Administrative Law Division of the Dutch Council of State – helped by preliminary rulings of the European Court of Justice[6] – halted this renewal practice because of a conflict with the freedom to provide services. Other companies must also be given the opportunity to compete for obtaining these limited licences, although room is left for an exception.[7]

The consequence of the Betfair case is that the Dutch procedure for granting certain kinds of limited gambling licences is considered to be improper, because the procedure is not transparent enough and the opportunities for third parties to compete for a licence are insufficient.[8] Consequently the Dutch Gambling Act – also called the Law on Games of chance (*Wet op de kansspelen*) – needs to be amended.

The main cause of the absence of opportunities to compete for an authorisation is that a kind of backdoor licensing procedure – "by direct agreement" – had been a continuous practice for decennia. I could give many other examples of this common practise, not only at a national level, but also at a regional and local level.

There are many sound legal reasons why this practise should change. Moreover, the Dutch administration also shows – on various political, economical and social grounds – an increasing preference for procedures that offer the opportunity to compete for a limited authorisation or grant.

At the same time is it important to keep in mind that a requirement of ex ante transparency probably doesn't always make sense for so called *un*limited licences. To grant an unlimited licence, it is sufficient that the applicant fulfils all the qualitative conditions to obtain the licence. The requirement that third parties should be informed about the available licence – to get the opportunity to compete for this licence – applies to limited licences only.

In the Betfair case the administration chose a temporary way out. In his judgment the Court left room for an exception in case the operator is a public operator whose management is subject to direct State supervision or a private operator whose activities are subject to strict control by the public authorities. Because of this the Minister appointed a so-called "*state commissioner*" – with extreme veto powers – in the supervisory board of Lotto.[9] The consequence of this solution is that there is no obligation anymore to offer the opportunity for third parties to compete for a licence.

6 Case C-203/08, *Sporting Exchange* [2010] ECR I-4695.

7 ABRvS (Administrative Law Section of the Dutch Council of State) 23 March 2011, LJN BP8768, AB (Administrative Law Reports) 2011, 230 m.nt. Wolswinkel.

8 See the contribution of M. Olfers, 'The Allocation of Limited Authorisations in the Netherlands: the Gambling Industry', in P. Adriaanse, F. van Ommeren, W. den Ouden and J. Wolswinkel, *Scarcity and the State II. Member State Reports on Gambling Licences, Radio Frequencies and CO_2 Emission Permits*, Intersentia, Antwerp 2016.

9 Kamerstukken II (Parliamentary Documents, Second Chamber) 2011/12, 32 264, nr. 25, p. 3.

3. A General Regulatory Framework

3.1. Regulation of Scarcity

Now it is time to take a look at the consequences for the legislator. In harmony with the topic of this book (see also the introductory Chapter) I write about *limited* authorisations and grants. As mentioned, a public right is limited when there are more applicants than available rights. The hazard of this starting point is that we are inclined to ignore the preliminary question of *when* the legislator should choose for a limited or maximized scheme of authorisation or grants.

Markets can be conceived as a mode or a means of regulation.[10] Scarcity is a relative notion that binds supply and demand. There are many other ways to regulate scarcity than by a scheme of authorisation or grants. Scarcity can be regulated at an abstract and a concrete level. A licence ceiling focuses primarily on the application of the rule; in other words: it focuses on the issuing of the licence or grant (against the background of certain general rules). But scarcity itself could also be regulated on the level of the general rules itself.[11] When the scarcity is regulated at an *abstract* level, is it not a necessity (although a possibility) that the licences and grants are limited in the sense that there are more applicants than available rights. For instance, in the Netherlands, environmental licences as such are not limited in this sense. The scarcity is rather regulated at the higher level of environmental policy plans. This means that every applicant who meets all of the requirements receives the environmental licence, regardless the number of applicants. However, this is different with the tradable CO_2-emission permits, which are limited indeed.[12]

The point here is to make clear that – before the legislator or the administrative authority have got round the question whether a limited authorisation scheme is necessary – the preceding question is on what level the scarcity should be regulated. A choice for a limited or maximized scheme of authorisations and grants implies a choice for a *concrete* level of regulation of the scarcity, the level of application.[13] I am afraid that the legislator often overlooks this important issue or at least does not make this choice deliberately. In my opinion this is a legislative practice that should change. The general regulatory framework of which I will sketch the main outlines hereinafter, is based on the premise that the legislator intentionally aspires to regulate the scarcity at a concrete level and therefore deliberately decides to opt for a limited or maximized scheme of authorisations and grants.

10 See profoundly: E.L. Rubin, *Beyond Camelot. Rethinking Politics and Law for the Modern State*, Princeton University Press, Princeton and Oxford 2005, pp. 308 ff.

11 Van Ommeren 2004, p. 70, 71 and F.J. van Ommeren, 'Bestuursrecht is verdelingsrecht', in: T. de Gier a.o. (eds.), *Goed verdedigbaar*, Kluwer, Deventer 2011, p. 100.

12 See J.R. van Angeren & L. Westendorp, 'The Allocation of CO_2 Permits in the Netherlands', in P. Adriaanse, F. Van Ommeren, W. den Ouden and J. Wolswinkel, *Scarcity and the State II. Member State Reports on Gambling Licences, Radio Frequencies and CO_2 Emission Permits*, Intersentia, Antwerp 2016.

13 This seems also presupposed in the interesting analytical approach of Arroyo and Utrilla in Chapter 2 of this book.

3.2. *Different Legislative Techniques*

The legal problems encountered by Betfair and others could have largely been prevented if the legislation would have shed a brighter light on how to deal with limited authorisations and grants. To accommodate the gambling legislation it is useful to learn from *other regulatory regimes*: what provisions do they offer on limited authorisations? Notably, in the Netherlands, as far as the area of gambling is concerned, the minister for Justice has indicated that for the amendment of the Gambling Act, he wants to learn from the experiences with the transparent allocation procedures in the field of radiofrequencies.[14]

It is very important to gain insight from other areas of regulation. However, this mutual exchange of knowledge is extremely hard in our sectioned and categorized society and legal system. In the world of environmental law, for instance, there is abundant ignorance of what happens in the world of telecommunications – and in the circle of telecommunications there is almost no understanding of what happens in the world of education or public health. General administrative law and general social and economic regulation help to bridge these gaps.[15] General overarching regulation could be regarded as a kind of an *intermediary* between more divided regulatory regimes. To accomplish more general legislation – like a general regulatory framework for limited authorisations and grants – the role of general regulatory regimes and general administrative law is of the greatest importance.

There are several ways of realizing a general regulatory framework for limited authorisations and grants. We can think of a separate general act on limited authorisations and grants or of a special regulation contained within a piece of legislation such as a General Administrative Law Act. The difference between a separate general act and a chapter in a General Administrative Law Act is not fundamental. Both are general pieces of legislation. And in both systems complementary rules, which can show differences in every sector, are necessary. That is why I will not pay attention to the differences between these two systems.

What should a general regulatory framework contain in order to improve the allocation of limited authorisations and grants? I think about two different kinds of legislative techniques: principles-based regulation and rules-based regulation. First of all, a set of overarching principles could be codified, which are meaningful for the allocation of limited rights. A second possibility is to codify a set of detailed prescriptive rules about the allocation of limited authorisations and grants. Although it is important to distinguish clearly between the applicable principles and rules, it is of course possible to combine both kinds of legislative techniques. This last option has my distinct preference; I will come back to that in Section 7.

14 Kamerstukken II (Parliamentary Documents, Second Chamber) 2008/09, 24 557, nr. 93, p. 7.

15 See for a classic general approach on social and economic regulation: A.I. Ogus, *Regulation: Legal Form and Economic Theory*, Hart Publishing, Oxford – Portland Oregon 2004.

4. Principles-Based Regulation

4.1. *Which Overarching Legal Principles?*

Which overarching legal principles could be codified, which the authorities should comply with when they issue limited licences or grants? I am thinking in particular here of the principle of equal treatment and the principle of transparency. After all, both principles also play an important part in European case law. Other legal principles are conceivable as well however.[16] For instance, in Dutch case law the principle of due care, the principle of proportionality and the principle of legal certainty are also at stake.[17] Nevertheless, I consider the principle of equal treatment and the principle of transparency to be the most significant for a general regulatory framework. The advantage is, moreover, that this reduces the risk of unnecessary differences arising between limited authorisations and grants that are covered by national law only and those also covered by European law.

4.2. *The Principle of Equal Treatment*

The principle of equal treatment manifests itself in many forms and variations and can be elaborated in many different ways. In many legal systems the principle of equal treatment is already established in some way. But the question is rather to what extent it is possible to establish it as a useful overarching principle for the *allocation* of public rights and to improve the allocation of limited authorisations and grants.

Applied to the allocation of limited authorisations and grants, the principle of equal treatment has a much broader scope than a prohibition to discriminate on certain grounds only.[18] The principle of equal treatment compels authorities to offer potential candidates and (in a later stage) the actual applicants an equal opportunity. This principle works here in two directions: it reduces the chance that certain candidates and applicants will be disadvantaged while encouraging (other) candidates and applicants to be favoured. The principle of equal treatment is considered an overarching principle that should be applied in *all* allocation procedures, irrespective of the sort of allocation procedure.

But this is not the whole story. There are many ways to realize equal treatment. This is related to the goal of the allocation. Principles-based regulation is also of a goal-based character. Equal treatment can be achieved both in a procedural and a substantive way.

16 Dutch legal doctrine shows various opinions about the fundamental principles that govern the allocation of limited authorisations and the obligation of transparency, see Wolswinkel 2013, p. 73 ff opting for the principle of equality and the principle of legal certainty in contrast to A. Drahmann, *Transparante en eerlijke verdeling van schaarse besluiten,* (diss. Leiden), Kluwer, Deventer 2015, pp. 367 ff who opts for the principle of equality only.

17 F.J. van Ommeren, 'Schaarse publieke rechten: een verplichting tot het creëren van mededingingsruimte?', in: F.J. van Ommeren, W. den Ouden & C.J. Wolswinkel (eds.), *Schaarse publieke rechten,* The Hague, Boom Juridische uitgevers 2011, pp. 255 ff.

18 See for a clear explanation why discrimination is usually not an appropriate term in law: J.H. Gerards, *Judicial Review in Equal Treatment Cases*, Leiden/Boston: Martinus Nijhoff Publishers 2005, chapter 2, section 1.1.2.

The choice for this depends mainly on the purpose of the allocation. A substantive fulfilment of the principle of equal treatment gives insight in the *differentiation criteria,* which might or might not justify a certain decision. The question what constitutes equal treatment depends on the goal of the allocation. It is the goal or objective of the allocation procedure that makes it possible to distinguish between relevant and irrelevant differences amongst candidates and applicants.[19]

The principle of equal treatment can be elaborated and codified in many ways – also as an allocation principle – but the question arises whether it might be more useful to include a strict *rule* in the general regulatory framework, which states that the *goal* of the allocation should always be expressed. So then we would shift to a regulatory framework that is more rules-based. I will pay attention to rules-based regulation hereinafter; but first the other principle.

4.3. The Principle of Transparency

The other principle – which, at first glance, presents itself as an overarching principle to be codified in legislation – is, as mentioned above, the principle of transparency. This principle is closely related to the principle of equality. The European Court of Justice even ruled that the principle of equal treatment and non-discrimination *implies* an obligation of transparency.[20] (It also speaks of the principles of equal treatment and of non-discrimination on the ground of nationality and "with the *consequent* obligation of transparency";[21] or of the obligation of transparency "which *flows* from" the principle of equal treatment.)[22] The idea that these principles are closely related is understandable in so far as the principle of transparency is considered as a procedural principle. Transparency is required not only to place potential candidates on an equal footing but also to facilitate the control of compliance.[23] Transparency makes it possible to review whether the principle of equal treatment has been observed.

The obligation of transparency requires especially the administrative authority to ensure, for the benefit of any potential candidate and applicant, a degree of publicity or advertising, sufficient to enable the market in question to be opened up to competition and the impartiality of the allocation procedures to be reviewed. These purposes of the obligation of transparency are well known from the case law of the European Court of Justice.[24]

19 The idea that the principle of equality itself is empty of content and must incorporate some external values to have meaning, is rather widespread; see e.g. already Peter Westen, 'The Empty Idea of Equality', (1982) 95 *Harv L Rev*, 537, who pushes this idea extremely far.

20 For instance Case C-19/00, *SIAC Construction* [2001] ECR I-7225 para. 41.

21 For instance Case C-203/08, *Sporting Exchange* [2010] ECR I-4695 para. 39.

22 For instance Case C-470/11, *Garkalns,* [2012], para. 42.

23 Cf. S. Prechal & M. de Leeuw, 'Dimensions of Transparency: The Building Blocks for a New Legal Principle?' (2007) 0 (1) *REALaw (Review of European Administrative Law)* 59.

24 Case C-324/07, *Coditel Brabant* [2008] ECR I-8457 para. 25; Case C-91/08, *Wall* [2010] ECR I-2815 para. 36; Case C-203/08, *Sporting Exchange* [2010] ECR I-4695 para. 41; Case C-64/08, *Engelmann* [2010] ECR I-8219 para. 50; Joined Cases C-72/10 and C-77/10, *Costa and Cifone* [2012] ECR para. 55.

The question arises to what extent it is useful to include this obligation of transparency in a general act of national law. There are a few difficulties. The principle is applicable in any event when *limited* authorisations of grants are concerned. But outside this area, this principle of transparency is not automatically at stake.[25] So it is rather difficult to determine the scope of this principle. This invokes (again) the question of the scope of the term "limited authorisations and grants": this concept has to be defined as concise as possible.[26] That is more than merely a technical complication.

Furthermore, a difficult aspect of codification is that the principle of transparency has also different and broader meanings than the ones just mentioned here, like the access to documents and openness of government. For the legislator this could be a problem as well, although these different kinds of transparency have recently been clearly disentangled in legal literature[27] Moreover, the principle of transparency seems to overlap, partially, with other legal principles: not only with the principle of equal treatment but also with the principle of legal certainty and the principle of due care. This makes it even more complicated to codify this principle in a general sense.

Right now, the question arises whether it would be preferable to break down the principle of transparency into several more detailed, strict prescriptive rules, which can be adopted in legislation. Again, we would then shift to a rule-based regulatory framework.

5. General Prescriptive Rules

5.1. The Core Elements

Although codification of these two legal principles in a principles-based general regulatory framework would be an improvement, I think it would be useful to take a further step: we should try to develop a more detailed set of general prescriptive rules on how to allocate limited authorisations and grants.

The advantage of a rule-based regulatory framework would be that the public authorities get more of a grip on the allocation problem and know – with more certainty – in advance how to act. Again, my aim is to develop overarching general rules that are applicable irrespective of the social or economical sector in which they will be applied. Without going into too much detail, I would like to sketch a few possibilities.

First of all, it is very well possible to stay close to the principle of transparency in the sense we have just touched upon. Potential candidates and applicants should be adequately informed in due time. It is probably easier to express more accurately in a general act about *what* these interested parties should be informed and furthermore *when* and *how* this should be done. What does this mean more precisely? There are, I think, quite a few different topics of which interested parties should have knowledge in advance, before the launch of the allocation procedure.

25 See however Case C-470/11, *Garkalns*, [2012].

26 See for an early, instrumental attempt: Ogus 2004, p. 214, 318.

27 See Anoeska Buijze, *The Principle of Transparency in EU Law*, dissertation Utrecht University, BOXPress, 's-Hertogenbosch 2013.

To start with, interested parties should know in advance that a limited authorisation or grant is available! We should not underestimate the impact of such a strict and simple rule. At this moment it is often a real deficiency that potential third parties have no idea that a limited licence has become vacant. Governmental authorities often do not have the necessary insight to inform potential candidates. Neither do they have the required culture, habit or attitude for sharing this kind of information with them. The explanation for this is that for *un*limited licences and grants it is often not necessary to inform third parties in Advance. After All, when there is no limitation each potential applicant can apply for a licence at the very moment that suits him best. But with *limited* authorisations and grants this is very different of course. The obligation to inform potential third parties in due time about the availability of a free limited licence, involves ensuring that third parties get the same chance to compete for this licence.

Although this would be a big step forward, it is not enough in my opinion. The interested parties should also know what kind of *allocation procedure* the authorities will follow to issue the licence. Furthermore, they should be timely informed about the *selection and award criteria* that will be used. This demands that the authority determines the kind of allocation procedure on time and that this choice should be sufficiently advertised in advance of the procedure. It also means that adding new criteria or specifications at a later stage is not permissible. These are all prescriptive rules that can be deducted from the principle of transparency.

Furthermore, a general prescriptive rule should express that the *objective* of the allocation should be stated as unambiguous and sharp as possible. We can think of some rather different goals of allocation. They can have an economical nature, like the promotion of the free-market mechanism in a certain area or the enhancement of the position of newcomers at the relevant market. But they are certainly not restricted to economical purposes. They can also have a social, cultural or other character, for instance focussed on the protection of environmental interests. It is usually not sufficient to state a goal as "effective competition" or something alike. After all, effective competition is not a goal in itself but a means to a certain end. Therefore it is necessary to state the underlying objective of the competition too. One should not underestimate how difficult it is to apply this simple rule. Often regulations are rather vague about the purpose of the allocation; and when they try to be more explicit it seems not so easy to find a correct and univocal phrasing.[28] However, it is very important that this is taken seriously, because without a clear objective it is impossible to choose the appropriate allocation procedure and perform a fair comparison.

There are other requirements that are necessary for a general regulatory framework for limited authorisations and grants. It is important that the power to set a ceiling is conferred upon the administrative authorities. For reasons of legitimacy, clearness and accessibility a general legal framework should express that the power to set a ceiling of authorisations and grants can only be created by law. That a ceiling can be established, under certain conditions, and how this should be done, is – again – a big step forward. It

[28] This is not only true at a national but also at European level, see the chapter by Oberst in this book, section 3.5, about the difficulties to formulate the "competition standards" of radio spectrum policy.

will reduce quite some uncertainties of the administrative authorities. Such a rule purports to end the somewhat misty practice of ceilings that – at least in the Netherlands – are created by public policy only.[29]

Of course, in the European Union it is important that on the grounds of internal market law the national legislator is not allowed to call a ceiling for a prior authorisation scheme into being without an adequate justification. According to Union law an authorisation scheme is considered to be a restriction on the freedom of establishment or service provision (art. 49 and 56 TFEU). As is well-known, it is settled case-law that these restrictions must be applied without discrimination; must be justified by imperative requirements in the general interest; must not go beyond what is necessary in order to attain it; and must be suitable for achieving the objective which they pursue.[30] The fact that the authorisation is of a *limited* nature is considered to be an *additional* restriction on free movement, since it tends to limit the number of service providers. Therefore an additional justification by an overriding reason relating to the public interest is required to set a ceiling. This is not the place to elaborate on the nature of this additional justification, but it is very interesting to see how these general overriding reasons relating to the public interest are being translated into more specific "allocation objectives" in order to justify a limitation to the number of authorisations.[31] At the same time it seems that European case law shows that if limited authorisations classify as exclusive or special rights, this limitation might be quite easily justified with reference to the need of provision of services of general economic interest.[32]

5.2. *Types of Allocation Procedures*

Legislation which limits the number of authorisations and grants, but at the same time does not express how these authorisations and grants should be allocated – nor with which objectives this should be done – has to be considered incomplete.

So a general legal framework should give an overview of the most important available allocation procedures for limited authorisations and grants. These procedures can be categorized in different ways. The question is therefore which types of allocation procedures we wish to distinguish.[33] To start with, I think – for the time being: tentatively – of the following types of procedures.

29 For instance for certain games of chance, see ABRvS (Administrative Law Section of the Dutch Council of State) 18 july 2007, AB (Administrative Law Reports) 2007, 302, fn. J.H. Jans (Schindler).

30 See already Case C-55/94, *Gebhard* [1995] ECR I-4165, para. 37 and Case C-243/01, *Gambelli* [2003] ECR I-13031, para. 65. See for in-depth elaborations the chapters by Hatzopoulos and Wolswinkel in this book.

31 J. Wolswinkel, From Public Contracts to Limited Authorisations and Vice Versa: Exploring General Award Requirements from the EU Court's Corollary Approach, (2015) 24 *PPLR (Public Procurement Law Review)* 148, referring inter alia to Joined Cases C-570/07 and C-571/07, *Blanco Pérez and Chao Chómez* [2010] ECR I-4629, para 78, see also his chapter in this book.

32 Wolswinkel 2015, p. 150.

33 See also Chapter 1 by Adriaanse, van Ommeren, den Ouden and Wolswinkel.

As to the first procedure – the order of the receipt of the applications: *first come first served* – the question arises whether this procedure is suitable for the allocation of limited authorisations and grants: is this a procedure suitable to realize a kind of competition? There are different opinions about this.[34] However, in a general regulatory framework this kind of procedure should be mentioned, because it would be going too far to exclude it. It is up to the administrative authority to determine whether a certain kind of limited licence could be allocated by this type of procedure.

The second method – a *proportional division* – is mainly suitable for an allocation of divisible public rights, like grants or subsidies.

The option of a *lottery* implies that the administrative authority looses the possibility to use comparative criteria. A lottery is often used in combination with another allocation method. A lottery is mainly suitable as a final procedure after a comparative test, to choose between the remaining applicants.

The *comparative test* is also called the 'competitive test', 'beauty contest' or 'tender'.[35] A comparative test in a general sense can serve many different goals. The purpose of the comparison could be the *economically most advantageous* application, but it can also serve other goals, like the interest of the environment or cultural issues.

The *auction* is, strictly speaking, a special kind of comparative test. The same goes for the public procurement setting. A public procurement procedure has to be regarded as a *reverse* auction. These procedures are particularly suitable for stimulating a competitive setting.

To prevent misunderstandings, it seems necessary to pay a bit more attention to the public procurement procedure. It follows from the applicable EU directives when the authorities are obliged to apply this kind of procedure. However, it is also possible to apply this kind of procedure in cases that are not covered by these directives. The national legislator can choose to prescribe the public procurement procedure in cases outside the scope of these directives. The Dutch Act on the Transport of Passengers 2000 (*Wet personenvervoer 2000*), which requires the authorities to use the public procurement procedure to award concessions for the services of public transport offers an example. Instead of the lowest price or the most economically advantageous tender the highest price might be used as the award criterion. All in all, whether the public procurement procedure is used to grant a concession, authorisation, governmental commission or other object is also up to the legislator.

These allocation procedures have a basic structure in common.[36] The allocation of limited authorisations and grants basically takes place through a *phased decision-making process*. Apart from the procedure of first come first served they consist of a two-stage mechanism: first the selection stage and then the award stage. It is essential for limited authorisations and grants that it is not enough for the applicants to meet with all of the (selection) criteria, but that thereafter the applicants who were successful in the first stage have to compete between themselves. This makes a substantial difference with

34 Wolswinkel 2013, pp. 150 ff.

35 The term 'tender' should not be confused with the specific use of this term in public procurement settings.

36 Van Ommeren 2004, p. 23 ff.

non-limited public rights, where the public authorities are after all legally obliged to grant the authorisation or grant to all the applicants that comply with all the granting criteria. This essential feature should be expressed in the general regulatory framework.

The question arises whether a general regulatory framework should offer more than merely an overview of the possible allocation procedures from which a public authority could choose. From the perspective of the legislator it would be ideal if this framework could prescribe under which conditions and circumstances a certain allocation procedure should be applicable. However, this ambition seems to be too great. The differences between economic or social sectors are simply too large. It is primarily up to the *sector-specific* legislator or the administration to determine how to make the right choice for the adequate allocation procedure.[37]

The advantage of this legislative overview in a general regulatory framework is that it promotes coherence, consistency and uniformity without being a straightjacket. Even more important is that it explicitly brings to an end the bias or prejudice that most administrative procedures implicitly rest on the system of first come first served.

6. Other General Prescriptive Rules?

6.1. Nature of the Regulatory Framework

It is not my intention here to give a complete overview of what a general regulatory framework on limited authorisations and grants could contain. But the topics just mentioned – (1) the announcement of the vacancy of a limited licence, (2) including the obligation to inform interested parties on time, (3) the ceiling, (4) including the obligation to state explicitly the objective or goal of the allocation and (5) the choice of allocation procedures – are surely the most urgent ones.

This is already a high standard. It is obvious that quite some national statutory law does not meet these requirements. A clear example is the Dutch Gambling Act, which enables authorisations to be limited without offering an allocation mechanism.[38]

Apart from these fundamental ones mentioned above, there are at first glance rather a few topics one can think of to include in this general regulatory framework. We can think of the duration of the authorisation (temporal scope), the way to deal with incomplete applications, amendments after the award or the renewal of the authorisation, the transferability and tradability of the authorisation, the special role of advisors (referees, experts etc.), judicial protection, etc. It is impossible – and given the intentions of this piece: not necessary – to give a detailed elaboration of all of these topics. The main question is what should be a good reason to decide that a topic should be part of the general regulatory framework of authorisations and grants. To determine what topic should be included in this framework, the main focus should be the fact that these

[37] Wolswinkel concludes in Chapter 8 that in general EU law does not include any general preference rule.

[38] See on the consequences of this system the contribution of M. Olfers in P. Adriaanse, F. van Ommeren, W. den Ouden and J. Wolswinkel, *Scarcity and the State II. Member State Reports on Gambling Licences, Radio Frequencies and CO_2 Emission Permits*, Intersentia, Antwerp 2016.

public rights are *limited*, which gives sound reasons to draft legislation with specific provisions.

Moreover, once a topic is chosen, it is meaningful to regulate this topic only as far as is determined by its limited character. Take, for instance, the judicial protection against authorisations and claims. A number of legal systems already have a finely-woven administrative law system of judicial protection against authorisations. It is not useful to adopt these rules again in a general regulatory framework for limited authorisations and grants. That would result in double work. On the contrary, the question is which rules for the judicial protection of limited authorisations and grants should be added. Which *additional* rules are necessary because of the fact that the object of regulation, the public right, is limited?

It has been suggested that a distinction between the classical *bipolar* citizen-state model of administrative law on the one hand and a new *multipolar* model of the law of the allocation limited rights on the other, could show more insight into the new provisions which are necessary for the judicial protection.[39] However, administrative law concerning *non*-limited rights is essentially of a multipolar nature too, in the sense that the decision of a public authority not only establishes a legal relationship between the administration and the citizen who is directly involved, but is also legally relevant for interested third parties. We can think of the broader access to justice that interested third parties usually enjoy in administrative law procedures (compared to their legal position in private law), especially in spatial planning for instance. So it is rather questionable whether a conceptual distinction between bipolar and multipolar administrative law could be considered suitable to serve as a guideline for the development of additional legal rules on limited rights regarding judicial protection. However, this does not impede that it is very well possible to make additional rules that are especially relevant for the judicial protection of the allocation of limited authorisations and grants (see hereafter Section 6.5).

A general regulatory framework on limited authorisations and grants should only consist of the rules that are not already part of general administrative law (of unlimited authorisations). In my opinion this is a much more useful approach than trying to regulate nearly completely everything for the topic which is at stake. This approach is also of a much more confined character, which probably improves the chances of realisation. To get an idea about what this kind of legislative provision could mean, I will offer here a brief illustration of a few of these topics.

6.2. *Duration of the Authorisation*

Unless there is a statutory provision, it is up to the competent authority to decide whether it will grant a licence for a determined or an undetermined period. Often the legislator leaves the duration of the authorisation aside. However, this does not exclude that the legislator has the possibility to start from two different basic starting points, which are diametrically opposed to each other.

[39] See the chapter by Wollenschläger in this book.

From a point of view of diminishing unnecessary or excessively and burdensome procedures it is that preferable that an authorisation is granted for an *unlimited* period of time. The idea behind this is that this causes the fewest administrative burdens ("red tape"). The granting of authorisations demands a lot of efforts, both from the government as well as from the citizen. It is very important to keep these efforts as low as possible.[40] However, when the number of the public right is limited, this is supposed to be an inferior starting point, because another (economic) interest carries more weight.

When there is scarcity, it is preferable that the limited authorisation should be granted for a *limited* period of time. The idea behind this is to support the free market mechanism. The assumption is that the market is changing permanently and that this characteristic involves that, after a while, all the parties on the relevant market should be able to compete again for the limited public right. Especially newcomers should get the opportunity to enter the market. The case law of the European Court of Justice shows that the starting point is that the licensing of an (exclusive) limited public right for an unlimited period or a very long time means a limitation of the freedom of other parties to perform the relevant activity.[41]

These two points of view are both recognizable in the Services Directive (art. 11). The Services Directive puts forward that an authorisation granted to a provider shall *not* be for a *limited period* (art. 11(1)), except in certain situations that are explicitly stated. Such an important exception is made where 'the *number* of available authorisations is *limited* by an overriding reason relating to the public interest' (art. 11(1) sub b). In addition the Services Directive (art. 12) determines that 'Where the number of authorisations available for a given activity is limited because of the scarcity of available natural resources or technical capacity' (art. 12(1)), 'the authorisation shall be granted for an *appropriate limited period*' (art. 12(2)).[42] These two articles of the Services Directive establish that in principle limited authorisations should be granted with a limited duration.[43]

Of course, the Services Directive applies only in so far as the authorisation concerns services in the sense of this directive. The national legislator is confronted with the important question of how far the legislation for other situations, outside the scope of the Services Directive, should be attuned to this system. In other words: should the national legislator – taking the European case law into account – prescribe that limited authorisations in general should in principle only be granted for a limited period? In my opinion it seems reasonable to include such a provision in a general statutory framework.

40 Cf *Smart Regulation in the European Union*, Com (2010), 543 final and *EU Regulatory Fitness* COM (2012), 746 final. Because of this reason, the implementation of the Services Directive required a thorough screening of the existing national legislation, see e.g.: M.R. Botman, *De Dienstenrichtlijn in Nederland*, diss. VU, Boom Juridische uitgevers, Den Haag 2015, p. 69 ff and p. 509 ff.

41 Case C-454/06, *Pressetext Nachrichtenagentur* [2008] ECR I-4401 paras. 73–74; Case C-451/08, *Helmut Müller* [2010] ECR I-2673 para. 79. See also Case C-389/05, *Commission v France* [2008] ECR I-5337, para. 53; Case C-323/03, *Commission v Spain* [2006] ECR I-2161 para. 44 and Case C-64/08, *Engelmann* [2010] ECR I-8219 para. 46. Cf Wolswinkel 2013, pp. 275 ff and Wolswinkel 2015, pp. 159, 160.

42 The relationship between these two articles is not very clear, see: Botman 2015, p. 293 ff.

43 ECJ Joined Cases C-340/14 and C-341/14, *Trijber and Harmsen* [2015] nyp.

6.3. *Renewal and Prolongation*

When an authorisation or authorisation scheme is limited, it is considered to be problematic to renew or prolong the authorisation. The reason for this is that with the renewal of a limited authorisation the potential changes that could occur at the relevant market during the duration of the initial authorisation are not taken into account. The initial licensing is extended for a period for which it is not meant to apply. Because of the renewal, potential newcomers do not get an opportunity to enter the market. In other words: the renewal thwarts the reason for which in the initial stage certain (relatively short) period of duration is chosen. After the initial authorisation has expired, the main rule is that in case of scarcity renewal is in principle prohibited. A limited authorisation should be granted by a new allocation procedure.

What are the consequences for the legislator? For the legislator this means that it is reasonable to impose a general prohibition on automatic renewals of limited authorisations. The Services Directive for instance prescribes that authorisations that are limited because of the scarcity of available natural resources or technical capacity 'may not be open to automatic renewal' (art. 12(2)).

On the other hand, an absolute prohibition could be too rigid. An alternative possibility for the legislator is to accept a renewal when this is in the public interest. In that case the period of prolongation should be limited as well. To justify the renewal it should be based on a legitimate goal of prolongation.[44] That goal of prolongation – the grounds of that goal included – should outweigh the reason of the limited term of the initial authorisation. In the Netherlands it is prescribed by law (Article 18(2) Frequency Decree) that a limited frequency licence shall not be renewed, unless the renewal is in 'the general societal, cultural or economic interest'. When the licensee has paid a fee for the initial authorisation, this should also be the case for the renewal. The amount of this additional fee should be based on the value of the licence for an averagely efficient entrant.[45]

6.4. *Transferability and Tradability*

One of the distinctive features of a real open market is the possibility to transfer scarce goods. Limited authorisations might be followed by a transfer from the initial licensee to a third party. Because of their scarcity they often represent a certain value, which makes them attractive for others than the initial licensee. This is especially true for those limited authorisations that are not strictly personal by their nature but could also be exercised by others. For the legislator the risk of leaving the possibility of transferability aside, is that this absence already gives rise to uncertainties as to the existing or non-existing

44 Cf Wolswinkel 2013, p. 619, 620.

45 See the contribution of J. Wolswinkel, 'The Allocation of Radio Frequencies in the Netherlands. An Introductory Overview of the Dutch Approach', section 4.5, in P. Adriaanse, F. Van Ommeren, W. den Ouden and J. Wolswinkel, *Scarcity and the State II. Member State Reports on Gambling Licences, Radio Frequencies and CO_2 Emission Permits*, Intersentia, Antwerp 2016.

possibility of transferability and leaves room for an increasing number of illegal transfers. Even when nothing is arranged, it is not unthinkable that the initial licensee wishes to transfer his limited public right against a certain fee to a beneficiary third party.

The transferability of an authorisation (public right) is not a recognized legal instrument in every jurisdiction, certainly not without an explicit statutory provision. However, with the introduction of a system of tradable emissions rights, the transferability is almost nowhere a totally foreign concept.[46] With the rather fast development of the case law on Article 1 of Protocol No. 1 of the European Convention on Human Rights the insight has grown that even an authorisation represents a certain value.[47] Because of that development it has become less unthinkable that such a public right is transferable.

That is why in most jurisdictions it is necessary that the legislator explicitly stipulates whether or not the transfer of the authorisation is possible. Leaving this unclear provokes illegal transfers. When the transfer is legally allowed it often takes place by means of registration; often the permission of the public authority or public regulator is required as well.

Finally, a very special instrument is the so-called obligatory transfer. When the public authorities have a legal ground to withdraw the licence, they can instead oblige the licensee to transfer (part of) his licence to another party with the consent of the authorities. When this transfer does not happen voluntarily, the authorities will take up this transfer by executing an allocation procedure on their own behalf. This is considered to be a rather new instrument, which was for instance recently introduced in de Dutch Telecommunications Act.[48]

6.5. Judicial Protection

The judicial protection of the allocation of limited authorisations and grants has its own noticeable characteristics, which ask for a provision of the national legislator. I merely discuss the most apparent ones.[49]

A characteristic feature of the allocation of limited authorisations and grants is that the final award to one applicant automatically involves the rejection of the unsuccessful applicants. The question is whether the award by the public authority requires only one decision or requires more separate decisions, one for each applicant. The traditional answer is that every distinct applicant receives one decision (of a positive or negative nature) from the allocating public authority. However, this multiplicity of decisions causes a number of practical (judicial) problems. It would be an improvement if there would be an arrangement to combine all these separate decisions. A general regulatory

46 See the chapter by Rønne in this book.

47 See the chapter by Den Ouden & Tjepkema in this book.

48 See J. Wolswinkel, 'The Allocation of Radio Frequencies in the Netherlands. An Introductory Overview of the Dutch Approach', section 4.4, in P. Adriaanse, F. Van Ommeren, W. Den Ouden and J. Wolswinkel, *Scarcity and the State II. Member State Reports on Gambling Licences, Radio Frequencies and CO2 Emission Permits*, Intersentia, Antwerp 2016.

49 See more extensively the chapter by Wollenschläger in this book.

framework of limited authorisations and grants should contain a provision for this. At the same time it should state what this provision means for questions of standing. Is it necessary to give extra rules for this too?

Not only the final award decision by which the authorisation will be granted, but also the earlier steps of the allocation procedure deserve our attention. After all, an essential characteristic of the allocation procedure is that it consists of rather a few different parts, which are all separate steps of a more comprehensive and phased decision-making process. The question is which separate steps should be amenable to judicial protection. Are there, from an economical point of view, not too many possibilities to lodge an appeal? What could be a solution for this? Is it reasonable and possible to take one or more of these steps together for purposes of judicial protection? In this regard, the Alcatal case law and the mandatory standstill period of public procurement law should be mentioned.[50] Is this kind of provision necessary for every authorisation or grant that is granted by a competitive allocation procedure?

Finally, probably the most complicated problem is the permanent movement of the relevant market. When one or more decisions are legally annulled, the question arises how these decisions could be restored while taking the judicial judgement into account. After all, in the meantime the relevant market will already have changed again. Could the legislator provide a solution for this by offering additional rules? Is it in essence possible that judicial protection provides a real recovery?

7. An Integrated Approach

The advantage of a regulatory framework is that it is the pre-eminent instrument to decrease legal uncertainties. A general regulatory framework on limited authorisations and grants intends to support the sector-specific legislator, the granting public authorities, the applicant, the interested third parties and the courts as well.

However, at the same time there are some risks involved. The downside is the risk of overregulation and the risk that, despite all the legal rules, what is intended is not achieved. This is a well-known problem in regulatory doctrine, which asks for more attention nowadays. Public procurement law offers an outstanding example.[51] The European and national laws on public procurement now form such a complex legal system, that in the eyes of many the original objectives of equal opportunities and "value for money" have become hard to realize. Contracting authorities complain that although they applied the demanding strict and fatal rules, they did not gain what was hoped for. However, to begin with, it is not true that the public procurement law is entirely so tightly regulated. The rules in public procurement law know different levels in detail. The award

50 See already: C-81/98, *Alcatel Austria* [1999] ECR I-7693. See Directive 2007/66/EC of the European Parliament and of the Council of 11 December 2007 amending Council Directives 89/665/EEC and 92/13/EEC with regard to improving the effectiveness of review procedures concerning the award of public contracts.

51 S. Arrowsmith, 'Modernising the EU's Public Procurement Regime: a Blueprint for Real Simplicity and Flexibility', (2012) 3 *PPLR* 71–82.

of concession contracts and social services are submitted to a lighter regime.[52] For the nucleus of public procurement law this is rather more exhaustive indeed.

It is exactly to prevent this danger – from overregulation and non-achievement of goals – that a general regulatory framework should in my opinion *also* be of a principles-based nature. This general regulatory framework on limited public rights should be an integrated system of principles and rules. Principles-based regulation is, as stated, goal based oriented.[53] A primary feature of principles-based regulation is the focus on so-called "outcomes that matter".[54] Principles-based regulation intends to impede the non-realisation of the objectives.

This raises the question how the relationship between principles and rules should be conceived. In recent years this thorny question evoked much attention in the regulatory literature of different sectors, like financial law and tax law.[55] What we can learn from this research is that principles and rules in a regulatory framework might theoretically have rather different kinds of relationships, but that an *integrated* approach of principles and rules is fairly advocated. When a legal rule does not provide for an answer, the integrated approach facilitates a fall back on the legal principle. This is less self-evident than it may seem: in this approach the principles have a far-reaching and more comprehensive function than merely to serve as a legitimate source to deduct the rule from or assist as a guideline for interpreting the rule. When there is a conflict between the principle and the rule it is the principle that prevails and not the rule (in other approaches it is usually the other way around). For instance, when in a certain case a limited licence becomes available and this is – in accordance with the applicable rules – sufficiently published, but at the same time the method of publication is in fact insufficient to adequately reach the potential candidates, the principle of transparency provides a solution to repair this deficiency in the rules and oblige the public authority to a better method. The advantage of an integrated approach is that it leaves less room for loopholes in the framework and that it at the same time makes it less necessary to include a provision for every possible, thinkable or unthinkable, problem in advance.[56]

In my view the right combination of principles-based regulation and rules based regulation provides the optimal mix. On the one hand it offers the advantage of the

52 Cf Directive 2014/23/EU of the European Parliament and of the Council of 26 February 2014 on the award of concession contracts and art. 74 ff Directive 2014/24/EU of the European Parliament and of the Council of 26 February 2014 on public procurement.

53 See for critical reflections: P. Westerman, 'The Emergence of New Types of Norms', in L.G. Wintgens (ed.), *Legislation in Context: Essays on Legisprudence*, Aldershot, Ashgate 2007, pp. 117 ff; P. Westerman, 'Governing by Goals: Governance as a Legal Style', (2007) 1 (1) *Legisprudence: International Journal for the Study of Legislation* 51–72 and S.J.A. ter Borg & W.S.R. Stoter, Is Goal-Based Regulation Consistent with the Rule of Law? in M. Sellers & T. Tomaszewski (eds.), *The Rule of Law in Comparative Perspective*, (Ius Gentium: Comparative Perspectives on law and Justice 3), Springer, Heidelberg 2010, pp. 57 ff.

54 E.g. the British Financial Services Authority, *Principles-based regulation. Focusing on the outcomes that matter*, London 2007.

55 J. Black, 'The Rise, Fall and Fate of Principles Based Regulation', in: K. Alexander & N. Moloney (red.), *Law Reform and Financial Markets*, Cheltenham, Edward Elgar 2011, p. 3 ff and J. Braithwaite, *Markets in Vice, Markets in Virtue*, Oxford, Oxford University Press 2005, p. 144 ff.

56 Cf Braithwaite 2005, p. 149.

sufficient certainty of the legal rules and on the other hand the advantage of the economical, flexible and goal-orientated nature of the legal principles.

8. To Conclude

Until now, general administrative law – as a separate field of law – includes relatively few general applicable rules to allocate limited public rights. Public procurement law is often considered to be a source of inspiration.[57] However, a general regulatory framework abstracts from the concerning economical or social sector. Although this contribution focuses on the national legislator, the 'Model Rules on EU Administrative Procedure' of ReNEUAL may serve as an example. One of the interesting features of these model rules is that they include a general provision for the allocation of limited public rights: where the number of applications to be granted is limited and a competitive award procedure is used the rules on competitive award procedures for contracts shall apply *mutatis mutandis* on single case decision-making.[58]

An important strand of discussion in this contribution was about the topics that a general regulatory framework should include. The core elements concern the announcement of the vacancy of a limited licence, including the obligation to inform interested parties on time, the ceiling, including the obligation to state explicitly the objective or goal of the allocation and the choice of allocation procedures. In addition a whole range of topics is conceivable. One should fear that sector-specific legal rules do not apply to all of these requirements. A general regulatory framework might help to prevent this.

At the same time a serious warning should be given: overregulation could be the trap. In the modern regulatory state it would be naive not to take the risk of overregulation into account. A balanced, middle course might be found in an integrated approach of principles-based and rules-based regulation. In this respect other fields of law, like financial law and even tax law, might show us the way. As regards procurement law, the call from Arrowsmith to consider the applicable general legal principles of greater importance again, speaks volumes.[59] From the perspective of the legislator it is important to already take this course into account in an early stage of the drafting process.

57 See, however, the chapter by Jansen in this book, who warns against overblown expectations.

58 Art. III-6(4) ReNEUAL Model Rules on EU Administrative Procedure. These model rules are developed by the Research Network on EU Administrative Law (ReNEUAL). See http://reneual.eu.

59 S. Arrowsmith, *The Law of Public and Utilities Procurement. Regulation in the EU and UK*, Volume 1, Sweet & Maxwell, London 2014, pp. 234, 235.

Ferdinand
Wollenschläger*

CHAPTER 5. THE ALLOCATION OF LIMITED RIGHTS BY THE ADMINISTRATION: CHALLENGES OF LEGAL PROTECTION*

1. Allocation Decisions and Legal Protection: The Challenge of Multipolarity

Allocation procedures, i.e. administrative procedures aiming at granting limited public rights, are not characterised by the classic bipolar citizen-state paradigm which may be found for instance in police law. Rather, a multipolar conflict has to be resolved: The competing interests of a multitude of applicants to win the competition and the interest of the allocating authority in realising effective distribution must be accommodated. From the perspective of legal protection this implies that challenging an allocation decision not only means challenging an administrative decision concerning the relationship between the acting public authority and the addressee, but also challenging a decision in favour of the initially successful applicant (who might even have received the good in line with legal requirements so that the action is unfounded).

This background entails certain consequences and poses specific challenges. For instance, to secure an efficient allocation, administrative decisions granting limited public rights often take on particular stability, i.e. the possibility to challenge such decisions may be restricted or even ruled out and substituted by a claim to damages. The question therefore arises as to whether, and if so to what extent, such limitations are in line with the guarantees of effective legal protection that are enshrined in national constitutional law, in EU law and in the European Convention on Human Rights (ECHR). Moreover, when challenging allocation decisions, we are dealing – at least according to the traditional understanding – with third party actions. Hence, the issue of standing arises: Under what conditions may an interested party challenge the allocation in favour of another person? The design of the allocation procedure also has repercussions on legal protection. We can distinguish between a multipolar and a bipolar structure, depending on whether the scarce good is allocated by a single administrative decision addressed to all applicants, or by a multitude

* Ferdinand Wollenschläger is Professor of Public Law, European Law and Public Economic Law at the University of Augsburg, Germany.

of positive/negative decisions addressed to the individual applicants. In the latter case, to take the German example, applicants usually have to combine an action for the annulment of the allocation of the good to the successful competitor with an action to receive the good themselves.[1] This multiplication of actions however entails negative procedural consequences (increase in court costs and legal fees; possible information deficit regarding the positive decision, in particular the name of the successful applicant and the reasons for their success). In the case of a multipolar decision, challenging a single allocation decision would be sufficient. A further question is whether particular difficulties arise when challenging a contract. Finally, to conclude this outline, decision-making in quite a number of administrative procedures granting limited public rights is phased in order to rationalise it, to enhance transparency and to reduce complexity. In terms of legal protection, this requires determining at what juncture(s) in the allocation procedure interested parties may lodge an appeal. To give an example: The principles of transparency and equal opportunities require the public authority to advertise the allocation including the award criteria and the procedure to be followed in order to enable persons interested in receiving the limited public right to apply.[2] If a (potential) applicant now considers an award criterion published in the call for applications unlawful – is she/he entitled to challenge already the advertisement or is judicial review limited to the final allocation decision?

Against this background, the chapter will address issues of legal protection raised by allocation procedures. Once the framework of constitutional law, EU law and the European Convention on Human Rights (ECHR) has been explored (2.), specific subject-matters will be addressed, namely jurisdiction (3.1.), available (primary) remedies and the stability of the allocation decision (3.2.), standing before the court (3.3.), when to lodge an appeal (3.4.), the role of interim relief (3.5.) and secondary remedies, i.e. damages (3.6.). A final part will draw some conclusions (4.). It needs to be pointed out at the outset that the chapter will focus, when a national legal order has to be considered, on the legal situation in Germany, which may however be considered as exemplary in terms of the issues mentioned above. This focus is to be understood as a starting point for further comparative research on EU and national level.

2. Framework of Constitutional Law, EU Law and the European Convention on Human Rights (ECHR)

The standards for legal protection in the context of granting limited public rights by means of an allocation procedure are determined by national constitutional law, EU law and the ECHR. All these levels encompass a guarantee of effective legal protection:

1 To mitigate the negative procedural consequences, some courts and authors consider it to be sufficient to challenge the negative decision; this approach has to be rejected, however, cf. in more detail F. Wollenschläger, *Verteilungsverfahren*, Mohr Siebeck, Tübingen 2010, pp. 636 ff.

2 Cf. F. Wollenschläger, 'EU Law Principles for Allocating Scarce Goods and the Emergence of an Allocation Procedure. Identifying Substantive and Procedural Standards and Developing a New Type of Administrative Procedure' (2015) 8 *REALaw* 205, 222 ff.; F. Wollenschläger 2010, pp. 38 ff., 126 ff.

On national level, to take the German example, Article 19 paragraph 4 sentence 1 GG ('Grundgesetz' = Basic Law; Constitution of Germany) guarantees as follows:

> Should any person's rights be violated by public authority, he may have recourse to the courts.[3]

Furthermore, a general guarantee of effective legal protection ('Allgemeiner Justizgewährleistungsanspruch') has been acknowledged as an unwritten constitutional principle. It mainly applies with regard to litigation under private law. The German Federal Constitutional Court ('Bundesverfassungsgericht') has however extended it to public procurement which, according to a questionable jurisprudence of the court, does not qualify as an exercise of public authority within the meaning of Article 19 paragraph 4 GG.[4]

On European (EU) level, Article 47 CFR stipulates:

> Everyone whose rights and freedoms guaranteed by the law of the Union are violated has the right to an effective remedy before a tribunal in compliance with the conditions laid down in this Article.

Moreover, it is well established that the fundamental freedoms encompass not only material rights, e.g. the right to non-discrimination and to unrestricted market access (cf. e.g. Article 45 TFEU), but also the requirement of effective legal protection in case of an infringement.[5]

Finally, the ECHR encompasses two guarantees of legal protection. Article 6 §1 sentence 1 ECHR guarantees as follows:

> In the determination of his civil rights and obligations or of any criminal charge against him, everyone is entitled to a fair and public hearing within a reasonable time by an independent and impartial tribunal established by law.

Furthermore, Article 13 ECHR stipulates as follows:

> Everyone whose rights and freedoms as set forth in this Convention are violated shall have an effective remedy before a national authority notwithstanding that the violation has been committed by persons acting in an official capacity.

3 In German, Article 19 para. 4 sentence 1 GG reads: 'Wird jemand durch die öffentliche Gewalt in seinen Rechten verletzt, so steht ihm der Rechtsweg offen.'

4 BVerfGE (reports of the decisions of the Bundesverfassungsgericht) 116, 135, 149 f. Cf. in detail and with further references Wollenschläger 2010, pp. 88 ff.; A. Leibohm, *Einstweiliger Rechtsschutz im Vergabeverfahren unterhalb der Schwellenwerte in Deutschland und Frankreich*, Nomos, Baden-Baden 2012, pp. 107 ff.

5 Cf. only Case 222/86, *Heylens* [1987] ECR 4097, paras. 14 f.; Case C-340/89, *Vlassopoulou* [1991] ECR I-2357, para. 22; Case C-91/08, *Wall AG* [2010] ECR I-2815, paras. 61 f.; Wollenschläger 2010, pp. 131 f.

As a framework for assessing existing legal protection schemes, but also in order to be able to design new schemes, the requirements and relevance of these guarantees have to be elaborated. The following points shall be highlighted: First, is there any discussion on the relevance of these guarantees for granting limited public rights by means of an allocation procedure on the national level? Do particular subject-matters raise specific issues in this respect? Has the right to effective legal protection had an impact on the standards of legal protection in certain subject-matters? And finally with regard to administrative procedure: Has the right to effective legal protection had any impact on administrative procedure, e.g. the requirement of motivating administrative decisions to facilitate judicial review?

2.1. *Constitutional Law*[6]

The constitutional guarantee of effective legal protection takes on two-fold significance in the context of allocation procedures: Not only does it determine to what extent and under which conditions allocation decisions are subject to judicial review, but it also has implications for administrative procedure. This is because the latter must be designed in such a way that effective legal protection is secured.[7] This particularly implies motivated allocation decisions as well as adequate documentation of the procedure.[8]

In terms of challenging an allocation decision, the requirement of effective legal protection not only demands access to the courts but also that 'judicial review should be as effective as possible',[9] meaning that there should be a comprehensive examination of the facts of the case and of the legal issues involved.[10] Understanding the requirement of effectiveness as a 'requirement to avoid irreparable decisions as far as possible',[11] it is

6 This section follows Wollenschläger 2010, pp. 89 ff. For reflections on the constitutional approach see also Arroyo and Utrilla Fernandez-Bermejo in this book.

7 BVerfGE 61, 82, 110; E 69, 1, 49; *NJW (Neue Juristische Wochenschrift)* 1990, 501, 501; E 116, 135, 156; cf. further E 22, 49, 81 ff.; E. Schmidt-Aßmann, 'Der Verfahrensgedanke im deutschen und europäischen Verwaltungsrecht' in W. Hoffmann-Riem, E. Schmidt-Aßmann and A. Voßkuhle (eds.), *Grundlagen des Verwaltungsrechts, vol. 2*, 2nd ed., C.H. Beck, Munich 2012, §27, para. 68; E. Schmidt-Aßmann, *Das allgemeine Verwaltungsrecht als Ordnungsidee. Grundlagen und Aufgaben der verwaltungsrechtlichen Systembildung*, 2nd ed., Springer, Berlin 2004, pp. 374 f.; F. Schoch, 'Gerichtliche Verwaltungskontrollen' in W. Hoffmann-Riem, E. Schmidt-Aßmann and A. Voßkuhle (eds.), *Grundlagen des Verwaltungsrechts, vol. 3*, §50 para. 353.

8 Cf. only BVerfGE 103, 142, 160 f.; K 2, 310, 315; E. Schmidt-Aßmann, 'Article 19 IV GG' in T. Maunz and G. Dürig (eds.), *Grundgesetz-Kommentar*, C.H. Beck, Munich 2014, paras. 253 ff.

9 BVerfG, *NVwZ (Neue Zeitschrift für Verwaltungsrecht)* 2009, 977, 977; also BVerfGE 35, 263, 274; E 40, 272, 275; *NZBau (Neue Zeitschrift für Baurecht und Vergaberecht)* 2004, 564, 565; P. M. Huber, 'Article 19 GG' in H. v. Mangoldt, F. Klein and C. Starck (eds.), *Kommentar zum Grundgesetz, vol. 1*, 6th ed., Franz Vahlen, Munich 2010, paras. 459 f.; Schmidt-Aßmann in Maunz and Dürig 2014, para. 229; Leibohm 2012, pp. 102 f.

10 BVerfGE 35, 263, 274; E 61, 82, 111; E 101, 106, 123 f.; Huber in Mangoldt, Klein and Starck 2010, para. 460.

11 BVerfG, *NVwZ* 2009, 977, 977; BVerfGE 35, 263, 274; also cf. M. Morlok, *Die Folgen von Verfahrensfehlern am Beispiel von kommunalen Satzungen*, Duncker & Humblot, Berlin 1988, pp. 69 f.

clear that primary legal protection, i.e. the availability of actions to quash illegal allocation decisions violating the rights of an individual, must be the rule, and that secondary legal protection, i.e. the award of compensation for damage, should be the exception.[12] Established case-law confirms the importance of this requirement, but one reservation has yet to be made: The multipolar conflict inherent in allocation procedures has to be reflected when determining the scope of the guarantee of legal protection.[13] In contrast to standard administrative procedure, as pointed out in the introduction, granting limited public rights by public authorities is not characterised by the classic bipolar citizen-state paradigm, but by a competitive relationship between several private individuals. Consequently, fundamental rights, including the guarantee of legal protection, cannot be understood as requiring maximised protection, but rather a sound balance has to be struck between the conflicting interests. For, challenging an allocation not only affects the relationship between the acting public authority and the addressee, but also the distribution of the good in favour of the initially successful applicant whose interest in stability must thus also be considered (all the more since the initial decision might have been lawful so that the action is unfounded from the outset).

Hence, the Bundesverfassungsgericht formulated as follows in its *Telekom* decision:

> The rules that have been developed for bipolar conflicts in order to assess the proportionality of an interference cannot be applied without alignment to the special characteristics of a multipolar conflict, and therefore not without considering the possibility of different interferences and privileges in each case.[14]

12 See BVerfGE 53, 300, 324; E 100, 226, 246; *NJW* 2000, 1402, 1402; BGH, *NJW* 1991, 1168, 1170; W. Erbguth, 'Primär- und Sekundärrechtsschutz im Öffentlichen Recht' (2002) 61 *VVDStRL (Veröffentlichungen der Vereinigung der Deutschen Staatsrechtslehrer)* 221, 229 ff., 238 ff.; S. Gers-Grapperhaus, *Das Auswahlrechtsverhältnis bei Auftragsvergaben unterhalb der Schwellenwerte*, Nomos, Baden-Baden 2009, p. 215; Huber in Mangoldt, Klein and Starck 2010, paras. 455, 458; Schmidt-Aßmann in Maunz and Dürig 2014, paras. 28, 283; E. Schmidt-Aßmann, 'Einleitung' in F. Schoch, E. Schmidt-Aßmann and R. Pietzner, *Verwaltungsgerichtsordnung, vol. 1*, C.H. Beck, Munich 2011, para. 231; with differentiations W. Höfling, 'Primär- und Sekundärrechtsschutz im Öffentlichen Recht' (2002) 61, *VVDStRL* 260, 278 ff.

13 R. Gaier, 'Verfassungsrecht – Fesseln und Freiheiten für das (Kartell-)Vergaberecht' (2008) *NZBau*, 289, 292 f.; W. Kahl, 'Begriff, Funktionen und Konzepte von Kontrolle' in Hoffmann-Riem, Schmidt-Aßmann and Voßkuhle 2012, §47 para. 130; T. Pollmann, *Der verfassungsrechtliche Gleichbehandlungsgrundsatz im öffentlichen Vergaberecht*, Duncker & Humblot, Berlin 2009, pp. 159 ff.; M. Ronellenfitsch, 'Der vorläufige Rechtsschutz im beamtenrechtlichen Konkurrentenstreit' (1991) 82 *VerwArch (Verwaltungsarchiv)* 121, 133; Schmidt-Aßmann in Maunz and Dürig 2014, para. 22. With reserves J. Gundel, 'Neue Entwicklungen beim Konkurrentenstreit im öffentlichen Dienst: Perfektionierung des bestehenden Systems statt grundsätzlicher Überprüfung' (2004) 37 *DV (Die Verwaltung)* 401, 426 f.; Leibohm 2012, pp. 104 f.

14 BVerfGE 115, 205, 234: '[D]ie für bipolare Konfliktlagen entwickelten Regeln zur abwägenden Prüfung der Verhältnismäßigkeit eines Eingriffs [können] nicht ohne Anpassung an die Besonderheiten der Mehrpoligkeit, und damit nicht ohne Beachtung der Möglichkeit jeweils unterschiedlicher Beeinträchtigungen und Begünstigungen, angewendet werden.'

Thus, in cases of administrative allocation decisions, the guarantee of effective legal protection can require a limitation of the remedies accruing to individual parties.[15] This is illustrated by two decisions of the Bundesverfassungsgericht: In BVerfGE 116, 1, the Court held that the exclusion of an action for annulment of the nomination of a liquidator brought by a competing applicant was necessitated by the Constitution. In this respect, the interest of the conflicting parties – considered by the Court not as individuals but rather as a group – was in fact not held to outweigh the interest of the creditors in making rapid progress in the insolvency proceedings.[16] In BVerfGE 116, 135, the Court underlines that the guarantee of legal protection 'in situations in which a multipolar conflict arises between different interests does not ensure or require simply maximising the remedies of the individual staking the claim. In fact, it requires the legally-protected competing interests to be balanced in an appropriate way'.[17] It is incumbent on the legislature to establish such a proportionate balance of interests. The legislature thus enjoys a margin of appreciation regarding 'the evaluation of the advantages and disadvantages for the rights concerned, as well as the balancing in view of the consequences for the different interests protected by law'.[18] The Court sums up as follows:

> Whether the guarantee of legal protection stipulates special demands for the legislature developing remedies in cases where different interests are concerned can only be decided with respect to the interests concretely affected. The legislature must consider the fundamental rights of the claimant as well as of third parties whose interests are concerned by granting legal protection and the specific characteristics of the subject-matter in question. When extending or limiting remedies in the public interest, the weight of these interests has to be taken into account as well.[19]

15 Kahl in Hoffmann-Riem, Schmidt-Aßmann and Voßkuhle 2012, §47 para. 130; Ronellenfitsch (1991) 82 *VerwArch* 121, 133; Schmidt-Aßmann in Maunz and Dürig 2014, para. 22. For example see BVerwGE (reports of the decisions of the Bundesverwaltungsgericht) 60, 297, 307, considering the foreclosure of substantive objection 'balancing and putting into an adequate relation the opposite interests influencing a multipolar legal conflict and originating from different substantive basic right positions'; also BVerfGE 61, 82, 113 f.

16 BVerfGE 116, 1, 19 ff. Consenting M. Martini, *Der Markt als Instrument hoheitlicher Verteilungslenkung. Möglichkeiten und Grenzen einer staatlichen Verwaltung des Mangels durch Marktmechanismen*, Mohr Siebeck, Tübingen 2008, p. 130.

17 BVerfGE 116, 135, 154: 'Der Justizgewährungsanspruch ermöglicht und verlangt in Lagen, in denen unterschiedliche Interessen Mehrerer betroffen sind, keine schlichte Maximierung der Rechtsschutzmöglichkeiten des einzelnen Rechtsuchenden. Er zielt vielmehr auf eine sachgerechte Gewichtung und Zuordnung der betroffenen rechtlich geschützten Belange.'

18 BVerfGE 116, 135, 155: 'Der Gesetzgeber ist auch bei der Ausgestaltung des Rechtsschutzes dazu berufen, die miteinander kollidierenden und verflochtenen Interessen in einen Ausgleich zu bringen, der allen in verhältnismäßiger Weise gerecht wird ... Dabei kommt ihm ein Einschätzungs- und Beurteilungsspielraum zu, der sich auf die Beurteilung der Vor- und Nachteile für die jeweils betroffenen Güter sowie auf die Güterabwägung mit Blick auf die Folgen für die verschiedenen rechtlich geschützten Interessen bezieht.'

19 BVerfGE 116, 135, 155: 'Ob besondere Maßgaben aus dem allgemeinen Justizgewährungsanspruch für den Gesetzgeber folgen, wenn er den Rechtsschutz in einer Situation ausgestaltet, durch die

Applying these general considerations, the Bundesverfassungsgericht – unlike the General Court (cf. below, 2.2.) – has accepted the de facto exclusion of primary legal protection in the field of public procurement not falling under the EU directives since it has not held the contracting authorities to be obliged to inform unsuccessful bidders of the intended conclusion of the contract in order to enable them to lodge an appeal:

> The legislature enjoys discretion regarding contracting decisions. Therefore it is possible to favour the interest of the contracting authority in an expedited execution of the contract and the interest of the successful bidder in legal certainty over the interest of the unsuccessful bidder in primary legal protection by limiting the latter to enjoy secondary legal protection.[20]

In other areas, however, the Bundesverfassungsgericht reached the contrary conclusion, e.g. in cases of distribution of posts in the public sector[21] or of stands at exhibitions and

unterschiedliche Interessen betroffen sind, lässt sich nur mit Rücksicht auf die Eigenart gerade der konkret betroffenen Interessenlage beurteilen. Der Gesetzgeber hat insbesondere grundrechtliche Schutzaussagen zugunsten des Rechtsuchenden, aber auch zugunsten Dritter, deren Belange durch den begehrten Rechtsschutz berührt werden, zu beachten und hierbei bereichsspezifischen Besonderheiten Rechnung zu tragen. Sollen Rechtsschutzmöglichkeiten aufgrund öffentlicher Belange erweitert oder beschränkt werden, muss auch das Gewicht dieser Belange in die Abwägung eingestellt werden.'

20 BVerfGE 116, 135, 156: 'Es liegt im Hinblick auf Vergabeentscheidungen im gesetzgeberischen Gestaltungsspielraum, das Interesse des Auftraggebers an einer zügigen Ausführung der Maßnahmen und das des erfolgreichen Bewerbers an alsbaldiger Rechtssicherheit dem Interesse des erfolglosen Bieters an Primärrechtsschutz vorzuziehen und Letzteren regelmäßig auf Sekundärrechtsschutz zu beschränken.' Also cf. (2008) *ZfBR (Zeitschrift für deutsches und internationales Bau- und Vergaberecht)* 816, 816 – with another focus (2004) *NZBau* 564, 565. Consenting OLG Brandenburg, 13 W 79/09 – juris, para. 5; Gaier (2008) *NZBau*, 289, 292 f.; J. Gundel, 'Rechtsschutz und Rechtsweg bei der Vergabe öffentlicher Aufträge unterhalb der Schwellenwerte' (2008) *JURA (Juristische Ausbildung)* 288, 290 f.; similar R. Ortner, *Vergabe von Dienstleistungskonzessionen. Unter besonderer Berücksichtigung der Entsorgungs- und Verkehrswirtschaft*, Carl Heymanns Verlag, Cologne 2007, pp. 186 f. See also BVerwGE 129, 9, 20 considering 'prompt information of the competitors about the intended contracting' as 'crucial for the effectiveness of legal protection'. Approving an obligation to inform M. Burgi, 'Die Vergabe von Dienstleistungskonzessionen: Verfahren, Vergabekriterien, Rechtsschutz' (2005) *NZBau* 610, 617; J. Englisch, 'Effektiver Primärrechtsschutz bei Vergabe öffentlicher Aufträge'(2007) 98 *VerwArch* 410, 441; W. Frenz, 'Unterschwellenvergaben' (2007) *VergabeR (Vergaberecht)* 1, 13; Gers-Grapperhaus 2009, pp. 219 ff.; K. Rennert, 'Konkurrentenklagen bei begrenztem Kontingent' (2009) *DVBl. (Deutsches Verwaltungsblatt)* 1333, 1337; H. C. Röhl, 'Verwaltung und Privatrecht – Verwaltungsprivatrecht?' (1995) 86 *VerwArch* 531, 561 f.; W. R. Schenke, 'Article 19 IV GG' in W. Kahl, C. Waldhoff and C. Walter, *Bonner Kommentar zum Grundgesetz*, C. F. Müller, Heidelberg 2014, para. 746. In contrast M. Dreher, 'Vergaberechtsschutz unterhalb der Schwellenwerte' (2002) *NZBau* 419, 426; J. Englisch, 'Effektiver Primärrechtsschutz bei Vergabe öffentlicher Aufträge' (2007) 98 *VerwArch* 410, considering the limitation to secondary legal protection in public procurement law as generally possible (425), but not over the thresholds because of the principle of equality (430); Kahl in Hoffmann-Riem, Schmidt-Aßmann and Voßkuhle 2012, §47 para. 130; J. Knöbl, *Rechtsschutz bei der Vergabe von Aufträgen unterhalb der Schwellenwerte*, Duncker & Humboldt, Berlin 2009, pp. 125 ff.; Schoch in Hoffmann-Riem, Schmidt-Aßmann and Voßkuhle 2012, §50 para. 10.

21 BVerfG, *NJW* 1990, 501, 501 f.; with restrictions in a later decision regarding the nomination of notaries (*NJW* 2006, 2395, 2396). In this decision the BVerfG declined an annulment of the nomination and limited the unsuccessful applicant to secondary legal protection.

markets,[22] but without engaging in any discussion of the multipolarity of the allocation conflict.

This illustrates the fact that the standards of legal protection have to be determined with regard to the interests at stake in the specific case.[23] Nonetheless, primary legal protection is the rule and any limitations are in need of a justification.

Aspects that are relevant when balancing the conflicting interests are the nature of the public right in question and the weight of the interest in having the contract awarded.[24] Moreover, the interest of the allocating authority, the general public and the successful bidder in holding up the initial allocation decision have to be considered. Against this background, a limitation to secondary legal protection may be justified more easily if only pecuniary interests are affected than in cases where limited rights are granted that are relevant for personal development (e.g. a post in the public service or places at university). Consequently, the Bundesverfassungsgericht has justified the limitation to secondary legal protection in public procurement law by arguing that the interest in legal protection is limited to an 'interest in damages pure and simple'.[25] A proportionate balance of interests might also entail modifying the general model of ex-post review, namely by substituting the ex-post remedy with a preventive expedited remedy[26] or with a right to be considered in a subsequent allocation procedure[27] (cf. 3.2. for the models in detail). It is however questionable whether an additional interest of the state in benefiting from the allocated good, namely from the performance of an awarded contract or of an employment relationship, can be counted in favour of limiting the possibilities for legal protection since a public interest in rapid allocation proceedings applies in almost every area, such as the interest in an effective public transport system, when allocating respective concessions.[28]

Finally, for cases in which primary legal protection may be excluded in line with constitutional requirements, the Bundesverfassungsgericht has assigned a compensatory function to secondary legal protection and to an action for a declaratory judgment. These must be effectively available.[29]

22 BVerfG, *NJW* 2002, 3691, 3692. Cf. further regarding the distribution of accounts for shares: VGH Kassel, 6 TG 540/07, p. 5.

23 Pollmann 2009, pp. 159 ff.; H. C. Röhl, 'Ausgewählte Verwaltungsverfahren' in Hoffmann-Riem, Schmidt-Aßmann and Voßkuhle 2012, §30 para. 20; also cf. BVerwGE 67, 206, 209 f.

24 Cf. Gundel (2008) *JURA* 288, 291.

25 BVerfG, *ZfBR* 2008, 816, 816. Cf. also Pollmann 2009, p. 160.

26 For example in the distribution of posts in public service.

27 For example in the allocation of places at university.

28 See also Gundel (2004) 37 *DV* 401, 426 f.

29 BVerfGE 116, 1, 22; E 116, 135, 159.

2.2. *EU Law*[30]

Being able to verify alleged violations of the market freedoms is vital to their effectiveness. Accordingly, a corresponding guarantee of legal protection is regarded as constituting an integral component of these guarantees.[31] With the Court of Justice, and in line with the situation under national constitutional law (cf. 2.1.), this is fundamentally orientated towards primary legal protection since not only individual legal protection interests, but also the internal market goal of the Union, is satisfied to a greater degree by reducing obstacles to mobility than by providing financial compensation for violations of the law.[32] That the priority of legal protection under primary legislation is however also not a dogma in Union law is made clear by the case of Unibet. In this case, the ECJ did not consider national legislatures and the judiciary to be obliged to create new legal remedies providing primary legal protection if the compatibility of national measures with Union law could be effectively reviewed within compensation actions.[33] Additionally, in the

[30] This section follows Wollenschläger (2015) 8 *REALaw* 205, 226 f., 238, and Wollenschläger 2010, pp. 131 f.

[31] Case 222/86, *Heylens* [1987] ECR 4097, paras. 14 ff.; Case C-340/89, *Vlassopoulou* [1991] ECR I-2357, para. 22; Case C-91/08, *Wall AG* [2010] ECR I-2815, paras. 61 ff.; Advocate General Bot, ibid., paras. 124 ff.; EC, Communication on the application of Community law on Public Procurement and Concessions to Institutionalised Public-Private Partnerships (IPPP) of 05.02.2008, C (2007) 6661, pp. 6 f. Cf. now also Article 47 CFREU. In the literature: Englisch, (2007) 98 *VerwArch* 410, 431; Wollenschläger, (2015) 8 *REALaw* 205, 226 f.

[32] In this vein Case C-265/95, *Commission v. France* [1997] ECR I-6959, paras. 59 f.: '*As regards the fact that the French Republic has assumed responsibility for the losses caused to the victims, this cannot be put forward as an argument by the French Government in order to escape its obligations under Community law. Even though compensation can provide reparation for at least part of the loss or damage sustained by the economic operators concerned, the provision of such compensation does not mean that the Member State has fulfilled its obligations*'; further – for public procurement – Case C-81/98, *Alcatel Austria* [1999] ECR I-7671, paras. 37 ff.; Düsseldorf Higher Regional Court, 27 U 1/09 – juris, para. 41. In the same vein K. Bitterich, 'Rechtsschutz bei Verletzung aus dem EG-Vertrag abgeleiteter Grundanforderungen an die Vergabe öffentlicher Aufträge' (2007) *NVwZ* 890, 893 f.; C. Braun, 'Europarechtlicher Vergaberechtsschutz unterhalb der Schwellenwerte' (2007) *VergabeR* 17, 19; C. Braun, 'Zivilrechtlicher Schutz bei Vergaben unterhalb der Schwellenwerte', (2008) *NZBau* 160, 161; M. Bungenberg, 'Rechtsschutz im Vergaberecht und Einsichtnahme in Vergabeakten' (2008) *SächsVBl. (Sächsische Verwaltungsblätter)* 53, 56 f.; M. Burgi, 'Von der Zweistufenlehre zur Dreiteilung des Rechtsschutzes im Vergaberecht' (2007) *NVwZ* 737, 742; Frenz (2007) *VergabeR* 1, 9 f. and 13; Gers-Grapperhaus 2009, pp. 246 ff.; F. Wollenschläger, 'Das EU-Vergaberegime für Aufträge unterhalb der Schwellenwerte' (2007) *NVwZ* 388, 395. With regard to the party seeking legal protection: R. Streinz, 'Primär- und Sekundärrechtsschutz im Öffentlichen Recht' (2002) 61 *VVDStRL* 300, 351 f.

[33] Case C-432/05, *Unibet* [2007] ECR I-2271, paras. 36 ff., in particular 53 ff.; cf. further Case C-91/08, *Wall AG* [2010] ECR I-2815, paras. 61 ff.; CFI, Joined Cases T-172/98 and T-175/98 to T-177/98, *Salamander AG et al.* [2000] ECR II-2487, paras. 77 f.; Joined Cases T-377/00, T-379/00, T-380/00, T-260/01 and T-272/01, *Philip Morris et al.* [2003] ECR II-1, para. 123; Advocate General Bot in Case C-91/08, *Wall AG* [2010] ECR I-2815, paras. 136 ff.; cf. also Bitterich, *NVwZ* 2007, 890, 893 f.; O. Dörr, 'Die Gewährleistung von Gerichtsschutz als menschenrechtliche Verpflichtung' in E. Klein (ed.), *Gewaltenteilung und Menschenrechte*, Berliner Wissenschafts-Verlag, Berlin 2006, 129, 139 f.; Gundel, *JURA* 2008, 288, 293 f.; F. Huerkamp, *Gleichbehandlung und Transparenz als gemeinschaftsrechtliche Prinzipien der staatlichen Auftragsvergabe*, Mohr Siebeck, Tübingen 2010, pp. 338 f. Dissenting Braun, *VergabeR* 2007, 17, 19 and 22 ff.; Englisch, *VerwArch* 98 (2007), 410, 433 f.

context of the multipolar conflict situation of access to employment with a recruitment practice that is in violation of Anti-Discrimination Directive 76/207/EEC, the European legislature did not consider primary legal protection to be absolutely necessary, but regarded effective compensation as being sufficient (Article 6 of Directive 76/207/EEC). The ECJ has not objected to this.[34] It remains to be seen how far-reaching are the consequences that can be drawn from this.[35] It can however be observed that restrictions in the guarantee of legal protection are permissible in multipolar legal relationships if important reasons apply.[36]

Furthermore, the case-law on gambling[37] demonstrates that it may be sufficient in terms of effective legal protection not to repeat an unlawful allocation procedure, but to grant chances in a new procedure (cf. also the model of substituting the ex-post remedy by a prospective remedy explained below, 3.2.4.): 'both the revocation and redistribution of the old licences and the award by public tender of an adequate number of new licences could be appropriate courses of action. In principle, those courses of action are both capable of remedying, at least as regards the future, the unlawful exclusion of certain operators, by allowing them to engage in their activity on the market under the same conditions as existing operators.'[38] The newcomers must, however, not be unduly disadvantaged vis-à-vis existing operators, by e.g., requiring a minimum distance between the establishment of new applicants and those of the former.[39]

Just as the guarantee of legal protection under national constitutional law (cf. 2.1.), the guarantee provided by Union law ultimately produces advance effects for the administrative procedure: The procedure must be sufficiently documented and the allocation decision must be reasoned in order to guarantee effective legal protection.[40] In this context, the General Court has stressed:

34 Case 14/83, *von Colson and Kamann* [1984] ECR 1891, paras. 8 ff. and 22 ff.; Case 79/83, *Harz* [1984] ECR 1921, paras. 16 ff.; Case C-380/01, *Schneider* [2004] ECR I-1389, paras. 27 f.; Bitterich, *NVwZ* 2007, 890, 894.

35 Far-reaching Gundel, *JURA* 2008, 288, 293 f. More restrictive C. Weißenberger, 'Die Zweistufentheorie im Wirtschaftsverwaltungsrecht – Teil 1' (2009) *GewArch (Gewerbearchiv)* 417, 426.

36 Cf. also F. Huerkamp/J. Kühling, 'Primärrechtsschutz für Unterschwellenvergaben aus Luxemburg?' (2011) *NVwZ* 1409, 1410 f.

37 See on the case-law on gambling also the chapter by Van den Bogaert and Cuyvers in this book.

38 Case C-463/13, *Stanley International Betting Ltd* ECLI:EU:C:2015:25, paras. 34 seq.; further joined Cases C-72/10 and C-77/10, *Costa and Cifone* ECLI:EU:C:2012:80, para. 52.

39 Joined Cases C-72/10 and C-77/10, *Costa and Cifone* ECLI:EU:C:2012:80, paras. 53 ff.; further Case C-463/13, *Stanley International Betting Ltd* ECLI:EU:C:2015:25, paras. 36 ff.

40 ECJ, Case 222/86, *Heylens* [1987] ECR 4097, para. 15; Case C-340/89, *Vlassopoulou* [1991] ECR I-2357, para. 22; Case C-75/08, *Mellor* [2009] ECR I-3799, para. 59; further the Commission Interpretative Communication of 24 July 2006 on the Community law applicable to contract awards not or not fully subject to the provisions of the Public Procurement Directives [2006] OJ C179/7; W. Frenz, *Handbuch Europarecht, Beihilfe- und Vergaberecht, vol. 3*, Springer, Berlin 2007, paras. 1824 and 1844; W. Frenz, 'Allgemeine Grundsätze des Vergaberechts – Das EuGH-Urteil ANAV/Comune di Bari' (2006) *EWS (Europäisches Wirtschafts- und Steuerrecht)* 347, 349; Ortner 2007, pp. 181 f.

> [I]n order to ensure that the requirement of effective judicial protection is satisfied, the contracting authority must comply with its duty to give reasons … by providing an adequate statement of reasons to any unsuccessful tenderer who so requests, in order to ensure that the latter may rely on that right under the best possible conditions and have the possibility of deciding, with full knowledge of the facts, if there is any point in his applying to the court having jurisdiction. The duty to state reasons for a contested decision is an essential procedural requirement, intended inter alia to ensure that the person adversely affected by the measure in question has the right to an effective remedy.[41]

In addition to the market freedoms, the EU's fundamental rights also comprise a guarantee of effective legal protection (cf. Article 47 CFR). The role of EU fundamental rights in the context of allocation procedures however remains to be further developed; compared to the market freedoms, they play only a limited role.[42] Yet, in a procurement case, the General Court has derived from this guarantee an obligation incumbent on the contracting authority to inform unsuccessful bidders of the decision to award the contract in order to facilitate primary legal protection. This is all the more remarkable if one considers that this interpretation of the guarantee of effective legal protection deviates from the Bundesverfassungsgericht's balancing of interests (cf. 2.1.).

> As regards, first of all, the purported infringement of the principle of the right to an effective remedy, it should be borne in mind that access to the courts is one of the essential elements of a community based on the rule of law and is guaranteed in the legal order based on the EC Treaty, inasmuch as the Treaty established a complete system of legal remedies and procedures designed to permit the Court of Justice to review the legality of acts of the Community administration … Moreover, the Court of Justice bases the right to an effective remedy before a court of competent jurisdiction on the constitutional traditions common to the Member States and on Articles 6 and 13 of the European Convention for the Protection of Human Rights and Fundamental Freedoms, signed in Rome on 4 November 1950 … Lastly, the right to an effective remedy for every person whose rights and freedoms guaranteed by the law of the European Union are infringed has also been reaffirmed by Article 47 of the Charter.
>
> Moreover, in tendering procedures, tenderers must be protected against arbitrary decisions by the contracting authority by ensuring that unlawful decisions taken by that authority may be reviewed effectively and as rapidly as possible …
>
> Full legal protection against arbitrary decisions on the part of the contracting authority therefore presupposes, first, the obligation to inform all the tenderers of the decision to award the contract before the contract is concluded, so that they may have a real possibility of initiating proceedings for annulment of that decision, where the requisite conditions are met.

41 Case T-461/08, *Evropaïki Dynamiki v. EIB* [2011] ECR II-6367, para. 122.

42 Cf. in more detail and with further references Wollenschläger 2010, pp. 107 ff.

Such full legal protection requires, next, that the unsuccessful tenderer should have the opportunity to examine in sufficient time the validity of the award decision, which means that there must be a reasonable period of time between communication of the award decision to the unsuccessful tenderers and the signature of the contract, in order inter alia to enable the latter to lodge an application for interim measures, under Articles 242 EC and 243 EC in conjunction with Article 225(1) EC, so that the judge hearing the application for interim measures may order suspension of the operation of the contested decision until the court adjudicating on the substance rules on the main action for annulment of that decision ... The right to full and effective judicial protection means that individuals must be granted interim protection if this is necessary to ensure the full effectiveness of the judgment to be given in the main proceedings, in order to prevent a lacuna in the legal protection afforded by the courts having jurisdiction ...[43]

2.3. European Convention on Human Rights (ECHR)[44]

The ECHR provides two guarantees regarding legal protection: Articles 6 and 13 ECHR. Article 6 §1 ECHR entitles everyone

> in the determination of his civil rights and obligations or of any criminal charge against him, ... to a fair and public hearing within a reasonable time by an independent and impartial tribunal established by law.

Referring to the Court's case-law, the concept of 'civil rights and obligations' cannot be interpreted by reference to the domestic law of the respondent state, but rather this concept is 'autonomous' within the meaning of Article 6 §1 ECHR.[45] There are two cases which the Court especially considers as covered by the notion of 'civil rights and obligations': First, if the outcome of the proceedings is decisive for private rights and obligations or second, property interests are in question. On the other hand, disputes between administrative authorities and their employees who occupy posts connected with the exercise of public authority definitely do not fall under the 'civil head' of Article 6 §1 ECHR.[46] For example, the ECtHR applied Article 6 §1 ECHR to cases regarding the sale of land, the running of a private clinic and the granting of administrative authorisations relating to the conditions of professional practice or of a licence to serve alcoholic beverages.[47] Furthermore, public procurement is seen as a question of civil

43 Case T-461/08, *Evropaïki Dynamiki v. EIB* [2011] ECR II-6367, paras. 118 f. Cf. further Case T-199/14 R, *Vanbreda Risk & Benefits v. EC* ECLI:EU:T:2014:1024, paras. 162, 172.

44 This section follows Wollenschläger, (2015) 8 *REALaw* 205, 241 f., and Wollenschläger 2010, pp. 112 ff.

45 See only *Benthem v. Netherlands*, ECtHR, no. 8848/80, series A, no. 97, para. 34; *Pudas v. Sweden*, ECtHR, no. 10426/83, series A, no. 125, para. 35; *Ferrazzini v. Italy*, ECtHR, no. 44759/98, rep. 2001-VII, para. 24; C. Grabenwarter and K. Pabel, *Europäische Menschenrechtskonvention*, 5th ed., C.H. Beck, Munich 2012, §24, paras. 7 ff.

46 See for example *Ferrazzini v. Italy*, ECtHR, no. 44759/98, rep. 2001-VII, paras. 25 ff.; Grabenwarter and Pabel 2012, §24, paras. 8 ff.; D. Kunz, *Verfahren und Rechtsschutz bei der Vergabe von Konzessionen*, Stämpfli, Bern 2004, p. 310.

47 *Ferrazzini v. Italy*, ECtHR, no. 44759/98, rep. 2001-VII, para. 27.

rights.[48] In respect of access to the civil service, the ECtHR declines the applicability of Article 6 §1 ECHR if the conflict refers to posts in the public sector connected with the exercise of powers intrinsic to state sovereignty.[49] In the case of *Kübler vs. Germany* the ECtHR clarifies that

> [i]t is thus for the Contracting States, in particular the competent national legislature, and not the Court, to identify expressly those areas of public service involving the exercise of the discretionary powers intrinsic to State sovereignty where the interests of the individual must give way. If a domestic system bars access to a court, the Court will verify that the dispute is indeed such as to justify the application of the exception to the guarantees of Article 6. If it does not, then there is no issue and Article 6 §1 will apply irrespective of whether the applicant seeks reinstatement or some other form of pecuniary redress.[50]

In case of interim proceedings, Article 6 §1 ECHR only applies if 'the right at stake in both the main and the injunction proceedings (is) ... "civil" (and the) ... interim measure can be considered effectively to determine the civil right or obligation at stake'.[51] Parallel to constitutional law, Article 6 §1 ECHR embraces not only access to the courts, but also an effective legal remedy.[52] Of course, proportionate restrictions of the guarantee of legal protection are possible,[53] so that secondary legal protection may be sufficient.[54]

48 ÖVfGH (Austrian Constitutional Court), judgment of 28 November 2005, B 817/05-8, p. 6; M. Bungenberg, *Vergaberecht im Wettbewerb der Systeme. Eine rechtsebenenübergreifende Analyse des Vergaberechts*, Mohr Siebeck, Tübingen 2007, pp. 247 ff., with reference to further judgements of the ÖVfGH and the 'Eidgenössische Rekurskommission' (Swiss Federal Appeals Commission); M. Holoubek, 'Grundrechtsschutz im österreichischen Beschaffungswesen unter besonderer Berücksichtigung der EMRK' (2008) *WiVerw (Wirtschaft und Verwaltung)* 273, 275 – also referring to the question of the application of Article 6 §1 ECHR to the contracting procedure itself (275 ff.); A. R. Ziegler, 'Die Bedeutung von Art. 6 Abs. 1 EMRK für das Rechtsmittelverfahren im Rahmen des öffentlichen Beschaffungswesens in der Schweiz' (2008) *WiVerw* 285, 292.

49 *Pellegrin v. France*, ECtHR, no. 28541/95, rep. 1999 – VII, paras. 58 ff. Stricter now *Eskelinen a.o. v. Finland*, ECtHR, no. 63235/00, not published yet, paras. 42 ff. Cf. regarding this Grabenwarter and Pabel 2012, §24 para. 11. For a general applicability J. Meyer-Ladewig, *EMRK – Europäische Menschenrechtskonvention, Handkommentar*, 3rd ed., Nomos, Baden-Baden 2011, Article 6, para. 19.

50 *Kübler v. Germany*, ECtHR, no. 32715/06, not published, para. 45.

51 *Kübler v. Germany*, ECtHR, no. 32715/06, not published, para. 47.

52 Instead of many *Veeber v. Estonia*, ECtHR, no. 37571/97, not published, para. 70; Grabenwarter and Pabel 2012, §24 para. 48; Meyer-Ladewig 2011, Article 6 para. 31; Streinz, *VVDStRL* 61 (2002), 300, 306 ff. Regarding consequences for contracting law in the judicature of the ÖVfGH: Holoubek, *WiVerw* 2008, 273, 278 ff.

53 *Lithgow a.o.*, ECtHR, no. 9006/80, 9262/81, 9263/81, 9265/81, 9266/81, 9313/81 and 9405/81, series A, no 102, para. 194; Dörr in Klein 2006, p. 129, 141; Grabenwarter and Pabel 2012, §24 paras. 49 ff.; Meyer-Ladewig 2011, Article 6 paras. 36 f.

54 Affirming: Dörr in Klein 2006, p. 129, 139 f.; Streinz, *VVDStRL* 61 (2002), 300, 311. However, the ECtHR has not ruled on this issue yet, cf. Grabenwarter and Pabel 2012, §24 para. 58. But see – in regard to Article 13 ECHR –*Kudla v. Poland*, ECtHR, no. 30210/96, rep. 2000 – XI, para. 159; furthermore *Mifsud*, ECtHR, no. 57220/00, rep. 2002 – VIII, para. 17: 'a remedy is "effective" if it can be used either to expedite a decision by the courts dealing with the case, or to provide the litigant with adequate redress for delays that have already occurred'; also *Mitev*, ECtHR, no. 40063/98, not published, para. 156.

Article 6 §1 ECHR furthermore influences the selection procedure which must not preclude the possibility of legal protection. As a result, the authority is obliged to give reasons for its final decision.[55]

Apart from the guarantee of legal protection in Article 6 §1 ECHR, Article 13, finally, provides that

> (e)veryone whose rights and freedoms as set forth in this Convention are violated shall have an effective remedy before a national authority notwithstanding that the violation has been committed by persons acting in an official capacity.

The effectiveness of the remedy available at national level must again be assessed in view of the circumstances of the particular case.[56]

3. Specific Subject-Matters

3.1. Jurisdiction

The variety of allocation decisions not only in terms of substance, but also in terms of legal form (notably administrative act and public or private law contract) immediately raises the question of jurisdiction: Which courts are competent to review these acts? Moreover, this section addresses the issue of whether there is an opportunity or even an obligation to challenge allocation decisions before the competent administrative authority before addressing a judge.

The German judicial system is divided up into various branches, a distinction being made between ordinary (civil and criminal cases), administrative, financial, labour and social courts. Jurisdiction is determined according to the subject-matter concerned, usually on the basis of a general norm and only exceptionally on the basis of a specific allocation. §40 paragraph 1 sentence 1 of the Code of Administrative Court Procedure (VwGO – 'Verwaltungsgerichtsordnung'), governing the jurisdiction of administrative courts, stipulates:

> Recourse to the administrative courts shall be available in all public-law disputes of a non-constitutional nature insofar as the disputes are not explicitly allocated to another court by a federal statute.[57]

55 Holoubek, *WiVerw* 2008, 273, 279.

56 *Kudla v. Poland*, ECtHR, no. 30210/96, rep. 2000-XI, para. 157; *Mitev*, ECtHR, no. 40063/98, not published, para. 155. More detailed regarding the extent of Article 13 Grabenwarter and Pabel 2012, §24 paras. 174 ff. Cf. in regard to the question of excluding primary remedies already above n 54.

57 In German, this provision reads: 'Der Verwaltungsrechtsweg ist in allen öffentlich-rechtlichen Streitigkeiten nichtverfassungsrechtlicher Art gegeben, soweit die Streitigkeiten nicht durch Bundesgesetz einem anderen Gericht ausdrücklich zugewiesen sind.'

According to §13 of the Courts Constitution Act (GVG – 'Gerichtsverfassungsgesetz'), the corresponding provision for the ordinary jurisdiction,

> [t]he ordinary courts shall have jurisdiction over the civil disputes, family matters and non-contentious matters (civil matters) as well as criminal matters for which neither the competence of administrative authorities nor the jurisdiction of the administrative courts ['Verwaltungsgerichte'] has been established and for which no special courts have been created or permitted by provisions of federal law.[58]

The majority of disputes concerning the grant of limited public rights by means of an allocation procedure refer to public-law matters, and thus fall within the jurisdiction of the administrative courts, e.g. gambling licences, CO_2 emission permits or radio and telecommunication frequencies. As it is the nature of the dispute and not the fact that the administration has acted that is decisive for determining jurisdiction, ordinary courts may be competent for reviewing administrative action if the latter may be considered to be of a private-law nature. The award of contracts by public authorities (below the threshold of EU public procurement law) has been a difficult case in this respect. In a controversial ruling,[59] the Federal Administrative Court ('Bundesverwaltungsgericht') has opted for a private-law qualification:

> Contracts of work and services concluded by public authorities belong to private law ... The same applies to the award procedure preceding the conclusion of the contract and aiming at selecting an applicant. A private legal relationship arises between the contracting authority and the applicant when the negotiations for the contract are commenced. This legal relationship lasts until the day when the contract is awarded to the successful applicant. The allocation decision shares the legal nature of the intended civil-law transaction and in that regard is to be considered as a private-law declaration of intent. All in all, public procurement has to be assigned to private law ...[60]

58 In German, this provision reads: 'Vor die ordentlichen Gerichte gehören die bürgerlichen Rechtsstreitigkeiten, die Familiensachen und die Angelegenheiten der freiwilligen Gerichtsbarkeit (Zivilsachen) sowie die Strafsachen, für die nicht entweder die Zuständigkeit von Verwaltungsbehörden oder Verwaltungsgerichten begründet ist oder auf Grund von Vorschriften des Bundesrechts besondere Gerichte bestellt oder zugelassen sind'.

59 Cf. Wollenschläger 2010, pp. 229 ff.

60 BVerwGE 129, 9, 13: 'Die von der öffentlichen Hand abgeschlossenen Werk- und Dienstverträge gehören ausschließlich dem Privatrecht an ... Das gleiche gilt für das dem Abschluss des Vertrages vorausgehende Vergabeverfahren, das der Auswahl der öffentlichen Hand zwischen mehreren Bietern dient. Mit der Aufnahme der Vertragsverhandlungen entsteht zwischen dem öffentlichen Auftraggeber und den Bietern ein privatrechtliches Rechtsverhältnis, welches bis zur Auftragsvergabe an einen der Bieter andauert. Die öffentliche Hand trifft in diesem Vergabeverfahren eine Entscheidung über die Abgabe einer privatrechtlichen Willenserklärung, die die Rechtsnatur des beabsichtigten bürgerlich-rechtlichen Rechtsgeschäfts teilt. Die Vergabe öffentlicher Aufträge ist als einheitlicher Vorgang insgesamt dem Privatrecht zuzuordnen.'

Moreover, in view of the procedural design, the Bundesverwaltungsgericht has also rejected a distinction between an award decision governed by public law and its subsequent execution by a private-law contract [such an approach would correspond to the 'Zwei-Stufen-Theorie' (two-step theory) developed by *H. P. Ipsen*[61] and applied especially in cases regarding public grants]:

> The process of contracting is not constructed as a two-phased decision. Rather, the award decision consists of the conclusion of a private law contract with the successful bidder (see §28 number 2 paragraph 1 Code for Awarding Construction Contracts, Part A (VOB/A) [former version]). Hence, there is no basis for assuming a 'first step' and thus a separate allocation decision governed by public law. Applying the two-step theory to public procurement cases would thus mean artificially splitting up one single procedure into two parts. Public authorities are subject to public law obligations, especially to the principle of equality. This does not require, however, assuming a 'first step' in the shape of a separate award decision governed by public law. The public law obligations of the contracting authority may also be secured within the framework of private law according to the principles of private administrative law ('Verwaltungsprivatrecht'). Hence, the ordinary courts have to consider necessary amendments of private law rules in view of public law requirements.[62]

A specific jurisdiction – including a specific procedure (cf. 3.2.3.) – has only been established in public procurement cases falling under the harmonised EU regime (cf. §102 et seqq. Act Against Restraints of Competition [GWB – 'Gesetz gegen Wettbewerbsbeschränkungen']). Finally, as social and health law matters quite often imply granting limited public rights by means of an allocation procedure, the social courts also have some jurisdiction in this regard.

In administrative law cases, there is usually not only an opportunity, but indeed an obligation to challenge allocation decisions before the competent administrative authority before starting court action. According to §68 paragraph 1 sentence 1 VwGO, '[p]rior to

61 H.P. Ipsen, *Öffentliche Subventionierung Privater*, Carl Heymanns Verlag, Berlin 1956, p. 64 ff. Cf. further Wollenschläger 2010, pp. 235 ff., 572 ff.

62 BVerwGE 129, 9, 19: 'Das Vergabeverfahren ist nämlich seiner Struktur nach gerade nicht zweistufig; vielmehr erfolgt die Entscheidung über die Auswahl zwischen mehreren Bietern im Regelfall unmittelbar durch den Abschluss eines privatrechtlichen Vertrages mit einem der Bieter durch Zuschlag (vgl. §28 Nr. 2 Abs. 1 VOB/A [a.F.]). Hiernach fehlt es an einem Anknüpfungspunkt für eine "erste Stufe", auf der eine – nach öffentlichem Recht zu beurteilende – selbstständige "Vergabeentscheidung" fallen könnte. Durch die Anwendung der Zweistufentheorie auf die Vergabe öffentlicher Aufträge würde vielmehr ein einheitlicher Vorgang künstlich in zwei Teile aufgespalten. Die öffentlich-rechtlichen Bindungen, vor allem die Bindung an den Gleichheitssatz, denen die öffentliche Hand bei der Vergabe öffentlicher Aufträge unterliegt, zwingen nicht zur Annahme einer "ersten Stufe" bei der Auftragsvergabe in Form einer gesonderten "Vergabeentscheidung". Die öffentlich-rechtliche Überlagerung der privatrechtlichen Auftragsvergabe kann vielmehr ohne Weiteres nach den Grundsätzen des Verwaltungsprivatrechts bewältigt werden, indem die ordentlichen Gerichte über die Ergänzungen, Modifizierungen und Überlagerungen des Privatrechts durch öffentlich-rechtliche Bindungen mit zu entscheiden haben.'

lodging a rescissory action, the lawfulness and expedience of the administrative act shall be reviewed in preliminary proceedings.' The same is true for enforcement actions (§68 paragraph 2 VwGO). There are however exceptions to this rule, e.g. for administrative acts 'handed down by a supreme federal authority or by a supreme *Land* authority, unless a statute prescribes the review' (§68 paragraph 1 sentence 2 number 1 VwGO) or for specific subject-matters in which an expedited legal review is considered vital, for example in the context of allocating telecommunication frequencies (§§132 and 137 paragraph 2, §61 of the Telecommunications Act [TKG – 'Telekommunikationagesetz']).[63] Moreover, award decisions in public procurement law falling under the harmonised EU regime have to be challenged before an independent administrative tribunal ('Vergabekammer' [public procurement tribunal]) in first instance.[64]

3.2. *Remedies (Primary Legal Protection)*

Except for public procurement cases falling under the harmonised EU regime, no specific remedies exist for challenging allocation decisions in German administrative law. Rather, the ordinary rules of the respective procedural code apply. They have nonetheless been modified in certain areas in order to accommodate the specific needs of allocation procedures. After an outline of the standard model of repressive primary legal protection (3.2.1.), the issue of conferring particular stability on (some) allocation decisions will be introduced (3.2.2.). As a consequence of this stability, modifications of the standard model of ex-post remedies have emerged, namely the substitution of the ex-post remedy by a preventive remedy (3.2.3.) or by a prospective remedy (3.2.4.) and the complete exclusion of primary remedies with a limitation to secondary legal protection (damages; 3.2.5.).

3.2.1. Ex-post remedies: the standard model of repressive primary legal protection

When granting limited public rights by means of an allocation procedure, the administration often acts via administrative acts (§35 of the Administrative Procedure Act [VwVfG – 'Verwaltungsverfahrensgesetz']) containing the negative and/or positive decision. Hence, jurisdiction is exercised by the administrative courts on the basis of the Code of Administrative Court Procedure (VwGO). The type of action to be pursued depends on whether decision-making is structured in a bipolar or multipolar way, i.e. whether there is an individual (positive or negative) decision for each applicant or a single allocation decision addressed to all applicants. In the former case, the unsuccessful applicant has to combine an action for annulment of the allocation of the good to the successful competitor (rescissory action = 'Anfechtungsklage', §42 paragraph 1 alternative 1 VwGO) with an action to receive the good her/himself (enforcement action,

[63] Cf. for further exceptions §68 para. 1 sentence 2 number 2 VwGO and further specific provisions.

[64] In more detail C. F. Germelmann, 'Die Vergabekammern im System des vergaberechtlichen Rechtsschutzes' (2013) *DÖV (Die Öffentliche Verwaltung)* 50.

'Verpflichtungsklage', §42 paragraph 1 alternative 2 VwGO).[65] The disadvantages of this model are obvious: The multiplication of actions entails negative procedural consequences (increase in court costs and legal fees; possible information deficit regarding the positive decision, in particular the name of the successful applicant and the reasons for her/his success). In the latter case, challenging the single allocation decision by means of an enforcement action (§42 paragraph 1 alternative 2 VwGO) is sufficient.[66]

In case of a contractual allocation, the nullity of a contract resulting from the fact of it infringing individual rights can be established with an action for a declaratory judgment ('Feststellungsklage'); it is available in administrative law (§43 VwGO) as well as in civil law (§256 Civil Procedure Act [ZPO – 'Zivilprozessordnung']) cases.[67]

The principle of legal certainty and of protecting the legitimate interests of the successful bidder call for time limits to be imposed on the possibility to challenge an allocation decision by unsuccessful competitors. In terms of general administrative procedural law, §74 paragraphs 1 and 2 VwGO require lodging the rescissory and enforcement actions within one month of announcement of the administrative act. In case of (allocation) contracts, however, no specific rules exist and proposals to oblige affected third parties to object within one month have not been realised;[68] applying the general principle of forfeiture, or limiting the consequence of nullity, may be a way to introduce any time limits. A further possibility to achieve legal certainty at an early stage is to require bidders to lodge an action or at least to notify the administrative authority as soon as an error becomes manifest (cf. 3.4.).

Despite these time limits, once an appeal has been lodged, the lawfulness of an allocation decision remains open until the court of last instance has ruled on the issue (plus a possible constitutional complaint before the Bundesverfassungsgericht, Article 93 paragraph 1 number 4a GG) which will take years. Moreover, the suspensive effect of an appeal being the rule in administrative court proceedings (§80 paragraph 1 VwGO), it is also not legally possible for the authority to execute the allocation decision, at least until the first-instance ruling is non-contestable or, 'if the rescissory action has been rejected at first instance', until 'three months after expiry of the statutory deadline for reasoning of the appeal available against the negative decision' (cf. §80b VwGO). This delay is problematic in view of the public interest and the interest of the successful bidder in holding up the initial allocation decision, in particular since its lawfulness cannot be excluded from the outset. This situation may be mitigated only to a certain extent by excluding the suspensive effect of an appeal either by statute or by administrative decision (cf. §§80a, 80 paragraph 2 VwGO). For, the lawfulness of the allocation decision, even if

65 Some courts and authors consider challenging the negative decision to be sufficient to mitigate the negative procedural consequences; this approach has to be rejected, however, cf. in more detail Wollenschläger 2010, pp. 636 f.

66 Cf. Wollenschläger 2010, pp. 635 ff., and on the notion 'Verteilungsverwaltungsakt' ibid., pp. 575 ff.

67 Cf. in more detail Wollenschläger 2010, pp. 645 ff.

68 Cf. Wollenschläger 2010, pp. 622 ff.

the suspensive effect of an appeal against it has been excluded and even if, moreover, an interim court decision has confirmed the legality of the exclusion, remains to be assessed in the main proceedings. Thus, if the applicant wins the case, the court (of last instance) will rescind the allocation decision and re-distribute the good to the successful applicant or, at least, order the allocation procedure to be repeated (cf. §113 VwGO). The situation is only different in cases of time-dependent allocation decisions, e.g. the allocation of a stand at a market taking place on a specific date. For, after this date, the administrative decision (and the appeal against it) have been settled so that only an action for damages or for a declaratory judgment (§113 paragraph 1 sentence 4 VwGO) remains possible; in this case, if the suspensive effect of the appeal has been excluded, the administrative authority may execute the allocation and the execution cannot be revoked anymore so that the allocation might be considered stable.[69] This situation, however, is the exception. In order to nonetheless permit a fast execution of allocation decisions (also beyond this exceptional situation), a doctrine of particular stability of (some) allocation decisions has been established which rules out their ex-post repeal once they have been executed. This leads over to the next section.

3.2.2. Stability of allocation decisions

Beyond the general rules of administrative procedure which have just been sketched, particular stability is conferred on some allocation decisions which rules out their ex-post repeal once they have been executed. This is generally accepted – though criticised by some voices in academia – in the case of public procurement contracts, admission to universities and the award of posts in the public service, but also claimed beyond this (e.g. sale of property, medical care contracts between public health insurance funds and hospitals).[70] In practice, this means that once a procurement contract has been concluded or a civil servant appointed or promoted, unsuccessful competitors are precluded from challenging this administrative action even if they had been entitled to receive the limited public right in question if a lawful procedure had been followed.

Some even consider stability as one of the key characteristics of allocation procedures.[71] Yet, having said that, the exclusion of an ex-post repeal of allocation decisions cannot be considered to be inherent in such procedures.[72] In contrast, limiting the possibility to challenge an administrative action before the courts constitutes a restriction of the fundamental right of effective legal protection. For, these guarantees enshrined in national constitutional law, EU law and the ECHR demand primary legal protection as the general rule. Hence, stability of an administrative decision granting

69 In this case, the unsuccessful applicant may request the court dealing with the main proceedings to order or restitute the suspensive effect (cf. §80 para. 5, §80a VwGO).

70 Cf. Wollenschläger 2010, pp. 621 ff., with further references.

71 Cf. U. Stelkens, 'Primärrechtsschutz trotz Zuschlagserteilung? – oder: Warum nach wirksamer Zuschlagserteilung trotz §114 II 1 GWB ein Nachprüfungsverfahren möglich sein kann' (2003) *NZBau* 654, 655 f., though with a critical assessment; Gers-Grapperhaus 2009, p. 149.

72 Such approaches claiming the impossibility or limited administrative competences to repeal a decision have to be rejected, cf. Wollenschläger 2010, pp. 623 f.

limited public rights has to be justified in view of these guarantees by overriding public and private interests like legal certainty, efficient procurement or the interest of the competitor in a fast allocation (cf. 2.). Against this background, various models balancing these competing interests in different ways have become established in practice. They will be discussed in the following sections.

3.2.3. Substitution of the ex-post remedy by a preventive remedy

In public procurement procedures falling under the EU directives, and in procedures allocating posts in the public service, ex-post remedies are substituted by a preventive remedy expediting the process.[73] To introduce the former example: After the contract is awarded, the allocation decision can no longer be challenged (cf. §114 paragraph 2 sentence 1 GWB: 'Once an award has been made, it cannot be cancelled.').[74] In order to nonetheless secure effective legal protection, the contracting authority is obliged to inform the unsuccessful bidders of the imminent award and to 'stand still' for a certain period in order to give them the opportunity to lodge a complaint before the Public Procurement Tribunal ('Vergabekammer') and prevent the execution of the allocation decisions (cf. the information and standstill obligation stipulated by §101a GWB). The lawfulness of the allocation procedure and/or of the decision is examined in an accelerated procedure (§§110 and 113 GWB), including the right to an appeal (§§116 et seq. GWB). If the contracting authority fails to fulfil its information and standstill obligations (§101a GWB), the contract may be declared void within certain time limits in order to secure effective legal protection (and, considering the time limits, also legal certainty). §101b GWB stipulates as follows in this respect:

> (1) A contract shall be deemed ineffective ab initio if the contracting entity 1. has violated §101a or 2. has awarded a public contract directly to an undertaking without inviting other undertakings to participate in the award procedure and without this being expressly permissible in accordance with the law and this violation has been established in review proceedings in accordance with paragraph 2.
>
> (2) Ineffectiveness pursuant to paragraph 1 can only be established if this is claimed in review proceedings within 30 calendar days after knowledge of the infringement, however at the latest six months after conclusion of the contract. If the contracting entity has published the award of the contract in the Official Journal of the European Union, the time limit for claiming ineffectiveness shall end 30 calendar days after publication of the notice of the award in the Official Journal of the European Union.[75]

73 Cf. in more detail Wollenschläger 2010, pp. 251 ff., pp. 307 ff., pp. 625 ff. and pp. 647 f.

74 In German, §114 para. 2 sentence 1 GWB reads: 'Ein wirksam erteilter Zuschlag kann nicht aufgehoben werden.'

75 In German, §101b GWB reads: '(1) Ein Vertrag ist von Anfang an unwirksam, wenn der Auftraggeber 1. gegen §101a verstoßen hat oder 2. einen öffentlichen Auftrag unmittelbar an ein Unternehmen erteilt, ohne andere Unternehmen am Vergabeverfahren zu beteiligen und ohne dass dies aufgrund Gesetzes gestattet ist und dieser Verstoß in einem Nachprüfungsverfahren nach Absatz 2 festgestellt

If the award of a contract is particularly urgent, §115 paragraph 2 and §121 GWB enable the public procurement tribunal or the court, respectively, based on a balancing of the interests at stake, to allow the contracting authority to award the contract.[76]

Legal review in procedures allocating posts in the public service follows a similar pattern,[77] which has been established in the Bundesverfassungsgericht's case-law.[78] One important difference has to be noted, though. Unlike in public procurement law, the expedited procedure is not the only and final procedure. Rather, the interim procedure in civil service law is limited to the question of whether the administration is (temporarily) prevented from executing its allocation decision by appointing the successful applicant, but does not substitute the main proceedings. Hence, as well as securing her/his position by applying for such an injunction, the unsuccessful applicant has to challenge the negative allocation decision in the main proceedings. If an injunction is issued in favour of the unsuccessful applicant, the administration must not appoint the initially successful applicant and the legality of the award decision will be examined in the main proceedings. It is evident that in this case, the gain in expediting the procedure is limited since all then depends on the result of the main proceedings; the public authority may, however, in view of the probable unlawfulness of its decision and under certain conditions, decide to terminate the current procedure and initiate a new one.[79] If the court rejects an injunction in favour of the initially unsuccessful applicant (and, if appealed against, further court instances confirm this), the public authority may appoint the initially successful applicant. In this case, an acceleration *vis-à-vis* the standard model of ex-post repeal is achieved. Since a negative decision in the interim procedure is final in the sense that a subsequent appointment is permissible and cannot be challenged ex-post, the court is obliged to apply strict scrutiny, unlike in ordinary interim procedures.[80]

3.2.4. Substitution of the ex-post remedy by a prospective remedy

In a further model, applied in the field of admission to universities, the ex-post (primary) remedy is substituted by a prospective remedy. Again, the allocation decision in favour of a competitor cannot be challenged ex post. Having said that, if the successful applicant succeeds in establishing that she/he should have received the good, but had

worden ist. (2) Die Unwirksamkeit nach Absatz 1 kann nur festgestellt werden, wenn sie im Nachprüfungsverfahren innerhalb von 30 Kalendertagen ab Kenntnis des Verstoßes, jedoch nicht später als sechs Monate nach Vertragsschluss geltend gemacht worden ist. Hat der Auftraggeber die Auftragsvergabe im Amtsblatt der Europäischen Union bekannt gemacht, endet die Frist zur Geltendmachung der Unwirksamkeit 30 Kalendertage nach Veröffentlichung der Bekanntmachung der Auftragsvergabe im Amtsblatt der Europäischen Union.'

76 Cf. in more detail Wollenschläger 2010, pp. 254 f.

77 Cf. in more detail Wollenschläger 2010, pp. 307 f. Cf. further Case T-199/14 R, *Vanbreda Risk & Benefits v. EC* ECLI:EU:T:2014:1024, paras. 162, 172.

78 BVerfG, 2 BvR 706/09 – juris, para. 4; cf. further Wollenschläger 2010, pp. 313 f.

79 Cf. in more detail Wollenschläger 2010, pp. 298 ff.

80 BVerfGK 1, 292, 297 f.; BVerwGE 124, 99, 106; *NVwZ* 2011, 358, 361.

been unlawfully disregarded, she/he has a right to receive a similar good in a future allocation procedure.

This model is based on, and hence justified in terms of, constitutional and Union law primarily by the consideration that a subsequent challenge to the allocation – arising from an error for which the successful applicant is not responsible – is unreasonable for the successful applicants, and that this moreover constitutes a waste of resources. Furthermore, it does not appear possible to correct the error in good time and in a manner that is permanent in view of the fact that an offer of a place at university is urgent in terms of time: Even if the unsuccessful competitor were to obtain a provisional allocation by means of an injunction, this allocation would be constantly precarious given that it could be corrected in the main proceedings. One should furthermore take into account the level of complexity of the mass awarding procedure the functionality of which would be placed in jeopardy were there to be large numbers of challenges, as well as considering the low level of propensity for error resulting from the schematic awarding criteria. True, this kind of model is conditional on homogeneous rights being continuously distributed, as is the case when awarding university places. Its disadvantage would be, firstly, the loss of time for the wrongly disregarded applicant, and secondly the fact that the amount available for distribution in later procedures is reduced, which however is less significant where the supply is plentiful. This means that the risk of error affects subsequent applicants, hence requiring a special justification which, whilst it does apply under the law on higher education for the reasons which have been put forward, cannot necessarily be presumed to be necessitated in other cases.[81]

3.2.5. Complete exclusion of primary remedies and limitation to secondary legal protection (damages)

Despite the general primacy of primary legal protection, the guarantee of effective legal protection allows, if sufficiently justified, to completely rule out ex-post remedies and to limit the unsuccessful competitor to secondary legal protection, i.e. to damages (cf. 2.).[82] Such a model has been held constitutional by the Bundesverfassungsgericht in the case of public procurement not falling under the co-ordinated EU regime,[83] but not without stressing that the exclusion of primary legal protection has to be compensated for by effective secondary legal protection.[84] This model, notably the issue of effectiveness of damages, will be considered below (3.6).

81 Also cf. M. Schmidt-Preuß, *Kollidierende Privatinteressen im Verwaltungsrecht. Das subjektive öffentliche Recht im multipolaren Verwaltungsrechtsverhältnis*, 2nd ed., Duncker & Humboldt, Berlin 2005, pp. 469 f., 483 f., 489 ff. and 494.

82 Wollenschläger 2010, pp. 87 f. and 131 f.

83 BVerfGE 116, 135, 156.

84 BVerfGE 116, 135, 159.

3.3. *Standing before the Court*[85]

Unlike for instance in the French legal system, the primary task of the German administrative courts is not to review the lawfulness of administrative action as such, but (only) to protect individual rights. Hence, to have standing before the court, a violation of a subjective right must be asserted. §42 paragraph 2 VwGO stipulates as follows in this respect:

> Unless otherwise provided by law, the action shall only be admissible if the plaintiff claims that his/her rights have been violated by the administrative act or its refusal or omission.[86]

Moreover, to succeed with an action to quash an administrative decision also in substantive terms, it has to be established not only that the latter is unlawful, but also that it has violated a subjective right of the plaintiff. §113 paragraph 1 sentence 1 VwGO stipulates in this respect:

> Insofar as the administrative act is unlawful and the plaintiff's rights have been violated, the court shall rescind the administrative act and any ruling on an objection.[87]

In the context of allocation decisions this means that, to win the case, it has to be established not only that the decision was unlawful, but also that the plaintiff either may claim the good for her/himself or – in case of administrative discretion – has a chance to be considered when redistributing the good in line with the court's findings.[88] A mere violation of procedural requirements must have had an effect on the applicant's position.[89]

Finally, it shall be noted that in a potentially far-reaching ruling, the Belgacom case handed down on 14 November 2013, the ECJ has blurred the distinction between objective lawfulness of an allocation decision and its violating subjective rights at least as far as the principle of transparency is concerned. For, the court has stressed that 'the obligation of transparency to be complied with by the concession-granting authority benefits any potential tenderer ..., *even where it is established in the same Member State as those authorities*.'[90] Hence, 'Articles 49 TFEU and 56 TFEU must be interpreted as meaning that an economic operator in a Member State may, before the courts of that

85 This section follows Wollenschläger 2010, pp. 610 ff.

86 In German, §42 para. 2 VwGO reads: 'Soweit gesetzlich nichts anderes bestimmt ist, ist die Klage nur zulässig, wenn der Kläger geltend macht, durch den Verwaltungsakt oder seine Ablehnung oder Unterlassung in seinen Rechten verletzt zu sein.'

87 In German, §113 para. 1 sentence 1 VwGO reads: 'Soweit der Verwaltungsakt rechtswidrig und der Kläger dadurch in seinen Rechten verletzt ist, hebt das Gericht den Verwaltungsakt und den etwaigen Widerspruchsbescheid auf.'

88 Cf. in more detail Wollenschläger 2010, pp. 643 f.

89 Cf. in more detail Wollenschläger 2010, pp. 603 ff.

90 Case C-221/12, *Belgacom* ECLI:EU:C:2013:736, para. 32 (emphasis added).

Member State, allege an infringement of the obligation of transparency under those articles occurring at the time of conclusion of an agreement whereby one or more public entities of that Member State have either granted to an economic operator of that same Member State a licence for services of certain cross-border interest or granted an economic operator the exclusive right to engage in an economic activity of cross-border interest.'[91] According to the orthodox understanding, however, an economic operator applying for the award of a contract in her/his Member State would not be entitled to invoke a violation of the market freedoms since she/he is not engaged in a cross-border economic activity in this context, notwithstanding the fact that the non-advertisement of an award constitutes an infringement of the principle of transparency following from the market freedoms.[92]

A specific rule for standing before the court in the context of granting limited public rights by means of an allocation procedure can be found in the area of public procurement falling under the EU directives. §107 paragraph 2 GWB stipulates as follows:

> Every undertaking which has an interest in the contract and claims that its rights under §97 (7) were violated by non-compliance with the provisions governing the awarding of public contracts has the right to file an application. In doing so, it must be shown that the undertaking has suffered a loss, or may be about to suffer a loss, in consequence of the alleged violation of provisions governing the awarding of public contracts.[93]

3.4. *Phased Decision-making: When to Lodge the Appeal?*[94]

Decision-making in quite a number of administrative procedures granting limited public rights by means of an allocation procedure is phased in order to rationalise it, to enhance transparency and to reduce complexity. Therefore, before awarding a contract, for instance, public authorities first have to define the contractual object, award criteria and procedure, then to publish a contract notice, and next to evaluate the tenders in a multi-step procedure. In case an error becomes manifest, such phased decision-making procedures raise the question of when to lodge an appeal: Is court action only admissible

91 Case C-221/12, *Belgacom* ECLI:EU:C:2013:736, para. 34.

92 Cf. in more detail and for a critical view F. Wollenschläger, 'Binnenmarktrelevanz statt grenzüberschreitender Aktivität – eine Neujustierung in der Dogmatik der Grundfreiheiten?' in C. Baldus, F. Kainer and C. Stumpf (eds.), *Privatrecht, Wirtschaftsrecht, Verfassungsrecht: Privatinitiative und Gemeinwohlhorizonte in der europäischen Integration, Festschrift für Peter-Christian Müller-Graff*, Nomos, Baden-Baden 2015, pp. 435 f., forthcoming; cf. further F. Wollenschläger, *REALaw* 8 (2015), 205, 211 f.; M. Gabriel and M. Voll, 'Das Ende der Inländerdiskriminierung im Vergabe(primär)recht' (2014) *NZBau* 155.

93 In German, §107 para. 2 GWB reads: 'Antragsbefugt ist jedes Unternehmen, das ein Interesse am Auftrag hat und eine Verletzung in seinen Rechten nach §97 Absatz 7 durch Nichtbeachtung von Vergabevorschriften geltend macht. Dabei ist darzulegen, dass dem Unternehmen durch die behauptete Verletzung der Vergabevorschriften ein Schaden entstanden ist oder zu entstehen droht'.

94 This section follows Wollenschläger 2010, pp. 654 ff.

against the final decision, or have preparatory acts to be challenged as soon as an error becomes manifest?

Legal protection in the context of public procurement is based on the latter model. In accordance with §107 paragraph 3 GWB[95], an application to review the lawfulness of the award of a contract

> 'is inadmissible if
>
> 1. the applicant became aware of the violation of provisions governing the awarding of public contracts during the award procedure and did not object to the contracting entity without undue delay,
>
> 2. violations of provisions governing the awarding of public contracts which become apparent from the tender notice are not notified to the contracting entity by the end of the period specified in the notice for the submission of a tender or application,
>
> 3. violations of provisions governing the awarding of public contracts which only become apparent from the award documents are not notified to the contracting entity by the end of the period specified in the notice for the submission of a tender or application,
>
> 4. more than 15 calendar days have expired since receipt of notification from the contracting entity that it is unwilling to redress the complaint.'[96]

The general rule of the German Code of Administrative Court Procedure, however, reflects a different approach, namely the former one. According to §44a sentence 1 VwGO, '[a]ppeals against procedural acts by authorities may only be asserted at the same time as appeals which are admissible against the factual decision.'[97]

95 It is controversial if §107 para. 3 sentence 1 number 1 (obligation to object without undue delay) is in line with the requirements of effective legal protection set out by the ECJ in the cases Uniplex and NRA (C-406/08, *Uniplex* [2010] ECR I-840 and C-456/08, *NRA* [2010] ECR I-883). Cf. in detail C. Stumpf, 'Die Obliegenheit zur unverzüglichen Rüge von Vergaberechtsverletzungen vor dem Hintergrund des Europarechts' (2014) *EuZW (Europäische Zeitschrift für Wirtschaftsrecht)* 337 arguing in favour of introducing a new uniform but short deadline for an objection by the legislature (339).

96 In German, §107 para. 3 GWB reads: 'Der Antrag ist unzulässig, soweit 1. der Antragsteller den gerügten Verstoß gegen Vergabevorschriften im Vergabeverfahren erkannt und gegenüber dem Auftraggeber nicht unverzüglich gerügt hat, 2. Verstöße gegen Vergabevorschriften, die aufgrund der Bekanntmachung erkennbar sind, nicht spätestens bis Ablauf der in der Bekanntmachung benannten Frist zur Angebotsabgabe oder zur Bewerbung gegenüber dem Auftraggeber gerügt werden, 3. Verstöße gegen Vergabevorschriften, die erst in den Vergabeunterlagen erkennbar sind, nicht spätestens bis zum Ablauf der in der Bekanntmachung benannten Frist zur Angebotsabgabe oder zur Bewerbung gegenüber dem Auftraggeber gerügt werden, 4. mehr als 15 Kalendertage nach Eingang der Mitteilung des Auftraggebers, einer Rüge nicht abhelfen zu wollen, vergangen sind'.

97 §44a sentence 2 VwGO allows for the immediate challenge of acts which 'may be executed or are handed down against a party which is not involved.' Cf. for the relevance of this provision in the context of granting

Since the decisions being made during the award procedure – for example the determination of the award criteria or the call for bids – prepare the final allocation decision, the majority opinion considers them to be procedural acts within the meaning of §44a sentence 1 VwGO. Hence, they can only be challenged together with the final administrative decision.[98]

For the allocation of telecommunication frequencies, the Bundesverwaltungsgericht came to the opposite conclusion in its ruling of 1 September 2009. In this context, the administration's decision to opt for an allocation procedure as well as the determination of the award criteria and procedure have to be challenged immediately since they do not constitute procedural acts within the meaning of §44a sentence 1 VwGO. The Court's reasoning stresses that the Telecommunications Act (TKG) aims at immediately clarifying the lawfulness of procedural acts in order to have a stable basis for the further procedure and to avoid having to repeat the whole procedure after the final decision has been successfully challenged. This concept has been derived from the fact that the Telecommunications Act requires the abovementioned procedural steps to be taken in the form of administrative acts (cf. §132 paragraph 1 sentence 2 TKG) and that appeals against them do not have a suspensive effect (§137 paragraph 1 TKG).[99]

A comparison of the two models in terms of effectiveness leads to an ambivalent finding: There is no doubt that the standard model of the VwGO precludes a prompt clarification of the lawfulness of procedural acts and thus the continuation of the further procedure on a stable basis. A critique of this[100] has to consider, though, that allowing for an immediate remedy also endangers an efficient administrative procedure.[101] Moreover, the relevance of procedural errors usually requires an effect on the outcome of the procedure which can only be determined in view of the final decision.[102] Finally, the content of the final decision might render remedies superfluous.

limited public rights by means of an allocation procedure Wollenschläger 2010, pp. 654 ff. In German, §44a VwGO reads: 'Rechtsbehelfe gegen behördliche Verfahrenshandlungen können nur gleichzeitig mit den gegen die Sachentscheidung zulässigen Rechtsbehelfen geltend gemacht werden. Dies gilt nicht, wenn behördliche Verfahrenshandlungen vollstreckt werden können oder gegen einen Nichtbeteiligten ergehen'.

98 Wollenschläger 2010, pp. 320, 442 f. and 460 f.

99 BVerwG, *NVwZ* 2009, 1558, 1560 f. Cf. in more detail Wollenschläger 2010, pp. 442 f., 544 f. and 654 f.

100 V. Jenny, 'Rechtsschutz gegen die Anordnung eines Vergabeverfahrens nach §55 Abs. 9 TKG' (2009) *CR (Computer und Recht)* 502, 504 ff.; H.A. Wolff, 'Die dienende Funktion der Verfahrensrechte – eine dogmatische Figur mit Aussagekraft und Entwicklungspotential' in R. Pitschas and A. Uhle (eds.), *Wege gelebter Verfassung in Recht und Politik, Festschrift für Rupert Scholz zum 70. Geburtstag*, Duncker & Humblot, Berlin 2007, pp. 977, 983 f. Also W. Brohm, 'Die Konkurrentenklage' in H.-U. Erichsen, W. Hoppe and A. von Mutius (eds.), *System des verwaltungsgerichtlichen Rechtsschutzes, Festschrift für Christian-Friedrich Menger*, Heymann, Cologne 1985, pp. 235, 255; J. Pietzcker, 'Verwaltungsverfahren zwischen Verwaltungseffizienz und Rechtsschutzauftrag' (1983) 41 *VVDStRL* 193, 227.

101 Cf. Huber in Mangoldt, Klein and Starck 2010, para. 465; H.-J. Piepenbrock and U. Müller, 'Rechtsprobleme des UMTS-Versteigerungsverfahrens' in H.-J. Piepenbrock and F. Schuster (eds.), *UMTS-Lizenzvergabe, Rechtsfragen der staatlichen Versteigerung knapper Ressourcen*, Nomos, Baden-Baden 2001, pp. 8, 31 f.

102 Cf. also VG Köln, *CR* 2009, 513, 516; M. Geppert, '§61 TKG' in M. Geppert and R. Schütz (eds.), *BeckTKG-Kommentar*, 4th ed., C.H. Beck, Munich 2013, para. 21.

3.5. *Interim Relief*

Since the execution of many allocation decisions is urgent and/or time-bound, interim relief does play an important role (cf. also 3.2.1.).[103] One field of application concerns cases in which the suspensive effect of remedies is ruled out either by a legal norm (e.g. allocation of telecommunication frequencies, §137 paragraph 1 TKG) or by an administrative decision in the individual case (§80 paragraph 1 sentence 1 number 4 VwGO); further examples are cases in which the allocation is imminent (e.g. access to a public institution on a specific date, like places at university or at a public market/trade fair). In this regard, the goal of the applicant might be, first, only to stop the imminent grant of a limited public right and leave the issue of the lawfulness of the allocation procedure to be addressed in the main proceedings. If, however, reaching an allocation decision in favour of the applicant is urgent, an injunction requiring the administrative authority to grant the limited right for an interim period (or at least to decide on this issue) or even an injunction granting the limited right by the court itself (again for an interim period) might be applied for.[104] In cases of time-bound allocation decisions, such an injuction might mean that the main proceedings at least as far as primary legal protection is concerned become settled; then, strict scrutinity is required since the interim decision will become final. Moreover, a specific expedited procedure has been established in public procurement cases falling under the harmonised EU regime (cf. 3.2.3.). Expedited procedures also apply in cases in which the usual ex-post remedy is substituted by a preliminary ruling procedure (cf. 3.2.3.).

3.6. *Damages (Secondary Legal Protection)*[105]

In addition to actions to annul allocation decisions infringing individual rights (primary legal protection), legal protection may also be afforded by awarding damages (secondary legal protection). The latter form of redress does play an important role in the context of allocation procedures, in particular if the possibility of annulment actions is restricted. It must however be pointed out at the outset that awarding damages is secondary to an action for annulment of an allocation decision for two reasons. First, the constitutional and EU law guarantees of effective legal protection establish the primacy of quashing unlawful decisions over awarding damages for having to tolerate them since the former has to be considered more effective than the latter. Exceptions to this rule have to be justified; moreover, adequate redress has to be secured (cf. 2.). Second, liability is ruled out if a claimant of damages for breach of official duty has failed to avert the damage by not having had recourse to available actions to quash administrative decisions infringing an individual's rights. §839 paragraph 3 Civil Code (BGB – 'Bürgerliches Gesetzbuch'), dealing with liability in case of breach of official duty and reflecting a general principle of law, rules out liability 'if the injured person has intentionally or negligently failed to

103 Cf. in more detail Wollenschläger 2010, pp. 651 f.
104 Cf. in more detail Wollenschläger 2010, pp. 651 f.
105 This section follows Wollenschläger 2010, pp. 656 ff.

avert the damage by having recourse to appeal'[106].[107] In the following section, an overview of the various legal foundations for damages (3.6.1.) will be followed by an examination of the core issue of effectiveness (3.6.2.).

3.6.1. Legal basis for damages

In Germany, only the rules governing public procurement offer a limited claim in case of infringement; §126 sentence 1 GWB stipulates as follows:

> If the contracting entity violates a provision intended to protect undertakings, and if the undertaking would have had a real chance without this violation of being granted the award upon an assessment of the tenders, which, as a consequence of that infringement, was adversely affected, the undertaking may demand compensation for the costs of preparing the tender or of participating in an award procedure.[108]

Apart from this specific norm, damages are awarded on the basis of the general rules of the law on government liability. The specific basis for claims for damage caused by state action depends on the latter's legal nature. Liability for actions taken as a public authority is provided for by §839 BGB in conjunction with Article 34 GG. In addition, claims based on violations of obligations in the context of special public legal relationships are possible, as is the case with allocating posts in the public service.[109] If such agencies act not as a public authority, but under private law, the ordinary rules of contract and/or tort law are held to be applicable.[110] If they act within the scope of competition and antitrust law[111],

106 §839 para. 3 BGB reads in German: 'Die Ersatzpflicht tritt nicht ein, wenn der Verletzte vorsätzlich oder fahrlässig unterlassen hat, den Schaden durch Gebrauch eines Rechtsmittels abzuwenden'.

107 Erbguth, *VVDStRL* 61 (2002), 221, 229; Wollenschläger 2010, pp. 634 f. The ECJ has pointed out in this respect: 'In particular, in order to determine the loss or damage for which reparation may be granted, the national court may inquire whether the injured person showed reasonable diligence in order to avoid the loss or damage or limit its extent and whether, in particular, he availed himself in time of all the legal remedies available to him. Indeed, it is a general principle common to the legal systems of the Member States that the injured party must show reasonable diligence in limiting the extent of the loss or damage, or risk having to bear the damage himself' (Joined Cases C-46/93 and C-48/93, *Brasserie du Pêcheur SA* [1996] ECR I-1029, paras. 84 f. Cf. further Case C-445/06, *Danske Slagterier* [2009] ECR I-2119, paras. 58 f.).

108 In German, §126 sentence 1 GWB reads: 'Hat der Auftraggeber gegen eine den Schutz von Unternehmen bezweckende Vorschrift verstoßen und hätte das Unternehmen ohne diesen Verstoß bei der Wertung der Angebote eine echte Chance gehabt, den Zuschlag zu erhalten, die aber durch den Rechtsverstoß beeinträchtigt wurde, so kann das Unternehmen Schadensersatz für die Kosten der Vorbereitung des Angebots oder der Teilnahme an einem Vergabeverfahren verlangen'.

109 BVerwGE 80, 123, 124 f.; in addition *NVwZ* 1999, 424, 424; *NVwZ* 2009, 787, 788.

110 The literature partly considers §839 BGB in conjunction with Article 34 GG to be applicable in cases in which public authority is acting privately, for example F. Ossenbühl and M. Cornils, *Staatshaftungsrecht*, 6th ed., C.H. Beck, Munich 2013, pp. 27 f. But declining BGH, *NJW* 2000, 2810, 2810 f.; OLG Zweibrücken, *ZfBR* 2009, 202, 203; H. Maurer, *Allgemeines Verwaltungsrecht*, 18th ed., C.H. Beck, Munich 2011, §26 para. 56; P. Reinert, '§839 BGB' in H.G. Bamberger and H. Roth (eds.), *BGB – Kommentar, vol. 2*, 3rd ed., C.H. Beck, Munich 2012, paras. 2, 15.

111 Cf. Wollenschläger 2010, pp. 183 f.

§33 paragraphs 3–5 GWB and §9 Act against Unfair Competition (UWG – 'Gesetz gegen den unlauteren Wettbewerb') may apply. Finally, Union law requires state liability for infringements of EU law; this claim is independent of the legal nature of the selection procedure.[112]

3.6.2. Effectiveness of damages

A key issue in secondary legal protection is the effectiveness of damages.

If the unsuccessful applicant seeks damages for the economic loss resulting from the non-allocation of the desired asset, such as income as a public servant that is not received, or the loss of profit from a public contract, it is incumbent on her/him to particularly explain and prove that she/he did indeed suffer damage as a result of the violation of the right; this is conditional on whether she/he would indeed have received the allocation had the selection been carried out properly. This proof of causality triggering liability is very difficult to furnish where a margin of appreciation exists for administrative decisions, as well as in constellations in which the causality of the error committed in awarding the contract can be neither confirmed nor ruled out (e.g. alleged lack of suitability leading to the consequence of non-admission to the drawing or auction).[113]

This is the dilemma of secondary legal protection. Unlike in primary legal protection, there is no possibility – as would do justice to remedying such rights violations – to repeal the awarding decision and order it to be repeated; this procedure would then reveal the prospects of success of the applicant who was (initially) unsuccessful.[114] In secondary legal protection, by contrast, it is only possible to award or deny compensation claims, frustration however being the potential result of its too restrictive treatment, but excessive liability arising if this treatment is overgenerous. The dilemma is exacerbated by the fact that, in some allocation procedures, exclusively secondary legal protection is available, and this must therefore – also for constitutional reasons[115] – compensate for the refused primary legal protection. The question thus arises of how to deal adequately with such frustrated opportunities.

Where proof of the causality of the rights violation is demanded in order to receive damages and causality is then negated where a margin of appreciation exists for

112 Case C-6 and C-9/90, *Francovich* [1991] ECR I-5357, para. 31 ff.; Case C-46 and 48/93, *Brasserie du Pêcheur SA*, [1996] ECR I-1029, para. 51.

113 BVerwGE 118, 370, 378 f.; E 124, 99, 108; *NVwZ* 2009, 787, 789; BGH, *NJW* 1995, 2344, 2345.

114 The BVerfG (2 BvR 811/09 – juris, para. 8) rightly states as follows: 'In regard to the promotion decision which – in accordance with the principle of the stability of offices – is irreversible as a matter of principle, the primary claim which applies regardless of fault aims – prior to this decision – to halt application procedures in which procedural violations have occurred and where the respective claimant is one of the candidates to be considered. Primary legal protection as manifested in conflict between rivals permits, in this regard, damage to be limited at an early stage, or rather the risk originating from a basis for decision-making which may still be unsure to be minimised.'

115 BVerfGE 116, 135, 159; in addition E 116, 1, 22. The fact that this is not true whether or not adequate primary legal protection is available is underlined by BVerfG, 2 BvR 811/09 – juris, paras. 6 ff.

administrative decisions and no decision could have been reached in favour of the claimant, claims for damages are ruled out from the outset.[116] This view, however, appears to be too restrictive for reasons lying in the interest of effective legal protection. Rather, in the view of the Bundesverfassungsgericht, in any case where primary legal protection is not available, this guarantee certainly impacts 'the interpretation and application of the provisions of private and civil procedure law which an unsuccessful bidder can invoke in order to obtain legal protection against being unlawfully disregarded. The factual preconditions and legal consequences of the provisions from which the unsuccessful bidder can derive a claim to damages must be determined in a manner which adequately does justice to their interest in legal protection aiming to comply with Article 3 paragraph 1 GG.'[117] On the other hand, it also does not appear reasonable to permit the mere possibility of being taken into account as a sufficient basis for total compensation as this would lead to limitless liability.[118]

As is recognised in the law on the public service, it is however possible to do justice to legitimate legal protection interests by reversing the burden of providing evidence and the burden of proof, assuming that a breach of the law and a damage have been established.[119] True, 'the party who has been injured by a breach of official duty must as a matter of principle also provide proof of having suffered damage as a result. If however the breach of official duty and the damage which subsequently resulted from it have been established, the injured party may leave it up to the public body to prove that the damage was not caused by the breach of official duty; this however only applies if experience shows that a de facto presumption or an actual probability of the causative connection exists, otherwise the burden of proof continues to be incumbent on the injured party.'[120] The relaxation of the burden of proof under §287 ZPO also applies if difficulties in investigation result from a breach of official duty.[121] The objection can be put forward against this solution in terms of the law on evidence – apart from the vagaries which it entails – that it is based merely on the alternative between full and denied liability, thus it constitutes an 'all or nothing'-approach.[122] This gives rise to reservations not only in terms of the lack of legal protection if the compensation claim is turned down; it is rather also particularly questionable in multipolar allocation conflicts in terms of the threat of overcompensation in the event of there being more than one applicant with chances of success, to whom compensation must hence be awarded although there is no doubt that only one applicant may be successful.

116 See LG Berlin *NVwZ-RR (Neue Zeitschrift für Verwaltungsrecht – Rechtsprechungs-Report)* 1997, 35, 36.

117 BVerfGE 116, 135, 159.

118 Also cf. BVerfG, 2 BVR 811/09 – juris, paras. 6 ff.

119 BGH, *NJW* 1982, 2241, 2242; *NJW* 1995, 2344, 2345; BVerwGE 124, 99, 108 f.; W. Spoerr, *Treuhandanstalt und Treuhandunternehmen zwischen Verfassungs-, Verwaltungs- und Gesellschaftsrecht*, Verlag Kommunikationsforum Recht, Wirtschaft, Steuern, Cologne 1993, p. 187. Facilitating the review of the handling of frustrated chances in the law of evidence G. Mäsch, *Chance und Schaden, Zur Dienstleisterhaftung bei unaufklärbaren Kausalverläufen*, Mohr Siebeck, Tübingen 2004, pp. 127 ff.

120 BGH, *NJW* 1982, 2241, 2242.

121 BGH, *NJW* 1995, 2344, 2345; in addition *NJW* 1986, 2829, 2832.

122 Mäsch 2004, p. 143 ff.

Against this background, the question arises of whether the missed opportunity itself is not to be regarded as damage that is amenable to compensation.[123] A provision which appears to go in this direction is contained in a provision of public procurement law covered by the EU directives, namely §126 sentence 1 GWB, which hence resolves the dilemma of furnishing proof by granting a right to compensation for expenditure incurred through participation in the procedure unless the bid had no reasonable chance from the outset. §126 sentence 1 GWB reads as follows: 'If the contracting entity violates a provision intended to protect undertakings, and if the undertaking would have had a real chance without this violation of being granted the award upon an assessment of the tenders, which, as a consequence of that infringement, was adversely affected, the undertaking may demand compensation for the costs of preparing the tender or of participating in an award procedure.' A bid had a 'real' chance, and this is the crux of the issue, if 'the contracting entity would have been entitled to award the contract within its margin of appreciation.'[124] However, this specific provision, which ultimately provides for a compensation entitlement with a relaxed burden of proof in comparison to general law on compensation, does not establish a right to compensation for missed opportunities, as it does not compensate for these because of its being limited to the negative interest.[125]

Such a right however appears to be justified in view of the fact that it is incumbent on the public authority, stemming from the constitutional right to participation, to refrain from frustrating the opportunities of the applicants participating in the procedure.[126] When it comes to liability for missed opportunities, the problem of causality becomes the problem of determining the damage incurred. In this regard, the damage incurred is calculated by multiplying the anticipated profit by the chances of acquiring that profit.[127] This also ensures that there is no overcompensation; what is more, the prospects for success of an opportunity are to be valued at 0% if consideration of the bid is ruled out for instance because there are grounds for its exclusion.

4. Conclusions

By not following the classic bipolar citizen-state paradigm on which many rules and institutions of administrative law are based, allocation procedures pose a challenge to legal doctrine and jurisprudence. It is essential to develop differentiated solutions acknowledging the multipolar conflict with which allocation procedures have to deal. This desired effect has already been achieved in certain respects. For instance, when determining the requirements of the guarantee of effective legal protection enshrined in

123 Comprehensively Mäsch 2004. Also cf. Pollmann 2009, p. 165.

124 BGH, *WRP (Wettbewerb in Recht und Praxis)* 2008, 370, 373.

125 Also Mäsch 2004, pp. 153 ff.

126 Cf. Mäsch 2004, pp. 145 f., 240 ff.; pp. 266 ff. also regarding objections. In light of the constitutional entitlement to ensure a reaction to the exclusion of liability for lost opportunities – in the opinion of Mäsch 2004, pp. 302 f., justified because of systematic reasons – out of the scope of protection according to §823 para. 2 BGB, cannot be supported in this context; besides there is a quasi-contractual relationship – also in the opinion of Mäsch 2004, pp. 312 ff. – legitimating liability.

127 In detail Mäsch 2004, pp. 320 ff.; regarding procedural implications ibid., pp. 317 ff.

national constitutional law, EU law and the ECHR, it is well established that the standards for judicial review have to be developed by balancing the interests in a comprehensive way, i.e. not only the interests of the unsuccessful applicant seeking redress have to be considered, but also those of the administration and of the successful competitor. Moreover, various models of legal protection have been developed against this background, each reflecting a different weighting of the interests at stake. In this context, the concept of the stability conferred on the allocation decision has been acknowledged, and with it modifications of the standard model of ex-post remedies have emerged, namely the substitution of the ex-post remedy by a preventive remedy or by a prospective remedy as well as the complete exclusion of primary remedies with a limitation to secondary legal protection (damages). It however remains to be examined in each subject-matter whether the balance of interests is sound. Notwithstanding these positive examples, there is still room for developing legal doctrine and jurisprudence in the context of allocation procedures. To give one concrete example: The debate on how to secure effective damages has to be continued, in particular in view of the deficits in primary legal protection in some procedures.

PART II

EU LAW PERSPECTIVES

Jacobine van den Brink*

CHAPTER 6. REQUIREMENTS UNDER EU LAW ON THE ALLOCATION OF SCARCE EUROPEAN SUBSIDIES

1. Introduction

For years, the European Union (hereinafter: the EU) has tried to achieve its policy objectives partly through the provision of European subsidies. These subsidies are not only provided by the European Commission and European executive agencies, but also by national authorities. Examples of European subsidies are the subsidies from the Structural Funds,[1] which aim among other things to reduce the economic differences between EU regions, and the research and development grants that are provided under the so-called Horizon 2020 programme.[2]

European subsidies qualify as public rights as this concerns individual rights which are granted by administrative authorities.[3] More specifically it concerns claims to governmental support. Because there is a limited amount of funding available for most of the European subsidy programmes,[4] as is the case for most national subsidies, it concerns limited public rights.[5]

Because it is likely that the amount of European subsidies requested will exceed the limited budget,[6] both European and national authorities responsible for the allocation of

* Jacobine van den Brink is Assistant Professor at the Department of Constitutional and Administrative Law of Leiden University, the Netherlands.

1 The European Social Fund (ESF) and the European Regional Development Fund (ERDF).

2 See Regulation No 1291/2013 of the European Parliament and of the Council of 11 December 2013 establishing Horizon 2020 – the Framework Programme for Research and Innovation (2014–2020) and repealing Decision No 1983/2006/EC [2013] OJ L347/104. This programme is the successor to the Seventh Framework programme in 2007–2013. See Decision No 1982/2006 [2006] OJ L412/1.

3 See Chapter 1, Section 4.

4 An exception exists for certain European subsidy schemes that are funded by the European Agriculture Guarantee Fund (EAGF). This concerns the export refunds and the single payment. For these schemes, anyone who meets the subsidy conditions and abides by the obligations, qualifies for European subsidy. These European subsidies can therefore not be classed as scarce.

5 See Chapter 1, Section 4.

6 In the Netherlands this is usually the case.

European subsidies will have to consider what requirements exist under European law in this allocation procedure. What allocation mechanism should be chosen, to what extent do the European general principles of equal treatment and transparency developed in procurement law apply and, if so, what obligations arise from these? These questions are considered for both the European subsidies that are provided by the European Commission and the European executive agencies, as well as the European subsidies that are provided by national authorities.[7] This chapter will go on to demonstrate that for each category of European subsidies, differences exist with regard to the requirements for the allocation.

As a starting point the European rules applying in the programme period 2007–2013 have been chosen. This is due to the fact that there has not been much experience so far with the regulations for the current programme period 2014–2020 concerning the allocation of EU subsidies. Because these regulations were not adopted before December 2013, the Member States could only then start drafting their own obligatory national programmes on the basis of which they intend to grant European subsidies. This means that most Member States allocated EU subsidies in the current programme period not earlier than the end of 2014. It remains to be seen what problems will occur in the coming years. The above also has the consequence that Financial Regulation No 1605/2002 will be taken as a starting point.[8] When I use the term Financial Regulation, I mean therefore Regulation 1605/2002. Although the new Financial Regulation has been applicable since 1 January 2013, it did not apply to European subsidies which were granted in the programme period 2007–2013.[9] However, interesting changes in the Financial Regulation as well as the regulations for the current programme period that are relevant for the topic of this chapter will be mentioned.

Before the question can be addressed concerning the requirements that have to be met under European law on the allocation of scarce European subsidies, Section 2 first discusses what can be understood under the term 'European subsidy'. Attention is paid to the distinction between European subsidies that are provided by the European Commission and European executive agencies on the one hand, and by the national authorities on the other hand. Section 3 then goes on to discuss which allocation mechanism should be chosen for the allocation of European subsidies, to what extent the principles of equal treatment and transparency apply and if so, what the resulting obligations are. Section 4 provides a conclusion.

7 Concerning the provision of European subsidies by Dutch authorities and the problems that occur see J.E. van den Brink, *De uitvoering van Europese subsidieregelingen in Nederland. Juridische knelpunten en uitdagingen*, Kluwer, Deventer 2012.

8 Council Regulation No 1605/2002 of 25 June 2002 containing the Financial Regulation applicable to the general budget of the European Community [2002] OJ L248/1.

9 Regulation No 966/2012 of the European Parliament and the Council of 25 October 2012 on the financial rules applicable to the general budget of the Union and repealing Council Regulation No 1605/2002 [2012] OJ L298/1 and the accompanying Commission delegated Regulation No 1268/2012 on the rules of application of Regulation No 966/2012 [2012] OJ L362/1. The new Financial Regulation came into force on 1 January 2013. However, the provisions concerning the implementation methods of the budget will come into force on 1 January 2014. See Article 214, opening words, under a, of the new Financial Regulation.

2. European Grants in Various Shapes and Sizes

2.1. The Concept of European Subsidy

Before dealing with the question of what requirements under European law have to be met on the allocation of European subsidies, this paragraph will look at the actual concept of European subsidies. How should this term be understood and what kinds of European subsidies exist? Since 2002 a definition of the concept of European subsidy has been included in the Financial Regulation, the European legislative instrument for the implementation of the EU budget. The old as well as the new Financial Regulation[10] refers to direct financial contributions, by way of donation, from the budget in order to finance a) an action intended to help achieve an objective forming part of a European Union policy; or b) the functioning of a body that pursues an aim of general European interest or has an objective forming part of a European Union policy.

The most important category of European funding does not fall within this definition. It concerns funding that, although paid from the EU budget, is provided through the intervention of the Member States. Examples are the important agricultural subsidies and subsidies that are provided from the Structural Funds, the European Social Fund (ESF) and the European Regional Development Fund (ERDF). In budget terms these subsidies are provided 'under shared management'. The section on Grants in the Financial Regulation – listing various conditions for the provision of European subsidies – does not apply to the provision of these 'European subsidies'.[11] However, the focus of this chapter does not only concern the direct financial contributions charged to the central EU budget, but also the 'European subsidies' provided by national authorities under shared management. The definition of European subsidy of the Financial Regulation is therefore too limited in the context of this chapter. The only difference with European funding provided by national authorities under shared management is that it doesn't concern a *direct* financial contribution from the EU budget. Apart from this, it matches the description of the Financial Regulation. To avoid having to distinguish between European subsidies in the sense of the Financial Regulation and European funding provided by national authorities under shared management, I have opted in this chapter for a broader definition of the term 'European subsidy', but will as much as possible keep to the description of European subsidy contained in the Financial Regulation:

> *A European grant is a financial contribution directly or indirectly financed by the EU budget, by way of donation to finance an action intended to help achieve an objective forming part of an EU policy.*

10 See Article 8 of Council Regulation No 1605/2002 and Article 121 of Regulation 966/2012.

11 This follows on from the word 'direct' contained in Article 108(1) of the Financial Regulation. The second paragraph stating what does not qualify as a grant within the meaning of the Grants title refers under (e) to the European subsidies provided under shared management, in other words European subsidies that are first paid into the budget of the Member State. These subsidies are explicitly excluded from the concept of European subsidy. See in the new Financial Regulation Article 121(1) and Article 121(2)(e).

The term *financial contribution* indicates that European subsidies are not just about the payment of money; they can also be contributions that may be perceived as monetary. For example, the provision of a loan at a favourable rate or a guarantee. Secondly, the above definition shows that the contribution is paid for from the EU budget; so it does not concern subsidies that are paid for from a national treasury. Thirdly, the financial contribution can be both direct, i.e. from the European Commission and European executive agencies, and indirect, i.e. provided by Member States. Fourthly, it concerns a donation; a European subsidy is not the same as a public contract which involves payment for the delivery of movable or immovable property, the performance of work or services. Such considerations are indeed absent in the context of a European subsidy. It concerns, after all, the funding of an action that is intended to help achieve an objective that is part of an EU policy. These EU objectives are contained in Article 3 of the Treaty on European Union (TEU). For example, the realisation of freedom, security and justice, a broadly competitive social market economy aimed at full employment and social progress and economic, social and territorial cohesion.

Note, however, that the concept 'European subsidy' is nowhere to be found in European law pertaining to the provision of European subsidies. This refers, among other things, to 'community support' – to be distinguished from national support,[12] premium,[13] 'subsidy',[14] 'support' and 'aid'.[15] If the definition formulated above has been met, then in the context of this chapter a European subsidy is intended.

The next paragraphs take a closer look at the various types of European subsidies that fall under the definition formulated above. For the purpose of this chapter this is relevant, because the requirements under EU law on the allocation of these various types of European subsidies vary. Paragraph 2.2 looks at the European subsidies provided by the European Commission and the European executive agencies. These are the European subsidies that also fall under the subsidy definition contained in the Financial Regulation to which the section Grants therefore (directly) applies. Paragraph 2.3 looks at the European subsidies that are provided via the Member States. In that context, a distinction should be made between European subsidies that are provided under shared management (paragraph 2.3.1.) and that therefore do not fall under the grant definition of the Financial Regulation on the one hand, and the European subsidies that are provided by

12 See Article 1, opening words and under 1, of Council Regulation No 1698/2005 of 20 September 2005 on support for rural development by the European Agricultural Fund for Rural Development (EAFRD) [2015] OJ L277/1.

13 See Article 79 of Council Regulation No 73/2009 of 19 January 2009 establishing common rules for direct support schemes for farmers under the common agricultural policy and establishing certain support schemes for farmers [2009] OJ L254/73 (EAGF).

14 See Article 14(1) of Decision No 573/2007 of the European Parliament and the Council of 23 May 2007 establishing the European Refugee Fund for the period 2008 to 2013 as part of the General programme 'Solidarity and Management of Migration Flows' (ERF).

15 See Council Regulation No 1083/2006 of 11 July 2006 laying down general provisions on the European Regional Development Fund, the European Social Fund and the Cohesion Fund and repealing Regulation (EC) No 1260/1999 [2006] OJ L210/25 (Structural Funds), version 01.07.2013.

organisations of the Member States under public and private law on the other hand. The section Grants of the Financial Regulation No 1605/2002 does apply to this latter category of European subsidies. Paragraph 2.4 looks briefly at the new Financial Regulation No 966/2012, which has the consequence that commitments made as of 1 January 2014 concerning subsidies that are provided by organisations of the Member States under public and private law no longer fall under the grant definition.[16]

2.2. *European Subsidies provided by the European Commission and European Executive Agencies*

The first category of European subsidies to be discussed are the subsidies that are provided directly by the departments of the European Commission, and subsidies which are delegated to be provided by European executive agencies.[17] In budget terms, these European subsidies are provided on a centralised basis.[18] Examples of these are the 'Seventh Framework'[19], 'Life+',[20] and 'Progress'.[21] An example of a European

16 See Article 58 to 63 in conjunction with Article 214, opening words and under a, of Regulation No 966/2012.

17 European executive agencies are legal persons under European law to whom – for the account and under the responsibility of the Commission – the implementation of a European programme or project can be delegated either in whole or in part, pursuant to Regulation No 58/2003. See Article 55 of the Financial Regulation. See also Council Regulation No 58/2003 of 19 December 2002, which determines the status of the executive agencies to which certain management tasks in the community programmes have been delegated [2003] OJ L11/1. On European executive agencies see for example P.P. Craig, 'The constitutionalisation of Community administration' (2003) *ELRev.* 840 and Wolfgang Schenk, *Strukturen und Rechtsfragen der gemeinschaftlichten Leistungsverwaltung*, Mohr Siebeck, Tübingen 2006, p. 183 f.

18 See Article 53 of the Financial Regulation which states that the budget of the Commission can be implemented a) on a centralised basis, b) by shared or decentralised management and c) by shared management with international organisations.

19 See Decision No 1982/2006 of the European Parliament and of the Council of 18 December 2006 concerning the Seventh Framework Programme of the European Community for research, technological development and demonstration activities (2007–2013) [2006] OJ L412/1. The procedure for the provision of grants can be found in Regulation No 1906/2006 of the European Parliament and of the Council of 18 December 2006 laying down the rules for participation of undertakings, research centres and universities in actions under the Seventh Framework Programme and for the dissemination of research results (2007–2013) [2006] OJ L391/1. In the current program period the programme has been renamed into Horizon 2020 from the programme period 2014–2020. See the Regulation No 1291/2013 of the European Parliament and of the Council of 11 December 2013 establishing Horizon 2020 – the Framework Programme for Research and Innovation (2014–2020) and repealing Decision No 1983/2006/EC [2013] OJ L347/104.

20 See Regulation No 614/2007 of the European Parliament and of the Council of 23 May 2007 concerning the Financial Instrument for the Environment (LIFE+) [2007] OJ L149/1. For the current programme period this regulation has been replaced by Regulation No 1293/2013 of the European Parliament and of the Council of 11 December 2013 on the establishment of a Programme for the Environment and Climate Action (LIFE) and repealing Regulation No 614/2007 [2013[OJ L347/185.

21 See Decision No 1672/2006 of the European Parliament and of the Council of 24 October 2006 establishing a Community Programme for Employment and Social Solidarity – Progress [2006] OJ L315/1. In the programme period 2014–2020 Progress has been integrated into the European Union Programme for Employment and Social Innovation ("EaSI") (see Regulation No 1296/2013 [2013] OJ L347/238).

programme for which the implementation is delegated to an executive agency is the programme 'Europe for citizens'. This programme is managed by the Education, Audiovisual & Culture Executive Agency (EACEA).[22] In these cases, through the provision of the European subsidy a relationship arises between the European Commission and the executive agency respectively on the one hand and the final beneficiary of the European subsidy on the other hand.[23]

The section Grants of the Financial Regulation applies to the European subsidies that are provided directly by the European Commission and the European executive agencies.[24] In both the Financial Regulation and the regulation of the European Commission[25] based on it, rules are laid down in connection with the form in which a grant can be provided,[26] the principles upon which they are provided,[27] the award procedure[28] and payment and control.[29] The European subsidies that are provided directly by the Commission or the European executive agencies are usually provided via a contract.[30]

22 This was done by Commission Decision of 26 April 2007 to transfer authority to the Education, Audiovisual and Culture Executive Agency (EACEA), with the aim of implementing activities connected to the implementation of community programmes in the area of education, audiovisual means and culture, particularly including the implementation of grant awards, as established in the budget of the Community under No C(2007) 1842, in accordance with the amendments of 26 May 2008. The Agency was established by the Commission Decision of 14 January 2005 establishing the Education, Audiovisual and Culture Executive Agency, for the management of community action in the fields of education, audiovisual media and culture in application of Council Regulation No 58/2003 [2005] OJ L24/35. This decision was amended on several occasions. Therefore Decision 2005/56 has been replaced in 2009 by Commission Decision of 20 April 2009 setting up the Education, Audiovisual and Culture Executive Agency for the management of Community action in the fields of education, audiovisual and culture in application of Council Regulation No 58/2003 [2009] OJ L101/26. In 2013 this Decision has been repealed by Commission Implementing Decision of 18 December 2013 establishing the 'Education, Audiovisual and Culture Executive Agency' [2013] OJ L232/46.

23 When European executive agencies entered into a subsidy relationship with final beneficiaries of European subsidies, the question arose in the practical implementation to what extent legal protection was possible in the European courts. To solve this problem Article 22 of Regulation No 58/2003 establishes administrative appeal at the European Commission against acts of an executive agency. If the European Commission rejects the administrative appeal, an action for annulment may be brought before the Court of Justice in accordance with Article 263 TFEU (see Article 22(5) of Regulation No 58/2003).

24 See Article 108 of the Financial Regulation and thereafter.

25 See Commission Regulation No 2342/2002 of 23 December 2002 laying down rules for the implementation of Council Regulation No 1605/2002 of 25 June 2002 on the Financial Regulation applicable to the general budget of the European Communities [2002] OJ L357/1 (hereafter: the Commission Regulation).

26 See Article 108*bis* of the Financial Regulation.

27 See Article 109 f. of the Financial Regulation.

28 See Article 114 f. of the Financial Regulation.

29 See Article 117 f. of the Financial Regulation.

30 See Article 108(1), second para. of the Financial Regulation in conjunction with Article 164 of the Commission Regulation.

2.3. *European Subsidies provided by National Administrative Bodies*

2.3.1. Subsidy provision under shared management

When European subsidies are provided under shared management, it means that the European subsides are granted through Member States intervention to final beneficiaries of the subsidies.[31] The Member States appoint the national authorities – in this chapter referred to as national administrative bodies – charged with the implementation of the European subsidy scheme in question. Originally the method of shared management only applied to the Structural Funds,[32] the European Fisheries Fund,[33] the European Agricultural Guarantee Fund (EAGF)[34] and the European Agricultural Fund for Rural Development (EAFRD).[35] Currently, this method is applied on a larger scale, for example through the Migration Funds[36] and the European Globalisation Fund.[37]

31 See the Second report of the Committee of Independent Experts on Reform of the Commission, Analysis of current practice and proposals for tackling mismanagement, irregularities and fraud, Volume I (10 September 1999), p. 78 and also Article 53 ter of the Financial Regulation. According to Craig 'shared management' is equal to 'shared administration'. See P.P. Craig, 'Shared administration, disbursement of community funds and the regulatory state', in H.C.H Hofmann and A.H. Türk (eds.), *Legal Challenges in EU Administrative Law: Towards an Integrated Administration*, Edward Elgar, Cheltenham 2009, p. 34. I make a distinction between both terms. 'Shared management' pertains to the joint implementation of the budget by the Member States and the EU, while 'shared administration' also pertains to other forms of cooperation.

32 European Social Fund and European Regional Development Fund. See Council Regulation No 1083/2006 (Structural Funds). For the new programme period 2014–2020 a new umbrella regulation has been adopted which also sees on the EAFRD and the EMFF. See Regulation No 1303/2013 of the European Parliament and of the Council laying down common provisions on the ERDF, the ESF, the Cohesion Fund, the EAFRD and the EMFF covered by the Common Strategic Framework and laying down general provisions on the ERDF, the ESF and the Cohesion Fund and repealing Council Regulation No 1083/2006 [2013] OJ L347/320.

33 In the programme period 2014–2020 this fund has been replaced by the European Maritime and Fisheries Fund. See Regulation No 508/2014 of the European Parliament and of the Council of 15 May 2014 on the European Maritime and Fisheries Fund, [2014] OJ L149/1.

34 See for example Council Regulation No 73/2009 of 19 January 2009 establishing common rules for direct support schemes for farmers within the framework of the Common Agricultural Policy and establishing a number of support schemes for farmers [2009] OJ L30/16. For the new programme period this Regulation has been replace by Regulation No 1307/2013 of the European Parliament and of the Council of 17 December 2013 establishing rules for direct payments to farmers under support schemes within the framework of the common agricultural policy and repealing Council Regulation No 637/2008 and Council Regulation No 73/2009.

35 See Article 53(1) in conjunction with Part II, Titles I and II, of the Financial Regulation. See Council Regulation No 1698/2005 (EAFRD). For the programme period 2014–2020 this Regulation has been replaced by Regulation No 1305/2013 of the European Parliament and of the Council of 17 December 2013 on support for rural development by the European Agricultural Fund for Rural Development (EAFRD) and repealing Council Regulation No 1698/2005 [2013] OJ L347/487.

36 In the new programme period these funds have been integrated into the Asylum, Migration and Integration Fund. See Regulation No 516/2014 of the European Parliament and of the Council of 16 April 2014 establishing the Asylum, Migration and Integration Fund [2014] OJ L150/168.

37 See 6.3 under a of the Commission Staff Working Document on the Review of the Financial Regulation. This document can be found via <www.europa.eu/comparl/cont/site/topics/regulation/5dec05_

In the case of shared management, the Commission and the Member States have distinct administrative tasks which are inter-dependent and set down in legislation and where both the Commission and the national administrative bodies need to discharge their respective tasks for the European policy to be implemented successfully.[38] The rules governing the relationship between the European Commission and the Member States have been laid down in specific European regulations and decisions. The most important matter in these regulations and decisions is that in the first instance the Members States are responsible for the provision of the European subsidies.[39] The rules on how these are provided, however, are mainly to be found in the aforementioned European regulations and decisions.[40] The responsibility of the Members States is therefore very much subject to European regulation.

In short, the system of the provision of subsidies under shared management is that the Member States draw up a long-term programme in which they indicate – within the limits of the applicable European regulations and decisions of course – what kind of projects they want to have considered for European subsidies and how they think they will realize the implementation of the European regulations and decisions at a national level.[41] These programmes are named, depending on the European subsidy scheme in question, operational programmes,[42] rural development programmes[43] or long-term programmes.[44] The programmes are submitted to the European Commission for approval before the national administrative body can proceed with the provision of European subsidies. The approval of the European Commission is usually combined with the establishment of the maximum amount of European funding that is available

en.htm>. See Regulation No 1927/2006 of the European Parliament and of the Council of 20 December 2006 on establishing the European Globalisation Adjustment Fund [2006] OJ L406/1. In the new programme period this Regulation has been replaced by Regulation No 1309/2013 of the European Parliament and of the Council of 17 December 2013 on the European Globalisation Adjustment Fund (2014–2020) [2013] OJ L347/855.

38 See the second report of the Committee of Independent Experts on the reform of the Commission, Analysis of current practice and suggestions for dealing with mismanagement, irregularities and fraud Volume I (10 September 1999), p. 78. See also the proposal for a Decision (EU, ECSC, Euratom) of the Council containing the Financial Regulation applicable to the general budget of the European Communities, 17 October 2000, COM (2000) 462 final. See furthermore P.P. Craig, *EU administrative law*, OUP, New York 2012, p. 80.

39 See for example Article 70(1) of the Regulation No 1083/2006 (Structural Funds).

40 For the sake of completeness, please note that the rules in many cases are laid down in European soft law. For example working documents and interpretative statements stating how certain articles in European Regulations should be explained. Strictly speaking, European soft law is not legally binding, but in practice it can have legal effects. The concept of European soft law will not be discussed here further. See H.C.H. Hofmann, G.C. Rowe and A.H. Türk, *Administrative Law and Policy of the European Union*, OUP, Oxford 2011, p. 536 f and L.A.J. Senden, *Soft Law in European Community Law*, Hart Publishing, Oxford and Portland Oregan 2004.

41 This does not apply to European subsidies provided from the EAGF.

42 The Structural Funds and the European Fisheries Fund.

43 The EAFRD.

44 The Migration Funds.

for the programme in question.[45] On the basis of these approved programmes, the appointed national administrative bodies provide the European subsidies to national beneficiaries, topped up with a compulsory national subsidy. This supplement, paid for with national money, is referred to as national co-financing. Normally obligatory, a 50% level of co-financing is required. The reason for this is that the EU does not wish to spend European subsidies for which the national authorities themselves have no national subsidy available. The payments made to national beneficiaries within the framework of a European subsidy are invoiced by the national administrative bodies to the European Commission by means of so-called payment requests on the grounds of which intermittent payments are made.[46] Checks are carried out by the national administrative bodies on the beneficiaries of the European subsidies both during the period when the subsidy is provided and at the time the European subsidy is determined. If irregularities are found, the European subsidy must be withdrawn and reclaimed. The Member State can submit a payment request for the final balance of the programme in question until the date stated in the European subsidy scheme.[47] The programme is terminated after being audited by the European Commission.

If a European subsidy is provided under shared management, two subsidy relationships arise: one between the European Commission and the Member State, on the basis of a programme approved by the Commission, and one between the national administrative body and the final beneficiary of the European subsidy.[48] If no European rules exist, this latter subsidy relationship is governed by the national law (procedural autonomy).[49] This national law must fulfil the given European principles of equivalence and effectiveness.[50]

45 See for example Article 70(1) of Regulation No 1698/2005 (EAFRD) and Article 53(6) of Regulation No 1083/2006 (Structural Funds).

46 The European Commission does pay advances to Member States before the first payment requests are submitted. See for example Article 82 of Regulation No 1083/2006 (Structural Funds). In addition, the European Commission can decide to delay or suspend payments. See Articles 91 and 92 of Regulation No 1083/2006 (Structural Funds).

47 In Article 89(1) of Regulation No 1083/2006 (Structural Funds) this date is set at 30 March 2017.

48 See also H.P. Nehl, *Europäisches Verwaltungsverfahren und Gemeinschafsverfassung. Eine Studie gemeinschafsrechtlicher Verfahrensgrundsätze unter besonderer Berücksichtigung "mehrstufiger" Verwaltungsverfahren*, Duncker & Humblot, Berlin 2002, p. 75 f. In this respect he refers to a 'Mehrstufige Verwaltungsverfahren'.

49 On the concept of procedural autonomy see for example P.P. Craig and G. de Búrca, *EU Law, Text, Cases and Materials*, UOP, York 2011, p. 219–220; D.U. Galetta, *Procedural Autonomy of EU Member Statse: Paradise Lost? A Study on the "Functionalized Procedural Competence" of EU Member States*, Springer, Berlin Heidelberg 2010 and P. Haapaniemi, 'Procedural Autonomy: A Misnomer?' in L. Ervo, M. Gräns and A. Jokela (eds.), *Europeanization of Procedural Law and the New Challenges to Fair Trial*, Europa Law Publishing, Groningen 2009.

50 On the principles of equivalence and effectiveness see J.H. Jans, S. Prechal and R.J.G.M. Widdershoven (ed.), *Europeanisation of Public Law*, Europa Law Publishing, Groningen 2015, p. 43 f.

2.3.2. Provision of subsidies by Member State bodies governed by public law or private law

The provision of European subsidies by national administrative bodies is not only carried out in the context of shared management. On the grounds of Article 54(2)(c) of the Financial Regulation, the European Commission can have European subsidies provided by national bodies governed by public law or private law that have a public service mission, providing adequate financial guarantees and complying with the conditions provided for in the implementing rules.[51] Despite national administrative bodies being engaged for the execution of such European subsidy schemes, this concerns European subsidies that are provided (indirectly) on a centralised basis. Since the European subsidies are not first paid into the budget of the Member State, this is a *direct* financial contribution paid by the European budget. The section Grants of the Financial Regulation is therefore applicable to these European subsidies. However the payments of the operational costs to the aforementioned national bodies do not fall within the subsidy definition.[52]

The most important European subsidies that are provided by national bodies governed by public law on the grounds of Article 54(2)(c) of the Financial Regulation, are the subsidies relating to the Lifelong Learning and Youth in Action Programmes.[53] The implementation of the European subsidy schemes Lifelong Learning and Youth in Action is done on the grounds of the European subsidy legislation partly by the executive agency EACEA[54] and partly by national agencies. According to decisions of the Commission in which the responsibilities of the Member States, the Commission and the national agencies concerning the implementation of the Lifelong Learning and Youth in Action Programmes are laid down respectively, the national agencies are responsible for the provision of European subsidies.[55] Once again two subsidy relationships exist: one

51 In this respect see the Statement of the Commission to the Council and the European Parliament, management of the community programmes by networks of national agencies, COM (2001) 648 (final). In addition see Craig 2003 and Schenk 2006, p. 207 f.

52 It should be noted that Article 108(2) opening words and under f, of the Financial Regulation is not very clear. According to the European rules applicable to the indirect centralized subsidies such as the Lifelong Learning and Youth in Action Programmes, Article 108 of the Financial Regulation f. is applicable. As a result, this must constitute a subsidy in the sense of Article 108(1) of the Financial Regulation.

53 See Decision No 1720/2006 of the European Parliament and of the Council of 15 November 2006 establishing an action programme in the field of lifelong learning [2006] OJ L327/45 and Decision No 1719/2006 of the European Parliament and of the Council of 15 November 2006 establishing the 'Youth in Action' programme for the period 2007 to 2013 [2006] OJ L327/30. In the new programme period 2014–2020 both programmes have been integrated into Erasmus+. See Regulation No 1288/2013 of the European Parliament and of the Council of 11 December 2013 establishing 'Erasmus+': the Union programme for education, training, youth and sport [2013] OJ L347/50.

54 See the Commission Decision of 20 April 2009 setting up the Education, Audiovisual and Culture Executive Agency for the management of Community action in the area of education, audiovisual and culture in application of Council Decision No 58/2003, [2009] OJ L101/26.

55 See Article 4(1) and appendix 2 of the Commission Decision of 26 April 2007, C(2007) 1807 final (Lifelong Learning) and Article 4(1) and appendix 2 of the Decision of 30 April 2007, C(2007) 2828 final (Youth in Action).

between the European Commission and the national agencies and one between the national agencies and the final beneficiaries of the European subsidies. As a result, there is no subsidy relationship between the European Commission and the final beneficiary. The subsidy relationship between the European Commission and the national agency is arranged on the basis of the guides for national agencies and annual financial agreements.[56] If there are no European rules, the subsidy relationship between the national agencies and the final beneficiaries of the European subsidy is governed by national law (procedural autonomy).[57] This national law must also fulfil the already mentioned European principles of equivalence and effectiveness. However, the provision of European subsidies by the national agencies is more Europeanised compared to European subsidies provided under shared management. For example, the calls for proposals are published in the European official journal, also concerning the applications that must be submitted to the national agencies. Also, the annual programme guides issued by the European Commission state exactly which projects are eligible to receive European subsidies.[58] And contrary to the European subsidies provided under shared management, the Member States do not draw up programmes that are approved by the European Commission. However, it appears from legislation on European subsidies that the national agencies select subsidy applications and enter into a subsidy relationship with final beneficiaries under their own responsibility. Disputes in the context of this relationship are eventually resolved in a national court.[59] Decisions made by national agencies are therefore not attributed to the European Commission.[60]

2.4. *Recent Developments*

In 2012 the European Parliament and the Council adopted a revision of the Financial Regulation.[61] The subsidy definition remains unchanged. However, the methods for the implementation of the European budget have been simplified. As stated by the Commission itself in a version of the proposal for a new Financial Regulation, the provisions of the former Financial Regulation on indirect, centralised, and shared management were so complex that no one knew what the original objective of these

56 See Articles 4 and 5 of the Commission Decision of 26 April 2007, C(2007) 1807 final (Lifelong Learning).

57 See Article 4(1) and appendix 2 of the Commission Decision of 26 April 2007, C(2007) 1807 final (Lifelong Learning) and Article 4(1) and appendix 2 of the Commission Decision of 30 April 2007, C(2007) 2828 final (Youth in Action).

58 See for example the Lifelong Learning Programme Guide 2012, parts 1, II a and II b: <http://ec.europa.eu/education/llp/doc848_en.htm>.

59 See for example Article VII of the standard Grant Agreement for an Erasmus Intensive Programme under the Lifelong Learning Programme, version 2010, made available by the European Commission.

60 Schenk 2006, p. 214.

61 See Regulation No 966/2012 on the financial rules applicable to the general budget of the Union and repealing Council Regulation No 1605/2002 [2012] OJ L298/1 and the accompanying Commission delegated Regulation No 1268/2012 on the rules of application of Regulation No 966/2012 [2012] OJ L362/1.

was.[62] This explains why the Commission in the proposal for a new Financial Regulation opted for a simplification of the methods of implementation of the budget. This proposal had as a consequence that a distinction was to be made only between European subsidies that are provided according to the method of direct management on the one hand and subsidies that are provided according to the method of indirect management on the other hand.[63] The European subsidies granted through the services of the European Commission and through intervention of European executive agencies were to be granted according to the method of direct management.[64] The category indirect management was intended to include firstly the European subsidies that are currently provided under shared management. Secondly, contrary to the old Financial Regulation, the European subsidies granted by the current national agencies Lifelong Learning and Youth in Action will be provided according to the method of indirect management.[65] However, due to amendments by the European Parliament[66] the final new Financial Regulation still makes a distinction between three ways of implementation of the budget by the Commission: direct management by the Commission's departments and executive agencies, under shared management with Member States and indirect management by entrusting budget implementation tasks to amongst others bodies governed by the private law of a Member State.[67] These amendments though do not change the fact that the consequence is that the section Grants in the Financial Regulation in the current programme period 2014–2020 is no longer applicable to the provision of European subsidies by national agencies concerning Erasmus+, in which Lifelong Learning and Youth in Action are integrated.[68]

For the rest of this chapter, however, the situation in the programme period 2007–2013 is taken and a distinction is made between European subsidies that are provided by the European Commission, European executive agencies and national agencies on the one hand and European subsidies provided under shared management on the other hand. In this programme period, the section on subsidies in the Financial Regulation applies to the first category of European subsidies. It will become clear in the next section that this

62 This follows on from para. 5.2.1 of the Proposal for a regulation of the European Parliament and of the Council establishing that the Financial Regulation is applicable to the general budget of the EU of 28 May 2010, COM (2010) 260 final. This concerns a different version than the proposal of 22 December 2010.

63 See Article 55 of the Proposal for a regulation of the European Parliament and of the Council on the financial rules applicable to the annual budget of the EU of 22 December 2010, COM (2010) 815 final.

64 See Article 108 in conjunction with Article 55(1), under 1, of the Proposal for a regulation of the European Parliament and of the Council on the financial rules applicable to the annual budget of the EU of 22 December 2010, COM (2010) 815 final.

65 See Article 55(1)(b) of the Proposal for a regulation of the European Parliament and of the Council on the financial rules applicable to the annual budget of the EU of 22 December 2010, COM (2010) 815 final.

66 See the position of the European Parliament adopted at first reading on 23 October 2012 with a view to the adoption of Regulation No 966/2012 of the European Parliament and of the Council on the financial rules applicable to the general budget of the Union and repealing Council Regulation No 1605/2002 (EP-PE_TC1-COD(2010)0395).

67 See Article 58(1) under a, b and c, of the new Financial Regulation.

68 See Article 121(2)(e) of the new Financial Regulation.

has consequences for the European requirements set on the allocation of the European subsidies.

3. Requirements under European Law for the Allocation of Scarce European Subsidies

3.1. General

The introduction already briefly mentioned that there is a limited budget available for most European subsidies. This limited budget is reflected, in the case of the European subsidies that are granted by the European Commission and the European executive agencies in the applicable European subsidy scheme.[69] In the case of Youth in Action and Lifelong Learning the level of the European subsidy available for a Member State is determined in an annual agreement between the European Commission and the national agencies.[70] In the case of the European subsidies provided under shared management, the Commission states how much European funding is available for a programme in separate decisions in which the programmes discussed above drawn up by the Member States are approved.[71] Ultimately, the available European subsidies are based on the long-term financial framework that is drawn up by virtue of Article 312 of the Treaty on the Functioning of the European Union (TFEU). Within this framework it is laid down how many funds the EU will have available during seven years to finance among other things European subsidies.[72]

In the current legislation on European subsidies, no provision can be found that states that subsidy applications have to be declined if there is insufficient budget available. Of course the fact that the budget is limited implies that not every application for European subsidy can be granted; the available amount should be divided among the various subsidy applications. Section 3.2 first looks at the extent to which European law prescribes a particular system for the allocation of European subsidies. Next, Section 3.3 goes on to discuss the European requirements on the division of European subsidies granted in a centralised (indirect) manner. This concerns the European subsidies that are provided by the European Commission, the European executive agencies and the national agencies. To illustrate this, the award procedure for the European subsidy programmes Lifelong Learning and Youth in Action will be looked at. It will become clear that the allocation

69 For example, Article 10(2) of the European subsidy regulation Life+ states that the financial award for the execution of this scheme in the period 2007 to 31 December 2013 amounts to 2,143,409,000 euro.

70 See section 3.2 of the agreement between the European Commission and the National Agency Lifelong Learning 2011 which pertains to 2011 (not published).

71 See for example Article 53(1) of the Regulation No 1083/2006 (Structural Funds).

72 In the programme period 2007–2013 this concerns the interinstitutional agreement between the European Parliament, the Council and the Commission of 17 May 2006 [2006] OJ C139/1. The interinstitutional agreement for the programme period 2014–2020 dates from 2 December 2013 ([2013] OJ C373/1). The multiannual financial framework for the years 2014–2020 has been laid down in Council Regulation No 1311/2013 (2013] OJ L347/884).

procedure required for European subsidies provided in a centralised (indirect) manner is founded on the principles of equal treatment and transparency. Section 3.4 is concerned with the extent to which these principles also apply to the division of European subsidies provided under shared management. Finally, Section 3.5 discusses the extent to which the European subsidy legislation places requirements on legal protection against violations of the principles of equal treatment and transparency in the division of scarce European subsidies.

3.2. Requirements under EU Law on the Allocation System for Subsidies

This section examines the allocation system that must be applied according to European subsidy legislation when European subsidies have to be divided. Several systems can be envisaged, such as a 'first come, first served' system, a tender procedure, allocation by lots or the equal division of the European subsidies over all applications.

With regard to the European subsidies that are provided by the European Commission, European executive agencies and national agencies, it is explicitly required that they are awarded by means of a tender procedure.[73] A tender procedure under European law entails that only the applications that score best after certain award criteria have been compared will be honoured.[74] Dutch literature on this matter also refers to the tender procedure as a 'beauty contest'.[75]

For the European subsidies provided under shared management, in many cases national administrative bodies are required to set up procedures for the selection of projects to be considered for subsidies.[76] This also includes the system in which scarce European subsidies are allocated. However, it is not possible to distinguish a specific prescribed allocation system.[77] So, unlike the European subsidies that are provided on a centralized

73 Articles 115 and 116 of the Financial Regulation.

74 Articles 115 and 116 of the Financial Regulation.

75 See for example M.J. Jacobs and W. den Ouden, 'Eerlijk zullen wij alles delen..., Ontwikkelingen in de jurisprudentie over de verdeling van de subsidiepot' (2011) *JBPlus* 35, 39 and F.J. van Ommeren, *Schaarse vergunningen. De verdeling van schaarse vergunningen als onderdeel van het algemeen bestuursrecht*, Kluwer, Deventer 2004, p. 12.

76 See Article 5(2)(c) of the Commission Regulation No 1828/2006 of 8 December 2006 setting out rules for the implementation of Council Regulation No 1083/2006 and of Regulation No 1080/2006 of the European Parliament and of the Council on the ERDF (Structural Funds); ANNEX VI of Commission Regulation No 1974/2006 of 15 December 2006 laying down detailed rules for the application of Council Regulation No 1698/2005 (EAFRD); Article 27(1)(d) of the Decision ERF (Migration Funds).

77 In the European subsidy legislation concerning the Migration Funds though, it is also prescribed that an assessment of the quality should also be carried out. See Article 9(3) of the Commission Decision of 19 December 2007 laying down rules for the implementation of Decision No 573/2007/EG (ERF) as regards Member States' management and control systems, the rules for administrative and financial management and the eligibility of expenditure on projects co-financed by the Fund [2008] OJ L7/1. Although the quality of applications is only *compared* in tender procedures, an *assessment* of quality is also possible in other allocation systems. For example, in a 'first come, first served' system, quality threshold criteria could be applied.

basis, in the European subsidy legislation in the case of the Migration Funds, the Structural Funds, the European Fisheries Funds and the EAFRD, there is currently no explicit obligation to use a tender procedure.

Within the framework of the allocation of European subsidies from the European Orientation and Guarantee Funds for Agriculture (section Orientation) – the forerunner of the EAFRD – in the *JK Otsa Talu* ruling, the Court of Justice found that the Member States should endeavour to provide European subsidy to every eligible applicant.[78] In the same ruling, it appears that this can be difficult, certainly if the Member State does not have sufficient resources to fund the required national co-finance. It that case, according to the Court it is permissible that the national administrative body limits the circle of national beneficiaries to only those farmers who received a subsidy in the past budgetary year.[79] So from European case law, it is again not possible to deduce a preference for one of the aforementioned allocation systems.

The above indicates that it does not matter to the EU what system is applied to allocate the European subsidies that are provided under shared management. All aforementioned allocation systems therefore appear to be possible. As will be discussed in the coming sections, there is much to recommend an allocation system that meets the requirements based on the principles of equal treatment and transparency. However, these principles say nothing about which allocation system should be used. They only demand that the rules which arise out of these principles have to be obeyed when implementing the chosen system.[80]

However, the conclusion that national administrative bodies are not required to apply a tender procedure in the provision of European subsidies does not hold in all cases. In the explanatory notes on the Netherlands' decisions in which Expert Committees are set up to allocate ESF subsidies, it appears that in the Commission's view the selection methods 'first come, first served' and/or 'drawing lots' are not permitted in principle.[81] This view seems to be based on the principle of sound financial management which has been laid down in Article 27 of the Financial Regulation. Considering Article 48(2) of the Financial Regulation and the specific European subsidy regulations this principle is also applicable to the granting of European subsidies by the Member States.[82] According to Article 27(1) of the Financial Regulation the principle of sound financial administration consists of three principles, that is the principle of economy, efficiency and effectiveness. The

78 Case C-241/07, *JK Otsa Talu* [2009] ECR I-4323, para. 38.

79 Case C-241/07, *JK Otsa Talu* [2009] ECR I-4323, para. 54.

80 For example a 'first come, first served' system can also meet the requirements arising from the principles of equal treatment and transparency.

81 See for example the explanatory notes to the Regulation of the Secretary for State for Social Affairs and Employment of 23 September 2009 to set up a Committee of Experts subsidy regulation ESF 2007–2013/ Actie E, *Stcrt.* 2009/14711, p. 3.

82 See for example Article 14(1) and 60, opening words, of Regulation 1083/2006.

principles of efficiency and effectiveness imply it should be guaranteed that only the best projects will receive a European grant. Only in a tender procedure this can be guaranteed, which also appears from the fact that a tender procedure is prescribed for the allocation of the European subsidies that are provided by the European Commission. Although in a 'first come, first served' system quality can be tested, no comparison of the various projects takes place.

In spite of the aforementioned position taken by the Commission, for the time being the European subsidy legislation on the allocation of European subsidies under shared management does not contain an explicit obligation to use a tender procedure. The question arises whether the principle of sound financial management is sufficient to oblige the Member States to apply a tender procedure. In my opinion explicit legislation should have to come from the EU. However, also the regulations concerning the granting of European subsidies by the Member States in the programme period 2014–2020 do not contain such an explicit obligation.[83]

3.3. *Requirements under EU Law for the Allocation of Scarce European Subsidies that are provided by the European Commission, European Executive Agencies and National Agencies on a Centralised (Indirect) Basis*

3.3.1. General

The allocation of European subsidies provided on a centralised (indirect) basis by the European Commission, European executive agencies and national agencies is, by virtue of Article 109 of the Financial Regulation, subject to the principles of transparency and equal treatment. These principles evolved in procurement law, among other things, which also deals with the division of scarce rights, but then in the case of public contracts.[84] In the procurement procedure, the principle of equal treatment has to be

83 Article 125(1) of Regulation 1303/2013 of the European Parliament and of the Council laying down common provisions on the ERDF, the ESF, the Cohesion Fund, the EAGF and the European Maritime and Fisheries Fund (EMFF) covered by the Common Strategic Framework and laying down general provisions on the ERDF, the ESF and the Cohesion Fund and repealing Council Regulation No 1083/2006 ([2013] OJ L347/320) only states that the managing authority shall be responsible for managing the operational programme in accordance with the principle of sound financial management. Neither an obligation to apply a tender procedure has been integrated in the various delegated and implementing acts of the Commission.

84 See for a good comparison of the award of public contracts and the award of scarce public rights: C.E.C. Jansen, 'De gereguleerde aanbesteding en de verdeling van schaarse publieke rechten: een vergelijking', in F.J. van Ommeren, W. den Ouden and C.J. Wolswinkel, *Schaarse publieke rechten*, Boom Juridische Uitgevers, Den Haag 2011, p. 293–322. With regard to the transparency principle as a Union general principle of Union law see A. Buijze, *The Principle of Transparency in EU law*, BOXPress, 's-Hertogenbosch 2013 and A. Buijze, 'The Six Faces of Transparency' (2013) *Utrecht Law Review*, 3.

observed so that all tenderers have an equal opportunity to obtain a European subsidy.[85] In order to create these equal opportunities on the one hand[86] and to monitor the observance of the principle of equal treatment on the other hand, the total procurement procedure – from announcement to award – must be 'transparent'.[87] The objective of the principles of equal treatment and transparency is to eliminate favouritism and arbitrariness on the side of the procuring body.

In this section, each stage of the tender procedure will be discussed as it applies to the allocation of European subsidies provided by the European Commission, European executive agencies and national agencies. The point of departure will be the rules that have been laid down in the Financial Regulation 1605/2002 and the European Commission regulation based on this. It is interesting to see how these rules are worked out in the regulations and decisions that apply to the separate European subsidies.

However, it would go too far in this chapter to discuss every European subsidy that is provided by the European Commission, European executive agencies and national agencies. Therefore only the subsidy programmes Lifelong Learning and Youth in Action in the programme period 2007–2013 will be taken as an illustration.

These European subsidies are particularly interesting, because national administrative bodies had to obey the principles of equal treatment and transparency when allocating these European subsidies.[88] They offer therefore a good illustration of the consequences of the applicability of the principles of equal treatment and transparency on the allocation of European subsidies by national authorities in the current programme period.

3.3.2. Pre-announcement of the opportunity to apply for a European subsidy, the procedure and conditions for entitlement to a subsidy

Firstly, the body that provides the European subsidy should publish the call for proposals on the internet site of the European institutions and perhaps in other suitable media, such as the official EU Journal.[89] The final date for submitting subsidy applications is

85 Case T-50/05, *Evropaïki Dynamiki/Commissie* [2010] ECR I-01071, para. 55; Case C-496/99P, *Succhi di frutta* [2004] ECR I-3801, para. 108; Case C-384/07, *Wienstrom* [2003] ECR I-14527, para. 47; Case C-87/94, *Waalse bussen* [1996] ECR I-2043, para. 54.

86 Case C-470/99, *Universale Bau* [2002] ECR I-11617, para. 93; Case C-87/94, *Waalse bussen* [1996] ECR I-2043, para. 54.

87 See for example Case C-260/04, *Commission v. Italy* [2007] ECR I-7083, para. 24; Case C-496/99P, *Succhi di frutta* [2004] ECR I-3801, para. 109; Case C-470/99, *Universale Bau* [2002] ECR I-11617, para. 91; Case C-19/00, *SIAC* [2001] ECR I-7725, para. 41. Case C-324/98, *Telaustria* [2000] ECR I-10745, para. 62.

88 This was caused by the fact that the section on Grants in the Financial Regulation applied to them until 1 January 2014 even though they are provided by national administrative bodies.

89 See Article 110(1)of the Financial Regulation and Article 167 of the Commission Regulation. See also the Guide for National Agencies Lifelong Learning Programme 2012, section 3.2.

indicated. In addition, the calls include criteria on eligibility,[90] exclusion,[91] selection,[92] and award,[93] as well as the corresponding supporting documentation and also the procedure to be followed.[94] In the case of the Lifelong Learning and Youth in Action Programmes, the calls for proposals – published in the official EU Journal – also refer to the annual programme guides drawn up by the European Commission.[95] All aforementioned criteria are incorporated. The weighting of the various award criteria should be published on the websites of the national agencies.[96] In this way it is guaranteed that all potential applicants will be afforded equality of opportunity in formulating the terms of their applications to take part.

3.3.3. Equal treatment of applications received

After the applications received have been registered,[97] the national agency should make a selection of those eligible for a European subsidy. The principles of equal treatment and transparency require among other things that the criteria on eligibility, exclusion, selection and award may not be changed during the procedure.[98] In addition, applications that are received too late are rejected.[99] Restraint is exercised with regard to changes and additions to (incomplete) subsidy applications. This means in concrete terms that the national agency will only accept modifications or complements of information with regard to specific grant applications sent spontaneously by applicants until the closing date for submission.[100] Modifications or complements of information sent after the closing date that change the nature of the grant application by providing new essential elements, are not taken into consideration.[101] In case of doubt with regard to any of the exclusion or eligibility criteria a national agency may request further proof from the

90 The eligibility criteria contain the formal requirements that have to be met by a subsidy application. See also Article 175a(2) of the Commission Regulation.

91 The exclusion criteria pertain to situations in which the subsidy applicant finds itself and on the grounds of which they are not entitled to a European subsidy. See also Article 114 of the Financial Regulation.

92 Selection criteria make assessable to what extent the organisation/partnership that submits the application possesses the financial and operational capacity to perform the proposed activities. See Article 115(1) of the Financial Regulation. See also the Lifelong Learning Programme Guide 2012, p. 24–26.

93 The award criteria are used to assess the quality of the grant applications; the applications are compared to each other on the basis of these criteria. See the Lifelong Learning Programme Guide 2012, p. 26.

94 This follows on from Article 167(1) of the Commission Regulation.

95 See for example the call for proposals 2012, Life Long Learning Programme [2011] OJ C233/15, p. 16.

96 See for example the Lifelong Learning Programme Guide 2012, p. 26. It should be noted that in procurement law the mutual weighting of criteria does not have to be published in advance. It is also permitted that the weighting of the criteria is decided on after receipt of the tender. See Case C-226/09, *Commission v. Ireland* [2010] ECR I-11807, paras. 43 and 44.

97 See the Guide for National Agencies Lifelong Learning Programme 2012, 3.5.1.

98 See Article 116(1) of the Financial Regulation and the Guide for National Agencies Lifelong Learning Programme 2012, 3.6.1.2 and 3.6.2.2.1.

99 See Lifelong Learning Programme Guide 2012, p. 22.

100 Guide for National Agencies Lifelong Learning Programme 2012, 3.5.5.

101 Guide for National Agencies Lifelong Learning Programme 2012, 3.5.6.

applicant (e.g. on date of submission).[102] The Youth in Action Programme Guide offers the possibility to the national agency to give the applicant the opportunity to rectify formal and manifest errors in the application within a reasonable deadline.[103] But the national agency is not obliged to do so. The basic rule is that after an application has been submitted, nothing can be changed.[104] In view of the principles of equal treatment and transparency, the subsidy provider should in any case be cautious in its contacts with subsidy applicants. The Youth in Action Programme Guide states in this respect that although the national agency can offer support during the application procedure, this may not be in contradiction with fair and transparent selection procedures.[105] On the other hand, the same Programme Guide also shows that the equal treatment of applicants is not always sufficient to guarantee that applicants actually have equal chances to obtain a European subsidy. Sometimes it can be necessary in certain categories of applicants – newcomers for example – to provide more assistance because these categories would otherwise have less chance of having their application honoured.[106] Reticence in contacts with subsidy applicants is therefore not always the rule in the tender procedure.

3.3.4. Evaluation committees and experts

For the assessment of subsidy applications evaluation committees are established for both the Lifelong Learning and the Youth in Action Programmes.[107] Evaluation committees are responsible for the evaluation process of submitted proposals,[108] in particular to guarantee the equal treatment of all applications through a fair and transparent procedure.[109] The committees are not concerned with an individual assessment of the applications received.[110] In the case of the Lifelong Learning Programme, the evaluation committees can be composed of members of the national agency, external experts and stakeholder representatives.[111]

The assessment of whether the applications received meet the criteria on exclusion, selection, eligibility and award is done by the national agency and by experts.[112] For the Lifelong Learning Programme the quality of each subsidy application that meets the

102 See Guide for National Agencies Lifelong Learning Programme 2012, 3.6.2.1.3.
103 Youth in Action Programme Guide 2012, p. 124.
104 Youth in Action Programme Guide 2012, p. 124.
105 Youth in Action Programme Guide 2012, p. 20.
106 Youth in Action Programme Guide 2012, p. 20.
107 See Article 178 of the Commission Regulation.See Lifelong Learning Programme Guide 2011, p. 21. See also Guide for National Agencies Lifelong Learning Programme 2012, 3.6.2.3;.
108 See Article 178(1) of the Commission Regulation.
109 See Lifelong Learning Programme Guide 2011, p. 21.
110 This is pursuant to Article 178(1) of the Commission Regulation, which sets down a general description of the task of the evaluation committee.
111 See Lifelong Learning Programme Guide 2011, p. 21.
112 The experts decide on the score of the subsidy application submitted.

eligibility and exclusion criteria must normally be assessed by at least two experts.[113] From the document 'Minimum requirements for assessors' it appears that at least one of the two experts must be an external expert.[114] These are experts not employed by the national agency that has organized the European grant award procedure.[115] But in the framework of the Youth in Action Programme external experts are appointed as an exception in the procedure allocating European subsidies.[116]

On the basis of the assessment by the national agency and the experts the evaluation committees put forward a proposal indicating which applications should be honoured, rejected or placed on a reserve list.[117] In this context, they should guarantee that all applicants have been treated equally by a fair and transparent application of the procedures.[118] The procedure rules that apply to the working method of the evaluation committees must also contain an objective method for classifying the applications that are of equal quality.[119]

The working method of the experts and the evaluation committee is described in the Guide for National Agencies implementing the Lifelong Learning programme 2012 which has been issued by the European Commission, but not published.[120] A reference can also be found in the Commission Regulation corresponding to the Financial Regulation.[121] The national agency is obliged to establish procedural rules,[122] assessment forms and checklists. In addition, the experts and the evaluation committees must be informed by the national agency about the process of subsidy provision and about the

113 See Article 178(1) of the Commission Regulation. See also Lifelong Learning Programme Guide 2012, p. 21. From the Guide for National Agencies Lifelong Learning Programme 2012 it appears that there is a minimum number of experts. In general it is advised to appoint as many external experts as possible. See 3.6.2.2.3.

114 "Minimum requirements for assessors", version December 2010.

115 Lifelong Learning Programme Guide 2011, p. 21.

116 Guide for National Agencies Youth in Action 2011, p. 21–22.

117 See the Guide for National Agencies Lifelong Learning Programme 2012, 3.6.2.3.6.

118 See Lifelong Learning Programme Guide 2012, p. 21.

119 See the Guide for National Agencies Lifelong Learning Programme 2012, 3.6.2.3.6.

120 Article 4(3) of the Commission Decision of 26 April 2007 on the responsibility of the Member States, the Commission and the national agencies respectively during the implementation of the Lifelong Learning programme (2007–2013) stipulates that the national agency carries out its tasks in accordance with the 'Guide for National Agencies', which contains the minimum conditions for internal audit standards that are applicable to national agencies and their management of the projects that are financed. For the working method of experts and evaluation committees in particular, see point 3.6.2 and 3.6.1 of the Guide for National Agencies Lifelong Learning Programme 2012.

121 For example, on the grounds of Article 178(2) the evaluation committee can request the applicant to provide additional information or an explanation of the supporting documentation submitted with regard to the application, particularly in the case of apparent written errors.

122 Guide for National Agencies Lifelong Learning Programme 2012, 3.6.2.3.4. The procedure rules must be established and the evaluation committee must be informed of these before the assessment starts. The procedure rules contain at least a detailed working method of the evaluation committee and the formal decision-making rules. On the grounds of Article 178(1a) the procedure for calling for proposals and submitting them is also notified.

various activities that could be subsidised. In that context, it is prescribed that the national agency gives courses to experts and members of the evaluation committee. The experts and the evaluation committees are of course bound to the criteria incorporated by the European Commission in the Programme Guide and to the weighting of each criterion.

Appointing an evaluation committee and experts ensures that all applications are treated impartially, objectively and equally. To guarantee that the experts and the members of the evaluation committee really are independent, the Guide for National Agencies implementing the Lifelong Learning programme states that they must sign a formal declaration to avoid a conflict of interest.[123] In addition, persons who have been involved in the assessment or in the criteria on eligibility, exclusion, selection or award are not permitted to have a deciding role in the evaluation committee.[124] Furthermore, to guarantee that the experts give their assessment individually and independently, they use a separate assessment form.[125] Moreover, they are not allowed to receive subsidy in the selection round where they take part in the assessment.[126] The Dutch contract entered into with experts adds that the expert is obliged to carry out the assessments completely independently without any restrictions from influences, irrespective of the nature or the type, and will inform the national agency immediately of any attempt to influence or exert pressure.[127] The Guide for National Agencies implementing the Lifelong Learning Programme requires that external experts must be recruited in a transparent manner, preferably by means of a public tender procedure.[128] Experts in the Netherlands appear to receive a fee for their services rendered,[129] which also prevents conflicts of interest. However, European subsidy legislation pertaining to the Youth in Action and Lifelong Learning Programmes does not require that the names of the external experts are made public. This means it is difficult for applicants to check whether the experts are really independent. Employees of the national agency can be experts or have a seat on an evaluation committee. Once again, they are then not allowed to apply for subsidy in the case of the Lifelong Learning Programme.[130]

123 See the Guide for National Agencies Lifelong Learning Programme 2012, 3.6.3.

124 See the Guide for National Agencies Lifelong Learning Programme 2012, 3.6.3.5.

125 See the Guide for National Agencies Lifelong Learning Programme 2012, 3.6.1.5.

126 Guide for National Agencies Lifelong Learning Programme 2012, 3.6.3.1.

127 See the contract for independent experts for the assessment of project proposals submitted in the framework of the European action programme Lifelong Learning, Leonardo da Vinci.

128 Guide for National Agencies Lifelong Learning Programme 2012, 3.6.3.3.

129 From the Call for Nominations for the Netherlands National Agency of the Lifelong Learning Programme, it appears that a fee is awarded varying between 75 to 125 euros. The EACEA also appoints experts in the assessment of the applications that are submitted at European level within the framework of the Lifelong Learning Programme. They also receive compensation for this. See the call for expressions of interest for the establishment of a list of experts responsible for assisting the Education, Audiovisual and Culture Executive Agency in the framework of the management of the Community programmes in the fields of education, audiovisual media, culture, youth and citizenship [2008] OJ C67/51.

130 See the Guide for National Agencies Lifelong Learning Programme 2012, 3.6.3.1.

As already mentioned, the evaluation committees put forward a proposal on the basis of the assessment by the national agency and the experts, which indicates which applications should be honoured, rejected or placed on a reserve list. In the end, the national agency takes the decision regarding the submitted subsidy applications. If a national agency deviates from the advice of the evaluation committee, a clear justification for this must be provided in the decision on the subsidy application.[131] It is therefore assumed that the advice of the evaluation committee will be accepted. There is good reason for this: if there is an independent evaluation committee which bases its conclusion on independent experts, it cannot be justified without reason that a national administrative body would conclude that the advice of the evaluation committee is unsound. It is advisable that national agencies only deviate from the advice if it is established that the evaluation committee has not followed the procedures or has used incorrect information.

3.3.5. Monitoring the observance of the principles of equal treatment and transparency

In order to ensure that the selection procedures can be monitored to see if they meet the principles of equal treatment and transparency, all stages of the subsidy provision process must be documented. Firstly, the body that provides the European subsidy must keep a suitable register containing all contacts with the applicants during the procedure.[132] Secondly, following the completion of their activities the members of the evaluation committee sign a report containing all proposals examined and the quality of these and stating which proposals are entitled to European subsidy.[133] This report is kept so that it can be consulted at a later stage.[134] It is not clear if this report is made public, or if the subsidy applicants are notified of it. The obligation to observe the rights of defence, which has been recognized as a general principle of EU law, does not appear to require this. After all, a decision about the quality of a subsidy application at the very worst leads to its rejection. The rights of defence only apply if a private individual is disadvantaged through the action of a national administrative body.[135] This will not often be the case when a subsidy application is rejected.[136] This section will examine whether the principle of transparency in combination with the rights of defence can lead to this becoming a requirement.

131 See Article 178(4) of the Commission Regulation and the Guide for National Agencies implementing the Lifelong Learning Programme, 3.6.2.4.4.

132 See Article 178(2) of the Commission Regulation.

133 Article 178(3) of the Commission Regulation.

134 Article 178(3) of the Commission Regulation.

135 See Case C-32/95, *Lisretal* [1996] ECR I-5373 in which the withdrawal of an awarded European subsidy is deemed to be an incriminating action.

136 Van Rijn van Alkemade refers to the situation in which the rejection marks the end of a long-term subsidy relationship. Zie J.M.J. van Rijn van Alkemade, 'Rechtsbescherming bij de verdeling van schaarse subsidies: motivering en (processuele) openbaarheid', In F.J. van Ommeren, W. den Ouden and C.J. Wolswinkel, *Schaarse publieke rechten*, Boom Juridische Uitgevers, Den Haag 2011, p. 379–409, p. 403.

The *Fisher* case is interesting in this context.[137] The Fishers – farmers – were required to have information about the use of their land in previous years in order to apply for a European subsidy for arable crops. But the national administrative body providing the subsidy refused to provide the information required. Because the Fishers did not have the correct information, their subsidy application contained mistakes which led to a fine being imposed. Because the rights of the defence in an incriminating action must be safeguarded, as a result of the fine being imposed, the required information was provided to the Fishers after all. Buijze and Widdershoven correctly note that this is an unsatisfactory outcome.[138] If the administrative body had allowed for inspection of the information, the Fishers could have submitted a correct subsidy application, the fine would not have been imposed and the Fishers would not have had to defend themselves.[139] In the end, the case came before the Court of Justice. The opinion of the advocate general is particularly interesting. It states that the authority is required, even before the application is submitted to actively cooperate in ensuring that the details are accurate, if need be through a corresponding disclosure of information.[140] According to the advocate general, in some cases this can lead to a duty to disclose information if the applicant unconditionally requires the data for his aid application and in order to avoid penalties, and if no third-party rights – in particular rights covered by data protection – constitute an obstacle in that regard. This must be resolved in each individual case by balancing the relevant interests. The transparency of the public administrative may be restricted only if special grounds of justification are shown to exist, the advocate general stated, following a detailed weighting of interests. The advocate general then formulates the prior conditions which according to him must be satisfied before protected data can be made public without the express approval of the involved party. In this case, the advocate general comes to the conclusion that the interests of the Fishers prevail above those of the person the protected data is related to. Buijze and Widdershoven conclude from this that the advocate general believes that when European law acknowledges a certain interest – in this case the economic and financial interests of the subsidy applicant which are apparent in the European regulations – transparency is required when this is necessary to protect that interest.[141] The Court also comes to the conclusion that the information should have been provided to the Fishers, but it does not explicitly base the ruling on the principle of transparency.[142] It applies a teleological interpretation; the objective of the regulation is best achieved by providing the Fishers access to the information in an early stage.[143] According to the Court besides a material obligation there is also a transparency obligation to the extent that the objective of the European regulation is achieved.[144] Buijze and Widdershoven conclude from the ruling

137 Case C-369/98, *Fisher* [2000] ECR I-6751.

138 A. Buijze & R.J.G.M. Widdershoven, 'De Awb en EU-recht: het transparantiebeginsel', in: T. Barkhuysen, W. den Ouden and J.E.M. Polak (red.), *Bestuursrecht harmoniseren: 15 jaar Awb*, 's-Gravenhage: BJU 2010, p. 589-607, p. 604.

139 Buijze and Widdershoven 2010, p. 604.

140 See the opinion of the advocate general Alber in Case C-369/98, *Fisher* [2000] ECR I-6751, para. 43.

141 Buijze and Widdershoven 2010, p. 604.

142 Case C-369/98, *Fisher* [2000] ECR I-6751, para. 36 f.

143 See Buijze 2013, p. 255.

144 Buijze and Widdershoven 2010, p. 604.

that the citizen has an individual right to the public access of documents on the grounds of the principle of transparency, when this is necessary to achieve an interest acknowledged by European law.[145] The Court of Justice does point out, however, that in this process account must always be taken of the fundamental right to the protection of personal data.[146]

I believe that the Fisher ruling is also relevant in the question of whether an applicant for a European subsidy whose application has been rejected, should be able to inspect the report which contains the quality assessment of all applications submitted. The applicant needs this information to be able to dispute his quality assessment in the case of legal proceedings against the rejection of his subsidy application. This interest is explicitly acknowledged in the European subsidy regulations for the Youth in Action and Lifelong Learning Programmes, since the applicable regulations require that the procedure must be fair and transparent.[147] From the *Fisher* ruling it can be deduced that in the case of an applicant for a European subsidy whose application is rejected, there is an individual right to public access of documents, though account must be taken of the fundamental right to the protection of the personal data of the other applicants.

Not allowing public access to the abovementioned report is also at odds with the principle of effective legal protection. If an applicant has insufficient access to the documents related to the ranking order and the drafting of these, then it becomes difficult to dispute the rejection of the relative subsidy applications.[148] There are enough reasons, therefore, under EU law to accept that providing public access to the evaluation committee's report containing the ranking order and the motivation should be a requirement.

This does not hold, however, if the reasoning of the decision of the national executive organ sufficiently enables the applicants of the rejected application to dispute the rejection decision. In this respect it is relevant that it follows on from the Financial Regulation that the body providing the European subsidy must inform the applicant in writing of the outcome of the application submitted.[149] In the decision not to award the European subsidy, the body should also give reasons why the application is rejected in relation to the pre-announced criteria and priorities.[150] By virtue of Article 178(4) of the Commission Regulation on the Financial Regulation, the body providing the subsidy should state in the decision the names of the beneficiaries, the titles of the actions, the

145 Buijze and Widdershoven 2010, p. 604–605. Also see Buijze 2013, p. 255.

146 Case C-369/98, *Fisher* [2000] ECR I-6751, para. 32 f. The right to the protection of personal data is currently laid down in Article 8 of the European Charter and the privacy directive (directive 95/46 of the European Parliament and of the Council of 24 October 1995 on the protection of individuals with regard to the processing of personal data and on the free movement of such data [1995] OJ L281/31).

147 Lifelong Learning Programme Guide 2012, p. 21.

148 See in this respect Van Rijn van Alkemade 2011, p. 407.

149 See Article 116(3) of the Financial Regulation and the Guide for National Agencies Lifelong Learning Programme 2012, 3.6.2.4. Pursuant to Article 179 of the Commission Regulation, this should be carried out within 15 calendar days after the award decision has been sent to the beneficiaries.

150 See Article 116(3), of the Financial Regulation and Guide for National Agencies Lifelong Learning Programme 2012, 3.6.4.3.

amounts accepted and the reasons for that choice and the names of any applicants rejected and the reasons for that rejection. This provision indicates that one decision is taken which is sent to all applicants. The guide for National Agencies implementing the Lifelong Learning programme, however, seems to assume that separate decisions are taken,[151] so that publication of the report is necessary to find out why other applicants were successful or unsuccessful. The above means that each case must be examined to see whether publication of the report is necessary.

3.3.6. Changes due to the entering into force of the new Financial Regulation

The section Grants of the new Financial Regulation and the Commission delegated regulation on the rules of application of the new Financial Regulation (hereafter: the Commission delegated regulation) does not seem to bring big changes in the requirements for the allocation procedure concerning scarce European subsidies that are provided by the European Commission and European executive agencies. Article 125(1) of the new Financial Regulation declares the principles of transparency and equal treatment applicable to grants, just like the former Article 109. However, the thing to notice is that the new Financial Regulation emphasises the importance of those two principles. First of all, the two principles are mentioned as a unity of two parts in Article 125(1). Furthermore, contrary to the former Article 110, in Article 128 it is explicitly stated that the work programmes to which grants shall be subject to have to be published prior to its implementation. Thirdly, Articles 132 and 133 lay down clearly the requirement that the selection as well as the award criteria shall be announced *in advance* in the call for proposals. This is new in comparison to the former Articles 115 and 116. Overall the new Financial Regulation emphasises the relevance of the twin principles. However, as has already been discussed the most important change is that the section Grants does not apply anymore to European subsidies that are provided by national agencies, for example Erasmus+ in which the programmes Lifelong Learning and Youth in Action have been integrated.

3.3.7. Intermediate conclusion

The above paragraphs show that there are all sorts of requirements set under EU law with regard to the allocation of European subsidies provided on a centralised (indirect) basis. Many of these requirements can be traced back to the principles of equal treatment and transparency. They are intended to ensure that every potential applicant has an equal opportunity to obtain a European subsidy. It is not surprising that these principles do not only have significance in procurement law, but are also applicable to the allocation of European subsidies.[152] After all, there is no fundamental difference between the allocation

[151] See 3.6.2.4.2.

[152] Note that the principles of procurement law and European subsidy regulations are not interpreted in the same way. For example, in European subsidy regulations I cannot see that the selection criteria have to be formulated in such a way that every reasonably well-informed and careful subsidy applicant will interpret them in the same way. To me, it is self-evident that the selection criteria that are used for the award of European subsidies also have to meet this requirement.

of scarce contracts and scarce European subsidies. Subsidy regulations are increasingly guided by economic considerations: subsidy applicants are increasingly have to compete against each other.[153] The next paragraph examines whether similar requirements are set under EU law on the allocation of European subsidies that are provided under shared management.

3.4. *Requirements under EU Law on the Allocation of Scarce European Subsidies provided under Shared Management*

3.4.1. Legal requirements on the allocation of scarce European subsidies provided under shared management in the programme period 2007–2013

Far fewer regulations have been set at EU level with regard to the allocation of European subsidies provided under shared management. The Financial Regulation and the related Commission Regulation applicable in the programme period 2007–2013 contain no rules at all on the allocation of such European subsidies.[154] However, in the specific European legislation pertaining to the allocation of European subsidies under shared management there are a number of regulations to be found. Firstly, that the national administrative body sets up the procedures for the selection of projects to be considered for European subsidies and establishes selection criteria.[155] Secondly, to a greater or lesser extent it is required that the opportunity to apply for European subsidies is widely published.[156] The European subsidy regulations pertaining to the Migration Funds furthermore require that the selection criteria are made known (in advance),[157] set requirements for the motivation of the decision to award a subsidy[158] and also require that the reasons why projects are not selected be noted down.[159] In the case of ESF and

153 See in this respect the case note of W. den Ouden on the judgment of the Administrative Jurisdiction Division of the Council of State of 20 October 2010, *AB* 2011, 232, with note by W. den Ouden.

154 See Article 53b of the Financial Regulation.

155 See with respect to the procedures to be set up for example Article 27(1) opening words and under d, of Decision No 573/2007 (ERF) and Article 5(2), under b, of Commission Regulation 1828/2006 (Structural Funds). On the selection criteria, see Article 75(1), under a, of Regulation No 1698/2005 (EAFRD); Article 59, opening words and under a, of Regulation No 1198/2006 (European Fisheries Funds) and Article 60, opening words and under a, of Regulation No 1083/2006 (Structural Funds).

156 In the case of the Migration Funds, it is explicitly required that calls for proposals must be published containing, among other things, the objectives, selection criteria and the relevant supporting documents, see for example Article 9(1) of the Commission Decision ERF. Also any substantial change to the content of the calls for proposal should be published. As far as other European subsidy regulations are concerned, the Member States must at least publish the possibility of being considered for European subsidies. See Article 5(1) of the Commission Regulation No 1828/2006 (Structural Funds), Article 29(1) of Commission Regulation No 498/2007 (European Fisheries Funds), ANNEX VI, under 1.1, of the Commission Regulation No 1974/2006 (EAFRD) and Article 8(1) of the Commission Regulation 501/2008 (information and sales promotion actions).

157 See Article 9(1), under b, of the Commission Decision ERF.

158 Selection decisions must be explained: see Article 9(6) of the Commission decision ERF.

159 See Article 9(3) of the Commission Decision ERF. It is not clear if this also means that these reasons must be communicated to the subsidy applicant.

ERDF, the European Fisheries Funds and the EAFRD it is explicitly stipulated that the national executive body provides clear and detailed information to potential beneficiaries concerning at least the description of the procedures for the handling of subsidy applications, the time required for this and the criteria for the selection of the projects to be subsidized.[160] The above requirements can be traced back to the principles of equal treatment and transparency. These principles, however, are not explicitly declared as being applicable to the national procedure that national executive bodies apply in the selection of applications for European subsidies.

3.4.2. Applicability of the principles of equal treatment and transparency to the provision of scarce European subsidies under shared management

The question arises whether the fact that in the programme period 2007–2013 the principles of equal treatment and transparency have not been declared explicitly applicable to the allocation of European subsidies provided under shared management, also entails that these principles and the requirements following on from these – to the extent that these requirements are not prescribed in European subsidy legislation – do *not* have to be observed by national executive bodies. In this section, a number of arguments are discussed which can lead to the conclusion that the aforementioned principles also apply when national administrative bodies provide European subsidies under shared management.

If no rules regarding the allocation of European subsidies have been prescribed in European legislation, the basic rule is that national law shall apply. However, the application of national law is restricted by the principles of equivalence and effectiveness. To the extent that the allocation of national subsidies is not governed by the principles of equal treatment and transparency, it is not problematical that these principles are also not applied to the allocation of European subsidies in view of the principle of equivalence. However, another requirement is that the application of national law is not contrary to the principle of effectiveness. For this purpose, it should be examined whether not applying the principles of equal treatment and transparency does not make the implementation of European law practically impossible or extremely difficult. In this context, it could be claimed that the non-observance of these principles results in a situation where it is impossible to monitor if the authority providing the subsidy is guilty of favouritism and arbitrariness. The result is that it is not guaranteed that each applicant has an equal opportunity to obtain a European subsidy and that the European subsidies do not therefore necessarily go to the best projects. Incompatibility with the principle of effectiveness could therefore be a first reason to put forward the proposition that the

160 See Article 5(2), opening words and under b and c, of the Commission Regulation No 1828/2006 (Structural Funds); Article 29(2), opening words and under b and c, of the Commission Regulation No 498/2007 (European Fisheries Funds) and Annex VI to the Commission Regulation No 1974/2006 (EAFRD).

principles of equal treatment and transparency are applicable in full to European subsidies provided by national administrative bodies.

Secondly, the general principles of Union law acknowledged by the Court of Justice and which are partly also enshrined in the Charter apply to the actions of the Member States if they are acting within the scope of EU law.[161] This is the case for example when national administrative bodies implement EU law including legislation on European subsidies.[162] This is not affected by the fact that national law is also applicable. The situation that no common European rules have been laid down concerning the applicability of the principles of equal treatment and transparency and that also the national law does not provide for such rules, does not therefore result in the general principle in question acknowledged by the Court of Justice not being fully applicable.[163] This means that even if according to national law a national administrative body is not obliged to apply the principles of equal treatment and transparency and the ensuing requirements to the provision of subsidies, it is obliged to do so under EU law if European subsidies are at stake.

In European case law, the applicability of the principles of equal treatment and transparency to the allocation of European subsidies for which no common European regulations exist, has not yet been explicitly confirmed.[164] In the *IPK International* ruling the General Court found that the principles of transparency and equal treatment apply in general to the procedure for the allocation of subsidies from the EU budget, irrespective of the fact that the old Financial Regulation that applied in that case did not mention these principles.[165] The General Court even rules that in the selection of subsidy applications, any undermining of equality of opportunity and of the principle of

161 See Case C-349/07, *Sopropé* [2008] ECR I-10369, *AB* 2009, 29, with note by R.G.J.M. Widdershoven. See more recently Case C-617/10 *Akerberg Fransson* [2013], not yet reported.

162 See Joined cases 201 and 202/85, *Klensch* [1986] ECR 3477, para. 10. See also Case C-241/07, *Otsa Talu/ Pollumajanduse* [2009] ECR 2009 I-04323, para. 46; Case C-181/04-C-183/04, *Elmeka* [2006] ECR I-8167, para. 31; Case C-376/02, *Goed Wonen* [2005] ECR I-3445, para. 32; Case C-381/97, *Belgocodex* [1998] ECR I-8153, para. 26; Case 5/88, *Wachauf* [1989] ECR 2609, para. 19. See also S. Prechal, 'Competence Creep and General Principles of Law' (2009) *REALaw* 5, 8 and T. Tridimas, *The General Principles of EU Law*, UOP, Oxford 2006, p. 36 f.

163 From Case C-349/07, *Sopropé* [2008] ECR I-10369, *AB* 2009, 29, with note by R.G.J.M. Widdershoven, para. 38, it follows that the Court in the enforcement of that principle, gives priority to the procedural autonomy of the Member State, if no common European rules exist on a certain aspect of the principle. The enforcement of the principle in that case is determined by the national law, provided the principles of equivalence and effectiveness are satisfied.

164 For this, the Court of Justice did have the opportunity in the *JK Otsa Talu* ruling (Case C-241/07 [2009] ECR I-4323). The Court finds – as discussed – only that the Member States must make an effort to manage their financial resources so that they can provide support to every entitled applicant for rural development within the meaning of the regulation.

165 Case T-297/05, *IPK International* [2007] ECR I-7467, *AB* 2011, 285, with note by A. Drahmann, *SEW* 2012, 49, with note by J.C.A. van Dam and J.E. van den Brink, para. 123. The old Financial Regulation dates back to 21 December 1977 [1997] OJ L356/1. The Financial Regulation at that time was not laid down in a regulation.

transparency constitutes an irregularity invalidating the award procedure.[166] From this, of course, it follows – and also from the current Article 109 of the Financial Regulation – that the European institutions and the bodies that provide European subsidies are bound to the principle of transparency.[167] But in view of the wording 'subsidies from the community budget', the ruling can also be understood to mean that all European subsidies are subject to the principle of transparency, even if they are provided by national administrative bodies. This is not certain, because European subsidies provided under shared management – discussed in Section 2.1 – do not fall under the definition of Article 108(1) of the Financial Regulation.

If the above Court ruling is interpreted less widely, then there would also now be another argument on the grounds of which it is conceivable that the provision of subsidies by national administrative bodies must meet the principles of equal treatment and transparency. This argument does not only apply to European subsidies provided under shared management, but also to subsidies that are paid from national funding. The tandem of both principles is increasingly applied by the Court of Justice to procedures outside the area of public procurement. The principles of equal treatment and transparency are no longer only applicable if a tender obligation applies to the national administration, but also if it concerns public contracts under the threshold or the provision of concessions or scarce service licences.[168] A national authority that awards a scarce licence, must also guarantee an appropriate measure of publicity, so that the right to competition exists and the allocation procedure can be tested for impartiality.[169] The Court of Justice considers the principles of equal treatment and transparency to be applicable to the allocation of increasingly scarce public rights. Consequently, the principle of transparency has developed at a European level into a general principle of EU law.[170] This means that the principle can possibly be extrapolated to areas other than procurement law, concessions and scarce licences.[171] The principle

166 Case T-297/05, *IPK International* [2007] ECR I-7467, *AB* 2011, 285, with note by A. Drahmann, *SEW* 2012, 49, with note by J.C.A. van Dam and J.E. van den Brink, para. 125.

167 See in this respect also F.J. van Ommeren, W. den Ouden and C.J. Wolswinkel, 'Schaarse publieke rechten. Wat Bard, Betfair en BNR met elkaar gemeen hebben' (2011) *NJB (Nederlands Juristenblad)*, 1858-1866, 1864.

168 Case C-64/08, *Ernst Engelmann* [2010] ECR I-8219; Case C-91/08, *Wall* [2010] ECR I-02815; Case C-260/04, *Commission v. Italy* [2007] ECR I-7083; Case C-410/04, *ANAV* [2006] ECR I-3303; Case C-231/03, *Coname* [2005] ECR I-7287; Case C-324/98, *Telaustria* [2000] ECR I-10745, para. 60–62; Case C-275/98, *Unitron* [1999] ECR I-8291, para. 31. See also Buijze and Widdershoven 2010, p. 593.

169 This follows on from the so-called *Betfair* ruling (Case C-203/08, *Betfair* [2010] ECR I-4695, *AB* 2011, 17, with note by A. Buijze, *JB* 2010/171, with note by C.J. Wolswinkel, *NJ* 2010/490, with note by M.R. Mok, *NJ* 2010/491, with note by A.J.C. de Moor-van Vugt, *SEW* 2011/33).

170 Compare Buijze 2013, p. 73 f. The Court of Justice recognized the principle as such for the first time in Case C-260/04, *Commission v. Italy* [2007] ECR I-7083.

171 R.J.G.M. Widdershoven, M.J.M. Verhoeven, S. Prechal, A.P.W. Duijkersloot, J.W. van de Gronden, B. Hessel and R. Ortlep, *Derde evaluatie van de Algemene wet bestuursrecht. De Europese agenda van de Awb*, Boom Juridische Uitgevers, 's-Gravenhage 2007, p. 90. Drahmann believes that the principle of transparency should also apply to the award of European subsidies besides under European law. See A.

of transparency is slowly finding its way from public procurement law into other areas of (European) administrative law.[172]

In this context, it is important that most (European) subsidies are regarded as limited public rights.[173] I see no principle difference between allocating contracts, concessions and permits on the one hand and allocating scarce subsidies on the other hand. After all, in both cases it concerns rights having an economic value.

However, from the case law of the Court of Justice on the allocation of public contracts, concessions and scarce licences, it appears that the principles of equal treatment and transparency are only applicable under European law if a cross-border interest is involved.[174] This is the case if a business could be interested in a concession or licence that is provided in a Member State other than where the business is established.[175] In that case, it must be possible for other European players to compete for the national concession or licence. From the *SECAP* ruling it appears that – applied to subsidy law – the estimated value of the subsidies to be provided and the place of implementation could be relevant as well.[176] It would appear that it should probably not be concluded too hastily that there is no cross-border interest involved. Moreover, in the provision of scarce European subsidies by national administrative bodies – other than just national subsidies – the question arises if the criterion that there must be a cross-border interest present is relevant. The allocation of European subsidies, after all, definitely falls within EU law because it concerns the implementation of EU law. This indicates that the European principles of equal treatment and transparency are applicable without a doubt. Insofar as there are consequences for the criterion of cross-border interest in the allocation of European subsidies by national administrative bodies, it is also not out of the question that international organizations could be interested in implementing these projects with European subsidies. In this context, it is relevant that it appears from European subsidy regulations that final beneficiaries of European subsidies that fall under procurement

Drahmann, 'Is het strikte onderscheid tussen subsidie- en opdrachtverlening nog houdbaar?' (2011) *Gst. (Gemeentestem)* 620 and A. Drahmann, 'Kan het subsidierecht transparanter?' (2011) *Gst.* 672.

172 See the case note of W. Den Ouden under the judgment of the Administrative Jurisdiction Division of the Council of State of 15 December 2010, *AB* 2011, 87, point 3, last para.

173 Compare A. Drahmann, 'Streven naar een transparante (her)verdeling van schaarse publieke rechten', in F.J. Van Ommeren, Den W. Ouden and C.J. Wolswinkel (eds.), *Schaarse publieke rechten*, Boom Juridische Uitgevers, Den Haag 2011, p. 267–292, p. 285–286.

174 See for example F.J. Van Ommeren, Den W. Ouden and C.J. Wolswinkel 2011, p. 1863–1864. In other cases there is a so-called 'internal situation'. See also E.H. Pijnacker Hordijk, G.W. van der Bend and J.F. van Nouhuys, *Aanbestedingsrecht, Handboek van het Europees en het Nederlandse aanbestedingsrecht*, Sdu Uitgevers, Den Haag 2009, p. 16 f.

175 See for example Case C-64/08, *Ernst Engelmann* [2010] ECR I-8219, paras. 50 and 53 and Case C-203/08, *Betfair* [2010] ECR I-46955, *AB* 2011, 17, with note by A. Buijze, *JB* 2010/171, with note by C.J. Wolswinkel, para. 47. In previous case law the Court refers to a 'clear cross-border interest'. It has not yet become apparent to what extent the criterion 'businesses established in other Member States with a possible interest' requires refining. See H.M. Stergiou, 'Het Hof van Justitie: Engelbewaarder van het transparantiebeginsel' (2011) *NtER* 77, 85.

176 Joined cases C-147/06 and C-148/06, *SECAP en Santorso* [2008] ECR I-3565.

law – normally government bodies – must observe the procurement regulations, including the principles of equal treatment and transparency when they have projects – financed with European subsidies – executed by third parties. In addition to this, the criterion is also applied that businesses from other Member States could be interested in executing the project concerned.[177] In this context, the Commission takes into account the nature of the contracts, the interests involved and the geographical location where the contracts will be executed and believes that if amounts are concerned close to the threshold, the cross-border interest will depend on the amount itself.[178] In many cases, however, no third party at all is involved, but projects or parts of projects are executed by the final beneficiaries of the European subsidies themselves. This mainly concerns subsidy beneficiaries who are not part of any government body. It is unlikely that the principles of equal treatment and transparency are not considered in cases where the national administrative bodies provide the European subsidies to final beneficiaries that implement the projects themselves, but it's a different matter when the final beneficiary involves a third party to execute the project.

In view of the above, there is much to recommend the notion that the principle of transparency as a guarantee for the fulfilment of the principle of equal treatment, also applies to the allocation of scarce European subsidies that are provided by national administrative bodies under shared management. In this way, national administrative bodies for example may no longer change the criteria to be considered for a European subsidy after the applications have been submitted. Furthermore this means that changes and amendments to the applications may not be accepted without reason, and that, in so far as experts and commissions are appointed, they must perform the assessment of applications independently. In addition it must be possible to check whether the selection procedure satisfied the principles of equal treatment and transparency. It is a fact, however, that there is not yet any European case law in this respect. This section does though demonstrate that the Court of Justice will need few reasons to declare the principles of equal treatment and transparency also applicable to the provision of other European and national subsidies.[179]

3.4.3. Changes in the programme period 2014–2020

Due to the new Financial Regulation there can be no doubts anymore on the applicability of the principle of transparency on the allocation of European subsidies by national administrative bodies under shared management from the programme period 2014–2020. This regulation states that the Member States shall respect the principles of sound

177 For example this appears from the point of view of the Commission in Case T-70/09, *Netherlands v. Commission* [2011] ECR II-114, *AB* 2011, 368, with note by J.E. van den Brink and C. de Kruif.

178 See also the point of view of the Commission in Case T-70/09, *Netherlands v. Commission* [2011] ECR II-114, para. 33–34, *AB* 2011, 368, with note by J.E. van den Brink and C. de Kruif.

179 In Case T-297/05, *IPK International* [2007] ECR I-7467, *AB* 2011, 285, with note by A. Drahmann, *SEW* 2012, 49, with note by J.C.A. van Dam and J.E. van den Brink, paras. 122–126, the link is made between procurement law and case law in this respect.

financial management, transparency and non-discrimination.[180] However, it is not totally clear what is meant by 'transparency' in this context. In view of Chapter 8 of the new Financial Regulation, the principle of transparency may only refer to the publication of accounts, budgets and reports, and of information on recipients. Nevertheless, in the Regulations concerning the programme period 2014–2020[181] it is explicitly stated that the national authority that provides the European subsidies draws up and once approved, applies the appropriate selection procedures and criteria for choosing specific operations that are non-discriminatory and transparent.[182] However, neither the Regulations concerned nor the corresponding delegated and implementing acts make these provisions more concrete. It has to be seen what exactly these provisions demand from national authorities. In my opinion it is likely that national authorities in drawing up and applying selection procedures and criteria should be inspired by the requirements following from the principles of equal treatment and transparency concerning the allocation of European subsidies in direct management and public procurement, including the case law of the Court of Justice in that respect.

3.5. Legal Protection against a Breach of the Principles of Equal Treatment and Transparency in the Allocation of Scarce European Subsidies

Assuming that the European principles of equal treatment and transparency are applicable to the allocation of all European subsidies – regardless of whether they are provided on a centralised (indirect) basis or under shared management – the question arises to what extent the European subsidy regulations place demands on the legal protection against breaches of these principles in the allocation of scarce European subsidies. This normally involves an applicant whose application for a European subsidy has been denied and who believes that these principles have not been observed in the allocation of the European subsidy. There are no specific rules in this respect in the European subsidy regulations on the provision of European subsidies by the European Commission, European executive agencies and national agencies. The same applies for the European subsidy regulations on the provision of European subsidies under shared management. Contrary to the European directives on public procurement, the European subsidy regulations do not provide an effective and fast opportunity for appeal against

180 See Article 59(1) of the new Financial Regulation.

181 Most proposals had an update in April 2013.

182 See Article 125(3) under a, opening words and under i, Regulation No 1303/2013 of the European Parliament and of the Council laying down common provisions on the ERDF, the ESF, the Cohesion Fund, the EAFRD and the EMFF covered by the Common Strategic Framework and laying down general provisions on the ERDF, the ESF and the Cohesion Fund and repealing Council Regulation No 1083/2006 [2013] OJ L347/320. The provision concerned pertains to the ERDF, ESF and the Cohesion Fund. Concerning the EAFRD Article 49(1) Regulation No 1305/2013 of the European Parliament and of the Council of 17 December 2013 on support for rural development by the EAFRD and repealing Council Regulation No 1698/2005 states that selection criteria defined by the managing authority shall aim to ensure equal treatment of applicants. Furthermore the member state authority responsible for project selection shall ensure that projects are selected in accordance with the selection criteria and according to a transparent and well documented procedure. See Article 49(2).

the decisions taken by the subsidy provider after it has been announced which projects will be subsidized.[183] European procurement law also requires – contrary to the European subsidy regulations – that the Court must have the possibility to take provisional measures in order to declare illegal decisions invalid and to award damages.[184] In the case law by the Court of Justice it appears that an appeal for a dismissal must be lodged against the decision to award a public contract, before the contracting authority and the particular private individual can enter into a contract.[185] This possibility must exist beside the possibility to receive damages following the conclusion of the contract.[186] This case law has now been codified in directive no. 665/1989.[187] Codification entails that before the conclusion of the contact, a standstill period of 10 days applies (when sent by fax of email) or 15 days (when sent by other means).[188] As long as the Court has not decided against the award decision or the request to take a provisional measure, the contract may not be concluded.[189] Buijze and Widdershoven correctly deduce from the above that European procurement law favours 'remedies' that redress the illegal award of public contracts above alternative compensation.[190]

European subsidy regulations do not provide for such a standstill period. It is also unclear whether – in the event the European or national court[191] rules that the subsidy award conflicts with the principles of equal treatment and transparency – the European subsidy must be provided anyway, or that the comparative test will have to be repeated, or if just damages will suffice.[192] If both the decision to refuse the subsidy and the decision to award the subsidy are dismissed by the national court, a new decision on the applications will have to be taken. But it would be a thorny issue for the (European) Court to rule that the comparative test had to be repeated, if years after the subsidies had been allocated the conclusion is taken that the allocation procedure at the time had been unlawful. In that case damages would seem to be the better solution. There are (still) no indications in European case law that the requirements for legal protection laid down in European procurement law, arise from the principle of effective legal protection.

183 See Article 1(1) of Directive No 665/1989.
184 See Article 2(1) of Directive No 665/1989. See also on this subject Buijze and Widdershoven 2011, p. 419.
185 Case C-81/98, *Alcatel* [1999] ECR I-7671, para. 43.
186 Case C-81/98, *Alcatel* [1999] ECR I-7671, para. 43.
187 See also on this subject Buijze and Widdershoven 2011, p. 419.
188 See Article 2a(2) of Directive 665/1989.
189 See Article 2(3) of Directive 665/1989.
190 Buijze and Widdershoven 2011, p. 419.
191 Insofar as the European subsidy is provided by the Commission and European executive agencies, it will be the European Court. Insofar as the European subsidies are provided by national agencies or under shared management, the national courts are authorized to take cognizance of appeals against the award of the subsidy.
192 This is also illustrated by the Baltlanta case (Case C-410/13, *Baltlanta*, *AB* 2015, 116, with note by J.E. van den Brink and J.C.A. van Dam). On issues concerning the settlement of disputes under administrative law on the award of scarce rights because a comparative test is concerned, see B.J. Schueler, 'Bestuursrechtelijke beslechting van geschillen over de verdeling van schaarse publieke rechten', in F.J. Van Ommeren, W. den Ouden and C.J. Wolswinkel (eds.), *Schaarse publieke rechten*, Boom Juridische Uitgevers, Den Haag 2011, p. 363–378.

It is doubtful whether proceedings for damages will eventually lead to payment. European case law on European subsidies provided by the European Commission shows that merely the dismissal of the decision to refuse subsidy, does not mean a claim for damages exists.[193] Damages are only considered if it is established that without the breach of the principles of equal treatment and transparency, a positive decision on the application would have been taken.[194] This means that, apart from the question if a European subsidy should be provided ultimately, to assess the damages the application must be reassessed.

To guarantee that the principles of equal treatment and transparency actually provide protection during the allocation of scarce European subsidies, more specific rules will have to be laid down in European subsidy legislation in respect of legal protection against award decisions that breach these principles. Insofar as legal protection is available in the national courts, minimum requirements could be considered.

4. Conclusion

This chapter has examined what requirements exist under European law for the allocation of scarce European subsidies. It would appear that at a European level in particular, requirements exist on the allocation of European subsidies that are provided on a centralised (indirect) basis; for example, subsidies provided by the European Commission, by European executive agencies and by national agencies. The allocation should be carried out by a tender procedure. The requirements that exist for this procedure can be traced back to the principles of equal treatment and transparency that are declared explicitly applicable in the section on Grants of the Financial Regulation. The aim of these principles is to ensure that every potential applicant has an equal opportunity to obtain a European subsidy.

For the other European subsidies provided by national administrative bodies under shared management, matters were not quite so clear. At a European level in the programme period 2007–2013 it was not explicitly stated which methodology should be applied in the allocation of European subsidies. In addition, there were some European rules about the procedure on the provision of subsidies that could be traced back to the principles of equal treatment and transparency, but these principles were not declared explicitly applicable. However, in Section 3.4.2 a number of arguments were put forward on the grounds of which it can be assessed that in the programme period 2007–2013 the aforementioned principles should also have been observed by the national administrative bodies that provide European subsidies under shared management. However, the lack of clarity in the European regulations in that regard bore the risk that national authorities

193 See Case T-478/93, *Wafer Zoo* [1995] ECR II-1497. In this case the Court came to the conclusion that contrary to the principle of legal certainty, the selection criteria were not published. Instead of the principle of legal certainty, the principle of transparency could be filled in.

194 In the *Wafer Zoo* ruling the Court finds that it must be certain that the applicant would have been entitled to subsidy without the application of a criterion that he was not informed about, because he satisfied the other criteria. However, in this ruling no comparative test was carried out.

did not obey these principles when allocating European subsidies. For that reason it is a good thing that in any event the principles of equal treatment and transparency in the current programme period 2014–2020 apply in full to all European subsidies provided by national administrative bodies. However, it is unclear what this means exactly for national authorities when allocating European subsidies.

In my opinion it is likely that national authorities in drawing up and applying selection procedures and criteria should be inspired by the requirements following on from the principles of equal treatment and transparency concerning the allocation of European subsidies in direct management and public procurement, including the case law of the Court of Justice in that respect. This means, for example, that national administrative bodies cannot change the criteria for entitlement to a European subsidy without reason after the applications have been submitted, that changes and amendments to applications submitted may not be accepted without reason and that, insofar as experts and committees are appointed, they are obliged to carry out the assessment of applications independently. Moreover, it must be possible to check whether the selection procedure satisfied the principles of equal treatment and transparency.

Unfortunately, also in the regulations concerning the programme period 2014–2020 there is – contrary to procurement law – at a European level no provision for fast and effective proceedings in which a breach of the principles of equal treatment and transparency in the allocation of scarce European subsidies can be dealt with. In order to guarantee that the principles of equal treatment and transparency actually offer protection, more detailed regulations on legal protection will have to be incorporated in the European regulations. That does not alter the fact that on the basis of this chapter it can be concluded that the significance of the principles of equal treatment and transparency in the allocation of European subsidies is becoming increasingly important, also for subsidies allocated by national authorities. And that is a good thing. Only then can it be guaranteed that scarce European subsidies will be allocated fairly.

Vassilis
Hatzopoulos*

CHAPTER 7. THE ALLOCATION OF LIMITED AUTHORISATIONS UNDER EU INTERNAL MARKET RULES

Introduction

That the requirement of a prior authorisation, as a precondition for the exercise of any economic activity, may restrict the freedom of establishment and the free provision of services is a truism. If an authorisation is required in the Member State where establishment is to take place or the service is to be offered (host Member State), then operators who lack such authorisation are in no right to proceed to the projected activity. Therefore, as soon as it is being accepted that the EU Internal Market rules are not only about discriminatory measures, but also cover mere restrictions, it comes as no surprise that national authorisation systems come to be scrutinised under the Internal Market rules.

This has been acknowledged by the Court in an explicit manner already in its 1986 Insurance cases[1] and constantly thereafter. The idea that authorisations restrict the provision of services has been enshrined into secondary legislation in many sector-specific texts starting with the "passport" systems in the field of insurance, banking and financial services.[2] The 'Internal Market clause' introduced by the Television without Frontiers (TVWF) Directive and the e-Directives also tries to side-step the need for obtaining a fresh authorisation in the host state. The sector-specific directives for the network-bound industries also describe several conditions for the authorisation of

* Vassilis Hatzopoulos is Professor at the Democritus University of Thrace, Greece and Visiting Professor at the College of Europe, Bruges, Belgium; Honorary Ast Professor at the University of Nottingham, UK; Attorney-at-Law, Member of the Athens Bar; the author may be contacted at vasshatz@socadm.duth.gr.

1 See most prominently Case C-205/84, *Commission v. Germany (insurance)* EU:C:1986:463, paras. 42 f.

2 For which see broadly E. Lomincka, 'The Home Country Control Principle in the Financial Services Directives and the Case Law' in M. Andenas and W.H. Roth (eds.), *Services and Free Movement in EU Law*, OUP, Oxford 2002, pp. 295–319; and before that V. Hatzopoulos, *Le principe communautaire d'équivalence et de reconnaissance mutuelle dans la libre prestation de services*, Sakkoulas/Bruylant, Athènes/Bruxelles 1999, pp. 414–449.

operators in order to curb Member State discretion.[3] More importantly and in a horizontal way, authorisations are solemnly held to be against the free provision of services by Articles 9–13 of the Services Directive. The fact, therefore, that national authorisation systems may fall foul of the Internal Market rules is granted.[4]

This, however, does not lead to all national authorisation systems being struck down. On the contrary, the recent case law of the Court of Justice of the EU (CJEU) offers extremely interesting indications as to the situations where an authorisation system could be accepted (1), the conditions that such a system should fulfill in order to comply with the Internal Market requirements (2) and the extent to which the host Member State is obliged to take into account authorisations delivered in other Member States (3).

1. When may an Authorisation System be Justified?

The answer to the above question calls for the exploration of two further questions, i.e. what are the grounds on which a Member State may introduce an authorisation system (1.1) and to what extent does the Member State in question has to prove that such a system is necessary and proportional (1.2).

1.1. Grounds for Justification of an Authorisation System

1.1.1. The Provision of some Service of General Economic Interest (SGEI)

Services of general economic interest have historically been offered by the State, especially within the continental tradition.[5] The trend in the last twenty years, however, has been to entrust private entities with the accomplishment of several such services. In doing so,

3 See in particular European Parliament and Council Directive 2002/20/EC of 7 March 2002 on the authorisation of electronic communications networks and services (Authorisation Directive) [2002] OJ L108/21.

4 European Parliament and Council Directive 2006/213/EU on services in the internal market, OJ L 376/36. Indeed, the applicability of the Internal Market rules may offer not only a different specter of analysis than the application of the competition rules, especially since public measures are at stake. What is more it may allow the CJEU to tackle technical issues even though it is lacking the technical information that an appreciation under the competition rules would require; see e.g. Case C-380/05, *Centro Europa 7 Srl* EU:C:2008:59 for an example where the Court declared inadmissible a preliminary question for the application of Art 106(2) TFEU in conjunction with Art 102 TFEU, for lack of sufficient information contained in the preliminary ruling, but did go on and discussed the issues under the Internal Market rules; the same approach was followed in Case C-384/08, *Attanasio Group Srl* EU:C:2010:133.

5 For an excellent comparison of the continental to the anglosaxon tradition in relation to the provision of services of general interest see C. Harlow, 'Public service, market ideology and citizenship' in M. Freedland and S. Sciarra (eds.), *Public services and citizenship in European law: Public and labour law perspectives,* Clarendon Press, Oxford 1998, pp. 48–56. Please note that the conversation which follows only concerns services of general economic interest, as opposed to non-economic services of general interest, over which EU law has, in principle, no impact.

States have been awarding exclusive or special rights to several undertakings. Such grant of exclusive or special rights is generally accepted under EU law. While at first Member States seemed to enjoy seamless discretion as to when/where they would award exclusive rights,[6] more recent case law suggests that the grant of exclusive rights should be objectively justified and should not lead to an abuse of dominant position by the beneficiary undertaking.[7] The Court's ambivalent approach has been recently resumed as follows:[8]

78 [...] the Treaty does not require national monopolies having a commercial character to be abolished completely, but requires them to be adjusted in such a way as to ensure that no discrimination regarding the conditions under which goods are procured and marketed exists between nationals of Member States [...].

79 However, Article 49 EC [56 TFEU] precludes the application of any national rules which have the effect of making the provision of services between Member States more difficult than the provision of services purely within one Member State [...].

If exclusive and special rights are accepted, then the less restrictive authorisation systems – which only exceptionally entail exclusivity – should raise no worries under EU law, when justified by the provision of some SGEI. Therefore, in *BUPA*, the General Court accepted that a system of authorisation of several operators in the field of healthcare going 'beyond ordinary conditions of authorisation [...] satisfies the condition of a clear and precise definition of the SGEI obligations in question within the meaning of the first *Altmark* condition'.[9] Thus, not only did the General Court accept that the system of prior authorisation established by the Irish legislation did not infringe the Internal Market rules, it also held that it qualified under the *Altmark* first condition, thus also allowing for the circumvention of the State aid rules.[10]

In a similar fashion in *ASM Brescia* the Court in the name of legal security approved of the extension, by way of a transitional period, of the exclusive public service licences for the distribution of natural gas in southern Italy.[11] Although the licences already in place had been granted without following the EU public procurement principles (of transparency etc.)[12] and thus constituted 'indirect discrimination on the basis of nationality, prohibited under Articles 43 EC and 49 EC'[13], the Court accepted that 'the

6 Case C-155/73, *Giuseppe Sacchi* EU:C:1974:40.

7 Case C-260/89, *ERT v. DEP and Sotirios Kouvelas* EU:C:1991:254; Case C-41/90, *Klaus Höfner and Fritz Elser v. Macrotron GmbH* EU:C:1991:161.

8 *Centro Europa 7* above n 4, paras. 78–9.

9 Case T-289/03, *BUPA* EU:T:2008:29, paras 182–3.

10 Case C-280/00, *Altmark Trans* EU:C:2003:415; although this finding may have been reversed by the Court in Case C-57/12, *Femarbel* EU:C:2013:171, paras. 48–49.

11 Case C-347/06, *ASM Brescia SpA v Comune di Rodengo Saiano* EU:C:2008:416.

12 For which see below n 18 and the corresponding text.

13 *ASM Brescia* para. 60.

principle of legal certainty not only permits but also requires that the termination of such a concession be coupled with a transitional period which enables the contracting parties to untie their contractual relations on acceptable terms both from the point of view of *the requirements of the public service* and from the economic point of view'.[14]

1.1.2. The allocation of scarce resources

The Court's lenient approach in *ASM Brescia* is to be contrasted with its judgment in *Centro Europa 7*, where it condemned Italy for not taking the necessary legislative measures to ensure that operators who had previously obtained authorisations for radio broadcasting (according to the relevant EU directive[15]) do obtain the corresponding radio frequencies. Contrary to the situation in *Brescia* the Court held that 'the Italian legislation [...] does not merely allocate to the incumbent operators a priority right to obtain radio frequencies, but reserves them that right exclusively, without restricting in time the privileged position assigned to those operators and without providing for any obligation to relinquish the radio frequencies'.[16]

The above case lies half-way between the organisation of public service (of radio broadcasting) and the allocation of scarce resources (of radio frequencies). In this latter case, the institution of a system of authorisations is inevitable.

In relation to radio frequencies the grant of authorisation is organised by the relevant directive. For other scarce resources, for which there is no sector-specific legislation, Article 12(1) of the Services Directive provides that 'Member States shall apply a selection procedure to potential candidates which provides full guarantees of impartiality and transparency, including, in particular, adequate publicity about the launch, conduct and completion of the procedure.'

The principle remains, however, that scarce resources not only tolerate, but also call for a system of authorisations.

1.1.3. The protection of public policy, public security and public health

The above rule of the Services Directive draws its inspiration in the Court's judgment in *Placanica*, while at the same time complementing it. In this judgment the Court held that where a Member State decides to limit the number of authorisations/licences granted for a given activity, *in casu* gambling, it should proceed to the 'revocation and redistribution of the old licences or the award by public tender of an adequate number of new licences'.[17] The reference to a 'public tender' is a clear indication that the award of new licences should take place in accordance with the 'public procurement principles' based on transparency, which have been developed in the meantime by the Court of Justice.[18]

14 Ibid, para. 71, emphasis added.

15 European Parliament and Council Directive 2002/20/EC of 7 March 2002 on the authorisation of electronic communications networks and services (Authorisation Directive) [2002] OJ L108/21.

16 *Centro Europa 7* above n 4, para. 115.

17 Joined cases C-338 and C-359 and C-360/04, *Criminal Proceedings against Massimiliano Placanica ea* EU:C:2006:71, para. 63.

18 By 'procurement principles' reference is made to the extremely reach body of case law, starting with Case C-324/98, *Telaustria Verlags GmbH and Telefonadress GmbH v. Telekom Austria AG*

The ruling in *Placanica* is different from the rule of Article 12(1) of the Services Directive in that it acknowledges that an authorisation system may be justified not only in cases of natural/technical scarcity, but also where the 'artificial' restriction of a given economic activity is justified by reasons of public policy, public security or public health. Indeed, all the subsequent gambling and gaming cases iteratively confirm the discretion left to Member States to adopt systems of legal monopolies,[19] or of strict (and even discriminatory) authorisation conditions, in order to combat fraud, protect consumers, restrain the propensity for gambling and the like. Such a system of authorisations, however, in order to be proportional should fulfil a further condition: it 'must be accompanied by a legislative framework suitable for ensuring that the holder of the said monopoly [or authorisations] will in fact be able to pursue, in a consistent and systematic manner, the objective thus determined by means of a supply that is quantitatively measured and qualitatively planned by reference to the said objective and subject to strict control by the public authorities.'[20]

Therefore, where the imposition of a system of authorisations/licences is not dictated by objective (natural/technical) necessity but corresponds to the legitimate exercise of discretionary power by the Member States, such system should a) be part of a broader series of measures that pursue the same objective[21] and b) be subject to control by the public authorities as to the actual achievement of the fixed objective. By this latter requirement authorisations justified by public policy rejoin those connected to the provision of some SGEI, who need also be subject to a system of supervision/evaluation – and possibly review.

EU:C:2000:669; Case C-234/03, *Contse SA, Vivisol Srl and Oxigen Salud SA v. Instituto Nacional de Gestion Sanitaria (Ingesa), formerly Instituto Nacional de la Salud (Insalud)* EU:C:2005:644; and Case C-458/03, *Parking Brixen GmBH v. Gemeinde Brixen and Stadtwerke Brixen AG* EU:C:2005:605, whereby the Court acknowledges that the principle of non-discrimination and of equal treatment, and the principle of transparency that these entail, should apply to all procedures of award of some contract/ authorisation by the public authorities, even if these do not fall within the scope of the public procurement directives; this is also known as 'the transparency case law'; for a brief discussion of the above developments see C. Bovis, 'Developing Public Procurement Regulation: Jurisprudence an its Influence on Law Making' (2006) 43 *CML Rev* 461 and more recently C. Bovis, 'Public Procurement in the EU: Jurisprudence and Conceptual Directions' (2006) 49 *CMLRev* 247.

19 Case C-67/98, *Questore di Verona v. Diego Zenatti* EU:C:1999:514, para. 35, and Case C-6/01, *Associação Nacional de Operadores de Máquinas Recreativas (Anomar) eo* EU:C:2003:446, para. 74, Case C-42/07, *Liga Portuguesa de Futebol Profissional and Bwin International Ltd v Departamento de Jogos da Santa Casa da Misericórdia de Lisboa* EU:C:2009:519; Joined cases C-316/07 and C-409–410/07 and C-358–360/07, *Markus Stoß ea* EU:C:2010:504; Case C-347/09, *Jochen Dickinger and Franz Ömer* EU:C:2011:582.

20 *Markus Stoss* para. 83.

21 For an analysis of the requirements that measures be 'coherent and systematic' see G. Mathisen, 'Consistency and Coherence as Conditions for Justification of Member State Measures Restricting Free Movement' (2010) 47 *CML Rev* 1021; my view is somehow different, since I understand this test as follows. Coherence is an internal test and looks into the very content of the measure under scrutiny, essentially asking the question 'does it make sense?' or 'is it logical?'. It looks into the restrictive measure and enquires whether the restriction is a standalone rule or, whether, on the contrary, it forms part of a coherent system. Consistency, on the other hand, is an external test and refers to the way the contemplated measure relates to other policies affecting the same legitimate objective; see Hatzopoulos *Regulating Services*, above n. 2, pp 176–8.

1.1.4. The pursuance of other Overriding Reasons of Public Interest (ORPIs)

If public policy and other express justifications foreseen in the Treaty allow Member States to put into place authorisation systems, the same is not clear in relation to ORPIs. The fact that up till now the Court has accepted ORPIs as the basis for justifying authorisation schemes could be undermined by recent case law.

Indeed, the Court has not only accepted ORPIs as the basis of imposition of an authorisation system,[22] but it has occasionally used ORPIs indistinctively together with the protection of public policy, an express exception foreseen by the Treaty. Hence in *Stoss*,

> the Court has observed that the objectives pursued by national legislation adopted in the area of gambling and bets, considered as a whole, usually concern the protection of the recipients of the services in question and of consumers more generally [two ORPIs], and the protection of public order [an express exception under Article 52 TFEU]. It has also held that such objectives are amongst the overriding reasons in the public interest capable of justifying obstacles to the freedom to provide services'.[23]

What is more, Article 9(1) of the Services Directive specifically provides that authorisation requirements may be justified by ORPIs.

This solution, systematically followed by the Court and expressly enshrined into the Services Directive, should be considered as the current state of the law.

This, however, should not veil the hints in the Court's case law which could eventually lead to dismissing ORPIs as a ground for upholding authorisation systems. Indeed, according to the Court's well-established – and yet non-systematic – case law, ORPIs may only serve as justifications to non-discriminatory restrictions, while discriminatory ones may only be saved by some of the express Treaty provisions (essentially public policy, public security and public health). It is true that several judgments deviate from this general rule,[24] but overall the Court seems still to be attached to it.[25]

If this is so, then the judgments in which the Court implies that authorisation procedures are not merely restrictive, but plainly discriminatory should raise the question of whether they could validly be upheld by virtue of some ORPI. Such judgments

22 See e.g. recently Case C-400/2008 *Commission v Spain (Shopping Centers)* EU:C:2011:172, para. 80, where the Court accepted that 'restrictions relating to the location and size of large retail establishments appear to be methods suitable for achieving the objectives relating to town and country planning and environmental protection'.

23 *Stoss* para. 74; this confusion is not uncommon in the case law; for a discussion see V. Hatzopoulos, 'La justification des atteintes aux libertés de circulation: cadre méthodologique et spécificités matérielles' in A. Dubout and A. Lemaire, (eds.) *L'unicité des libertés fondamentales du traité*, Bruylant/Larcier, Brussels, under press; see also V. Hatzopoulos, *Regulating Services in the EU*, OUP, Oxford 2012, pp. 146–79.

24 See in the previous n.

25 See e.g. Case C-341/05, *Laval un Partneri Ltd* EU:C:2007:809, para. 117; Case C-219/08, *Commission v. Belgium (posted workers)* EU:C:2009:599; Case C-153/08, *Commission v Spain (gambling tax)* EU:C:2009:618.

are all but rare. If in the early *German Insurance* case the element of discrimination was looming, since *Placanica,* and even more since the recent *Costa and Cifone* judgments,[26] the Court has made it clear that under certain circumstances the requirement of an authorisation/licence will be discriminating in favour of the national undertakings already present in the market and against free movers from other Member States. It is in order to redress this discrimination that the Court suggested, in *Placanica*, that the Italian Government should either proceed to the 'revocation and redistribution of the old licences or [to] the award by public tender of an adequate number of new licences'.[27] Discrimination will be more pronounced whenever the delivery of a new authorisation/ licence is conditional upon some territoriality or other restrictive clause. In *Attanasio Group*, concerning the delivery of new authorisations for petrol stations in Italy subject to a territoriality clause, the Court held that[28]

> [s]uch a rule, which applies only to new service stations and not to service stations already in existence before the entry into force of the rule, makes access to the activity of fuel distribution subject to conditions and, by being more advantageous to operators who are already present on the Italian market, is liable to deter, or even prevent, access to the Italian market by operators from other Member States.

Similarly in the *Spanish Shopping Centres* case, the Court, while hinting to some kind of discrimination, held the authorisation procedures, in general, and the territoriality clause, in particular, to restrict market access for free movers from other Member States.[29]

In *Costa and Cifone*, however, a follow-up case to the *Placanica* litigation, the Court opted for a more radical condemnation of the territoriality clause attached to the new licences. It held that

> The very fact that the existing operators have been able to start up several years earlier than the operators unlawfully excluded, and have accordingly been able to establish themselves on the market with a certain reputation and a measure of customer loyalty, confers on them an unfair competitive advantage. To grant the existing operators even greater competitive advantages over the new licence holders has the consequence of entrenching and exacerbating the effects of the unlawful exclusion of the latter from the 1999 tendering procedure, and accordingly constitutes a new breach of Articles 43 EC and 49 EC and of the principle of *equal treatment*.[30]
>
> [...]
>
> In consequence, such a measure entails *discrimination* against the operators which were excluded from the 1999 tendering procedure.[31]

26 Joined Cases C-72/10 and 77/10, *Marcello Costa, Ugo Cifone* EU:C:2012:80.
27 *Placanica* above n 17, para. 63.
28 *Attanasio Group* above n 4, para. 45.
29 Case C-400/08, *Commission v Spain (shopping centres)* EU:C:2011:172, para. 64.
30 *Costa and Cifone* para. 53, emphasis added.
31 Ibid para. 58, emphasis added.

In this more recent case, therefore, the Court's analysis clearly moved from the logic of restrictions to market access, and identified a measure which is discriminatory (at least) in fact. The fact that in this very case the Court did accept ORPIs such as 'the reduction of betting and gaming opportunities, and the combating of criminality by making the operators active in the sector subject to control'[32] as justifications, does not necessarily grant that ORPIs will be admitted in the future without more ado.

1.2. *Burden of Proof*

Since any authorisation system constitutes a restriction for – if not a discrimination against – free movers, its imposition by a Member State need be justified. Such justification does not take place *in abstracto*, but needs be substantiated by the Member State concerned, against the allegations of the plaintiff undertaking (in preliminary rulings) or the Commission (in direct actions). Hence, the allocation of the burden of proof has a direct incidence on the kinds of authorisation systems which will be allowed by the Court. In this respect the Court's case law is clear in some respects and less clear in others.

1.2.1. Clear rules

1.2.1.1. *Prima facie* restriction: for the Commission or the plaintiff

In direct actions, it is clear that the Commission has to make a *prima facie* case by demonstrating that the contested authorisation scheme has as its object or effect to block market access or else to hinder free movement.[33] Over fifty-five years after the creation of the EEC, very few national measures will have as their proclaimed object the restriction of free movement; what becomes crucial, therefore, are the effects of any given measure. The Court will go as far as to ignore the expressed protectionist intent of any measure and will focus on its effects.[34]

Similarly, in preliminary rulings, it is for the plaintiff to propose and for the referring court to substantiate the way in which the contested measure may affect free movement. Failing which the Court will reject the preliminary question as being inadmissible, either on the ground that it is purely hypothetical or that it is purely internal to the Member State concerned and bears no relationship with any of the Treaty freedoms.[35] In view of the well-established case law and the texts of secondary legislation discussed above,[36] however, it is highly unlikely that the Court will ever reject any preliminary question concerning some authorisation scheme.

32 Ibid para. 61.

33 See e.g. Case C-565/08, *Commission v Italy (Lawyer's fees)* EU:C:2011:188, para. 52.

34 Case C-438/05, *Viking Line ABP and OÜ Viking Line Eesti* EU:C:2007:772.

35 See G. Davies, 'Abstractness and concreteness in the preliminary ruling procedure: implications for the division of powers and effective market regulation' in N.N. Shuibhne (ed.), *Regulating the Internal Market*, Edward Elgar, Cheltenham/ Northampton 2006, pp. 210–43.

36 In the previous paras. of the present section.

1.2.1.2. The existence of justification: the Member State

Once this *prima facie* restriction has been established, then it is for the Member State to prove that its system of authorisations is justified by some objective interest. In this regard Member States enjoy unrestricted freedom to pick the policy objectives they consider fit, subject to minimal control by the CJEU. Indeed, in the fifty-five years of Internal Market case law, only in a handful of occasions has the Court second-guessed the national preferences.[37] Rather, the Court exerts all its diligence on the issue of proportionality.

1.2.2. Less clear rules: proportionality

One would expect that the Member State which seeks to introduce a measure restrictive of some fundamental freedom should bear the burden of proving the proportionality of such measure. Indeed, in many cases the Court is quite demanding and requires that

> the reasons which may be invoked by a Member State in order to justify a derogation from the principle of freedom of establishment must be accompanied by an analysis of the appropriateness and proportionality of the restrictive measure adopted by that Member State, and by *precise evidence enabling its arguments to be substantiated*.[38]

Or that

> In this connection, it is the Member State wishing to rely on an objective capable of justifying the restriction of the freedom to provide services which must supply the court called on to rule on that question with *all the evidence of such a kind* as to enable the court to be satisfied that the measure does indeed comply with the requirements deriving from the principle of proportionality[39]

This seemingly heavy burden of proof, however, is being mitigated by three 'correctives'.

First, the Court admits that 'that burden of proof cannot be so extensive as to require the Member State to prove, positively, that no other conceivable measure could enable that objective to be attained under the same conditions'.[40] What is more, a claim that a measure is proportional may not be dismissed 'solely on the ground that that Member State is not able to produce studies serving as the basis for the adoption of the legislation at issue'.[41]

[37] See C. Barnard, 'Restricting Restrictions: Lessons for the EU from the US?' (2009) 68 *Cambridge Law Journal*, 575; V. Hatzopoulos, 'Exigences essentielles, impératives ou impérieuses: une théorie, des théories ou pas de théorie du tout?' (1998) 34 *RTDEur*, 191.

[38] See e.g. *Spanish Shopping Centres* above n 29, para. 83, emphasis added.

[39] See e.g. *Stoss* n 19, para. 71 *in fine*; and Case *Dickinger and Ömer* n 19, para. 54, emphasis added.

[40] Case C-518/06, *Commission v. Italy (motor insurance)* EU:C:2009:270, para. 84.

[41] *Stoss* n 19, para. 72.

Second, in an effort to dissipate fears of regulatory competition nurtured by its own case law i.a. on posted workers, the Court has repeatedly held in its recent case law that 'it is in particular not necessary, with regard to the criterion of proportionality, that a restrictive measure decreed by the authorities of one Member State should correspond to a view shared by all the Member States'.[42]

Therefore, not only is the 'precise' evidence required by the Court's earlier judgments emptied from much of its substance, but also the comparison with other Member States' practices which (as was the case in *Stoss*) may be more advanced and/or more efficient for securing the same interest, is not conclusive.

Third, in at least one case, concerning the shareholding of biomedical laboratories in France, the Court has even mooted the idea that it is for the Commission to prove 'that the risks for the profession of biologist [or any other protected interest] could be removed with the same degree of effectiveness' by other less restrictive measures.[43]

It need not be stressed here that such a requirement, if it were to be generalised, would require from the Commission a *probatio diabolica* and that it would significantly impair the Commission's capacity in direct actions against Member States. What is more, such a position would be in clear retreat in relation to the proof requirements imposed under WTO law, and the GATS in particular. In the *US/Gambling* case, where the issue was extensively debated by the Appelate Body, a fine equilibrium has been traced, whereby if the complainant raises a WTO-consistent alternative measure, it is up to the respondent 'to demonstrate why its challenged measure nevertheless remains "necessary" in the light of that alternative'.[44]

2. Conditions for the Admissibility of an Authorisation System: Authorisations as Public Procurement Contracts

2.1. *Procedural*

According to well-established case law any procedure for the delivery of authorisations should fulfill three requirements: a) it should be based on criteria which are objective, non-discriminatory and known in advance, b) it should be completed within reasonable time and c) it should be subject to review, either hierarchical or, wherever possible, judicial.[45]

42 See e.g. *Stoss* para. 80; in the same sense see *Liga Portuguesa* paras. 57–58 and *Dickinger and Ömer* paras. 46–47.

43 Case C-89/09, *Commission v France (medical laboratories)* EU:C:2010:772, para. 83.

44 See AB report in US/Gambling, WT/DS285/AB/R, para. 311.

45 See e.g. the judgments on patient mobility, such as Case C-157/99, *B.S.M. Geraets-Smits v. Stichting Ziekenfonds VGZ and H.T.M. Peerbooms v. Stichting CZ Groep Zorgverzekeringen* EU:C:2001:404, para. 90; more recently see, Case C-203/08, *Sporting Exchange Ltd v Minister van Justitie* EU:C:2010:307, para. 50, where it is made clear that negative decisions should be subject to judicial – as opposed to other types of – review.

In the field of free movement of services, in particular, the Court has gone further by demanding that 'the authorisation procedure set up by the host Member State must neither delay nor complicate exercise of [the free provision of services]';[46] it has even specified that where the conditions for the delivery of the authorisation are similar in the home and host States, and therefore open to mutual recognition[47] 'any entry required on the trades register of the host Member State cannot be other than automatic, and [...] cannot constitute a condition precedent for the provision of services, result in administrative expense [...] or give rise to an obligation to pay subscriptions to the chamber of trades'.[48]

These requirements have been fleshed out in the Services Directive. Indeed, Article 9(2) foresees that the criteria for the delivery of any authorisation should be objective, known in advance etc., 9(3) that similar delivery conditions in the home and host States should be mutually recognised, 9(5) that the authorisation should be delivered without delay and 9(6) that negative decisions should be fully motivated and 'open to challenge before the courts or other instances of appeal'. What is more Article 13, bears the title 'Authorisation procedures' and further details the conditions for the delivery of the authorisations. A very important rule is contained in Articles 13(3) and (4), whereby the host State authorities should respond to the application within a set timeframe, failing which an authorisation 'shall be deemed to have been granted'. This possibility of 'tacit acquiescience' which reverses the age-old rule in force in most continental countries, whereby 'silence means dismissal', could revolutionise the way public administrations deal with applications.[49]

Next to this first series of obligations, which tend to frame the discretion of national administrations and to offer minimal procedural guarantees to undertakings, a second set of procedural requirements has been progressively developed, aimed at securing effective competition between undertakings. Starting in *Placanica,* becoming more explicit in *Sporting Exchange* and *Engelmann*[50] and even more so in *Costa and Cifone,* the Court has put into place quite detailed rules concerning the conditions for the delivery of authorisations; rules which are derived from the ones applicable in the field of public procurement.[51] Hence 'without necessarily implying an obligation to call for tenders, that obligation of transparency [...] requires the licensing authority to ensure, for the benefit of any potential tenderer, a degree of publicity sufficient to enable the licence to be opened up to competition'.[52]

46 Case C-58/98, *Josef Corsten* EU:C:2000:527, para. 47; and Case C-215/01, *Bruno Schnitzer* EU:C:2003:662, para. 36.

47 For which see below under 3.

48 See e.g. *Schnitzer* para. 37.

49 This issue was extensively debated by the Court in the *Spanish Shopping Centers* case, above n. 29, where the Court found that no such obligation could stem directly from the Treaty rules themselves.

50 Case C-64/08, *Criminal proceedings against Ernst Engelmann* EU:C:2010:506.

51 *Sporting Exchange* para. 46 and on identical terms *Engelmann*, para. 52.

52 *Costa and Cifone* para. 55.

Therefore, the 'revolution' started over ten years ago, whereby the Court actively completed the public procurement rules and imposed a 'transparency principle'[53] applicable in all situations where the State is to choose a co-contractor (such as concession contracts, public-private partnerships and below-the-threshold public contracts)[54] is being extended to situations of delivery of authorisations. As with public procurement, this transparency case law only concerns situations of potentially trans-border interest.[55]

This case law has prompted the Commission to come up with an interpretative Communication 'on the community law applicable to contract awards not or not fully subject to the provisions of the public procurement directives' (the so called *de minimis* Communication).[56] It further pushed for a large consultation to take place in relation to concession contracts and public-private partnerships (PPPs).[57] All this, in turn, has led to fresh texts in order a) to reshuffle the existing legislative framework for public procurement and b) to adopt legislation in relation to concession contracts.[58]

Presumably, therefore, all the rules and principles set out by the Commission in the above texts of soft law also apply to the grant of authorisations. These also may be seen to flesh up the rule of Article 12(1) of the Services Directive, whereby a requirement of minimal publicity ensuring impartiality and transparence should apply in situations of natural and technical scarcity. What is more, they apply to situations where the limited number of authorisations to be delivered results from a deliberate political decision of the Member State concerned and not from natural/technical constraints.[59]

53 For the transparency principle see briefly above n 18 and the literature quoted there.

54 For which see above n 18.

55 See *Costa and Cifone* para. 55; the requirement that the situation has to present some trans-border interest was spelled out in Case C-507/03, *Commission v Ireland (An Post)* EU:C:2007:676 and further explained in Joined Cases C-147–148/06, *SECAP SpA and Santorso Soc. coop. arl v. Comune di Torino* EU:C:2008:277, para. 24: 'the estimated value [of the contract] in conjunction with its technical complexity or the fact that the works are to be located in a place which is likely to attract the interest of foreign operators'.

56 [2006] OJ C179/2.

57 Communication COM (2005) 569 final, 'on Public-Private Partnerships and Community Law on Public Procurement and Concessions'; and, as a follow up, Communication 2008/C 91/02 'on the application of Community law on Public Procurement and Concessions to Institutionalised Public-Private Partnerships (IPPP)' [2008] OJ C91/4.

58 European Parliament and Council Directives 2014/24/EU (the general directive) and 2014/24/EU (the utilities directive) of 26 February 2014 on public procurement and repealing Directive 2004/18/EC Text with EEA relevance [2014] OJ L94/65 and L94/243; these directives are to fully enter into force and repeal Directives 2004/18/EC and 2004/17/EC, respectively, on 18.04.2016; see also European Parliament and Council Directive 2014/23/EU (concessions) of 26 February 2014 on the award of concession contracts Text with EEA relevance [2014] OJ L94/1.

59 European Parliament and Council Directive 2006/123/EC of 12 December 2006 on services in the internal market [2006] OJ L376/36, art. 12(1); for a brief discussion of this provision and its relationship with the *Placanica* case law, see V. Hatzopoulos, 'Que reste-t-il de la Directive Services' (2008) 43 *Cahiers de Droit Européen*, 299, 333–334.

2.2. *Substantial*

2.2.1. Extending non-discrimination from the delivery of the authorisation to the delivery of the service itself

As explained above, the Court has come to treat several 'objective' conditions for the delivery of an authorisation as being discriminatory against operators from other Member States. This tendency has been floating in the Court's case law for some time, until it found a clear expression in *Costa and Cifone*.[60] This tendency seems confirmed by *Susisalo*, a more recent judgment concerning the Finnish system of delivery of authorisations for branch pharmacies, whereby the University of Helsinki was subject to more favourable conditions than private parties.[61] Without ever using the 'd' word, the Court held that 'the fact that the restrictive effects of that preferential system affect home country nationals and those from other Member States alike is not such as to exclude that *preferential* system from the scope of Article 49 TFEU'[62] and therefore identified a restriction by accepting that the 'licensing scheme for the operation of branch pharmacies specific to the [University] is *more favourable* than that applicable to private pharmacies'.[63] A restriction which was found to be justified, in view of the educational and other functions performed by the University hospitals. This judgment beefs up the finding in *Costa and Cifone: Costa* stands for the idea that authorisation conditions may be *de facto* discriminatory when they entail restrictions which were not applicable to the operators already in place, while *Susisalo* makes clear that the operators discriminated against need not be exclusively, or even essentially, from other Member States.[64]

In *Costa and Cifone*, where the Court identified a discrimination in the above-mentioned terms,[65] it did so at the price of a logical leap: it moved from the formal/procedural conditions for the delivery of an authorisation to the material conditions of delivery of the service itself. According to the Court 'the principle of equal treatment requires moreover [on top of objective, non-discriminatory criteria which are known in advance, as described in the previous para of the Court's judgment] that all potential tenderers be afforded equality of opportunity and accordingly implies that all tenderers must be subject to the same conditions' for the delivery of services.[66] This is not the case, however, where '[t]he very fact that the existing operators have been able to start up

60 For a brief discussion of this trend see above the text accompanying n 27–31.

61 Case 84/11, *Susisalo ea* EU:C:2012:374.

62 Ibid para. 34, emphasis added.

63 Ibid para. 44 and operative part, emphasis added.

64 See, recently, in the same logic Case 542/09, *Commission v. The Netherlands (student grants)* EU:C:2012:346, para. 38.

65 See the text of n 30 and 31.

66 *Costa and Cifone* para. 57; the fact that the Court is concerned with the conditions of the delivery of services is confirmed by the following para. of the judgment where the Court notes that 'the effect of that measure is to protect the market positions acquired by the operators who are already established to the detriment of new licence holders, who are compelled to open premises in less commercially attractive locations than those occupied by the former. In consequence, such a measure entails discrimination against the operators which were excluded from the 1999 tendering procedure'.

several years earlier than the operators unlawfully excluded, and have accordingly been able to establish themselves on the market with a certain reputation and a measure of customer loyalty, confers on them an unfair competitive advantage'.[67]

Therefore, by virtue of the principle of non-discrimination, not only the purely procedural conditions for the delivery of the authorisation, but also the substantial conditions for the delivery of the service in question should not entail any discrimination. This is a clear spill-over, in two ways: from procedural to substantive rules, and from Internal Market to competition law objectives.

2.2.2. Better regulation in the Member States?

The principle of non-discrimination does not only cover the issuance of the authorisation as well as the conditions of exercise of the activity; it also extends to the circumstances in which such authorisation may be withdrawn, since 'those situations also correspond in practice to conditions for obtaining a licence'.[68] Hence, 'the principle of transparency, which is a corollary of the principle of equality, [...] implies that all the conditions and detailed rules of the award procedure must be drawn up in a clear, precise and unequivocal manner'.[69] By way of extension, also 'the circumstances [of revocation] be set out in a clear, precise and unequivocal manner'.[70]

In this way the Internal Market rules impact on the quality of national regulation, since they require it to be clear, precise and unequivocal, so as to secure legal certainty. By the same token the Court judges of the quality of national regulation, since it may decide to set it aside (as, indeed, it did in *Costa and Cifone*), if it does not fulfil the above criteria. This, combined to the age-old principle that compliance with EU law may not be secured through circulars or other acts of uncertain legal value and/or visibility,[71] may impact severely on the administrative practices of several Member States (essentially in the south of the EU), where the actual content of EU regulation is being specified by way of non-binding acts. It may, therefore, be said that the Court is pushing towards 'better regulation'.[72]

2.3. *Judicial Control: Withdrawal of Licences Subject to a 'Remedies' Directive?*

Next to better regulation, the second aspect in which EU Internal Market law impacts on the way national administrations run the various authorisation procedures, is by imposing extensive and effective judicial review obligations. Indeed, the Court finds that the principle of transparency requires any decision that revokes an authorisation or

67 *Costa and Cifone* para. 53.
68 Ibid para. 68.
69 Ibid para. 73.
70 Ibid para. 78.
71 See e.g. Case C-167/73, *Commission v France (code du travail maritime)* EU:C:1974:35.
72 For the concept of better regulation see the various contributions to s. Weatherill (ed.), *Better Regulation*, Hart, Oxford/ Portland 2007.

imposes a heavy sanction (such as a heafty fine) 'may only [be] based on a judgment which has the force of *res judicata* and concerns a sufficiently serious offence'[73] and, that any 'legislation which provides for operators to be excluded, even temporarily, from the market can be regarded as proportionate only if it provides for an effective legal remedy *and* compensation for any loss suffered'.[74]

By asking for the above, the Court pushes beyond its well-established requirement for judicial review, in three ways. *First*, it requires that any exclusion from the market only becomes effective once the judgment pronouncing it becomes definitive. Therefore, it seems to be running against the generally accepted presumption of legality of administrative acts, whereby an appeal against an administrative decision or a judgment does not, on its own, suspend the effects of that very act. *Second*, by asking for 'an effective legal remedy *and* compensation' the Court seems to be insisting on 'primary' judicial protection (direct challenge of an administrative decision) co-existing with the possibility 'secondary' judicial protection in the form of damages. Although the general tendency of the Court's case law has consistently been to secure a 'droit au juge',[75] such right may be satisfied by the existence of an action in damages and does not necessarily require the availability of a direct action.[76] In the field of delivery of authorisations, however, the above quotation of the Court may be suggesting that *both* direct and secondary judicial protection should be available. By insisting on these two elements, *third*, the CJEU seems to be insisting on judicial control being more than a procedural formality and offering effective redress for any damage unduly suffered. In this way the Court seems to be pin-pointing at extremely short limitation rules, as well as at restrictive proof rules concerning the damage suffered, common to most national legal orders.

The above requirements call for two observations. Firstly, that, if the Court decides to push these requirements further, they may radically reform the way that justice is being delivered within Member States. Indeed, Member States' procedural autonomy is being framed – if not tamed – in view of securing the full *effet utile* of the Internal Market rules. If the consequences seem far-reaching, the logic of the Court is compelling. What is more, the Court's role as the EU's Constitutional Court, does call for unification of the law; and after fifty five years of bringing closer the substantive rules, it may be that some approximation of procedural rules is not completely misplaced.

Secondly, one may not miss the link between these two requirements and the public procurement 'Remedies Directive' 2007/66.[77] Indeed, what the Remedies Directive does, among other things, is that it sets clear periods during which the award procedure is being suspended and it makes sure that unduly excluded tenderers may receive just

73 *Costa and Cifone* para. 81.

74 Ibid, emphasis added.

75 Already in Case C-222/86, *Heylens* EU: C:1987:442; and Case C-271/91, *Marshall* EU:C:1993:335.

76 See e.g. Case C-432/05, *Unibet* EU:C:2007:163 and Case C-91/08, *Wall* EU:C:2010:182; on this issue see the discussion by F. Wollenschläger, 'EU Law Principles for Allocating Scarce Goods and the Emergence of an Allocation Procedure' (2015) 8 (1) *Review of European Administrative Law*, 205, 226–229.

77 European Parliament and Council Directive 2007/66/EC of 11 December 2007 amending Council Directives 89/665/EEC and 92/13/EEC with regard to improving the effectiveness of review procedures concerning the award of public contracts [2007] OJ L335/31.

compensation.[78] The parallelism between the Court's judgment in *Costa and Cifone* and the Remedies Directive is further fleshed out by the fact that in the judgment in question, the plaintiff was admitted before the Court (and the preliminary question was not dismissed as inadmissible following the relevant argument by the Italian Government) despite the fact that it had not participated in the award procedure for the authorisations. This draws a clear parallel with Article 1(3) of the Remedies Directive and the Court's well-established case law according to which the procedures put into place by the Directive are available also to tenderers who have not participated to a given procedure, provided they can show some interest.[79]

In this way a full circle is drawn and the transposition of public procurement rules and principles to the delivery of authorisations, under the Internal Market rules, seems to be perfect. Based on a general principle of non-discrimination and of transparency, supposedly governing the first stage of the award procedure and aimed at securing adequate publicity, the Court does much more: it circumscribes not only the material conditions for the award of the authorisation – and even the conditions for the exercise of the activity in question – but also sets extremely high review standards. Therefore, not only the requirements of Directives 2004/18, 2004/17 and the corresponding interpretative Commission Communications may be of relevance – if not directly, at least as yardsticks – for authorisation procedures, but also the very Remedies Directive.

3. Mutual Recognition of Authorisations

Mutual recognition has always occupied a core role in the creation of an Internal Market for services.[80] It has served as the foundation of services liberalisation, by the judiciary, especially at times when secondary legislation in the field of services was scarce. Further, it has been put to work by the legislature, in different variants: EU passports for banks, insurance and financial service providers; Internal Market clause for ISP and e-commerce

78 For a brief presentation of this Directive see, among many, E. Chitti 'Directive 2007/66 and the Difficult Search for Balance in Judicial Protection Concerning Public Procurements' [2010] *Italian Journal of Public Law,* 125–53, also available at <www.ijpl.eu/assets/files/pdf/2010_volume_1/E.%20Chiti%20-%20Directive%202007-66%20and%20the%20difficult%20search%20for%20balance%20in%20judicial%20protection.pdf> last accessed 08/12/15; see also E. Olsson 'The Full Force and Effect of Public Procedure Remedies – the general principles of directive 2007/66, available at <http://lup.lub.lu.se/luur/download?func=downloadFile&recordOId=1560955&fileOId=1565479> last accessed 08/12/15, who in his concluding section specifically addresses the question of whether the directive satisfies to the principles of effectiveness and effective judicial protection – and finds to the positive.

79 Case C-230/02, *Grossmann* EU:C:2004:93.

80 For an early analysis see V. Hatzopoulos, *Le principe communautaire de reconnaissance et d'équivalence mutuelle dans la libre prestation de services,* Sakkoulas/Bruylant, Athènes/Bruxelles 1999; for an updated evaluation see, by the same author 'Le principe de reconnaissance mutuelle dans la libre prestation de services' (2010) *CDE* 47; and for slightly different focus, by the same author, 'Forms of Mutual Recognition in the Field of Services' in I. Lianos and O. Odudu (eds.), *Regulating Trade in Services in the EU and the WTO: Trust, Distrust and Economic Integration*, CUP, Cambridge 2012, pp. 59–98; see also K. Nicolaidis, 'Trusting the Poles? Constructing Europe through mutual recognition' (2007) 15 *JEPP* 682, who also uses the terms 'managed' and 'pure' mutual recognition, in the way they will be used hereunder.

providers; home country control for TV broadcasters. The fact that the Services Directive was adopted only after the country-of-origin principle was dropped, means that, but for few sector-specific activities, there is no such thing as automatic recognition of authorisations of service providers (a). Indeed, if mutual recognition of authorisations in the field of goods is, henceforth, an issue extensively dealt with by secondary law, in the field of services the role of the Court continues being core (b).

3.1. *Managed Mutual Recognition: Passports and Internal Market Clauses*

The fact that authorisations at the national level create obstacles to free movement has prompted the EU legislature to intervene in key areas of economic activity and to put into place a system of managed mutual recognition. Hence, following some (more or less extensive) harmonisation, the authorisations delivered by the one Member State would be valid in all other Member States. The first areas in which such a system has been followed were financial and banking services, as well as insurance, by way of the so called 'European Passports'.[81] These Passports, initially issued and monitored by national authorities, have progressively been subject to extensive harmonisation[82] and, lately, also to monitoring, at the EU level, in a way that nowadays one can talk of a centralised system of authorisation and control of the main (also called 'systemic') financial institutions.[83]

More ambitious than the 'passport' system, has been the introduction of the 'Internal Market clause', to the extent that it was based on very light prior harmonisation. An early version of this clause was used in the 'Television Without Frontiers' (TVWF) Directive, adopted as far back as in 1989 and amended several times ever since, for the last time through the adoption of the so called 'Audio Visual Media Directive' (AVMS).[84]

[81] For which see, among many, Lomincka above n 2.

[82] Especially so since the adoption of the MiFiD, European Parliament and Council Directive 2004/39/EC of 21 April 2004 on markets in financial instruments [2004] OJ L145/1. The MiFiD itself was further modified by successive in the sense of further centralisation, before being repealed by European Parliament and Council Directive 2014/65/EU of 15 May 2014 on markets in financial instruments and amending Directive 2002/92/EC and Directive 2011/61/EU (MiFiD 2 – Updated rules) [2014] OJ L173/349 and the other rules establishing the 'single resolution mechanism'.

[83] For this evolution see, briefly V. Hatzopoulos, *Regulating Services in the EU*, pp. 231–238 and the literature cited there.

[84] Council Directive 89/552/EEC of 3 October 1989 on the coordination of certain provisions laid down by Law, Regulation or Administrative Action in Member States concerning the pursuit of television broadcasting activities [1989] OJ L298/23; modified by the European Parliament and Council Directive 97/36/EC [1997] OJ L202/60 and repealed by the European Parliament and Council Directive 2010/13/EU [2010] OJ L95/1. European Parliament and Council Directive 2007/65/EC of 11 December 2007 amending Council Directive 89/552/EEC on the coordination of certain provisions laid down by law, regulation or administrative action in Member States concerning the pursuit of television broadcasting activities [2007] OJ L332/27; on the AVMS see N. Geach, 'Converging Regulation for Convergent Media: an overview of the AVMS' (2008) 1 *J of Information L and Technology* 1, also available at <http://go.warwick.ac.uk/jilt/2008_1/geach> last accessed on 08/12/15; see also P. Valcke, D. Stevens, E. Lievens and E. Werkers, 'AVMS in the EU, Next Generation Approach or Old Wine in New Barrels?' (2008) 71 *Communications and Strategies* 103.

Alongside this 'media' Directive are the two e-Directives, adopted during the dot-com bubble, with the aim of encouraging the emergence of pan-European providers of electronic services (e-services) that would be in a position to compete on the international scene. The first text concerns the provision of electronic signatures,[85] while the second is more concerned with content and e-commerce in general.[86]

Internal Market Clauses take the form of a *quid pro quo*: home state authorities make sure that service providers established in their territory satisfy the minimum coordinated rules, which are essentially connected to the protection of general interest. In return, host state authorities cannot exclude such 'compliant' service providers, for any reason falling within the coordinated field. Internal Market clauses are based on strict 'nationality' requirements intended to restrict arbitrary or otherwise abusive 'regulatory shopping' by service providers.[87]

The extent to which the Court is attached to the proper and effective application of Internal Market Clauses may be illustrated by reference to its judgment in *Mesopotamia*.[88] Was at stake the prohibition, by the German authorities, of the activities on German territory of two Danish companies who used to broadcast emissions and footages in favour of the Kurdish PKK, a terrorist organisation. The companies in question were authorised under Danish law, in compliance with the TVWF Directive. Therefore, despite the fact that the Court accepted the German view that the contested emissions did constitute incitation to hatred and thus could justify measures based on public order, morality and security, it held that such measures could not hinder retransmission itself (covered by the Directive), but could only concern other related activities (such as the production of broadcasts and the organisation of events and sympathy actions) carried out on German territory. Hence, although the Court was openly sympathetic towards the German government's worries, it was not ready to loosen up the application of the Internal Market Clause.

This is a strong sign that in areas where the delivery of authorisations is subject to some EU harmonisation and/or overview, it will be extremely difficult for Member States to invoke national interests – unless these have been completely ignored by the EU legislature at the first place. 'Managed' mutual recognition is likely to be effective even in areas where authorisations are being delivered for scarce resources, such as radio and TV

85 E-signature Directive (European Parliament and Council Directive 1999/93/EC of 13 December 1999 on a Community framework for electronic signatures [2000] OJ L13/12), repealed by European Parliament and Council Regulation (EU) 910/2014 of 23 July 2014 on electronic identification and trust services for electronic transactions in the internal market and repealing Directive 1999/93/EC [2014] OJ L257/73.

86 E-Commerce Directive (European Parliament and Council Directive 2000/31/EC of 8 June 2000 on certain legal aspects of information society services, in particular electronic commerce, in the Internal Market [2000] OJ L178/1).

87 The trend is for such requirements to become increasingly strict, as can be witnessed in the AVMS Directive.

88 Joined Cases C-244–245/10, *Mesopotamia Broadcast and Roj* EU:C:2011:607.

frequencies. The opposite solution may prevail where 'pure' mutual recognition is being put to work by the Court.

3.2. *Pure Mutual Recognition*

In areas not covered by any text of secondary law, where mutual recognition only delves on the Court's determinism, the Court has followed an ambivalent approach.

3.2.1. General trend: recognition of everything but the authorisation

According to well-established case law mutual recognition covers all the elements leading to the authorisation, *but* the authorisation itself. Therefore, the host Member State is supposed to recognise documents irrespective of whether these are harmonised[89] or not,[90] as well as conformity certificates and assimilated documents.[91] It is also supposed to recognise the professional qualifications acquired in any other Member State, irrespective of whether such qualifications fall within the relevant Directive[92] (which the Court interprets in an extensive manner)[93] or not.[94] What is more, guarantee deposits with Banks in other Member States should always and under any circumstance be recognised. Any opposite solution would violate simultaneously a) the free movement of service providers (being an indirect discrimination), b) the free movement of banking services (being an absolute prohibition) and c) the free movement of capital (being an absolute prohibition).[95]

Any other element which has been taken into account by the home Member State in order to deliver its authorisation should be duly taken into account by any other Member State. Two recent cases illustrate this obligation. In *Commission v Italy (sanitary services)*,[96] Italy was found in breach of Article 56 TFEU because the registration system it imposed did 'exclude from its scope a provider of services who is established in a

89 See e.g. Case C-326/00, *IKA v Ioannidis* EU:C:2003:101 and Case C-202/97, *Fitzwilliam* EU:C:2000:75, for documents E 111 (covering urgent medical care) and E 102 (certifying affiliation to a compulsory pension scheme), respectively; see also Case C-476/01, *Kapper* EU:C:2004:261, concerning driving licences.

90 See e.g. Case C-274/05, *Commission v. Greece (University Degrees)* EU:C:2008:585.

91 See e.g. Case C-6/05, *Medipac* EU:C:2007:337; Case C-489/06, *Commission v. Greece (EC markings)* EU:C:2009:165; see also Case C-432/03, *Commission v. Portugal, plastic pipes* EU:C:2005:669.

92 The Professional Qualifications Directive (European Parliament and Council Directive 2005/36/EC of 7 September 2005 on the recognition of professional qualifications [2005] OJ L255/22), codifying various pre-existing texts; itself amended by European Parliament and Council Directive 2013/55/EU of 20 November 2013 amending Directive 2005/36/EC on the recognition of professional qualifications and Regulation (EU) No 1024/2012 on administrative cooperation through the Internal Market Information System ('the IMI Regulation') [2013] OJ L354/132.

93 See e.g. Case C-313/01, *Morgenbesser* EU:C:2003:612 and Case C-234/97, *Bobadilla* EU:C:1999:367.

94 See e.g. Case C-222/86, *Unectef v. Georges Heylens ao* EU:C:1987:442; Case 71/76, *Jean Thieffry v. Conseil de l'ordre des avocats à la cour de Paris* EU:C:1977:65; and Case C-340/89, *Vlassopoulou* EU:C:1991:193.

95 Case C-263/99, *Commission v. Italy (transport consultants)* EU:C:2001:293; Case C-279/00, *Commission v. Italy (temporary labour agencies)* EU:C:2002:89.

96 Case C-358/98, *Commission v Italy (sanitary services)* EU:C:2000:114, para. 13.

Member State other than the Italian Republic and who [...] under the legislation of its Member State of establishment, already satisfies formal requirements equivalent to those under the Italian Law'. The Italian authorities should, before imposing any of the sanctions foreseen for breach of the registration procedure, examine whether the same or similar conditions as the ones required for registration were not already satisfied by the service providers in their home states.

In *Commission v Portugal (construction)* was at stake the system of prior authorisation of all construction workers operating in this country for a period exceeding a year.[97] The Court reminded that a service provision may go on for periods longer than a year, and repeated its settled case law according to which any prior authorisation requirement constitutes a restriction to Article 56 TFEU. It then went on to the control of proportionality of the measure. In this context it stated that 'a national authorisation scheme goes beyond what is necessary where the requirements to which the issue of authorisation is subject duplicate the equivalent evidence and safeguards required in the Member State of establishment, *inferring in particular an obligation on the part of the host Member State to take account of controls and verifications already carried out in the Member State of establishment*'.[98] The Court, thus, found that the Portuguese scheme could not be upheld since it 'precludes the possibility of account being duly taken of equivalent obligations to which such an undertaking is subject in the Member State of establishment or of the verifications already carried out in that regard by the authorities of that Member State'.[99] In this way the Court drew a very close line to the country of origin principle, vilified and abandoned by the Services Directive. Indeed, if the authorisation delivered by the home State of the service provider is not recognized as such by the host State authorities, all the elements leading to such authorisation should be. To the extent that, by virtue of the Services Directive, Member States need to justify all the authorisation schemes that they seek to maintain by reference to objective criteria, they are likely to end up imposing similar requirements for similar activities. Such requirements should, according to the above case law, be subject to mutual recognition, thus leading to *de facto* recognition of the authorisation itself.

The same idea is also expressed in Article 10(3) of the Services Directive, according to which '[t]he conditions for granting authorisation for a new establishment shall not duplicate requirements and controls which are equivalent or essentially comparable as regards their purpose to which the provider is already subject in another Member State or in the same Member State.'

3.2.2. Sensitive areas: no mutual recognition at all!

A second, and opposing, tendency, however, may be identified in the Court's recent case law, whereby the very foundations of mutual recognition are being questioned. This

97 Case C-458/08, *Commission v Portugal (construction)* EU:C:2010:692.
98 Ibid para. 100, emphasis added.
99 Ibid para. 101.

'assault' on mutual recognition has been essentially staged in the area of gambling and gaming, but 'collateral damages' may not be excluded.

Liga Portuguesa,[100] concerned the exclusive right given under Portuguese law to a single, state-controlled, operator to run all games of chance in the country. The Court reminded that in relation to gaming, an area where any harmonisation is lacking, Member States enjoy wide discretion. It held that

> a Member State is therefore entitled to take the view that the *mere fact* that an operator such as Bwin lawfully offers services in that sector via the internet in another Member State, *in which it is established and where it is in principle already subject to statutory conditions and controls* on the part of the competent authorities in that State, cannot be regarded as amounting to a sufficient assurance that national consumers will be protected against the risks of fraud and crime.[101]

This is a striking finding since it questions the fundamentals of mutual recognition, at least whenever such recognition is not 'managed', i.e. organised by some text of secondary legislation proceeding to some degree of harmonisation. A first remark concerns the language used by the Court. What has been the quintessential condition on which mutual recognition has been grounded ever since *Van Binsbergen* and *Cassis de Dijon*,[102] i.e. the fact that the operator/product has been lawfully authorised in another Member State is here described as a 'mere fact'. Second, it is clear from this very passage that the Court does not allude to any situation of abuse of rights or *fraude à la loi*, since it clearly states that the operator *is* established and *is* subject to statutory conditions and controls. Third, the Court states that the above holds true in the absence of harmonisation, but it is unclear how much harmonisation would be enough for mutual recognition to be operational: if full harmonisation, by definition, does not leave any place for mutual recognition, and no harmonisation at all excludes it (according to the above finding) then a grey area of 'partial' harmonisation is being designed by the Court and needs to be further clarified.

In the immediately following paragraph of the same judgment the Court makes reference to the specific nature of the internet and to risks associated with the lack of direct contact between the parties – a reference repeated in other gambling judgments.[103] It could be thought, therefore, that the above negation of the principle of mutual recognition could be limited to situations where delicate services are offered over the internet. Such an

100 Case C-42/07, *Liga Portuguesa de Futebol Profissional and Bwin International Ltd v Departamento de Jogos da Santa Casa da Misericórdia de Lisboa* EU:C:2009:519.

101 Ibid para. 69, emphasis added.

102 Case 33/74, *Johannes Hervicus Maria van Binsbergen v. Bestuur van de Bedrijfsvereniging voor de Metaalnijverheid* EU:C:1974:131; Case 120/78, *Rewe-Zentral AG v Bundesmonopolverwaltung für Branntwein (Cassis de Dijon)* EU:C:1979:42.

103 See e.g. Case C-258/08, *Ladbrokes Betting & Gaming Ltd and Ladbrokes International Ltd v Stichting de Nationale Sporttotalisator* EU:C:2010:308, para. 55; Case C-212/08, *Zeturf Ltd* EU:C:2011:437, para. 80.

explanation, however, has been tacitly dismissed by the Court. In *Dickinger and Ömer*, a case concerning the Austrian system of authorisations for online games, the Court without any reference to the internet solemnly stated that[104]

> no duty of mutual recognition of authorisations issued by the various Member States can exist in the current state of European Union law' since 'the mere fact that an operator lawfully offers services in one Member State, in which it is established and is in principle already subject to statutory conditions and controls on the part of the competent authorities of that State, cannot be regarded as a sufficient assurance that national consumers will be protected against the risks of fraud and crime.

As if this were not clear enough, the Court further explained that[105]

> A Member State may legitimately wish, moreover, to monitor an economic activity which is carried on in its territory, and that would be impossible if it had to rely on checks done by the authorities of another Member State using regulatory systems which it itself does not grasp.

It is the first time to the knowledge of the present author that the Court pronounces such an outspoken negation of mutual recognition.[106] If it is precise that no mutual recognition of authorisations, as such, has ever been imposed by the Court, it has been explained above that the Court's general case law pointed in the direction of recognizing everything *but* the authorisation itself. In these cases, however, the trend is clearly reversed: since mutual recognition is in principle dismissed, Member States are unconstrained to choose not only the level of protection but also the means appropriate for attaining it – excluding by the same token any alternative means. Hence in *Dickinger and Ömer* the Court accepted that Austria could freely opt for the more 'archaic' means of control instead of being forced into considering the efficiency of the (presumably better-performing) ITC-based means of control pioneered by Malta.[107] This is questionable on two accounts. First, because it approves of artificial and unnecessary grounds for partitioning the Internal Market since it allows full 'sovereignty' to national controls, however inefficient and/or arbitrary these may be. Second, because, contrary to previous case law where the Court pushes Member State authorities to improve and to rationalize their practices by reference to international practices,[108] here the Court readily settles for inefficiency. What is more, the above statements seem to be denying the idea that

104 Ibid para. 96.

105 Ibid para. 98.

106 This pronouncement should be seen in combination with the finding in *Stoss*, above n 19 para. 109, according to which mutual recognition of authorisations is '*ex hypothesi*' excluded in areas where the Member State concerned has opted for the existence of a monopoly.

107 Ibid para. 98.

108 See e.g. in the field of healthcare, Case C-157/99, *Smits and Peerbooms* EU:C:2001:404; Case C-368/98, *Vanbraekel* EU:C:2001:400; Case C-372/04, *The Queen, on the application of Yvonne Watts v Bedford Primary Care Trust and Secretary of State for Health* EU:C:2006:325.

mutual recognition constitutes a general principle of law, applicable in all circumstances.[109]

This, in turn, could mean that, in the absence of any specific text of secondary legislation (such as e.g. in the field of TV frequencies),[110] mutual recognition would not be operational for authorisations mandated by scarcity, as it would be putting into question national choices on delicate, or even strategic, issues.

Conclusion

Authorisation systems offer efficient ways of regulating economic activities. Regulating through the delivery of authorisations may be justified either by natural/technical reasons, or by political choices; the EU may not change the former nor second-guess the latter. It has, therefore, to put up with authorisation regimes put into place by Member States, even though these may constitute restrictions – and even discriminations – prohibited by the Internal Market law.

In doing so, however, the EU does impact on such regimes, in four ways. *First*, the EU Courts, prompted by the Commission, may exercise some (limited) control over the objective necessity for establishing an authorisation system. *Second*, and more spectacularly, the Court together with the Commission have been actively defining the conditions, procedural and material, for the delivery of authorisations. By so doing they have been actively interfering not only with the supposed 'procedural autonomy' of Member States, but also with the way national administrations operate. The Services Directive is also expected to have a very important input in this direction. *Third*, the Court and the legislature have been imposing quite extensive mutual recognition obligations. Mutual recognition may cover the authorisation itself, when it is managed through some text of secondary legislation, or all the elements but the authorisation itself, when it imposed directly by the Court. In the absence of any harmonisation, however, and in view of considerable differences between the Member States, mutual recognition may be altogether inoperative; similarly, authorisations delivered in areas characterised by scarcity, may not be recognized in other Member States. *Fourth*, where mutual recognition proves not to be effective, the EU may take over from the Member States and fully regulate specific activities, such as financial services. These four developments have been briefly presented in the present contribution.

The germs of such developments were present in the early case law of the Court, starting with *Van Binsbergen* and *Cassis de Dijon*.[111] The fact, however, that EU law would have such a profound impact on the way authorisation systems are designed, implemented and monitored by the Member States could have been hardly foreseen. Indeed, this outcome stems from several concurring developments: the expansive definition of the concept of restriction and/or discrimination by the Court, as well as the

109 Idea explained by Hatzopoulos above n 80.
110 For which see above n 88, the discussion of Case *Mesopotamia*.
111 Above n 102.

express consecration of the 'market access' criterion for the violation of the Internal Market rules; progressive recognition of the non-discrimination and transparency principles as guiding all 'public procurement like' procedures; the adoption of the Services Directive; the regulatory adjustments made essential in order to tame the financial and economic crisis. These are just few of the jigsaw pieces which brought things where they stand today. The need for structural reforms in order to re-launch the European economy may only push further in the direction of Europeanisation of authorisation regimes.

Johan Wolswinkel*

CHAPTER 8. THE NEED FOR OPTIMAL CHOICE: EXPLORING A HIERARCHY BETWEEN ALLOCATION PROCEDURES FOR LIMITED AUTHORISATIONS UNDER EU LAW

1. Introduction

If the number of authorisations available for grant has been limited to a maximum, these 'limited authorisations' need to be granted by means of an 'allocation procedure' in which applications are being compared with each other. Among the most well-known allocation procedures are the auction, the comparative assessment ('beauty contest'), the lottery and allocation in order of receipt of the allocations ('first come, first served'). It should be clear from the outset that the chosen allocation procedure might have important consequences for the final outcome of the allocation.

The issue of the (optimal) choice of the allocation procedure can be approached from among various disciplines and, within the discipline of law, from among various perspectives. This chapter explores whether EU law contains any preferences for allocation procedures or criteria to be applied and, if so, on which grounds.[1] An example of such a preference might be that an auction is being preferred to a lottery. Thus, there might exist some kind of *hierarchy* between allocation procedures: some allocation procedures are considered 'better' than other allocation procedures from the perspective of EU law.

In order to unveil this possible hierarchy between allocation procedures from an EU law perspective, this chapter will first provide for some conceptual preliminaries necessary to understand the idea of a hierarchy between allocation procedures (Section 2). Next, this chapter will identify so-called 'baseline' requirements, *i.e.* minimal requirements that all allocation procedures should satisfy (Section 3). This chapter will then examine whether *additional* requirements can be imposed on allocation procedures. To that end,

* Johan Wolswinkel LLM, MSc, PhD is Associate Professor of administrative law at Tilburg University, the Netherlands. Any comments or thoughts on this article can be addressed to c.j.wolswinkel@uvt.nl.

1 On this issue, see also the chapter by Buijze in this book.

Section 4 adopts a bottom-up approach, identifying preferences for specific allocation procedures in sector-specific EU legislation. Complementarily, Section 5 will discuss whether EU law also provides for general guidance as to the choice of allocation procedures. In that respect, the areas of internal market law (fundamental freedoms), competition law and state aid law will be distinguished. Finally, the conclusion will discuss to what extent there exists some hierarchy between allocation procedures from the perspective of EU law (Section 6).

2. Conceptual Preliminaries

In order to clarify the line of reasoning to be followed in this chapter, some central terms need to be defined in advance. First of all, a distinction needs to be made between, on the one hand, *limitation* of the number of authorisations and, on the other hand, *allocation* of these 'limited authorisations'.[2] Although limitation is a preliminary condition for allocation ('no allocation without limitation'), limitation and allocation are two different decisions that should be distinguished conceptually. In fact, a limitation to the number of authorisations available for grant, adds a 'refusal ground' or 'granting criterion' to the authorisation scheme: the authorisation shall be refused if the granting of this authorisation would result in the maximum number of authorisations being exceeded. However, this 'granting criterion' does not make clear to which applicant or application this refusal ground should apply. This latter question needs to be answered by the outcome of the allocation procedure.

The term 'allocation procedure' covers all elements relevant for the comparison of applicants. This *relative* comparison can be considered the key characteristic of allocation decisions. Compared with this broad definition of 'allocation procedure', the term 'allocation criterion' merely refers to the dimension(s) on which applications are being compared, e.g. the offered price or the moment of receipt of the applications.[3] As such, this understanding of 'allocation criteria' resembles the public procurement notion of 'award criteria' (as opposed to 'selection criteria'),[4] although terminology is not univocal throughout EU law.[5] Anyway, every allocation procedure contains one or more allocation criteria, *i.e.* dimensions on the basis of which the applications are compared with each other.

2 Into more detail on this terminology, see also C.J. Wolswinkel, 'An allocation perspective to public law: limited public rights and beyond' (2014) *Law & Method* (DOI: 10.5553/REM/.000004), and C.J. Wolswinkel, 'From public contracts to limited authorisations and vice versa. Exploring general award requirements from the EU Court's corollary approach' (2015) 24 *Public Procurement Law Review* 137, 142.

3 Cf. the distinction in Directive 2006/123/EC of the European Parliament and of the Council of 12 December 2006 on services in the internal market [2006] OJ L376/36 (hereinafter: Services Directive) between 'authorisation procedure' (Article 13) and 'authorisation criteria' (Article 10).

4 Cf. Article 53 Directive 2004/18/EC of the European Parliament and of the Council of 31 March 2004 on the coordination of procedures for the award of public works contracts, public supply contracts and public service contracts [2004] OJ L134/114 (hereinafter 2004 Public Sector Directive).

5 For example, Article 12(1) Services Directive refers to 'selection procedure' instead of 'allocation procedure'.

Following the distinction made above between limitation and allocation, an 'allocation objective' is defined as the objective that is being pursued by the allocation procedure. There might be good reason to distinguish this allocation objective from the 'limitation objective', *i.e.* the objective that is being pursued by the limitation of the number of authorisations available for grant. Although these two kinds of objectives may coincide, this is not necessarily the case, as the following analysis will show.

3. Defining the Baseline: Objective and Non-Discriminatory Allocation Criteria Known in Advance

3.1. *General*

According to settled case-law of the Court of Justice of the European Union (CJEU), a prior authorisation scheme constitutes a restriction to the fundamental freedom of establishment or service provision (Articles 49 and 56 TFEU respectively).[6] First, any undertaking interested in carrying out the economic activity at stake, may have to bear the additional administrative and financial costs which any such grant of authorisation entails. Secondly, the system of prior authorisation acts as a bar to self-employed activity for economic operators who do not satisfy predetermined requirements, since compliance with these requirements is a condition for the issue of that authorisation.[7] If such an authorisation scheme applies to all persons and undertakings pursuing an economic activity in the territory of the host Member State,[8] it constitutes a non-discriminatory restriction to service provision. Such a restriction may be justified by overriding reasons relating to the public interest. However, in order to be so justified, the authorisation scheme should also be *suitable* for securing the attainment of the legitimate objective which it pursues and should not go beyond what is *necessary* in order to attain this objective.[9] According to recent case-law, an authorisation scheme is suitable to ensuring attainment of the objective pursued *only* if it genuinely reflects a concern to attain it in a consistent and systematic (coherent) manner.[10]

6 The concept of establishment as defined in Article 49 TFEU, means that the operator offers its services on a stable and continuous basis from an establishment in the Member State of destination, whereas every provision of services that are not offered on a stable and continuous basis from an establishment in the Member State of destination constitutes a 'provision of services' within the meaning of Article 56 TFEU. Cf. Joined Cases C-357/10, C-358/10 and C-359/10, *Duomo* ECLI:EU:C:2012:283, para. 31.

7 Joined Cases C-570/07 and C-571/07, *Blanco Pérez and Chao Gómez* [2010] ECR I-4629, para. 54. See also Case C-169/07, *Hartlauer* [2009] ECR I-1721, paras. 34 and 35, and Article 9 Services Directive.

8 Cf. Case C-323/03, *Commission v. Spain* [2006] ECR I-2161, para. 45, and Case C-64/08, *Engelmann* [2010] ECR I-8219, para. 47.

9 Case C-55/94, *Gebhard* [1995] ECR I-4165, para. 37.

10 Case C-243/01, *Gambelli and others* [2003] ECR I-13031, para. 67; Joined Cases C-338/04, C-359/04 and C-360/04, *Placanica and others* [2007] ECR I-1891, para. 53; Case C-169/07, *Hartlauer* [2009] ECR I-1721, para. 55, and Case C-169/08, *Presidente del Consiglio dei Ministri* [2009] ECR I-10821, para. 42. Into more detail on the justification of authorisation schemes, see the chapter by Hatzopoulos in this book.

The CJEU seems to consider any *limitation* to the number of available authorisations as an *additional* restriction to the freedom of establishment or service provision, since any such measure makes the pursuit of an economic activity subject to a condition which is linked to the economic or social needs for that activity and thereby tends to *limit* the number of service providers.[11] Such a non-discriminatory[12] restriction needs to be justified separately by an overriding reason related to the public interest and should comply with the proportionality requirements of suitability and necessity.[13]

In addition to the standard justification scheme applying to any restriction to a fundamental freedom, the CJEU requires additionally with regard to prior authorisation schemes derogating from a fundamental freedom, that these schemes should be based on 'objective, non-discriminatory criteria known in advance to the undertakings concerned, in such a way as to circumscribe the exercise of the authorities' discretion so that it is not used arbitrarily'.[14] These case-law requirements have been codified already in Article 10 Services Directive, which contains an extensive set of requirements that authorisation criteria should meet.[15] While these three requirements of objectivity, non-discrimination and publicity in advance can be considered minimal requirements applying to any authorisation scheme, the relevant question for this chapter is whether these requirements have some specific meaning in case of *limited* authorisation schemes, thereby providing for some (minimal) guidance as to the choice of allocation procedures or allocation criteria.

3.2. *Criteria Known in Advance*

In its hallmark judgment *Sporting Exchange*,[16] the CJEU combined its case-law on authorisation schemes with its case-law on the obligation of transparency, emerging from the area of procurement law.[17] This obligation of transparency requires the awarding authority with regard to the award of service concessions, without necessarily implying an obligation to launch an invitation to tender, to ensure, for the benefit of any potential applicant, 'a degree of advertising sufficient' to enable the service concession to

11 Case C-169/07, *Hartlauer* [2009] ECR I-1721, para. 36, and Joined Cases C-570/07 and C-571/07, *Blanco Pérez and Chao Gómez* [2010] ECR I-4629, para. 55.

12 Usually, such a limitation will apply to all undertakings interested in these 'limited authorisations'. See however the *Bressol* judgment in section 5.1.2.

13 Joined Cases C-570/07 and C-571/07, *Blanco Pérez and Chao Gómez* [2010] ECR I-4629, para. 61.

14 See for example Case C-205/99, *Analir* [2001] ECR I-1271, para. 38, and Case C-203/08 *Sporting Exchange* [2010] ECR I-4695, para. 50.

15 According to Article 10(2) Services Directive, authorisation criteria should be (a) non-discriminatory, (b) justified by an overriding reason relating to the public interest, (c) proportionate to that public interest objective, (d) clear and unambiguous, (e) objective, (f) made public in advance and (g) transparent and accessible. Into more detail on these additional requirements, see below section 5.1.

16 Case C-203/08, *Sporting Exchange* [2010] ECR I-4695.

17 Into more detail, see G.S. Ølykke, 'Is the granting of special and exclusive rights subject to the principles applicable to the award of concessions? Recent development in case law and their implications for one of the last sanctuaries for protectionism' (2014) 23 *P.P.L.R.* 1 and Wolswinkel 2015, pp. 150–152.

be opened up to competition and the impartiality of the procurement procedures to be reviewed.[18] According to the CJEU, this obligation of transparency appears to be a mandatory prior condition of the right of a Member State to award to an operator the exclusive right to carry on an economic activity, irrespective of the method of selecting that operator, because the effects of a single licence on undertakings established in other Member States and potentially interested in that activity are the same as those of a service concession contract.[19] When applying this obligation of transparency to exclusive authorisation schemes, the Court held that compliance with the principle of equal treatment and with the consequent obligation of transparency in case of exclusive authorisations necessarily means that *the objective and non-discriminatory criteria* circumscribing the competent authorities' discretion, *must be sufficiently advertised.*[20] Thus, following *Sporting Exchange*, the existing requirement that authorisation criteria should be 'known in advance to the undertakings concerned' seems to be replaced by the more demanding requirement of 'sufficient advertising' in case of *limited* authorisation schemes.[21]

According to the CJEU, the award of an exclusive authorisation in the absence of any transparency, *i.e.* in the absence of any prior call for competition, to an undertaking located in the Member State of the authorising authority amounts to a difference in treatment to the detriment of undertakings located in another Member State. Unless justified by objective circumstances, such a difference in treatment, which operates mainly to the detriment of undertakings located in another Member State, amounts to indirect discrimination on the basis of nationality.[22] Hence, the complete absence of transparency with regard to the allocation criteria may amount to indirect discrimination, even though the allocation criteria themselves are not discriminatory.[23]

18 Case C-324/98, *Telaustria* [2000] ECR I-10745, para. 62; Case C-324/07, *Coditel Brabant* [2008] ECR I-8457, para. 25; Case C-91/08, *Wall* [2010] ECR I-2815, para. 36; Case C-203/08, *Sporting Exchange* [2010] ECR I-4695, para. 41, and Case C-64/08, *Engelmann* [2010] ECR I-8219, para. 50 ('a degree of publicity sufficient'). See on possible differences between 'publicity' and 'advertising' the opinion of Advocate General Sharpston delivered on 18 January 2007 in Case C-195/04 (*Commission v. Finland*), arguing that 'advertising' implies an obligation to publish, where 'publicity' only implies an obligation to do more than simply contacting a single potential tenderer and awarding the contract to that undertaking (point 82).

19 Case C-203/08, *Sporting Exchange* [2010] ECR I-4695, para. 47.

20 Case C-203/08, *Sporting Exchange* [2010] ECR I-4695, para. 50. See also Case C-470/11, *Garkalns* ECLI:EU:C:2012:505, para. 42.

21 See also Case C-64/08, *Engelmann* [2010] ECR I-8219, para. 57.

22 Case C-231/03, *Coname* [2005] ECR I-7287, paras. 17 and 19.

23 Article 10 Services Directive requires the granting criteria to be both 'made public in advance' and 'transparent and accessible'. These requirements seem to be strongly interrelated. Cf. Case C-231/03, *Coname* [2005] ECR I-7287, para. 21: '*transparency* requirements [...], without necessarily implying an obligation to hold an invitation to tender, are, in particular, such as to ensure that an undertaking located in the territory of [another] Member State [...] can have *access to* appropriate information regarding that concession before it is awarded, so that, if that undertaking had so wished, it would have been in a position to express its interest in obtaining that concession.'

At the same time, this obligation of transparency does not seem to affect the application of the other baseline requirements of 'objective criteria' and 'non-discriminatory criteria'. Instead, since this obligation of transparency does not relate to the *contents* of the allocation procedure,[24] this requirement does not prescribe or exclude certain allocation procedures: as long as the allocation procedure at issue has been sufficiently advertised, the obligation of transparency does not impede the application of this procedure.

3.3. *Objective Criteria*

The second baseline requirement is that authorisation criteria should be 'objective'. However, this requirement does not have an absolute character. In *Commission v. Spain*, the Court of Justice acknowledged that it is sometimes impossible to specify precise thresholds *in advance* without introducing a degree of rigidity likely to be even more restrictive of the freedom of establishment.[25] A similar conclusion can be derived from the Court's ruling in *Sokoll-Seebacher*. In this case, the Court considered that an authorisation criterion relating to 'the connections' of people with the area concerned, is not completely unambiguous. Nevertheless, if that criterion is not the main criterion for determining the number of 'people remaining to be served' and if these different connections are defined in an objective manner and are verifiable, *inter alia*, by means of statistical data, then this criterion is 'sufficiently objective in nature'.[26] However, even when authorisation criteria are sufficiently objective, these criteria can still be unsuitable to attain the legitimate objective at issue, in particular in case of a uniform application of those objective criteria without any possibility of derogation.[27]

There are good reasons to strengthen the objectivity test in case of *limited* authorisation schemes, since the absence of a second chance to obtain limited authorisations puts pressure on public authorities to design an allocation procedure as objectively as possible in advance. The CJEU's judgment in *Costa and Cifone* provides some support for this argument. Instead of referring to the general requirement of objective authorisation criteria, the CJEU considered, with reference to public procurement law, that all the conditions and detailed rules of the award procedure must be drawn up in a clear, precise and unequivocal manner, to make it possible for all reasonably informed tenderers exercising ordinary care to understand their exact significance and interpret them in the

24 See for example C.J. Wolswinkel, 'The Allocation of a Limited Number of Authorisations. Some General Requirements from European Law' (2009) 2 *Review of European Administrative Law* 61, 92–93. See also M. Szydlo, 'The Process of Granting Exclusive Rights in the Light of Treaty Rules on Free Movement' (2011) 12 (7) *German Law Journal* 1408, 1437; F. Wollenschläger, 'EU Law Principles for Allocating Scarce Goods and the Emergence of an Allocation Procedure' (2015) 8 (1) *Review of European Administrative Law* 205, 222.

25 Case C-400/08, *Commission v. Spain* [2011] ECR I-1915, para. 117. In this case, the CJEU concluded that the authorisation criteria at stake were not so imprecise as to render them *inappropriate* for the achievement of the objectives or disproportionate in relation to those objectives. See more recently Case C-470/11, *Garkalns* ECLI:EU:C:2012:505, para. 46.

26 Case C-367/12, *Sokoll-Seebacher* ECLI:EU:C:2014:68, paras. 31 and 32.

27 Case C-367/12, *Sokoll-Seebacher* ECLI:EU:C:2014:68, para. 41.

same way, and to circumscribe the contracting authority's discretion and enable it to ascertain effectively whether the tenders submitted satisfy the criteria applying to the relevant procedure.[28] However, even when applying an increased objectivity standard, it is still impossible to require complete preciseness of the allocation criteria in advance. In *Naftiliaki Etaireia Thasou*, the CJEU ruled, on the one hand, that the need to circumscribe the exercise of the administration's power by objective and non-discriminatory criteria known in advance *also* applies when, in a situation which concerns the sharing of timeslots between a number of interested shipowners in competition with each other, the national administration *decides between* the candidates where reasons of safety of ships and ports prevent a number of departures at the same time or require spacing between them. On the other hand, however, the Court considered that although the general authorisation criteria relating to the safety of ships and the order of ports did not define in detail the safety and order reasons which could justify a change in timeslots, they seemed to provide an *objective* framework of a 'sufficiently precise nature known in advance' for the exercise of the national authorities' discretion.[29]

To conclude, it is important to point out that the requirement of objective criteria does not seem to restrict the material range of possible allocation criteria, since this requirement does not concern the contents of criteria, but only their (lack of) precision.[30] Hence, any 'imprecise' allocation criterion might be replaced by a 'proxy' allocation criterion satisfying the requirement of objectivity. Consequently, this requirement of objective criteria does only exclude certain allocation criteria in as far as it is possible to redraw these criteria in an objective manner.

3.4. *Non-Discriminatory Criteria*

According to *Analir* and following case-law, criteria for the grant of an authorisation should not only be objective, but also be non-discriminatory. Since the very aim of any allocation criterion is to make distinction between applications by ranking them, any criterion is to some extent 'discriminatory'. However, this case-law requirement of non-discriminatory criteria should be understood such as to prohibit discrimination *on grounds of nationality*, which is the cornerstone of the fundamental freedoms of movement.[31] This principle of non-discrimination prohibits not only direct or overt discrimination on grounds of nationality, but also all covert or indirect forms of discrimination which, by the application of other distinguishing criteria, lead to the

[28] Joined Cases C-72/10 and C-77/10, *Costa and Cifone* ECLI:EU:C:2012:80, para. 73, with reference to Case C-496/99 P, *Commission* v *CAS Succhi di Frutta* [2004] ECR I-3801, para. 111, and Case C-250/06, *United Pan-Europe Communications Belgium and Others* [2007] ECR I-11135, paras. 45 and 46. Whereas Article 10 Services Directive requires authorisation criteria to be both 'clear and unambiguous' and 'objective', these requirements seem to overlap partly, if not entirely.

[29] Joined cases C-128/10 and C-129/10, *Natfiliaki Etaireia Thasou*, [2011] ECR I-1885 paras. 49 and 50.

[30] See clearly Case C-400/08, *Commission v. Spain* [2011] ECR I-1915, para. 117.

[31] C. Barnard, *The Substantive Law of the EU. The Four Freedoms*, 3rd ed., OUP, Oxford 2010, p. 223.

same result.[32] Authorisation criteria must be regarded as indirectly discriminatory, *unless* objectively justified and proportionate, if they are intrinsically liable to affect the nationals of other Member States more than the nationals of the host Member State and if there is a consequent risk that these criteria will place the former nationals at a particular disadvantage.[33] Again, this requirement allows for exceptions: whereas *direct* discrimination on grounds of nationality, e.g. with the nationality of the applicant as authorisation criterion,[34] can be justified only by an express derogating provision in the TFEU,[35] *indirect* discrimination can also be justified by (other) overriding reasons relating to the public interest.[36]

This general legal framework holds in particular for allocation procedures, as can be derived from the CJEU's judgment in *Blanco Pérez and Chao Gómez*. This case dealt with a procedure of 'competitive examination' for the grant of authorisations for the establishment of pharmacies in the region of Asturias (Spain).[37] The most important allocation criterion in this examination was the professional experience of the applicants, which was measured in points by the period during which applicants had been active as a pharmacy holder. Two elements in this points system related explicitly to the region of Asturias: (i) points for professional experience were increased by 20% for professional experience within the region of Asturias, and (ii) in the event that several applicants would score an equal number of points ('tie'), priority was given to pharmacists who had pursued their professional activities within the region of Asturias. With regard to both 'allocation criteria', the Court assessed that these criteria could be more easily met by national pharmacists, who more often pursue their economic activities on the national territory, than by pharmacists who are nationals of other Member States, who more frequently pursue those activities in another Member State. Since this difference in treatment could not be justified by the need that pharmacists should be immediately capable of providing pharmaceutical services in the region of Asturias, the CJEU concluded that these allocation criteria amounted to indirect discrimination.[38]

In general, it should be realized that some allocation criteria might be more easily met by applicants from the host state, thereby amounting to indirect discrimination. This holds, for example, in case of allocation on a 'first come first served' basis, if it impossible for

32 Joined Cases C-570/07 and C-571/07, *Blanco Pérez and Chao Gómez* [2010] ECR I-4629, para. 118.

33 Joined Cases C-570/07 and C-571/07, *Blanco Pérez and Chao Gómez* [2010] ECR I-4629, para. 122.

34 According to advocate general Sharpston, discrimination on grounds of nationality can be considered to be *direct* where the difference in treatment is based on a criterion which is either explicitly that of nationality or necessarily linked to a characteristic indissociable from nationality (see para. 53 of the opinion delivered on 25 June 2009 in Case C-73/08 (*Bressol*)).

35 Case C-153/08, *Commission v. Spain* [2009] ECR I-9735, para. 37. In case of the freedom of establishment and the freedom to provide services, the main derogations are public policy, public security or public health (Article 52 TFEU and Article 62 TFEU respectively).

36 See clearly Case C-388/01, *Commission v. Italy* [2003] ECR I-721, distinguishing between distinction on the basis of nationality (para. 19) and distinction on the basis of residence (para. 21).

37 Joined Cases C-570/07 and C-571/07, *Blanco Pérez and Chao Gómez* [2010] ECR I-4629, para. 17.

38 Joined Cases C-570/07 and C-571/07, *Blanco Pérez and Chao Gómez* [2010] ECR I-4629, para. 124.

foreign applicants to submit applications electronically or if the announcement of the allocation procedure has been published in a national medium first, thereby allowing applicants in the host state to submit their applications earlier. Whether a particular allocation procedure amounts to (indirect) discrimination, will depend, however, on the specific design of the allocation procedure. Thus, it cannot be concluded in advance that allocation on a first come first served basis always gives an advantage to undertakings in the host state. Moreover, even if allocation criteria are directly or indirectly discriminatory, e.g. criteria relating to the nationality of applicants, the residence of applicants or the experience of applicants in a certain region, then these criteria might still be justified.

3.5. *Conclusion*

In sum, the triad that the allocation criteria of an authorisation scheme should be objective, non-discriminatory and known in advance (or sufficiently advertised), constitutes minimal requirements any allocation procedure should comply with. Deviation from these baseline requirements, however, is still possible if this deviation can be justified objectively and if this deviation is both suitable and necessary with regard to that legitimate objective. At most, it can be argued that possibilities for deviation might be more limited in case of *limited* authorisation schemes than in case of *open* authorisation schemes, since the absence of a second chance to obtain limited authorisations strengthens the need for a 'fair' allocation in advance.

What is more important, though, is that in general these baseline criteria do not seem to exclude certain allocation procedures from being applied. Instead, given these requirements, public authorities can still choose from among a wide range of allocation procedures. Only in particular circumstances, the baseline requirements of objective and non-discriminatory criteria known in advance might exclude the application of a particular allocation procedure.

4. Beyond the Baseline: Allocation Preferences in Secondary EU Law

4.1. *Introduction*

After having established the baseline requirements any allocation procedure should satisfy, it is necessary to explore whether EU law provides more guidance as to the choice of the allocation procedure. To that end, this section will briefly sketch various secondary EU legislation with specific attention for provisions on allocation criteria. This description does not only take into account the three central examples of this book (radio frequencies, greenhouse gas emission allowances and gambling licences),[39] but also deals with some other directives which can be considered even more important for identifying preferences for certain allocation criteria.

39 Since gambling activities are not subject to secondary EU legislation, these activities will be dealt with in section 5.1.2.

4.2. *Telecommunications Law*

4.2.1. Allocation procedure

As part of the common regulatory framework for electronic communications networks and services, the Authorisation Directive[40] deals with the assignment of rights of use for radio frequencies and numbers.[41] According to Article 5(1), Member States may grant such individual rights of use, where necessary, in order to (a) avoid harmful interference, (b) ensure technical quality of service, (c) safeguard efficient use of spectrum, or (d) fulfil other objectives of general interest as defined by Member States in conformity with Community law. Moreover, according to Article 5(5), Member States shall not *limit* the number of rights of use to be granted except where this is necessary to ensure *the efficient use of radio frequencies* in accordance with Article 7. Thus, an efficient use of radio frequencies is the *limitation objective* for limiting the number of rights available for grant. Article 7 contains the procedure for limiting the number of rights of use to be granted for radio frequencies. According to its third paragraph, where the granting of rights of use for radio frequencies needs to be limited, Member States shall grant such rights on the basis of selection criteria which must be objective, transparent, non-discriminatory and proportionate. Besides, any such selection criteria must give 'due weight' to the achievement of the objectives of Article 8 of the Framework Directive.[42] These objectives are – in general – (a) promoting competition in the provision of electronic communications networks and services, (b) contributing to the development of the internal market and (c) promoting the interests of the citizens of the European Union.

Article 7 should be read in conjunction with Article 5(4) Authorisation Directive, according to which Article 7 shall apply with regard to 'competitive or comparative selection procedures' for radio frequencies. However, the wording of the Authorisation Directive is not entirely clear on the issue whether 'competitive or comparative selection procedures' *should* always be applied after having limited the number of rights of use to be granted for radio frequencies.[43] The relevant recitals of the Authorisation Directive are not conclusive either:

> (22) Where the demand for radio frequencies in a specific range exceeds their availability, *appropriate and transparent* procedures should be followed for the assignment of such frequencies in order to avoid any discrimination *and* optimise use of those scarce resources.

40 Directive 2002/20/EC of the European Parliament and of the Council of 7 March 2002 on the authorisation of electronic communications networks and services (Authorisation Directive) [2002] OJ L108/21. This directive has been adopted on the basis of (ex) Article 95 EC (Article 114 TFEU).

41 Into more detail, see the chapter by Oberst in this book.

42 Article 7(3) Authorisation Directive.

43 According to Article 7(4) Authorisation Directive, *where* competitive or comparative selection procedures are to be used, Member States may extend the maximum period necessary to decide on applications for rights of use for radio frequencies.

> (23) National regulatory authorities should ensure, in establishing criteria for *competitive or comparative selection procedures*, that the objectives in Article 8 of Directive 2002/21/EC (Framework Directive) are met. [...]

On the one hand, it can be argued that selection criteria should be objective, transparent, non-discriminatory and proportionate and that the procedure for granting rights of use *may* include *'competitive or comparative selection procedures'*.[44] Recital 21 of the Framework Directive supports this argument by considering that Member States may use, *inter alia*, competitive or comparative selection procedures for the assignment of radio frequencies.[45] However, the opposite view can be adopted as well: since national regulatory authorities should ensure – according to recital 23 Authorisation Directive – that the objectives of Article 8 Framework Directive are met, there is an obligation to apply competitive of comparative procedures in case of a limited number of radio frequencies. It should be realized that the exact consequences of this debate depend on the understanding of 'competitive or comparative procedures'. However, the Authorisation Directive does not define the concept of 'competitive or comparative selection procedures'.[46] It is clear that this term includes at least an auction,[47] but it is less clear which other allocation procedures are covered by this term. If a procedure is competitive or comparative merely because it has been initiated by a call for competition or a general invitation to submit applications, then any allocation procedure might be considered as competitive or comparative: a relative comparison of applications is the key characteristic of any allocation procedure, even allocation on a 'first come first served' basis or a lottery.[48] A more restrictive interpretation, which gives the species 'competitive or comparative selection procedure' added value next to the genus 'selection

44 See for this argument B. Vesterdorf, 'Radio spectrum licence renewals', *Spectrum: renewal and pricing in Europe*, Moving the debate forward – The Policy Paper Series, number 14, Vodafone Group, May 2012, p. 20: "It follows from the wording of Article 7 and the Recitals [22 and 23] that when an NRA has decided to grant a limited number of rights of use, the central obligation on the NRA is to ensure that it uses selection criteria which are objective, transparent, non-discriminatory and proportionate. It further follows from the Directive that the procedure for granting rights of use *may* include "*competitive or comparative selection procedures*" as referred to in Article 7(4). [...] In summary, therefore, Article 7(4) does not *require* competitive or comparative selection procedures, but *allows* for such procedures in circumstances where the NRA has concluded, on the basis of the factors referred to in Articles 7(1) and 7(3), that such a procedure is appropriate and proportionate."

45 Directive 2002/21/EC of the European Parliament and of the Council of 7 March 2002 on a common regulatory framework for electronic communications networks and services (Framework Directive) [2002] OJ L108/33.

46 Vesterdorf 2012, p. 20.

47 See Vesterdorf 2012, p. 20, and A. Brandenberg, 'Authorisations' in C. Koenig and A. Bartosch (eds.), *EC competition and telecommunications law*, 2nd ed., Kluwer Law International, Alphen aan den Rijn 2009, p. 495, concluding that both auctions and administrative processes are admissible allocation methods.

48 For example, according to Electronic Communications Committee, *Number assignment practices in CEPT countries*, EEC-report 60 (May 2005), p. 11, *lotteries* can be considered competitive or comparative procedures as well.

procedure', requires bids of applicants to be compared,[49] as a result of which this term may only cover the auction and other procedures of 'comparative selection' ('beauty contest').[50] Moreover, one might wonder whether the requirement to give 'due weight' to the objectives of the Framework Directive can be reconciled with allocation procedures such as a lottery or 'first come, first served' allocation.

Irrespective of a broad or restrictive interpretation of 'competitive or comparative selection procedure', it is clear that national regulatory authorities have at least some discretion in the choice of the allocation procedure to be applied. This is confirmed by Article 7(1), obliging Member States, *inter* alia, to invite applications for rights of use *after having determined the procedure.* Thus, the Authorisation Directive does neither prescribe nor prefer a certain allocation procedure to be applied. Even if 'competitive or comparative procedures' (interpreted restrictively) should be applied, then the Authorisation Directive does not express any preference for either an auction or another method of 'comparative selection'. However, since – according to recital 22 – appropriate and transparent procedures should be followed for the assignment of such frequencies in order to avoid any discrimination *and* to optimise use of those scarce resources, there is a need to give due weight to an efficient or optimal use of scarce resources in the design of the allocation procedure. Thus, this 'limitation objective' turns out to be relevant for the choice of the allocation procedure as well.

4.2.2. Financial fees

In addition to the choice of the allocation procedure in Article 7, Article 13 Authorisation Directive stipulates that Member States may allow the relevant authority to impose fees for the rights of use for radio frequencies which reflect the need to ensure *the optimal use of these resources.* Member States shall ensure that such fees shall be objectively justified, transparent, non-discriminatory and proportionate in relation to their intended purpose and shall take into account the objectives in Article 8 of the Framework Directive. In *Telefónica Móviles España*, the Court considered that it is apparent that the authorisation to use public property which constitutes a scarce resource enables the holder of that authorisation to make significant economic gains and grants that holder advantages as compared with other operators who are also seeking to use and exploit that resource, which justifies imposing a charge which reflects, *inter alia*, the value of the use of the scarce resource at issue.[51] Therefore, the purpose of ensuring that operators make optimal use of scarce resources to which they have access means that the charge must be set at an appropriate level to reflect inter alia *the value of the use of those*

[49] The initial Commission proposal referred to 'comparative bidding procedures' in Article 7(4). See Proposal for a Directive of the European Parliament and of the Council on the authorisation of electronic communications networks and services (COM 2000/386/final).

[50] See for this terminology of 'comparative selection', sometimes referred to as 'competitive tendering', C-431/07 P, *Bouygues and Bouygues Télécom* v *Commission* [2009] ECR I-2665, paras 91–92. On this case, see below section 5.3 on State aid.

[51] Case C-85/10, *Telefónica Móviles España* [2011] ECR I-1575, para. 27.

resources, which requires account to be taken of the economic and technical situation of the market concerned.[52] An excessive charge is likely to discourage the use of the scarce resources at issue and thereby result in under-utilisation of those resources. Similarly, too low a charge risks undermining the efficiency of the use of those resources.[53] Thus, Article 13 Authorisation Directive has been interpreted such as to exclude the sole allocation objective of revenue maximisation, but to allow for the allocation objective of allocative efficiency, *i.e.* to award the authorisations to the undertakings that value them most.[54]

Since Article 13 Authorisation Directive does not provide explicitly for a specific method for determining the amount of such a financial charge,[55] the CJEU has further clarified in *Belgacom* that the fixing of a fee for rights of use for radio frequencies by reference *either* to the amount of the former one-off licence fee calculated on the basis of the number of frequencies and months to which the rights of use relate, *or* to the amounts raised through auction, may be an *appropriate* method for determining the value of the radio frequencies.[56] Thus, whereas an auction is a suitable method to determine the value of an authorisation, other allocation procedures may be equally suitable in attaining this objective. Again, there is no preference in the Authorisation Directive for the application of an auction instead of another financial instrument.

Finally, the CJEU has also clarified in *Telefónica Móviles España* with regard to the requirement that the need to foster the development of innovative services and competition should be taken into account, that the amount of the charge cannot have the effect of hindering the access of new operators to the market or of reducing the capacity of telecommunications service operators for innovation. Moreover, competition must not be distorted, which can be guaranteed only if *equality of opportunity* is secured as between the various economic operators.[57] Thus, Member States cannot, in principle, apply *different* charges to competing operators for the use of scarce resources whose values appear to be *equivalent* in economic terms.[58] This notion of 'equality of opportunity' is important, since even though it does not prescribe the application of a certain allocation procedure, it requires at least some elementary consistency once a specific allocation procedure has been chosen.

52 Case C-85/10, *Telefónica Móviles España* [2011] ECR I-1575, para. 28.

53 Case C-85/10, *Telefónica Móviles España* [2011] ECR I-1575, para. 29.

54 See also M. Kerste, N.A.N.M. van Eijk and J.P Poort, 'Valuing commercial radio licences' (2015) 39 *European Journal of Law and Economics* 331, 333–334.

55 Case C-85/10, *Telefónica Móviles España* [2011] ECR I-1575, para. 25.

56 Case C-375/11, *Belgacom* ECLI:EU:C:2013:185, para. 52.

57 See also Joined Cases C-327/03 and C-328/03, *ISIS Multimedia Net and Firma O2* [2005] ECR I-08877, paras. 38 and 39.

58 Case C-85/10, *Telefónica Móviles España* [2011] ECR I-1575, para. 31, and Joined Cases C-327/03 and C-328/03, *ISIS Multimedia Net and Firma O2* [2005] ECR I-8877, paras. 40 and 41.

4.3. *Energy Law*

4.3.1. Production of minerals (hydrocarbons)

The objective of an efficient use of scarce resources is also a pre-eminent objective in the so-called Hydrocarbons Directive on the conditions for granting and using authorisations for the prospection, exploration and production of hydrocarbons.[59] The recitals of this directive point out that the Community largely depends on imports for its hydrocarbon supply. Consequently, it is advisable to encourage the best possible prospection, exploration and production of the resources located *in* the Community. Therefore, steps must be taken *to ensure the non-discriminatory access* to and pursuit of activities relating to the prospection, exploration and production of hydrocarbons under conditions which encourage greater competition in this sector *and thereby to favour the best* prospection, exploration and production of resources in Member States *and to reinforce* the integration of the internal energy market. Again, as in telecommunications law, the (primary) objective of non-discriminatory access goes hand in hand with an additional objective of efficient use of natural resources.

With regard to the design of the authorisation procedure, the Hydrocarbons Directive requires authorisations to be granted on the basis of criteria *concerning in all cases* (a) the technical and financial capability of the entities, (b) the way in which they propose to prospect, to explore and/or to bring into production the geographical area in question, and – where applicable – (c) if the authorisation is put up for sale, the price which the entity is prepared to pay in order to obtain the authorisations. Only if after an evaluation under these criteria two or more applications have equal merit, 'other relevant objective and non-discriminatory criteria' can be taken into account in order to make a final choice among these applications.[60]

These provisions in the Hydrocarbons Directive allow for some general observations. First, while recognizing the baseline requirements of objective and non-discriminatory criteria, this directive requires some allocation criteria to be taken into account: (i) the technical and financial capability of applicants and (ii) the feasibility of their proposal to prospect, explore or produce hydrocarbons. Both allocation criteria can be related easily to the additional objective of an optimal use of scarce resources.[61] Secondly, this directive makes clear that other allocation criteria can only be applied *after and in addition to* the criteria of financial and technical capability and feasibility of the business

59 Directive 94/22/EC of the European Parliament and of the Council of 30 May 1994 on the conditions for granting and using authorisations for the prospection, exploration and production of hydrocarbons [1994] OJ L 164/3 (hereinafter Hydrocarbons Directive). This directive has been adopted on the basis of ex Articles 57(2), 66 and 100a EC.

60 Article 5(1) Hydrocarbons Directive.

61 See also the recitals of the Hydrocarbons Directive: "For this purpose, it is necessary to set up common rules for ensuring that the procedures for granting authorizations for the prospection, exploration and production of hydrocarbons must be open to all entities possessing the necessary capabilities."

proposal. Last but not least, although the Hydrocarbons Directive explicitly allows for the application of the price as an allocation criterion, it does not express a *preference* for a price mechanism, as the wording 'where applicable' clarifies that Member States are free to choose this allocation criterion or not.

Compared with the Authorisation Directive, the Hydrocarbons Directive shows a more elaborated legal framework on the choice of the allocation criteria. It does not only establish which criteria should be taken into account, but also prescribes to some extent *the order* in which these criteria are to be applied.

4.3.2. Greenhouse gases

The directive on the EU Emissions Trading System (EU ETS)[62] prescribes the auction as the main allocation procedure for greenhouse gas emission allowances, at least for the future after a transitional period.[63] Whereas the recitals of the (amended) Directive 2003/87/EC remain rather silent about this preference for the auction, the subsequent Commission Regulation, establishing one uniform auction format for all participating Member States, is very clear in this respect: auctioning should be the basic principle for allocation, as it is the simplest and generally considered to be the most economically efficient means of doing so. Where the efficiency of the emissions trading scheme relies on a clear carbon price signal to achieve abatement of greenhouse gas emissions at least cost, auctioning supports this carbon price signal.[64] In fact, this 'carbon price signal' reflects the 'polluter pays principle'.[65]

Unlike the other directives in this section, the legal basis for Directive 2003/87/EC is Article 175 TFEU on environmental policy of the European Union instead of the establishment of the internal market (Article 114 TFEU).[66] This different legal basis might explain why EU law is more demanding as to the choice of the allocation procedure and even prescribes a uniform design of the auction format at an EU-wide level.

62 Directive 2003/87/EC of the European Parliament and of the Council of 13 October 2003 establishing a scheme for greenhouse gas emission allowance trading within the Community and amending Council Directive 96/61/EC [2003] OJ L275/32, as amended afterwards.

63 Article 10 Directive 2003/87/EC: 'From 2013 onwards, Member States shall auction all allowances which are not allocated free of charge in accordance with Article 10a and 10c [*i.e.* transitional regimes for free allocation].' Thus, Member States may not use any other procedure than the auction to allocate allowances which are not allocated free of charge.

64 See recital 1 of Commission Regulation (EU) No 1031/2010 of 12 November 2010 on the timing, administration and other aspects of auctioning of greenhouse gas emission allowances pursuant to Directive 2003/87/EC of the European Parliament and of the Council establishing a scheme for greenhouse gas emission allowances trading within the Community [2010] OJ L302/1.

65 Into more detail, please refer to the chapter by Rønne in this book.

66 Article 175 TFEU.

4.4. *Procurement Law*

4.4.1. Public contracts

Finally, it is worth discussing the directives on public procurement.[67] According to the 2004 Public Sector Directive,[68] the criteria for the award of public contracts are either (a) the most economically advantageous tender or (b) the lowest price only. Both criteria, 'the lowest price' and 'the most economically advantageous tender', are considered to be objective criteria which ensure compliance with the principles of transparency, non-discrimination and equal treatment *and* which guarantee that tenders are assessed in conditions of *effective competition*.[69] Even though the 2004 Public Sector Directive allows for only two allocation (award) criteria, it should be realized that in selecting the most economically advantageous tender, contracting authorities are free to choose the criteria to be used in awarding the contract, provided that these award criteria are 'linked to the subject-matter of the contract'.[70] Furthermore, these award criteria (i) should not confer an unrestricted freedom of choice on the authority, (ii) should be expressly mentioned in the contract documents and (iii) should comply with all the fundamental principles of EU law, in particular the principle of non-discrimination.[71] Whereas these last three requirements reflect the minimal baseline requirements of objective and non-discriminatory criteria known in advance, the requirement concerning *the link to the subject-matter of the contract* reflects an additional requirement of 'relevance'.[72] This requirement has been interpreted such as to exclude as award criteria *inter alia* criteria relating to the tenders' suitability to perform the contract; such criteria should be used as 'qualitative selection criteria', being applied *before* awarding the contract.[73]

In *Sintesi*, the CJEU held that the predecessor of Article 53 of the 2004 Public Sector Directive precludes national rules which, for the purpose of the award of public contracts

67 Into more detail, please refer to the chapter by Jansen in this book.

68 Directive 2004/18/EC of the European Parliament and of the Council of 31 March 2004 on the coordination of procedures for the award of public works contracts, public supply contracts and public service contracts [2004] OJ L134/114.

69 Recital 46 of the 2004 Public Sector Directive.

70 See also Case 31/87, *Beentjes* [1988] ECR 4635, para. 26. See also Article 53(1)(1) 2004 Public Sector Directive.

71 Case C-513/99, *Concordia Bus Finland* [2002] ECR I-7213, para. 69; Case C-448/01, *EVN and Wienstrom* [2003] ECR I-14527, para. 33. This does not mean that each of the award criteria to identify the economically most advantageous tender should necessarily be of a purely economic nature, since it cannot be excluded that factors which are not purely economic may influence the value of a tender (*Concordia Bus Finland*, para. 55; *EVN and Wienstrom*, para. 32).

72 Szydlo 2011, p. 1429–1430, establishes a link between this requirement of relevance and the principle of non-discrimination by arguing that award criteria should be 'mostly' linked to the subject-matter of the resource, since the farther and more loosely the criteria are connected with the subject-matter of the resource, the greater the risk that they would be set arbitrarily, being beneficial merely for some applicants.

73 Case C-532/06, *Lianakis* [2008] ECR I-251, para. 32.

following open or restricted tendering procedures,[74] impose *a general and abstract requirement* that the contracting authorities use only the criterion of the lowest price. According to the CJEU, it is true that a national provision which restricts the contracting authorities' freedom of choice in the context of 'open' or 'restricted' tendering procedures, by requiring that the lowest price be used as the sole criterion for the award of the contract, does not prevent those authorities from comparing the different tenders and from accepting the best one on the basis of an *objective* criterion fixed in advance and specifically included among those set out in the procurement directive at issue. However, this *abstract and general fixing* by the national legislature of a single criterion for the award of public contracts deprives the contracting authorities of the possibility of taking into consideration the nature and specific characteristics of such contracts, *taken in isolation*, by choosing for each of them the criterion most likely to ensure free competition and thus to ensure that the best tender will be accepted.[75]

This ruling of the CJEU does not apply, however, to the so-called 'competitive dialogue'.[76] With regard to this procurement procedure, the 2004 Public Sector Directive requires the allocation criterion of the most economically advantageous tender to be applied.[77] This exclusion of the lowest price as an allocation criterion can be understood from the condition of 'particularly complex contracts' which should be satisfied in order to apply a competitive dialogue. It would be inconsistent with this condition of particular complexity of the contract to award this contract on the basis of the lowest price only.

In the new 2014 Public Procurement Directive, the choice between 'lowest price and 'economically most advantageous tender' has been replaced by the sole award criterion of the 'most economically advantageous tender'.[78] This economic advantage must be identified on the basis of the price or cost, using a cost-effectiveness approach, such as life-cycle costing,[79] and may include the best price-quality ratio, which shall be assessed on the basis of criteria, including qualitative, environmental and/or social aspects, linked to the subject-matter of the public contract in question. As a result, this new provision does not intend to create any discontinuity with the previous Article 53 2004 Public

74 Into more detail on the difference between open and restricted procedure, refer to the chapter by f Jansen in this book.

75 Case C-247/02, *Sintesi* [2004] ECR I-9215, paras 40–42.

76 A competitive dialogue is a procedure in which any economic operator may request to participate and whereby the contracting authority conducts a dialogue with the candidates admitted to that procedure, with the aim of developing one or more suitable alternatives capable of meeting its requirements, and on the basis of which the candidates chosen are invited to tender (Article 2(11)(h) 2004 Public Sector Directive).

77 Article 29(1) 2004 Public Sector Directive.

78 Article 67(1) Directive 2014/24/EU of the European Parliament and of the Council of 26 February 2014 on public procurement and repealing Directive 2004/18/EC [2014] OJ L94/95 (hereinafter: 2014 Public Procurement Directive).

79 See Article 68 2014 Public Procurement Directive.

Sector Directive.[80] Moreover, it is worth emphasizing that the new 2014 Directive acknowledges that the cost element may also take the form of a *fixed* price or cost on the basis of which economic operators will compete on quality criteria only. Additionally, Member States may provide that contracting authorities may not use price *only* or cost *only* as the sole award criterion or *restrict their use* to certain categories of contracting authorities or certain types of contracts.[81] Finally, it is worth mentioning recital 93 of the new 2014 Directive, stating that given the numerous possibilities of evaluating value for money on the basis of substantive criteria, recourse to drawing of lots as the sole means of awarding the contract *should be avoided*.[82] This recital suggests that a lottery is not excluded in advance, but it can be questioned whether a lottery (as sole award criterion) is linked to the subject-matter of the contract.

To conclude, the discretion of contracting authorities to choose an award procedure that meets the specific demands in the circumstances of the case, should be highlighted. Consequently, there is no guarantee that the same allocation criterion or procedure will be used for similar works or services. This seems to contrast somehow with the approach in telecommunications law, emphasizing equality of opportunity between (all) economic operators.

4.4.2. Concessions

Apart from the new Public Procurement Directive, a new Concessions Directive[83] has been adopted as well. In many aspects, this Concessions Directive is a light version of the Public Procurement Directive. With regard to award criteria, this Concessions Directive does not prescribe the award criterion of the 'most economically advantageous tender'. Instead, this directive merely requires that concessions shall be awarded on the basis of objective criteria which comply with the principles of equal treatment, non-discrimination and transparency *and* which ensure that tenders are assessed in conditions of effective competition so as to identify an *overall economic advantage* for the contracting authority.[84] In this respect, the award criteria must be 'linked to the subject-matter of the concession' and may not confer an unrestricted freedom of choice on the contracting

80 See also recital 89 of the 2014 Public Procurement Directive: "The notion of award criteria is central to this Directive. It is therefore important that the relevant provisions be presented in as simple and streamlined a way as possible. This can be obtained by using the terminology 'most economically advantageous tender' as the overriding concept, since all winning tenders should finally be chosen in accordance with what the individual contracting authority considers to be the economically best solution among those offered."

81 See also recital 90 of the 2014 Public Procurement Directive.

82 In section 2.2.2 of its Interpretative communication on the Community law applicable to contract awards not or not fully subject to the provisions of the Public Procurement Directives [2006] OJ C179/4, the Commission listed the lottery as a suitable method to limit the number of applicants invited to submit an offer.

83 Directive 2014/23/EU of the European Parliament and of the Council of 26 February 2014 on the award of concession contracts [2014] OJ L94/1 (hereinafter: Concessions Directive).

84 Article 41(1) Concessions Directive.

authority or the contracting entity. Moreover, the directive puts beyond doubt that the award criteria may include, inter alia, environmental, social or innovation-related criteria.[85] In sum, even though the provisions in the Concessions Directive are not as detailed as their counterparts in the Public Procurement Directive, they seem to reflect at least that the criteria for the award of concessions should have an economic dimension as well.

4.5. *Conclusion*

EU secondary legislation shows a rich diversity as to the regulation of allocation procedures. In fact, the several directives outlined above show various degrees of preferences for certain allocation procedures or criteria. In general, all directives aim at preventing discrimination on grounds of nationality. In some directives, however, this primary objective is accompanied by additional *allocation objectives*, such as an efficient use of natural resources (frequencies, minerals) or an economic advantage for public authorities (public contracts). The underlying question *why* efficient use of natural resources is important, can be answered differently, from the need to guarantee EU independence as to natural resources (minerals) to the need to prevent a 'tragedy of the commons' (frequencies). After all, an optimal or efficient use of scarce resources can be considered a legitimate allocation objective.

Some additional observations can be made. First, EU law shows that a *general and abstract* choice of an allocation procedure may be even more restrictive of the fundamental freedoms than a case-by-case approach, identifying the 'optimal' allocation procedure for each allocation issue separately. Secondly, EU law shows the importance of the connection between the allocation criterion and the allocation objective: allocation criteria should be 'relevant' to attain the underlying objectives of the authorisation system. As a result, there is no general preference for the allocation criterion 'price' or the allocation procedure 'auction', since other allocation procedures might be able to contribute to the allocation objective of 'economic advantage' or 'optimal use' as well. In other words, there is no one-to-one connection between the 'auction' and 'efficient use'. Thirdly, when identifying the relevant allocation objectives, the 'limitation objectives' of the authorisation scheme remain relevant. Fourthly, EU law requires some consistency in the choice of the allocation procedure in order to ensure equality of opportunity of operators. This might imply that once a particular allocation procedure has been chosen and applied to some operators, this procedure should be applied to other operators as well.

In addition to these findings, the following section will address the question whether preferences for the choice of allocation procedures can also be derived from primary EU law (instead of sector-specific EU legislation). This question will be dealt with separately for internal market law (fundamental freedoms), competition law and State aid law, although these areas are closely interrelated.

85 Article 41(2) Concessions Directive.

5. Beyond the Baseline: Towards Additional General Requirements in EU Law?

5.1. *Internal Market Law (Fundamental Freedoms)*

5.1.1. Services Directive

Given the *Analir* baseline requirements of objective and non-discriminatory criteria known in advance, the question is whether additional *general* requirements apply to the choice of the allocation procedure as well. A natural starting point for this analysis is the Services Directive which 'establishes general provisions facilitating the exercise of the freedom of establishment for service providers and the free movement of services, while maintaining a high quality of services'.[86] Unlike the directives analyzed in the previous section, this Services Directive has a rather general scope, applying to any service activity, unless this service activity has been excluded from the scope of the directive.[87]

In order to identify general rules on allocation procedures, Article 12 Services Directive might be a useful starting point. This article deals with 'limited authorisation schemes' where the number of authorisations available for a service activity is limited 'because of the scarcity of available natural resources or technical capacity'.[88] In those circumstances, a selection procedure should be applied which provides full guarantees of impartiality and transparency, including, in particular, adequate publicity about the launch, conduct and completion of the procedure.[89] Subject to this requirement of an impartial and transparent selection procedure, Member States *may* take into account, in establishing the rules for the selection procedure, considerations of overriding reasons relating to the public interest, in conformity with EU law.[90] However, this article does not contain any preference for certain allocation procedures to be applied, provided that these procedures are impartial and transparent.

Unlike Article 12, Article 10 Services Directive applies to all kinds of authorisation schemes, both 'open' and limited authorisation schemes.[91] This article contains several

86 Article 1(1) Services Directive.

87 This holds, for example, for gambling and pharmaceutical activities (Article 2 Services Directive).

88 An example of a service authorisation falling within the scope of Article 12 Services Directive is the authorisation for the *storage* of hydrocarbons or other minerals. Electronic communications services involving the use of radio frequencies have been excluded from the scope of the Services Directive (Article 2(2)(c) Services Directive).

89 Article 12(1) Services Directive. See Wolswinkel 2009, pp. 90–94, for a detailed analysis of Article 12 Services Directive.

90 Article 12(3) Services Directive.

91 See also recital 62, stressing that Article 12 Services Directive should not prevent Member States from limiting the number of authorisations for reasons other than scarcity of natural resources or technical capacity. These 'other' limited authorisations should remain in any case subject to the other provisions of the Services Directive relating to authorisation schemes.

requirements that the authorisation criteria should satisfy. In general, these criteria should preclude the competent authorities from exercising their power of assessment in an arbitrary manner. Therefore, these criteria should be (a) non-discriminatory, (b) justified by an overriding reason relating to the public interest, (c) proportionate to that public interest objective, (d) clear and unambiguous, (e) objective, (f) made public in advance, and (g) transparent and accessible.[92] It can be safely assumed that *allocation* criteria, as a species of authorisation criteria, should satisfy these general requirements as well. Since several of these requirements have been discussed already in Section 3 as baseline requirements, this subsection will only examine the specific meaning of the requirement that an allocation criterion should be justified by an overriding reason relating to the public interest and should be proportionate, *i.e.* suitable and necessary, with regard to that legitimate objective. In order to unveil the specific meaning of this general requirement when being applied to allocation criteria, it is necessary to resort to relevant case-law under the fundamental freedoms.

5.1.2. Case-law

First of all, the CJEU has considered more than once that grounds of an economic nature, such as the need to ensure continuity, financial stability and a proper return on past investments for licence holders, cannot be accepted as overriding reasons in the general interest justifying a restriction of a fundamental freedom.[93] The same holds for grounds of an administrative nature.[94] This may already exclude the choice for an auction mainly because of revenue maximization or the choice for a lottery mainly to avoid a complex comparison of applications.

As for the application of the requirements of suitability (and necessity) to allocation criteria, the most clarifying judgment of the CJEU is (again) the *Blanco Pérez and Chao Goméz* judgment on authorisations for the establishment of pharmacies.[95] In this case, the number of authorisations available had been limited to a maximum by two quantitative restrictions: first, the number of pharmacies was based on a unit of population of 2 800 inhabitants per pharmacy and, second, the minimum distance between pharmacies was 250 metres. We saw already in subsection 3.4 that whenever new authorisations were to be granted, these authorisations were allocated by means of a 'competitive examination' which was based primarily on the criterion of professional

92 Cf. A. Prechal and M. de Leeuw, 'Dimensions of Transparency: The Building Blocks for a New Legal Principle' (2007) 0 *Review of European Administrative Law* 51, 60, pointing out that these criteria do not always have added value.

93 See for example C-260/04, *Commission v. Italy* [2007] ECR I-7083 para. 35, and Joined Cases C-72/10 and C-77/10, *Costa and Cifone* ECLI:EU:C:2012:80, para. 59.

94 Case C-463/13, *Stanleybet* ECLI:EU:C:2015:25, para. 50.

95 For case-law on authorisation criteria for gambling activities, see for example Joined Cases C-338/04, C-359/04 and C-360/04, *Placanica and others* [2007] ECR I-1891, and Case C-64/08, *Engelmann* [2010] ECR I-8219.

experience of the applicants.[96] This allocation criterion of professional experience, however, did not have to be justified before the CJEU. Instead, the CJEU merely evaluated three specific allocation rules that were used to score the professional experience of applicants into points: (i) professional experience was not taken into consideration if this experience has previously been used to obtain a licence to set up a pharmacy, (ii), in case of a tie, priority was given to pharmacists who had never held a licence to operate a pharmacy, and (iii) again in case of a tie, priority was given to pharmacists who had held a licence to operate a pharmacy in pharmaceutical areas or towns with a population of fewer than 2800 inhabitants.

The CJEU classified these three allocation criteria[97] as restrictions applying *without* discrimination on grounds of nationality.[98] Such restrictions may be justified by overriding reasons relating to the general interest, provided that these restrictions are appropriate for securing attainment of the objective pursued and do not go beyond what is necessary for attaining that objective.[99] As the overriding reason relating to the general interest, the CJEU identified the protection of public health and – more particularly – the objective of ensuring that the provision of medicinal products to the public is reliable and of good quality.[100] By doing so, the Court translated a general legitimate objective ('public health') into a more concrete 'allocation objective' (territorial distribution of pharmacies). Next, when evaluating the justification of the maximum number of licences available, the CJEU concluded that these three allocation criteria contributed to the attainment of the allocation objective of territorial distribution. On the one hand, rule (iii) encourages pharmacists to set up in those areas, with a view to being rewarded later, when licences are again granted for the opening of new pharmacies.[101] On the other hand, rules (i) and (ii) favour pharmacists who have never held a licence to operate a pharmacy, thereby ensuring that *more* pharmacists have access to independent professional activity and preventing that pharmacists already established on the market would benefit from disproportionate advantages.[102]

Hence, the CJEU considered the justification of the allocation criteria *as part of* the justification of the maximum number of authorisations. In particular, the allocation criteria were evaluated in the light of the *suitability* of this limitation. However, the opinion of Advocate General Poiares Maduro shows that the exact *boundaries* of this suitability test are unclear, since it put into doubt two elements of the authorisation system which the Court did not consider explicitly. First, according to the Advocate

96 Joined Cases C-570/07 and C-571/07, *Blanco Pérez and Chao Gómez* [2010] ECR I-4629, para. 17.

97 In fact, the first rule is a 'scoring rule' with regard to the allocation criterion of 'professional experience' rather than an allocation criterion itself.

98 Joined Cases C-570/07 and C-571/07, *Blanco Pérez and Chao Gómez* [2010] ECR I-4629, paras. 116 jo. 62.

99 Joined Cases C-570/07 and C-571/07, *Blanco Pérez and Chao Gómez* [2010] ECR I-4629, para. 61.

100 Joined Cases C-570/07 and C-571/07, *Blanco Pérez and Chao Gómez* [2010] ECR I-4629, paras. 63 en 64.

101 Joined Cases C-570/07 and C-571/07, *Blanco Pérez and Chao Gómez* [2010] ECR I-4629, paras. 86 and 87.

102 Joined Cases C-570/07 and C-571/07, *Blanco Pérez and Chao Gómez* [2010] ECR I-4629, paras. 92 and 93.

General, the authorisation system should have to benefit those who open pharmacies in underserved areas over those who simply wait for an opening in a lucrative area, whereas, in case of a tie, higher priority is given to unaccredited pharmacists than to those accredited to operate in zones with populations under 2 800 inhabitants. Moreover, once a pharmacist opens a pharmacy in an underserved area, he loses the benefit of his prior professional experience when attempting to open another pharmacy. Although the impacts of these provisions are mitigated somewhat by the provision giving more points for practice in an underserved area, they still raise concerns as to the coherence and consistency of the provision.[103] Thus, the Advocate General concluded that the design of the allocation procedure was inconsistent with the objectives of the limited authorisation scheme. Secondly, again according to the Advocate General, authorisations in well-populated areas should be available to those who have practised in under-populated areas when the holders of the more lucrative authorisations for well-populated areas wish to cease to operate their pharmacies. The current system, however, permits holders of authorisations for pharmacies to *transfer* these authorisations to the person of their choice, thereby limiting the number of authorisations available to those who have 'served their time' in under-populated areas.[104] The possibility to transfer authorisations therefore undermined the coherence and consistency of the authorisation scheme as well, according to the Advocate General. The CJEU, however, did not take into account these elements when considering the consistency and coherence as part of the suitability of the authorisation system.

This *Blanco Pérez and Chao Gómez* judgment shows that the CJEU is prepared to evaluate (non-discriminatory) allocation criteria as part of the evaluation of the limitation to the number of available authorisations. In particular, it turns out to be insufficient for allocation criteria not to impede the attainment of the objectives justifying the limitation of the number of available authorizations. Instead, they should even contribute to the attainment of these 'limitation' objectives. Hence, although the CJEU seems to adopt no strict preference for a certain allocation procedure, the chosen allocation criteria should at least be *consistent with* the objectives underlying a limitation to the number of authorisations and should even *contribute to* the attainment of this objective. Since this 'objective-oriented approach' does not concern the allocation objectives as such, but the objectives justifying the limitation of authorisations, the CJEU can be said to have adopted a 'maximum oriented approach'.

In *Bressol*, the Court seemed to adopt a similar maximum oriented approach. This case dealt with access to higher education within the French Community of Belgium. Since the economic freedoms of service provision and establishment do not apply to these education activities, the registration system at issue was evaluated under Article 18 TFEU and Article 21 TFEU, ensuring the right for each EU citizen to move and reside

[103] See para. 32 of the conclusion of advocate general Poiares Maduro delivered on 30 September 2009 in Joined Cases C-570/07 and C-571/07, *Blanco Pérez and Chao Gómez*.

[104] See para. 33 of the conclusion of advocate general Poiares Maduro delivered on 30 September 2009 in Joined Cases C-570/07 and C-571/07, *Blanco Pérez and Chao Gómez*.

freely within the territory of EU Member States. Whereas resident students, *i.e.* students who have their principal residence in Belgium,[105] enjoyed access to (para)medical courses without any restriction to the number of students to be registered, non-resident students were confronted with restricted access to these courses: the total number of non-resident students was limited to 30% of all registrations in the preceding academic year. Once that percentage had been reached, the non-resident students were selected by drawing lots.[106]

In response to the question whether this registration system constituted indirect discrimination on grounds of nationality, the CJEU emphasized that Member States are free to choose for an education system based on free access – without restriction on the number of students to be registered – or on limited access. In both cases, nonetheless, the rules of the chosen system should comply with the principle of non-discrimination on grounds of nationality.[107] Since the residence condition is more easily satisfied by Belgian nationals than by nationals of other Member States, whose residence is generally in a Member State other than Belgium,[108] the difference in treatment between resident and non-resident students amounted to indirect discrimination on the ground of nationality which is prohibited, unless objectively justified.[109] With regard to the justification of the measure at stake, the CJEU accepted that a difference in treatment based indirectly on nationality may be justified by the (allocation) objective of maintaining a *balanced high-quality medical service open to all citizens*, in so far as it contributes to achieving a high level of protection of health.[110] Even then, however, this difference in treatment should comply with the requirements of suitability and necessity as well.[111] Most important for the purposes of this chapter is the Court's reflection on the allocation procedure to be applied: since non-resident students who are interested in higher education are selected by *drawing lots* which, as such, does not take into account their knowledge or experience, it should be ascertained whether the selection process for non-resident students by the drawing of lots – based not on the aptitude of the candidates concerned but on chance – is *necessary* to attain the objective of maintaining a balanced high-quality medical service open to all citizens.[112]

105 Case C-73/08, *Bressol and others* [2010] ECR I-2735, para. 9.
106 Case C-73/08, *Bressol and others* [2010] ECR I-2735, para. 43.
107 Case C-73/08, *Bressol and others* [2010] ECR I-2735, para. 29.
108 Case C-73/08, *Bressol and others* [2010] ECR I-2735, para. 45.
109 Case C-73/08, *Bressol and others* [2010] ECR I-2735, para. 47.
110 Case C-73/08, *Bressol and others* [2010] ECR I-2735, para. 62.
111 Case C-73/08, *Bressol and others* [2010] ECR I-2735, paras. 66–78.
112 Case C-73/08, *Bressol and others* [2010] ECR I-2735, paras. 80 and 81. The referring constitutional court of Belgium assessed in the end that the original system of 'first come, first served' was unsuitable because of implementation difficulties. A comparative assessment on the basis of a diploma involved difficulties as well because of the comparison between diplomas of different education systems. Similarly, a comparative entry examination would require considerable human and financial efforts. Therefore, the lottery caused least dispute by providing every non-residing student equal treatment (chances). Consequently, the constitutional court of Belgium considered the lottery necessary to attain the objectives pursued.

This consideration seems to suggest that, at least according to the CJEU, a selection procedure based on the aptitude of the candidates, like a diploma comparison or an entry examination, is less restrictive from the perspective of the freedom of movement than an allocation procedure that is not based on the aptitude of the candidates, like a lottery. However, it would go too far to derive from this *Bressol* judgment a *general* preference for a procedure of qualitative or competitive selection instead of a lottery. Actually, the CJEU seems to point out the need to take into account the aptitude of the candidates, just because of the *specific* objective underlying the limitation of the number of non-resident students, being the maintenance of a balanced high-quality medical service open to all citizens. In order to maintain this 'high quality' medical service, priority should be given to a selection procedure based on the aptitude of the candidates, since these qualified candidates might contribute better to the attainment of the limitation objective of medical service of high quality. Hence, the CJEU is willing to accept a difference in treatment between resident and non-resident students, provided that the allocation procedure for non-resident students contributes to the attainment of this 'limitation objective'.

Thus, in both *Blanco Pérez and Chao Gómez* and *Bressol*, the evaluation of the allocation procedure is *part* of the evaluation of the limitation. In particular, the allocation criteria are considered in the light of the suitability and necessity of this limitation. In fact this 'maximum oriented' approach reflects a consistency requirement: *if* a maximum can be justified by a legitimate objective, then the corresponding allocation criteria should contribute to the attainment of this objective as far as possible. If not, another allocation procedure could be said to be less restrictive from the perspective of the fundamental freedoms. To some extent, this maximum oriented approach seems to be at odds with the approach adopted in *Engelmann*, in which the CJEU held that each restriction must be examined *in turn* in order to determine in particular whether the restriction is suitable for achieving the objective or objectives invoked by the Member State concerned and whether it goes beyond what is necessary in order to achieve those objectives.[113] However, since limitation and allocation cannot be isolated from each other (cf. Section 2), the requirement of consistency and coherence requires to take into account the limitation and the allocation objectives together.

5.2. *Competition Law*

5.2.1. Exclusive and special rights

The competition law provisions of the TFEU might be relevant as well for the allocation criteria that Member States may adopt. According to Article 106(1) TFEU, Member States shall neither enact nor maintain in force any measure contrary to the rules contained in the Treaties – in particular to those rules provided for in Article 18 (prohibition of discrimination on grounds of nationality) and Articles 101 to 109 – in the

[113] Case C-64/08, *Engelmann* [2010] ECR I-8219, para. 43.

case of public undertakings or undertakings to which Member States grant *special or exclusive rights*. The TFEU does not contain a general definition of 'special or exclusive rights'. However, this notion has been defined several times in secondary legislation. Since the aim of these definitions in secondary legislation has always been to limit the scope of this legislation, these definitions have not always been identical ever since.

A useful definition of exclusive and special rights can be found in the recent Concessions Directive. On the one hand, an *exclusive* right is defined as a 'right granted by a competent authority of a Member State by means of any law, regulation or published administrative provision which is compatible with the Treaties the effect of which is to limit the exercise of an activity to a single economic operator and which substantially affects the ability of other economic operators to carry out such an activity'.[114] On the other hand, a *special* right is defined as a 'right granted by a competent authority of a Member State by means of any law, regulation or published administrative provision which is compatible with the Treaties the effect of which is to limit the exercise of an activity to two or more economic operators and which substantially affects the ability of other economic operators to carry out such an activity'.[115] Unlike definitions in previous directives, these definitions in the Concessions Directive do not pay attention to the procedure of allocation.[116] Although all these definitions of exclusive or special rights in secondary legislation may provide guidance for the interpretation of Article 106(1) TFEU,[117] these definitions may never exceed the limits inherent to Article 106(1) TFEU.[118] Therefore, it seems safe to consider 'exclusive or special rights' broadly as rights that are granted to a *limited* number of undertakings. Consequently, 'limited authorisation schemes', either limited to 'one' or to 'two or more', may come within the scope of Article 106(1) TFEU.

5.2.2. Allocation criteria

Now we arrive at the question whether EU competition law prefers the application of certain allocation procedures when awarding limited authorisations. First of all, it should be recalled that Article 106(1) TFEU should be applied in conjunction with another Treaty provision. For this analysis, 102 TFEU seems most relevant,[119] according to which any abuse by one or more undertakings of a dominant position within the internal market is prohibited.

114 Article 5(10) Concessions Directive.

115 Article 5(11) Concessions Directive.

116 See for example Articles 2(f) and 2(g) Commission Directive 2006/111/EC of 16 November 2006 on the transparency of financial relations between Member States and public undertakings as well as on financial transparency within certain undertakings [2006] OJ L 318/17: if two or more rights have been granted according to objective, proportional and non-discriminatory criteria, then these rights are not considered special rights within the scope of this directive.

117 B.J. Drijber and H.M. Stergiou, 'Public procurement law and internal market law' (2009) 46 *Common Market Law Review* 805, 822–823.

118 Szydlo 2011, p. 1413–1414.

119 For the conjunction of Article 106(1) TFEU with the prohibition of discrimination on grounds of nationality (Article 18 TFEU) and the resulting fundamental freedom of movement, see section 5.2.

Whereas not every grant of an exclusive or special right will automatically result in a dominant position, even the mere creation of a dominant position through the grant of special or exclusive rights is not in itself incompatible with Articles 106 jo. 102 TFEU. A Member State will be in breach of the prohibitions laid down by those provisions only (i) if the undertaking in question, merely by exercising the special or exclusive rights conferred upon it, is led to abuse its dominant position or (ii) where such rights are liable to create a situation in which that undertaking is led to commit such abuses.[120] Although such a situation of abuse of a dominant position might be expected in particular if exclusive or special rights are not being granted according to objective, proportional and non-discriminatory allocation criteria, this does not mean that the grant of exclusive or special rights according to objective, proportional and non-discriminatory criteria, will never lead to abuse of a dominant position. Thus, it is impossible to conclude in advance that the application of certain allocation criteria or procedures will always result in abuse of a dominant position, whereas other allocation criteria will never do so.

Instead, competition law stresses 'equality of opportunity' in the award of limited authorisations, irrespective of the chosen allocation procedure. According to the CJEU in *Connect Austria*, a national measure is not contrary to Articles 102 and 106(1) TFEU if, taking into account the fees imposed on the different operators involved for their respective licences, the allocation of additional frequencies, without the imposition of a separate fee, to an undertaking with an exclusive or special right in a dominant position must be considered to comply with the requirement to ensure *equality of opportunity* for different economic operators and therefore to guarantee undistorted competition. If the fee imposed on this undertaking in a dominant position for its original licence, including subsequent allocations of additional frequencies without additional payment, appears to be *equivalent in economic terms* to the fee imposed on the new competitor which was granted a licence, national legislation must be deemed to ensure equality of opportunity for different economic operators and therefore guarantee undistorted competition.[121] Thus, the CJEU puts forward the concept of 'economic equivalence' between competitors, which seems to be a more practical test in case of limited authorisation schemes than the general test of distortion of competition.

To conclude, competition law has no preference for the application of a certain allocation procedure, provided that 'equality of opportunity' is guaranteed. Therefore, as long as the imposed payments are equivalent in economic terms, there can be no abuse of a dominant position merely because of the grant of special or exclusive rights. This has two important consequences. First, equivalence between operators can exist both when authorisations are being awarded by means of an auction and when authorisations are being awarded free of charge. Secondly, equality of opportunity prevents public authorities from merely focusing on the allocation at stake: once a certain allocation

120 See e.g. Case C-475/99, *Ambulanz Glöckner* [2001] ECR I-8089, para. 39; Case C-462/99, *Connect Austria* [2003] ECR I-5197, para. 80; Case C-380/05, *Centro Europa* 7 [2008] ECR I-349, para. 60.

121 Case C-462/99, *Connect Austria* [2003] ECR I-5197, paras. 89–90.

procedure has been applied, there may be good reason to apply this procedure in future allocations as well in order to ensure equality of opportunity.

5.3. *State Aid Law*

Finally, the existence of a preference for certain allocation procedures can be examined from the point of view of State aid.[122] According to settled case-law, for a measure to be categorised as State aid, each of the four cumulative conditions laid down in Article 107 TFEU must be fulfilled: (i) there must be an intervention by the State or through State resources, (ii) the intervention must be liable to affect trade between Member States, (iii) the intervention must confer an advantage on the recipient, and (iv) the intervention must distort or threaten to distort competition.[123] A measure which, although conferring an advantage on its recipient, is justified by 'the nature or general scheme of the system' of which it is part, does not fulfill the third condition of selectivity.[124]

For the purposes of this chapter, the Court's case-law with regard to the first and third requirement is most relevant. First, with regard to an intervention of State resources, the preliminary point is whether the limited authorisations at issue represent market value. The underlying argument seems to be that in the absence of such economic value, the State does not waive revenues when it awards these limited authorisations free of charge or at least below market value. For example, in *Bougyues Télécom*, the issue was whether a reduction of fees for UMTS frequencies to be paid after a procedure of comparative selection by two 'incumbents' up to the level of the fee to be paid by a new entrant, amounted to State aid, since these two incumbents could have profited from a time advantage because of the earlier grant of their authorisations.[125] The Court of First Instance explicitly put forward that these UMTS licences had an economic value: the exercise of State functions (official authority) by granting licences did not preclude the State – in her capacity of a manager of public assets – from taking into account economic facts in connection with the management of a scarce public resource.[126] Therefore, by reducing the fees to be paid by the incumbents, the national authorities may have waived their right to a significant part of State resources.[127] In another judgment, dealing with the Dutch scheme of NO_x emission allowances, the Court of First Instance noted that these emission allowances represented economic value and conferred an advantage to the holder thereof, because they were tradable: in the absence of the possibility to trade

122 Into more detail, see the chapter by Adriaanse in this book.

123 Case C-169/08, *Presidente del Consiglio dei Ministri* [2009] ECR I-10821, para. 52; Case C-237/04 *Enirisorse* [2006] ECR I-2843, paras. 38 and 39.

124 Case C-143/99, *Adria-Wien Pipeline* [2001] ECR I-8365, para. 42.

125 Into more detail on this case, see the chapter by Adriaanse.

126 Case T-475/04, *Bouygues Télécom* [2007] ECR II-2097, para. 101.

127 Case T-475/04, *Bouygues Télécom* [2007] ECR II-2097, paras. 106 and 107. Since only the Commission's finding of absence of a selective advantage had been disputed by the new entrant, the judgment did not deal explicitly with the requirement of a transfer of State resources.

those allowances, they would be worthless on the market.[128] Next, the Court of First Instance considered that the State had in principle a choice between allocating NO_x emission allowances free of charge or selling or auctioning them.[129] Consequently, whenever these allowances are put at the disposal of the undertakings free of charge, *whereas they could have been sold or put up for auction*, the State has foregone State resources.[130] Thus, whereas State aid seems to be neutral as to the choice of the allocation procedure, the chosen allocation procedure may have important consequences for the applicability of the State aid regime: under some market-oriented allocation procedures, like an auction, there may be no transfer of State resources.[131]

Even if an allocation procedure involves a transfer of State resources, there still needs to exist a selective advantage in order to qualify as State aid. In this respect, the argument that limited authorisations would confer a selective advantage to their recipients merely because of the application of an allocation (selection) procedure, is insufficient. In fact, this requirement of the existence of a selective advantage seems to be neutral as to the chosen allocation procedure, as long as the operators involved are treated equally. For example, in *Bouygues Télécom*, the Court of First Instance noted that the community framework for telecommunications services rests on *equality of treatment* between operators for the award of licences and leaves the Member States *free to choose* the procedure for the award of licences, provided that the principles of freedom of competition and equality of treatment are respected. Hence, while the Member States may use auctions, they may *equally opt* for a comparative selection procedure, the essential point being that the operators are accorded the same treatment, in particular as regards fees.[132] Thus, although the UMTS licences had an economic value, the amount payable as a fee *could constitute State aid only if*, all other things being equal, there was a difference

128 Case T-233/04, *Commission v. Netherlands* [2008] ECR II-591, paras. 70–72, and Case C-279/08 P *Commission v. Netherlands* [2011] ECR I-7671, paras. 88 and 106.

129 Case T-233/04, *Commission v. Netherlands* [2008] ECR II-591, para. 75. See also Case C-279/08 P, *Commission v. Netherlands* [2011] ECR I-7671 paras. 106–107 and 111, and point 87 of the opinion of advocate general Mengozzi delivered on 22 December 2010 in Case C-279/08 P, stating that Member States are free in the choice of their allocation system, hence an allocation free of charge, by sale or by auction. However, this freedom does not exclude the possibility of State aid elements in the chosen system.

130 Case T-233/04, *Commission v. Netherlands* [2008] ECR II-591, para. 75. See also Case C-518/13, *Eventech* ECLI:EU:C:2015:9, para. 44, in which the Court concluded that the public authorities were *not*, under the bus lanes policy including preferential access to these lanes for some taxi undertakings, foregoing revenue which they would have received in the absence of that policy.

131 In this respect, it is interesting to note that the Commission assumes in its Communication on State aid elements in sales of land and buildings by public authorities [1997] OJ C209/3, that a sale of land and buildings following a sufficiently well-publicized, open and unconditional bidding procedure, comparable to an auction, accepting the best or only bid is *by definition* at market value and consequently does not contain State aid. Alternatively, an independent evaluation should be carried out by one or more independent asset valuers prior to the sale negotiations in order to establish the market value on the basis of generally accepted market indicators and valuation standards. The market price thus established is the minimum purchase price that can be agreed without granting State aid.

132 Case T-475/04, *Bouygues Télécom* [2007] ECR II-2097, paras. 108 and 109, with reference to Case C-462/99, *Connect Austria* [2003] ECR I-5197, paras. 92 and 93 (section 5.2).

between the price paid by each of the operators concerned (and therefore selective advantage for some operator). By contrast, if the national authorities decide as a general principle that licences will be awarded (i) free of charge, (ii) by means of public auctions or (iii) at a standard price, *there is no aid element, provided* these terms are applied to all the operators concerned without distinction.[133] Consequently, the mere fact that the State may have waived resources and that this may have created an advantage for the beneficiaries of the fee reduction, is not sufficient to prove the existence of State aid incompatible with the common market, given the specific provisions of Community law on telecommunications. In this respect, it is worth emphasizing that the Court of First Instance concluded that the abandonment of the claim at issue here was inevitable 'because of the general scheme of the system': this abandonment was the only way both to prevent a late launch of UMTS services (in breach of the deadline established by the community framework for telecommunications) *and* to ensure the operators to be treated without discrimination.[134] Thus, the Court of First Instance combined the general objective of non-discrimination with the additional regulatory objective of a quick release of UMTS services. This approach has been followed by the Commission in its recent draft Commission Notice on the notion of State aid: when the State acts as a *regulator*, it can decide legitimately not to maximise the revenues which could otherwise have been achieved, without falling under the scope of State aid rules, provided that all the operators concerned are treated equally, and that there is an inherent link between achieving the regulatory purpose and the foregoing of revenue.[135]

Thus, the prohibition of State aid may be relevant for the evaluation of allocation criteria in different ways. However, first of all, it should be assessed, *independent from* the allocation procedure at stake, whether the limited authorisations have economic value: only then the award of these authorisations free of charge may be classified as a transfer of State resources. Case-law shows that this economic value can be derived from the object of the authorisation, e.g. the use of a scarce public resource, or from its tradability. Because of this case-law, it is not clear whether *every* limited authorisation awarded free of charge, *e.g.* a non-tradable authorisation not concerned with the use of a scarce public resource (like the establishment of a pharmacy), will classify as a State resource. State aid law seems to be neutral as to the chosen allocation procedures: where some allocation procedures do not result in the transfer of State resources, a selective advantage does only exist, irrespective of the allocation procedure at stake, if there is a difference in the treatment of the operators concerned which cannot be justified by the nature or general scheme of the system.

133 Case T-475/04, *Bouygues Télécom* [2007] ECR II-2097, para. 110. See also Case C-431/07 P, *Bouygues Télécom* [2009] ECR I-2665, paras. 90 and 91.

134 Case T-475/04, *Bouygues Télécom* [2007] ECR II-2097, para. 111. This judgment of the Court of First Instance was confirmed by the European Court of Justice in Case C-431/07 P, *Bouygues Télécom* [2009] ECR I-2665, paras. 93–96.

135 See the 2014 draft Commission Notice on the notion of State aid pursuant to Article 107(1) TFEU, pp. 15–16.

6. Concluding Remarks

The central question in this chapter is whether EU law contains any preferences as to the choice of allocation procedures or – conversely – whether EU law is neutral with regard to this choice. Such preferences might imply that some allocation procedures can never be applied under EU law or – in a more mitigated form – that some allocation procedures can be applied only if the application of other allocation procedures is considered inappropriate.

The baseline requirement any allocation procedure should meet, is that the allocation criteria should be objective, non-discriminatory and made known in advance to the undertakings concerned. In particular, in order to meet this latter requirement, the allocation criteria should be sufficiently advertised. It has been argued that both the requirement of objectivity and the requirement of non-discrimination do not have an absolute character, but allow for some deviation and relaxation: where objectivity might result in a (too) rigid application of allocation criteria, there might be an objective justification for discriminatory allocation criteria, provided that these criteria satisfy the requirements of suitability and necessity as well. Thus, although these baseline requirements seem to provide only little guidance as to the contents of allocation criteria, they may exclude the application of certain allocation procedures in specific circumstances, e.g. if allocation on a 'first come first served' basis would put foreign undertakings at a disadvantage.

Various secondary EU legislation shows that the primary objective of non-discrimination on grounds of nationality, which is the cornerstone of the fundamental freedoms, is often accompanied by an additional regulatory objective, like efficient use of resources. This additional objective explains why the EU legislator has sometimes made more detailed choices with regard to the design of allocation procedures. More than once, secondary legislation indicates that there should be a connection between the chosen allocation criterion and the regulatory objectives, including not only the allocation objectives but also the objectives underlying the limitation to the number of authorisations and the authorisation system as such. At the same time, secondary legislation turns out to be concerned about a (too) general fixation of allocation procedures that need to be applied in a particular case.

From a more general perspective, internal market law (in particular the freedoms of establishment and service provision) seems to be more demanding with regard to the justification of a chosen allocation procedure than competition law or state aid law. First of all, the need to justify allocation criteria by overriding reasons relating to the public interest, excludes any justification on purely economic or administrative grounds. Next, with regard to the suitability of the allocation procedure, the CJEU seems to require that the choice of the allocation criteria is not only consistent with the 'allocation objective', but should even contribute to the attainment of the 'limitation objective' underlying the limitation of the number of rights. Finally, with regard to the necessity of the allocation procedure, it turns out that an allocation procedure which does not take into account the characteristics of the applicants (e.g. a lottery) might go beyond what is necessary to attain the legitimate regulatory objectives if these objectives can be attained by means of a comparative selection procedure as well. Besides, the requirement of necessity seems to prevent a too general and abstract fixing of the allocation procedure to be applied, since such a general fixing (instead of a tailor-made choice) might be even more restrictive of the fundamental freedoms.

Competition law, however, adds an interesting perspective to the legal framework as provided for by the fundamental freedoms. Instead of prescribing certain allocation procedures to be applied, competition law requires some kind of 'temporal' coherence or consistency in the choice of allocation procedures: equality of opportunity for all competitors in a certain sector needs to be ensured. This competition law perspective of 'temporal consistency of allocation procedures' might conflict sometimes with the internal market perspective, emphasizing the need to fine-tune the choice of the allocation procedure in a particular case in order to avoid restrictions to fundamental freedoms as far as possible.

State aid law shows a similar neutral position as to the choice of allocation procedures: irrespective whether limited authorisations are awarded free of charge, by means of auctions or at a standard price (in a procedure of comparative selection), this award does not amount to State aid, provided that these terms are applied to all the operators concerned without distinction. However, under some allocation procedures, a transfer of State resources is lacking, whereas under other allocation procedures, the absence of a selective advantage needs to be ensured in order to avoid State aid. Moreover, State aid law makes clear that additional elements of the limited authorisation scheme, e.g. the tradability of the authorisations, should be taken into account as well when evaluating allocation procedures, whereas these elements are still sometimes absent in the analysis of the suitability (consistency and coherence) of allocation procedures under the fundamental freedoms.

In general, although EU law does not contain general preferences prescribing or precluding certain allocation procedures and is even reluctant to establish such preferences, EU law is gradually developing some general indicators and tools guiding a legitimate choice of allocation procedures. In particular, it can be observed that the CJEU has started to translate general requirements like 'suitability', 'necessity', 'distortion of competition' and 'selective advantage', into more concrete 'allocation requirements' which bridge the gap between general legal principles and the allocation of limited authorisations. As this translation process is still far from complete, further steps of the CJEU are to be welcomed.

Paul Adriaanse*

CHAPTER 9. THE INFLUENCE OF EU STATE AID LAW ON THE ALLOCATION OF LIMITED RIGHTS BY NATIONAL AUTHORITIES

1. Introduction

When allocating and granting limited rights, national authorities within the EU Member States should be aware of the possible influence of EU State aid law. The same applies to the national legislatures, when creating the underlying schemes for such limited rights. In fields in which regulation at EU level exists, e.g. in the field of CO_2 emissions, the role of EU State aid law may be mentioned explicitly and clarified in the applicable EU legislation or guidelines.[1] However, also by lack of such explicit reference in secondary EU regulation or soft law documents, the EU State aid rules, as laid down in the Treaty on the Functioning of the European Union (hereinafter: TFEU), may be applicable when dealing with limited authorisations or claims within the scope of this book, for example in the field of the allocation of limited gambling licences. According to consistent case law of the European Court of Justice the concept of State aid embraces all measures 'which, in various forms, mitigate the charges which are normally included in the budget of an undertaking and which, therefore, without being subsidies in the strict sense of the word, are similar in character and have the same effect (…).'[2] Although the concept of State aid is interpreted and applied broadly, little literature exists on the application of EU State aid rules to the allocation of limited rights by administrative authorities.

The aim of this chapter, therefore, is twofold. First, to explore to what extent the EU State aid law requirements could influence the allocation of limited rights by national

* Paul Adriaanse is Associate Professor of constitutional and administrative law at Leiden University and practising lawyer at Justion Advocaten, the Netherlands.

1 E.g. paragraph 49 of the preamble of Directive 2009/29/EC of the European Parliament and the Council of 23 April 2009 amending Directive 2003/87/EC so as to improve and extend the greenhouse gas emission allowance trading scheme of the Community [2009] OJ L140/63: 'The application of this Directive is without prejudice to Articles 87 [now 107] and 88 [now 108] of the Treaty.' See also the Communication from the Commission – Guidelines on certain State aid measures in the context of the greenhouse gas emission allowance trading scheme post-2012 [2012] OJ C158/4.

2 See Case C-73/11 P, *Frucona Košice a.s v. Commission* ECLI:EU:C:2013:32, para. 69.

authorities or the legislature (hereinafter generally referred to as: the allocation of limited rights). The second aim of this chapter is to contribute to the central question of this book. Based on the explorative analysis of the role of EU State aid law with regard to the allocation of limited rights, an answer is sought to the question what could be learned from EU State aid law with a view to the development of a consistent and general legal theory of the allocation of limited rights by national authorities. To do so, Section 2 first deals with the conditions which should be met in order to qualify a specific measure as State aid in the sense of the TFEU. Only if a measure can be qualified as State aid, according to these conditions, will the EU State aid rules be applicable. In Section 3 these conditions will be applied to various examples of limited rights, based on an analysis of leading case law from the European Courts and given the Commission's policy. The necessity for this extensive case-based analysis follows from the lack of literature on this theme, as mentioned above. Section 4 further describes the consequences in terms of procedural aspects and the compatibility assessment which should be taken into account, given the possible applicability of EU State aid rules when dealing with limited rights. Conclusions will follow in Section 5, given the twofold aim of this contribution.

2. The Concept of State Aid in the Sense of Article 107(1) TFEU

The EU State aid rules only apply if a measure qualifies as State aid in the sense of Article 107(1) TFEU. According to consistent case law of the European Courts this is the case if the measures cumulatively satisfy four conditions. First, there must be an intervention by the State or through State resources. Secondly, the measure must confer a selective advantage on the recipient (being an undertaking or a production). Thirdly, the intervention must be liable to affect trade between Member States and fourthly, it must distort or threaten to distort competition.[3] These four conditions will be further explained below, only as far as necessary for a better understanding of the concept of State aid within this chapter. The purpose of this explanation is not to give a detailed overview here of the relevant case law on the concept of State aid.

The concept of State aid is according to the Court of Justice a legal concept which must be interpreted on the basis of objective factors.[4] In order to qualify a measure as State aid in the sense of Article 107(1) TFEU, only the effects of the measure will be relevant, not the name, its causes or its aims.[5]

As regards the first condition of the concept of State aid, two subconditions have in fact to be met. First, the advantage must be granted directly or indirectly through State resources and, secondly, it must be attributable to the State.[6] Relating to the

3 See Case C-690/13, *Trapeza Eurobank Ergasias AE v. Agrotiki Trapeza tis Ellados AE (ATE), Pavlos Sidiropoulos*, n.y.r., para. 17.

4 See e.g. Case C-83/98 P, *France v. Ladbroke Racing and Commission* ECLI:EU:C:2000:248, para 25.

5 See e.g. Case C-159/01, *Netherlands v. Commission* ECLI:EU:C:2004:246, para. 51.

6 Case C-262/12, *Vent De Colère e.a.* ECLI:EU:C:2013:851, para. 16.

commitment of State resources, the Court recalled in the *Eventech* case (to be discussed further in Section 3.5) 'that the concept of aid embraces not only positive benefits, such as subsidies, but also measures which, in various forms, mitigate the charges which are normally included in the budget of an undertaking and which, therefore, without being subsidies in the strict sense of the word, are similar in character and have the same effect.'[7] According to consistent case law, it is necessary to establish a sufficiently direct link between, on the one hand, the advantage given to the beneficiary and, on the other, a reduction of the State budget or a sufficiently concrete economic risk of burdens on that budget.[8] The Court has further made clear in the *Bouygues* case (to be discussed further in Section 3.2) that 'it is not necessary that such a reduction, or even such a risk, should correspond or be equivalent to that advantage, or that the advantage has as its counterpoint such a reduction or such a risk, or that it is of the same nature as the commitment of State resources from which it derives.'[9]

As regards the second condition of the concept of State aid, it follows from consistent case law that an advantage exists if the recipient undertaking, in circumstances which correspond to normal market conditions, could not obtain the same advantage as that which has been made available to it through State resources.[10] The advantage will be selective, if it is such as to favour certain undertakings or the production of certain goods 'in relation to other undertakings which, in light of the objective of the measure at issue, are in a comparable factual and legal situation'.[11]

As regards the third and the fourth condition of the concept of State aid, relating to an effect on trade between Member States and on competition, the Court recalled in the case *Ministerio de Defensa and Navantia SA v. Concello de Ferrol* that 'for the purposes of categorising a national measure as State aid, it is necessary, not to establish that the aid has a real effect on trade between Member States and that competition is actually being distorted, but only to determine whether that aid is liable to affect such trade and to distort competition.'[12] According to consistent case law, competitors must be regarded as affected by aid, if the aid granted by a Member State strengthens the position of the recipient undertaking as compared with that of other undertakings competing in intra-Community trade.[13]

7 Case C-518/13 *Eventech Ltd v. Parking Adjudicator* ECLI:EU:C:2015:9, para. 33.
8 Ibid. para. 34.
9 Joined Cases C-399/10 P and C-401/10 P, *Bouygues SA and Bouygues Télécom SA v. Commission* ECLI:EU:C:2013:175, para. 110.
10 Case C-124/10 P, *EDF* ECLI:EU:C:2012:318, para. 78.
11 Case C-672/13, *OTP Bank v. Magyar Állam*, n.y.r., para. 45.
12 Case C-522/13, *Ministerio de Defensa, Navantia SA v. Concello de Ferrol* ECLI:EU:C:2014:2262, para. 51.
13 Ibid. para. 22.

3. The Application of the Concept of State Aid in Cases Concerning the Allocation of Limited Rights

3.1. General

Given the broad interpretation of the four conditions of the concept of State aid in the sense of Article 107(1) TFEU, as explained above, various measures relating to the allocation of limited rights by national authorities may involve State aid. Most clearly this could be the case when the limited right itself consists of a claim towards national authorities for the payment of an amount of money, which is the case for subsidies. A State aid risk could also exist when in addition to a concession contract or the award of any exclusive or special rights to the undertaking to carry out a public service obligation public funding is granted to offset the costs involved in the performance of that obligation.[14] Apart from these scenarios in which at least the transfer of State resources will be assumed quite easily, the granting of limited or exclusive rights, such as licences, might also be subject to the State aid rules.

It will depend on the circumstances of the given case, if a concrete measure relating to the allocation of limited rights by national authorities includes State aid. It should be recalled in that respect that, according to consistent case law of the European Courts, Article 107(1) TFEU does not distinguish between measures of State intervention by reference to their causes or their aims, but defines them in terms of their effects.[15] In order to get a better understanding of the application of the concept of State aid to the allocation of limited rights by national authorities, four cases will first be discussed below where this relationship was disputed before the European Courts. These cases illustrate how the European Courts deal with this interesting, but also complex relationship. After this case law analysis, the actual approach taken by the Commission will be discussed.

3.2. Bouygues Télécom

In 2000 the French authorities organised a call for the award of four licences for the introduction of third generation mobile and wireless communication systems (UMTS, Universal Mobile Telecommunications System). The award of these limited authorisations would be accompanied by the obligation for the selected operators to pay a fee totalling EUR 4,954,593,000 payable over the lifetime of the licence, which was set at 15 years. Since only two applications had been received, a supplementary call for applications was organised, setting different conditions. Without waiting for the launch of the supplementary call for applications, two initial licences were issued in July 2001 to Orange and SFR. As a result of the supplementary call Bouygues Télécom also obtained

14 The issue of compensation for the performance of Services of General Economic Interest will not be dealt with further in this chapter.

15 Case C-522/13, *Ministerio de Defensa, Navantia SA v. Concello de Ferrol* ECLI:EU:C:2014:2262, para. 28.

a licence. At the same time, the French authorities decided to change the conditions for the fees payable by Orange and SFR for their UMTS licences, in order to act in accordance with the relevant secondary EU legislation, applicable at that time,[16] in particular the requirements of equality with respect to public contracts and of effective competition between operators when deciding the terms on which to grant the licences. As a result of this amendment, the three companies would have to pay the same, lower fees for their UMTS licences. However, Bouygues Télécom lodged a complaint with the Commission. It raised objections to the claim being waived by the State towards Orange and SFR.

The Commission came to the conclusion that Orange and SFR derived no advantage from the amendment in question. Bouygues Télécom contested the decision of the Commission. In the procedure before the General Court, they maintained first 'that the measure of which they complain entails a selective advantage, primarily temporal in nature and granted without consideration, as the French authorities waived their right to collect what for Orange and SFR was a normal expense, corresponding to the market value of the licences.'[17] Secondly, they argued 'that the amendment of the disputed fee could not be justified by the principle of non-discrimination, since on the contrary it discriminated against Bouygues Télécom.'[18]

It should be noted, that the question whether the waiving of a claim by the State, which aims to demonstrate the existence of a transfer of State resources within the meaning of Article 107(1) TFEU, was not explicitly dealt with in this case.[19] The Commission did not rule on this question, nor did the General Court, although the Court seems to assume that in such a case a transfer of State resources could be assumed.[20] The dispute merely focused on the question whether, by amending the fees payable by Orange and SFR for their UMTS licences, the French authorities granted these two operators an advantage that constituted State aid within the meaning of Article 107(1) TFEU.[21]

It is important to note that the Court started by recognising the economic value of the licences. It ruled: 'Similarly, UMTS licences, which authorise economic activities consisting in the provision of mobile telephony services in the wireless spectrum and are interpreted as conferring the right to occupy or use the corresponding public domain, have an economic value that the manager of that domain is bound to take into account when he determines the amount of fees to be paid by the operators involved.'[22]

16 Directive 97/13/EC of the European Parliament and of the Council of 10 April 1997 on a common framework for general authorisations and individual licences in the field of telecommunications services ([1997] OJ L117/15) and Decision No 128/1999/EC of the European Parliament and of the Council of 14 December 1998 on the coordinated introduction of a third generation mobile and wireless communications system (UMTS) in the Community ([1999] OJ L17/1).

17 Joined Cases T-425/04 et al, *France and Others v. Commission* ECLI:EU:T:2010:216, para. 85.

18 Ibid.

19 Ibid. para. 55.

20 Ibid. para. 106.

21 Ibid. para. 84. See also in appeal Case C-431/07 P, ECLI:EU:C:2009:223, para. 149.

22 Ibid. para. 101.

The Court considered further: 'Hence, the exercise of State functions does not preclude the taking into account of economic facts in connection with the management of a scarce public resource such as the radio frequencies constituting the public airwaves, to which a right of access or a right of usage may be granted. Hence, the Member States simultaneously perform the roles of telecommunications regulator and manager of the public assets that constitute the wireless airwaves.'[23]

However, this does not necessarily lead to the conclusion that the French authorities, by waiving their right to a significant part of State resources in the present case, resulted in the granting of State aid. The Court ruled that, 'even if, taking into account the economic value of the licences, it must be conceded to the applicants that the national authorities waived their right to a significant part of State resources in the present case, this conclusion must be tempered in the light of the claim in question and, moreover, this loss of resources does not necessarily constitute a State aid by reason of the nature and general scheme of the system.'[24]

The EU framework for telecommunications service, applicable at that time, rests on equality of treatment between operators for the award of licences and the calculation of any fees. It leaves the Member States free to choose the procedure for the award of licences, provided that the principles of freedom of competition and equality of treatment are respected. The Court considered that 'the Member States may use public auctions, they may equally opt for a comparative selection procedure, as in the present case, the essential point being that the operators see that they are accorded the same treatment, in particular as regards fees.'[25]

Hence, according to the Court, 'although the right to use the wireless space granted to the operators has an economic value, the amount payable as a fee can constitute State aid only if, all other things being equal, there is a difference between the price paid by each of the operators concerned, it being recalled that, according to the Court of Justice, it is the time when each of the operators concerned entered the market that must be taken into account (the Connect Austria judgment[26], paragraph 93). On the other hand, if the national authorities decide as a general principle that licences will be awarded free of charge, or awarded by means of public auctions or awarded at a standard price, there is no aid element, provided these terms are applied to all the operators concerned without distinction.'[27]

The Court then concluded: 'Consequently, the fact that the State may have waived resources and that this may have created an advantage for the beneficiaries of the

23 Ibid. para. 104.
24 Ibid. para. 106.
25 Ibid. para. 108.
26 Case C-462/99, *Connect Austria* ECLI:EU:C:2003:297.
27 General Court 21.05.2010, Joined Cases T-425/04 et al. *France and Others v. Commission* ECLI:EU:T:2010:216, para. 110.

reduction in the fee is not sufficient to prove the existence of a State aid incompatible with the common market, given the specific provisions of Community law on telecommunications in the light of common law on State aid. The abandonment of the claim at issue here was inevitable because of the general scheme of the system, apart from the fact that the claim was not certain, as noted in paragraph 107 above.'[28]

Furthermore, the Court ruled that the Commission had rightly found that Orange and SFR, had not, in practice, profited from the temporal advantage of having been awarded their licences before Bouygues Télécom. Consequently, the Commission was, according to the Court, able to consider that Orange and SFR did not in fact have a competitive advantage over Bouygues Télécom.[29]

The second argument raised by Bouygues Télécom, that the amendment of the disputed fee could not be justified by the principle of non-discrimination, since on the contrary it discriminated against Bouygues Télécom, was also dismissed. The Court came to the conclusion that the new system of fees did not discriminate against Bouygues Télécom. On the contrary, according to the Court, 'in the circumstances of the case, the requirement of Directive 97/13 to treat operators equally necessitated the alignment of the fees payable by Orange and SFR with those payable by Bouygues Télécom.'[30]

The judgment of the General Court was confirmed by the Court of Justice.[31] Nevertheless, it is interesting to quote one particular consideration of the Court of Justice with regard to the economic value of a licence and the related fee. The Court observed: 'In the present case, the fact that UMTS licences were awarded to Orange and SFR at an earlier date can justify, or even require, that the related fees be set higher than the fees charged to Bouygues Télécom only if the economic value of those licences could be regarded, by dint merely of having been awarded earlier, as being of greater value than the licence awarded to the latter undertaking.'[32]

3.3. *Commission v. The Netherlands (The Dutch NOx Emission Trading Scheme)*

The second case to be discussed concerns *Commission v. The Netherlands*. The case deals with the question whether a measure by the Dutch authorities, establishing an emission trading scheme for nitrogen oxides (NOx), constituted State aid in the sense of Article 107(1) TFEU. The Commission found that this was the case, while adding that the measure could be considered to be compatible with the internal market in accordance with Article 107(3) TFEU. The General Court, however, annulled the Commission's

28 Ibid. para. 111.
29 Ibid. para. 122.
30 Ibid. paras. 152–153.
31 Case C-431/07 P, *Bouygues SA and Bouygues Télécom SA v. Commission* ECLI:EU:C:2009:223, para. 103.
32 Ibid. para. 115.

decision, holding that the measure in question could not be classified as State aid.[33] A few years later, the Court of Justice came to the opposite conclusion, ruling that the Commission was right in its assessment that the Dutch measure resulted in State aid in the sense of Article 107(1) TFEU and set aside the judgment of the General Court.[34]

What was the measure about? In the framework of the NOx national emission ceiling for the Netherlands established by Directive 2001/81[35], the Dutch authorities set a target of 55 kilotons of NOx emissions for its large industrial facilities, approximately 250 undertakings, to be attained by 2010.[36] The measure concerned the award by the State of NOx credits free of charge as intangible assets to that specific group of undertakings. Other companies were also bound by the obligations regarding the limitation or reduction of those emissions, but could not participate in the trading system.

According to the Court of Justice, the Dutch measure concerned resulted in a loss of State resources and, therefore, meets the first requirement of the State aid concept in the sense of Article 107(1) TFEU. This was the case, since the Dutch authorities, by conferring on those emission allowances the character of tradable intangible assets and by making them available to the undertakings concerned free of charge instead of selling those allowances or putting them up for auction, forwent public resources.[37] Moreover, the Court of Justice held that the applicable system in the Netherlands offered a legal framework for limiting the discharge of NOx emissions in a profitable manner for undertakings with large facilities, which then have an alternative to the imposition of a fine by the State.[38] According to the Court of Justice, the foregoing of resources in this case cannot be considered as 'inherent' in any instrument designed to regulate emissions of atmospheric pollutants by an emission allowance trading scheme. The Court of Justice held: 'Where it has recourse to those instruments, the State has in principle a choice between allocating those allowances free of charge or selling or auctioning them.'[39]

The measure in this case, comprising the tradability of emission allowances, also met the second condition of the concept of State aid in the sense of Article 107(1) TFEU, which is the granting of an economic advantage which the recipient undertakings would not have obtained under normal market conditions. The Court of Justice considered that 'it must be held that the right of those undertakings to choose between the costs of acquiring the emission allowances and the costs linked to measures intended to reduce NOx emissions, constitutes an advantage for them. Also, the right, for the undertakings covered by the

33 Case T-233/04, *The Netherlands v. Commission* ECLI:EU:T:2008:102.
34 Case C-279/08, P *Commission v. the Netherlands* EU:C:2011:551.
35 Directive 2001/81/EC of the European Parliament and of the Council of 23 October 2001 on national emission ceilings for certain atmospheric pollutants [2001] OJ L309/22.
36 C-279/08 P *Commission v. the Netherlands* ECLI:EU:C:2011:551, para. 10.
37 Ibid. para. 107.
38 Ibid. para. 108.
39 Ibid. para. 111.

measure in question, to trade all the emission allowances and not only the credits resulting at the end of the year from the positive difference between the authorised emission and the emission obtained, constitutes an additional advantage for those undertakings. The latter can enjoy liquidity by selling the emission allowances before the conditions for their final allocation have arisen, irrespective of the fact that a ceiling is applicable to them, and the undertakings which exceed the emission norm laid down must compensate for that surplus the following year.'[40]

The Court of Justice also found the Dutch measure to be selective. The Court of Justice observed that every undertaking which produces NOx emissions through its operations must comply with obligations regarding the limitation or reduction of those emissions, whether or not it falls within the measure in question. However, the aforementioned advantages granted to the specific undertakings that could obtain NOx credits within the measure concerned were not available to other undertakings. Therefore, the Court of Justice ruled that the measure constituted a selective advantage in favour of the undertakings concerned compared to other undertakings in a comparable situation.[41]

The Court of Justice concluded its judgment by observing that the Commission's decision had been sufficiently reasoned with regard to how trade between Member States is affected and the distortion of competition.[42]

3.4. *Club Hotel Loutraki and Others v. Commission*

The third case to be discussed on the applicability of the State aid concept to the allocation of limited rights by the national authorities concerns *Club Hotel Loutraki and others v. Commission*.[43] The case deals with exclusive gambling licences that the Greek government had granted to a public company, called OPAP. The Greek authorities had taken two measures. The first measure consisted of a prolongation of OPAP's exclusive right to operate 13 games of chance, by any means, for a period of 10 years, against the payment to the State of a consideration (fee). The second measure was the award of an exclusive licence to operate 35,000 gaming machines of the Video Lottery Terminal type for a period of 10 years against the payment to the State of a consideration (fee).

The Greek authorities had notified these measures in favour of OPAP to the Commission. After a preliminary procedure the Commission took the view that the measures, evaluated separately and jointly, did not, on average, confer an advantage on OPAP and therefore did not contain any elements of State aid within the meaning of Article 107(1)

40 Ibid. para. 90.
41 Ibid. paras. 63–64.
42 Ibid. para. 133.
43 Case T-58/13, *Club Hotel Loutraki AE and Others v. Commission* ECLI:EU:T:2015:1.

of the TFEU. The Commission took the view that OPAP would pay the Greek State a higher amount than the cumulated values of the exclusive rights granted to OPAP.

Club Hotel Loutraki and others, concurrent casino operators in Greece, claimed that the Greek State would have been able to receive an amount higher than the received € 560 million if it had granted more than one licence to operate Video Lottery Terminals and if it had organised a public international call for tenders for their allocation. They brought an action before the General Court against the Commission's decision. Among other pleas, they claimed that the Commission did not correctly assess the question of the existence of an advantage for OPAP, since the Commission jointly assessed the measures to reach the conclusion that they did not confer an economic advantage on OPAP. According to Club Hotel Loutraki et al. the measures referred to distinct markets. They claimed that an advantage, for the purpose of Article 107(1) TFEU must be assessed for each market and not on the basis of joint consideration of similar measures concerning different markets. The fact that the measures concern the same recipient should not be relevant in that respect.[44] They also claimed that in this case the measures covered different periods. The first measure referred to the period from 2020–2030, whereas the second measure covered the period from 2012 to 2022.

The General Court came to the conclusion that the claimants had failed to demonstrate the existence of an error of law when the Commission carried out a joint assessment of the two measures.[45] In the first place, the contested decision, according to the Court, did not establish that the two measures related to different markets. The Commission had only mentioned that the measures concern similar activities, namely games of chance.[46] Moreover, the Commission is not required to define the relevant markets to determine whether the State measures constituted State aid within the meaning of Article 107(1) TFEU.[47] In the second place, the Court ruled that the Commission, like it had stated, is required to take into account the context in which a transaction takes place.[48] The Commission, therefore, was entitled to jointly assess the two measures. The Court held that the two measures were adopted at the same time. The Commission was 'entitled to consider that the two notified measures were part of a single privatization transaction, that they took place within the same economic context and that it was therefore appropriate and necessary to consider them jointly, in the context of a single notification.'[49] In the third place, the Court ruled that, although the measures applied to different periods, it was confirmed that the levies payable by OPAP for the award of the two categories of exclusive rights were due at the same time.[50] The Commission, therefore, was indeed entitled to assess the measures jointly.

44 Ibid. para. 79.
45 Ibid. para. 96.
46 Ibid. para. 87.
47 Ibid. para. 89.
48 Ibid. para. 91.
49 Ibid. para. 92.
50 Ibid. para. 93.

It is not sure if the General Court's judgment will be upheld, since at the time of writing, the appeal is pending before the Court of Justice.[51]

3.5. *Eventech v. Parking Adjudicator*

The fourth case worth discussing concerning the possible relationship between the concept of State aid and the allocation of limited public rights by the national authorities deals with a dispute between a firm called Eventech and the Parking Adjudicator in London. The dispute concerns the lawfulness of a local policy in London which consists of permitting London taxis, the so-called Black Cabs, to use most London bus lanes during the hours when the bus lane restrictions are operational, while prohibiting private hire vehicles, so-called minicabs, from using those bus lanes, except for the purpose of picking up and dropping off passengers who have pre-booked such a vehicle.[52] The preferential right for the Black Cabs to use bus lanes on public roads during the hours when traffic restrictions with respect to those lanes are operational, is granted in the interests of establishing a safe and efficient transport system. This preferential right may be considered as a limited right in the sense of this book. Eventech, a private firm which keeps a fleet of minicabs in London, started proceedings before the national court, claiming, inter alia, that the bus lanes policy constitutes un-notified State aid to the operators of Black Cabs, which is contrary to Article 108(3) TFEU and Article 107(1) TFEU.[53] By way of preliminary questions, the national court asked the Court of Justice, whether the bus lanes policy involves a commitment of State resources and confers on taxis a selective economic advantage for the purposes of Article 107(1) TFEU.[54]

The Court of Justice first dealt with the question whether State resources are involved. Eventech had argued that this was the case, since the Black Cabs are exempted from any liability to pay fines when they use the bus lanes, whereas the minicabs risk the imposition of fines. Eventech referred to the judgment of the Court of Justice in the case *Commission v. The Netherlands* on the Dutch NOx emission trading scheme, in which the Court of Justice considered, as discussed above, that the applicable system in the Netherlands offered a legal framework for limiting the discharge of NOx emissions in a profitable manner for undertakings with large facilities, which then have an alternative to the imposition of a fine by the State.[55] However, in the Eventech case, the Court of Justice came to another reasoning, stating that the circumstances of the case *Commission v. The Netherlands* are different to those of the Eventech case. According to the Court of Justice, in the Eventech case the authorities have not put in place any means of evading payment

51 Appeal lodged on 16.03.2015, Case C-131/15 P. See for a critical analysis of the 'cross-overpayment' acceptance by the General Court A. Sánchez Graells, *Exclusive rights, State aid and lottery: a winning ticket worth an extended monopoly? (T-58/13)*, blog at How to Crack a Nut at <http://howtocrackanut.blogspot.nl/2015/01/exclusive-rights-state-aid-and-lottery.html>.

52 Case C-518/13, *Eventech Ltd v. Parking Adjudicator* ECLI:EU:C:2015:9, para. 2.

53 Ibid. para. 26.

54 Ibid. para. 31.

55 Ibid. para. 108.

of fines, since each unauthorised use of the bus lanes constitutes an offence punishable by a fine. The reason why the Black Cabs are not subject to fines is that such taxis are permitted to use the bus lanes.[56] For that reason, the Court of Justice ruled 'that the fact that Black Cabs are not obliged to pay fines because of their use of bus lanes does not involve additional burdens on the public authorities which might entail a commitment of State resources.'[57] One could question, however, if the reasoning of the Court of Justice on this point is convincing, while in both cases the possibility for the selected group to escape the imposition of a fine, was in fact created by either a legislative or an administrative measure.[58]

The Court of Justice also considered that the public authorities in this case are not forgoing revenue which they would have received in the absence of the bus lanes policy, because of the preferential access for the Black Cabs to the bus lanes.[59] The Court came to this conclusion, because it considered that the traffic routes at issue, in general, and the bus lanes which are part of them, in particular, are not operated commercially by the public authorities.[60] Use of those routes and those lanes is free of charge.[61]

The Court of Justice then moves on to the question whether the authorities, in the circumstances of this case, are nevertheless obliged to impose on the users entitled to the privileged access to the public infrastructure a charge which corresponds to the economic value of that privilege. It is recognised namely, that the preferential right for the Black Cabs to use the bus lanes has an economic value.[62] In the context of the allocation of limited rights this is an interesting question. The Court of Justice, however, came to a negative conclusion to this question. The Court considered that where authorities, in order to pursue the realisation of an objective laid down by that State's legislation, grant a right of privileged access to public infrastructure which is not operated commercially, they do not necessarily confer an economic advantage in the sense of Article 107(1) TFEU.[63]

The Court of Justice further considered 'that the identification of the objective pursued is, in principle, a matter within the prerogative of the competent national public authorities alone and they must have a degree of discretion both as regards whether it is necessary, in order to achieve the regulatory objective pursued, to forgo possible revenue and also as regards how the appropriate criteria for the granting of the right, which must be determined in advance in a transparent and non-discriminatory manner, are to be identified.'[64]

56 Ibid. para. 40.
57 Ibid. para. 41.
58 See also B. Nijhoff, *On Black Cabs and bus lanes: a middle-of-the-road judgment by the CJEU in Eventech*, European Law Blog at: <http://europeanlawblog.eu/?p=2701#sthash.sY2FXron.dpuf>.
59 Case C-518/13, *Eventech Ltd v. Parking Adjudicator* ECLI:EU:C:2015:9, para. 44.
60 See Case C-288/11 P, *Mitteldeutsche Flughafen AG and Flughafen Leipzig-Halle v. Commission* ECLI:EU:C:2012:821.
61 Case C-518/13, *Eventech Ltd v. Parking Adjudicator* ECLI:EU:C:2015:9, para. 43.
62 Ibid. paras. 46 and 50.
63 Ibid. para. 48.
64 Ibid. para. 49.

In the *Eventech* case the Court of Justice came to the conclusion that the decision to forgo revenues in the given circumstances could be justified by the fact that the realisation of the objectives pursued with the bus lane policy might be jeopardized, if a charge was imposed on Black Cabs corresponding to the economic value of their right of access to the bus lanes.[65]

As far as the requirement of selectivity is concerned, the Court of Justice considered that it depends on the concrete circumstances of the case whether the measure at issue introduces distinctions between operators who are, in light of the objective pursued, in a comparable factual and legal situation. The decision on this issue was left to the national court. The Court of Justice, however, provided guidance for the national court by considering that the Black Cabs and minicabs are in factual and legal situations which are sufficiently distinct to permit the view that they are not comparable.[66]

3.6. *The Approach taken by the Commission*

The approach taken by the Commission towards the applicability of EU State aid rules to the allocation of limited (or even exclusive) rights can be derived from concrete decisions as well as from policy documents of the Commission.

In a decision on alleged unlawful State aid by the Slovakian authorities to Imuna Pharm by granting the undertaking a limited export licence, the Commission applied the above-mentioned lines from the case law of the European Courts. The Commission was of the opinion that the Slovak Republic did not directly forgo any State resources which it should otherwise receive when granting such a licence. Therefore, the sole act of granting and/or extending an exclusive licence did not constitute an act by which the State forgoes its resources. For this conclusion, the Commission took into account that the export licence applicable in Slovakia was not granted in exchange for any fee and the applicable legal framework in Slovakia was based on objective eligibility criteria which do not include the payment of any fee, whether based on prospective profits or auctioned to the highest bidder among applicants for the licence(s). Moreover, the licence was not tradable on any market.[67]

In another decision on alleged unlawful aid from the Split Port Authority to the State-owned Croatian ferry operator Jadrolinija, the Commission further clarified that the mere fact that a private undertaking has an exclusive right does not entail that the State aid rules apply to that private undertaking. The Commission considered that State aid

65 Ibid. para. 51.
66 Paras. 57–61.
67 Decision of 15.10.2014, SA. 37624 – Slovakia – Alleged illegal State Aid to Imuna Pharm SA, C(2014) 7286 final, paras. 11–17. See also Ph. Nicolaides, *Exclusive Rights*, in a blog at StateAidHub.eu at <http://stateaidhub.eu/blogs/stateaiduncovered/post/1553#_ftn2>.

rules can apply to public undertakings, since their resources can be considered State resources. On the contrary, the resources of private undertakings are not considered State resources.[68]

In its Draft Notice on the notion of State aid pursuant to Article 107(1) TFEU the Commission has explained in general its view on the relationship between the concept of State aid and the granting of limited rights.[69] This view is in line with the above-mentioned case law from the European Courts, as appears from the various references to the case law in the footnotes of this Notice. The Commission states:

> 'Granting access to public domain or natural resources or granting special or exclusive rights without adequate remuneration in line with market rates can constitute foregoing State revenues (again, as well as the granting of an advantage).
>
> In these cases it needs to be established whether the State, in addition to its role of manager of public assets, acts as a regulator that pursues policy objectives by making the selection process of the undertakings concerned subject to qualitative criteria (established ex ante in a transparent and non-discriminatory manner). When the State acts as a regulator, it can decide legitimately not to maximise the revenues which could otherwise have been achieved, without falling under the scope of State aid rules, provided that all the operators concerned are treated equally, and that there is an inherent link between achieving the regulatory purpose and the foregoing of revenue.
>
> In any event, a transfer of State resources is present if, in a given case, the public authorities do not charge the normal amount under their general system for access to the public domain or natural resources or for granting certain special or exclusive rights.'[70]

So, the Commission appears to be of the opinion that it cannot automatically be presumed that State aid is at stake when allocating limited rights which have an economic value. The State may act as a regulator and decide legitimately not to maximise the revenues which could otherwise have been achieved. However, in order to exclude the applicability of the State aid rules, the State, by doing so, shall treat all operators equally and there should be an inherent link between achieving the regulatory purpose and the foregoing of revenues.[71] This requires a careful analysis in every particular case.

68 Decision of 15.10.2014, SA.37265 (2014/NN) – Croatia – Alleged aid to Jadrolinija, C (2013) 7285 final, para. 41.

69 Draft Commission Notice on the notion of State aid pursuant to Article 107(1) TFEU at <http://ec.europa.eu/competition/consultations/2014_state_aid_notion/draft_guidance_en.pdf>. At the time of writing the final version is still to be expected. The text of the final version may vary from the cited text of the draft version.

70 Ibid. paras. 55–57.

71 See also the chapter by Wolswinkel in this book.

3.7. *Conclusion on the Application of the Concept of State Aid to the Allocation of Limited Rights*

As far as the application of the concept of State aid to the allocation of limited rights by the national authorities is concerned, it follows from both the case law of the European Courts and Commission practice, that various situations can occur in which State aid is involved. In each situation, however, it should be carefully assessed whether all four conditions of Article 107(1) TFEU have been fulfilled.

The *Bouygues* case makes clear that the allocation of limited rights by national authorities, like the UMTS licences, which have an economic value, could result in State aid, if the conditions on which fees for such rights have to be paid, do not equally apply to all applicants, who are in a comparable factual and legal position. However, the case also makes clear that the mere fact that the State waves resources which may lead to an advantage for the beneficiaries, is not sufficient to prove the existence of State aid, if the abandonment of the claim at issue is inevitable because of the requirements which may follow from the applicable EU law framework.

The judgment of the Court of Justice in the case *Commission v. The Netherlands* provides further clarity on the explanation of the condition of State resources, as well as of an advantage and the concept of selectivity when dealing with the allocation of limited rights by national authorities, such as the measure in question in the field of CO_2 emission reduction. As soon as limited rights involve the character of tradable intangible assets, the authorities cannot make these rights available free of charge to a separate group of undertakings. The fact that these undertakings, by obtaining tradable rights, get the opportunity to escape the imposition of a fine by the State, might also involve State aid.

From the judgment of the General Court in the case *Club Hotel Loutraki AE and others v. Commission* it seems to follow that, when allocating limited rights (in the given case exclusive rights) the granting of an advantage can be avoided if on balance, even considered jointly with other measures, the payment for such rights is in accordance with market conditions, or higher. However, it is not sure if the General Court's judgment will be upheld, since at the time of writing the appeal is pending before the Court of Justice.[72]

The judgment of the Court of Justice in the *Eventech* case makes clear that the allowance of preferential rights which as such have an economic value, do not necessarily involve the granting of State aid, as long as they are linked to infrastructure which is not to be commercially operated. The national authorities might then, within the sphere of its discretionary powers to pursue public policy goals, decide to forgo revenues, without acting in breach of EU State aid rules. We have to wait to see if this line will be followed and confirmed in later judgments.

72 Appeal lodged on 16.03.2015, Case C-131/15 P.

Also from the decisions and policy documents of the Commission, as mentioned above, it follows that in every case a careful analysis has to be made whether the allocation of limited rights might involve State aid, based on the State aid conditions of Article 107(1) TFEU. It cannot automatically be presumed that State aid is at stake. The State may act as a regulator and decide legitimately not to maximise the revenues which could otherwise have been achieved. However, in order to exclude the applicability of the State aid rules, the State, by doing so, shall treat all operators equally and there should be an inherent link between achieving the regulatory purpose and the foregoing of revenues.[73]

Note that the analysis made in this chapter is not exhaustive. There may be other scenarios in which State aid can be involved, e.g. when the allocation of limited rights is based on discretionary powers without objective rules or criteria or based on preferential terms for certain undertakings or sectors.[74]

4. Consequences of the Applicability of EU State Aid Rules[75]

EU State aid control is based on Articles 107, 108 and 109 TFEU. The control system consists of the constant review of all existing aid in the Member States, combined with a system of preventive control exercised by the Commission on any new plans to grant or alter aid measures. The concept of State aid, as defined in Article 107(1) TFEU, has been explained in Section 2.

Various reasons can be mentioned to support legitimising a transnational monitoring system for aid measures undertaken by Member States. First, such a regime would protect competition in interstate trade (so-called cross-border externalities).[76] Secondly, it would counter protectionism and a subsidy race.[77] Thirdly, a transnational regime of State aid control would guarantee the protection of Member States transcending European interests, in particular that of the internal market,[78] and according to the Commission's Modernisation Communication of 2012,[79] it would also prevent inefficient spending of taxpayers' money, which in the literature is described as solving national commitment problems.[80]

73 See also the chapter by Wolswinkel in this book.

74 See A.T. Seinen, 'State aid aspects of the EU Emission Trading Scheme: the second trading period' 2007 3 *Competition Policy Newsletter*, p. 100–105.

75 The text of this section has partly been derived from P.C. Adriaanse, 'Legitimising Transnational Decision-making in the EU State Aid Regime', to be published in H.M.Th.D. Ten Napel and W.J.M.Voermans (eds.), *The Powers that Be*, Leiden University Press.

76 H.W. Friederiszick, L.H. Röller & V. Verouden, 'European State Aid Control: An Economic Framework', in: P. Buccirossi (ed.), *Handbook of Antitrust Economics*, MIT Press, Cambridge MA 2007, pp. 638–640.

77 J. Haucap and U. Schwalbe, *Economic Principles of State Aid Control*, Discussion Paper No. 11, Düsseldorf Institute for Competition Economics, 2011, pp. 2–5.

78 Friederiszick, Röller & Verouden 2007, p. 641.

79 Communication from the Commission to the European Parliament, the Council, the European Economic and Social Committee and the Committee of the Regions, *EU State Aid Modernisation* (SAM), COM/2012/0209 final, para. 5.

80 Friederiszick, Röller & Verouden 2007, p. 640–641.

State aid in the sense of Article 107(1) TFEU is in principle prohibited, since it is deemed to be incompatible with the common market. However, it is recognised that in some circumstances, government interventions are necessary for a well-functioning and equitable economy. The second and third paragraph of Article 107 TFEU therefore provide for several grounds to consider State aid measures as being compatible with the common market.

It is the exclusive task of the Commission to examine the compatibility of State aid measures on the basis of the provisions of Article 107 TFEU.[81] Neither Member State authorities, nor national courts are allowed to perform this task. According to Article 108(2) TFEU, however, the Council may also in exceptional circumstances decide that aid which a State is granting or intends to grant shall be considered to be compatible with the common market, in derogation from the provisions of Article 107 TFEU or from the regulations provided for in Article 109 TFEU.

In order to make it possible for the Commission to fulfil its supervisory task within EU State aid control, several obligations rest upon the Member States. They shall, according to Article 108(1) TFEU, constantly inform the Commission of relevant developments or changes in existing aid measures. They shall also inform the Commission, in sufficient time to enable it to submit its comments, of any plans to grant new aid or alter existing aid. This notification obligation is laid down in Article 108(3), first sentence, TFEU. According to the last sentence of this provision, the Member States shall not put proposed measures into effect until the investigation procedure of the Commission has resulted in a final decision authorising the aid concerned, which is called the standstill obligation.

Based on these basic Treaty provisions, over the years many acts of secondary legislation have been adopted both by the Council and the Commission. Besides, the Commission has issued various communications and other soft law documents in which it has explained its State aid policy to the main actors concerned. Many of these documents have been revised within the context of the State aid modernisation, started in 2012.[82] This complex framework of State aid law has given rise to many preliminary questions by national courts and, as a consequence, many judgments by the European Courts, resulting in a comprehensive body of case law concerning various subjects related to State aid.

It appears that EU State aid control applies to a broad range of measures in many sectors of society. In order to keep this far-reaching control mechanism manageable in a growing European Union, the Commission has adopted various *de minimis* regulations and group exemption regulations. Except for certain sensitive sectors, *de minimis* aid is considered

81 See Case C-39/94, *SFEI et al.* ECLI:EU:C:1996:285, para 42.

82 Communication from the Commission to the European Parliament, the Council, the European Economic and Social Committee and the Committee of the Regions, *EU State Aid Modernisation* (SAM), COM/2012/0209 final.

not to affect trade between Member States and/or not to distort or threaten to distort competition, and therefore not to fall under Article 107(1) TFEU, as long as it does not exceed a fixed ceiling over a given period of time. Aid granted to a particular enterprise by any State authority or organ should be taken into account for this purpose even when financed entirely or partly from Union resources.[83] Group exemption regulations have been adopted in order to simplify State aid control. Most common is the General Block Exemption Regulation.[84] The Member States are allowed to grant aid measures that fulfil the criteria of this regulation without prior notification to the Commission.

It follows from the above that if a measure relating to the allocation of limited rights by national authorities qualifies as State aid, a whole set of rules, procedures and powers enter into force. This may cause a delay, especially when such a measure has to be notified to the Commission. The whole procedure may take a few months or, in case the Commission has started a formal investigation procedure, much longer. Especially in allocation procedures on limited public rights, in which different parties with parallel or opposite interests often have an interest in a timely outcome, this delayed decision-making may cause problems. Until now, State aid law offers no solution for this procedural implication.

However, breaching the procedural State aid rules by granting the aid without notification and standstill could cause even bigger problems. The unlawful State aid plus interest may have to be recovered from the beneficiaries in that scenario.[85] A breach of the standstill obligation laid down in Article 108(3) TFEU might also give rise to claims for damages or other private enforcement actions before national courts by interested parties involved.[86]

More and more State aid law stresses the importance of an open, transparent, sufficiently well-publicised, non-discriminatory and unconditional tender procedure, in compliance with the principles of the Public Procurement Directives in order to presume that a given transaction will be in line with market conditions and therefore, that State aid could be excluded.[87] Until now, in State aid cases the Court of Justice of the EU has not ruled on

83 See in particular the general *de minimis* regulation Commission Regulation (EC) No 1407/2013 of 18 December 2013 on the application of Articles 107 and 108 of the Treaty on the Functioning of the European Union to de minimis aid [2013] OJ L352/1 which sets a ceiling of Euro 200,000 for de minimis aid to an undertaking in a period of three years.

84 Commission Regulation (EU) No 651/2014 of 17 June 2014 declaring certain categories of aid compatible with the internal market in application of Articles 107 and 108 of the Treaty Text with EEA relevance [2014] OJ L187/1.

85 See Article 16 of Council Regulation (EU) 2015/1589 of 13 July 2015 laying down detailed rules for the application of Article 108 of the Treaty on the Functioning of the European Union [2015] OJ L248/9.

86 See Case C-690/13, *Trapeza Eurobank Ergasias AE v. Agrotiki Trapeza tis Ellados AE (ATE) and Pavlos Sidiropoulos*, n.y.r., paras. 47–53.

87 See e.g. para. 91 of the Draft Commission Notice on the notion of State aid pursuant to Article 107(1) TFEU at: <http://ec.europa.eu/competition/consultations/2014_state_aid_notion/draft_guidance_en.pdf>. See also Articles 55 and 56 of the General Block Exemption Regulation [2014] OJ L187/1.

this particular procedural issue, but it can be presumed that if such a procedure has not been followed, the risk of being considered State aid increases. This will also be the case with regard to the allocation of limited rights by administrative authorities.

5. Conclusion

The aim of this chapter was twofold: to explore to what extent the EU State aid law requirements could influence the allocation of limited rights by national authorities or the legislature and to see what can be learned from EU State aid law with a view to the development of a consistent and general legal theory on the allocation of limited rights by national authorities.

It follows from the case law analysis applied in this chapter, as well as from the Commission practice, that various situations can occur in which State aid is involved in the allocation of limited rights.

In each situation, it should be carefully assessed whether all four conditions of Article 107(1) TFEU have been fulfilled. State aid is only at stake if a measure with regard to the allocation procedure cumulatively satisfies four conditions: First, there must be an intervention by the State or through State resources; secondly, the measure must confer a selective advantage on the recipient (being an undertaking or a production); thirdly, the intervention must be liable to affect trade between Member States; and fourthly, it must distort or threaten to distort competition.

From the Court's case law with regard to the allocation of limited rights, discussed in this chapter, it follows that in particular the first two State aid conditions may give rise to legal dispute. It can further be concluded that, when dealing with the allocation of limited rights, the State can only forego revenues in the sense of State aid law, if the limited right has economic value. Such an economic value can be derived from both the object of the limited right, for example in the case of a scarce public resource like the UMTS licences, and the tradability of rights, like emission allowances.

However, the case law also makes clear that the mere fact that the State waves resources which may lead to an advantage for the beneficiaries, is not sufficient to prove the existence of State aid, if the abandonment of the claim at issue is inevitable because of the requirements which may follow from the applicable EU law framework. The judgment of the Court of Justice in the *Eventech* case makes clear that the allowance of preferential rights which as such have an economic value, do not necessarily involve the granting of State aid either, as long as they are linked to infrastructure which is not to be commercially operated. The national authorities might then, within the sphere of their discretionary powers to pursue public policy goals, decide to forgo revenues, without acting in breach of EU State aid rules. We have to wait to see if this line will be followed and confirmed in later judgments.

From the *Club Hotel Loutraki* case it follows that the granting of an advantage may also be avoided if on balance, even considered jointly with other measures, the payment for such rights is in accordance with market conditions, or higher. However, it is not sure if the General Court's judgment will be upheld, since at the time of writing the judgment is pending appeal before the Court of Justice.

When allocating limited rights, a selective advantage can be presumed, however, if given the economic value of a limited right, a differential treatment between operators is applied which cannot be justified by the nature or general scheme of the underlying system.[88]

Given these various possible influences of EU State aid law on the allocation of limited rights, the following remarks can be made with regard to the elaboration of a consistent and general theory on the allocation of limited rights. First, it is important to note that the allocation of limited rights by administrative authorities, even when acting in accordance with the transparency principle, might in certain circumstances involve State aid which, as a rule, will be incompatible with the internal market unless an exception applies. The impact on competition and trade between EU Member States, which the allocation of limited rights involving State aid will have, should therefore be considered as one of the relevant aspects in deciding upon the allocation of limited rights. This is particularly true, since the applicability of the EU State aid rules involves certain procedural safeguards, which, if not obeyed, could have negative consequences for the acts by which the aid was carried out and therefore influence the outcome of the allocation process.

Secondly, it should be noted that various State aid law documents stress the importance of an open, transparent, sufficiently well-publicised, non-discriminatory and unconditional tender procedure, in compliance with the principles of the Public Procurement Directives in order to presume that a given transaction will be in line with market conditions and to avoid State aid. However, apart from these requirements, State aid law seems to be neutral as to the specific allocation procedure to be applied.

Thirdly, also if the State aid rules are applied correctly, the procedural State aid requirements may have an important impact on the allocation procedure. In particular, if the aid measure has to be notified to the Commission, this procedural requirement may cause a serious delay in the allocation procedure. State aid law offers no solution for this procedural implication.

It may be concluded, therefore, that State aid law could have an important influence on the allocation of limited rights by administrative authorities, but is not yet tailored to the particularities and interests involved in such allocation procedures.

88 See also the chapter by Wolswinkel in this book.

Chris Jansen*

CHAPTER 10. ALLOCATION OF LIMITED RIGHTS FROM A EUROPEAN PUBLIC PROCUREMENT LAW PERSPECTIVE

1. Introduction

This contribution departs from the assumption that the allocation of limited (public) rights in the EU and its Member States is in need of a consistent and general legal theory.[1] The editors of this book assume that inspiration for such an approach may be drawn from the phenomenon of public procurement and its EU regulation.[2] The question dealt with in this contribution is whether and to what extent this is indeed possible. In order to answer that question, and for the purpose of a better understanding of the subject matter, I will first briefly explain what 'public procurement' is and how it is generally being organised having regard to both the objectives that can be pursued with it, and the interests that can be affected by it (Section 2). This will provide a basis to answer the question what 'EU public procurement *law*' is, what type of decisions in an ordinary public procurement process it seeks to regulate and, having regard to its objectives, what the content of the regulation in essence is (Section 3). The information gathered in Sections 2 and 3 will thereupon be considered in order to determine whether and to what extent public procurement and its regulation can serve as a source of inspiration for a consistent and general legal theory on the allocation of limited rights. The analysis will start by making some general comments on the position and relevance that the editors have granted to both public procurement and its regulation in this book (Section 4), having regard to their threefold approach of the subject matter of the allocation of limited rights: a conceptual approach (definitions and characteristics), a

* Chris Jansen is full professor of private law at VU University Amsterdam, professor of construction law at Tilburg University and vice-chairman of the Dutch Public Procurement Ombudsman.

1 Adriaanse, Van Ommeren, Den Ouden & Wolswinkel, Chapter 1 (Section 1). Compare also F. Wollenschläger, 'EU Law Principles for Allocating Scarce Goods and the Emergence of an Allocation Procedure', [2015/1] *REALaw (Review of European Administrative Law)*, pp. 205–256.

2 Adriaanse, Van Ommeren, Den Ouden & Wolswinkel, Chapter 1 (Section 5.3.1). Compare also J. Wolswinkel, 'From Public Contracts to Limited Authorisations and Vice Versa: Exploring General Award Requirements from the EU Court's Corollary Approach', (2015) 24 *P.P.L.R. (Public Procurement Law Review)*, pp. 137–163.

top-down approach (EU law perspectives) and a bottom-up approach (comparative law perspectives). Subsequently, this contribution will analyse what probably can – and cannot – be learned from public procurement and its regulatory framework with a view to the development of a consistent and general legal theory on the allocation of limited rights, having regard to public procurement's generic and particular characteristics, objectives, interests involved, and organisation (Section 5). The analysis will deal with issues that have been selected and organised according to the following distinction helpfully provided by the editors: (i) the object of allocation (limited rights), (ii) allocation procedures, and (iii) their legal form.[3] In conclusion, this contribution will provide an answer to the question raised at the beginning of this section and offer a recommendation for the purpose of developing a consistent and general legal approach of the phenomenon of allocation of limited rights (Section 6).

2. Public Procurement

2.1. Public Procurement: What are the Objectives and Interests at Stake?

The notion of 'public procurement' or 'government procurement' can be explained as the procurement of works, goods and services on behalf of a public authority from an external source.[4] Although the notion of 'procurement' has much in common with 'purchasing' or simply 'buying', procurement is generally considered to relate to a more or less elaborate and formalised staged process of decisions, eventually resulting in works, goods or services to be supplied in accordance with the public authority's expectations as to quality, delivery time and budget. A particular feature of this staged process is, for instance, selection on the basis of *supplier* quality, not to be confused with the selection on the basis of quality of the *performance* offered by a supplier in order to meet the authority's expectations.[5] Although the procuring authority will in many cases issue public tenders, it is to be noted that this is not a constituent feature of public procurement.[6]

The primary goal that a public authority will aim for with the procurement of works, goods or services is probably self-evident. The authority's task is to deliver services to the public at large. In doing so, he might encounter a specific problem that needs to be solved. That solution can be obtained from the market through the procurement of works, goods or services. A public authority may, however, pursue additional goals through public procurement also. Some of these goals are hardly to be discerned from the aforesaid primary goal. One could think of the desire of the authority to achieve better value for taxpayers' money when procuring works, goods or services. He will then try to satisfy his

3 Adriaanse, Van Ommeren, Den Ouden & Wolswinkel, Chapter 1 (Section 4).

4 See also Article 1(2) Directive 2014/24/EU: '(...) the acquisition by means of a public contract of works, supplies or services by one or more contracting authorities from economic operators chosen by those contracting authorities (...).' See also S. Arrowsmith, *The law of public and utilities procurement. Regulation in the EU and UK*, Volume 1, Sweet & Maxwell, London 2014, p. 1.

5 See also Section 2.2.

6 See previous footnote.

needs against the lowest possible total cost by the delivery of a high-quality performance with an eye to the optimal life cycle. In line with this is the aim of the authority to keep the transaction costs involved with the procurement process as low as possible. Other additional policy goals that can be pursued with public procurement have a more secondary character. Here one could think of public authorities acting as launching customers in promoting the development of innovative market solutions and in encouraging environmental and social sustainability as regards products and services to be supplied. The idea is that this could increase the prosperity and welfare of society at large.

Public procurement will also affect the interests of economic operators in the supply market of works, goods and services. Obvious interests that are at stake relate to business continuity and the desire to obtain maximum return on investment. In the event that an economic operator is granted access to a particular contract without having to compete with other economic operators – at least not in a direct manner – the public authority and the economic operator involved will be able to safeguard and balance their mutual interests in direct negotiations with one another. From the perspective of the aforesaid public authority's primary and additional goals it could be profitable, however, to provoke direct competition in the supply market through the issuing of public tenders. This will obviously cause effects to the interests of the preferred supplier, but it will at the same time foster the business interests of other economic operators in the sense that they too will be granted access to the contract. It is even possible that public authorities – in addition to their primary goal pursuit – use public procurement through competitive tendering as a means to pursue the additional goal of facilitating access to the contract for local economic operators ("buy national"), particularly if these have a weak market position such as small and medium enterprises (SME's). From this perspective public procurement can also affect the interest of opening-up of the EU market – and even the global market – of public supply contracts, as part of the overall objective of the EU to establish an internal market without internal frontiers in which the principles of free movement of goods, persons, services and capital are ensured.[7]

2.2. *Public Procurement: How is It Generally being Organised?*

Public procurement is in essence a decision-making process. The process will be designed and completed starting from the objectives a public authority aims to achieve and taking into account the interests that are likely to be affected as a result of the procurement. As explained above (Section 2.1), the decision to issue public tenders is not a constituent feature of that process. Nevertheless, although many of the decisions explained in this section are an indispensable part of the decision-making process public procurement in essence is – even if a public authority decides *not* to issue public tenders – the following analysis will be based on the assumption that the authority *does* decide to do so. This assumption is needed for the purpose of facilitating the analysis in Section 5 below.

7 See Article 3(3) Treaty on European Union (TEU) *jo.* Article 26 Treaty on the Functioning of the European Union (TFEU).

At the very beginning of the procurement process, the public authority will have to decide on the objectives he aims to achieve with that process, particularly as regards quality, delivery time and available budget. He will start by generally describing these objectives and subsequently convert them into technical specifications. At a later stage of the process, these technical specifications will serve as a basis for the submission of tenders. The winning tenderer will have to perform the contract in accordance with the technical specifications. Depending on the objectives the public authority aims to achieve and the interests likely to be affected, the technical specifications can be formulated either in terms of functional and performance-related requirements – to put it simply: the "what" that is to be supplied – allowing sufficient freedom to tenderers to decide on "how" to supply the "what", or in terms of genuine detailed technical requirements barely allowing tenderers to determine how they will supply the works, goods or services.

The public authority will further have to decide on the award criteria he will apply upon receipt of the tenders in order to determine which tender he thinks best, for instance "the lowest price" or "the best price-quality ratio". The nature and content of the award criteria will again depend on the objectives he aims to achieve and have to be decided upon in close connection with the aforesaid requirements to be determined in the technical specifications starting from the same objectives.

Subsequently, the public authority will have to consider what skills and competences his future counterpart is required to possess in order to be able to meet the requirements in the technical specifications in such a manner that this will cause the objectives of the procurement process to be achieved. On the basis of the outcome of this analysis, he will have to convert these skills and competences into criteria for qualitative selection, which will be applied later on in the process in order to determine whether an economic operator may continue to participate in the process, or is to be excluded therefrom. Here too it shows that the nature and content of these criteria for qualitative selection – given their close connection with the technical specifications – strongly depend upon the objectives the public authority aims to achieve with the procurement process.

Given the above assumption that the public authority has decided to call for tenders, he will further have to decide on the type of tendering procedure he intends to follow. Starting from the objectives he aims to achieve, and having regard to the interests that are likely to be affected, he can decide between either an open procedure, whereby any interested economic operator may submit a tender, or a restricted procedure, whereby any economic operator may request to participate as candidate and whereby only those candidates who meet the criteria for qualitative selection are invited by the public authority to submit a tender.[8] Again, both the choice of the particular tendering procedure to be followed and all other process decisions explained above have to be

8 The public authority can also decide to equip the restricted procedure with the possibility to shortlist the amount of candidates meeting the qualitative selection criteria, prior to inviting them to submit a tender. This will require him, however, to decide on the criteria and rules to apply for the purpose of shortlisting when designing the procedure. Again, the decision to equip the procedure with the possibility to shortlist as well as the nature and content of the criteria and rules to do so, depend on the

tailored to one another from the perspective of the objectives and interests the authority pursues with the procurement process as a whole.[9]

Once the technical specifications, contract award criteria, and the criteria for qualitative selection have been designed and formulated, and once the tendering procedure to be followed has been selected, the public authority will make known his intention to award a contract by means of that procedure with the publication of a contract notice. Depending on the nature of the tendering procedure applied, economic operators will either put themselves forward as candidates (restricted procedures) or submit tenders directly (open procedures). In the case of restricted procedures, only those candidates who meet the criteria for qualitative selection will be invited to submit a tender. By the same token, in the case of open procedures, the public authority will only assess tenders received from tenderers who meet the aforesaid criteria for qualitative selection. To the extent that candidates or tenderers meet these latter criteria, their (subsequent) tenders will first be assessed on the basis of the requirements set in the technical specifications. Only tenders that are in accordance with these requirements will be further assessed on the basis of the award criteria in order to determine the winning tender. Unless the public authority decides not to award the contract at all, he will award it to the tenderer who submitted the winning tender who will thereupon start with the performance of the contract.

3. EU Public Procurement Law

3.1. EU Public Procurement Law: What are Its Objectives?

As was explained in Section 2.1, public authorities may pursue many differing goals when procuring goods, works and services.[10] By the same token, their decisions in the framework of the design and completion of a procurement process may affect many differing interests. The essence of public procurement *law* in general is that it regulates this decision-making process with the objective of striking a balance between (some of) those interests.

Although EU public procurement law[11] *recognises* that public procurement can affect many interests, it is important to note that it *regulates* basically only *one particular*

goals the public authority aims to achieve having regard to other decisions to be taken in the procurement process.

9 Depending on the applicable regulatory framework, variations on restricted procedures also exist, allowing the public authority more flexibility than the basic procedures when it comes to bilateral communication with individual economic operators in the course of the tendering procedure.

10 Compare also Arrowsmith 2014, pp. 150 ff.

11 Sources of EU public procurement law are: the principles of the Treaty on the Functioning of the European Union (TFEU), and in particular the free movement of goods, freedom of establishment and the freedom to provide services, as well as the principles deriving therefrom, such as equal treatment, non-discrimination, mutual recognition, proportionality and transparency, and the relevant Directives, in particular 2014/23/EU, 2014/24/EU, 2014/25/EU, and 2009/81/EC.

interest: the opening-up of the EU market of public supply contracts and concessions,[12] as part of the overall objective of the EU to establish an internal market without internal frontiers in which the principles of free movement of goods, persons, services and capital are ensured.[13] The regulation certainly *recommends* public authorities to use public procurement as a means to pursue all kind of policy goals,[14] but the primary focus of the regulation is to restrict the authorities' freedom of choice regarding the design and completion of the overall decision-making process from the perspective of the opening-up of the EU internal market. The corollary of this is that EU public procurement law hardly imposes any positive duties upon either Member States or public authorities to pursue additional policy objectives and interests, other than those that involve safeguarding the aforesaid internal market interest.[15] Such additional policy objectives may of course be pursued by public authorities on a national level, and they may even be stimulated actively by positive duties in national public procurement regulation,[16] as long as both such policy initiatives as well as regulation comply with the boundaries that are set by EU public procurement law from the aforesaid perspective of safeguarding the internal market objective.

The following section will take the typical decision-making process as explained in Section 2.2 as a starting-point and will deal with the question to what extent EU public procurement law seeks to regulate this process and what the content of the regulation in essence is, having regard to the aforesaid primary objective.

12 A 'public contract' is a contract to which at least one of the parties is a public body. It encompasses, among other contracts, both 'supply contracts' and 'concessions'. In this paper the notion of 'supply contracts' is used as the collective term for all contracts involving the supply of works, goods and services, falling within the ambit of the Directives 2014/24/EU and 2014/25/EU. The notion of 'concessions' is used to indicate all contracts falling under the scope Directive 2014/23/EU.

13 Arrowsmith 2014, pp. 2–10.

14 See for instance Recital (4), second paragraph, Directive 2014/23/EU: 'A uniform application of the principles of the TFEU across all Member States and the elimination of discrepancies in the understanding of those principles is necessary at Union level in order to eliminate persisting distortions of the internal market. *That would also favour the efficiency of public spending, facilitate equal access and fair participation of SMEs in the award of concession contracts, both at local and Union level, and support the achievement of sustainable public policy objectives*' (my italics, CJ). Compare also Recital (4) Directive 24/24/EU and Directive 24/25/EU. See also M.E. Comba, 'Variations in the scope of the new EU public procurement Directives of 2014: Efficiency in public spending and a major role of the approximation of laws', in: F. Lichère, R. Caranta & S. Treumer (eds.), *Modernising Public Procurement. The New Directive*, Djøf Publishing, Copenhagen 2014, pp. 29–48.

15 See however Article 18(2) Directive 2014/24/EU: 'Member States shall take appropriate measures to ensure that in the performance of public contracts economic operators comply with applicable obligations in the fields of environmental, social and labour law established by Union law, national law, collective agreements or by the international environmental, social and labour law provisions listed in Annex X.' See also D.C. Dragos & B. Neamtu, 'Sustainable public procurement in the EU: experiences and prospects', in: F. Lichère, R. Caranta & S. Treumer (eds.), *Modernising Public Procurement. The New Directive*, Djøf Publishing, Copenhagen 2014, pp. 301–336.

16 It is beyond the scope of this contribution to deal with the question whether and to what extent national public procurement law of the Member States of the EU regulates additional policy goals that can be achieved by means of public procurement.

3.2. *EU Public Procurement Law: How does It Regulate the Decision-Making Process?*

When performing its task to deliver services to the public at large, a public authority may encounter a specific problem that needs solving.[17] He will then first have to decide whether to obtain that solution from an 'in-house' source or to procure the works, goods or services from an external supplier. This decision is outside the domain of EU public procurement law: the rules do not interfere with the freedom of public authorities to deal with their needs without procuring solutions from the market.[18] It is noted, however, that EU public procurement imposes duties upon a public authority to prevent distortion of competition in relation to private economic operators, in the event that he decides to obtain works, goods or services from 'in-house' sources or via legal co-operation with other entities within the public sector.[19] This subject matter involves issues that fall outside the scope of this contribution, and the aforesaid rules will therefore not be dealt with.[20]

In the event that a public authority decides to procure works, goods or services from the market, he will further have to decide whether or not to call for tenders. Depending on the circumstances of the case, he will be under an obligation to do so on the basis of EU public procurement law. Basically, this obligation exists whenever a public authority qualifies as an entity that is instructed by the EU public procurement Directives to call for tenders and decides to procure from the market works, goods or services representing a certain financial value. There is a lot that can be said about the criteria that have to be met in order for an entity to fall under the scope of the Directives.[21] The same goes for the types of contracts these entities must put out to tender on the basis of a tendering procedure provided for in the Directives, in the event that their financial value exceeds the relevant thresholds referred to in the Directives.[22] For the purpose of this contribution, however, it is not considered necessary to deal with these issues in detail either. In the

17 See Section 2.1.

18 See Recital (5) Directive 2014/24/EU: 'It should be recalled that nothing in this Directive obliges Member States to contract out or externalise the provision of services that they wish to provide themselves or to organise by means other than public contracts within the meaning of this Directive.'

19 See particularly Article 12 Directive 2014/24/EU. See also Recital (30) and following.

20 See extensively and with further references Arrowsmith 2014, pp. 497 ff.

21 See particularly the definition of 'contracting authorities' in Article 6 Directive 2014/23/EU, Article 2(1)(1) Directive 2014/24/EU and Article 3 Directive 2014/25/EU. See also the definition of 'contracting entities' in Article 7 Directive 2014/23/EU and in Article 4 Directive 2014/25/EU. See extensively and with further references on the concept of 'contracting authorities' in Directive 2014/24/EU, Arrowsmith 2014, pp. 339 ff. See also S. Arrowsmith, *The law of public and utilities procurement*, Sweet & Maxwell, London 2005, pp. 841 ff. on the concepts of 'contracting authorities' and 'contracting entities' in the predecessor of Directive 2014/25/EU.

22 Directive 2014/23/EU applies to both 'works concessions' and 'services concessions', see Article 1(1) and 5(1)(a) and 5(1)(b). Directive 2014/24/EU applies to a 'public contract of works, supplies or services' according to Article 1(2). Directive 2014/25/EU is applicable to a 'supply, works or service contract of works, supplies or services', see Article 1(2). The limits of these concepts can be problematized on the basis of numerous provisions in the Directives. See extensively and with further references on Directive 2014/24/EU, Arrowsmith 2014, pp. 385 ff. See also Arrowsmith 2005, pp. 899 ff. regarding the predecessor of Directive 2014/25/EU.

following, it will therefore be assumed that both public authorities as well as the works, goods or services they intend to procure from the market, are within the ambit of the said Directives. It is noted that the Directives only apply to procurements with a value net of value-added tax (VAT) estimated to be equal to or greater than the thresholds mentioned in the Directives.[23] The assumption is that such procurements will have a cross-border dimension. This does not mean, however, that procurements with a value under the relevant thresholds are considered to be irrelevant from the perspective of EU public procurement law. Provided that they too have a cross-border dimension, these procurements must comply with the principles of the TFEU despite their relatively low value, and in particular with the free movement of goods, freedom of establishment and the freedom to provide services, as well as the principles deriving therefrom, such as equal treatment, non-discrimination, mutual recognition, proportionality and transparency.[24] Finally, if a public authority decides to procure works, goods or services from the market, which have *no* cross-border dimension at all, an obligation to call for tenders may be imposed on the basis of the national law of the Member States, depending on the circumstances of the case.

Prior to the issuing of tenders, a public authority will determine the objectives he aims to achieve with the procurement process and subsequently convert these into technical specifications. EU public procurement law does not restrict the authorities' freedom to decide whether to formulate the technical specifications in terms of functional and performance-related requirements allowing sufficient freedom to tenderers to decide on "how" to supply the "what", or to formulate them in terms of detailed technical requirements barely allowing tenderers to determine how they will supply the works, goods or services. They are under an obligation however, to formulate the technical specifications in such a manner that these will afford economic operators equal access to the tendering procedure and shall not have the effect of creating unjustified obstacles to the opening up of public procurement to competition.[25] This rule is a specific application of the principles of public procurement law to be found in the Directives: public

23 See Article 8 Directive 2014/23/EU (EUR 5.186.000 for works and services concessions), Article 4 Directive 2014/24/EU (EUR 5.186.000 for public works contracts; EUR 134.000 for government authorities and design contests organised by such authorities; EUR 207.000.000 for public supply and service contracts awarded by sub-central contracting authorities and design contests organised by such authorities; EUR 750.000 for public service contracts for social and other specific services. See Article 15 Directive 2014/25/EU (EUR 414.000 for supply and service contracts as well as for design contests; EUR 5.186.000 for public works contracts; EUR 1.000.000 for service contracts for social and other specific services).

24 Compare Recital (1) Directive 2014/24/EU. See also Recital (3) Directive 2014/25/EU: 'For procurement the value of which is lower than the thresholds triggering the application of the provisions of Union coordination, it is advisable to recall the case-law of the Court of Justice of the European Union regarding the proper application of the rules and principles of the TFEU.' See for example the Joined Cases C-147/06 and C-148/06, *SECAP and Santorso v Commune di Torino* [2008] E.C.R. I-03565, paras 20–21. See for further references Arrowsmith 2014, pp. 245 ff. and particularly at pp. 264 ff. dealing with the question what precise requirements the positive obligation of transparency entails according to the case law of the Court of Justice.

25 See for instance Article 42 Directive 2014/24/EU, particularly paragraph (2). Compare also Article 60 Directive 2014/25/EU and Article 36 Directive 2014/23/EU.

authorities must treat economic operators equally and without discrimination and shall act in a transparent and proportionate manner.[26]

The public authorities' decision on the nature and content of the award criteria to be applied upon receipt of the tenders is also subject to specific rules derived from the aforesaid principles of public procurement law.[27] A public authority must base the award of a contract on the most economically advantageous tender, which shall be identified on the basis of the price or cost, using a cost-effectiveness approach, such as life-cycle costing, and may include the best price-quality ratio, which shall be assessed on the basis of criteria, including qualitative, environmental and/or social aspects, linked to the subject-matter of the public contract in question.[28] This shows that a public authority has ample freedom of choice as regards the award criteria, as long as these criteria are linked to the subject matter of the relevant contract[29] and ensure the possibility of effective competition.[30] They must be accompanied by specifications that allow the information provided by the tenderers to be effectively verified in order to assess how well the tenders meet the award criteria.[31] A public authority must specify, in the procurement documents, the relative weighting which he gives to each of the award criteria chosen to determine the most economically advantageous tender, except where this is identified on the basis of price alone.[32]

Likewise, the freedom of a public authority to decide on the skills and competences his future counterpart is required to possess is also restricted in the EU public procurement Directives. Firstly, if the authority decides to formulate qualitative selection criteria, these criteria may only relate to the economic operators' suitability to pursue the professional activity, their economic and financial standing, and their technical and professional ability.[33] Secondly, these criteria too must be formulated in accordance with the aforesaid principles of public procurement law. It is further noted that a public

26 See Article 3 Directive 2014/23/EU, Article 18(1) Directive 2014/24/EU, and Article 36(1) Directive 2014/25/EU.

27 See Article 67 Directive 2014/24/EU and Article 82 Directive 2014/25/EU. Compare also Article 41 Directive 2014/23/EU.

28 See Article 67(2) Directive 2014/24/EU and Article 82(2) Directive 2014/25/EU. See however Article 41(1) Directive 2014/23/EU: 'concessions shall be awarded on the basis of objective criteria, which comply with the [principles of public procurement law] so as to identify an overall economic advantage for the contracting authority or the contracting entity.' See also Article 41(2): 'They may include, inter alia, environmental, social or innovation-related criteria.'

29 See Article 41(1) Directive 2014/23/EU, Article 67(3) Directive 2014/24/EU and Article 82(3) Directive 2014/25/EU.

30 See Article 41(1) Directive 2014/23/EU, Article 67(4) Directive 2014/24/EU and Article 82(4) Directive 2014/25/EU.

31 See Article 41(2) Directive 2014/23/EU, Article 67(4) Directive 2014/24/EU and Article 82(4) Directive 2014/25/EU.

32 See Article 67(5) Directive 2014/24/EU and Article 82(5) Directive 2014/25/EU. Compare however the Directive on concessions: Article 41(3) Directive 2014/23/EU states that the public authority must list the criteria in descending order of importance.

33 See Article 38(1) Directive 2014/23/EU and Article 58(1) Directive 2014/24/EU. See however Article 36(1) Directive 2014/25/EU: 'Contracting entities may establish objective rules and criteria for the exclusion and selection of tenderers or candidates; those rules and criteria shall be available to interested economic operators.'

authority is not allowed to use qualitative selection criteria as contract award criteria, although the rule is not completely without exception.[34]

Given the above assumption that a public authority has decided to call for tenders, EU public procurement law further limits the authorities' freedom to decide on the type of tendering procedure he intends to follow. Basically, he can decide between either an open procedure whereby any interested economic operator may submit a tender, or an ordinary restricted procedure, whereby any economic operator may request to participate as candidate and whereby only those candidates who meet the criteria for qualitative selection are invited by the public authority to submit a tender. Depending on the applicable Directive, variations of the ordinary restricted procedure – such as the competitive procedure with negotiation, the competitive dialogue, and the innovation partnership, each with their own characteristics[35] – may be applied in limited situations only.[36]

Once the technical specifications, contract award criteria, and the criteria for qualitative selection have been designed and formulated, and once the tendering procedure to be followed has been selected, the public authority will have to make known his intention to award a contract by means of that procedure with the publication of a contract notice in accordance with the formal requirements stipulated in the Directives.[37] Depending on the type of tendering procedure applied, he will either receive requests of candidates for an invitation to tender (restricted procedures) or receive tenders (open procedures). In the case of restricted procedures, EU public procurement law does not allow him to invite candidates to tender if they do not meet the criteria for qualitative selection. By the same token, in the case of open procedures, the public authority will only be allowed to assess tenders received from tenderers who meet the aforesaid criteria for qualitative selection. To the extent that candidates or tenderers meet these latter criteria, the authority will have to assess the (subsequent) tenders on the basis of the requirements set in the technical specifications. He can only further assess tenders on the basis of the award criteria if they are in accordance with the aforesaid requirements. EU public procurement law does not impose a duty upon the authority to conclude the tendering procedure with a contract award decision: he has a broad discretion whether or not to terminate the procedure.[38] But if he decides to award the contract, he will have to award it to the tenderer who submitted the winning tender who will thereupon start with the performance of the contract.

34 See for instance Article 67(2) Directive 2014/24/EU. See also Arrowsmith 2014, pp. 749 ff.

35 See Article 29–31 Directive 2014/24/EU and Article 47–49 Directive 2014/25/EU.

36 See Article 26 Directive 2014/24/EU and Article 44 Directive 2014/25/EU. See however Article 30(1) Directive 2014/23/EU: 'The contracting authority or contracting entity shall have the freedom to organise the procedure leading to the choice of concessionaire subject to compliance with this Directive.' See also Article 30(2): 'The design of the concession award procedure shall respect the [principles of public procurement law].'

37 See Article 31 Directive 2014/23/EU; Article 49 Directive 2014/24/EU and Article 69 Directive 2014/25/EU.

38 See Arrowsmith 2014, p. 856.

4. Public Procurement (Law): Top-Down or Bottom-Up Approach?

The editors of this book have developed a threefold approach in their introductory chapter, in order to address current legal questions regarded relevant to find the rules and principles for a consistent and general legal theory on the allocation of limited rights in the EU and its Member States: a conceptual approach (definitions and characteristics), a top-down approach (EU law perspectives) and a bottom-up approach (comparative law perspectives).[39] It is beyond doubt that they think European public procurement law is relevant particularly in the context of the second approach.[40] This does not only follow from the placing of the underlying contribution in Part II of this book, but also from the content of Section 5.3.1 of the introductory chapter, where public procurement law is presented as a constituent part of the body of (general principles of) European Union law that could provide for the elements of a consistent and general legal theory on the allocation of limited rights.[41] Although it is true that public procurement involves an example of a limited right of which the allocation is probably regulated more detailed by the European Union than any other example, it is suggested here to consider its importance with care when contemplating a consistent and general legal theory on the allocation of limited rights. In this section I will briefly elaborate on this suggestion, prior to the detailed analysis provided in Section 5.

Firstly, the editors sketch out some important developments in EU law that they regard most relevant to a generalized approach to the allocation of limited rights, both at EU level and at national level.[42] In this respect, and focussing on the specific EU rules for such allocation by Member States, they particularly deal with public procurement law, internal market law, and competition law (including State aid law).[43] One could question, however, whether public procurement belongs on this list. The rules that are part of the other fields of EU law are generic in the sense that their ambit is not restricted to one or more specific limited rights. Contrary, public procurement law involves an area of law that has as its object the allocation of *one particular* limited right only: the right to remuneration in exchange for the supply of works, goods or services to the government.[44] Moreover, the generic character of the rules belonging to the other fields of (primary) EU law is reflected by the fact these rules – particularly internal market law and competition law[45] – provide the very basis for public procurement law itself, mainly to be found in secondary EU law.[46]

39 Adriaanse, Van Ommeren, Den Ouden & Wolswinkel, Chapter 1 (Section 3).
40 See also Wollenschläger 2015/1 *REALaw*, 250–251.
41 See also Adriaanse, Van Ommeren, Den Ouden & Wolswinkel, Chapter 1 (Section 3).
42 Adriaanse, Van Ommeren, Den Ouden & Wolswinkel, Chapter 1 (Section 5.1). See also Wollenschläger [2015/1] *REALaw*, 209 ff.
43 Adriaanse, Van Ommeren, Den Ouden & Wolswinkel, Chapter 1 (Section 5.3).
44 See Section 5.2.1 below.
45 The editors acknowledge this in their statement that 'the specific two-fold objective of the EU rules in the field of public procurement has always been to ensure the free movement of services and the opening-up to undistorted competition in the Member States', see Adriaanse, Van Ommeren, Den Ouden & Wolswinkel, Chapter 1 (Section 5.3.1). See also B.J. Drijber & H.M. Stergiou, 'Public procurement law and internal market law', 46 *CML Rev. (Common Market Law Review)* (2009), pp. 805–846; Wollenschläger 2015/1 *REALaw*, 209 ff.
46 See Section 3.2 above.

Secondly, in order to support their argument that 'public procurement law might be a very useful starting point to explore the possibilities for a generalised legal theory on the allocation of limited rights', the editors refer to the so-called 'process of generalisation' in order to characterise the development of EU public procurement law in the past decades: 'While starting in the 1970s with some (general) requirements on the award of public contracts, the 1990s showed not only a modernised and detailed update of the old directives, but also an extension of these rules to public contracts for the provision of services.'[47] Despite the enormous practical impact both this expansion of the ambit of EU public procurement law as well as its further elaboration in detailed rules indeed has had in the Member States, one has to understand, however, that it has not resulted in a fundamental extension of the type of limited right that is the object of allocation. That right remains in essence the same: the right to remuneration in exchange for the supply of works, goods or services to the government. By the same token, the recent adoption of a Directive for the award of concession contracts does neither imply that the allocation of a fundamentally different type of limited right is brought within the ambit of public procurement law:[48] the economic operator still obtains a right to remuneration in return for the execution of works or the provision and the management of services. The fact that this right to remuneration consists either solely in the right to exploit the works or the services that are the subject of the contract or in that right together with payment,[49] does not make it in essence a different limited right from the one that is being allocated under the rules of the Directives dealing with public procurement in the framework of traditional supply contracts.[50]

A third comment to be made in this respect relates to what has been stated in Section 3.1. There it has been argued that the government, when procuring works, goods or services, will pursue certain objectives. The specific nature of these objectives and the fact that their pursuit will affect specific interests will have implications for the specific design of the decision-making process that a public procurement process in essence is. The same goes for the fact that an applicant of a payment right in public procurement, unlike the applicants of many other limited rights, must give valid consideration for the public authority's promise to grant the payment right. One has to bear in mind that these objectives, interests, peculiarities, and the decision-making process designed to take them all into account may differ within the framework of public procurement – in some cases even fundamentally – from the ones that relate to the allocation of other limited rights. The corollary of this is that one has to be careful with estimating the importance of public procurement *law* in the framework of a generalised approach to the allocation of limited rights in the EU and its Member States. The nature of public procurement law seems *specific* rather than *generic*. Within the framework of the allocation of limited rights it regulates the specific decision-making process regarding *one particular* right only. To the extent that the objectives, interests, and peculiarities of public procurement

47 Adriaanse, Van Ommeren, Den Ouden & Wolswinkel, Chapter 1 (Section 5.3.1).

48 Directive 2014/23/EU. See Adriaanse, Van Ommeren, Den Ouden & Wolswinkel, Chapter 1 (Section 5.3.1).

49 Article 5(1) Directive 2014/23/EU.

50 See Directive 2014/24/EU and Directive 2014/25/EU.

as well as their translation into a decision-making process design differ from the ones to be found in other areas of allocation of limited rights, these differences will have to be taken into account when developing a consistent and general legal theory on the allocation of limited rights on the basis of EU public procurement law. Rather than assigning an important position to public procurement law from a EU law perspective (top-down) only, I would recommend to embed its analysis in the comparative perspectives (bottom-up) as well.[51] It is with this preliminary recommendation in mind that I will analyse public procurement (law) in more detail in the following section, in order to answer the question whether and to what extent a consistent and general legal theory on the allocation of limited rights in the EU and its Member States may draw inspiration from the phenomenon of (European) public procurement and its regulatory framework.

5. A Consistent and General Legal Theory on the Allocation of Limited Rights: What We can (not) Learn from Public Procurement (Law)

5.1. *Introductory Remarks*

In the following subsections, I will try to establish what probably can – and cannot – be learned from public procurement and its regulation with a view to the development of a consistent and general legal theory on the allocation of limited rights. The analysis will take into account issues that have been selected and organised on the basis of the following distinction provided by the editors in the introductory Chapter of this book: limited rights as the object of allocation (Section 5.2), allocation procedures (Section 5.3), and legal form of limited rights (Section 5.4). In each of these subsections, I will first reflect on the introductory remarks the editors have made on the aforementioned topics. I will do this by focussing, from a comparative perspective, on some of the generic and particular characteristics of public procurement, and on the manner in which these characteristics have been taken into account in the (regulation of the) decision-making process public procurement in essence is. Subsequently, I will conclude each subsection with an attempt to answer some of the questions the editors have raised in light of their introductory remarks.

5.2. *The "What" Question: The Object of Allocation*

5.2.1. Rights

Limited (public) *rights* are defined as individual rights granted by a public authority. These rights can be subdivided into 'authorisations' and 'claims'.[52] According to the editors, the procurement of works, goods and services by public authorities clearly falls

51 Adriaanse, Van Ommeren, Den Ouden & Wolswinkel, Chapter 1 (Section 3). Compare also Wolswinkel 2015 24 *P.P.L.R.*, 140. See also Section 6 of this contribution.

52 Adriaanse, Van Ommeren, Den Ouden & Wolswinkel, Chapter 1 (Section 4.1). Compare also Wolswinkel 2015 24 *P.P.L.R.*, 140.

within the ambit of the concept of 'claims': 'Governmental commissions (...) create a claim for a private party against the commissioning government to something in return for the supply of goods and services.'[53]

In public procurement, the economic operator becomes the beneficiary of a payment duty owed by the public authority in consideration of the operator's duty owed to the authority to supply works, goods or services in accordance with the awarded contract. It is this 'payment right' – linked to the aforesaid duty to supply – that is the object of allocation. In the event that such payment right turns out to be *limited* – an issue to be dealt with in Section 5.2.2 below – there would be no principal objection to approach the allocation of limited rights in general in the same way as the allocation of payment rights in public procurement. One could perhaps argue that these payment rights differ from other limited rights, in the sense that in many cases an applicant becomes entitled to a limited right without having to give valid consideration for the public authority's promise.[54] This is obviously not the case in public procurement, where an economic operator is bound to supply works, goods or services in order to be entitled to payment.[55] It is true that this difference – depending on the nature of the right, the interests involved, and the objectives the public authority aims to achieve with its allocation – might influence the design and completion of the allocation process.[56] The difference does not, however, alter the fact that in either case the *right* as such has economic value and that its allocation – in the event that the right turns out to be *limited* – can be problematized in the same way as a matter of principle.

The editors further acknowledge that the manifestation of the object of allocation in public procurement – a 'payment right' – can be twofold: 'Usually this reciprocity or consideration consists of payment, but this reciprocity may also consist of the right to exploit these goods or services.'[57] The idea that such payment right may also consist of an exploitation right, confirms that there is no need – at least not from the perspective of the concept of 'limited rights' – to make a distinction between public procurement in the framework of a traditional supply contract and procurement of works and services on the basis of a concession contract:[58] what they have in common is that payment rights are

53 Adriaanse, Van Ommeren, Den Ouden & Wolswinkel, Chapter 1 (Section 4.1). See also C.E.C. Jansen, 'De gereguleerde aanbesteding van overheidsopdrachten en de verdeling van schaarse publieke rechten: een vergelijking', in: F.J. Van Ommeren, W. Den Ouden & C.J. Wolswinkel (eds.), *Schaarse publieke rechten*, Boom Juridische uitgevers, Den Haag 2011, pp. 303–304.

54 One could think for instance of the grant of subsidies by public authorities.

55 I accept that in the example mentioned in the previous footnote – once the subsidy has been granted – the economic operator will have to live up to certain conditions imposed upon by the public authority in order not to lose the grant. The nature and purport of the duty to observe these conditions differs, however, fundamentally from the duty of an economic operator in public procurement to supply works, goods or services.

56 See Section 5.3.

57 Adriaanse, Van Ommeren, Den Ouden & Wolswinkel, Chapter 1 (Section 4.2). See also Jansen (2011), pp. 303–304.

58 See Section 4 above and Jansen 2011, pp. 303–304. I exclude concessions regarding the exploitation of tangible goods to be supplied under the contract. It might be concluded from the ambit of Directive 2014/23/EU – which only deals with works or services concessions – that such concessions have no practical relevance. Compare also Arrowsmith 2005, p. 307.

being allocated. In the event that the regulation of the allocation of these rights can indeed be based on the same principles, the distinction between 'authorisations' and 'claims' does not seem to add much relevance – at least not within the domain of public procurement – to the debate on the need of a consistent and general legal theory on limited rights. One might even argue that EU public procurement law shows that the distinction between 'authorisations' and 'claims' – if its presence is felt at all within the domain of public procurement – does not seem to prevent the development of such a theory as a matter of principle.

5.2.2. Limited

Public rights are *limited*, if they are available in limited quantity. They presuppose a maximum – a 'ceiling' – indicating the maximum number of rights that can be granted (within a given period).[59] How does this relate to the allocation of the aforesaid 'payment rights' in the context of public procurement?

First of all, it is noted that payment rights are available in abundant quantity on the market of public contracts for works, goods and services.[60] That being the case, it could still be argued however – and this is what the editors probably must have had in mind – that whenever a particular public authority decides to bring a particular contract involving the supply of particular works, goods and services on the market, a limited right is thus "created" in the sense that the availability of (a) payment right(s) under *that* particular contract will generally attract the attention of more than one single economic operator, depending of course on whether and how the public authority has called for tenders.

Secondly, whenever a public authority decides to create a limited right – consisting of a *payment* right – in the framework of public procurement, he will occasionally decide to create another – *preliminary* – limited right: the right *to submit a tender.* For as was explained before,[61] a public authority may opt for a restricted procedure when issuing tenders, allowing *any* economic operator to request to participate as candidate. In the event that *all* candidates meet the criteria for qualitative selection, the default rule is that they will *all* have to be invited by the public authority to submit a tender. In such a case, the right to submit a tender is not to be qualified as a *limited* right. That right will become limited, however, when the authority has further decided to equip the restricted procedure with the possibility to shortlist the amount of candidates meeting the qualitative selection criteria – a 'ceiling' – prior to inviting them to submit a tender.

Thirdly, whether or not a public authority has decided to create a preliminary limited right *to submit a tender*, the maximum available number of *payment rights* that can be granted in an ordinary case of public procurement, once tenders have been submitted, seems to be *one*. This proposition has to be nuanced, however, for two reasons.

59 Adriaanse, Van Ommeren, Den Ouden & Wolswinkel, Chapter 1 (Section 4.1).
60 Jansen 2011, p. 305.
61 See Section 2.2.

A first reason relates to the practice where a public authority decides to divide a particular contract into separate lots and to bring these lots on the market by a single call for tenders. When doing so, the authority can further decide to limit both the number of lots for which an economic operator may tender, and the number of lots that may be awarded to any one tenderer.[62] In such a case, multiple payment rights are in fact made available in one single allocation procedure at the same time. It is noted, however, that each of these parallel payment rights will usually not attract the attention of all and the same economic operators. The reason for this is that the duties to supply works, goods or services that correspond with each of these parallel payment rights, will in practice differ as regards content. It can therefore be argued that whenever multiple payment rights are being allocated within the framework of one single allocation procedure at the same time, each of these payments rights still remains the object of a unique allocation procedure from the perspective of the uniqueness of the group of economic operators deciding to try to obtain the particular payment right related to a particular lot.

A second reason relates to the practice where a public authority decides to bring to the market a framework agreement with the intention to conclude such agreement with more than one economic operator, and subsequently to award several individual contracts for the supply of works, goods or services under that agreement during a given period of time, following the terms and conditions of the framework agreement. These terms and conditions may stipulate that such contracts are to be awarded after reopening competition amongst the economic operators parties to the framework agreement.[63] It is argued here that in such a case two types of limited rights are in fact being allocated. The *first* right – *i.e.* the right to become a party to the framework agreement – is not a payment right. It basically involves the right to submit a tender in order to obtain a *second* right – a genuine payment right – in return for the supply of works, goods or services. Both types of rights are *limited* in the sense that they are only available in limited quantity whenever a public authority decides to bring a particular framework agreement on the market. The number of *primary* rights available depends on the amount of economic operators the authority grants access to the framework agreement. The number of *secondary* (payment) rights available depends on the amount of supply contracts the authority decides to award under the framework agreement during a given period of time. However, given that each of these secondary (payment) rights will be the object of a separate allocation procedure, each time competition is reopened and following the terms and conditions of the framework agreement, it can – again – be argued that the number of genuine payment rights that can be granted in each allocation procedure, seems to be *one*.

5.2.3. Duration

In public procurement (law), the *duration* of a limited right can only become an issue once a public authority has decided to procure works, goods or services from the market

62 See Recitals (78) and (79) Directive 2014/24/EU. This exception is not discussed in Jansen (2011).

63 See Article 33 Directive 2014/24/EU, in particular paragraphs 1 and 4(b).

and to do so by calling for tenders.[64] It is noted, however, that the duration of the limited payment right thus created will not be regarded as an issue in *all* of these cases. The reason for this is that in the bulk of cases, public procurement will involve the one off supply of works, goods or services under a traditional supply contract. This means that reallocation of payment rights will become obsolete once these works, goods or services have been supplied to the public authority. Reallocation of payment rights may be a relevant issue in public procurement (law), however, in the following situations.

First of all, not every traditional supply contract will have a one off character. Such contract can also have the character of a continuing performance agreement. This could mean, in theory, that if the maximum duration of the contract is not limited, other economic operators will not have access to the relevant payment right for an indefinite period of time once the contract has been awarded. In practice, however, the likelihood of a contract of excessive duration will be limited by the fact that public authorities will be reluctant to accept binding obligations and run the operating risk stemming from factors outside their control for a long period of time.[65] This is probably why it is not considered necessary under the relevant EU public procurement Directives to impose a duty upon public authorities to limit the duration of a traditional supply contract.[66] In the event that a public authority, despite the aforesaid, decides to enter into such contract for a (too) long or even unlimited period of time, this may result in distortions of the free movement of goods and services and amount to a violation of the general principles and rules of the EU, depending on the circumstances of the case.

Secondly, reallocation of payment rights is considered to be a relevant issue whenever a public authority decides to bring a framework agreement to the market and subsequently to award several individual traditional supply contracts under that agreement.[67] Given that the framework agreement – unlike the traditional supply contract discussed under the previous situation – does not impose binding obligations upon the public authority,[68] it is argued that the latter will not be deterred from concluding indefinite agreements when it comes to framework agreements.[69] This is why the relevant EU public procurement Directives stipulate that the term of a framework agreement shall not exceed four years, save in exceptional cases duly justified, in particular by the subject of

64 See Section 3.2.

65 Compare Arrowsmith 2005, p. 688.

66 Although the Directives provide rules on methods for calculating the estimated value of traditional supply contracts that are based on their estimated value during a certain period of time, these rules are not to be interpreted as imposing a duty upon the public authority to limit the duration of contracts. See for example Article 5(11) ff. Directive 2014/24/EU.

67 See Section 5.2.2.

68 Obviously, the public authority will be bound by the relevant public procurement regulation as well as the terms and conditions of the framework agreement. This means that, *when* he decides to procure works, goods or services falling within the ambit of the framework agreement, he must procure them from his contractual counterpart(s) in accordance with the said regulation, terms, and conditions. But he is under no obligation to actually *decide* to procure.

69 Arrowsmith 2005, p. 688; Arrowsmith 2014, p. 1175. See also Explanatory Note of the Commission of 24 July 2005 (CC/2005/03), Framework Agreements Classic Directive, p. 5.

the framework agreement.[70] It is argued that a period longer than four years might be justified, for example, for frameworks involving significant initial investments by the parties to the framework agreement for the purpose of being able to participate in fulfilling orders.[71]

Thirdly, in the event that a public authority decides to procure works and services on the basis of a concession contract, he must limit the duration of the concession on the basis of the works or services requested.[72] The reason for this is to be found in the nature of the concession contract. An important distinction between a traditional supply contract and a concession contract, from the perspective of EU public procurement (law), is that operating risks stemming from factors outside the parties' control are imposed upon the economic operator under the latter type of contract. This might cause public authorities to enter into long term or even indefinite concession contracts, particularly if they are able to strike a (relatively) good deal, in order to shield their interests from the financial consequences of future developments that would make the operation of the works or services more costly.[73] It can be assumed on the basis of the relevant Directive that a concession contract with a fixed term of five years is not regarded as problematic from the aforesaid perspective.[74] For concessions lasting more than five years: 'the maximum duration of the concession shall not exceed the time that a concessionaire could reasonably be expected to take to recoup the investments made in operating the works or services together with a return on invested capital taking into account the investments required to achieve the specific contractual objectives. The investments taken into account for the purposes of the calculation shall include both initial investments and investments during the life of the concession.'[75]

What can be learned from public procurement (law), having regard to the above, with a view to the development of a consistent and general legal theory on the issue of the limited duration of limited rights, allowing for reallocation of such rights after a certain period of time?[76] Before answering this question, it is noted that the issue of duration is problematized in European public procurement (law) from the perspective of market foreclosure and restriction of competition.[77] The following suggestions are therefore considered relevant whenever the allocation of other limited rights can be problematized from the same perspective. Secondly, although the rules to be found in

70 See for example Article 33(1) Directive 2014/24/EU.

71 Arrowsmith 2014, p. 1175, with reference to Recital (62) Directive 2014/24/EU: 'Such cases (...) might for instance arise where economic operators need to dispose of equipment the amortisation period of which is longer than four years and which must be available at any time over the entire duration of the framework agreement.'

72 See Article 18(1) Directive 2014/23/EU.

73 See also Recital (52) Directive 2014/23/EU: 'The duration of a concession should be limited in order to avoid market foreclosure and restriction of competition. In addition, concessions of a very long duration are likely to result in the foreclosure of the market, and may thereby hinder the free movement of services and the freedom of establishment.'

74 See Article 18(2) and Recital (52) Directive 2014/23/EU.

75 See Article 18(2) and Recital (52) Directive 2014/23/EU.

76 Adriaanse, Van Ommeren, Den Ouden & Wolswinkel, Chapter 1 (Section 4.1).

77 See also Section 3.1.

the EU public procurement Directives, dealing with the above specific situations,[78] are all based on the same general principles underlying the TFEU and its rules regarding the prevention of distortions of the free movement of goods and services, it is not easy to grasp their coherence. It is tentatively suggested, however, that the following principles can be derived from public procurement (law), which might be helpful in the development of a consistent and general legal theory on the issue of duration for all limited rights.

First of all, in cases where it can reasonably be expected from the nature of the limited right at hand, and from the interests of public authorities involved, that the latter will receive sufficient incentives *not* to grant limited rights for a (too) long or even indefinite period of time, there seems to be no need to problematize and regulate the issue of duration. Conversely, if it is likely – again: based on the nature of the limited right at stake, as well as the interests involved – that public authorities will grant these rights for such a period of time that market distortions contemplated by the TFEU are expected to occur, this could justify regulatory action. Such action would then have to result in a rule imposing an obligation upon public authorities to limit the duration of the said limited right.[79] That rule would have to take into account, however, that market parties must be allowed a reasonable time to earn back investments reasonably made in order to be able to exercise the rights allocated to them.

It is not possible to give guidance from the perspective of public procurement (law) as to what the aforementioned rule should hold regarding the maximum duration of limited rights. Apart from the fact that this will very much depend on the nature of the right at hand, in connection with the specific possibilities for market parties to recoup their investments, the above analysis of situations shows that the EU public procurement Directives do not take a consistent approach as regards this matter. Although payment rights created in the context of traditional supply contracts with

78 The three situations I have dealt with above are considered to be of particular importance in practice. In addition to these situations, one could further think of the situation where it is allowed to use the negotiated procedure without prior publication for contracts for the traditional supply of goods in the event that the public authority would like to obtain additional deliveries from the original supplier which are intended either as a partial replacement of supplies or installations or as the extension of existing supplies or installations and where a change of supplier would oblige the public authority to acquire supplies having different technical characteristics which would result in incompatibility or disproportionate technical difficulties in operation and maintenance. According to Article 32(3)(b) Directive 2014/24/EU, the duration of such contracts as well as that of recurrent contracts shall not, as a general rule, exceed three years. See also Article 32(5), which allows the public authority to use the aforesaid procedure for new works or services consisting in the repetition of similar works or services entrusted to the economic operator to which he awarded an original contract, provided that such works or services are in conformity with a basic project for which the original contract was awarded pursuant to a procedure in accordance with Article 26(1) of the Directive. The basic project must indicate the extent of possible additional works or services and the conditions under which they will be awarded. As soon as the first project is put up for tender, the possible use of negotiated procedure without prior notification shall be disclosed and the total estimated cost of subsequent works or services shall be taken into consideration by the public authority when applying the rules of Article 4 on threshold amounts.

79 Compare Wolswinkel 2015 24 *P.P.L.R.*, 159.

the character of a continuing performance agreement cannot be granted for an indefinite period of time, the Directives silently leave it to the procurement policy of public authorities to determine the maximum duration of such rights.[80] By the same token, but less silently, the maximum duration of a payment right is left for them to decide in principle, in the event that works and services are procured on the basis of a concession contract.[81] This approach differs from the one chosen for framework agreements, given that the Directives stipulate that such agreements shall not exceed four years in principle.[82]

5.2.4. Tradability

Given that the object of allocation consists of a payment right, it is argued here that its tradability is not a particular issue in public procurement.[83] As said, these rights involve normal payment duties owed by the public authority. The law generally allows that such rights are either traded by means of assignment or encumbered with a security right for the benefit of a third party, unless the economic operator and the public authority agree on a prohibition or restriction to do so. This, however, will normally not be in the interest of the parties involved – particularly when it comes to prohibitions – given that it would limit the operator's possibilities to pre-finance the performance of his duty owed to the authority to supply the works, goods or services.[84] To the extent that limited rights outside the scope of public procurement merely consist of genuine payment rights, the preceding insights might be helpful in the search for a consistent and general legal theory when it comes to the tradability of these rights. The corollary of this is, however, that there is not much to learn from public procurement (law) when the question of tradability involves a particular limited right to performance by the public authority which the latter, by reason of the nature of the performance or the relationship between the authority and the beneficiary of the limited right involved, could not reasonably be required to render to anyone except that beneficiary.

80 See Directive 2014/24/EU and Directive 2014/25/EU.

81 See Article 18(1) Directive 2014/23/EU.

82 See for example Article 33(1) Directive 2014/24/EU.

83 Jansen 2011, p. 304. This issue is not to be confused with the question whether the economic operator is allowed to 'trade' its *duty* owed to the public authority to supply works, goods or services. This issue is problematic in public procurement for several reasons. First of all, the public authority will generally be allowed to refuse performance from a third party given that personal performance by the debtor – the economic operator – will be required in many cases. Secondly, the economic operator will generally require consent of the authority for the substitution of a new debtor of the duty to supply. Thirdly, 'trading' the duty to supply owed to the public authority is problematic from the perspective of public procurement law itself having regard to the concept of "substantial modification of contract", see Article 72 Directive 2014/24/EU, in particular paragraph 4 (d).

84 (Contractual) restrictions seem less of a problem if they would merely require the economic operator to either give notice to the public authority or ask for consent, prior to assigning the payment debt or to encumber it with a security right.

5.2.5. The object of allocation: questions of the editors

In light of their introductory remarks in the introductory Chapter as regards the object of allocation – limited rights – the editors raise the following questions:[85] (i) when may or should a number of public rights be limited; (ii) how are these limitations constructed legally; and (iii) does it make any legal difference, which subject (e.g. radio frequencies, CO_2 emissions or gambling activities) these limited rights concern? In this subsection I will try to answer these questions from the perspective of European public procurement (law). I will further try to determine, on the basis of the answers to these questions, what could be learned from public procurement and its regulation with a view to the development of a consistent and general legal theory on the allocation of limited rights.

Starting with the first question, it follows from what has been explained in Section 5.2.2 that a limited right – in public procurement: a payment right – is created whenever a particular public authority decides to bring a particular contract involving the supply of particular works, goods and services on the market. This decision does neither result from scarcity of natural resources, like the radio spectrum or mineral resources or (clean) water, nor does it seem to be inspired by 'artificial' reasons, like consumer protection or public order.[86] Moreover, as has been explained in Section 3.2, European public procurement law leaves the decision whether or not to create a limited payment right – *i.e.* whether to obtain works, goods or services either 'in-house' or from an external supplier – to the authority's discretion. It could be argued that this latter principle is something that public procurement law could contribute to the development of a consistent and general legal theory on the allocation of limited rights.

Given the answer to the first question, the second question on how limitations are constructed legally becomes however irrelevant, that is to say: from the perspective of EU public procurement law. The question is probably also not relevant from the perspective of the Member States' national public procurement law. For whenever a public authority contemplates the creation of a limited payment right by procuring from an external supplier, the decision whether or not to do so will usually depend on policy considerations only. It may very well be the case that national law occasionally governs the decision-making process as well. But whether or not this is indeed the case – as well as the lessons that could be learned from it, with a view to the development of a consistent and general legal theory on limited rights allocation – is a question that could be investigated in the future, by comparing the Member States' national public procurement policy and regulation. It is repeated, however, that no inspiration can be drawn from EU public procurement law in this respect.

As regards the third question – does it legally make any difference, which subject limited rights concern? – I would like to suffice with the interim conclusion that payment rights in public procurement are not considered relevant from a legal perspective prior to their creation. They become of legal interest, once a public authority has decided to exercise his freedom to procure particular works, goods and services from the market,

85 Adriaanse, Van Ommeren, Den Ouden & Wolswinkel, Chapter 1 (Section 4.1).

86 Adriaanse, Van Ommeren, Den Ouden & Wolswinkel, Chapter 1 (Section 4.1).

either by means of a traditional supply contract, a framework agreement, or a concession contract. It could be the case, however, that it makes a legal difference from the perspective of their *allocation procedure* which subject limited rights concern. And that brings me to the following subsection.

5.3. *The "How" Question: Allocation Procedures*

5.3.1. Allocation procedures and allocation methods

When a public authority decides to bring a contract involving the supply of works, goods or services on the market, he creates a limited right: a payment right. This payment right will generally be of interest to more than one single economic operator.[87] If the public authority further decides to attract the attention of these economic operators by means of a competitive method,[88] he will do so by calling for tenders.[89] Hence in public procurement payment rights are allocated by means of a tendering procedure.

In their introductory chapter, the editors of this book distinguish the following allocation procedures: (1) the order of receipt of the applications ('first come first served'); (2) the drawing of lots; (3) an auction; (4) a comparative assessment (also called 'beauty contest' or 'tender'); and (5) a proportional division.[90] What these allocation procedures have in common is that they all represent unique allocation *methods*: each method stands for the application of one or more unique allocation *criteria*. A tendering procedure in public procurement does *not* represent such a unique allocation method with its own unique allocation criteria.[91] As will be explained below, the design of a tendering procedure in public procurement is based on one or more of the allocation methods already mentioned on the above list.[92]

In public procurement, the qualification of a tendering procedure in terms of one or more of the aforementioned allocation procedures depends on the contract award criterion a public authority will use in a particular case. Current European public procurement *law* allows public authorities to opt for either one of the following two criteria:[93] (i) the most economically advantageous tender, where price or cost-effectiveness is the only relevant criterion; and (ii) the most economically advantageous tender, where price or cost is a relevant award criterion next to qualitative, environmental and/or social

87 See Sections 5.2.1 and 5.2.2.

88 As is explained in Section 3.2, EU public procurement law regulates *this* decision.

89 See Section 2.2.

90 Adriaanse, Van Ommeren, Den Ouden & Wolswinkel, Chapter 1 (Section 4.2).

91 The editors suggest that 'it is sometimes useful to distinguish public procurement as a separate allocation procedure, because it is the most regulated and detailed procedure to allocate limited rights', see Adriaanse, Van Ommeren, Den Ouden & Wolswinkel, Chapter 1 (Section 4.2).

92 See on this issue more extensively Wolswinkel 2011, pp. 195–196 and Jansen 2011, pp. 312–315.

93 See Article 67 Directive 2014/24/EU and Article 82 Directive 2014/25/EU. See, however, Article 41 Directive 2014/23/EU: 'Concessions shall be awarded on the basis of objective criteria which comply with the [principles of public procurement law] and which ensure that tenders are assessed in conditions of effective competition so as to identify an overall economic advantage for the contracting authority or the contracting entity.'

aspects of the tenders (the best price-quality ratio). Another award criterion that can be identified – but which does no longer seem to be allowed by European public procurement law[94] – is (iii) the most economically advantageous tender, where the award decision is based on non-cost criteria only. From the perspective of the aforesaid distinction between allocation procedures, the tendering procedure in the first option is to be qualified as a (reversed) auction. In the third option it would qualify as a comparative assessment, whereas in the second option the procedure has features of both an auction as well as a comparative assessment. In the latter procedure, all tenders will be evaluated on the basis of price or cost on the one hand, and on the basis of non-cost criteria on the other. The results of these two distinctive evaluations will then have to be merged in an overall evaluation of each individual tender, in order to be able to rank them. European public procurement law does not prescribe what method a public authority should use in this respect. Obviously, the method must ensure compliance with the principles of transparency, non-discrimination and equal treatment, with a view to ensuring an objective comparison of the relative value of the tenders in order to determine, in conditions of effective competition, which tender is the most economically advantageous tender.[95] This will require the non-cost aspects of tenders to be sufficient specific and objectively measurable, and to express the value judgment of each non-cost aspect of each individual tender in terms of a grade or a sum of money. In order to objectively determine the overall value judgment of each tender as well as their ranking, the price offered by the tenderer can either be deducted from the outcome of the evaluation of the non-cost aspects – a total amount of points calculated on the basis of the grades that have been awarded, or a total sum of money – or the said outcome can be divided by that price. Hence the overall evaluation of a tender in the aforesaid second option takes place on the basis of a mathematical equation of grades or sums of money identical to what happens in the first option, where price or cost-effectiveness is the only relevant contract award criterion. It could then be argued that whenever a public authority has opted for the contract award criterion of the most economically advantageous tender, and where price or cost is a relevant award criterion next to qualitative, environmental and/or social aspects of the tenders (the best price-quality ratio), the tendering procedure primarily qualifies as a (reversed) auction which is partly facilitated by a (qualitative) comparative assessment of the tenders.

In addition to what has been stated above, another particular feature of public procurement can be mentioned from the perspective of the qualification of a tendering procedure in terms of one or more of the aforementioned allocation procedures identified by the editors. For as was explained in Section 5.2.5, whenever a public authority decides

94 See for instance Recital (90) ('should always include a price or cost element') and Recital (92) ('To identify the most economically advantageous tender, the contract award decision should not be based on non-cost criteria only. Qualitative criteria should therefore be accompanied by a cost criterion that could, at the choice of the contracting authority, be either the price or a cost-effectiveness approach such as life-cycle costing') Directive 2014/24/EU. Arrowsmith questions whether the option is indeed banned by Directive 2014/24/EU, see Arrowsmith 2014, p. 762–763. See also the previous footnote as regards Article 41 Directive 2014/23/EU.

95 See for instance Recital (90) Directive 2014/24/EU.

to create a limited payment right in public procurement, he will occasionally decide to create another – preliminary – limited right: the right to submit a tender. This limited right will be created whenever the authority applies a restricted procedure and decides to shortlist the amount of candidates meeting the qualitative selection criteria prior to inviting them to tender. This latter decision will give rise to questions of allocation too. And again, dependent on the allocation *criterion* applied in a particular case, the *procedure* that is used for shortlisting the amount of candidates can be qualified in terms of one or more of the aforementioned allocation procedures as well. European public procurement law does not prescribe which criterion should be used for shortlisting. Obviously, the rules impose a duty upon the public authority to observe the general principles of public procurement law in this respect.[96] In practice, public authorities will shortlist the amount of candidates on the basis of (additional) qualitative selection criteria that are related to the candidates' skills and competences.[97] The shortlist procedure is then to be qualified as a comparative assessment. But it also seems possible to apply other objective procedures to allocate the right to submit a tender among those candidates who meet the minimum qualitative selection criteria: the drawing of lots, the procedure based on the order of receipt of the applications ('first come first served'), and a proportional division.[98]

The preceding analysis confirms that a 'public procurement procedure' cannot be distinguished from other allocation methods as a *unique* method. One might regard it as a unique feature of a tendering procedure that it occasionally consists of two separate allocation procedures: one procedure to allocate the limited right to submit a tender and another procedure to allocate a limited payment right. And one might further regard it as a unique feature that the latter procedure sometimes qualifies as a combination of already existing allocation *methods* (in the second option that was analysed above). But even if these features would be unfamiliar to any other allocation procedure – which is doubted here – one has to admit that, in the end, a tendering procedure in public procurement involves the use of one or more allocation *criteria* that are not unique to it: they are derived from other, genuine allocation methods.

Obviously, it will be interesting to determine what could be learned from European public procurement (law) in this respect, with a view to the development of a consistent and general legal theory on the allocation of other limited rights. That is one of the questions raised by the editors that will be dealt with in Section 5.3.3 below.

96 See Article 65(2) Directive 2014/24/EU: 'The contracting authorities shall indicate, in the contract notice or in the invitation to confirm interest, the objective and non-discriminatory criteria or rules they intend to apply, the minimum number of candidates they intend to invite and, where appropriate, the maximum number.'

97 In that case, it is argued that they may only use (additional) qualitative selection criteria within the boundaries of the European Directives. See Arrowsmith 2014, pp. 686 ff. See Article 38(1) Directive 2014/23/EU and Article 58(1) Directive 2014/24/EU. See however Article 36(1) Directive 2014/25/EU.

98 Compare Arrowsmith 2014, p. 689–690, who mentions the drawing of lots as well as rotation. The latter procedure can be qualified as an example of the allocation procedure referred to by the editors as proportional division.

5.3.2. Newcomers

In Chapter 1 of this book, the editors also mention the phenomenon of "newcomers" as part of the overall issue of allocation procedures: 'In particular, in relationship to the duration of limited rights mentioned above, the issue of prolongation turns out to be highly relevant: as a result of prolongation, newcomers who will reckon with the limited duration of limited rights, might (once again) not be able to compete for these rights in the future. Finally, after the expiry of limited rights, these rights become available again to grant, provoking the debate whether new entrants should be put at an advantage *vis-à-vis* incumbents.'[99] Here the editors raise two issues regarding the case where a limited right has already been allocated in the past: firstly, the issue of prolonging the allocated right, possibly to the detriment of newcomers and, secondly, the availability for newcomers to obtain such right once its duration has expired. I will not deal with these issues in this section, given that they seem more related to the "what" question instead of the "how" question. From a European public procurement (law) perspective, they involve matters of reallocation and that is why I have already dealt with them in Section 5.2.3 on the duration of limited rights.[100]

The phenomenon of newcomers can nevertheless be problematized in the context of the overall issue of allocation *procedures* from a European public procurement (law) perspective. This will be possible whenever an economic operator is interested in obtaining a specific limited payment right in return for the supply of specific works, goods or services under a traditional supply contract or a concession contract, and where the said operator has never before supplied works, goods or services of the same quality, in the same quantity and under the same conditions. In such a case, the economic operator can be regarded as a "newcomer" from the perspective of the duties that need to be performed by the winning tenderer under the traditional supply or concession contract that is the object of the tendering procedure. From what has been explained earlier on, it follows that the public authority will consider what skills and competences the winning tenderer is required to possess in order to be able to perform the said duties in such a manner that this will cause the objectives of the procurement process to be achieved.[101] The authority will use the outcome of this analysis for the purpose of formulating qualitative selection criteria related to the economic operators' suitability to pursue the professional activity, their economic and financial standing, and their technical and professional ability.[102] Obviously, there is a risk that he will do so in such a manner that newcomers will not be able to meet these criteria. That would prevent them from having access to the tendering procedure, and hence to the limited payment right that is at stake. In order to control this risk, however, European public procurement law imposes a duty upon public authorities to formulate the qualitative selection criteria

99 Adriaanse, Van Ommeren, Den Ouden & Wolswinkel, Chapter 1 (Section 4.2).

100 The reason for this is that the editors too recognize the issue of "duration" of limited rights to be part of the overall issue of the *object* of allocation, see Adriaanse, Van Ommeren, Den Ouden & Wolswinkel, Chapter 1 (Section 4.1).

101 See Section 2.2.

102 See Section 3.2.

in accordance with the general principles of public procurement law, in particular the principle of proportionality.[103] This will prevent them from applying qualitative selection criteria that can only be met by those economic operators that have proven past experience with the supply of works, goods or services of the quality and quantity that is identical to the quality and quantity of the ones the authorities intend to obtain with the tendering procedure at stake and that are supplied under exactly the same conditions.

5.3.3. Allocation procedures: questions of the editors

In light of their introductory remarks as regards allocation procedures, the editors raise the following questions in Chapter 1 of this book:[104] (i) when should limited rights be allocated by a competitive method; (ii) what kind of objective allocation criteria are used in order to prevent favouritism and nepotism; and (iii) how can the equal treatment of long-established parties and newcomers be ensured? In this subsection I will try to answer these questions from the perspective of European public procurement (law). I will further try to determine, on the basis of the answers to these questions, what could be learned from public procurement and its regulation with a view to the development of a consistent and general legal theory on the allocation of limited rights.

As regards the answer to the first question, it is necessary to distinguish between *public procurement* and European public procurement *law*, starting from what has been explained in Section 3.2 above: in public procurement, a limited right – a payment right – is created whenever a public authority decides to bring a particular contract involving the supply of particular works, goods and services on the market. From a mere *public procurement* perspective it will subsequently be wise for the authority to call for tenders by applying a competitive tendering procedure whenever the competition between suppliers resulting therefrom is expected to positively contribute to the objectives the authority aims to achieve with the procurement process. But apart from this general and rather self-evident observation, public procurement *as such* has not much to offer when it comes to the answer to the question when limited rights should be allocated by means of a competitive method. The reason for this is that the objectives a public authority aims to achieve with the allocation of payment rights in public procurement may differ substantially from the ones he has in mind with the allocation of other types of limited rights.

If one approaches the first question from a European public procurement *law* perspective, however, it is first to be repeated that the law does not impose a duty upon a public authority to actually procure his needs from an external supplier.[105] However, once a public authority has decided to do so, the law may impose a duty to call for tenders through the application of a competitive tendering procedure, depending on the circumstances of the case. This duty will become relevant when the authority's procurement decision affects the interest of the opening-up of the EU market of public

103 See Section 3.2. See also Arrowsmith 2014, p. 1192–1194 and 1213–1214.
104 Adriaanse, Van Ommeren, Den Ouden & Wolswinkel, Chapter 1 (Section 4.2).
105 See Section 3.2.

supply contracts and concessions, as part of the overall objective of the EU to establish an internal market without internal frontiers in which the principles of free movement of goods, persons, services and capital are ensured.[106] This interest is considered affected whenever a payment right has a cross-border dimension. Such payment right is deemed to have a cross-border dimension when it relates to a contract within the ambit of one of the EU public procurement Directives and with a value net of value-added tax (VAT) estimated to be equal to or greater than the thresholds mentioned in that Directive. Given that a particular payment right has a cross-border dimension, the Directive imposes a duty upon the public authority to allocate the payment right in accordance with the principles of equal treatment, non-discrimination, mutual recognition, proportionality and transparency, all to be derived from the aforesaid principles of the TFEU, and in particular the free movement of goods, freedom of establishment and the freedom to provide services. Having regard to the aforesaid, it could be argued that a consistent and general legal approach would require a public authority to allocate *other* limited rights by means of a competitive method too, whenever his decision to bring such rights to the market is expected to have a cross-border impact on the aforesaid overall objective of the EU to establish an internal market without internal frontiers.[107] But again, apart from this general observation, I doubt whether it is possible to determine on the basis of European public procurement law the conditions that need to be fulfilled in order for other types of limited rights to have a cross-border dimension. Obviously, one cannot simply copy the rules of the European public procurement Directives on financial thresholds. Likewise, it can be questioned whether the criteria developed by the Court of Justice of the European Union for contracts with a value under the relevant thresholds can be used as a source of inspiration.[108] The reason for this is that the nature of a payment right in public procurement, as well as the (cross-border) interests involved in it, may differ substantially from the nature of other types of limited rights that are outside the domain of public procurement.

That brings me to the second question: What kind of objective allocation criteria are used in order to prevent favouritism and nepotism? It has been explained in Section 5.3.1 that the use of a particular allocation *criterion* implies the use of a particular allocation *method* represented by a particular allocation *procedure*. Hence the second question departs from the editors' assumption that a public authority has decided to allocate a limited right by means of a competitive allocation method as referred to in their first question. It then follows from Section 5.3.1 that limited payment rights are being allocated in European public procurement (law) by means of a competitive tendering procedure. From a *limited rights* perspective, two types of tendering procedures can be identified.[109] The first and most common procedure will involve the allocation of a

106 See Section 3.1.

107 Compare Wolswinkel 2015 24 *P.P.L.R.*, pp. 150–152.

108 See Section 3.2.

109 This perspective is not to be confused with the *European public procurement law* perspective, on the basis of which a distinction between *open* procedures and *restricted* procedures can be made. See Section 3.2 above.

limited *payment right* only.[110] The second tendering procedure consists of two separate allocation procedures: one to allocate the limited right to *submit a tender*, and another procedure to allocate the *payment right*.[111] It subsequently follows from the EU public procurement Directives that a public authority can opt for only two allocation methods in the aforesaid tendering procedures: a (reversed) auction or a (reversed) auction facilitated by a (qualitative) comparative assessment. If the first method is applied, the allocation criterion allowed is the most economically advantageous tender, where price or cost-effectiveness is the *only* relevant criterion. If the authority opts for the second allocation method, the criterion to be used is the most economically advantageous tender, where price or cost is a relevant award criterion *next to* qualitative, environmental and/or social aspects of the tenders (the best price-quality ratio). When a public authority decides to assess tenders on the basis of one of these allocation criteria, he can only do so to the extent that tenders are in conformity with the authority's technical specifications. In addition to this, given that *supplier* quality is an important feature of public procurement next to *performance* quality,[112] the authority will usually have set minimum criteria for qualitative selection. In that case he is only allowed to assess those tenders that have been submitted by economic operators who meet these criteria. In the occasional event that the tendering procedure consists of two separate allocation procedures as explained above, the procedure that is used to allocate the limited right to submit a tender will usually be designed on the basis of a (qualitative) comparative assessment, although other allocation methods, such as the drawing of lots, 'first come first served', or a proportional division, are also possible in theory.

So what can be learned from the above answer to the second question, in light of the development of a consistent and general legal theory on the allocation of limited rights? From a European public procurement *law* perspective, one might first of all argue that – similar to a tendering procedure in public procurement – any procedure involving the allocation of a limited right by means of a competitive method based on a particular allocation criterion will require a public authority to act in accordance with the principles of non-discrimination, equal treatment, transparency, and proportionality. This might particularly be argued whenever the allocation procedure is expected to have a cross-border impact on the overall objective of the EU to establish an internal market without internal frontiers in which the principles of free movement of goods, persons, services and capital are ensured.[113] It follows from the above answer to the first question, however, that it is not possible to derive inspiration from the detailed rules and criteria to be found in the EU public procurement Directives for the purpose of developing a standard that can be used to determine when other types of limited rights are considered to have a cross-border impact.[114]

110 And this can be done either by means of an open procedure or a restricted procedure. See also the previous footnote.

111 And this will imply that the authority has opted for a restricted procedure. See also the previous footnotes.

112 See Section 2.1.

113 Compare Wolswinkel 2015 24 *P.P.L.R.*, 145.

114 See on this topic also Wolswinkel 2015 24 *P.P.L.R.*, 146.

A second observation concerns the restrictions to be found in the EU public procurement Directives as regards the allocation methods the authority is allowed to apply for the purpose of allocating payment rights. It could be argued that if he would be allowed to use an allocation method *other* than a (reversed) auction or a (reversed) auction facilitated by a (qualitative) comparative assessment, he would still be able to design a decision-making process in accordance with the aforesaid principles of non-discrimination, equal treatment, transparency and proportionality. It could be questioned in such a case, however, whether the use of such other allocation methods would enable the authority to achieve the (other) objectives he has in mind with the procurement process, having regard to the interests that are likely to be affected as a result of it. Clearly, a tendering procedure representing an allocation method based on the drawing of lots or the principle 'first come first served' would run the risk of resulting in a suboptimal grant of a limited payment right from the perspective of these other objectives. A lesson that can be drawn from this, having regard to the further development of a consistent and general legal approach, is that the nature of the limited right to be allocated, as well as the interests inherent in it, are probably decisive factors when it comes to the choice of the allocation method to be applied. If the outcome of the allocation procedure is irrelevant from the perspective of the authority's objectives and interests involved, there will be no reason to prevent him from using any of the procedures identified by the editors to allocate a limited right, given that all these procedures represent allocation methods that will enable him to prevent favouritism and nepotism. Conversely, if the outcome of the procedure *is* relevant to the authority, given the objectives he aims to achieve, it would seem proper to restrict his options as to what allocation procedures he may apply. Assuming that the achievement of these objectives depends on the quality of the *application*, it is advised to allow the authority to use only those procedures that represent allocation methods that will enable him to grant a limited right on the basis of such quality: a (reversed) auction, a (qualitative) comparative assessment, or a combination of these allocation methods. Obviously, in cases where the beneficiary of the right will have to offer valid consideration for the authority's promise to grant that right, and where the quality of such offer may differ for each applicant – as is the case in public procurement – there is evidence that the quality of the application and hence the outcome of the procedure is relevant to the authority.

Thirdly, in cases where it seems proper to use only those procedures that represent allocation methods enabling a public authority to grant a limited right on the basis of the quality of the *application*, he will further have to decide whether to apply either (i) a (reversed) auction with the allocation criterion of price (or cost) only; or (ii) a (qualitative) comparative assessment based on non-financial criteria only; or (iii) a (reversed) auction which is partly facilitated by a (qualitative) comparative assessment based on financial and non-financial allocation criteria. Apart from the fact that the EU public procurement Directives now ban the second option, European public procurement *law* does not give any further guidance as to what option would be best in a particular case. It is argued here that the choice to be made will eventually have to depend on the exact nature of the objectives – financial, non-financial, or a combination – the authority aims to achieve.

Another issue that needs attention in this respect concerns the quality of the *applicant* of a limited right. What can be learned from European public procurement (law) is that the applicant's quality might be a relevant factor to be taken into account in the design of the allocation procedure. However, the fact that supplier quality is an important feature of public procurement does not necessarily mean that this will similarly be the case with other limited rights. The need to take the quality of the applicant into account will depend on, again, whether such quality may influence the outcome of the allocation procedure and whether such outcome is relevant to the authority, given the nature of the right and the interests involved, particularly the objectives the authority aims to achieve with the procedure. By the same token, the fact that supplier quality – the quality of the *applicant* – is an important feature in public procurement *in addition to* performance quality – the quality of the *application* – does neither have to imply that allocation procedures regarding other types of limited rights need to combine these features also. In this respect it is also relevant to remember that European public procurement law generally prevents a public authority from allocating payment rights on the basis of supplier quality as allocation criterion.[115] The decision to grant a payment right to a particular economic operator is solely to be based on the quality of his tender, whereas the comparative assessment of his skills and competences on the basis of minimum qualitative selection criteria will only be relevant in order to determine whether his tender may subsequently be assessed at all. This too seems to be a particular feature that will not necessarily have to be dealt with (in the same way) when regulating the allocation of other limited rights is contemplated, given that it is feasible that the quality of the *application* of these other rights will be irrelevant to a public authority, contrary to the quality of the *applicant*.

A final observation from the perspective of European public procurement regarding the answer to the second question involves the occasional situation where a public authority opts for a tendering procedure consisting of two separate allocation procedures. One procedure relates to the allocation of a limited right to *submit a tender*, whereas the other concerns the allocation of a corresponding limited *payment right*. European public procurement law generally allows a public authority to create a limited right to submit a tender once he has decided to bring a corresponding payment right to the market by means of a competitive tendering procedure. The law also gives guidance as to the procedural requirements that need to be observed when designing the allocation procedure involving the limited right to submit a tender. European public procurement law does not give guidance, however, as to the question when it is considered proper to create such a limited right. It is argued here that it may be sensible to do so from a perspective of administrative convenience in cases that meet the following cumulative criteria: (i) it is expected that there will be many applicants for a particular limited right; (ii) in the event that minimum qualitative selection criteria have been set by the public authority, it is further expected that many of the applicants will meet these criteria; (iii) the quality of the applications is relevant from the perspective of the authority's objectives and interests involved; and (iv) both the drafting of the applications as well as the comparative assessment of their quality is expected to take a disproportionate amount of time and generate disproportionate transaction costs.

115 See Section 3.2.

As regards the third and final question of the editors – how can the equal treatment of long-established parties and newcomers be ensured? – I just wish to refer to what has been argued in Section 5.3.2 in this respect. The editors approach the issue of newcomers from the perspective of the reallocation of a limited right that has already been allocated once in the past. Taken from this perspective, the third question has already been dealt with in Section 5.2.3 on the duration of limited rights. However, the issue can also be approached from the perspective that an applicant of a limited right is to be regarded as a "newcomer" in cases where he applies for a limited right of such a nature, quality or quantity that has never been acquired by him before. What can be learned from European public procurement (law) is how to control the risk of excluding such newcomers from the allocation of a limited right, whenever the quality of the applicants is a relevant factor for a public authority to be taken into account in the design of the allocation procedure.

5.4. *The "Form" Question: Legal Form of Limited Rights*

5.4.1. Legal form

It is pointed out by the editors in Chapter 1 of this book that '(G)enerally, administrative authorities grant public rights by unilateral single case decision-making or by a contract. Although a public right will usually be allocated unilaterally, it is sometimes necessary that the other (receiving) party agrees with this grant and that there is some kind of bilateral or multilateral legal form to express this reciprocity. In particular, this kind of agreement – a bilateral or multilateral "public" contract – is needed when the administrative authority lacks the power to grant the public right unilaterally. "Public" contracts in this broad sense, i.e. contracts of which at least one of the parties is a public authority, are conceptualised very differently in separate EU Member States: in some jurisdictions, these public contracts are understood to be administrative agreements under public law while in other jurisdictions as civil law contracts.'[116] According to the editors, '(T)his definition of public contracts includes, but does not coincide with the definition of 'public contracts' in Article 1(2a) Directive 2004/18/EC (...):[117] contracts for pecuniary interest concluded in writing between one or more economic operators and one or more contracting authorities and having as their object the execution of works, the supply of products or the provision of services'.[118] They further argue that 'the public procurement procedure (...) most often (...) results in a bilateral public contract, but this is not necessarily the case; the public procurement procedure may also be used in the case of unilateral decision-making.'[119]

116 Adriaanse, Van Ommeren, Den Ouden & Wolswinkel, Chapter 1 (Section 4.3).
117 The definition provided by Article 2(1)(5) Directive 204/24/EU is identical. See also Article 2(1) Directive 2014/25/EU. Compare the definition of "concessions" in Article 5(1) Directive 2014/23/EU.
118 Adriaanse, Van Ommeren, Den Ouden & Wolswinkel, Chapter 1 (Section 4.3), footnote 35.
119 Adriaanse, Van Ommeren, Den Ouden & Wolswinkel, Chapter 1 (Section 4.3).

Although I agree with the editors' proposition that 'a certain kind of limited right does not automatically imply a certain allocation procedure, nor does a certain kind of allocation procedure imply a certain legal form',[120] I find it difficult to frame the grant of a payment right in public procurement, by means of a competitive tendering procedure, in a legal form other than a bilateral agreement between a public authority and an economic operator. For even if one would isolate the authorities' final decision to grant such payment right from the overall decision-making process public procurement in essence is, and subsequently qualify that particular decision – dependent on its legal framing within a particular Member State – as a case of unilateral decision-making, one cannot deny that such decision is always preceded by a voluntarily expression of willingness of the economic operator to become the beneficiary of a payment duty owed by the authority. One might argue that this line of reasoning would make the above distinction between "unilateral single case decision-making" and "public contract" obsolete within the overall domain of the grant of limited rights, given that a public authority's decision to grant any such right will always be based on an implied or express application by its counterpart to become the beneficiary of that right. And the further implication of this would be that one could suffice with unilateral decision-making as the legal form to accommodate limited rights. One has to understand, however, that this line of reasoning only holds true in cases where the legal effect of the application – when granted – is that the applicant becomes entitled to the limited right without having to give valid consideration. In cases where consideration has to be given in return for the authority's promise to grant the limited right, the voluntary expression of willingness of the applicant is a necessary requirement in order for him to become bound to a duty to give such consideration. This latter legal effect cannot be achieved by means of unilateral decision-making on the authority's behalf. As has been explained in Section 5.2.1 above, the grant of a payment right in public procurement belongs to this latter type of cases. In cases like these – to put it in the words used by the editors – the public authority lacks the power to unilaterally both grant such right *and* become the beneficiary of the economic operator's duty to supply works, goods or services in return.[121] Obviously, the preceding analysis does not imply that it is problematic to qualify isolated decisions made by a public authority in the course of an application procedure in terms of unilateral decision-making with legal effect. The point I am trying to make is that if the objective of the overall decision-making process resulting in the grant of a limited right is to impose a duty upon the beneficiary of that right to give consideration, there is more required from a legal perspective than mere unilateral decision-making.

120 Adriaanse, Van Ommeren, Den Ouden & Wolswinkel, Chapter 1 (Section 4.3).

121 And this will not be different in the case mentioned by the editors where a "public service contract", according to Article 2(i) Regulation (EC) No 1370/2007 of the European Parliament and of the Council of 23 October 2007 on public passenger transport services by rail and by road and repealing Council Regulations (EEC) Nos 1191/69 and 1107/70, may also consist of 'a decision adopted by the competent authority taking the form of an individual legislative or regulatory act', depending on the law of the Member State, see Adriaanse, Van Ommeren, Den Ouden & Wolswinkel, Chapter 1 (Section 4.3), footnote 37.

5.4.2. Legal form: questions of the editors

The editors raise the following questions in Chapter 1 in light of their introductory remarks as regards the legal form of limited rights:[122] (i) does EU law prescribe a preferred legal form of limited rights; (ii) which judge (civil, administrative or otherwise) has jurisdiction with regard to the various legal forms of limited rights; and (iii) to what extent do the various legal forms of limited rights entail specific problems of legal protection? In this subsection I will try to answer these questions from the perspective of European public procurement (law). I will further try to determine, on the basis of the answers to these questions, what could be learned from public procurement and its regulation with a view to the development of a consistent and general legal theory on the allocation of limited rights. The analysis will be brief, given that European public procurement law hardly deals with the issues raised in the questions.

Starting with the first question, European public procurement law does not impose a duty upon the Member States regarding the legal form of payment rights granted in public procurement. On the other hand, it follows clearly from the definitions provided in the Directives of the concepts "public contracts",[123] "supply, works and service contracts",[124] and "concessions"[125] that these concepts fit the definition of "public contracts" used by the editors as opposed to the concept of "unilateral decision-making".[126] Be that as it may, I don't think European public procurement *law* gives much guidance as to the question how to deal with the issue of legal form with a view to the development of a consistent and general legal theory. The approach of the subject matter by the editors, including the distinction they make between the concepts of unilateral decision-making on the one hand and public contracts on the other, seems to provide a proper basis for further analysis of the law of the various Member States from the perspective of the said issue. This further analysis might establish – based on what has been stated in Section 5.4.1 in the framework of public procurement – whether or not the concept of public contract used by the editors is indeed the proper legal form to accommodate limited rights in cases where consideration is given for the public authority's promise to grant such rights.

That brings me to the second question, which can be answered as follows. European public procurement law does not deal with the issue which judge will have jurisdiction with regard to the various legal forms of payment rights in public procurement. The Remedies Directives merely require that decisions taken by public authorities in the framework of a tendering procedure under one of the EU public procurement Directives may be reviewed by review bodies.[127] The Member States must ensure that these bodies as well as their review procedures are in accordance with minimum requirements

122 Adriaanse, Van Ommeren, Den Ouden & Wolswinkel, Chapter 1 (Section 4.3).

123 Article 2(1)(5) Directive 2014/24/EU.

124 Article 2(1) Directive 2014/25/EU.

125 Article 5(1) Directive 2014/23/EU.

126 The editors also recognize this, see the citation in Section 5.4.1.

127 Directives 89/665/EC and 92/13/EC as amended by Directive 2007/66/EC.

stipulated in the Remedies Directives.[128] The Directives allow review procedures to be carried out by a body that is not judicial in character, provided that any measure taken by such body or any exercise of power conferred on it can be the subject of judicial review or review by another body which is a court or tribunal within the meaning of Article 267 TFEU, and independent of both the public authority and the review body.[129] As to the nature of such court or tribunal - civil, administrative or otherwise - the Directives remain silent.

The third and final question cannot be answered from the perspective of European public procurement *law* either, given that the EU public procurement Directives do not impose a duty upon the Member States regarding the legal form of payment rights granted in public procurement. Hence the question as to what extent the legal form of these payment rights entails specific problems of legal protection is to be answered on the basis of a further analysis of the law of the various Member States as suggested above. When the subject matter is approached from the perspective of *public procurement*, and taking into account what has been argued in Section 5.4.1, it is also difficult to see what can be learned from it with a view to answering the third question. I wonder whether problems of legal protection related to the fact that payment rights in public procurement are granted by a public authority in consideration for the economic operator's promise to supply works, goods or services, are *specific* in comparison to other cases where limited rights are granted in consideration for a promise by the beneficiary of such right.

6. Conclusions and Recommendation

Public procurement represents an important example of the phenomenon of allocation of limited public rights. From a contractual point of view, the limited right being allocated is the financial benefit the applicant obtains under a traditional supply or a concession contract, in return for the performance of a duty to supply works, goods or services to a public authority. Hence the term 'payment rights' used in this contribution to distinguish limited rights in the framework of public procurement.

Is it possible to draw inspiration from European public procurement (law) for the purpose of a general legal approach to the allocation of limited rights in the EU and its Member States? I think the analysis carried out in the previous sections shows that this is indeed possible, at least to some extent.

First of all, European public procurement law leaves the decision to obtain works, goods or services either 'in-house' or from an external supplier - and thus creating a limited payment right - at the public authority's discretion.[130] It could be argued that a general legal approach should reflect the principle that it is for public authorities to decide whether or not to create limited rights, that is to say: in cases where they have the ability to do so.[131]

128 See Article 1(1) Directive 89/665/EC as amended by Article 1(1) Directive 2007/66/EC.

129 See Article 2(9) Directive 89/665/EC as amended by Article 1(1) Directive 2007/66/EC.

130 See Section 3.2.

131 See Section 5.2.5. The creation of a limited right will not always be the result of a decision of a public authority, as it may also result from scarcity of natural resources.

Secondly, when a public authority decides to procure works, goods or services from an external supplier, it may follow from the fundamental rules and general principles of the TFEU that he has a duty to advertise the contract to enable the market to be opened up for competition. In addition to this, it is even possible that the authority is under a further duty to call for competitive tenders in accordance with the provisions of one of the European public procurement Directives. These duties will become relevant, depending on the circumstances of the case, when the authority's procurement decision is considered to affect the interest of the opening-up of the EU market of public supply contracts and concessions, as part of the overall objective of the EU to establish an internal market without internal frontiers in which the principles of free movement of goods, persons, services and capital are ensured. Consequently, it can be argued from the perspective of a general legal approach that the aforesaid duties will *also* become relevant when a public authority decides to bring *other* limited rights to the market and where this decision is expected to have a cross-border impact on the aforesaid overall objective of the EU. However, I doubt whether it is possible to determine solely on the basis of European public procurement law the conditions that need to be fulfilled in order for these other types of limited rights to have a cross-border dimension. Obviously, one cannot simply follow the rules of the European public procurement Directives on financial thresholds. Likewise, it can be questioned whether the criteria developed by the Court of Justice of the European Union for contracts with a value under the relevant thresholds can be used as a source of inspiration.[132] The reason for this is that the nature of a payment right in public procurement, as well as the (cross-border) interests involved in it, may differ substantially from the nature of other types of limited rights that are outside the domain of public procurement.

Thirdly, when a public authority is under the aforesaid duty to advertise a traditional supply contract or a concession, and perhaps even under a further duty to call for competitive tenders in accordance with the provisions of the relevant Directive, European public procurement law requires him to design and perform a decision-making process – eventually resulting in the allocation of a limited payment right – in accordance with the principles of non-discrimination, equal treatment, transparency, and proportionality. The underlying idea is that whenever allocation decisions are being made in conformity with these principles, the authority will contribute to the overall objective of the opening-up of the internal market. This is the essence of European public procurement law, which explains what is probably the most important lesson a general approach to the allocation of limited rights can learn from it: whenever a procedure is used to allocate any limited right, that procedure must be designed and carried out in accordance with the aforesaid principles.

The previous shows that a general legal approach to the allocation of limited rights can indeed draw inspiration from European public procurement (law) to a considerable extent. But what more can be learned from it, besides what has been argued above? I think there are two issues that need to be addressed in this respect.

132 See Section 3.2.

Firstly, although it would indeed seem logic to design and carry out allocation procedures for *other* limited rights in accordance with the aforesaid principles of non-discrimination, equal treatment, transparency, and proportionality, it is questioned whether the underlying design of a tendering procedure in European public procurement (law) can generally be used as a model for that purpose. The reason for this is that the said design is very much tailored to the characteristics that are typical for the allocation of a limited payment right in public procurement. Obviously, these characteristics are inherent in the particular objectives a public authority aims to achieve with the procurement, having regard to the interests involved in it. It is important to recall in this respect that a tendering procedure is a means for the authority to become the beneficiary of a duty owed by the winning tenderer to supply works, goods or services in accordance with the awarded contract. The authority will generally not be interested in 'just any' tenderer, offering 'just any' solution to fulfil his needs. On the contrary, it will be of particular interest to the authority to find a supplier who does not only have the skills and competences that are required for the supply of the works, goods or services, but who is also capable of providing him with the best offer to fulfil his needs. This particular interest is first of all reflected by the typical design of the various stages of a tendering procedure, which enables the authority to select on the basis of both supplier quality and the quality of the performance offered by a supplier. The said interest is further reflected by the closed system and the specific nature of both the qualitative selection and award criteria which European public procurement law allows the authority to apply when taking selection decisions in the course of a tendering procedure.[133] Assuming that the objectives which a public authority aims to achieve with the allocation of *other* limited rights may differ substantially from those pursued in public procurement, it can be argued that the characteristics of the procedures to be designed for the allocation of such other rights will not necessarily have to resemble the characteristics of a tendering procedure.

Secondly, although European public procurement law may illustrate and explain why it would indeed seem logic to design allocation procedures for *other* limited rights in accordance with the principles of non-discrimination, equal treatment, transparency, and proportionality, it is questioned whether it can be helpful in deciding what the nature of the general regulatory framework for the allocation of limited rights in the EU should be: a principle-based or a rule-based regulatory framework.[134] Apart from the fact that is it possible to find examples illustrating *both* approaches in European public procurement law,[135] the ratio underlying these differing approaches is also subject to debate.[136]

133 See Sections 3.2 and 5.3.3.

134 See also the chapter by Van Ommeren in this book.

135 The regulatory framework for traditional supply contracts to be found in Directive 2014/24/EU and – to some extent – Directive 2014/25/EU is rule-based, whereas the framework for social and other specific services (see Article 76 Directive 2014/24/EU) and for concessions (see Article 30 Directive 2014/23/EU) is principle-based.

136 Compare also Arrowsmith 2014, pp. 230 ff.

Having regard to these issues, it is argued here that the nature and characteristics of a limited right, as well as the interests inherent in it, are important factors to be taken into account when deciding on the proper design, not only of its allocation procedure, method, and criteria, but also of the nature and content of its regulatory framework. With regard to the further development of a consistent and general legal theory on limited rights, I would therefore recommend to take a bottom up approach and to analyse the allocation of each specific limited right – including payment rights in public procurement – starting from the specific objectives and interests involved as well as their translation into a specific decision-making process, a specific allocation procedure, allocation method, and allocation criteria. One cannot fully understand the regulation of the allocation of a specific limited right without its particular context, leave alone compare one regulation with another with a view to a consistent and general legal approach of all limited rights.

Willemien den
Ouden and
Michiel Tjepkema*

CHAPTER 11. THE ALLOCATION OF LIMITED LICENCES BY THE ADMINISTRATION – REQUIREMENTS UNDER THE EUROPEAN FUNDAMENTAL RIGHT TO PROPERTY

1. Introduction

This book deals with limited public rights, such as authorisations and subsidies. Limited public rights often represent a specific value for the holder of such rights, who commonly regards them as property. Authorisations are sometimes limited as a consequence of scare natural resources, but they also often concern intentionally created scarcity as a result of specific government policy objectives,[1] for instance gambling licences, parking licences or licences to operate a pharmacy. These policy objectives tend to change over time. If, for example, the government wants to pursue a stricter policy in the area of betting and gaming in order to reduce gambling addiction, this can have consequences for the holder of a gambling licence. What if this limited right, his 'property', is taken away and re-allocated or amended (for example in scope or conditions) to the detriment of the holder? What if the government takes other measures which result in the value of the licence decreasing? Can holders of limited public rights claim property rights in such cases in order to prevent changes to their rights?

In this book the authors seek to demonstrate the need for a consistent approach to the allocation of limited public rights from a legal perspective. The issues highlighted above show that when addressing the question of which rules and principles are relevant in a general legal theory on the allocation of limited public rights in the EU and its Member States, the right to property must be included. In this chapter we will focus on how the concept of the protection of property can be incorporated into a consistent legal framework.

To answer this question, we will take a closer look at the implications and influence of the European Convention on Human Rights (ECHR). The right to property as

* Willemien den Ouden is Professor of administrative law at Leiden University, the Netherlands. Michiel Tjepkema is Associate Professor of administrative law at Leiden University, the Netherlands. They both work as research fellows at Leiden Law School.

1 See further on this subject para. 4 (concepts and definitions) of Chapter 1 of this book.

governed by Article 1 of the First Protocol to the ECHR is much more developed in the case law on the revocation of authorisations than its mirror image laid down in Article 17 of the EU Charter of Fundamental Rights (CFR). In ECtHR case law, licences (and even subsidies[2]) are acknowledged to be property in certain circumstances. It is interesting to investigate what guarantees property rights can offer holders of limited licences pursuant to the case law against government decisions that are detrimental to their interests in relation to these licences. Do these guarantees fit easily into a general theory on limited public rights and what possible tensions are discernible?

When answering this question, we will limit our research to a discussion on limited authorisations for economic activities. There are two reasons for this. First, the case law of the ECHR on limited public rights and property is mainly related to licences (in the broadest sense). The case law on the withdrawal of licences provides valuable information on the way that holders of favourable decisions are protected by the right to property. In addition, the regulation of an economic activity through a system of licences forms without doubt a restriction on the freedom of movement under Union law, at least to the extent that there are or could be transboundary effects. This means that the related EU regulations on free movement are applicable. These have proven to be very significant in the legal approach towards (limited) licences in EU law. EU law and ECHR law come together here, giving rise to an interesting research area. Where do the similarities and tensions lie in these areas of case law? How can the two systems, where tension is observed, be reconciled with each other?

In the next section we will first discuss ECHR case law on the licence as a property. In other words: this section will first deal with the *object of the allocation:*[3] can the object of allocation, a limited authorisation, be qualified as a possession of the applicant to whom it was granted and under what conditions does this hold? Then the question is considered whether the right of possession pursuant to the ECHR can also be relevant in the procedure that is used to withdraw, amend or (re)allocate licences. Can preconditions be derived from Article 1 First Protocol ECHR that regulators and/or administrative authorities must observe when determining the method or procedure of allocation? There is no clear-cut answer to this last question, but the recent ruling in *Vékony v Hongary*[4] does provide new insights.

Having acquired an impression of which preconditions may arise from Article 1 First Protocol ECHR, in Section 3. we turn our focus to the EU law dimension. This is based on a different perspective, where every licence system is deemed to place restrictions on economic operators, which is not favourable to the common market. To the extent a restriction is permitted, licence systems must be based on objective, non-discriminatory criteria made known in advance. In this context, the Court of Justice of the European Union (CJEU) is of the opinion that 'the principle of equal treatment requires that all potential tenderers be afforded equality of opportunity and accordingly implies that all tenderers must be subject to the same conditions' and that preferred positions of

2 See for example *Plalam S.P.A. v. Italy*, ECtHR 18.05.2010, no. 16021/02.
3 See para. 4 (concepts and definitions) of Chapter 1 of this book.
4 *Vékony v. Hungary*, ECtHR 13.01.2015, no. 65681/13.

licence-holders already on the market is discriminative towards newcomers.[5] Are these requirements in line with the requirements formulated by the ECHR in the aforementioned *Vékony* case, where national authorities are actually requested to take into account the interests of former licence-holders during the re-allocation of limited licences based on new policy? This question is discussed in Section 4, where we consider, among other things, the recent ruling in *Berlington* et al.,[6] where the CJEU deals with the ruling in *Vékony*. Section 5. provides some cautious conclusions.

2. The Licence as (a Restriction on) Property in ECHR Case Law

There are many examples in the jurisprudence of the ECHR of cases in which the issue arose whether the withdrawal of a licence brought about an unacceptable violation of property rights. This section first establishes that a licence can qualify as 'property' (2.1) and that the ECHR considers the withdrawal of a licence to be a form of regulating property (2.2). We then go on to consider other conditions placed by the ECHR on the withdrawal of licences, namely that these have a legal basis and are in the general interest (2.3) and that proportionality exists between the general interest being served and infringement in individual cases (2.4). The *Vékony* ruling will be considered more closely in this respect (2.5).

2.1. The Licence as a Property Right?

It is not self-evident that a licence[7] can be deemed a property right. For example, the German *Bundesverfassungsgericht* refused to recognise the licence as property for a long time. The Courts stated that a licence did not have the constitutional protection of Article 14 of the Basic Law (which protects the right to property) when the licence-holder could not freely dispose of the licence, because, according to the law, it was not transferable to another person or company. Moreover, a licence was not considered to be the equivalent of a personal contribution of the owner; rather, it is issued and determined on the basis of public law.[8] The US Supreme Court for a long time also stated that a licence is not property and can be revoked without notice or a hearing. In its view, a licence was only a temporary permit to do something that would otherwise be unlawful – a mere privilege to be enjoyed when certain conditions are satisfactorily met. From the early 1970s, however, the Supreme Court began to acknowledge that a licence-holder did have a property interest in a licence once it had been issued.[9]

5 See for instance Joined Cases C-72/10 and C-77/10, ECLI:EU:C:2012:80, *Costa & Cifone*, para. 57 and more extensive on this topic: Hatzopolous in this book, par 1.1.4.

6 Case C-98/14, *Berlington Hungary and others v. Magyar Állam* [2015], ECLI:EU:C:2015:386.

7 Or similar authorisations such as entitlements, permissions or concessions.

8 M. Schröder, 'Property protection of public licenses and permits', *China-EU Law Journal* (2015), 4, pp. 104–120.

9 See the Supreme Court cases *Board of Regents of State Colleges v. Roth* (408, U.S. 564 (1972)) and *Perry v. Sindermann* (408 U.S. 593 (1973)).

This last view is also the view of the ECtHR. The ECtHR applies an autonomous notion of property and states in this regard:

> 'The Court reiterates that the concept of "possessions" in the first part of Article 1 of Protocol No. 1 has an autonomous meaning which is not limited to ownership of physical goods and is independent from the formal classification in domestic law: the issue that needs to be examined is whether the circumstances of the case, considered as a whole, may be regarded as having conferred on the applicant title to a substantive interest protected by that provision. Accordingly, as well as physical goods, certain rights and interests constituting assets may also be regarded as "property rights", and thus as "possessions" for the purposes of this provision (see Iatridis v. Greece [GC], no. 31107/96, §54, ECHR 1999-II, and Beyeler v. Italy [GC], no. 33202/96, §100, ECHR 2000-I).'[10]

The Court has never concerned itself with theoretical reflections on the issue of *why* a licence can be viewed as property. A cautious tendency towards considering a licence as property can, however, be inferred from the case *Benthem*, where the Court stated:

> 'The grant of the licence to which the applicant claimed to be entitled was one of the conditions for the exercise of part of his activities as a businessman. It was closely associated with the right to use one's possessions in conformity with the law's requirements. In addition, a licence of this kind has a proprietary character, as is shown, inter alia, by the fact that it can be assigned to third parties.'[11]

Therefore a number of considerations can lead to a licence being viewed as property: the fact that it was a necessary condition to promote business interests (and thus represents an asset value), its association with the possibility to use property in a legal way and the transferability of the licence itself.[12]

Thus in the *Benthem* ruling we see that the Court attaches relevance to the relationship between the licence and the business activities of the licence-holder. In subsequent rulings the Court again emphasised this relationship. This makes it sometimes difficult to determine the exact *object* of the property protection: the licence itself or the business that is operated with the assistance of the licence? The case *Tre Traktörer Aktiebolag* concerned the withdrawal of the alcohol licence of a business where it was established during an audit that the accounts were not in order. The Court took the view that the economic interests connected to running Le Cardinal (the restaurant of the applicants) were 'possessions' for the purposes of Article 1 of the Protocol. In the same vein, in the case of *Centro Europa 7 S.R.L. v. Italy*, the Court considered that 'the interests associated with exploiting the licence constituted property interests attracting the protection of

10 *Öneryildiz v. Turkey*, ECtHR 30.11.2004, no. 48939/99, para. 124.

11 *Benthem v. The Netherlands*, ECtHR 23.10.1985, no. 8848/80.

12 See furthermore: *Mullai and others v. Albania*, ECtHR 23.06.2010, no. 9074/07, para. 100, where the Court stated that a building permit 'generated a capital asset and had a definite economic value for the individual applicants'.

Article 1 of Protocol No. 1'.[13] In other cases, however, the Court qualified the licence itself as property, even though the licence was a prerequisite to running a business. Thus, in *Megadat.com* it said that the 'applicant company's licences constituted a possession for the purposes of Article 1 of Protocol No. 1'[14], which was repeated in later case law.[15]

2.2. The Withdrawal of Licences: Regulation or Deprivation of Property?

It is necessary to determine the object of the right to peaceful enjoyment of possessions, since this is connected to the question whether the withdrawal of a licence should be qualified as regulation or deprivation of property. This question is important with regard to the issue of which preconditions have to be met in a withdrawal procedure, in order for it to withstand the test of Article 1 First Protocol ECHR. If the authorisation itself qualifies as a possession, then its withdrawal, strictly speaking, must qualify as deprivation of property. That would imply far-reaching consequences in every situation where Member States issue general prohibitive regulations but want to make exceptions in individual cases. It would, after all, imply that the state is obliged in principle to reimburse the *full market value* if, as a result of the amended policy objectives, it decided to rearrange an existing allocation by withdrawing licences and possibly awarding other, perhaps more suitable, parties.[16] This consequence however was never accepted by the Court. The conditions which have to be met for an infringement to qualify as deprivation are strict. This includes all cases where a 'transfer of ownership' is involved. In such cases, expropriation for example, the Court sometimes qualifies an infringement as *de facto* deprivation, but even here the threshold is high: it must concern a loss of 'all essential elements of ownership' and that loss must be 'more or less irreversible'.[17]

When a licence is withdrawn, strictly speaking a possession 'disappears'. However, no transfer of ownership is actually involved since the government does not become the beneficiary of the rights that previously belonged to the licence-holder. Instead, a prohibitive situation that already existed comes into effect. And even in the event that it is possible to claim that the withdrawal of a licence leads to 'irreversible loss', the aggrieved party generally still remains the owner of the business and the assets belonging to the business. This consideration, in particular, was cause for the Court to qualify the withdrawal of a licence not as deprivation, but as regulation. So, although the licence

13 *Centro Europa 7 S.R.L and di Stefano v. Italy*, ECtHR 07.07.2012, no. 38433/09, para. 177. Compare *Posti & Rahko* v. *Finland*, ECtHR 24.09.02, no. 27824/95 where the Court states that the applicants' rights to engage in certain types of fishing in State-owned waters on the basis of their lease constituted a "possession" for the purposes of Article 1 of Protocol No.1.

14 *Megadat.com S.R.L. v. Moldova*, ECtHR 08.04.2008, no. 21151/04, para. 62.

15 *Vékony v. Hungary*, ECtHR 13.01.2015, no. 65681/13 and *Bimer v. Moldova*, ECtHR 10.07.2007, no. 15084/03, para. 49.

16 On the obligation to reimburse the full market value in cases of deprivation of property see for example *James v. United Kingdom*, ECtHR 21.02.1986, no. 8793/79, para. 54 and *Immobiliare Saffi v. Italy*, ECtHR 28.07.1999, no.22774/93, para. 57.

17 M. Pellonpää, 'Reflections on the notion of "deprivation of possessions" in Article 1 of the First Protocol to the European Convention on Human Rights', in P. Mahoney et al. (eds.), *Protecting Human Rights: the European Perspective*, CH Verlag KG, Köln 2000, p. 1101.

itself is qualified as an object of the interference, when it comes to the determination of the applicable protective regime the interference is aimed not at the licence, but at the other goods within the business for which the licence is used. When these goods retain their value, then the regulation of property is at stake, even if the withdrawal of a licence leads to a situation where a business can no longer be run profitably. This approach can also be detected in the *Megadat.com v. Moldavia* ruling, in which the Court stated:

> 'Although the applicant company could not carry on its business, it retained economic rights in the form of its premises and its property assets. In these circumstances, as in the *Bimer S.A.* case, the termination of the licences is to be seen not as a deprivation of possessions for the purposes of the second sentence of Article 1 of Protocol No. 1 but as a measure of control of use of property which falls to be examined under the second paragraph of that Article.'[18]

In the case *Capital Bank Ad. v. Bulgaria* the Court reasoned differently, by stating that the withdrawal led to a regulation of property. The case involved the withdrawal of a bank licence to an insolvent bank. The Court acknowledged that, if the licence were to be qualified as property, then it would be a matter of deprivation of a possession. However, the Court also found that 'in the circumstances the deprivation formed a constituent element of a scheme for controlling the banking industry.' So since the licence was part of a broader policy to regulate the financial sector, it was deemed a matter of regulation of property. Generally, this line is of interest in cases where – as is often the case in the withdrawal of licences – property is 'reallocated' on the basis of new legislation or policy. Even when this leads to the withdrawal of existing rights, this is still seen as the regulation of property. In the *Baner* case the Commission found that:

> 'Legislation of a general character affecting and redefining the rights of property owners cannot normally be assimilated to expropriation even if some aspect of the property right is thereby interfered with *or even taken away* (curs. WdO/MT). There are many examples in the Contracting States that the right to property is redefined as a result of legislative acts. Indeed, the wording of Article 1 para. 2 shows that general rules regulating the use of property are not to be considered as expropriation. The Commission finds support for this view in the national laws of many countries which make a clear distinction between, on the one hand, general legislation redefining the content of the property right and expropriation, on the other.'[19]

An important consequence of qualifying the withdrawal of property as regulation, is that the Court leaves the authorities a wide *margin of appreciation* to implement policy in the manner desired. The legislature not only has a wide margin of appreciation with regard to the existence of a problem of public concern warranting measures of control, but also in the choice of the detailed rules for the implementation of such measures. The

18 *Megadat.com S.R.L. v. Moldova*, ECtHR 08.04.2008, no. 21151/04, para. 65.

19 *Banér v. Sweden*, European Commission 09.03.1989, no. 11763/85.

Court will respect the legislature's judgment as to what is in the general interest unless that judgment be manifestly without reasonable grounds.[20]

After establishing the applicable property rule, the case law of the ECtHR then proceeds by means of a three-step test to consider whether this interference meets the conditions of Article 1 First Protocol and is therefore justified (legitimate):

1. Is the infringement legitimate i.e. provided for by law (the *lawfulness* test)?
2. If so, does the infringement have a legitimate goal in the general interest? (the *general interest* test)?
3. If so, is there a reasonable balance between the requirements of the general interest in society and the protection of the fundamental rights of the individual (the *fair balance* test)?

We will discuss questions 1. and 2. first, and then proceed to consider the proportionality of the infringement. After all, when the withdrawal of a licence is motivated by policy considerations, it often comes down to the proportionality test in order to determine whether there has been a breach of Article 1. First Protocol ECHR.

2.3. Lawfulness of the Withdrawal of Permits and the General Interest Test

The *lawfulness* test concerns the quality of the law in question, requiring that it is accessible to the persons concerned, precise and foreseeable.[21] In this respect, the Court found that it was contrary to the requirement of lawfulness that the applicants in the case *Mullai a.o. v. Albania* for ten years had to conduct all sorts of legal, and often contradictory, proceedings to obtain clarity about the legal status of a building permit granted to them. The role of the authorities was also criticised since their letters concerning the status of the building permit '*added further confusion to this continuous lack of clarity and certainty*'. This conflicted with '*the State's obligation to deal with the applicants' situation in a clear and coherent manner as possible and with the utmost consistency.*' We shall subsequently see that the requirement for clear and consistent policy concerning the withdrawal of permits can also play a role in the proportionality test. The lawfulness test also requires that the injured party is offered sufficient opportunity to plead their case in court. As the Court held in the case *Capital Bank Ad v. Bulgaria*, domestic law must provide a measure of legal protection against arbitrary interferences by the public authorities in matters safeguarded by the Convention. In this case, the Bulgarian National Bank (BNB) had ascertained that Capital Bank Ad was no longer solvent and consequently withdrew the bank's licence. Capital Bank was informed of this only after the withdrawal had taken place, so without the bank being given the opportunity to dispute the finding of insolvency. Also, in view of the fact that the withdrawal had serious and far-reaching consequences for the bank, which automatically ceased to operate as a going concern and was placed in compulsory liquidation, this meant that the withdrawal

20 *Mellacher et al. v. Austria*, ECtHR 19.12.1989, no. 11070/84.

21 *Beyeler vs. Italy*, ECtHR 05.01.2000. no. 33202/96.

could only be deemed legitimate if it had been adopted after, or had been subject to verification in, some sort of proceedings that afforded a reasonable opportunity to the bank to present its case to the competent authorities with a view to effectively challenging the revocation of its licence.

In the case of the *general interest* test, the Court acknowledges that national authorities have direct democratic legitimation and are in principle 'better placed' than the ECtHR to evaluate local needs and conditions.[22] The Court therefore grants the State an extremely wide margin of appreciation: it is primarily down to the State to determine the object of the infringement and also to determine whether a certain measure is necessary 'in the general interest'.[23] Thus in the *Broniowski* case the Court held:

> 'The Court has declared that, finding it natural that the margin of appreciation available to the legislature in implementing social and economic policies should be a wide one, it will respect the legislature's judgment as to what is *in the public interest* unless that judgment is manifestly without reasonable foundation.'[24]

Cases where the test of Article 1 First Protocol fails at this stage are therefore quite exceptional.[25] In cases involving the 'reallocation' of existing licences on the basis of general policy applying equally to all licence-holders, in principle little doubt will arise over the lawfulness of that policy or the question whether the policy is in the general interest. We shall thus turn our focus now towards the proportionality test.

2.4. *Proportionality: The Necessity of 'Genuine and Consistent Policy'*

It was established above that the withdrawal of a licence can often have serious consequences for the injured party, as the licence is often a necessary prerequisite for performing economic activities, and these consequences can entail substantial financial interests. Within the framework of the proportionality test it is, however, not the severity of the infringement alone that counts: this is a factor to be balanced against other circumstances. Thus the Court found with respect to the withdrawal of the licence of *Olbertz*, who ran a tax consultancy firm, that although this led to a 'heavy burden' for *Olbertz*, in the case in question a very wide margin of appreciation was appropriate in view of the special circumstances in the unified Germany. In addition, it was significant that *Olbertz* could not have the justifiable expectation that he could legally run an office, since he did not meet all the legal requirements to do so.[26]

Cases where the Court does find that on the basis of the proportionality test the withdrawal of a licence is contrary to Article 1 First Protocol ECHR, are mainly cases involving withdrawal in the form of a *sanction*. Here, the Court requires a convincing

22 S. Praduroux, *The Protection of Property Rights in Comparative Perspective*, Groningen: Europa Law Publishing 2013, p. 178 e.v.

23 *Former King of Greece v. Greece*, ECtHR 23.11.2000, no. 25701/94.

24 *Broniowski v. Poland*, ECtHR 22.06.2004, no. 31443/96.

25 Such a scarce example is *Tkachevy v. Russia*, ECtHR 12.02.2012, no. 35430/05.

26 *Olbertz v. Germany*, ECtHR 25.05.1999, no. 37592/97.

motivation from the authorities with regard to the question whether the violation justified the serious infringement of the property right, and whether a claim can justifiably be made on the grounds of the general interest. In this regard, the Court requires that specific negative consequences of the violation of the licence conditions are provided. It is not satisfied with 'theoretical and abstract negative consequences'.[27] When it is not deemed plausible that the applicant company was in breach of the law, the Court concludes that the requirements of Article 1 First Protocol ECHR have not been met.[28]

In a number of rulings the Court emphasised that the authorities must show that they followed *genuine and consistent policy considerations* when revoking and changing their decisions concerning the applicants' business operation.[29] The case law demonstrates that the Court takes into account the following criteria in order for a policy to be 'genuine and consistent':

- the policy is justified by a credible claim on the general interest served by it[30];
- the form of control is sufficient in order to reach the goals the government has set (thus, the government should not choose a severe measure such as a withdrawal when less severe measures are also available to reach the same goals);[31]
- the government applies the same rules to all companies; for example, the authorities can prove that licences of other companies were also withdrawn for similar reasons and that the applicant company was therefore not the only company that was subjected to such a severe measure;[32]
- the decision-making process is unambiguous: an initial withdrawal, for example, is not followed by a series of licence extensions.[33]

We ascertained these 'rules' from cases in which withdrawal occurred as a form of sanction, but the requirement of a 'genuine and consistent policy' is also of significance in situations (relevant to this chapter) where withdrawal is carried out on the basis of general policy considerations. A recent ruling in which this is explicitly mentioned is *Vékony v. Hungary*, which shows that the principle of transparency can play an important part in the question of whether a withdrawal is carried out within the framework of a 'genuine and consistent policy'.

27 See for example *Megadat.com S.R.L. v. Moldova*, ECtHR 08.04.2008, no. 21151/04 and *Donprut S.R.L. v. Moldova*, ECtHR 21.07.2015, no. 45504/09.

28 See *Rosenzweig and bonded warehouses ltd. v. Poland*, ECtHR 05.06.2012, no. 51728/99.

29 *Rosenzweig and bonded warehouses ltd. v. Poland*, ECtHR 05.06.2012, no. 51728/99, *Megadat.com S.R.L. v. Moldova*, ECtHR 08.04.2008, no. 21151/04, *Vékony v. Hungary*, ECtHR 13.01.2015, no. 65681/13.

30 *Rosenzweig and bonded warehouses ltd. v. Poland*, ECtHR 05.06.2012, no. 51728/99, para. 62, *Megadat.com S.R.L. v. Moldova*, ECtHR 08.04.2008, no. 21151/04, para. 68.

31 *Rosenzweig and bonded warehouses ltd. v. Poland*, ECtHR 05.06.2012, no. 51728/99, para. 56.

32 *Megadat.com S.R.L. v. Moldova*, ECtHR 08.04.2008, no. 21151/04, para. 75.

33 See *Tre Traktörer Aktiebolag v. Sweden*, ECtHR 07.07.1989, no. 10873.84, para. 61, *Rosenzweig and bonded warehouses ltd. v. Poland*, ECtHR 05.06.2012, no. 51728/99, para. 59.

2.5. *The Case of Vékony v. Hungary*

This case concerned the withdrawal of a licence to sell tobacco products in a shop. The applicant and his family had had such a licence for their shop since 1994. The sale of tobacco amounted to one third of the annual turnover. However, in 2012 the Hungarian parliament adopted a law that made the sale of tobacco a state monopoly. Shop owners lost their licence, but could obtain a new concession via a tender procedure. Vékony applied for a concession in good time, but this application was rejected. The rejection decision was not motivated and could not be contested in court. As a consequence of the rejection, the applicant had to stop selling tobacco, which eventually led to bankruptcy of the business. In Strasbourg he invoked Article 1 First Protocol ECHR.

The Court found, in accordance with established case law, that the licence constituted 'property' in the sense of Article 1 First Protocol ECHR, since it once guaranteed an important share of the applicant's turnover. In light of the above, it is not surprising that the Court qualifies the withdrawal as regulation of the use of property. In addition, the Court found that the desire to amend the licence policy clearly served the public interest, since the measure served the purpose of combatting underage smoking, an aim that was in accordance with the public interest. The Court subsequently stated first and foremost that the competent authorities in this field enjoy a wide margin of appreciation. Nevertheless, it found that Article 1 First Protocol had been violated for a number of reasons.

First, the Court held that the authorities had observed a transitional period that was too short. There were only ten months between the law coming into effect (11 September 2012) and the moment when the applicant had to stop selling tobacco (14 July 2013), or respectively three months from when the claim was dismissed (23 April 2013). Considering that the applicant had had a licence for no less than twenty years, the Court found that the transitional periods were too short for the business to be able to adjust to the new situation.

Second, in the event the authorities nevertheless wanted to adhere to the short transitional period, they should have provided reasonable compensation. This compensation – as noted by the judges in their concurring opinions – was not to serve to replace the economic value of the lost licence, but to ease the transition to a new system. This was also lacking in the case in question; the requirement that new licence-holders had to buy up the stocks of the former licence-holders was far too inadequate.

Third, there were no contraindications: it had not been suggested that the applicant, although his family business was active in lawfully selling products harmful to health, was in any way in breach of the law.

Having discussed the proportionality of the withdrawal decision specifically in the case of *Vékony*, the Court goes on to assess *the process* of granting new concessions. It states, in paragraph 36 of the ruling, that this process was arbitrary by nature. For the sake of convenience, we quote the entire passage:

> 'The Court finds that the measure did not offer a realistic prospect to continue the possession because the process of granting of new concessions was verging on arbitrariness, given that
>
> (i) the existence of the previous licence was disregarded;

(ii) the possibility of a former licence-holder to continue tobacco retail under the changed conditions accommodating the policy of protection of minors was not considered in the new scheme (...);
(iii) the concession system enabled the granting of five concessions to one tenderer which objectively diminished the chances of an incumbent licence-holder, in particular of those individuals, such as the applicant's family, whose livelihood had depended for many years on the possibility of tobacco sale, now lost (see, mutatis mutandis, Di Marco v. Italy, no. 32521/05, §65, 26 April 2011; and Lallement v. France, no. 46044/99, §§20–24, 11 April 2002) and, finally,
(iv) the lack of transparent rules in the awarding of the concessions, which took place
(v) without giving any privilege to a previous licence-holder, such as limiting the scope of the first round of tendering to such persons.'

The procedure for granting concessions bordered on arbitrariness according to the Court, because among other things it did not matter if an applicant had previously been granted a licence, and the regulations for granting concessions were not transparent. The position of the former licence holders was not taken into account sufficiently during the allocation of the new concessions according to the Court. In addition, the Court seems to have difficulty with the fact that more than one licence could be granted to a single applicant, which in turn reduced the chances of former licence-holders obtaining a new licence. As a result of the 'faults' in this allocation process, the Court also came to the conclusion that the applicant had been exposed to an excessive individual burden and a violation of Article 1 First Protocol was observed.

Judges Spano and Kjølbro wrote a joint concurring opinion in the ruling. They believe that in this case the Court should have limited itself to the question of whether the withdrawal of the licence of Vékony was a violation of Article 1 First Protocol. In this regard they stated that Vékony must have been aware that the retail of tobacco products in the future had become precarious, being conditional on obtaining a tobacco retail concession under the new law. However, they agreed on the finding of a violation of Article 1 First Protocol in light of the particularly short transitional period, the lack of reasons for not having been granted a new licence and the absence of a legal remedy to challenge the refusal to grant a new licence. They *disagreed* with the majority, however, by finding that the *process* for the allocation of the new tobacco retail concessions appears to be arbitrary. In their opinion, it is not the Court's task to tell the State what it could or should have done in implementing its policy in this area (ibid.), but rather to assess whether the way the applicant's licence was revoked in the specific circumstances of the case amounted to an unjustified interference with his property rights under Article 1 First Protocol.

2.6. *Some Concluding Remarks*

What lessons can be learned from the above in relation to property rights when we consider the Court's vision on the withdrawal of licences for economic activities as a result of new policies where a maximum is imposed and licences are reallocated? Generally, it can be concluded that the ECtHR is fairly quick to accept that the withdrawal of a licence provided for an economic activity forms an interference in property rights. This interference is then tested against the customary requirements of lawfulness, general interest and the fair balance requirement (proportionality). The lawfulness test requires, among other things, access to a legal remedy to challenge the revocation and the refusal to grant a new licence. The proportionality test produces the most interesting building blocks for a legal theory on the allocation of limited authorisations, because when ruling on the proportionality of the violation on the property right the Court takes into account both the withdrawal of the licence *and* the possibility to repair the consequences of the withdrawal in the subsequent allocation process. At least two points are of interest with regard to the proportionality test:

a. do justifiable expectations exist on the side of the licence holder? This is not the case if the withdrawal constitutes a sanction for not meeting the requirements attached to the licence, statutory or otherwise, and the same applies if the licence was granted for a specific period. However, if a justifiable expectation exists on the side of a licence holder with regard to his concession, this warrants the possibility of a transitional period until the time when the licence will be withdrawn or a financial compensation, which enables the former licence holder to prepare for the new situation without the licence.
b. Is there genuine and consistent policy for granting new licences? A consistent policy is not arbitrary. The Court found the licencing procedure in the *Vékony* case to be arbitrary since the procedure was not set up to be transparent and took insufficient account of the position of former licence holders.

When comparing the ECtHR case law with the case law of the Court of Justice, which we will do from the next section onwards, one has to bear in mind the 'human rights' perspective from which cases such as *Vékony* are generally viewed. The ECtHR's perspective commonly focuses on the severe consequences that the withdrawal of a licence might have for an individual. From this perspective, less attention has been paid so far to the perspective we have chosen in this book – the scarcity of rights, the necessity to grant the government a certain leeway in the redistribution of those rights and equal treatment c.q. fair competition between interested parties. We hope, however, that this case only goes to illustrate that the development of a theory on limited rights can benefit from both perspectives. With this in mind, we will now address the question of how the two aspects mentioned above under a and b are assessed under EU law, particularly with regard to free movement.

3. The Licence as a Restriction on Free Movement under EU Law

A prior authorisation scheme for economic activities is generally considered by the CJEU to be a restriction on the fundamental freedoms. More specifically, as a rule the Court considers such national measures to be a restriction on the freedom of services (Article 56 TFEU), or on the freedom of establishment (Article 49 TFEU). First, the undertaking may have to bear the additional administrative and financial burdens which any such granting of authorisation entails. Secondly, the system of prior authorisation acts as a bar to self-employed activity for economic operators who do not satisfy predetermined requirements, compliance with which is a condition for issuing that authorisation.[34]

Consequently it is settled case law that non-discriminatory[35] restrictions on market freedoms, such as prior authorisation schemes, must be justified by overriding reasons relating to the general interest.[36] Furthermore, a prior authorisation scheme must be appropriate for securing attainment of the objective it pursues and must not go beyond what is necessary to attain that objective.[37] To start with, the first requirement: purely economic objectives (such as the objective of maximising public revenue alone, or the purpose of offering the licence holder a guarantee of continuity, financial stability and an acceptable return on past investments) cannot constitute an overriding reason in the public interest.[38]

In addition, it is important to note that the CJEU has consistently stressed in past years that a licence system is only appropriate for achieving a policy objective if its realisation is pursued in a coherent and systematic manner.[39] This criterion is referred to as 'the principle of consistency' or the 'hypocrisy test'.[40]

Even when a system of prior authorisation can be justified by overriding reasons, there are other matters to consider. According to settled case law the procedure for granting authorisations for economic activities must be based on *objective, non-discriminatory criteria known in advance* to the applicant, in such a way as to circumscribe

34 See for instance Joined Cases C-338/04, C-359/04 and C-360/04, *Placanica et al. v. Italy* [2007], ECLI:EU:C:2007:133, para. 42; Case C-169/07, *Hartlauer Handelsgesellschaft v. Wiener Landesregierung and Oberösterreichische Landesregierung* [2009], ECLI:EU:C:2009:141, para. 34; Joined Cases C-570/07 and C-571/07, *Blanco Pérez and Chao Gómez* [2010], ECLI:EU:C:2010:300, para. 54 and Case C-470/11, SIA *Garkalns v. Rīgas Dome* [2012], ECLI:EU:C:2012:505, para. 34.

35 Direct discrimination on grounds of nationality can only be justified by an express derogating provision, e.g. public policy, public security or public health.

36 See on the question of what circumstances qualify as overriding reasons that may justify a prior authorisation scheme the Chapter by Hatzopolous in this book, para. 1.1.

37 Case C-169/07, *Hartlauer Handelsgesellschaft v. Wiener Landesregierung and Oberösterreichische Landesregierung* [2009], ECLI:EU:C:2009:141, para. 44; Joined Cases C-171/07 and C-172/07 Apothekerkammer des Saarlandes and others [2009], ECLI:EU:C:2009:316, para. 25; and Joined Cases C-570/07 and C-571/07, *Blanco Pérez and Chao Gómez* [2010], ECLI:EU:C:2010:300, para. 61. See also Article 9 of the Services Directive.

38 See for example Case C-352/85, *Bond van Adverteerders and others v. the Netherlands State*, ECLI:EU:C:1988:196, para. 34; Case C-260/04, *Commission v. Italy*, ECLI:EU:C:2007:508, para. 35; Case C-400/08, *Commission v. Spain*, ECLI:EU:C:2011:172, para. 74; Case C-98/14, *Berlington Hungary and others v. Magyar Állam* [2015], ECLI:EU:C:2015:386, para. 60.

39 See for example Case C-169/07, *Hartlauer Handelsgesellschaft v. Wiener Landesregierung and Oberösterreichische Landesregierung* [2009], ECLI:EU:C:2009:141, para. 55; Joined Cases C-570/07 and C-571/07, *Blanco Pérez and Chao Gómez* [2010], ECLI:EU:C:2010:300, para. 94; Case C-98/14, *Berlington Hungary and others v. Magyar Állam* [2015], ECLI:EU:C:2015:386, para. 64.

40 Opinion of the A-G Mengozzi in the Joined Cases C-316/07, C-358/07, C-359/07, C-360/07, C-409/07 and C-410/07, *Markus Stoß et al. v. Land Baden-Württemberg* [2010], ECLI:EU:C:2010:109, para. 50 and opinion of the A-G Gruz Villalón in Case C-577/10, *Commission v. Belgium* [2012], ECLI:EU:C:2012:477, para. 58.

the exercise of the authorities' discretion so that it is not used arbitrarily.[41] *Objective criteria* provide clarity to potential applicants about the requirements they have to meet in order to be considered for a licence, and at the same time are appropriate for achieving the underlying objective of the licence system.[42] The requirement of prior knowledge of the selection criteria serves to give the applicant the opportunity to estimate whether his application has a chance of being successful.

This last requirement is refined even further when it comes to limited authorisations. This is easily explained: when a national legislature limits the amount of authorisations to be granted, this constitutes an extra restriction on the fundamental freedoms. The opportunity to carry out economic activities is even further restricted as a result, so such a scheme tends to limit the number of providers of services.[43] It is therefore understandable that the CJEU tends to look critically at licence systems that contain strict thresholds and criteria. In the case *Sporting Exchange* the Court decided for the first time that in the event a single licence is awarded 'compliance with the principle of equal treatment and with the consequent obligation of transparency necessarily means that the objective criteria enabling the Member States' competent authorities' discretion to be circumscribed must be sufficiently advertised.'[44] The requirement of prior notification has therefore been changed to the requirement of being adequately advertised in the case of single or limited authorisations.[45]

Here the application of the principle of transparency consequently leads to stricter requirements. The principle of transparency has become quite developed in procurement law, where it is applied to preclude any risk of favouritism or arbitrariness on the part of the contracting authorities. What the transparency principle entails exactly for the allocation of limited authorisations has not been made quite clear yet.[46] The Services Directive, however, does now prescribe that in cases involving limited licences as a result of scarce resources or technical opportunities, the Member States must use an impartial and transparent selection procedure, including in particular sufficient notification of the opening, execution and closure of the procedure (Article 12(1)). Furthermore, such limited authorisations must be granted for an appropriate limited period[47] and cannot

41 See for example Case C-389/05, *Commission v. France* [2008], ECLI:EU:C:2008:411, para. 94; C-169/07, *Hartlauer Handelsgesellschaft v. Wiener Landesregierung and Oberösterreichische Landesregierung* [2009], ECLI:EU:C:2009:141, para. 64 and Case C-203/08, *Sporting Exchange Ltd v. Minister van Justitie* [2010], ECLI:EU:C:2010:307, para. 50. See also Article 10 of the Services Directive.

42 See for instance Case C-400/08, *Commission v. Spain* [2011], ECLI:EU:C:2011:172, para. 117–118 and Case C-470/11, *Sia Garkalns v. Rīgas dome* [2012], ECLI:EU:C:2012:505, para. 45–46.

43 Case C-63/99, *The Queen v. Gloszczuk*, ECLI:EU:C:2001:488, para. 59; Case C-169/07, *Hartlauer Handelsgesellschaft v. Wiener Landesregierung and Oberösterreichische Landesregierung* [2009], ECLI:EU:C:2009:141, para. 36 and Joined Cases C-570/07 and C-571/07, *Blanco Pérez and Chao Gómez* [2010], ECLI:EU:C:2010:300, para. 55.

44 Case C-203/08, *Sporting Exchange Ltd v. Minister van Justitie* [2010], ECLI:EU:C:2010:307, para. 51. See also Case C-64–09, *Engelmann* [2010], ECLI:EU:C:2010:506, para. 50.

45 See for instance Case C-72/10 and C-77/10, *Costa and Cifone* [2012], para 55.

46 See on this topic A.W.G.J Buijze, 'The principle of transparency in EU law', Utrecht University 2013. http://dspace.library.uu.nl.

47 Although the scope of Article 12 is limited to authorisations that are scarce due to limited natural resources or technical capacity, the *Trijber & Harmsen* Case made clear that the requirement of

be automatically renewed, nor may any other advantage be conferred on the provider whose authorisation has just expired (Article 12(2)).

One aspect of a transparent allocation procedure is therefore that it involves the granting of a licence for a limited period *and* that no special favours are given to persons who previously had an entitlement. This last requirement corresponds to case law by the Court which emphasises that the principle of equal treatment requires that all potential interested parties must be afforded equal opportunities and that accordingly implies that all tenderers must be subject to the same conditions.[48] All these rules are a logical consequence of the principle of free (or fair) access to the market.

Not much can be said on the issue of how these guiding principles are related to property law as protected by Article 17 of the Charter when it comes to former licence-holders. In the Services Directive no attention is paid to the property rights of former licence-holders and in CJEU case law little has been said until now on the subject. In the ruling in *Pfleger* the CJEU made it clear that a national rule which appears to obstruct the operation of free movement can only be justified to the extent that the fundamental rights guaranteed by the Court are complied with. It stated:

> "There is no doubt that where a Member State points at overriding requirements in the public interest in order to justify rules which are liable to obstruct the exercise of the freedom to provide services, such justification, provided for by EU law, must be interpreted in the light of the general principles of EU law and in particular the fundamental rights henceforth guaranteed by the Charter. The obligation to comply with fundamental rights manifestly comes within the scope of EU law and, consequently, within that of the Charter."[49]

However, until now the Court has not paid much attention to property law in cases where licences were revoked. It has limited itself to observing that an unjustified or disproportionate restriction on the freedom to provide services under Article 56 TFEU is also not permitted under Article 52(1) of the Charter in relation to Articles 15 to 17 of the Charter.[50] As a consequence, a breach of the right to property does not require to be examined separately. This approach was also applied in the recent *Berlington* Case where former licence-holders invoked a right to property and the Court explicitly referred to the *Vékony* ruling of the ECtHR.

granting a limited authorisation for an appropriate limited period applies also in situations in which the number of available authorisations was limited for overriding reason relating to the public interest: Case C-341/14, *Trijber and Harmsen* [2015], para. 62.

48 See for instance Joined Cases C-72/10 and C-77/10, ECLI:EU:C:2012:80, *Costa & Cifone*, para. 57 and more extensive on this topic: Hatzopolous in this book, para. 1.1.4.

49 See Case C-390/12, *Pfleger and others* [2014], ECLI:EU:C:2014:281, para. 35 and 36. See also Article 10 of the Services Directive.

50 See Case C-390/12, *Pfleger and others* [2014], ECLI:EU:C:2014:281, para. 59.

4. The *Berlington* Ruling[51]

In the recent *Berlington* ruling, the Court responds to a request for a preliminary ruling from the Budapest-Capital Regional Court. The request was made in proceedings concerning an action seeking compensation for damages that Berlington and other Hungarian companies allegedly suffered as a result of national legislation concerning slot machines which was in breach of EU law. They claimed their interests were damaged by two amendments to the law on games of chance which followed each other in rapid succession. In 2011, an amending law (to promote budgetary stability) required that as of 1 January 2013 slot machines operated in amusement arcades would be connected to a central server. It also introduced a five-fold increase in the previous amount of the monthly flat-rate tax in respect of the operation of slot machines installed in amusement arcades, together with a proportional tax in the form of a percentage of the net quarterly revenue from each machine. The implementation of the operating system for slot machines based on a central server never took place because the operation of slot machines outside casinos was prohibited entirely in an amending law in 2012. To justify the prohibition, the legislature cited the prevention of crime and gambling addiction and public health considerations related to the prevention of gambling addiction. The 2012 amending law was adopted by the Hungarian Parliament on 2 October 2012 and came into force on 10 October 2012, the day after its publication. The next day, on 11 October 2012, licences to operate slot machines in amusement arcades automatically expired without any compensation for the operators concerned. Berlington and other undertakings sought compensation for the losses they claimed to have suffered as a result of the imposition of the gambling taxes which they had paid, the depreciation of their slot machines and the costs of judicial proceedings. They invoked in particular the fundamental freedoms, the principles of legal certainty and the protection of legitimate expectations and the right to property.

When answering the questions referred by the Hungarian judge, the CJEU premises that the two amending laws constitute restrictions on the freedom to provide services. It handles the question of whether these restrictions can be justified in the customary way.[52] It recalls that legislation on games of chance is an area in which significant moral, religious and cultural differences exist between the Member States. In the absence of harmonisation at EU level, the Member States are, in principle, free to set their own objectives in policy on betting and gaming and to define in detail the level of protection sought. Nevertheless, restrictions imposed by the Member States in this area must satisfy the familiar conditions of proportionality (i.e. they must be suitable, necessary and coherent), aspects that the referring court must review.

After these considerations, the CJEU continues its judgment with an interesting examination of the justifications put forward in the light of fundamental rights.[53] It

51 Case C-98/14, *Berlington Hungary and others v. Magyar Állam* [2015], ECLI:EU:C:2015:386.

52 See also the Chapter by Van den Bogaert and Cuyvers in this book.

53 Case C-98/14, *Berlington Hungary and others v. Magyar Állam* [2015], ECLI:EU:C:2015:386, para. 74–92.

recalls that where a Member State relies on overriding requirements in the public interest in order to justify rules which are liable to obstruct the exercise of the freedom to provide services, such justification must also be interpreted in the light of the general principles of EU law, in particular the fundamental rights now guaranteed by the Charter of Fundamental Rights. Thus, the national rules in question can fall under the exceptions provided for only if they are compatible with the fundamental rights, the observance of which is to be ensured by the Court.

When examining the justification of the contested restrictions in the light of fundamental rights, the claims under the principle of legal certainty and the principle of legitimate expectations receive the most attention. This is understandable, since extensive case law now exists on these principles in relation to changes in policy and subsequent changes in legislation[54] and this can easily be referred to. For a long time the Court has found that although market participants may not assume that a law will not be amended, the legislature can be expected to take into account the special situation in which they may find themselves as a result. In that respect, the Court points out to the national courts, which will have to decide if the principles referred to have been breached by the national regulations, that the tax system, having not been changed for around twenty years, was all of a sudden substantially altered by the 2011 Amendment Act. Furthermore it notices that with the 2012 Amendment Act the exploitation licences for slot machines were almost immediately and automatically revoked, without providing for either a transitional period or compensation. In that regard, the Court notices that 'when the national legislature revokes licences that allow their holders to exercise an economic activity, it must provide, for the benefit of those holders, a transitional period of sufficient length to enable them to adapt or a reasonable compensation system' while referring to the *Vékony* case.[55]

This case shows that the automatic revocation of a licence without a transitional period or compensation is reviewed in the light of the principle of legal certainty and this also applies to costly investments that the traders had to make in order to comply with the online requirements for slot machines. The court states that the interests of the traders could be considerably affected by the early withdrawal of the scheme concerned, all the more so because that withdrawal was sudden and unforeseeable, leaving no time to adapt to the new legal situation.

The right to property, which plays a central role in the *Vékony* ruling by the ECtHR, receives just as little attention, as it was given in the *Pfleger* ruling: 'In that regard, it should be noted that national legislation that is restrictive from the point of view of Article 56 TFEU is also capable of limiting the right to property enshrined in Article 17 of the Charter. Likewise, the Court has already held that an unjustified or disproportionate restriction of the freedom to provide services under Article 56 TFEU is also not permitted under Article 52(1) of the Charter, in relation to Article 17 thereof.'

54 See more extensively on this subject: P. Craig, *EU Administrative Law*, Oxford University Press 2012, pp. 573–578.

55 See Case C-390/12, *Pfleger and others* [2014], ECLI:EU:C:2014:281, para. 85.

What conclusions can be drawn from the *Berlington* ruling? First and foremost, due care should be taken here. As in previous cases, the Court pays little attention to property law when it comes to licences that are restricted due to unfavourable conditions or that are withdrawn completely. Nevertheless, the Court does refer to the *Vékony* case, where the allocation procedure for limited authorisations was found to be in violation of property law. The CJEU, however, does not refer to this ruling under the heading of property law, but in light of the principle of legal certainty when assessing the contested restrictions. Furthermore, it places particular emphasis on the fact that there was no transitional period, nor was compensation offered to the former licence-holders which resulted in them having no opportunity to adjust to the new situation. No attention is paid to the position of former licence-holders in the allocation system for new licences. This is not surprising, though, since the licences for slot machines outside casinos would expire completely under the new policy of the Hungarian government. Nevertheless, with regard to this subject, we do not believe that it is likely that the CJEU will accept the findings of the ECtHR in the *Vékony* ruling concerning the preferred position that former licence-holders should have within a procedure for allocating new licences. As mentioned above, the Services Directive stresses that former licence-holders may not be given a preferred position when (certain) limited licences are reallocated. In addition, according to the case law of the CJEU, selection criteria should be linked to the policy objectives behind the licence system and a system of preferential treatment for former licence-holders is hardly compatible with this.

5. Closing Remarks

This chapter looked at the role property law plays in the withdrawal, reallocation or amendment of limited authorisations. Two recent cases were highlighted: the *Vékony* ruling by the ECtHR in January 2015 and the *Berlington* Case at the CJEU in June 2015. The facts of the cases were very similar. In both cases former licence-holders were confronted with their licences for economic activities being withdrawn as a result of changes in government policy that aimed to serve the general public interest. To address smoking and gambling addiction current licences were suddenly revoked and in both cases the appellants were not considered for a new licence. In both cases the former licence-holders believed that this procedure (among other things) constituted a violation of their property rights.

In view of the common features of the two cases, it is obviously worthwhile considering whether the legal protection of undertakings under Article 17 Charter and Article 1 First Protocol correspond with each other in substance. This question is all the more pressing since, to a certain extent, it is not clear to which court a dispute about limited licences should be referred. For example, a dispute could come before the CJEU following a request for a preliminary ruling, but if the judge does not make a request (and also when he *does* make a request), the course of the legal proceedings could lead to the same matter coming before the ECtHR. Vice versa the case *Vékony* could have come before the CJEU if transboundary effects of the national scheme to grant new authorisations could be made plausible, for instance because new authorisations could be granted to non-Hungarian market operators.

It should be realised that the exact content and scope of property protection in relation to limited rights under both treaties has not yet been considered extensively in case law.[56] That said, however, the CJEU and the ECtHR are unanimous in their judgment concerning the fact that the sudden revocation of licences without providing for either a transitional period or compensation is in breach of the law. But the actual approaches leading to this conclusion differ in an interesting way. The ECHR approaches the issue by considering trends in legal precedence on the regulation of property. According to legal precedence, this article sets procedural requirements, including the existence of sufficient possibilities to be able to challenge a breach in court. But the *Vékony* case adds a number of elements to this which the Court did not refer to in previous case law. The court stresses that a transitional period should be observed or that, if this is not possible, at the very least compensation should have been offered to *Vékony* so that he could prepare for the new situation without the licence. The ECtHR also rules in *Vékony* that in the procedure for granting new limited authorisations, national authorities should give a preferred position to former licence-holders who are dependent on the licence for their livelihood. In this regard, the ECtHR rules, among other things, that the first round of tendering could be limited in scope to previous licence holders.

This application of the principle of transparency with regard to the test of Article 1 First Protocol ECHR – though not explicitly referred to by the ECtHR – cannot count on broad support within the ECtHR itself, as is demonstrated by the *concurring opinion* in *Vékony*. The concurring judges question whether they have the task to prescribe in detail which specific procedural standards should be fulfilled in a scheme for the allocation of new authorisations. However, it is not just from the perspective of the definition of tasks between the ECtHR and national authorities that questions can be posed concerning whether the approach by the ECtHR is wise. We believe that it is not likely that the CJEU will follow the stance of the ECtHR in this area. The favouring of established parties in the internal market is severely frowned upon by the CJEU. This line of jurisprudence was codified in the Service Directive, which prescribes that former licence-holders may be handed no advantage whatsoever in a procedure to reallocate limited licences.

Thus the question arises whether problems are to be expected in this area in the near future. After all, in some cases it is not clear which European court former licence-holders will be dealing with and it is quite conceivable that the same case could come before both the ECtHR and the CJEU. However, we do not expect that a clash is imminent. For one thing, the CJEU ruled in the *Berlington* case by virtue of the principle of legal certainty, defending its stance by using its own line of legal precedence on this principle. And besides, situations where limited licences are revoked without prior warning are likely to occur less frequently now the Service Directive (and the case law of the CJEU) has made it clear that limited licences cannot be granted for an indefinite period of time.

56 Cf. more broadly on the subject of the (modest) role of fundamental rights within the framework for allocation activities by the state: F. Wollenschläger, 'EU Law Principles for Allocating Scarce Goods and the Emergence of an Allocation Procedure. Identifying Substantive and Procedural Standards and Developing a New Type of Administrative Procedure' *Review of European Administrative Law* 2015, pp. 236–242.

The ECtHR also assumes that the holder of a temporary licence can foresee that the licence will terminate at some point in the future. There can be no breach of property law in such cases. Furthermore, it can be presumed that the ECtHR will take the *Berlington* ruling seriously and – just like the two concurring judges – will reflect further on the question of whether general rulings can also be given on reallocation systems on the grounds of property law. If the answer to this question remains affirmative, then the perspective of the equal treatment of potential applicants will have to be considered further.

PART III

COMPARATIVE LAW PERSPECTIVES

Stefaan Van den
Bogaert and
Armin Cuyvers*

CHAPTER 12.
'LET IT BE'? THE REGULATION AND ALLOCATION OF GAMBLING LICENCES AT THE EU AND MEMBER STATE LEVEL

1. Introduction: The Trilemma of Gambling Regulation

For those looking for an on-line poker room right now, gambling opportunities will hardly appear scarce. For those looking for licences to legally offer such games of chance, scarcity is usually very real. Apparent incongruities like these lie at the heart of the legal dilemmas concerning gambling services in the EU and many individual Member States.

On the one hand, gambling poses serious risks relating to addiction, crime and fraud. Member States are rightly trying to protect their citizens from these risks. One of the main ways Member States try to do so is by limiting and regulating games of chance. Be it via a blanket prohibition, a monopoly or restrictive licensing, many Member States aim to create an artificial scarcity in games of chance. This scarcity can concern the *volume* of games of chance, such as, in particular, the amount of casino's, gaming machines or lottery draws allowed; it may also concern the *nature* of the games of chance offered, for example in terms of attractiveness, game dynamics or incentives offered.

On the other hand, games of chance bring in serious revenue for Member States and all kinds of good causes. A certain temptation to expand gambling may therefore exist. The desire of humankind to gamble seems almost unstoppable anyway. Certainly with the advent of the internet, entirely preventing people from betting seems to behave become 'virtually' impossible. So why not regulate what you cannot prevent, and make some money along the way, especially as revenue might otherwise 'leak' to illegal suppliers?

National regulation of games of chance typically tries to navigate this trilemma of protection, revenue and the reality of illegal supply.[1] How to balance protection versus revenue? How to make the legal supply, if any, attractive enough to fend of illegal

* Stefaan Van den Bogaert is professor of European Law and director of the Europa Instituut of Leiden University, the Netherlands. Armin Cuyvers is assistant professor of EU Law at the same Europa Instituut.

1 Cf in this regard also the German national report by M. Martini, 'The Allocation of Gambling licences, Radio Frequencies, and CO_2 emission permits in Germany' in P. Adriaanse, F. Van Ommeren, W. den Ouden and J. Wolswinkel, *Scarcity and the State II. Member State Reports on Gambling Licences, Radio Frequencies and CO_2 Emission Permits*, Intersentia, Antwerp 2016.

competition, but not so attractive so as to cause the very same harm that justifies prohibiting the unregulated and illegal supply? And how to find the right balance in the midst of an on-line revolution that may leave national borders meaningless?

In navigating this trilemma, states have to respect EU law, including the rules on equal treatment, free movement, fair competition and state aid. And these rules add an interesting twist. For although EU law is generally highly sympathetic towards the public policy concerns of the Member States, it abhors purely economic justifications for restrictions on free movement. As a result, in the European law arena, one core element of the gambling trilemma, money, may officially only play a secondary role in the gambling policy of Member States. States and public monopolies therefore often try, or are forced, to 'mask' their very real financial interest behind other objectives such as consumer protection.[2] In addition to this problematic role of money, the justification of national restrictions on gambling services under EU law is further strained by the exploding (illegal) online supply already mentioned. For though illegal online supply requires regulation, it also raises the question how one can justify a restriction on legitimate and licensed operators where an abundant supply is available online 24/7.

This contribution provides a European and comparative perspective on the allocation of gambling licences, and the challenges it raises. Firstly, the EU legal framework for the award of gambling licences as established by the CJEU is set out. This framework concerns both the limits set to the national system for regulating gambling (section two) and the concrete procedure for awarding any licences (section three). Section four then highlights several of the key trends we see emerging in the case law on both points. Subsequently, based on the different country reports received, section five highlights several of the main challenges facing Member States: where have Member State so far struggled to comply with EU law, and where may future conflicts arise? Taking stock of these remaining challenges, section six concludes with some reflections on the possibility and use of EU legislative activity, especially in relation to the major challenge of online gambling.

2. The EU Legal Framework for Regulating Games of Chance

Currently, there is no EU legislation directly harmonizing gambling services, even though the Commission is increasingly active, inter alia by developing proposals and coordinating soft law. So far, however, Gambling services have been so politically sensitive that they have been explicitly excluded from general legislation on services, such as the services directive or the electronic commerce directive.[3] As a result, gambling services are governed by EU primary law, especially the Treaty rules on free movement of services and the freedom of establishment.[4] It has been up to the CJEU to apply these Treaty provisions to the specific context of gambling services. The EU framework that

2 Obviously the CJEU itself is aware of this point as well. Cf in this regard Case C-212/08, *Zeturf* [2011] ECR I-5633, paras. 59–60 or Case C-347/09, *Dickinger and Ömer* [2011] ECR I-8185, para. 61.

3 See Article 2(2) Directive 2006/123/EC on services in the internal market [2006] OJ L376/36 and Article 1(5) Directive 2000/31/EC on Electronic Commerce in the Internal Market [2000] OJ L178/1.

4 See Articles 49 and 56 of the Treaty on the Functioning of the EU (TFEU). In the future we expect the Treaty rules on competition law, including the rules on state aid, to become more relevant as well.

emerges from its judgments displays all the typical characteristics of a judge-made body of law. What gradually becomes apparent is that the CJEU is remarkably lenient when assessing the overall system for regulation, be it a blanket prohibition, a monopoly or a licensing system, but far more strict when assessing the procedure for awarding licences.[5]

2.1. *Regulating Games of Chance*

Despite their morally contested character, the CJEU has consistently held that games of chance do qualify as a service under EU law.[6] As a result, gambling providers can rely on the freedom to provide services or the freedom to establishment as protected under Articles 49 and 56 of the Treaty on the Functioning of the EU (TFEU) respectively.[7] Moreover, even the lightest form of regulation will make it harder for providers to offer their gambling services in a Member State. As a result, almost all forms of national gambling regulation, ranging from total bans or monopolies to open-ended licensing schemes, will qualify as a restriction on free movement.[8] In principle, such restrictions are prohibited under EU law, unless they can be justified. Restrictions are only justified when they serve one or more important social aims in a proportionate manner.[9]

It is in the assessment of such justifications that the real legal action takes place, and where the legal framework on games of chance develops its own particular characteristics. The key characteristic of current EU gambling law is the enormous leeway left by the CJEU to the Member States. Establishing the core characteristics of the legal framework for gambling, therefore, can best be done by mapping the different layers of margin left to the Member States as compared to the 'standard' internal market approach.

2.1.1. The general margin to regulate gambling

Even before it applies the free movement test proper, the CJEU grants Member States a *prima facie general margin* when regulating games of chance. Already in *Schindler*, the CJEU held that the particular nature of games of chance, including the 'moral religious

5 For a deconstruction of this case law see S.C.G. Van den Bogaert and A. Cuyvers, 'Money For Nothing: The Case Law of the EU Court of Justice on the Regulation of Gambling' (2011) 48 *Common Market Law Review*, p. 1175.

6 Case C-275/92, *Her Majesty's Customs and Excise v Schindler* [1994] ECR I-1039, para. 25.

7 For the distinction between both, which is not always easy to make, see especially Case C-55/94, *Gebhard* [1995] ECR I-4165, and Case C-215/01, *Schnitzer* [2003] I-14847. Specifically in the gambling context see Case C-347/09, *Dickinger and Ömer*, para. 35 and Case C-470/11, *Garlkans* [2012] ECLI:EU:C:2012:505, paras. 26 and 27.

8 See for the standard formulation Case C-76/90, *Säger* [1991] ECR I-4221, para. 12, or in the gambling context Case C-98/14, *Berlington* [2015] ECLI:EU:C:2015:386, para. 35. Also note that the prohibition to advertise foreign gambling services also forms a restriction, as confirmed in Case C-176/11, *HIT LARIX* [2012] ECLI:EU:C:2012:454, paras. 17 and 18.

9 For the so called Treaty exceptions see art. 52 and 62 TFEU. For the so called 'Rule of Reason' exceptions developed by the CJEU see in the context of Gambling inter alia Joined Cases C-338/04, C-359/04 and C-360/04, *Placanica* [2007] ECR I-1891 and Case C-203/08, *Stichting de Nationale Sporttotalisator (Betfair)* [2010] ECR I-4695.

and cultural' factors involved, justifies a 'sufficient degree of latitude' for national authorities.[10] The CJEU continues to emphasize this particular nature of gambling before assessing national gambling regulations on the merits. In *Liga Portuguesa*, the CJEU formulated it as follows:

> 'the legislation on games of chance is one of the areas in which there are significant moral, religious and cultural differences between the Member States. In the absence of Community harmonisation in the field, it is for each Member State to determine in those areas, in accordance with its own scale of values, what is required in order to ensure that the interests in question are protected.'[11]

Evidently, this general margin does not equal a complete *carte blanche*. The CJEU always stresses that, within this margin, national regulation must still 'satisfy the conditions laid down in the case-law of the Court as regards their proportionality'.[12] In this context, the CJEU has granted the Member States further leeway.

2.1.2. Justification: take your pick or let us choose for you?

Restrictions on free movement may be justified if they serve a legitimate aim. These aims are either explicitly contained in the Treaty exceptions, or they may be created by the CJEU under the so called 'rule of reason' doctrine.[13] In the context of gambling, the CJEU has provided significant leeway concerning the grounds of justification in three ways. Firstly, the CJEU has been lenient in accepting particular overriding objectives. Secondly, the CJEU has been even more lenient in overlooking other, less acceptable, objectives also underlying national regulation. Thirdly, the CJEU has accepted the combination of different overriding objectives, even where these objectives might seem rather incompatible.

Firstly, the Court has traditionally accepted three distinct but related grounds for justifying restrictions on gambling, being 1) consumer protection; 2) the prevention of both fraud and incitement to squander on gaming and 3) the general need to preserve public order.[14] Since *Stoß*, the CJEU usually refers to two broad categories of grounds of

10 Case C-275/92, *Schindler*, para. 61.

11 Case C-42/07, *Liga Portuguesa* [2009] ECR I-7633, para. 57. This formulation links to the earlier formulations in *Schindler* para. 32 and *Placanica* para. 47. This formulation is also used verbatim in Joined Cases C-447/08 and C-448/08, *Sjöberg* [2010] I-6921, para. 37, *HIT LARIX* para. 24, *Garlkans* para. 36, Joined Cases C-186/11 and C-209/11, *Stanleybet* [2013] ECLI:EU:C:2013:33, para. 24, Case C-156/13, *Digibet* [2014] ECLI:EU:C:2014:1756, para. 24, and *Berlington*, para. 56, although there the 'scale of values' is replaced with the even more far reaching 'in principle, free'. For a mix of both lines see Joined Cses C-316/07, C-358/07, C-359/07, C-360/07, C-409/07 and C-410/07, *Stoß* [2010] ECLI:EU:C:2010:504, para. 76.

12 See for example *Liga Portuguesa* para. 59.

13 For the Treaty exceptions on services and establishment see Articles 51, 52, and 62 TFEU. For the Rule of Reason, which provides an open ended category of justifications, see generally Case 120/78, *Cassis de Dijon*, [1979] ECR-649, and in the context of gambling already *Schindler.*

14 This particular formulation was first used in *Placanica* para. 46, adding public order to the previous formulation in Case C-243/01, *Gambelli* [2003] ECR I-13031. These precise grounds were repeated

justification, namely consumer protection and protection of the public order (crime).[15] More specific national objectives are then rather easily brought under one of these two main general headings: protecting minors or other vulnerable groups and preventing addiction, for example, falls under the heading of consumer protection. Preventing money laundering, fighting organized crime or preventing fraud all fall under the general category of public order. The classification of a particular ground for justification under the 'consumer protection' or 'crime prevention' heading may impact on the proportionality test. As will be illustrated further below, the CJEU has especially developed crime and fraud prevention into a very broad and permissive objective.[16]

In addition to flexibly accepting specific objectives under these general headings, the CJEU has also demonstrated a willingness to accept other, less obvious, justification grounds. The high watermark in this regard undoubtedly is *Sjöberg*, in which the CJEU accepted the Swedish aim of the 'exclusion of private profit from the gambling sector' as a valid overriding objective.[17] Now it must be stressed that the Court is often rather lenient in accepting overriding objectives, also outside the gambling context. Nevertheless, the *Sjöberg* objective is particularly creative, also because it could be said to be a financial aim. The fact that there may be no private profit, after all, entails that there may only be public profit. Such public profit, moreover, was apparently morally acceptable. Interestingly, in *Sjöberg* the CJEU also focused solely on this particular objective of preventing private profit, and not on the other objectives also pursued by Sweden, even though this particular objective was not even mentioned in the Swedish legislation itself and had only been proffered by the referring Court.

Secondly, *Sjöberg* also demonstrates that the CJEU sometimes grants leeway by singling out acceptable objectives whilst overlooking less appropriate ones that also underlie the national regulation. For example, the CJEU itself has repeatedly stressed that purely financial aims may only form 'an ancillary beneficial consequence' of gambling regulation.[18] At the same time, however, the CJEU has seemingly been willing to ignore even rather obvious financial objectives and focus on the more EU-palatable ones, as long as these financial aims were not flagrantly driving national policy according to the referring court.[19] It is only where the referring courts indicate that, in their view,

verbatim in Case C-260/04, *Commission v. Italy* [2007] ECR I-7083, para. 27, *Liga Portuguesa*, para. 56, *Betfair*, para. 26, Case C-258/08, *Ladbrokes* [2010] ECR I-4757, para. 18 and *Sjöberg*, para. 36.

15 See *Stoß*, para. 74. For earlier roots of this basic dichotomy in objectives, already see *Schindler*, para. 58, Case C-124/97 *Läärä*, [1999] ECR I-6067 para. 32 and Case C-67/98, *Zenatti* [1999] ECR I-7289, para. 31.

16 Regarding suitability one curious discrepancy in *Ladbrokes* and *Betfair* should be mentioned. Ladbrokes and Betfair only wanted to provide on-line gambling services in the Netherlands. Both in *Betfair* and *Ladbrokes* the ECJ, however, worked from the (incorrect) assumption that there is a blanket ban on interactive gambling in the Netherlands. (*Betfair* Paragraph 11 and *Ladbrokes* par. 7.). As such complete bans have been accepted from *Läärä* and *Zenatti* onwards no further analysis would have seemed necessary, yet the Court still applied its single licence framework established in *Liga Portuguesa*.

17 *Sjöberg* paras 41 and 45. For an earlier allusion to private profit see *Schindler*.

18 See for example *Zenatti* para. 36 and 37, *Gambelli* para. 69, *Stoß* paras. 99 and 104.

19 See for example *Sjöberg*, *Ladbrokes*, *Betfair*, and *Liga Portuguesa*.

revenue generation in fact forms an overriding consideration that the CJEU includes this objective in its assessment. And even in such cases it leaves the final judgment on the real objectives to the referring court.[20] Member States can thus to a large extent pick and choose the objective they want to rely on to justify their gambling regulation. And even when they do not, the CJEU often focuses solely on the single most appropriate aim, often crime prevention.[21]

The third and last form of leeway regarding the objectives discussed here concerns the far fewer cases where the CJEU does not pick and choose the most acceptable aim, but instead allows Member States to combine objectives that in principle conflict with each other. The primary tension here is between protecting consumers against addiction and creating an attractive legal supply to combat illegal gambling services and the crime associated with it. Although *Gambelli* and *Placanica* seemed to indicate that Member States had to choose between such aims,[22] later case law has shown that they nevertheless may be combined. The leading case here is *Ladbrokes*.

In *Ladbrokes*, the CJEU first recognized that 'the objective of protecting consumers from gambling addiction is, in principle, difficult to reconcile with a policy of expanding games of chance characterised, inter alia, by the creation of new games and by the advertising of such games'.[23] Subsequently, however, it found that the contested national legislation aims not only to combat fraud and other crimes in the sphere of games of chance, but also to safeguard consumer protection. Thus, a fair balance had to be struck 'between demand for the controlled expansion of authorised games of chance with the aim of making the provision of such games attractive for the public and the need to reduce as far as possible consumer addiction to such games.'[24] This line has since been confirmed, *inter alia* in *Stoß*.[25] The combination of such conflicting objectives, furthermore, is further enabled by the significant leeway granted to the Member States in assessing the suitability of gambling regulations: for how to suitably achieve two conflicting aims at the same time?

20 See in this regard especially the 'Italian' cases of *Zenatti*, *Gambelli*, *Placanica* and Joined Cases C-72/10 and C-77/10, *Costa and Cifone* [2012] ECLI:EU:C:2012:80 where the National Courts really stressed the financial aims of Italian legislation. Also see the critical position of the Austrian and German Courts in this point in for example C-390/12, *Pfleger* [2014] ECLI:EU:C:2014:281, paras. 53–54 and *Stoß* paras. 39 and 100.

21 See in this regard also paras. 13, 30 and 36 in *Betfair*, where the CJEU decides solely under the objective of fighting crime and fraud, even though the legislation explicitly referred to multiple objectives as well as See similarly *Liga Portuguesa* para. 15, *Sjöberg* para. 4, Case C-46/08, *Carmen Media* [2010] ECR I-8149 para. 12, Case C-409/06, *Winner Wetten* [2010] ECR I-8015 para. 8, and *Stoß* para. 8 for national legislation referring to multiple objectives but the CJEU focusing only on one.

22 See A. Cuyvers, Case note to *Placanica*, (2008) 45 *Common Market Law Review*, 515.

23 *Ladbrokes* para. 30. See also para. 26 where the CJEU refers back to *Placanica*, acknowledging that here the CJEU chose to focus on a single justification.

24 *Ladbrokes* para. 32.

25 *Stoß* para. 102. Also note, however, that in the end the CJEU decided *Stoß* under the sole objective of consumer protection, including preventing addiction, because the referring courts indicated that this was the primary objective, or perhaps more correctly, should be the primary objective, of German gambling regulation (para. 106).

2.1.3. Suitability: Consistent and systematic discretion and devolution

Suitability concerns the question whether a national measure can actually achieve its objective. In the context of gambling, the suitability test centres around the now famous 'hypocrisy test' introduced in *Gambelli*:

> '(...) whilst (...) restrictions on gaming activities may be justified by imperative requirements in the general interest, such as consumer protection and the prevention of both fraud and incitement to squander on gaming, restrictions based on such grounds and on the need to preserve public order must also be *suitable* for achieving those objectives, inasmuch as they must serve to limit betting activities in a *consistent and systematic manner*.'[26]

This test essentially asks whether Member States are genuinely trying to achieve the stated aim in a consistent and systematic way, or whether in reality they also pursue other aims that *de facto* undermine the stated aim. Considering this focus on consistency, the expectation after *Gambelli* was that the CJEU would intensify is scrutiny. This did not happen, however. So far, the CJEU itself has refrained from finding national legislation inconsistent on its own accord. Rather, the *Gambelli* test functions as an invitation to national courts to critically assess the consistency of their national regulation. The CJEU can then back up national courts which indicate that, in their own assessment, national regulation does not genuinely serve the stated overriding objectives. *Dickinger and Ömer* and *Stoß* are exemplary in this respect. In both cases, the Austrian and German courts were very outspoken on the inconsistencies they perceived. In both cases, the CJEU provided back-up cover for the national courts to find a conflict with EU law, yet still left the final decision on consistency to the referring courts.[27]

The devolution of suitability to the national courts can add an important margin for Member States, especially where the national courts are more amenable to upholding national gambling regulation. Besides this procedural leeway, the CJEU has also clarified that Member States enjoy quite some leeway within the consistency test. For example, the possibility for Member States exists to allow some level of expansion and advertising even under the objective of consumer protection and preventing addiction. Because some legal supply can also be considered necessary to prevent addiction, 'a certain amount of measured advertising' should be allowed to 'direct' consumers to this safe and legal supply.[28] Such channelling, however, must remain limited:

> 'Such advertising cannot, however, in particular, aim to *encourage* consumers' natural propensity to gamble by stimulating their active participation in it, such as by trivialising gambling or giving it a *positive image due to the fact that revenues derived from it are used for*

26 *Gambelli* para. 67, our italics.

27 See *Dickinger and Ömer* para. 59, or *Stoß*, inter alia paras. 20, 25, 39, 100 and 106. Also see in this context *Pfleger* and *Stanleybet*.

28 *Stoß* para. 102. See also in this direction the opinion of AG Mengozzi in this case, paras. 59 – 61.

> *activities in the public interest,* or by increasing the attractiveness of gambling by means of enticing advertising messages depicting major winnings in *glowing colours.*'[29]

Where Member States rely on the objective of consumer protection and preventing addiction, therefore, the consistency of their national legislation is not automatically compromised where they allow a certain amount of attractive and advertised legal supply. Instead, it must be assessed, in practise by the national courts, whether the legal supply is sufficiently restrained and controlled to remain compatible with the objective of preventing addiction.

In addition to 'softening' the consistency test under the objective of consumer protection, the CJEU further increased the leeway of Member States by allowing them to combine multiple conflicting objectives.[30] The effect of serving conflicting or competing objectives is that each objective has less restricting effect over the consistency of national measures. Several inconsistencies can now be justified by pointing to the other objectives also being pursued, and by the need of finding a balance between the different objectives.[31]

Lastly, the CJEU has significantly reduced the potential bite of the suitability test for restrictions on online gambling by rejecting to include the existence of abundant illegal online supply into its suitability assessment. Parties and national courts have asked whether the reality of an abundant supply of illegal online games of chance does not undermine national gambling regulation. Essentially, this should be read as a suitability argument: national regulation cannot be expected to achieve its aim of controlling or limiting online gambling where there is a virtually uncontrollable illegal supply. Hence, such regulation is inherently unsuitable, and cannot be justified to restrict legal supply whilst illegal supply is rampant. For understandable reasons, the CJEU has somewhat shied away from this point, not willing to wholly surrender the internet. Yet from the viewpoint of consistency, the Courts reasoning is not fully satisfactory, *inter alia* because the desire for effective legal control is not the same as actual legal control, and in practise Member States seem to have very limited control indeed.[32] In any event, the reasoning of the CJEU here is again more lenient than in other sectors.

Conversely, whilst granting these different layers of discretion, the CJEU has also opened up one further avenue for national courts to become stricter on consistency, if they so desire, via the argument of cross-sector consistency. In *Stoß*, the referring courts pointed out that the regulation of gambling differed significantly across the different sectors such as casino games, slot machines, lotteries and sports bets. Moreover, some of

29 *Stoß* para. 103, our italics.

30 See the discussion in the previous section.

31 *Ladbrokes*, para. 32. For a more detailed analysis of how combining objectives increases the margin for Member States, see S.C.G. Van den Bogaert and A. Cuyvers, 'Money For Nothing: The Case Law of the EU Court of Justice on the Regulation of Gambling' (2011) 48 *Common Market Law Review*, p. 1192 et seq.

32 See especially *Stoß* para. 85–87, where the CJEU holds that 'Member States are not deprived of legal means enabling them to ensure, *as effectively as possible*, compliance with the rules which they lay down in relation to actors operating on the internet and falling, for one reason or another, within their jurisdiction.'

the sectors known to carry a relatively high risk of addiction, such as slot machines, were less strictly regulated than sectors with a significantly lower risk, such as lotteries. In light of these facts, the referring courts asked whether the suitability of the German regulation could also be undermined by inconsistencies *between* the regulations of these different sectors, especially as the prevention of addiction formed the primary objective.[33] In its reply, the CJEU first of all stressed that differences between the different sectors are not 'in itself capable of affecting the suitability'.[34] The mere fact that regulation differs per sector, therefore, is not sufficient to undermine consistency. Subsequently, however, the CJEU indicated that differences between sectoral regulation may undermine overall consistency, especially where in some sectors people are being excessively incited to gamble.[35] If they want to, national courts can therefore take cross-sector consistency into account when assessing national gambling regulation. If they start doing so, and they will undoubtedly be invited to do so by service providers, this would have the effect of significantly reducing Member State leeway in regulating gambling.

2.1.4. No need for necessity?

The necessity test inquires if a restrictive measure is really necessary to achieve a certain objective, or whether this objective may also be achieved via less far reaching measures.

Necessity often is a major hurdle for justifying restrictions on free movement, as the CJEU can be highly critical in its assessment. In the context of gambling, however, the CJEU has almost completely abandoned the necessity test, thereby significantly increasing the leeway left to Member States. The standard formulation of the CJEU in this regard goes as follows:

> 'In that regard, it should be recalled that the Court has previously held that it is for each Member State to assess whether, in the context of the legitimate aims which it pursues, it is necessary wholly or partially to prohibit activities of that nature, or only to restrict them and to lay down more or less strict supervisory rules for that purpose, the need for and proportionality of the measures thus adopted having to be assessed solely in relation to the objectives thus pursued and the level of protection which the national authorities concerned seek to ensure.
> It has also held that, in the context of legislation which is compatible with the Treaty, the *choice of methods* for organising and controlling the operation and playing of games of chance or gambling, such as the conclusion with the State of an administrative licensing contract or the restriction of the operation and playing of certain games to places duly licensed for that purpose, falls within the margin of discretion which the national authorities enjoy.'[36]

33 See the strong questions of the German courts to this extent in *Stoß*, paras. 24–25, and *Carmen Media*, para. 31.
34 *Stoß* para. 96.
35 *Stoß* para. 106.
36 *Stoß*, paras. 91 and 92. Similarly see *Läärä* paras. 35 and 36, *Zenatti*, paras. 33 and 34, *Liga Portuguesa* para. 58, *Carmen Media* para. 59 and *Berlington* para. 62.

In other words, Member States may themselves choose which system they want, whether this is a blanket ban, a monopoly or a limited licensing system. The CJEU invariably adds that the 'mere fact that a Member State has opted for a system of protection which differs from that adopted by another Member State cannot affect the assessment of the need for and proportionality of the relevant provisions.'[37] The CJEU thereby aims to preempt any necessity argument that would point out that other Member States regulate gambling in a less restrictive way. Such comparative arguments are covered with the mantle of national discretion. This entails that providers are essentially prevented from arguing that the same level of protection can also be achieved via less far reaching regulation. *Stoß* again provides a good illustration. One of the referring courts expressly doubted whether the aims of the German monopoly could not be equally pursued by other, less restrictive, means, such as effective supervision of licensed providers and rules on marketing and advertising.[38] In response, the CJEU referred to the margin of discretion left to Member States, and stressed that it is not necessary that 'a restrictive measure decreed by the authorities of one Member State should correspond to a view shared by all the Member States concerning the means of protecting the legitimate interest at issue.'[39] As a result, Member States 'may be entitled to take the view' that a monopoly is the only way to provide the level of protection they want.[40] In other, less sensitive, areas, the CJEU would arguably have shifted the burden of proof to the Member State, requiring the state to proof why a less far reaching restriction, in operation in another Member State, would not have sufficed. In *Stoß*, however, the CJEU, did not want to enter into a substantive debate on the necessity of individual measures. It simply accepted 'the view' that a monopoly is required, and deflected the real question by replacing it with the question if the mere difference between national regulations would suffice to challenge their proportionality. As a result, Member States are generally left free to choose the regulatory model for games of chance without any real necessity check.[41]

Another example of the lack of a real necessity test concerns mutual recognition. The court has reconfirmed several times that there currently is no mutual recognition in the context of gambling:

> 'the mere fact that an operator lawfully offers services in one Member State, in which it is established and is in principle already subject to statutory conditions and controls on the part of the competent authorities of that State, cannot be regarded as a sufficient assurance that national consumers will be protected against the risks of fraud and crime, in view of the difficulties liable to be encountered in such a context by the authorities of the Member State of establishment in assessing the professional qualities and integrity of operators).'[42]

37 *Dickinger and Ömer* paras. 46 and 47. Similarly see *Liga Portuguesa* paras. 58 and 59. For the roots of this leeway on necessity already see *Schindler* para. 61.

38 *Stoß*, para. 73.

39 *Stoß*, para. 80.

40 *Stoß*, para. 81.

41 See, however, section 4.1 below on the possible trend that the CJEU is increasing the threshold for justifying a full monopoly, as well as the reasoning on necessity in *Stoß* paras. 103 and 107.

42 *Dickinger and Ömer* para. 96. Also see *Stoß* par. 112 as well as *Liga Portuguesa* para. 69 for the original rejection of mutual recognition.

This rejection of mutual recognition, which is especially relevant in the context of online providers licensed in one Member State such as Malta, fits with the rejection of the CJEU to take the regulation of gambling in other Member Stated into account when assessing proportionality. The CJEU does not want to fit the shoes of the legislator, and leaves enormous leeway to Member States when regulating games of chance. As a result, one of the most stringent and restrictive elements of the standard free movement test has been virtually disarmed in the context of gambling.

2.1.5. Conclusion: regulating games of chance

When it comes to the regulation of gambling, Member States have a large, and almost unprecedented, leeway under EU law. On top of the *a priori* general discretion to choose a particular form of regulation, the CJEU is highly accommodating at every step of the internal market test, even prepared to virtually dismantle the often crucial necessity test. The Court consistently adopts a cautious approach, seems reluctant to find a conflict between national gambling regulation and EU law, and appears content to follow the lead of the referring courts. Where the referring courts are critical, as in Austria, Germany or Italy, the CJEU is supportive, and provides them with the tools required, such as the consistency test in *Gambelli* or the concept of cross-sector consistency in *Stoß*. Where the referring courts are not openly critical, or even indicate that in their perception national law complies with EU law, the CJEU seems equally willing to follow suit, even if this entails mooting some of the more thornier questions normally asked by EU free movement law.

3. Awarding Gambling Licences

Member States have an enormous, if not unlimited, leeway when designing their system for gambling regulation. Once they have chosen to award gambling licences in some way or form, however, the picture changes quite radically: the procedure of awarding these licences must strictly comply with the EU norms on equal treatment and transparency. The CJEU has made clear that the factors underlying Member State discretion when organizing games of chance do not pertain to the award procedure. Competition between providers for the award of a licence, for example, does not pose the same risks as providers competing for market share and developing even more attractive supply to that end.[43] Quite the opposite, providers could be made to compete on licence requirements such as prevention of addiction and limited advertising, only furthering the desired overriding objectives. Consequently, the CJEU has been much more willing to critically assess national law in the context of award procedures. The Court appears especially invested 'to preclude any risk of favouritism or arbitrariness on the part of the licensing authority.'[44] In a sector where there are understandably often close ties between the state and the existing licensee, some ties

43 See in this regard also *Commission v. Italy* paras. 32 and 33, as well as the convincing arguments of AG Bot in *Betfair*, para. 58.
44 *Costa and Cifone*, para. 73.

dating back to 1783, a strict application of transparency can have a major impact.[45] This impact is only increased because of the by now standard position of the CJEU that no sanctions may be imposed on illegal operators where the procedure for the award of licences violated EU law.[46] As long as the current licences have not been awarded in line with EU law, therefore, operators without a licence may not be penalized. As a result, the entire issue of transparency should be seen as a vital second dimension in the EU framework for the regulation of gambling. In a sense, transparency provides some counterbalance to the leeway of Member States in regulating gambling as such, and to a certain extent challenges the national champions that have developed over time in many Member States.

The issue of award procedures first became salient in *Placanica*.[47] In a series of earlier cases on the Italian regulation of gambling, including *Gambelli*, the CJEU had left a clear path for the Italian courts to find their national law inconsistent with EU law. The Italian supreme court consistently turned down this invitation.[48] In *Placanica*, two lower Italian courts once again referred questions on the Italian system to the CJEU, but this time also explicitly asked whether the procedure that had been used to award a large number of new licences complied with EU Law. The main problem in the procedure was the exclusion of companies quoted on the stock exchange, which incidentally happened to exclude all major international providers of gambling services. In reply to these questions, and rediscovering necessity in this different context, the CJEU found that the exclusion of quoted undertakings was not necessary to achieve the objectives of the Italian legislation, and hence conflicted with EU law.[49]

Six months after *Placanica*, transparency made its first appearance on the EU gambling stage in *Comission v. Italy*. This infringement action again concerned Italy, and more specifically its decision to renew 329 old licences for horse-race betting without inviting any competing bids.[50] The CJEU agreed with the Commission that these licences qualified as public service concessions, and hence were subject to the principles of non-discrimination and transparency. Importantly, these principles flow directly from Article 56 TFEU, and hence apply to all situations where a licence is not covered by (even more stringent) secondary legislation on public procurement.[51] Applying its previous case law on transparency to gambling the CJEU held that:

> ' (...) the principles of equal treatment and non-discrimination on grounds of nationality imply, in particular, a duty of transparency which enables the concession-granting public

45 Cf the factual position of the licensee in *Liga Portuguesa*.

46 See *Placanica*, as later confirmed in inter alia *Dickinger and Ömer* and *Costa and Cifone*.

47 See A. Cuyvers, Case note to *Placanica*, (2008) 45 *CMLRev*, 515.

48 See especially judgment 111/04 of 26 April 2004, *Gesualdo*, where the Italian supreme court held that the Italian regulation consistently and systematically pursued only the objective of preventing crime and fraud.

49 *Placanica* para. 62. Note that here the final decision on compatibility was not left to the national court. See in this regard also *Commission v. Italy* paras. 32 and 34.

50 Note that the other 671 licences that were open to competitive bids formed the subject matter of *Placanica*, and hence were also struck down, albeit because of the exclusion of quoted undertakings.

51 See for the relation between primary and secondary law in this regard Case 5/77, *Tedeschi* [1977] ECR 1555.

authority to ensure that those principles are complied with. That obligation of transparency which is imposed on the public authority consists in ensuring, for the benefit of any potential tenderer, a degree of advertising sufficient to enable the service concession to be opened up to competition and the impartiality of procurement procedures to be reviewed.'[52]

As there had been nothing close to a transparent procedure, the direct renewal of the licences constituted a restriction on the free movement of services. Italy, moreover, could not justify this restriction, as it could not demonstrate why a direct award of the licences was necessary to achieve any acceptable overriding objectives.[53] Consequently, *Commission v. Italy* confirms that both the award and the renewal of gambling licences must comply with the principles of equal treatment and transparency. Hence, at least some form of open and competitive procedure must be used when awarding gambling licences, even if a 'full tender' is not required.

Subsequently, the transparency requirement was markedly absent in *Liga Portuguesa*, even though the licence at issue had been directly awarded and renewed for several centuries. Since then, however, transparency has been confirmed and applied quite forcefully in multiple judgments. In *Betfair*, transparency was first applied in a preliminary reference. It was found that the direct award of a licence by the Netherlands in principle violated transparency, hence forming a restriction on free movement.[54] This restriction could, however, be justified if the direct award was to 'a public operator whose management is subject to direct State supervision or a private operator whose activities are subject to strict control by the public authorities.'[55] Considering the reliance of the CJEU on *Parking Brixen* in the overall judgment, arguably this exception to the transparency requirement is to be interpreted very strictly, in line with the criteria developed by the CJEU for in-house or pseudo-in-house situations.[56] Although not referring to *Teckal* or its offspring in its final judgment, the Dutch Council of State also applied a very strict test, holding that neither the Lotto nor SGR came close to meeting the 'strict control' required.[57]

Since *Betfair*, transparency has been successfully relied on in *Carmen Media*, *Engelmann*, *Dickinger and Ömer*, *Costa and Cifone*, *Stanleybet*, and *Biasci*. Only in *Garlkans* did the CJEU not find a problem with transparency, instead adopting a rather flexible approach to protect Member States' options to preserve public order. Transparency thus appears to be rapidly becoming a factor of significance in gambling case law.[58] This possible impact of transparency also becomes more readily apparent when one realizes that it does not only cover the procedure for the award itself (transparency in the

52 *Commission v. Italy* para. 24. For the general case law on transparency see especially Case C-324/98, *Telaustria and Telefonadress* [2000] ECR I-10745, paras. 61 and 62, Case C-26/03, *Stadt Halle* [2005] ECR I-1, par. 46, and Case C-458/03, *Parking Brixen* [2005] ECR I-8585, par. 63.

53 *Commission v. Italy* para. 38.

54 *Betfair* para. 53.

55 *Betfair*, paras. 59 and 60.

56 See Case C-107/98, *Teckal* [1999] ECR I-8121, para. 50, *Stadt Halle* par. 46, as well as Case C-458/03, *Parking Brixen* [2005] ECR I-8585.

57 See especially para. 2.10.7–2.10.12 of the judgment of the Council of State of 23 March 2011 in *Betfair*, nr. 200700622/1/H3-A, ECLI:NL:RVS:2011:BP8768.

58 See further below section 4 on recent developments.

narrow sense), but covers all elements of the national regulation that may affect the ability of providers to effectively compete for a licence, or even their reasonable desire to do so (transparency in the broad sense). Transparency can therefore be used to challenge a wide range of issues, including not just the procedure for the award itself, but also the number of licences awarded (why 20 and not 25?), the duration of the licences awarded, the process for renewal, additional requirements for licensees including seat requirements and requirements as to legal form or capital, the amount of discretion left to the awarding entity, the criteria used for the award, as well as the obligations and limitations attached to a licence, including the grounds for withdrawal. Mistakes on any of these issues may undermine the validity of the entire award procedure.

4. New Trends Emerging: More Limits?

By now the main characteristics of the EU framework for gambling appear relatively stable. Nevertheless, some important (emerging) trends can be discerned in the recent case law of the CJEU that could affect the scarcity of gambling licences in the future: 1) a seemingly stricter approach to justifying monopolies, 2) a strict approach against measures protecting incumbents, and 3) a further delineation of the advertising and expansion allowed under channeling approaches.

4.1. A Stricter Approach towards Monopolies?

In general, the CJEU used to simply accept monopolies as one of the policy options open to Member States, without really inquiring whether a less restrictive method might also suffice to reach the same objectives.[59] Although too far reaching conclusions should not be drawn at this stage, the CJEU now seems to be developing a somewhat stricter approach to monopolies, particularly under the objective of preventing incitement to squander money on gambling and combating addiction to gambling.

The beginning of this trend can be seen in *Stoß*, where the CJEU held that 'a measure as restrictive as a monopoly' can be 'justified only in order to ensure a particularly high level of consumer protection'.[60] In addition, a monopoly 'must be accompanied by a legislative framework suitable for ensuring that the holder of the said monopoly will in fact be able to pursue, in a consistent and systematic manner, the objective thus determined by means of a supply that is quantitatively measured and qualitatively planned by reference to the said objective and subject to strict control by the public authorities.'[61]

This seemingly stricter approach to monopolies was developed in *Zeturf*. The CJEU began by confirming that 'the establishment of a measure as restrictive as a monopoly can be justified only in order to ensure a particularly high level of protection with regard

59 See for example *Zenatti*, para. 35, *Anomar*, para. 74, *Commission* v *Italy*, paras. 83 and 84, and *Liga Portuguesa*, para. 58.

60 *Stoß* par. 83.

61 *Stoß* para. 83.

to those objectives'[62], before adding that it must be determined whether 'the establishment of a monopoly could actually be considered *necessary*.'[63] *Zeturf*, therefore, seems to reintroduce some measure of a necessity criterion for monopolies. In *Dickinger and Ömer*, the CJEU further added that, because a monopoly is an unusually restrictive measure, 'the imposition of certain restrictions on the holder of a monopoly of games of chance is consequently, in principle, not only compatible with European Union law but required by that law.'[64] Member States can thus only justify a monopoly where a high level of protection is sought, and sufficient restrictions are placed on the monopolist to effectively and consistently achieve this aim. The stricter line for gambling monopolies has been confirmed in *Stanleybet*.[65]

Taking all these cases together, the CJEU seems to be somewhat returning to the more standard internal market test when confronted with gambling monopolies: firstly, Member States must aim for a very high level of protection to make a monopoly necessary. Secondly, national courts can check whether the national regulation and policy consistently and systematically pursue this very high level of protection, or whether compromises are made, for example to safeguard revenue.[66] Thirdly, even the necessity test seems at least partially resurrected. If national law or policy fail on either of these grounds, the national monopoly in principle conflicts with EU law. If this trend were to be confirmed in later case law, this would be a welcome development. At the same time, for now, it is probably wise not to overrate the expected impact of this trend. It is yet still unlikely that the CJEU would itself find a national monopoly in conflict with EU law. Rather, this new stricter line on monopolies could be seen as an invitation for national courts to critically assess national monopolies. These recent cases give them further tools and support to determine whether national monopolies actually pursue and provide an especially high level of protection and whether they are necessary.

4.2. *No Protection for the Incumbent*

A second trend, highly relevant from the scarcity perspective, concerns transparency and the increasingly clear stance the CJEU is taking against protection of incumbents. Especially in Member States that have recently liberalized gambling or are in the process of doing so, former (exclusive) licensees will generally have a relatively strong or even dominant position. The question arises how to deal with their position under EU law.

In its recent case law, the CJEU seems quite willing to strike down national measures that offer added protection to incumbents. This trend builds on the strict line taken in *Placanica* and *Commission v. Italy* where Italy was not allowed to protect incumbents by indirectly excluding foreign providers or renewing licences without transparency.[67] In *Costa and Cifone*, again in the Italian context, the CJEU further developed this application

62 *Zeturf* para. 46, our italics. Also see para. 53.
63 *Zeturf* para. 47.
64 *Dickinger and Ömer* para. 72.
65 *Stanleybet* paras. 29 and 34.
66 Also see in this regard *Zeturf* paras. 58, 61 and 62.
67 Equally see *Betfair* paras. 48 and 53.

of transparency. This judgment actually concerns the licences that had been awarded by Italy to remedy the violation of EU law found in *Placanica*. In awarding these licences, Italy had included an obligation for new licensees to retain a minimum distance from existing licence holders. This obligation protected existing licensees who tended to have occupied the most attractive locations already. The CJEU rejected this protective requirement in rather strong and general terms:

> 'That is not the case, however, if the market positions acquired by the existing operators are protected by the national legislation. The very fact that the existing operators have been able to start up several years earlier than the operators unlawfully excluded, and have accordingly been able to establish themselves on the market with a certain reputation and a measure of customer loyalty, confers on them an unfair competitive advantage. To grant the existing operators even greater competitive advantages over the new license holders has the consequence of entrenching and exacerbating the effects of the unlawful exclusion of the latter from the 1999 tendering procedure, and accordingly constitutes a new breach of Articles 43 EC and 49 EC and of the principle of equal treatment. (...).'[68]

This clear and strict line was confirmed in *Biasci*, again concerning the same Italian context.[69] The CJEU further clarified, moreover, that a licence requirement which 'in fact precludes all cross-border activity in the betting and gaming sector, irrespective of the form in which that activity is undertaken' also violates EU law.

These recent judgments indicate a clear trend that, be it in the form of distance requirements, direct renewals or other creative rules, Member States are not allowed to, directly or indirectly, protect incumbents.[70] 'Favouritism or arbitrariness on the part of the licensing authority' are to be avoided.[71] This trend fits with the overall strict approach taken to transparency. It also easily sits together with the first trend concerning monopolies: when Member States no longer want to maintain a monopoly, they will have to carefully consider how to respect transparency in the transition from a monopoly to a multi-licence system, *inter alia* by not unduly protecting incumbents.

4.3. *Advertising and Expanding: Between Informing and Inviting?*

A third emerging trend is the further delineation of the possibilities for advertising and expansion of supply allowed under the objective of consumer protection, including the prevention of addiction. Initially, the CJEU required Member States relying on the

68 *Costa and Cifone*, para. 53. Also see paras. 89 and 90 for further violations of transparency because the terms of the licence were not clear, precise and unequivocal.

69 See Joined Cases C-660/11 and C-8/12, *Biasci* [2013] ECLI:EU:C:2013:550, paras. 32–37.

70 As confimred in *Berlington*, Member States may compensate incumbents or maintain their licence for a transitional period where legitimate expectations so require. These measures, however, may not further protect or strengthen the position of incumbents, but may only allow them to recuperate investments. See especially *Berlington* paras. 85 and 86.

71 *Costa and Cifone*, para. 73.

justification of consumer protection to reduce 'gambling opportunities'.[72] This seemed to exclude a national policy advertising attractive new gambling supply, for instance to channel players into legal and safe supply (active channeling).[73] In *Ladbrokes*, however, active channeling was subsequently allowed, albeit in the specific context where the Netherlands pursued the aims of preventing addiction *and* preventing crime at the same time.[74] This opening turned out to be the prelude to *Stoß*, where active channeling was also allowed under the sole objective of consumer protection and preventing addiction. The referring courts had indicated that the German authorities were developing or tolerating policies of expanding supply, which could be deemed problematic under the *Placanica* line. The CJEU, however, held that:

> 'It should be remembered that, giving its view in relation to the objective pursued by a national legislature consisting in preventing exploitation of gaming activities for criminal or fraudulent purposes, the Court has held that a policy of controlled expansion of the said activities may be consistent with the objective of channelling them into controllable circuits by drawing players away from clandestine, prohibited betting and gaming to activities which are authorised and regulated. In order to achieve that objective, authorised operators must represent a reliable, but at the same time attractive, alternative to a prohibited activity. This may as such necessitate the offer of an extensive range of games, advertising on a certain scale and the use of new distribution techniques.
> (...) such considerations may, in principle, also apply where restrictive internal measures pursue an objective of protecting consumers, preventing incitement to squander money on gambling and combating addiction to the latter, in that, in particular, a certain amount of advertising may, without prejudice to the requirements referred to in paragraphs 97 to 99 of this judgment, contribute in certain cases to directing consumers towards the offer emanating from the holder of the public monopoly, that offer being deemed to have been established and conceived precisely in order better to pursue the said objective.'[75]

Consequently, the acceptance of active channeling under the objective of crime prevention was extended to the object of preventing addiction. The CJEU immediately added, however, that such advertisement and expansion must 'remain measured and strictly limited to what is necessary (...).'[76] In any event, such advertising may not 'encourage consumers' natural propensity to gamble'. This precludes *inter alia* 'trivialising gambling or giving it a positive image due to the fact that revenues derived from it are used for activities in the public interest.' It equally precludes 'increasing the attractiveness of gambling by means of enticing advertising messages depicting major winnings in glowing colours.'[77] Considering the often close links between games of chance and good causes, these are important limitations.

72 Cf *Gambelli* para. 69 and *Placanica* paras. 52–54.
73 See on this need *Placanica* para. 55, and *Liga Portuguesa* para. 64.
74 *Ladbrokes* paras. 26 and 28.
75 *Stoß* paras. 101 and 102.
76 *Stoß* para. 103.
77 *Stoß* para. 103.

The emerging trend now seems to be that the CJEU is further delineating and narrowing the extent to which providers may advertise and develop new attractive supply under the objective of consumer protection and the prevention of addiction. After a confirmation of *Stoß* in *Zeturf*, this trend is especially visible in *Dickinger and Ömer*. This judgment concerned the Austrian monopoly on internet casino games and the claimed expansionist commercial policy of the monopolist. Although the CJEU again left the final judgment on suitability to the national court, it did stress two limits on advertising and expanding supply. Firstly, it repeated the *Gambelli* line that Member States cannot rely on consumer protection or preventing addiction where they 'incite and encourage consumers to participate in games of chance *so that the public purse can benefit*.'[78] This limitation thus specifically concerns the objective pursued. Active channeling measures may only aim to lure people away from illegal supply, and not to increase revenue. It is up to the national court to make this tricky factual assessment.

Secondly, and more novel, the CJEU introduced a distinction between *informing* customers on the one hand, and *inviting and encouraging* them on the other. To this end, the CJEU first combines the *Ladbrokes* position that 'the objective of protecting consumers from addiction to gambling is in principle difficult to reconcile with a policy of expanding games of chance',[79] with the *Stoß* limit that in any event any advertising by a monopolist must remain 'measured and strictly limited to what is necessary.'[80] It then added that:

> 'In particular, a distinction should be drawn between strategies of the holder of a monopoly which are intended solely to inform potential customers of the existence of products and serve to ensure regular access to games of chance by channelling gamblers into controlled circuits, and those which invite and encourage active participation in such games. A distinction must therefore be drawn between a restrained commercial policy seeking only to capture or retain the existing market for the organisation with the monopoly, and an expansionist commercial policy whose aim is to expand the overall market for gaming activities.'[81]

The CJEU here not just distinguishes between 'informing' and 'inviting and encouraging', but also between 'capturing or retaining the existing market' and 'expanding the overall market.' Apparently 'informing' the customer is presumed to be linked to capturing or retaining the existing market, whereas 'inviting and encouraging' is linked to expanding the overall market. The Court then, seemingly logically, allows Member States to direct consumers to existing legal supply so as to channel the already existing desire to gamble

78 *Dickinger and Ömer* para. 62, our italics. Cf also *Gambelli* para. 69.

79 *Dickinger and Ömer* para. 67, *Ladbrokes*, para. 30.

80 *Dickinger and Ömer* para. 68, and see also para. 100 where the CJEU further operationalizes this limit by holding that 'to be consistent with the objective of fighting crime and reducing opportunities for gambling, national legislation establishing a monopoly of games of chance which allows the holder of the monopoly to follow an expansionist policy must: (...) 2) allow only moderate advertising limited strictly to what is necessary for channeling consumers towards monitored gaming networks.' Cf further *Stoß* para. 103.

81 *Dickinger and Ömer* para. 69. NB. The misspelling of channeling is copied from the original.

(informing). It then prohibits them to actively increase the overall demand for gambling by advertising and expanding new and attractive supply (inviting and encouraging). In practice, however, this distinction may be hard to draw. Moreover, it does not seem to cover the *potential market*, i.e. the potential demand in a Member State that may be developed by illegal supply where there is no sufficiently attractive legal supply. In other words, will Member States be allowed to develop the market that would otherwise be developed by illegal supply, or do they have to wait until the market has expanded due to illegal supply before recapturing that market?

This third trend is – again – mostly discernible in cases where the national courts were highly critical of their national regulation. For now, it remains rather unlikely that the CJEU would apply the limits to active channeling in a given dispute. Even so, these limits are potentially far reaching, and may again inspire national courts to be more critical in their own assessment.[82] Further clarification is required, and it will be primarily up to the national courts to further develop these limits.

5. The National Dimension: Member States in Times of Trouble?

This section concerns the national dimension, and connects the framework and trends set out above to the developments reported at national level. An analytical approach is adopted. The focus will be on three cross-cutting developments and challenges that can be observed in all or most reports. The first is the apparent trend to liberalize or modernize games of chance. The second development concerns the difficulties all reported Member States seem to be having in meeting the transparency requirements, including the prohibition to protect incumbents, now that they have started to modernize their market. The third development is the shared struggle with rapidly developing online supply, and the challenges raised by separate regimes for games of chance, for example in terms of cross-sector consistency.

5.1. Increasing Liberalization

A first fundamental development, which may be so basic as to almost escape attention, is the fact that all six countries reported on – France, Germany, Greece, Romania, Spain and the Netherlands – have liberalized or are in the process of liberalizing their markets for games of chance. Most, except France, have gone or are still going from a system with one or more monopolies to a more liberalized system with multiple licences, especially in the field of online gambling and sports betting. Germany, for example, started key liberalizations in 2012 and 2013. Spain, Greece and Romania all started liberalizations, especially for online gambling, in 2011, with Romania introducing further liberalization

82 Note that on the other hand the CJEU has also been rather lenient on issues of proportionality in other cases. In *Digibet*, for example, the diverging legation between Schleswig-Holstein and the other *Länder* was held not to undermine the overall consistency of German gambling law. In effect, this allowed a transition period which prima facie sits uneasily with *Winner Wetten* and *Stanleybet*. In effect, par. 36 of *Digibet* even seems to formulate a kind of *de minimis* approach for consistency.

measures in 2014.[83] The Netherlands produced a draft law liberalizing online games of chance (*Kansspelen op Afstand*) in 2013, as part of a more general modernization of the regulation of games of chance.[84]

This clear trend towards liberalization prompts the question whether EU law has instigated this. Correlation must evidently not be confused with causation. Moreover, national choices to liberalize are undoubtedly affected my multiple factors, including the meteoric rise of online gambling, fiscal considerations in times of crisis and many other country specific determinants. Be that as it may, judging from the national reports, EU law does seem to be at least one of the driving forces behind liberalization. In Germany, Romania and The Netherlands, for example, EU law was explicitly mentioned in the draft legislation or preparatory documents as one of the reasons for modernizing, whereas in Greece and in Spain EU law also seems to have played a direct role. This apparently causal effect of EU law is not just interesting for the gambling sector, but for our understanding of EU law more generally. Even though the CJEU so far did not directly assess national regulation, but rather acted via the national courts, the framework developed by the CJEU still appears to have had a significant effect on national law. If verified, this might provide further insight into the channels through which the CJEU actually impacts on national legal systems, and on how an indirect, non-confrontational approach may also prove an effective catalyst for change.

Furthermore, the question arises as to what dynamic will ensue now that the EU legal framework will be applied and developed in an increasingly liberalizing context. Once states start to modernize, for example, the impact of requirements of consistency and transparency on the regulation of the gambling sector may further increase. The liberalization in one sector may affect the justification for more restrictive approaches in other sectors. Similarly, new licences that may be introduced must all be awarded in a transparent manner, which in turn requires that the licence requirements also meet transparency requirements and that the position of incumbents is carefully considered. As we have seen in other sectors, once the logic and law of liberalization is embraced, it becomes difficult to stop halfway. In any event, restrictions that are to be maintained must be designed to fit within the EU legal framework.

5.2. *Struggling with EU Law, especially Transparency*

Despite the clear trend toward liberalization, however, the process of liberalization is far from smooth. Member States are clearly struggling to successfully liberalize and fulfill the requirements of EU law, especially as far as transparency is concerned.

83 For further details, also in the interest of preventing duplication, we refer to the national reports in P. Adriaanse, F. van Ommeren, W. den Ouden en J. Wolswinkel, *Scarcity and the State II. Member State Reports on Gambling Licences, Radio Frequencies and CO_2 Emission Permits*, Intersentia, Antwerp 2016. Only for the Netherlands where we can draw on our own national expertise, we refer more concretely to primary sources where necessary.

84 *Wetsvoorstel Wijziging van de Wet op de kansspelen, de Wet op de kansspelbelasting en enkele andere wetten in verband met het organiseren van kansspelen op afstand*, published on 22 May 2013, available (in Dutch) via: www.internetconsultatie.nl/kansspelenop_afstand.

In Romania, for example, the 2011 legislation contained all kinds of problematic obstacles for foreign providers, including a necessary link to an offline licensee to acquire an online licence. The legislation also – problematically- explicitly identified revenue as an objective. The 2014 amendments remove some of the obstacles for foreign providers, but still, according to the report, retain several problems such as the requirement of an agent, vague and far reaching rules for withdrawal and rules that protect the incumbent. In general, moreover, the Romanian system and situation is apparently considered so unattractive that no provider has yet applied for a licence.

In France the report also indicates that the current system seems to protect incumbents, which still control 77% of some markets, despite the relatively long experience with liberalization. In addition, the current framework appears unable to actually deal with the reality of online supply and massive illegality, whereas there also are competition law concerns regarding the market power and behavior of the incumbents.

Greece probably tops the list of problems with liberalization, also due to the very special and powerful position of *ΟΠΑΠ* (or OPAP), the Greek Organisation of Football Prognostics which *de facto* controls many games of chance in Greece. The national report indicates multiple problems with transparency, including the lack of sufficiently clear and precise rules which leave too much discretion to the awarding authority, the fact that OPAP licences are awarded and renewed without transparency, and that generally the new procedure, especially for online licences, frankly does not seem up to any kind of standard. Revenue, furthermore, plays a central role in the Greek regulation, with OPAP currently being the third largest undertaking quoted on the Greek stock exchange. In this regard, the rather critical question referred by the majority of the Greek Council of State to the CJEU in *Stanleybet* is highly interesting, as is the apparently much softer final decision of the Council of State reported.

In the Netherlands, the new legislation designed to bring Dutch gambling law into compliance with EU law has been bogged down in Parliament, despite an attempt to fast-track those parts linked to on-line gambling and transparency. In the meantime, several existing licences have been renewed, seemingly without meeting the required standards of transparency.[85] This renewal has already been challenged before the courts by several large foreign providers actively trying to gain access to the Dutch market. In addition, cross-sector consistency in the Netherlands may be problematic as the difference in regulation between the different sectors does not seem grounded in the underlying objectives, the new draft legislation for online gambling still refers explicitly to financial objectives, and several measures that are planned or discussed to flank liberalization, such as a grace period for incumbents, may unduly protect the position of incumbents.

Even Germany, generally known for the sophistication of its legal system, is clearly struggling, and not just because regulatory competence is divided over the central government and the *Länder*. The elaborate German report is extremely critical of the German system, which echoes the highly critical views of referring German courts in,

85 See in this regard already the previous critical judgment of the Dutch Council of State in *Betfair*.

for instance, *Stoß*.[86] The author indicates, for example, that German law often fails to achieve its stated objectives, whereas revenue often forms the real objective. In addition, the author sees significant problems in the coherence of the German system, particularly across sectors. Germany is also struggling to organize a transparent licensing system. Due to several problems and challenges, no transparent procedure has yet been developed, and not a single new licence has been awarded so far. As in the Netherlands, this lack of a transparent procedure subsequently means that the incumbents retain their position, even though this position is not in line with transparency or the new objectives underlying the modernized gambling regulation. So far, therefore, the 2013 liberalization attempt has not yet translated into a consistent and transparent system.

Complying with EU law requirements, and especially establishing a consistent and transparent system, thus seems to be a major challenge for Member States liberalizing their gambling regulation. Considering the strict framework for transparency set out above, including the increasingly strict review of measures protecting incumbents, much work lies ahead, and many conflicts and courts cases seem likely. Moreover, the other trend of increasing scrutiny for monopolies may lead to further liberalization, and hence to even more pressure to develop transparent multiple licence schemes. In designing such schemes, attention should be paid to the third development, centering around the challenge of online supply and the clear trend to regulate online gambling separately from offline supply.

5.3. *A Separate Regime for Online Gambling?*

As indicated, the online revolution is one of the driving forces behind the liberalization of gambling and the evolution of gambling law. The different reports clearly support the conclusion that all states concerned are in the same boat when it comes to the challenge of dealing with online gambling: how to regulate and tax the seemingly uncatchable? The reports also indicate a further similarity: in responding to this challenge, all states concerned seem to opt for a separate regime for online and offline gambling. France perhaps goes furthest, even having a separate authority for online gambling (Arjel), but all other states also treat online gambling as a separate category. This treatment reflects the fact that online gambling is a relatively new phenomenon for which many states simply had no framework at all. As such it may also be the easiest path to develop separate legislation for online gambling instead of overhauling all gambling law. The separate treatment of online gambling may equally reflect the assumption, shared by the CJEU in *Liga Portuguesa*, that online gambling is somehow different, and may even carry higher risks, even though this assumption does not seem to be fully supported by the evidence.

Creating a special regime for online gambling, however, also raises several problems. To begin with, as evidenced by the reports, it increases the risks of cross-sector inconsistency. When regulating online gambling, Member States often opt for a relatively liberalized approach, because stricter approaches as monopolies or complete bans are

[86] Also see in this regard the judgment of the FCC of 28-3-2006, criticizing the German regulation from the perspective of German law itself.

considered to be unfeasible. If online gaming is indeed considered to be high-risk, however, this raises issues of cross-sector or online versus offline consistency. Why is it suitable, for example, to liberalize online casino-games, but to retain a monopoly on land-based casinos? Or why liberalize online sports betting, yet retain a monopoly on online lotteries for the incumbent, even though sports betting clearly forms a higher risk for addiction than lotteries? Often, differences in tax treatment are also included, so as to make registering attractive enough for online suppliers, which can lead to problems with consistency and state aid.[87] Separate online frameworks may also cause problems in terms of transparency, especially where interests of incumbents are actively protected, for example by granting them privileges in acceding to the online market or in protecting their offline activities against online developments.

In the end, the most fundamental question remains to which extent national policies are really capable of effectively regulating online supply by themselves. As most reports indicate, the current systems fail to really control and regulate (illegal) online supply. The CJEU may have sidelined this fact for its assessment of suitability, but national policies should address reality. And the reality seems to be that so far, special national regimes for online gambling seem unable to meet their double aim of controlling online supply while equally ensuring revenues from online gambling flow to Member States and good causes instead of illegal providers. This sobering reality should affect how the regulation of gambling is approached at the national and the European level.

6. Conclusion: Whispering Words of Wisdom ...

Taking one step back from legal tests and trends, a liberalizing gambling landscape can be observed, struggling to come to grips with a new, increasingly online, reality. This new reality is being guided and influenced by a still developing framework of EU law that is trying hard to find a balance between respecting Member States' regulatory choices and upholding internal market law. The result is a somewhat inconsistent whole that largely depends on national courts for its ultimate interpretation and application. As this EU framework is based on negative integration, it is inherently more suited to support liberalization than to support constructive regulation. After all, free movement law can tell Member States what not to do, but it cannot tell them what to do, or how to come to terms with the online revolution.

Member States are all engaged in a similar struggle to get a grip on online gambling, and to do so in a way that fits with their values, national traditions and interests. Control is crucial to protect consumers, prevent crime, and retain valuable revenue for good causes. For even if free market law cannot accept it as a justification, it makes perfect sense that Member States want to divert the income from illegal online gambling to public causes. It is evident, however, that individual Member States are currently not

87 The issue of potential state aid due to difference in tax regimes is an important one, but also one that requires a separate discussion. As a result, we here only point out the problems with state aid and competition law in a broader sense that surround gambling regulating, and that may well develop into epicenters of contention soon, but do not engage in a substantive discussion of them.

winning the struggle for control over online gambling. Online gambling opportunities are not exactly scarce at the moment, and the licensing systems developed so far by individual Member States are facing many problems.

Considering the fact that all Member States are struggling with the same challenge, and considering the inherent cross-border nature of online gambling, it would make sense to cooperate at European level to regain control over online gambling. This cooperation should focus on effectively controlling illegal supply, licensing and supervising legal supply, and ensuring that Member States receive maximum income from that legal supply. Considering the significant problems many Member States are reporting in actually establishing an effective licensing system for online gambling, an EU licensing procedure for online gambling could be an option to consider. Such a procedure would only cover the technical aspects surrounding the award of licences, leaving the Member States sufficient room for setting individual licensing requirements, such as the height and the recipients of gambling revenue. Not only would this share the burden and the expertise of licensing, providers with a European licence would also have an enormous incentive to respect their licence requirements, for example concerning advertisement and addiction prevention and guaranteeing that the agreed percentage of income is transferred to the national good causes specified: after all, a single mistake in one Member State could cost them their licence in the entire EU. Licensed providers could also be taxed more easily, and would form a natural ally in the digital fight against illegal supply. An additional benefit of European cooperation would be that Member States with less developed legal infrastructure, could benefit from EU expertise. Both the Romanian and the Greek report, for example, explicitly invite European support to overcome national challenges and gaps in expertise.

By cooperating as a block, Member States could better control supply, increase income and actually create the desired scarcity, whilst retaining the freedom to set their own national substantive policy. Cooperation would also increase the overall revenue, expanding the pie and hence the income of each Member State, whilst creating a European block of regulators and licensed suppliers that could together target illegal supply. In the context of positive integration, i.e. EU regulation, there is after all no barrier to openly consider financial interests, and hence escape the trilemma of current EU gambling law. The current cooperation between regulators and the different soft law instruments developed by the Commission provide logical and welcome starting points in this regard.[88] But common sense, which should not be scarce, would now seem to suggest that further steps are taken, so as to have a real scarcity of gambling instead of a *de facto* scarcity in effective control.

88 See for example the 2014 Commission Recommendation on protecting consumers and minors or the 2012 Communication 'Towards a comprehensive European framework for online gambling.'

Gerry Oberst*

CHAPTER 13. THE ALLOCATION OF RADIO FREQUENCIES; OVERVIEW OF SPECTRUM POLICY AND REGULATION IN EUROPE

1. Introduction

Legal theory and practice concerning radio frequencies are among the topics chosen by the editors of this book in the search for a general legal theory on allocation of limited authorisations and grants in the EU Member States. The topic is timely, as there have been substantial developments within the European Union (EU) over the last decade, even in the last few years. This period has seen a strong shift in emphasis in Europe from non-binding decisions reached by spectrum technical experts acting within the European Conference of Post and Telecommunication Administrations (CEPT), to EU law defined by directives and decisions of the European institutions in Brussels. This shift has occurred for many reasons, among them (a) an emphasis on EU policy guidelines supplanting purely technical decisions on radio spectrum and (b) the immense increase in the value and use of radio spectrum in general.

This overview first discusses certain critical terminology unique to the spectrum field. It then examines the following series of questions:

1. How is the limitation of... radio frequencies constructed legally? How is a maximum – a ceiling – to this public right created within a given period?
2. What kind of allocation procedure is being used? Are authorisations being allocated by a competitive method?
3. How are favoritism and nepotism being prevented? How is the equal/fair treatment of newcomers being approached?
4. Which general legal principles (e.g. of proper or good administration/transparency) play an important role in the national debate or jurisprudence concerning the allocation of... radio frequencies?

* Gerry Oberst is Senior Vice President, responsible for Global Regulatory and Governmental Strategy for the international satellite operator SES, Luxemburg. The views expressed in this paper are based on the author's experience as a lawyer in private practice prior to joining SES and are not necessarily the views of SES. For purposes of brevity, some EU legislation is cited in "short hand" form, which nevertheless should permit the reader to readily find these references.

5. Are there any national cases in which competition law (e.g. abuse of a dominant position or State aid) played an important role?
6. Which specific problems of legal protection might be considered to be the most important or interesting issues ...?

As shall be seen, this overview discusses most closely the first question, as it permits direct identification of EU legal standards that apply specifically to radio frequency use, which must be implemented by the EU Member States.

2. Telecoms Terminology and Main Actors

At the outset, it is necessary to get past the jargon, as the radio spectrum field, similar to many other fields, defines itself with a barrage of technical terms that can confound outsiders. Combined with the EU terminology, this thicket of acronyms for the main actors and other elements of the field would be impenetrable without an initial explication.

The starting point is the International Telecommunication Union (ITU), its Radiocommunication Bureau (BR) and the international Radio Regulations (RRs). The ITU RRs define an "allocation" as an entry into the ITU (or national or regional) Table of Frequency Allocations of a given frequency band for a particular purpose, whether it be for terrestrial or space radiocommunication services, radio astronomy, or other defined service categories. By contrast, "assignments" are the authorisations given by an administration (i.e., national regulator) to use a radio frequency within the allocation and under specified conditions.[1] The ITU is not in the business of handing out assignments – that is a national role. But allocations are made at the ITU level by the Member States, with refinements adopted at regional and national level so long as they are consistent with the ITU structure.

In the European context, we already have referred to the CEPT, which comprises 48 countries across Europe and thus extends beyond the 28 EU Member States. Acting through its Electronic Communications Committee (ECC) and various working groups, project teams and other groupings, the CEPT has served for years as a means to establish decisions, recommendations and other output concerning use of radio spectrum. These deliverables are non-binding, i.e., their legal effectiveness is only substantiated by adoption into national law by CEPT members, which leaves room for delay and inconsistency in application.

As already noted, there has been a substantial shift in EU spectrum regulation towards European institutions, led by the European Commission (EC or Commission). Radio spectrum use increasingly is seen as an important element in the EU internal market and a contributor to numerous EU policies. Nevertheless, there remains a tension between national regulators, seeking to retain their role in administration of critical radio frequency

1 ITU RR Article 1 sets forth a wide variety of terms and definitions. Allocations and assignments (as well as allotments, which are not pertinent to this discussion) are defined in RR 1.16 and 1.18 (and 1.17), respectively.

resources, and the EC, seeking to define EU internal market principles and make progress in the optimal use of these resources at a more or less uniform rate throughout the EU.

Among the important elements of EU legislation and regulation in this area is the overarching Electronic Communications Framework (the Framework), comprised of a suite of EU directives first adopted in 2002,[2] and substantially amended in 2009.[3] At the same time it adopted the Framework in 2002, the EU also adopted the Radio Spectrum Decision, which establishes a procedural structure for making technical implementing decisions by the EC through a Radio Spectrum Committee (RSC) comprised of Member State regulators.[4] Policy advice on the direction this regulation should take is supplied by the Radio Spectrum Policy Group (RSPG), comprised of Member State policy level representatives.[5]

Subsequent to the 2009 Framework amendments, the EU adopted a Radio Spectrum Policy Programme (RSPP) designed to set high level policy for spectrum regulation.[6] Subsequently, in 2013 the EC proposed extensive new measures affecting spectrum regulation, which would have even more vigorously moved regulatory decisions to the EU level.[7] That proposal became stalled in Brussels, however, and the ultimate regulation adopted in November 2015 contained no provisions on spectrum.[8]

2 The original suite of directives consisted of the Directive 2002/21/EC of the European Parliament and of the Council of 7 March 2002 (Framework Directive) [2002] OJ L108/33; Directive 2002/22/EC of the European Parliament and of the Council of 7 March 2002 (Universal Service Directive) [2002] OJ L108/51; Directive 2002/19/EC of the European Parliament and of the Council of 7 March (Access Directive) [2002] OJ L108/7 and Directive 2002/58/EC of the European Parliament and of the Council of 12 July 2002 (E-Privacy Directive) [2002] OJ L201/37.

3 The Framework directives were amended in 2009 by the "Better Regulation" Directive 2009/140/EC of the European Parliament and of the Council of 25 November 2009 (amending the Framework, Access and Authorisation Directives) [2009]OJ L 337/37 and the "Consumer Rights" Directive 2009/136/EC of the European Parliament and of the Council of 25 November 2009 (amending the Universal Service and E-Privacy Directives) [2009] OJ L337/11. All references to Framework directives in this paper are to the amended versions currently in force unless otherwise noted.

4 Decision No 676/2002/EC of the European Parliament and of the Council of 7 March 2002 on a regulatory framework for radio spectrum policy in the European Community [2002] OJ L108/1. A full list of technical implementing decisions taken by the Commission through the RSC, as well as other relevant legislation, is found at <http://ec.europa.eu/digital-agenda/en/radio-spectrum-policy-document-archive> accessed 10.07.2015>.

5 The European Commission created the RSPG in Commission Decision 2002/622/EC of 26 July 2002 [2002] OJ L198, amended in Commission Decision 2009/633/EC of 16 December 2009. The RSPG website contains a substantial amount of useful information at <http://rspg-spectrum.eu/category/news/> accessed 10.07.2015.

6 Decision No 243/2012/EU of the European Parliament and of the Council of 14 March 2012 establishing a multiannual radio spectrum policy programme [2012] OJ L81/7.

7 European Commission Communication, "On the Telecommunications Single Market", COM (2013) 634 final, 11.08.2013; and proposed regulation set forth in COM(2013) 627 final, 11.09.2013.

8 Regulation (EU) 2015/2120 (concerning open internet access and roaming on public communications networks) [2015] OJ L 310/1.

3. The Issues

3.1. How is the Limitation of Radio Frequencies Constructed Legally? How is a Maximum – A Ceiling – to this Public Right Created within a given Period?

Limits and ceilings on radio frequencies can take the form of regulations on what the spectrum can be used for, who gets to use it, at what cost and for how long. In this section we focus on the latter three issues, related to assignments, and leave the matter of allocations for subsequent sections.

The preliminary question concerning EU limits or a maximum on radio frequency usage is why such constraints are needed in the first place and why should Member States have the right to apply them. Theories abound, including concepts that spectrum is a public resource inherently limited in quantity by the laws of physics, spectrum is used for many important purposes, and regulation is necessary to avoid harmful interference from competing usages. Recitals of the Better Regulation Directive 2009/140/EC concisely express these concepts as the grounds for EU regulation:

> "24 Radio frequencies should be considered a scarce public resource that has an important public and market value. It is in the public interest that spectrum is managed as efficiently and effectively as possible from an economic, social and environmental perspective, taking account of the important role of radio spectrum for electronic communications, of the objectives of cultural diversity and media pluralism, and of social and terrestrial cohesion. ***
>
> 31 Radio frequencies should be managed so as to ensure that harmful interference is avoided. This basic concept of harmful interference should therefore be properly defined to ensure that regulatory intervention is limited to the extent necessary to prevent such interference."[9]

The RSPP adds color to these principles. In its recitals, the RSPP states:

> "3 Spectrum is a key public resource for essential sectors and services... Regulatory measures on spectrum therefore have economic, safety, health, public interest, cultural, scientific, social, environmental and technical implications."

In sum, radio spectrum is fairly important and a public resource. The latter point is important, as it implies that private property rights cannot be granted for spectrum; instead, private operators can be granted rights to use radio frequencies without holding

9 This recital reference to defining "harmful interference" is followed by a specific definition in Framework Directive Article 2(r), which in turn is derived from the ITU RR 1.169 definition. This linkage demonstrates the dependencies of EU and international law in the radio frequency area.

property rights in the normal sense of the term. For example, in France, radio frequencies are State assets: "[t]he radio electric frequencies available on the territory of the Republic are in the State's public domain"[10] and the use by authorisation holders of radio electric frequencies available on the territory of the Republic is a private utilization of the public domain.[11]

With these assumptions in place, the next question is how limits might be implemented. At the international level, ITU RR 4.1 provides that "Member States shall endeavour to limit the number of frequencies and the spectrum used to the minimum essential to provide in a satisfactory manner the necessary services. To that end they shall endeavour to apply the latest technical advances as soon as possible." This provision refers in turn to Article 195 of the ITU Constitution, in which the same principle is enshrined.

Article 18 of the ITU RR dealing with "Licences" provides that all transmitting stations (other than government stations) must operate with a licence issued "in an appropriate form and in conformity with the provisions of these Regulations by or on behalf of the government of the country to which the station in question is subject..." On its face, this provision would seem to indicate that each transmitting station must have a licence issued to the operator, but this is actually not true. Instead, there are various types of "licences," which can take the form of "class licences" issued to anyone who fits within the class of users defined by the regulator without further ado or filing, to "blanket licences" for an operator to transmit on multiple units, all the way to licence exemptions, typically applied for types of transmitters which are incapable of causing harmful interference if operated in compliance with technical rules.

In Europe, the basic tool set by the Framework is for national regulatory authorities (NRAs) to grant either *individual rights of use* as authorisations for radio frequency usage, or *general authorisations*. For the latter, normally there is no limit or pre-defined maximum on radio frequency use (and thus no need for individual rights of use) aside from compliance with technical rules. General authorisations can be administered as a form of declaration, a simple registration or a class licence. In the EU structure, the operator should not be required to obtain affirmative approval from the NRA before operating under a general authorisation. As such, this form of authorisation is not

10 Article L. 2111-17, code general de la propriété des personnes publiques (General Code of Property of Public Entities).

11 Article L.41-1(3), code des postes et des communications électroniques (Code of Postal Activities and Electronic Communications).This position was confirmed as a constitutional principle in a ruling of the Constitutional Council of 28 December 2000, *Loi de finances pour 2001*, n° 2000-442DC. The author thanks Professor F. Lafarge and colleagues for reference to these French law provisions. See F. Lafarge and A. Soldatenko, 'The Allocation of Gambling Licences, Radio Frequencies and CO_2 Emission Permits in France' in P. Adriaanse, F. Van Ommeren, W. Den Ouden and J. Wolswinkel, *Scarcity and the State II. Member State Reports on Gambling Licences, Radio Frequencies and CO_2 Emission Permits*, Intersentia, Antwerp 2016.

pertinent to our discussion of limits, but it is nevertheless an extremely important tool for many uses of radio frequencies.[12]

By contrast, individual rights of use do require an affirmative grant from the NRA and definitely involve limits, such as duration, fees, specified spectrum ranges and so on. Again, a useful recital from the Better Regulation Directive gives a rationale for limiting the duration of individual rights of use:

> "69 Considering its restrictive impact on free access to radio frequencies, the validity of an individual right of use that is not tradable should be limited in time. Where rights of use contain provision for renewing their validity, competent national authorities should first carry out a review, including a public consultation, taking into account market, coverage and technological developments. In view of spectrum scarcity, individual rights granted to undertakings should be regularly reviewed."[13]

A further recital expresses the rationale for maximum amounts of radio frequency, as a means of avoiding the hoarding of this resource:

> "71 Competent national authorities should have the power to ensure effective use of spectrum and, where spectrum resources are left unused, to take action to prevent anti-competitive hoarding, which can hinder new market entry."

The concepts set forth in these recitals are given legal force in Framework Directive Articles 8a, 9, 9a and 9b. A key element of Article 9(1) requires NRAs to grant rights of use on "objective, transparent, non-discriminatory and proportionate criteria." Further, Article 9(7) is designed to prevent spectrum hoarding, by requiring "strict deadlines for the effective exploitation of the rights of use by the holder..."[14]

Even more direct limits on radio frequency use are defined in the Authorisation Directive, which governs how rights (i.e., assignments) are granted and administered. Authorisation Directive Article 5 provides the general rules, including a provision in Article 5(2) (fourth paragraph) that "[w]here Member States grant rights of use for a limited period

12 For example, "short range devices" such as automotive radar, garage door openers and certain medical devices are operated under general authorisations that do not limit the number of operators or devices. There remain, however, significant technical limits on how and where such devices can be used, in order to avoid unacceptable or harmful interference. An extreme case was automotive radar in the 24 GHz range, which in Europe were only authorized to be implemented for a defined time period (i.e., certain automotive model years) and had to rely on automatic deactivation within certain distances of radioastronomy stations (based on GPS data).

13 Certain aspects of this recital, and of spectrum regulation under the Framework Directive Article 9b, relate to spectrum trading, a topic outside the scope of this discussion, but pertinent for radio spectrum theory in general.

14 See also RSPP Article 3(i) 'Policy objectives,' which establishes a policy to avoid 'excessive accumulations of rights of use of radio frequencies ...' and Article 5(2) 'Competition,' which permits limits on the amount of spectrum authorized to any particular undertaking.

of time, the duration shall be appropriate for the service concerned, in view of the objective pursued taking due account of the need to allow for an appropriate period for investment amortisation."

Authorisation Directive Article 7 directly addresses "procedure[s] for limiting the number of rights of use to be granted for radio frequencies." Notably, if a NRA is considering whether to limit the number of rights of use it will grant, or to extend the duration of authorisations already granted, it must "give due weight to the need to maximise benefits for users and to facilitate the development of competition."

The Authorisation Directive also defines in an annex the types of conditions that NRAs may attach to the rights of use they grant for radio frequencies. Annex section B specifically defines radio frequency conditions, and gives NRAs ample authority to limit spectrum use.

So far this discussion has focused on EU legal principles expressed in Framework directives. It is well known that directives can be implemented in widely different ways by Member States. This result is especially true in the radio frequency field, in which NRAs grant rights of use based on national circumstances and interpretations. Pragmatically, this approach means there can be substantial differences in the conditions that NRAs apply.

The author reviewed examples of these differences in two projects for the European Commission designed to assess Member State conditions for granting authorisations and enforcing conditions concerning systems in the Mobile Satellite Service (MSS) using radio frequencies in the 2 GHz range.[15] These projects presented a virtual case study in harmonisation versus variation in Member State practice, because they were conducted against the backdrop of a suite of EU legislation selecting two MSS operators, setting various conditions and milestones for their authorisations, directing the Member States to grant the authorisations promptly and setting (vague) rules for enforcement.

Despite the apparent EU-level harmonisation, the conclusion of the February 2012 report was that "[t]he approaches that Member States have taken towards authorisation of the MSS component of 2 GHz MSS networks vary considerably."[16] Fees for the satellite component of the MSS systems were "diverse"; fees for the terrestrial component of the systems were "extraordinarily diverse." Despite the EU structure specifying the service that could be provided, our conclusion was "authorisation structures for [terrestrial

15 G. Oberst, Hogan Lovells Int'l LLP, "*Study on MSS Authorisation Regimes and Authorisations in the EU Member States*," SMART N° 2011/0015, 20.02.2012; and SMART N° 2010/20, 04.01.2011. These studies provide extensive background on the 2 GHz MSS legal structure. The views expressed in these studies are not necessarily those of the European Commission for which the studies were conducted, and the author at the time of the projects was acting in private practice.

16 2012 Study, p. 1.

components] were technology and service neutral in 10 Member States. Another 11 were not neutral; for the remaining 6 it was not possible to say."[17]

This lack of harmonisation in spectrum decisions has not gone unnoticed by the European Commission. In support of a proposed new "Single Telecoms Market" regulation noted above, the Commission stated in September 2013 that:

> "Meanwhile differences in the timing, the conditions and the costs of procedures for acquiring spectrum chill investment, and make it hard to develop integrated wireless networks between countries. More timely and predictable spectrum availability would allow more widespread and affordable broadband connections in Europe, but remains too often locked into regulatory structures at national level.
>
> * * *
>
> In short, the sector suffers from fragmentation along national borders; a lack of regulatory consistency and predictability across the Union; unfairly high prices for specific services; and a lack of investment."[18]

The proposal included such changes as implementing a single EU authorisation and establishing a structure for harmonisation of spectrum inputs by such means as:

- Defining common regulatory principles applicable to Member States when defining conditions on the use of spectrum which is harmonized for wireless broadband communications
- Empowering the Commission to adopt implementing acts to harmonize spectrum availability, the timing of assignments and the duration of rights of use for spectrum
- A consultation mechanism enabling the Commission to review draft national measures concerning the assignment and the use of spectrum
- Simplifying conditions for the deployment and provision of low-power wireless broadband access ('Wi-Fi', small cells) to enhance competition and reduce network congestion.[19]

Subsequent developments indicated that this proposal was too radical a change for European Member States to accept, as all provisions on spectrum regulation were stripped from the final version adopted in 2015. Nevertheless, the issue of diverging practice at the Member State level for radio spectrum authorisations is well recognized.

17 Id., p. 3.
18 COM(2013) 634, pp. 4 and 5.
19 COM(2013) 627 at Explanatory Memorandum, p. 11.

3.2. *What Kind of Allocation Procedure is being used? Are Authorisations being Allocated by a Competitive Method?*

At the outset, the careful reader will note that the terms used in Chapter 1 of this book do not apply correctly to the radio frequency field. Terms defined at the international level separate "allocations," which define which services can use specific radio frequency bands, from "authorisations," which define who gets to use the radio frequencies to provide those allocated services. Extensive work goes into defining these allocations at all levels: the international (through the ITU), broadly regional (i.e., CEPT), European (EU) and national level.

Allocations are in effect another form of limit on the use of radio frequencies, but at the higher level of service definitions and conditions. The ITU RR define numerous services and where they can be used in particular radio frequency bands, subject to technical conditions. These definitions are made at regular World Radiocommunication Conferences (WRC's) in which all ITU administrations participate in lengthy "horse trading" sessions to determine which services should be allocated in the international Table of Frequency Allocations (RR Article 5) and to make other changes to the RR.

Historically, the CEPT has determined European positions for the WRCs through Conference Preparatory Group (CPG) work. The CEPT brings together NRA spectrum experts and policy officials, as well as industry and other interested parties, to determine European Common Proposals (ECPs) for each WRC.

In recent years, the European Commission has participated in or sought to guide some of this CPG work.[20] The Commission has determined that allocation decisions that affect EU internal policy should, at least in part, be an exclusive competency of the EU, rather than left to Member State determinations. In preparation of the 2009 Framework amendments, and again in preparation of the RSPP, the Commission sought to take this approach further to create greater competency for the EU in spectrum matters, with somewhat limited success due to opposition by the Council, representing Member States and their NRAs. The scope for exclusive versus shared competency, and thus the role of the European Commission, will continue to be a matter of controversy as the Commission seeks to move European participation in ITU activities from the Member States to the EU level in the future.

The Commission's proposed new regulation also would have centralized some aspects of spectrum management at the European level. Article 16 of the proposed regulation addressed both allocations and authorisations, by providing that Member States "shall in

20 See, e.g., European Commission Communication COM(2011) 180, 06.04.2011, "The European Union's policy approach to the ITU [WRC-12]," (*WRC-12 Communication*). More recently, see also European Commission, "Proposal for a Council Decision on the position to be adopted, on behalf of the European Union, in the [WRC-15]," COM(2015) 234, 29.05.2015.

particular take all necessary radio spectrum allocation or assignment measures" in order to avoid impeding use of spectrum by other Member States. The final paragraph of that article would possibly have led to further EU level activity in this respect, as it provided that "[t]he Commission may adopt implementing measures to ensure that coordinated outcomes respect the requirement of equitable access to radio spectrum among the relevant Member States, to resolve any practical inconsistencies between distinct coordinated outcomes between different Member States, or to ensure the enforcement of coordinated solutions under Union law." While this proposal was rejected in 2015, it is expected that the Commission has not given up and will set forth similar proposals in future proposals.[21]

3.3. *How are Favoritism and Nepotism being Prevented? How is the Equal/ Fair Treatment of Newcomers being Approached?*

As noted above, the Framework Directive requires NRAs to grant rights of use on "objective, transparent, non-discriminatory and proportionate criteria." At a more basic level, that directive in Article 3 requires that NRAs must be "legally distinct from and functionally independent of all organisations providing electronic communications networks, equipment or services." Member States must ensure that their NRAs exercise their power "impartially, transparently and in a timely manner." Further, Framework Directive Article 4(1) requires a right of appeal from NRA decisions to a body that is independent of the parties involved. These are general rules, designed to ensure that in all aspects of electronic communications there is no favoritism or nepotism.

There are various provisions to treat newcomers fairly, both in the Framework as a whole and specifically for use of radio frequencies. Mainly, these are provisions requiring adherence to competition standards, discussed below. There also is a specific provision in the RSPP on reserving bands for new users, in Article 5(2)(b), permitting the Member States to reserve, if appropriate, "a certain part of a frequency band or group of bands for assignment to new entrants."

Some Member States have sought directly to encourage newcomers, particularly in the provision of mobile communications, typically through reserving spectrum for new entrants or imposing caps on how much spectrum the incumbent users can obtain. These approaches do not always work. For example, in an Austrian auction of 800 MHz in late 2013, regulators originally were said to have reserved spectrum for new entrants but in the actual auction the incumbents successfully bid for it all. In the 2010 Dutch 2.6 GHz auction designed to encourage newcomers, certain bands were not sold. "Suggestions

21 When announcing the final EU agreement on its proposed regulation, in which the European Council had quite consciously stripped out spectrum provisions, the Commission nevertheless stated it would try again in another round of proposals. It stated "These measures will be completed by an ambitious overhaul of EU telecoms rules in 2016. This reform will include a more effective EU-level spectrum coordination." European Commission Memo 15/5275, unpaginated p. 4, updated 27.10.2015.

were made that one of the reasons why not all the spectrum [was] sold was the tight spectrum caps imposed on the three incumbent bidders who were limited to 20 MHz and 10 MHz respectively."[22] This Dutch situation was described in contributions to the Leiden University workshop, which highlighted that political efforts to encourage new market entry can result in failed auction design or results. Perhaps as a result, the German national regulator has chosen not to reserve spectrum for new entrants.[23]

Member States have not necessarily been as active in fostering new entry in other communications fields, such as competition to state-run broadcasters. A long series of Commission cases examining State aid to public broadcasters has occurred since the Commission issued a 2001 Communication on the application of state aid rules to public broadcasting.[24] The impact on newcomers have been limited, however, as technology and economic changes permitted a substantial increase in other methods of distributing broadcasting content to consumers, through cable, satellite and internet means. Nevertheless, a case involving Italy that we describe below in the section on State aid shows that there still can be resistance to granting spectrum resources to new broadcasting entrants.

The Commission's proposed new regulation could have had varying impact on entry of newcomers. On the one hand, the proposed effect of Article 3 would have absolved small newcomers from payment of administrative charges or universal service fees if their revenues in a particular Member States fell below certain thresholds. This provision is explicitly described as a means to avoid "hinder[ing] cross-border market entry, in particular of new entrants and smaller operators" in recital paragraph 14. On the other hand, the proposal also was touted as a means to foster large cross-border operators, to accomplish economies of scale that the Commission believes have been hampered by reliance on national operations.

3.4. *Which General Legal Principles (e.g. of Proper or Good Administration/ Transparency) Play an Important Role in the National Debate or Jurisprudence Concerning the Allocation of Radio Frequencies?*

This question essentially is answered above (for authorisations). General principles of the Framework require NRAs to grant rights of use on "objective, transparent, non-

22 "*RSPG Opinion on Strategic Challenges Facing Europe in Addressing the Growing Spectrum Demand for Wireless Broadband*," RSPG Doc. 13-521 rev. 1, 13.06.2013, p. 14. The RSPG also refers to a "Spanish 'super auction' in July 2011 [in which] several blocks of prime spectrum in the 900 MHz and 2.6 GHz bands were unsold." The explicit reason for the failure was that the incumbents reached their spectrum caps.

23 See M. Martini, 'The Allocation of Gambling licences, Radio Frequencies, and CO_2 emission permits in Germany' in P. Adriaanse, F. Van Ommeren, W. den Ouden and J. Wolswinkel, *Scarcity and the State II. Member State Reports on Gambling Licences, Radio Frequencies and CO_2 Emission Permits*, Intersentia, Antwerp 2016.

24 European Commission, "Communication from the Commission on the application of State aid rules to public service broadcasting" (2001/C 320/04) [2001] OJ C320/5.

discriminatory and proportionate criteria." The Framework Directive sets forth a series of policy objectives and regulatory principles for NRAs to follow in Article 8, which includes principles to promote regulatory predictability (Article 8(5)(a)); avoid discrimination (Article 8(5)(b)) and safeguard competition (Article 8(5)(c)), among others.

Also as noted above, procedures are in place for authorizing spectrum use in Authorisation Directive Article 7. Among the required procedures is the Article 7(1)(b) requirement that NRAs give all interested parties the opportunity to express their views.[25] This requirement gives a certain amount of transparency to the process.

One of the more important European court cases to apply these principles to the authorisation of frequencies is *Centro Europa 7 Srl*, which involved the granting of rights to use frequencies in order to broadcast media content.[26] In 1999, the Italian authorities granted Centro Europa 7 a national licence for terrestrial television broadcasting without, however, giving it the necessary radio frequencies. The Italian NRA was supposed to make transitional arrangements to award these frequencies to the newcomer by taking spectrum from incumbents who exceeded a cap on the number of national television channels they could operate on terrestrial frequencies. Political and administrative delays ensued, and after five years of inaction Centro Europa 7 sought a declaration before the national court that it was entitled to the frequency authorisation and to compensation for damages.

On appeal, an Italian court certified questions to the European Court under EU Treaty provisions on freedom to provide services and on competition, as well as the Framework, Authorisation and Competition Directives, and the principle of pluralism of information sources.

In its judgment of 31 January 2008, the Court found that the Italian transitional arrangements had the effect of preventing operators without radio frequencies from accessing the broadcast market. The Court held that:

> "97 First, by limiting de facto the number of operators able to broadcast on the market in question, those measures are and/or were likely to hinder the provision of services in the area of television broadcasting.
>
> 98 Secondly, those measures have and/or have had the effect of freezing the structures on the national market and protecting the position of the operators already active on that market.

25 Notably this requirement is only for NRAs to allow interested parties to express their view. There is no legal requirement in the Framework for NRAs to actually take those views into account. NRAs must nevertheless, publish any decision to limit the granting of rights of use or renewals, "stating the reasons therefor," Authorisation Directive Article 7(1)(c), which implies that the NRAs must review the interested parties' input.

26 Case C-380/05, *Centro Europa 7 Srl* [2008] ECR-I 349.

99 Consequently, Article 49 EC and, from the date on which they became applicable, Article 9(1) of the Framework Directive, Article 5(1) of the Authorisation Directive and point 1 of Article 4 of the Competition Directive preclude such measures unless they are justified.

100. In that respect, it is clear from the case-law of the Court that a licensing system which restricts the number of operators in the national territory is capable of being justified by general-interest objectives [references omitted], on condition that the restrictions resulting from them are appropriate and do not go beyond what is necessary to attain those objectives."

The ruling of the Court was essentially to uphold the basic provision of the Framework that requires "objective, transparent, non-discriminatory and proportionate criteria.[27]

3.5. *Are there any National Cases in which Competition Law (e.g. Abuse of a Dominant Position or State Aid) Played an Important Role?*

On the European level, the 2002 Framework contained mainly general references to the need to promote competition, with limited direct application to spectrum regulation. At the same time, the 2002 Competition Directive, adopted in parallel with the Framework, explicitly provided that "Member States shall not grant exclusive or special rights of use of radio frequencies [and the ...] assignment of radio frequencies for electronic communication services shall be based on objective, transparent, non-discriminatory and proportionate criteria."[28]

The 2009 amendments to the Framework greatly expanded rules for planning, management and review in spectrum policy, as well as expanded application of competition law concepts to spectrum. The RSPP further expanded application of these competition law concepts to spectrum and gave the Commission new tools for regulating and harmonizing in this field.

27 This 2008 decision of the European Court was followed by a proceeding before the European Court of Human Rights. After the 2008 decision, Italian authorities authorized Centro Europa 7 to operate on a single channel that covered less than 80% of national territory. Around the same timeframe, in a judgment of 20 January 2009, the Consiglio di Stato also ordered the Ministry to pay Centro Europa 7 slightly over € 1 million euros damages for the Ministry's negligence in not granting the necessary frequencies. Centro Europa 7 was not satisfied with the single frequency, the coverage or the award of damages, so it brought a further action that made its way to the ECHR. That Court, in a judgment of 7 June 2012, held that Article 10 ECHR and Article 1 of Protocol No. 1 had been violated. Referring to Article 41 ECHR, the Court awarded Centro Europa 7 damages of € 10 million plus tax (plus € 100,000 in costs). *Centro Europa 7 SRL and Di Stefano v. Italy*, 38433/09 [2012] ECHR 974. For general background and also questions whether either of the two remedies were effectively implemented see G. Andreoli, "*Trame televisive: il caso infinito Rete 4 – Europa 7*, 05.12.2104 <www.wilditaly.net/trame-televisive-il-caso-infinito-rete-4-europa-7–19515/> accessed 20.07.2015.

28 European Commission Directive 2002/77/EC of 16 September 2002 on competition in the markets for electronic communications networks and services, OJ L 249/21, 17.09.2002, Article 4. See also recital (11).

Analyzing this latest construct, RSPP Article 5 is entitled "Competition", and provides that Member States must promote effective competition and avoid distortions. The Member States are called on to adopt, *inter alia*, the following (paraphrased) measures:

- Spectrum caps or conditions
- Reserve bands for new entrants
- Conditions on transfers or accumulations
- Amend existing rights of use – anti-hoarding provisions

Moreover, Article 5(4) provides that Member States shall ensure that their authorisation and selection procedures for electronic communications services (in general) should promote effective competition "for the benefit of citizens, consumers and businesses in the Union."

These latest provisions create an issue of consistency which is worthwhile to discuss. The various provisions in the Framework and the RSPP require adherence to competition law concepts, but the requirement is expressed in slightly different ways. This lack of consistency could translate into awkward judicial interpretations or NRA applications if the meaning of the different expressions is parsed out thoroughly.

For instance, the RSPP contains three expressions of the standard for competition assessments with slightly different terms. It calls on Member States to undertake the following:

- "Promote effective competition" and avoid distortions of competition – Article 5(1);
- Regulate transfers "likely to result in significant harm to competition" – Article 5(2)(d); and
- Avoid accumulations that result in "significant harm to competition" Article 3(i) or which "distort competition" Article 5(2)(e)

To date, we have not seen national courts or regulators forced to interpret these terms precisely. Nevertheless, these terms are not exactly the same and could lead to difficulties in real world contexts.

Competition law considerations of radio spectrum resources have played a significant role in a number of mergers of large operators. For example, in 2010, the Commission cleared a joint venture between UK subsidiaries of Deutsche Telekom and France Telecom (T-Mobile and Orange, respectively), subject to conditions involving radio spectrum. Among many other conditions, the parties agreed to divest 15 MHz of spectrum in the 1800 MHz band.[29]

[29] *T-Mobile/ Orange* (Case COMP/M.5650) Commission Decision C(2010) 1274. See European Commission Press Release IP/10/208, 01.03.2010.

In an earlier decision, the Commission approved a 2006 merger between the Austrian subsidiary of T-Mobile and its direct competitor tele.ring, also with conditions that the parties sell the rights to use certain important radio frequencies together with certain mobile telephony sites to competitors with lower market shares.[30] To the extent radio frequencies are critical inputs to provision of communications services they are a clear subject for competition law assessments.

This question also invites analysis whether State aid principles have played an important role in national cases on spectrum policy or regulation. Application of these principles is a EU principle designed to avoid Member State distortions of the internal market. As a general matter, EU guidelines on State aid for broadband require that "[g]ranting authorities shall also take into account spectrum (re-) allocations leading to possible network roll-out in the target areas that could achieve the objectives of the granting authorities without the provision of direct grants."[31]

One of the most recent cases involving the intersection of State aid principles and radio frequency use arose in Spain, where the national authorities decided in 2005 to provide a subsidy of € 260 million for the transition to digital terrestrial television (DTT) in remote areas of Spain, but in a manner that benefited only terrestrial operators. SES Astra took the case to the EC on the grounds that the measure discriminated against satellite services. On 19 June 2013, the Commission issued a formal decision declaring that the Spanish State aids to DTT were illegal and ordered the beneficiaries of the aid to pay the money back to the government.[32] As Commission Vice-President in charge of competition policy, Joaquín Almunia, said at the time that the investigation was commenced: "The liberation of the digital dividend creates tremendous opportunities for a better use of spectrum, but we have to make sure that those opportunities are available fairly in compliance with EU State aid rules."[33]

Despite this recent example, it must be conceded that the majority of State aid cases that involve consideration of radio spectrum result in a finding that there is no violation of the rules.[34] There are numerous cases involving State aid to public broadcasters that

30 *T-Mobile Austria / Tele.ring* (Case COMP/ M.3916) Commission Decision C (2006) 1695 [2007] OJ L38/44. See European Commission Press Release IP/06/535, 26.04.2006.

31 EU Guidelines for the application of State aid rules in relation to the rapid deployment of broadband networks, [2013] OJ C25/1, at para. 44.

32 European Commission Decision of 19 June 2013 on State Aid SA.28599 (C 23/2010 (ex NN 36/2010, ex CP 163/2009)) C(2013) 3204 final (public version at <http://ec.europa.eu/competition/state_aid/cases/237770/237770_1459850_1036_2.pdf>). The Commission decision was upheld upon appeal. Judgment in Cases T-461/13 et seq, *Spain v. Commission*, 26 November 2015.

33 European Commission Press Release IP/12/401, 25.04.2012.

34 See, e.g., C. Hocepied and A. Held, "The Assignment of Spectrum and the EU State Aid Rules: the case of the 4th 3G license assignment in France" 2011 <http://ec.europa.eu/competition/publications/cpn/2011_3_6_en.pdf>. See also Commission Press Release IP/11/555, "State aid: the procedure for awarding France's fourth 3G mobile phone licence did not involve state aid", 10.05.2011. A Dutch case from 2007 explicitly held that granting the use of radio frequencies to a public service broadcaster at no

implicate the grant of rights of use, but these cases do not center on the use of radio frequencies so much as the cultural aspects of public broadcasters. Even in the Spanish case, the issue was over subsidies to different platforms and was not related to authorisations per se for the radio frequencies.

3.6. *Which Specific Problems of Legal Protection do you Consider to be the Most Important or Interesting Issues?*

One of the more interesting and yet unresolved issues involving European legal standards in the radio frequency area is the interaction between EU and international rules, and which institutions should be involved in shaping the latter to define legal protection for spectrum use. The RR are external treaty level obligations made by the Member States. This is recognized in Framework Directive Article 9(1) that provides "Member States shall respect relevant international agreements, including the ITU Radio Regulations..."[35] The Radio Spectrum Decision 676/2002/EC states that measures taken must be "without prejudice" to Member State obligations under international treaties (Article 6(4)) and work under the decision must take "due account" of ITU activities (Article 1(3)).

Member States always sign the results of ITU radiocommunication conferences subject to the reservation that they will apply revised RR "in accordance with their obligations under the Treaty on the European Union and the Treaty on the Functioning of the European Union."[36] Hence, even when adopting international treaty rules that govern spectrum matters, Member States agree that EU law must prevail in case of any conflict.

Further, the Commission has recently sought to become more active in ITU negotiations and conferences that amend the international RR and other treaties. For example, when the Commission first proposed the RSPP in September 2010 it initially included an aggressive expansion of its competence and role with respect to ITU matters.[37] The Member States blocked this expansionary tendency, with resulting provisions that sustain the longstanding practice of relying on the CEPT mechanism to involve national experts from the Member States, leaving the Commission to monitor developments and issue communications to set European policy objectives.[38] However, in a communication

charge was not a form of unlawful State aid. District Court Rotterdam ("Rechtbank Rotterdam") 12.03.2007, ECLI:NL:RBROT:2007:BA5115 (*Vereniging van Commerciële Radio v. Minister of Economic Affairs*). See on this case and other case-law on State aid in the Netherlands in the field of radio frequencies the chapter by Wolswinkel in this book.

35 See also Framework Directive Article 9(4) permitting Member States to apply proportionate and non-discriminatory restrictions on the types of service to be provided, as a limit to the otherwise policy objectivity of service neutrality, 'where necessary, to fulfill a requirement under the ITU Radio Regulations.'

36 E.g., WRC-12 Plenary Doc. 546 rev2, 05.04.2012, p. 8 (password protected).

37 European Commission, Proposal for a Decision of the European Parliament and of the Council establishing the first [RSPP], COM(2010) 471, 20.09.2010. Provisions on international negotiations were contained in Article 9.

38 G. Oberst, "European Union and the Results of WRC-12: the Space Perspective", in M. Hofmann (ed.), *International Regulations of Space Communications, Current Issues*, Larcier, 2013, pp. 121–136.

on the WRC-12, the Commission proposed raising the matter of the EU's status before the ITU, and in particular noted that this might be discussed at the ITU's next Plenipotentiary Conference, scheduled at the end of 2014.[39] Clearly the scope for EU (i.e., Commission) involvement in ITU treaty-making is not a settled story. As such, the level at which legal protection for spectrum allocations in Europe could be greatly affected in the future, in yet unresolved ways.

39 European Commission, '*WRC-12 Communication*', p. 10. The matter was in fact not raised at the ITU Plenipotentiary Conference, but the Commission has initiated new efforts in advance of the WRC-15 to define and expand its authority. See reference to the Commission's latest proposal at n 21.

Anita Rønne*

CHAPTER 14. THE ALLOCATION OF EMISSION RIGHTS

1. Introduction

This chapter will focus on the rules and principles to the allocation of CO_2 emission allowances in the EU and selected Member States i.e. France, Germany, Greece, Italy, Romania, Spain and the Netherlands. It will seek to address the conceptual distinctions as set out in Chapter 1(3) on *what* is allocated, *how* it is allocated and which *form* the allocated rights are granted in this specific field of law. Emission trading is characterised by an almost complete Europeanisation in the sense that European Union (EU) legislation governs almost completely the allocation of emissions rights and has during its existence been amended to leave very limited room for individual national legislation. Therefore this chapter devotes most attention to EU governance and gives a fairly detailed account of the EU emission trading system as developed under amended directives. It will, however, not consider the Member State reports separately but rather contextualize the EU rules and principles by providing examples of the implementation at the national level and practice based upon national reports.[1]

First this chapter will highlight briefly the policy developments within the area of climate change and emission trading (Section 2) and then focus on the emission trading concept as such (Section 3). The need for applying for an emission permit is examined under Section 4, whereas the allocation of allowances is discussed under Section 5. Then follows under Section 6, a description of the control and enforcement instruments, and thereafter under Section 7 the linking of the emission trading system to the international flexible mechanisms. Finally, Section 8 completes the chapter with a brief conclusion.

* Anita Rønne is Associate Professor of energy law at the Faculty of Law, University of Copenhagen, Denmark.

1 France prepared by F. Lafarge and A. Soldatenko; Germany prepared by M. Martini; Greece prepared by G. Dellis and N. Sakellariou; Italy prepared by F. Giglioni; Romania prepared by D.C. Dragos, B. Neamtu and R. Suciu; Spain prepared by I. Fernández Torres and D. Utrilla Fernández-Bermejo; and the Netherlands prepared by J.R. van Angeren and L. Westendorp. These national reports have been collected in P. Adriaanse, F. van Ommeren, W. den Ouden and J. Wolswinkel, *Scarcity and the State II. Member State Reports on Gambling Licences, Radio Frequencies and CO_2 Emission Permits*, Intersentia, Antwerp 2016.

2. Policy Developments

The United Nation Framework Convention on Climate Change (UNFCCC) was ratified by the then European Community in 1994 and the Kyoto Protocol in 2002.[2] The European Union (EU) has been at the forefront of international efforts towards the adoption of the global climate deal at the Paris climate conference (COP21) in December 2015. The Paris agreement will be opened for signature on 22 April 2016 and is due to enter into force in 2020. The EU made use of the Kyoto Protocol's possibility to fulfill the reduction targets jointly (Article 4) with a common reduction target of 8 per cent compared to 1990 levels for the first period 2008–2012 and reduction of 20 per cent in the second period lasting from 2013 to 2020. Many climate-related strategies and legislation have increasingly been adopted by the EU over the last two decades.[3] Importantly, the Lisbon Treaty in addition to reaffirming the EU commitment to protect the environment and to sustainable development included also a specific reference to "combatting climate change" in the environmental policy objectives in Article 191 of the Treaty on the Functioning of the European Union (TFEU). A special Climate and Energy Package included the target of reduction of CO_2 emissions by 20 per cent compared to 1990 levels by 2020 which has required the EU to put in place new legislation in order to achieve this target.[4] However, the EU has also offered to step up this cut to 30 per cent if other major economies agree to do their fair share of a global reduction effort.[5]

More recent policy documents of the Commission suggest that by 2050 the EU should cut its emissions to 80 per cent below 1990 levels through domestic reductions alone, as part of the mitigation effort needed from developed countries as a whole.[6] A policy framework for the period up to 2030 has been prepared which seeks to drive continued progress towards a low-carbon economy.[7] Central to this policy is the target to reduce

2 Cf. Decision 94/69, [1994] OJ L33/11 and Decision 2002/358, [2002] OJ L130/1 that also contains the so-called burden sharing agreement.

3 The first strategy was SEC(91)1744 "Community strategy to limit carbon dioxide (CO_2) emissions and improve energy efficiency". See also COM(2000) 88, on EU policies and measures to reduce greenhouse gas emissions: Towards a European climate change programme".

4 See in general for more details on the EU ETS the Commission's homepage: <http://ec.europa.eu/clima/index_en.htm> accessed 01.11.2015. See also M. Pohlmann, 'The European Union Emissions Trading Scheme', p. 337 and N.S. GHALEIGH, 'Emissions Trading before the European Court of Justice: Market Making in Luxembourg', p. 367, and C.F. Clarke and T. Chagas, 'Aviation and Climate Change Regulation, p. 606 – all in D. Freestone and C. Streck (eds.), *Legal Aspects of Carbon Trading – Kyoto, Copenhagen and beyond*, Oxford University Press, 2009; and M. Pallemaerts and R. Williams, 'Climate change: The international and European Policy Framework' in M. Peeters and K. Deketelaere (eds.), *EU Climate Change Policy: the Challenge of New Regulatory Initiatives*, Edward Elgar, 2006, p. 22; and J.H. Jans and H.H.B. Vedder *European Environmental Law* – 4th ed (Europa Law Publishing 2012), p. 431; L. KRÄMER, *EU Environmental Law*, 7th ed, Sweet & Maxwell, 2011, Ch. 9, p. 307 and E. Woerdman, M.M. Roggenkamp and M. Holwerda (eds.), *Essential EU Climate Law*, Edward Elgar, 2015.

5 Decision 406/2009 on the effort of Member States to reduce their greenhouse gas emissions to meet the Community's greenhouse gas emission reduction commitments up to 2020, [2009] OJ L140/136. This is also reflected in the amended Directive 2003/87, Article 1.

6 COM(2011)112, "A Roadmap for moving to a competitive low carbon economy in 2050 and COM(2011) 885, "Energy Roadmap 2050".

7 COM(2014) 15, "A policy framework for climate and energy in the period from 2020 to 2030".

EU domestic greenhouse gas (GHG) emissions by 40 per cent below the 1990 level by 2030, and that is seen as an important step on the course to cutting emissions by at least 80 per cent by 2050. The EU was among the first to submit its intended contribution to the new agreement in March 2015, that included a target to reduce emissions by at least 40 per cent by 2030.

Following the adoption of a Green Paper on GHG trading and of Directive 2003/87 establishing the EU Emission Trading Scheme (ETS), the EU ETS came into effect as from January 2005.[8] It is a prominent example of the application of market-based instruments to address environmental problems. While the EU originally followed a concept developed in the US,[9] the EU ETS has developed into the largest and first cross-border GHG emissions trading system in the world covering 31 countries[10] and more than 11,000 installations including a significant part of the energy sector as well as energy-intensive industries, the offshore sector and more recently aviation.[11] In total the EU ETS covers around 45 per cent of the EU's GHG emissions.

3. The Emissions Trading Concept

The EU ETS regime is based on the principle of "cap and trade" where a fixed limit is set for the total quantity of emissions of certain GHGs over a specified period and then tradable allowances equal to that limit are allocated or auctioned to the operators whose installations or activities are covered by the system. Every year these operators are required to surrender allowances equivalent to their emissions. If an operator foresees that it is likely to emit more than its allocation, it has the choice of either buying more allowances in the market or taking steps to emit less by for instance, replacing existing technology that will produce lower emissions. Within limits, it can also buy credits from certain types of approved emission-saving projects around the world. If a company reduces its emissions, it can retain the spare allowances to cover its future needs or else sell them to another company that is short of allowances. The flexibility that trading brings is supposed to ensure that emissions are cut where it costs least to do so. The cap is reduced over time so that total emissions fall, and the limit on the total number of allowances available ensures that they have a value.

The emissions trading mechanism has taken the EU more than a decade to put in place and has encountered a series of problems. It has been noted that the EU ETS has only delivered limited benefits in CO_2 reduction. Perhaps even more importantly, the market price has been too low partly due to over-allocation of allowances, and partly because of the economic crisis that caused a decrease in demand for allowances. Consequently, a

8 COM(2000) 87, "Green Paper on greenhouse gas emissions trading within the European Union".

9 ETS dates back to the 1970's when it was first applied in the US to implement the Clean Air Act. The success in reducing air emissions resulted in other countries' adoption of similar schemes.

10 The 28 EU Member States plus Iceland, Liechtenstein and Norway. See also factsheet at <http://ec.europa.eu/clima/publications/docs/factsheet_ets_en.pdf> accessed 01.11.2015.

11 COM(97)196, "Climate Change: The EU Approach for Kyoto", COM(97)48, "The energy dimension of climate change"; and COM(97)167, "An overall view of energy policy and actions".

sense of crisis has recently surrounded the system and some have advocated interim measures in response in the form of "back loading",[12] implying the temporarily holding allowances as a means of driving the carbon price up. The Commission has also proposed to establish a market stability reserve at the beginning of the next ETS trading period in 2021.[13] The reserve attempts to address the surplus of emission allowances that has built up in recent years.

Over the years, revisions of the legislation have been necessary to cope with issues of efficiency and transparency, price volatility, and the risk of fraud. The EU ETS is now in its third phase of operation and planning is already underway for the fourth phase that would begin in 2021. The first phase ran from 2005–2007, the second from 2008–2012 and the third commenced at the beginning of 2013 and will run until the end of 2020. In each successive phase, the aim has been to learn lessons from the previous one and improve and extend the scope of the system. Thus, Phase II saw the range of industries covered by the system extended to include, for example, offshore oil and gas production and petrochemicals, reduction of the number of allowances, the inclusion of EEA countries, and the development of the National Allocation Plans (NAPs). Aviation was included in the system from 1 January 2012. Phase III saw major reforms in the ETS. Importantly, the NAPS was replaced by a single EU-wide cap and is an evident confirmation of the Europeanisation that have taken place of the ETS and which have implied that there is less to compare between the national jurisdictions as an annual reduction has now been introduced to produce an overall reduction of over 20 per cent over the period. Another determining amendment is an increase in the use of auctioning over a cost-free allocation of allowances. These amendments are further elaborated upon in the following sections.

The original Directive 2003/87/EC established a scheme for GHG emission allowance trading within the EU in order to promote reductions of GHG emissions in a cost-effective and economically efficient manner (Article 1).[14] As indicated above, the Directive has been amended several times. The activities and the GHGs which the Directive applies to are listed in Annex I and Annex II, respectively. The activities include power and heat generation; energy-intensive industry sectors including oil refineries, steel works and production of iron, aluminum, metals, cement, lime, glass, ceramics, pulp, paper, cardboard, acids and bulk organic chemicals and civil aviation whereas the GHGs in addition to CO_2 are nitrous oxide (N_2O) and perfluorocarbons (PFCs) from aluminum production.

12 Implying the postponing of auctioning, see <http://ec.europa.eu/clima/policies/ets/reform/index_en.htm> accessed 01.11.2015.

13 COM(2014) 15, "A policy framework for climate and energy in the period from 2020 to 2030".

14 Directive 2003/87/EC of 13 October 2003 establishing a scheme for greenhouse gas emission allowance trading within the Community and amending Council Directive 96/61/EC, [2003] OJ L275/32; amended by Directive 2004/101/EC, [2004] OJ L338/18; Directive 2008/101/EC, [2009] OJ L8/3; and Directive 2009/29/EC [2009] OJ L140/ 63). The Directive is published in a consolidated version of 30 April 2014, cf. <http://eur-lex.europa.eu/LexUriServ/LexUriServ.do?uri=CONSLEG:2003L0087:20130701:EN:PDF> accessed 01.11.2015.

The 2008 amendment[15] to the ETS Directive included the aviation sector under the regime in view of the absence of an international agreement.[16] Since the start of 2012 emissions from all flights from, to and within the 28 EU Member States, plus Iceland, Liechtenstein and Norway (EEA) have been covered (Article 3 a–g). The EU ETS regime applies to EU and non-EU airlines alike and thus requires operators to surrender emission allowances for the relevant flight and including emissions generated outside EU airspace although some exceptions were allowed. This turned out to be very controversial and some US airlines and their trade association brought the case to CJEU. The Court concluded that the directive including aviation activities in the EU's ETS is valid and does not infringe the principles of customary international law or the Open Skies Agreement.[17] The Court stated that the extension of the EU ETS to aviation infringes neither the principle of territoriality, nor the sovereignty of third countries since the scheme is applicable to the operators only when their aircraft are physically in the territory of one of the Member States of the EU; that the EU ETS does not constitute a tax, fee or charge on fuel, which could be in breach of the EU-US Air Transport Agreement; and that the uniform application of the EU ETS to European and non-European airlines alike is consistent with provisions in the EU-US Air Transport Agreement prohibiting discriminatory treatment between aircraft operators on nationality grounds.

However, due to the pressure experienced and to allow time for negotiations on a global measure addressing international aviation emissions by 2016 and to apply it by 2020, the EU ETS requirements were suspended for flights in 2012 to and from non-European countries following an agreement by the ICAO Assembly in October 2013.[18] For the period 2013–2016 the legislation has also been amended so that only emissions from flights within the EEA fall under the EU ETS.[19] Exemptions for operators with low emissions have also been introduced.

A major revision of the ETS was adopted by the amending Directive 2009/29/EC[20] to improve and strengthen the emission allowance trading scheme. The ETS was among

15 Directive 2008/101/EC of 19 November 2008 amending Directive 2003/87/EC so as to include aviation activities in the scheme for greenhouse gas emission allowance trading within the Community.

16 Reflecting that the International Civil Aviation Organization (ICAO) had failed to adopt proper measures.

17 Case C-366/10, *Air Transport Association of America, American Airlines Inc., Continental Airlines Inc., United Airlines Inc.* v *Secretary of State for Energy and Climate Change*, of 21.12.2011. See S. BOGOJEVIC, 'Legalising Environmental Leadership: A Comment on the CJEU'S Ruling in C-366/10 on the Inclusion of Aviation in the EU Emissions Trading Scheme', *EJIL (European Journal of International Law)*, 2012, 24 (2): 345–356 and J. SCOTT and L. RAJAMANI, 'EU Climate Change Unilateralism', *EJIL*, 2012, 23 (2): 469–494.

18 See <www.icao.int/Newsroom/News%20Doc%202013/COM.36.13.A38.Closing.EN.pdf> accessed 01.11.2015.

19 Decision 377/2013/EU of 24 April 2013 derogating temporarily from Directive 2003/87/EC and Regulation (EU) No 421/2014 of 16 April 2014 amending Directive 2003/87/EC establishing a scheme for greenhouse gas emission allowance trading within the Community, in view of the implementation by 2020 of an international agreement applying a single global market-based measure to international aviation emissions.

20 Directive 2009/29/EC of 23 April 2009, amending Directive 2003/87/EC so as to improve and extend the greenhouse gas emission allowance trading scheme of the Community.

others critised for over-allocation of allowances that had resulted in a situation with too many allowances on the market compared to the actual demand and in a consequential drop in the price of allowances. Furthermore, a Europe-wide VAT fraud regarding emission allowances in the national registries had been detected. Therefore phase 3 starting in 2013 is significantly different from the previous 2 phases and is based on rules which are far more harmonised than before. The changes include first and foremost the introduction of an EU-wide quantity of allowances replacing the previous system of national caps combined with a centralized EU registry managed by the European Commission. Moreover, a decrease of the quantity of allowances is implemented. The improved efficiency measures include conditions of allocation via increased competitive auctions replacing free allocation. From 2013 more than 40 per cent of allowances are auctioned, rising progressively each year. For those allowances still given away for free, harmonised allocation rules apply which are based on EU-wide benchmarks of emissions performance. Finally, rules for new entrants have been adopted. These new entrant and closure rules have been criticised because companies that make losses could decide to maintain their unprofitable production capacity in order to continue receiving free allowances, which is inefficient from an economic point of view.[21] Allowances are set aside in a New Entrants Reserve to fund the deployment of innovative renewable energy technologies as well as carbon capture and storage.

4. Emission Permits

To emit GHGs from an installation, the operators must hold a GHG emission permit issued by the relevant national authority, unless the installation is excluded from the EU scheme pursuant to Article 27. Both the content of the application and the permit is further detailed. Applications for a permit must, among other issues, include the installation and its activities, the raw materials, and the sources of emissions of gases (Article 5).

As to the content of the permit, it must include the name and address of the operator; description of the activities and emissions from the installation; a monitoring plan, reporting requirements and the obligation to surrender allowances equal to the total emissions of the installation in each calendar year, within a time limit of four months (Article 6). The competent authority must be satisfied that the operator is capable of monitoring and shall, at least every five years, review the permit and make any amendments as are appropriate. The permit may cover one or more installations on the same site operated by the same operator. As many of the activities will also require an integrated pollution prevention and control (IPPC) permit, coordination must be ensured with the permit conditions and procedure under the IPPC Directive (Article 8).[22]

[21] Cf. E. Woerdman, 'The EU Greenhouse Gas Emissions Trading Scheme', in: E. Woerdman, M.M. Roggenkamp and M. Holwerda (eds.), *Essential EU Climate Law*, Edward Elgar, 2015, pp. 43–75.

[22] Directive 96/61/EC of 24 September 1996 is now replaced by Directive 2008/1/EC of 15 January 2008 concerning integrated pollution prevention and control, [2008] OJ L24/8.

5. Form and Allocation of Emission Allowances

In the EU ETS, one allowance permits the person holding it to emit one tonne of CO_2 (Article 3(a)) the main GHG gas, or the equivalent amount of two more powerful GHGs – nitrous oxide (N_2O) and perfluorocarbons (PFCs). Allowances can be used only once.[23]

The Directive only lays down some criteria for the allowances whereas the legal nature and status is not further defined and as such left for the transposition in national legislation. The allowances could be categorized as either a public administrative right, a private property right or solely a financial instruments. However, the national reports verify that the unsettled legal qualification of allowances resulted in heated doctrinal debates e.g. in France and Italy.[24] Allowances differ from the well-known public / administrative rights and financial instruments since they are allocated for trading, may be purchased, transferred and cancelled and thus allows the participants to choose the compliance method. There are therefore clear similarities to property rights. In France the allowances are defined as "movable property" and generally it is probably more to the point to talk about a novelty and a hybrid than to try to categorise the allowance as either public or private.

Until the end of 2012, the Member States had to allocate the allowances in national allocation plans (NAPs) based on objective and transparent criteria. It was the Member State that determined the quantity of allowances, but the Commission could reject the plan if it was incompatible with the Directive. Often the total amount of allowances was very high.[25] As mentioned above, the national plans have been replaced by an EU-wide cap.

From 2013 onwards, the EU-wide quantity of allowances issued each year is to decrease by 1,74 per cent every year and be compared to the average annual total quantity of allowances issued by Member States in accordance with the Commission Decisions on their NAPs for the period from 2008 to 2012 (Article 9) subject to some possible adjustments according to Article 9a. This means that in 2020, GHG emissions from the included sectors will be 21 per cent lower than in 2005. A separate cap applies to the

23 The legal status of an allowance is discussed by S. Goldberg, 'Emission Trading in the EU – Some Legal Issues in Relation to the Commitment Period 2005–2007' in M.M. Roggenkamp and U. Hammer (eds), *European Energy Law Report IV*, Intersentia, 2007, pp. 71–85.

24 Cf. F. Lafarge and A. Soldatenko in the French National Report and F. Giglioni in the Italian National Report.

25 Cf. well-illustrated in the National Report on Spain prepared by I. Fernández Torres and D. Utrilla Fernández-Bermejo: "In NAP I, the total amount of allowances allocated was even higher than gas emissions produced in the previous period (2000–2005). NAP II reduced the amount allocated by 16.4% over the previous one, but such amount was still too high." There are several court cases on the scope of the Commission's discretion and decisions on NAPs, e.g. *Romania* v *Commission* Case T-483/07 and T-484/07, T-183/07 T374/04 *Germany* v *Commission Poland* v *Commission*. All phase one and two NAPs including those of the selected Member States mentioned above are published at http://ec.europa.eu/clima/policies/ets/pre2013/nap/documentation_en.htm, accessed 01.11.2015.

aviation sector: for the whole 2013–2020 trading period, this is 5 per cent below the average annual level of emissions in the years 2004–2006.

The vast majority of emission allowances was previously given away free by governments based on historical emissions ("grandfathering"). The Directive did limit the free allocation to 95% and 90% in the 1st and 2nd phase but nevertheless eg Spain allocated all allowances got free, and France did not either make use of this auction possibility to the full extent. Likewise Germany decided to observe the experience of other Member States that had implemented auction models. Since 2013 auctioning has become the main method of allocation (Article 10). 88 per cent of the allowances to be auctioned are allocated to the Member States on the basis of their share of verified emissions under the EU scheme for 2005 or the average of the period from 2005 to 2007. 10 per cent are allocated to the least wealthy Member States and the remaining 2 per cent is given as a bonus to 9 Member States which by 2005 had reduced their GHG emissions by at least 20 per cent of levels in their Kyoto Protocol base year or period. Importantly, the goal is to phase out free allocation completely by 2027. However, eight of the Member States[26] which have joined the EU since 2004 have made use of a provision allowing them to continue granting limited numbers of free allowances to existing power plants until 2019, including Romania.[27] In return they will invest at least as much as the value of the free allowances in modernizing their power sector.

Over the period from 2013 to 2020, 5 per cent of the EU-wide quantity of allowances must be set aside for new entrants (Article 10(a)(7)). Up to 300 million allowances in the new entrants' reserve must be available until 31 December 2015 to help stimulate the construction and operation of up to 12 commercial CCS demonstration projects, that has, however, not materialized, as well as demonstration projects of innovative renewable energy technologies (Article 10(a)(8)).

From the beginning of the EU ETS, it was recognized that there is a risk that industries affected may find themselves at a competitive disadvantage compared with counterparts elsewhere in the world. There are exceptions provided for sectors and energy intensive industries that are subject to carbon leakage (Article 10(b)) an option for transitional free allocation for the modernisation of electricity generation.

Member States shall auction all allowances which are not allocated free of charge in accordance with Article 10(a) and 10(c). A detailed Auctioning Regulation (EU) No 1031/2010 implies that very limited measures are required to implement the timing, administration and other aspects of auctioning in the Member States. Auctions shall be designed to ensure that operators have full, fair and equitable access and access to the

26 Bulgaria, Cyprus, Czech Republic, Estonia, Hungary, Lithuania, Poland and Romania.

27 Cf. D.C. Dragos, B. Neamtu and R. Suciu, National Report Romania that also highlight that although the companies are aware the money from trading emission rights should be used for investments, the companies report that they sold allowances in order to have cash flows or for company consumption.

same information at the same time. Moreover, the organisation and participation in auctions must be cost-efficient and undue administrative costs must be avoided (Article 10(4)). Auctions are held by companies appointed by national governments but are open to buyers from any country participating in the EU ETS. Most governments use a common 'platform' for their auctions, but e.g. Germany have opted to use its own platforms. As a first step, Germany carried out a Europe-wide awarding procedure to establish a temporary auction platform. German emission allowances as well as the air traffic authorisations have been auctioned on this temporary platform until 31 December 2013. The European Exchange AG (EEX) in Leipzig prevailed in its bid to operate the auction, with its associated clearinghouse, European Commodity Clearing AG (ECC). After the granting of the award the platform needed to go through a test procedure conducted by the European Commission. EEX will serve as the German auction platform at least until autumn 2018. Poland didn't bring up its own platform yet, but has contracted the German platform (EEX) to auction on its behalf. In Greece, the Hellenic Exchanges Group (HELEX) supported the small percentage of auctioning of emission allowances during Phase II of the EU-ETS. However, according to press information, there were market operators who claimed that it was a rather closed auction with few participants and a process established under Greek State's pressure to generate revenues. In France activities were carried out by the largest CO_2 trading exchange platform, the Paris-based exchange: BlueNext.[28]

Member States shall determine the use of revenues generated from the auctioning of allowances. However, the Directive requires that at least 50 per cent of the revenues should be used to reduce GHG emissions through various mitigation and adoption measures, including but not limited to renewables, energy efficiency, Carbon Capture and Storage; deforestation; and to finance further research and development in these areas (Article 10(3)).

Allowances can be transferred between persons within the EU without restrictions and with persons in third countries where such allowances are recognised pursuant to a special procedure (Articles 12 and 25). National ETS systems are operating in several countries, including Japan, New Zealand, Switzerland and the US. The linking of the EU ETS with other emissions trading systems would enable participants in one system to use units from a linked system for compliance purposes.[29] A linking of emission trading systems between the EU and Australia agreed by mid-2018, with an interim link from 1 July 2015 has been abandoned by Australia.[30]

28 Cf. M. Martini, National Report Germany, the Greek Report by G. Dellis and N. Sakellariou, and French National Report by F. Lafarge and A. Soldatenko.

29 See the International Carbon Action Partnership (ICAP) that was established to provide an international forum for public authorities and governments that have established or are actively pursuing carbon markets through mandatory cap and trade systems, <https://icapcarbonaction.com/> accessed 01.11.2015.

30 See European Commission – IP/12/916 and MEMO/12/631 of 28 August 2012.

Following the revision of the ETS Directive, EU ETS operations have been centralised in a single EU registry operated by the Commission. The EU registry has replaced Member States' national registries. The revision followed the so-called 'phishing attacks' in 2010/2011 where millions of allowances were fraudulently obtained and resold. Allowances issued from 1 January 2013 onwards shall be held in the EU registry for the execution of processes related to holding accounts, allocation, surrender and cancellation of allowances under Regulation 389/2013 (Article (11). Any person may hold allowances, and the registry shall be accessible to the public and shall contain separate accounts to record the allowances held by each person to whom and from whom allowances are issued or transferred.

6. Monitoring, Control and Enforcement of Emissions Rights

Industrial installations and aircraft operators covered by the EU ETS are required to have an approved monitoring plan, according to which they monitor and report their emissions during the year (Article 10). Member States must submit an annual report to the Commission on the application of the Directive, including details of arrangements for the allocation of allowances, the application of the implementing measures on monitoring and reporting, verification and accreditation and issues relating to compliance with the Directive and on the fiscal treatment of allowances, if any (Articles 21 and 10(4)). The Commission is required to adopt a regulation for the monitoring and reporting of emissions (Article 14) and has done so regularly.[31]

The data in the Member States' annual emissions report for a given year must be verified in accordance with the criteria set out in Annex V and regulations adopted by the Commission (Article 14).[32] The verification process includes consideration of the report and of monitoring during the preceding year, and addresses the reliability, credibility and accuracy of the monitoring systems and the reported data and information relating to emissions (Annex V). Such verification must be carried out by an accredited verifier by 31 March of the following year. Once verified, operators must surrender the equivalent number of allowances by 30 April of that year.[33]

Member States should lay down rules on penalties applicable to infringements of the Directive and ensure that these are implemented. Such penalties must be effective,

31 See Regulation (EU) No 601/2012 of 21 June 2012 on the monitoring and reporting of greenhouse gas emissions and Regulation (EU) No 525/2013 of 21 May 2013 on a mechanism for monitoring and reporting greenhouse gas emissions and for reporting other information at national and Union level relevant to climate change.

32 Commission Regulation (EU) No 600/2012 of 21 June 2012 on the verification of greenhouse gas emission reports and tonne-kilometre reports and the accreditation of verifiers.

33 Regulations and guidance on verification and accreditation of verifers can be found at <http://ec.europa.eu/clima/policies/ets/monitoring/documentation_en.htm> accessed 01.11.2015. See also Commission Regulation (EU) No 600/2012 of 21 June 2012 on the verification of greenhouse gas emissions reports and tonne-kilometre reports and the accreditation of verifiers pursuant to Directive 2003/87/EC, OJ L81/1. Article 75 requires national accreditation bodies (NABs) to set up and manage a database which includes information on each verifier accredited.

proportionate and dissuasive and be notified to the Commission (Article 16). Member States shall also ensure publication nationally of the names of operators and aircraft operators who are in breach of requirements to surrender sufficient allowances – the so-called "naming and shaming". Germany has become the first EU country to publish a list of aircraft operators that have not complied with the EU ETS for emissions in 2012. According to the German Emissions Trading Authority, fines totalling € 5,363,400 have been levied and the 44 operators named. Other countries have not published lists, but the number not complying is thought to be quite high, and there can be observed a reluctance by States to publish publicly-available lists of non-compliant airlines, particularly those from outside Europe.[34]

Any operator or aircraft operator who does not surrender sufficient allowances by 30 April of each year to cover their emissions from the previous year shall pay a penalty of EUR 100 per tonne of CO_2 emitted for which the operator or aircraft operator has not surrendered allowances. However, payment of the excess emissions penalty is not releasing the operator from the obligation to surrender the amount of allowances equal to those excess emissions when surrendering allowances in relation to the following calendar year (Article 16) – meaning "both and". The excess emissions penalty relating to allowances issued from 1 January 2013 onwards shall increase in accordance with the European index of consumer prices.

7. Cooperation and Flexible Mechanisms

The Kyoto Protocol's flexibility mechanisms are integrated under the EU ETS by a so-called Linking Directive 2004/101/EC[35] amending the ETS Directive. For some sceptical countries like towards the European framework for limiting greenhouse gas emissions, due to its negative consequences for the domestic industry eg Italy has emphasized the importance of the linking directive to "soften" the cap criterion of allowances. Companies can thus use credits generated by certain types of emission-reducing projects around the world to cover a proportion of their emissions along with EU allowances. The purpose of linking the EU ETS scheme to the use of the flexible mechanisms under the Kyoto Protocol is to increase the cost-effectiveness of achieving the EU emission reduction targets, and at the same time promote technology transfer and contribute to sustainable development at the global level (Articles 11b).

These projects must be recognised under the Kyoto Protocol's Clean Development Mechanism (CDM) or Joint Implementation (JI) mechanism, as bringing real and genuinely additional emission reductions. In line with Article 11(b)(6) of the Directive,

34 "GreenAir" online reports in March 2015 that, see <www.airportwatch.org.uk/2015/03/germany-fines-aircraft-operators-e5-36-million-as-it-publishes-first-aviation-eu-ets-non-compliance-list/> accessed 01.11.2015.

35 Directive 2004/101/EC of 27 October 2004 amending Directive 2003/87/EC establishing a scheme for greenhouse gas emission allowance trading within the Community, in respect of the Kyoto Protocol's project mechanisms, [2004] OJ L338, p. 18. See the Italian National Report prepared by F. Giglioni.

Member States approving such projects must ensure compliance with international criteria and guidelines. Credits are accepted from all types of projects except nuclear energy projects, afforestation or reforestation activities and projects involving the destruction of industrial gases.[36] Acceptance in the EU ETS of credits from JI or CDM hydroelectric projects exceeding 20 MW of installed capacity is subject to certain conditions.

Unused allowances from the second phase (2008–2012) are transferred to phase 3 (2013–2020). The exact amount per operator for phase three is determined in line with the methodology set out in the revised EU ETS Directive (Article 11(a)(8)) and is further specified in a Regulation on determining international credit entitlements.[37] Overall, international credits can be used to cover emissions of some 1.6 billion tonnes of CO_2 (or the equivalent amount of N_2O or PFCs) between 2008 and 2020. This represents half the reduction in emissions that will be made under the EU ETS in that period. By allowing companies to buy international credits, the EU ETS is channeling substantial amounts of investment and clean technologies to promote low-carbon development in developing countries and economies in transition.

8. Conclusion

Due to the way the ETS has developed at the European level, today there is very little room and freedom for the national authorities to differentiate what is allocated, how it is allocated and in which form the allocated rights are granted.[38] Gradually, harmonization and centralization has taken place so today it is the European Commission and the EU as such that plays the central role in this specific field of law and not the individual Member States. Still, however, it is unsettled as to how an allowance should be defined legally or classified in the different national legal systems.

36 See Directive 2004/101/EC, recital 8 and 9 with reference to UNFCCC and the Kyoto Protocol and subsequent decisions e.g. Decision 17/CP.7 that in its preamble state "Recognizing that Parties included in Annex I are to refrain from using certified emission reductions generated from nuclear facilities to meet their commitments under Article 3, paragraph 1".

37 Commission Regulation (EU) No 1123/2013 of 8 November 2013 on determining international credit entitlements pursuant to Directive 2003/87/EC.

38 The Dutch national report prepared by J.R. van Angeren and L. Westendorp illustrates this in the following way: "The heart of the Dutch emissions trading rules is found in a single chapter of the Environmental Management Act and in a single ministerial regulation", and further "the national legislature had only limited freedom to make 'national choices' in implementing the ETS regulations". Likewise it is interesting to note from the Italian National Report that the Italian administrative judges have stated that the greenhouse gas emission allowance framework is a clear example of the existence of European Administrative Law. Finally, the Greek national report confirms that "a harmonised – at EU level – licensing regime in a specific sector clearly leads to a more consistent framework which, on the one hand, bridges the gaps between the different perspectives Member States may share and, on the other hand, seems to ensure a more efficient way of regulating economic activities."

LIST OF CONTRIBUTORS

Paul Adriaanse
Associate Professor of constitutional and administrative law at Leiden University and practising lawyer at Justion Advocaten, the Netherlands

Luis Arroyo Jiménez
Professor of administrative law at University of Castilla-La Mancha, Spain

Anoeska Buijze
Assistant Professor of administrative law at Utrecht University, the Netherlands

Armin Cuyvers
Assistant Professor of European law at Leiden University, the Netherlands

Willemien den Ouden
Dean of the Honours Academy of Leiden University and Professor of constitutional and administrative law at Leiden University, the Netherlands

Vassilis Hatzopoulos
Assistant Professor at the Democritus University of Thrace, Greece, Visiting Professor at the College of Europe, Bruges, Belgium and Attorney-at-Law, Member of the Athens Bar

Chris Jansen
Professor of private law at VU University Amsterdam, Professor of construction law at Tilburg University and vice-chairman of the Dutch Public Procurement Ombudsman, the Netherlands

Gerry Oberst
Senior Vice President, global regulatory and governmental strategy at SES, Luxemburg

Anita Rønne
Associate Professor of energy law at the Faculty of Law of University of Copenhagen, Denmark

Konrad Schiemann
Former Judge of the Court of Justice of the European Union

Michiel Tjepkema
Associate Professor of constitutional and administrative law at Leiden University, the Netherlands

Dolores Utrilla Fernández-Bermejo
Assistant of administrative Law and Research Fellow of the Center for European Studies at University of Castilla-La Mancha, Spain

Stefaan Van den Bogaert
Professor of European law and Director of the Europa Institute at Leiden Law School, the Netherlands

Jacobine van den Brink
Assistant Professor of constitutional and administrative law at Leiden University, the Netherlands

Frank van Ommeren
Professor of constitutional and administrative law at VU University Amsterdam, the Netherlands

Ferdinand Wollenschläger
Professor of Public Law, European Law and Public Economic Law at the University of Augsburg, Germany

Johan Wolswinkel
Associate Professor of administrative law at Tilburg University and senior member of the Tilburg Law and Economics Center (TILEC), the Netherlands

IUS COMMUNE EUROPAEUM

A peer-reviewed book series in which the common foundations of the legal systems of the Member States of the European Union are the central focus.

The *Ius Commune Europaeum* series includes horizontal comparative legal studies as well as studies on the effect of treaties within the national legal systems. All the classic fields of law are covered. The books are published in various European languages under the auspices of METRO, the Institute for Transnational Legal Research at Maastricht University.

Recently published:
Volume 137: *Who does What? On the Allocation of Competences in European Private Law*, B. Akkermans, J. Hage, N. Kornet and J.M. Smits
Volume 138: *The Nature of Mutual Recognition in European Law.* W. van Ballegooij
Volume 139: *Evidence in Contemporary Civil Procedure. Fundamental Issues in a Comparative Perspective*, C.H. van Rhee and A. Uzelac (eds.)
Volume 140: *The effect of D&O insurance on managerial risk taking*, Max Gaber
Volume 141: *Information and Notification Duties*, Ilse Samoy and Marco B. Loos
Volume 142: *The Application of the Theory of Efficient Breach in Contract Law. A Comparative Law and Economics Perspective*, Wenqing Liao
Volume 143: *A European Legal Framework for Nuclear Liability. Rethinking Current Approaches*, Tobias Heldt
Volume 144: *The Development of European Private Law in a Multilevel Legal Order*, Esther van Schagen
Volume 145: *Property Law Perspectives IV*, D. Gruyaert, E. Ramaekers and L. Rostill (eds.)
Volume 146: *The Citizen in European Private Law: Norm-Setting, Enforcement and Choice*, C. Cauffman and J. Smits (eds.)
Volume 147: *Legal Certainty in Real Estate Transactions. A Comparison of England and France,* Bertrand du Marais and David Marrani (eds.)

www.ingramcontent.com/pod-product-compliance
Ingram Content Group UK Ltd.
Pitfield, Milton Keynes, MK11 3LW, UK
UKHW051926100926
8556IPUK00022B/1387

9 781780 68347